Glencoe

Introduction to Business

Dr. Betty J. Brown

Dr. John E. Clow

McGraw Hill Education

COVER: Blend Images/DreamPictures/Getty Images

mheducation.com/prek-12

Copyright © 2016 McGraw-Hill Education

Send all inquiries to:
McGraw-Hill Education
8787 Orion Place
Columbus, OH 43240

ISBN: 978-0-02-140045-4
MHID: 0-02-140045-8

Printed in the United States of America.

7 8 9 10 QVS 22 21 20

Meet Our Authors

Dr. Betty J. Brown is a Professor of Business Information Systems Management and Coordinator of the Business and Marketing Education Program at Ball State University in Muncie, Indiana. She served on the faculty in business education and management at The University of Tennessee, Knoxville. In addition to teaching at the secondary and postsecondary levels, she has written articles and conducted workshops on the teaching of business and economic education. Dr. Brown has served as National President for Delta Pi Epsilon, national graduate honor society in business education, as Executive Director for the Policies Commission for Business and Economic Education, and is a recipient of the John Robert Gregg Award in business education.

Dr. John E. Clow is the Director of the Leatherstocking Center for Economic Education and Professor Emeritus of Business Education at the State University of New York, College at Oneonta. He has held professorial positions at a number of universities in Illinois and Iowa. He has been the Director of a number of national projects in personal finance and consumer economics for the National Council on Economic Education. He has held several college and university administrative positions, including president of Berkeley College in New York City. Dr. Clow has taught at the middle, high school, and college levels and has to his credit numerous speeches and publications in the areas of business and economic education.

Business and Career Education
Industry Advisory Board

Peggy Bradfield
Vons, A Safeway Co.
Burbank, CA

Andy Chaves
Marriott International Inc.
Washington, DC

Mike De Fabio
Otis Spunkmeyer
Torrance, CA

Brian Dunn
JD Power and Associates
Westlake Village, CA

Donna Farrugia
Carrie Nebens
Robert Half International
Westlake Village, CA

Mark Hatch
Ohio Association of Public
   School Employees
Columbus, OH

Mike Kulis
Sherwin Williams Co.
Cleveland, OH

Dr. David M. Mitchell
Johnson & Wales University
Providence, RI

Debbie Moreton
JCPenney
Dallas, TX

Joyce Winterton
USA Today
McLean, VA

We wish to acknowledge the contributions of the following reviewers:

Meredith H. Bell
Timberland High School
St. Stephen, SC

Barb Bielenberg
Sioux City Community
   Schools
Sioux City, IA

Jeremy Brady
Coleman High School
Coleman, WI

Jay S. Brown
Pleasant Valley Middle
   School
Brodheadsville, PA

Margaret Colvin
Southern Regional High
   School
Manahawkin, NJ

Cheryl Cooper
Southeast Career Center
Columbus, OH

Linda Cuppett
East Bay
Gibsonton, FL

Joy Davis
Delaware Area Career
   Center
Delaware, OH

Linda Davis
Jay High School
Jay, ME

Joe Deangelo
Badin High School
Hamilton, OH

Marta E. Diaz
Channelview High School
Channelview, TX

Brian Dudley
Wapahani High School
Selma, IN

Jody Forsythe
Northwestern High School
Maple, WI

Brian Gray
Myers Park High School
Charlotte, NC

Karen Griffith
Phoebus High School
Hampton, VA

Brad Hackworth
Central Washington
   University
Ellensburg, WA

Nancy J. King
Fairfax County Public
   Schools
Falls Church, VA

Vivian King
Independence High School
Columbus, OH

Brenda Knight
Cedar Park High School
Cedar Park, TX

Brad Knoche
South Milwaukee High
   School
South Milwaukee, WI

Sharon Larson
Prairie Ridge High School
Chrystal Lake, IL

Pamela LeCompte
Klein High School
Spring, TX

Lynore Levenhagen
Lyman High School
Longwood, FL

Lucinda Mason
Demopolis High School
Demopolis, AL

Timothy M. McCabe
Badin High School
Hamilton, OH

Cindy Miller
Frenship High School
Wolfforth, TX

Joan Miller
Darlington High School
Darlington, WI

Robert Moccia
Learey Technical Center
Tampa, FL

James Monroe
Greene Central High School
Snow Hill, NC

Cheryl A. Moore
Ellison High School
Killeen, TX

Vanessa Moorhead
Alonso High School
Tampa, FL

Beth Patzke
Baldwin-Woodville High
   School
Baldwin, WI

Deanna Peck
David W. Butler High School
Matthews, NC

Janet Richards
Riverview High School
Riverview, FL

Paul Richmond
Thomas Edison High School
Elmia Heights, NY

Tim Rohlinger
Kewaskum High School
Kewaskum, WI

Natalie Schaublin
Westerville North High
   School
Westerville, OH

Keith A. Schneider
Cambridge High School
Cambridge, WI

Michelle See
East Mecklenburg High
   School
Charlotte, NC

Donna Lee Sirkis
Myers Park High School
Charlotte, NC

Julie Smith
Southeast Career Center
Columbus, OH

Dale Snow
Illinois Business Education
   Association
Joliet, IL

Jaclyn Soles
East Bay High School
Tampa, FL

Joan Sountis
Cliffside Park High
Cliffside Park, NJ

Sandra Talley
Sunny Hill High School
Fullerton, CA

Karen Teach
Clear Spring High School
Clear Spring, MD

Vince Tesi
Colts Neck High School
Colts Neck, NJ

Victoria Vavricka
Washington Township Public
   Schools
Sewell, NJ

Joe Ward
Jackson High School
Jackson, MI

Liz Watt
North Education Center
   High School
Columbus, OH

April Winternheimer
Tampa Bay Technical High
   School
Tampa, FL

Nancy Yankee
Holden High School
Holden, MI

Table of Contents

Ilene MacDonald/Alamy

Table of Contents

Marc Romanelli/Blend Images LLC

Unit 3   Influences on Business   160

Table of Contents

Table of Contents

Table of Contents

Echo/Getty Images

Table of Contents

Table of Contents

Chris Ryan/age fotostock

Table of Contents

The Economy and You

P.B.Loco produces and sells gourmet peanut butter in cafés and online. At the end of this unit, you will learn about the founders of P.B.Loco and how they achieved their success.

Decision Making Do you use a decision-making process every time you buy something?

Courtesy of P.B.Loco

Unit 1   *Thematic Project Preview*

Trends in the World of Business After completing the unit, you will research trends in the world of business to find out how they can affect business and workers.

Project Checklist As you read the chapters in this unit, use this checklist to prepare for the unit project.

✔ Think about how economic events affect workers you know.

✔ Consider how technology has evolved during your lifetime.

✔ Look for cultural diversity in your community.

✔ Notice how globalization affects business.

Basic Economic Concepts

Chapter Objectives After completing this chapter, you will be able to:

▶ **Section 1.1** *A Look at Wants and Needs*
- **State** the differences between wants and needs.
- **Describe** how resources limit the number of wants people and businesses can satisfy.
- **Explain** how to use the decision-making process to make the most of your resources.

▶ **Section 1.2** *Business Activities*
- **Explain** how profit and competition motivate businesses.
- **List** the activities businesses undertake when developing products and services.
- **Explain** how business impacts you and how you impact business.

Ask

AN EXPERT

Investing in Stocks: Initial Investment, Capital Gains, and Dividends

Q: How do you build wealth by investing in stocks?

A: Stocks represent a partial ownership of a given company. To raise money for their current and future operations, "public" or "publicly traded" companies let anyone purchase a stake in their business. That's why one unit of stock is called a share. There are different types of stock, including common stock and preferred stock. Common stock is what most investors purchase—it gives the holder basic ownership of the company and a vote equivalent to the number of shares held. The key here is "ownership"—that's why stocks are considered equity investments—because as an owner of the company, you benefit or lose when the company benefits or loses.

Mathematics A friend of yours bought 100 shares of stock in the Greg Corporation for $48 each. She calls you up to tell you that the stock is now at $\frac{3}{4}$ of the price at which she bought it. If you buy 100 shares too, how much will you spend?

CONCEPT **Writing a Fraction as a Decimal** Any fraction $\frac{a}{b}$, where $b \neq 0$ can be written as a decimal by dividing the numerator by the denominator. So $\frac{a}{b} = a \div b$. If the division ends, or terminates, when the remainder is zero, the decimal is a terminating decimal. Not all fractions can be written as terminating decimals. Some have a repeating decimal element. A bar indicates that the decimal repeats forever. For example, the fraction $\frac{4}{9}$ can be converted to a repeating decimal, $0.\bar{4}$.

● **Choosing What Is Most Important** We cannot have everything we want and need. We must choose what we want or need the most. This man has chosen to spend time with his son. **Do you consider spending time with family a want or a need?**

A Look at Wants and Needs

Reading Guide

● Before You Read

Think about the difference between the things you want and the things you need.

Read to Learn

- State the differences between wants and needs.
- Describe how resources limit the number of wants people and businesses can satisfy.
- Explain how to use the decision-making process to make the most of your resources.

The Main Idea

Businesses make money by offering goods and services to satisfy the wants and needs of consumers and other businesses. In this way, wants and needs drive the U.S. economy.

Key Concepts

- Wants and Needs Drive the Economy
- How Resources Limit the Ability to Satisfy Wants and Needs
- Making the Most of Your Resources

Vocabulary

Key Terms

wants   services
needs   resources
goods

Academic Vocabulary

You will find these words in your reading and on your tests. Make sure you know their meanings.

determine   consider
identify   evaluate

Graphic Organizer

On a chart like this, list things you want in the WANTS column and things you need in the NEEDS column.

WANTS	NEEDS

 Go to **connectED.mcgraw-hill.com** to print out this graphic organizer.

Wants and Needs Drive the Economy

Every day you make decisions about how to spend your money. Suppose you have $10. You could use it to buy lunch or to go to a movie. Which of these things do you want, and which do you need? What is the difference between what you want and what you need?

An Abundance of Wants and Needs

Wants and needs determine what products and services businesses provide. **Wants** are things that you do not have to have to survive, but would like to have. You might want a mountain bike, while your best friend may want a new computer. **Needs** are things that you must have in order to survive. The basic needs of people include food, water, shelter, and clothing.

A group of people may share the same wants. A family may want a new kitchen table. A business may want an advanced computer system. Although these wants are shared, they are considered *private wants*. Individual people also have private wants.

Public wants are wants that are widely shared by many people. Examples include highways, public libraries, and parks. Local, state, and federal governments satisfy public wants.

✔ **Reading Check** **Contrast** How are public wants different from private wants?

● **As You Read**

Think about the last thing you bought. Was it a want or a need?

● **Goods and Services** Service businesses dominate the American economy. **Does this business offer goods, services, or both?**

ColorBlind Images/Blend Images LLC

Satisfying Wants and Needs

Businesses provide goods and services to satisfy wants and needs. **Goods** are physical products. Skates, groceries, and telephones are examples of goods.

Services are tasks that businesses perform for consumers. These include tasks that people or machines do. Like goods, services are provided for a fee. For example, when you pay H & R Block to prepare your taxes, you are buying a service. Insurance, sports and entertainment, tourism, banking, and education involve offering services. Most companies that sell goods also provide services to their customers.

How Resources Limit the Ability to Satisfy Wants and Needs

Most people have unlimited wants for goods and services. In the United States, most consumers are able to satisfy their basic needs. Marketers promote goods and services that will appeal to people's wants.

The more money you make, the more goods or services you can buy. However, few people have enough resources to satisfy all of their wants. **Resources** are items that people can use to make or obtain what they need or want. Examples of resources include money, fuel, and labor.

Resources limit the number of needs and wants people can satisfy. For example, you may want a new pair of jeans and a new camera. You may have only enough money to buy one of these things. Businesses and governments are influenced by the same problem. They lack the resources to do all the things that they want to do. To make the best use of limited resources, **determine** what your needs are and satisfy them first.

?ETHICS in Business

A Conflict of Interest

■ **Critical Reading** Life is full of important decisions. Think about the kinds of decisions that you make as you read the question below.

You work as an event planner for a local company. You are in charge of hiring a caterer for the company's 10th anniversary celebration. You have bids from four caterers in town. One of the bids is from a caterer who is an old friend. His bid is higher than the three others.

■ **Decision Making** Would your relationship with the caterer affect which company you would hire? Explain your answer.

Making the Most of Your Resources

Every day you make choices about how you will spend your resources to satisfy your needs and wants. You should make these important decisions carefully. You can make the most of your resources by making the best choices about what to buy.

✔ Reading Check   **Explain** How can you make the most of your resources?

The Decision-Making Process

The decision-making process can help you make good choices. It helps you to identify and consider your various alternatives and their consequences before you make a final decision. The essential steps of the process are outlined in **Figure 1.1**.

Figure 1.1 — *The Decision-Making Process*

Step 1: Identify the situation.
Whether the problem is one that occurs daily or comes up only a few times in a lifetime, identifying the problem is the first step.

Step 2: Identify possible courses of action.
Take time to think through the situation so you can identify and consider all the important alternatives.

Step 3: Determine the pros and cons.
Consider your values and goals when determining the advantages and disadvantages of each alternative. You can use this information to compare and evaluate your choices.

Step 4: Make a decision.
Use the information you gathered to rank the alternatives and make a decision. Once you have made your decision, you can plan how to reach your goal.

Step 5: Evaluate your decision.
Once your decision is put into effect, ask yourself whether you achieved the results you expected. Would you make the same choice again?

● **Making Better Choices** The decision-making process can be used to make all kinds of decisions. **What major decisions have you made recently?**

Personal Decision Making You may not use all of the steps of the decision-making process every time you buy something. When you decide to buy orange juice, you may always buy the same brand, such as Tropicana. However, many decisions need more careful thought. A bike can be an important purchase because you are likely to keep it for some time. When you consider what kind of bike to buy at what price, you will probably use all five steps of the decision-making process. The longer a decision will affect your life, the more you need to **evaluate** your options and consider the possible consequences.

Business Decision Making Competition among businesses is intense. For this reason, businesses must decide how to best use and conserve their resources. Businesses must make thoughtful decisions that are consistent with their goals. Business managers constantly make decisions. Most companies allow managers to make routine decisions independently. Higher-level business managers usually make more important decisions that affect the future of their companies.

Section 1.1

○ After You Read

Review Key Concepts

1. Describe the difference between public wants and private wants.
2. Define resources.
3. List the steps in the decision-making process.

Academic Skills

4. **Mathematics** In making a household budget, you determine that your basic needs require 75 percent of your monthly income. The items you listed as "wants" cost another 15 percent. If your monthly income is $2,500, how much are you spending on wants? How much do you have left to save?

CONCEPT **Number and Operations:**
Percents A percent is a ratio comparing a number to 100. It can also be represented as a fraction with 100 as the denominator. To find a decimal equivalent, divide the percent by 100. Multiply that decimal by the total amount to determine the dollar amount that it represents.

 For math help, go to the Math Appendix.

 Go to **connectED.mcgraw-hill.com** to check your answers.

Business Activities

Reading Guide

● Before You Read

Think about all the things a business must do in order to sell products and services.

Read to Learn

- Explain how profit and competition motivate businesses.
- List the activities businesses undertake when developing products and services.
- Explain how business impacts you and how you impact business.

The Main Idea

Businesses seek profit by providing goods and services in exchange for money. Companies thrive on competition, the contest between businesses to win customers. Competition and profit motivate businesses to continually strive to find new ways to satisfy customers.

Key Concepts

- How to Define Business
- Business Activities
- Business and You

Vocabulary

Key Terms

business
profit
competition
market research
consumer

Academic Vocabulary

You will find these words in your reading and on your tests. Make sure you know their meanings.

analyze
respond
affect
modify

Graphic Organizer

On a chart like the one below, list the six activities businesses undertake when developing products or services.

Business Activities
1 _____
2 _____
3 _____
4 _____
5 _____
6 _____

 Go to **connectED.mcgraw-hill.com** to print out this graphic organizer.

● **As You Read**

Think about the types of businesses in your community and the activities they do to sell their products and services.

How to Define Business

Whether you need to buy food for dinner or want a new bike, your wants and needs are usually satisfied by business. **Business** is any commercial activity that seeks profit by providing goods and services to others in exchange for money. **Profit** is the money left over after a business has paid the cost of providing its goods and services.

Businesses provide consumers and other businesses with necessities, such as food, clothing, housing, medical care, and transportation. Businesses also provide goods and services that make life easier and better. For entrepreneurs, owning a business also offers an opportunity to earn a good living.

✔ **Reading Check** **Apply** Think of your favorite retail store. What companies are its competition?

The Motive of Business: To Make a Profit

Businesses supply goods and services with the motivation of making profits. Without profit, a company cannot survive. Profit is the reward for satisfying the needs and wants of consumers and businesses. The wealth created by businesses benefits the entire community because businesses pay taxes and provide jobs.

Science/Tech TRENDS

The Green Revolution
In 1798, Thomas Malthus, the great social scientist, showed that even as population increases geometrically (2, 4, 8, 16,…), the food supply increases arithmetically (1, 2, 3, 4,…). He predicted that hunger and conflict would be the result. In the 1960s, the Green Revolution promised to eliminate hunger by increasing crop yields. This was accomplished by using genetics to develop new varieties of grains and educating farmers in the technology of agriculture. Between 1960 and 1990, food production increased 1,000 percent, famine decreased 20 percent, caloric consumption increased 25 percent, and people around the world saw a rise in their incomes and standard of living.

Locate Web sites where you can research how the technology of agriculture fueled the revolution in farming practices around the world. Look for information on irrigation strategies, the use of fertilizers and pesticides, and crop rotation. Write a few paragraphs about how farmers in countries, such as Mexico, increased their crop yields.

The Significance of Competition

Companies thrive on **competition**, the contest between businesses to win customers. For example, Skechers® competes with other shoe retailers, such as Foot Locker®, for business. Competition is a direct response to wants and needs.

Competition is possible because companies have the freedom to produce the products they think will be the most profitable. Because the American economy is based on freedom and voluntary exchange, buyers can compete to find the best products at the lowest prices. The result is that goods and services are produced and sold at the lowest possible cost.

Competition among businesses has never been greater than it is today. Some companies find a competitive edge by focusing on making high-quality products. Others compete by focusing on making products with no defects. However, simply making a high-quality, defect-free product is not enough to allow a company to stay competitive in the global marketplace. For companies to successfully compete in the global economy, they must offer quality products with outstanding service at competitive prices.

● **The Functions of Business** The success of a business depends on how well key activities are coordinated, managed, and performed. **Why should businesses use market research when making important decisions?**

Purestock/SuperStock

Business Activities

You might be surprised to know all the activities a business undertakes when developing products or services. They must:

- identify opportunities for products or services;
- evaluate the demand for products or services;
- obtain start-up money and operating capital;
- manage the production of goods and/or services;
- market the goods and/or services;
- keep records to satisfy government requirements and improve processes.

Some business activities should be supported by market research. **Market research** is the act of gathering and analyzing information about the wants, needs, and preferences of consumers in a certain market. Market research provides information that can help a business identify opportunities, **analyze** demand, and **respond** to consumer demand for goods and services.

Business Case Study

Surviving Tough Economic Times

To survive downturns, business owners must adapt—and get creative!

The Great Recession, which hit the United States in 2007, was the nation's worst economic slowdown since the Great Depression of the 1930s. Millions of Americans lost their jobs and had trouble finding new ones. Household wealth declined, and consumers severely cut back their spending. In the first two years, 170,000 businesses failed.

Longtime business owners' advice for surviving such a downturn? Take decisive action. Review expenses and make necessary cuts. Make sure staff are motivated and feel valued. Work hard to retain existing customers, and expand marketing efforts to attract new ones.

Creative business owners find ways to adapt, and even use the challenge to create the foundation for future growth. That's why 80 percent of business owners whose operations survived the Great Recession said it made them better entrepreneurs.

Active Learning

With a partner or in a team, identify a familiar local business and imagine you own it during tough economic times. Make a list of your customers' wants, needs, and preferences. Come up with three ideas for attracting customers to your business despite the recession. Present your list and ideas to the class.

Business and You

Businesses make many decisions that impact you, the consumer. A **consumer** is a person who uses goods or services. Businesses decide what goods and services to produce to meet the needs and wants of consumers. Businesses also **affect** consumers when they **modify** or discontinue products. The decision to stop manufacturing products is often because there is a decreasing demand for them. Businesses affect you as a wage earner. In order to make goods and provide services, businesses hire people to work.

Consumers also affect businesses. Consumers decide what kinds of goods and services they want and where they will buy them. You reward companies by making the decision to purchase their products. When consumers choose not to purchase a business's products or services, the business usually fails. To avoid failure, a business can modify its products, services, and business practices to satisfy consumers.

Section 1.2

After You Read

Review Key Concepts

1. Define business.
2. List the activities that every business undertakes when developing new products and services.
3. Describe why it is important to understand how business impacts you.

Academic Skills

4. **English Language Arts** Competition between similar businesses is one of the basic characteristics of the American economy. Competition is good for consumers because it provides choices. It also forces companies to improve quality and lower prices. Think of your favorite retail store. Write two or more paragraphs that describe the store and its competition, and explain how the competition among these businesses has affected you as a consumer.

5. **English Language Arts** In order to better understand the challenges and opportunities small businesses face, you decide to interview three business owners in your area. To prepare, identify three businesses that each provide a different type of product or service. Then write a series of questions that will help you understand how the products or services were chosen, whether they have changed in response to consumer demands, and how the business owner keeps in touch with consumers.

 Go to **connectED.mcgraw-hill.com** to check your answers.

Chapter 1 Review and Activities

Section 1.1 *Summary*	Section 1.2 *Summary*
A Look at Wants and Needs Everyone has wants and needs. Wants are things that you do not have to have to survive, but would like to have. Needs are things that you must have in order to survive. People use resources to make or obtain what they need or want. Resources limit the number of needs and wants people can satisfy. The decision-making process can help you make good choices and make the most of your resources by considering alternatives and their consequences. The longer a decision will affect your life, the more you need to consider all of the possible consequences.	**Business Activities** Businesses supply goods and services with the motivation of making profits. Companies thrive on competition, the contest between businesses to win customers. All businesses undertake these activities: identifying opportunities, evaluating demand, obtaining money, managing production, marketing to consumers and businesses, and keeping records. Consumers affect businesses by deciding what kind of goods and services to buy. Businesses affect consumers by making decisions about what products and services to offer and by providing jobs.

Vocabulary Review

1. On a sheet of paper, use each of these key terms and academic vocabulary terms in a sentence.

Key Terms

wants	business
needs	profit
goods	competition
services	market research
resources	consumer

Academic Vocabulary

determine	analyze
identify	respond
consider	affect
evaluate	modify

Review Key Concepts

2. Explain the differences between wants and needs.

3. Describe how resources limit the number of wants people and businesses can satisfy.

4. Explain how to use the decision-making process to make the most of your resources.

5. Explain how profit and competition motivate businesses.

6. List the activities businesses undertake when developing products and services.

7. Explain how business impacts you and how you impact business.

Critical Thinking

8. Explain how your wants and needs have changed over the years. How do you think they will change as you get older?

9. Consider the resources that you have that are limited and those that are plentiful. How do you decide to use your resources to get the things you want and need?

10. What do you think is the most important service available where you live? What would your life be like without this service?

11. Think of a small business in your community. What do you think that business could do to increase its profits?

12. A niche is a small, specialized segment of the market, usually based on customer needs discovered in market research. Think of a company that has succeeded by focusing on a niche market. What kinds of advantages and disadvantages does it have over a store that sells a variety of products?

13. As a consumer, what are some of the things about products and services that matter most to you? Explain your answer.

Write About It

14. Draw a Venn diagram of two overlapping circles. Label the left circle WANTS and the right circle NEEDS. Label the area where the two circles intersect BOTH. Then list your wants in the left circle and your needs in the right circle. List things that are both wants and needs in the area where the two circles overlap.

15. List three reasons why the decision-making process is important to use when making choices. Then describe a decision you recently made and explain how you made it.

16. Market research is the act of gathering and analyzing information about the wants, needs, and preferences of consumers in a certain market. Write two or more paragraphs to explain how market research can be used as a basis for business activities.

17. In a letter to your teacher, explain how the decisions businesses make affect you as a consumer.

18. Write a journal entry about how the decisions you make affect businesses.

19. Describe a situation in which you made a decision that greatly influenced your life.

Technology Applications

Spreadsheet

20. When there are limited resources, you need to make decisions about the best use of those resources. Imagine you are managing a concession stand at a school basketball game. Use a spreadsheet program to list and categorize all of the resources you will need to operate the concession stand for one day. Resources include equipment, money, supplies, and labor.

Business Ethics

Confidentiality Agreements

21. A confidentiality agreement is a contract that requires the employee or contractor not to reveal information that they acquire while working for an employer or client. Use library or Internet resources to research confidentiality agreements. Find several examples, and write a report detailing their similarities and explaining their importance.

Applying Academics to Business

English Language Arts

22. Select two words from this chapter that were unfamiliar to you or that you would like to know more about. Using your own words and ideas about how to represent sounds, write a pronunciation guide and a definition of each of the words. Then write two sentences using the words. Keep a personal glossary of words you have chosen and researched in this way.

Mathematics

23. When shopping for a new winter coat, you find one that suits your needs and costs $50. A more stylish coat that you want costs $65. Describe the difference between the two prices using a percentage.

CONCEPT **Number and Operations: Percents** To describe how much more the stylish coat costs, create a fraction using the difference in price as the numerator and the cost of the basic coat as the denominator. To convert the fraction to a percent, divide the numerator by the denominator and multiply the product by 100.

English Language Arts

24. Research and write a list of synonyms or closely related words and phrases for each of the following terms from the chapter: services, resources, business, and limit. For example, for the word goods, you might list merchandise, commodities, supplies, wares, and cargo. Choose two of the words in your list and write a sentence telling how their meanings are alike and different.

Mathematics

25. Imagine you have $100 for next month's expenses. Make a budget showing how you would spend the money on needs and wants. Express the relationship between needs and wants as a ratio. Compare your ratio with your classmates by writing equations or inequalities.

CONCEPT **Algebra: Equations and Inequalities** Equations and inequalities are used to describe the relationship between two algebraic expressions. Equations consist of two equivalent numbers or expressions with an equal sign between them. An inequality consists of two nonequivalent numbers or expressions with a "greater than" ($>$) or a "less than" ($<$) sign between them.

Active Learning

Write an Ethics Policy

26. Many problems and ethical conflicts can be avoided if business owners communicate their ethical expectations to their employees. Pair up with a classmate and imagine that you are the co-owners of a small accounting business. Work together to write an ethics policy that offers general ethical guidelines and specific ways to deal with different situations.

Business in the Real World

Making Business Decisions

27. Interview the manager or owner of a local small business. Find out about the sources of information he or she uses in making business decisions. Ask how he or she evaluates the information before acting upon it. Does he or she use the decision-making model described in this chapter? Write two or more paragraphs to describe the ways that person evaluates information.

Real LIFE skills

INTERPERSONAL SKILLS

28. The strength of your interpersonal skills can make or break how successful you are in the workplace. Interpersonal skills are essentially people skills—the nontechnical, intangible, personality-specific skills that determine your strengths as a leader, listener, negotiator, and conflict mediator. Write a one-page report that explains why it is important for businesses to have employees with good interpersonal skills.

 **Business CAREERS**

FIND YOUR DREAM JOB

29. Locate the Occupational Outlook Handbook Web site. Click on the "OOH Search/A-Z Index" link and enter the search term "Tomorrow's Jobs" to read about the future job market. Then write a one-page report about this topic. Conclude your report with a list of things you could do now to prepare yourself to pursue the occupation.

Role Play

THE IMPORTANCE OF BUSINESS

30. Situation You are an assistant manager for a company that makes household appliances. Your manager has asked you to put together a presentation about the activities of business for its new sales associates.

Activity Prepare a presentation that describes all of the activities that businesses undertake in order to sell products and services. Use magazines to find photos that represent all of the activities, and include the photos in your presentation. Then give the presentation to your classmates (sales associates).

Evaluation You will be evaluated on how well you meet the following performance indicators:

- Explain the motivations of business.
- Describe business activities.
- Discuss how competition impacts the company's decisions.
- Prepare a written report.

Standardized Test Practice

Directions Find the value of each algebraic expression. Write the letter of the answer on a separate piece of paper.

1. If $3x = 6x - 15$ then $x + 8 =$

- A 10
- B 11
- C 12
- D 13

2. Evaluate $5t + 4$ if $t = 3$.

- F 7
- G 13
- H 19
- J 21

 TEST-TAKING TIP When answering multiple-choice questions, read the question first, then read all the answer choices before choosing your answer. Eliminate answers you know are not right.

Economic Resources and Systems

> **Chapter Objectives** | After completing this chapter, you will be able to:

▶ Section 2.1 *Economic Resources*

- **Explain** how scarcity requires individuals and nations to make decisions about resources.
- **Describe** the four factors of production.

▶ Section 2.2 *Economic Systems*

- **Describe** the three basic economic questions each country must answer to make decisions about using its resources.
- **Contrast** the way a market economy and a command economy answer the three economic questions.

Ask AN EXPERT

Getting Your Financial Life in Order: The Proper Use of Credit Cards

Q: I know that many people have too much credit card debt. Why is credit card debt such a problem, and when is it appropriate to use a credit card?

A: The effect of compounding interest is to seriously increase the rate you are actually paying on credit card debt. For example, if you borrow $40,000 at an annual percentage rate of 5%, you'll pay almost $6,400, or 16% of the total if you make the minimum payment of $644 each month. Debt is generally a barrier to financial success. Use debt as an alternative to taking money out of savings or money tied up in another investment that earns more interest than the rate at which you are borrowing. When buying a home, keep in mind that interest on a mortgage loan is often tax deductible, allowing you to better manage a large loan.

Mathematics Franco borrowed $40,000 for four years at an annual percentage rate of 5%. He is scheduled to make a payment each month. His first payment includes interest due on the unpaid portion of the debt. The interest due is found by multiplying the unpaid amount by the annual rate divided by the number of payments made in a year.

How much of Franco's first payment is interest?

CONCEPT **Percents and Decimals** When solving real-life problems, it is often easier to convert percents to decimals. To convert, move the decimal point two places to the left, and drop the percent sign.

● **Scarcity** Many people have to deal with scarcity issues, such as having few funds to make purchases. Countries also deal with scarcity of resources. **How do you think nations deal with the problem of scarcity and determine how resources are to be used?**

Pixtal/AGE Fotostock

Economic Resources

Reading Guide

Before You Read

Think about the resources you use every day. Consider which resources are limited and which are not.

Read to Learn

- Explain how scarcity requires individuals and nations to make decisions about resources.
- Describe the four factors of production.

The Main Idea

Both people and countries must deal with the problem of scarcity. Nations do not have enough factors of production to produce everything that their population wants. Factors of production are all the economic resources necessary to produce a society's goods and services.

Key Concepts

- Making Economic Decisions
- Factors of Production

Vocabulary

Key Terms

- scarcity
- factors of production
- natural resources
- labor resources
- capital resources
- entrepreneurial resources
- entrepreneurship
- entrepreneur

Academic Vocabulary

You will find these words in your reading and on your tests. Make sure you know their meanings.

- factors
- processed
- labor
- individuals

Graphic Organizer

Write the four factors of production in a figure like the one below.

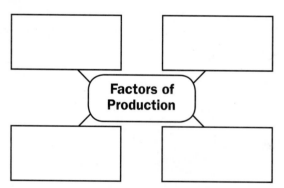

 Go to **connectED.mcgraw-hill.com** to print out this graphic organizer.

Making Economic Decisions

Just as individuals have to deal with a shortage of resources, so do societies. In this case resources are the items that go into the making of goods and services. This lack of resources is called scarcity. The principle of scarcity states that there are limited resources for satisfying unlimited wants and needs.

Because resources are in limited supply, to have one thing may mean giving up something else. For example, a restaurant owner may forgo plans for a costly new décor to have more money to put into kitchen equipment. A city government might decide to cut expenses for most services to be able to hire more police officers. When dealing with scarcity, it is important to think of the best way to use the item that is in short supply.

✔ **Reading Check** **Identify** What is scarcity?

Factors of Production

Factors of production are all the economic resources necessary to produce a society's goods and services, such as the wheat that grows in the ground, the tractor that harvests it, the labor that turns it into flour, and the distribution system that delivers it to the marketplace. There are four **factors** of production: natural resources, labor resources, capital resources, and entrepreneurial resources.

<aside>
● As You Read

Think of a product you own. What factors of production were involved in creating it?
</aside>

International Business

Global Marketplace
More businesses that used to operate exclusively within the United States now market their products around the world. From farmers to fast-food franchisees to theme-park operators, businesspeople in every sector of the economy are considering entering the global marketplace. Even though companies may operate successfully in the U.S. market, an increasing number of them are thinking about "going international."

Examples of Language Across Cultures
Q: In Italian, how do you say: "Hello, how are you?"
A: Salve, come sta? (pronounced: Sălvā, kōmā stă?)

What are some reasons a company might choose to enter a foreign market? What are some questions companies should ask before they enter a foreign market?

Natural Resources

Natural Resources are raw materials from nature that are used to produce goods. Trees, water, and grains are natural resources. Natural resources can often be **processed** in various ways to create goods. Even synthetic or artificially produced materials are made by combining or changing natural resources. For example, nylon is a synthetic material derived from coal, water, and air.

The economy of many countries is primarily based on its natural resources. For example, some Latin American countries rely on their coffee and banana crops. Other countries, such as Japan, have little land and scarce natural resources and must get them from somewhere else.

Some natural resources, such as wheat and cattle, are *renewable*. They can be reproduced. You can breed cattle to make more cattle. Other resources are limited, or *nonrenewable*. Coal, iron, and oil are nonrenewable. The amount of natural resources available to a society has a direct effect on its economy.

✔ **Reading Check**   **Contrast** How are renewable resources different from nonrenewable resources?

Business Case Study

The Technology and Innovation Economy

Science and math are keys to a competitive nation.

From the light bulb to the smartphone, innovations in science and technology have made the United States a leader in the global economy. But that leadership is slipping. To ensure a competitive workforce, U.S. schools must do a better job training students in skills necessary for technology work.

The STEM fields—science, technology, engineering, and math—provide the knowledge base for future tech innovations. Yet studies have shown that American-born college graduates are less proficient in STEM than students from many other nations. To address this gap, the President's Council of Advisors on Science and Technology has called for the creation of a Master Teachers Corps that would hire and develop 100,000 STEM teachers and pay the best-performing teachers higher salaries.

Immigration reform may be another key to solving the STEM gap. Over 50,000 foreign-born STEM graduates of American universities have moved abroad to work, leading to a tech "brain drain." Some experts are calling for changing immigration policies to make it easier for potential innovators to stay in the U.S. Together, they say, reforms in education and immigration would create a "brain gain," leading to continued U.S. competitiveness.

Active Learning

Your school offers many classes in STEM fields. Through your teacher or the school registrar, obtain a list of all the classes offered at your school. Read through the courses and compile your own list of all that are in STEM fields. Identify each course with S, T, E, or M (Science, Technology, Engineering, Mathematics). How many have you taken?

● An American Pastime
Capital goods are things used to create goods and services. The capital goods needed to create and sell the entertainment service of baseball include bats, balls, uniforms, and a ballpark. **Name two other capital goods in this picture.**

Labor Resources

Every type of business needs labor resources to produce goods and provide services. **Labor resources** are people who make the goods and services for which they are paid. Labor can be skilled or unskilled, physical or intellectual. Teachers, coal miners, bank managers, and farm workers are all human resources. Whether you are a cashier or a news anchor, you are a labor resource.

Capital Resources

Capital resources make up another factor of production. Capital resources are not the same as capital, or money. **Capital resources** are the things used to produce goods and services, such as buildings, materials, and equipment. They are also called capital goods. They include delivery trucks, supermarkets, cash registers, and medical supplies. A tractor that a farmer uses to harvest wheat is a capital resource. The headquarters of a major firm is a capital resource. If you are a writer or an accountant, the computer you use is a capital resource.

✔ **Reading Check** **Contrast** How are capital resources different from capital?

Entrepreneurial Resources

Entrepreneurial resources meet society's changing wants and needs. **Entrepreneurial resources** are used by the people who recognize opportunities and start businesses.

Entrepreneurship is the process of recognizing a business opportunity, testing it in the market, and gathering the resources necessary to start and run a business. An **entrepreneur** is an individual who undertakes the creation, organization, and ownership of a business. He or she accepts the risks and responsibilities of business ownership to gain profits and satisfaction. Being *entrepreneurial* means acting and thinking like an entrepreneur.

Entrepreneurial resources are different from **labor** resources, even though people provide both. Entrepreneurial resources are **individuals** who start and direct businesses to produce goods and services to satisfy needs or wants. Labor resources are people who produce the goods or services.

Section 2.1

After You Read

Review Key Concepts

1. Why do all nations face the problem of scarcity?
2. Identify one similarity and one difference between labor and entrepreneurial resources.
3. List five different natural resources.

Academic Skills

4. **Mathematics** Jeanne makes costume jewelry and sells it at art fairs. She has tried different pricing strategies and gets different results. Here is a chart of results over the last seven months:

Month	Price	Number of items sold
April	$10	300
May	$12	290
June	$14	280
July	$20	250
August	$15	280
September	$13	320
October	$12	340

Describe a graph that you might make from this data. Write a sentence or two about what it would show.

CONCEPT **Data Analysis and Probability: Line Graphs** A line graph is useful in displaying information about quantities that change over time. In this case, there are three variables to analyze: time, price, and quantity sold.

 For math help, go to the Math Appendix.

 Go to **connectED.mcgraw-hill.com** to check your answers.

Economic Systems

Reading Guide

● Before You Read

Consider the way you make decisions about how you will use your resources.

Read to Learn

- Describe the three basic economic questions each country must answer to make decisions about using its resources.
- Contrast the way a market economy and a command economy answer the three economic questions.

The Main Idea

Scarcity of economic resources forces every country to develop an economic system that determines how resources will be used. Each economic system has its advantages and disadvantages.

Key Concepts

- Basic Economic Questions
- Different Types of Economies

Vocabulary

Key Terms

economics
economic systems
market economy
price
supply

demand
equilibrium price
command economy
mixed economy

Academic Vocabulary

You will find these words in your reading and on your tests. Make sure you know their meanings.

relationship   observed
interact   control

Graphic Organizer

In the left oval, write notes about market economies. In the right oval, write notes about command economies. In the overlapping section, write notes that apply to both.

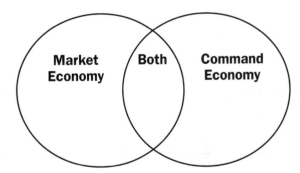

 Go to **connectED.mcgraw-hill.com** to print out this graphic organizer.

Basic Economic Questions

Economics is the study of how individuals and groups of individuals strive to satisfy their needs and wants by making choices. All societies have to make choices to deal with some form of scarcity. No society has enough productive resources available to produce everything people want and need. Societies make economic decisions about how to meet the needs of people by answering three basic economic questions.

What should be produced? Deciding to use a resource for one purpose means giving up the opportunity to use it for something else. This is called an *opportunity cost.*

How should it be produced? The methods and labor used as well as the quality of items produced are important factors. In a country with many workers but few capital resources, it is likely that little equipment and larger amounts of labor are used in producing goods.

Who should share in what is produced? In most societies, people can have as many goods and services as they can afford to buy. The amount of income people receive determines how many goods and services they can have.

● **As You Read**

People make choices every day. What economic decisions have you made recently?

Science/Tech TRENDS

Finding Natural Resources

Earth's crust contains more than 100 naturally occurring elements. For example, gold can be concentrated with other minerals in veins that form in igneous rocks deep underground. Forces related to plate tectonics uplift these rocks and form mountain ranges. Weathering and erosion expose the veins at Earth's surface, and some of the gold is eventually deposited as nuggets, flakes, or flour-size material in stream and river sediment. The gold is sometimes extracted directly from sedimentary rocks in the streambed. The use of satellite imagery has become a valuable tool for geologists. Geologists are now able to perform large-scale surveys of remote, unexplored regions for the presence of geologic structures and key minerals that may indicate areas favorable for mineral deposits.

WebQuest

Loacte Web sites where you can find satellite images of Earth's geologic structures. Look for companies whose business involves extracting natural resources from Earth's crust. List at least three companies. Write a paragraph or two about one of them, discussing how they might use satellite imagery to support research and exploration. Include a discussion about types of geologic structures.

Different Types of Economies

Economic systems are the methods societies use to distribute resources. Different economic systems answer the three basic economic questions in different ways. Two basic types of economic systems are a market economy and a command economy.

Market Economies

A **market economy** is an economic system in which economic decisions are made in the marketplace. The marketplace is where buyers and sellers meet to exchange goods and services, usually for money. A market economy can also be called a private enterprise system, the free enterprise system, or capitalism.

In a market economy, resources are privately owned. Citizens can own their own homes, land, and businesses. Business owners decide how their businesses will be run, what to produce and sell, and how much to charge. The government works to promote free trade and prevent unfair trade practices. Consumers choose their occupations and decide where to live, where to shop, and what to buy. People who have labor skills that are in demand earn higher incomes than those who do not. There is an uneven distribution of income. In a market economy, individuals are responsible for being informed and making careful decisions.

 **Reading Check** **Explain** What is the role of the individual within the free enterprise system?

Supply and Demand
The price of a TV set with a 3-inch screen was $125 in 1938, which would equal approximately $1,721 today. The cheapest model with a 12-inch screen was $445 ($6,256 today). Only 0.5% of U.S. households had a TV set in 1946, 55.7% had one in 1954, and 90% by 1962. *What factors do you think contributed to the large increase in TV ownership?*

Price, Supply, and Demand There is a **relationship** between price, supply, and demand. The price for an item is determined through the interactions of supply and demand. **Price** is the amount of money given or asked for when goods and services are bought or sold. **Supply** is the amount of goods and services that producers will provide at various prices. Producers want a price for their goods and services that will cover their costs and result in a profit. **Demand** is the amount or quantity of goods and services that consumers are willing to buy at various prices. The higher the price, the less consumers will buy. The lower the price, the more consumers will buy.

Supply and demand **interact** with each other, as shown in **Figure 2.1** on page 30. The **equilibrium price** is the point at which the quantity demanded and the quantity supplied meet.

Competition and Profit In a market economy, competition is **observed**. Competition between similar businesses is one of the basic characteristics of a free enterprise system. It encourages businesses to produce better products at lower prices to attract more customers. Entrepreneurs take risks to make profits. *Profit motive* is the desire to make a profit, and profit is the reward for taking a risk and starting a business.

● **The Effect of Price**
There is a direct relationship between price and the number of items produced and purchased. **What is the equilibrium price for DVDs? At that price, approximately how many DVDs will consumers demand?**

Figure 2.1 — *Supply, Demand, and Equilibrium*

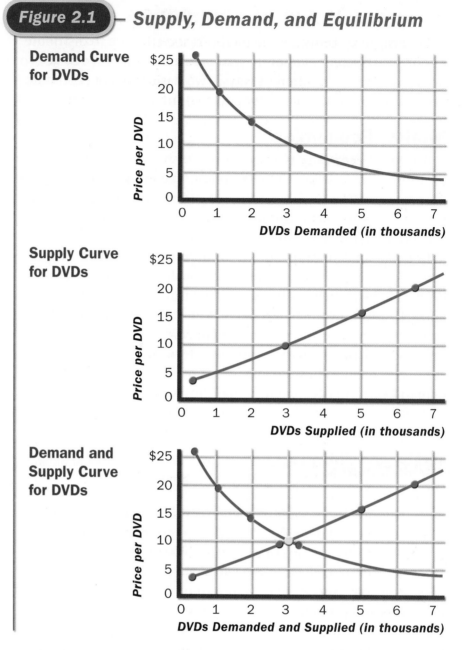

Demand Curve for DVDs

Price per DVD / DVDs Demanded (in thousands)

Supply Curve for DVDs

Price per DVD / DVDs Supplied (in thousands)

Demand and Supply Curve for DVDs

Price per DVD / DVDs Demanded and Supplied (in thousands)

Command Economies

A **command economy** is an economic system in which a central authority makes the key economic decisions. The government dictates what will be produced, how it will be produced, and who will get the goods. The government owns and controls all the resources and businesses. There is little choice of what to buy. Goods that are not considered necessities are often unavailable. Prices are controlled by the state. There is no incentive to produce a better product since there is no competition. Highly skilled workers may earn the same wages as low-skilled workers.

In a moderate command economy, also called *socialism,* there is some form of private enterprise. The state owns major resources, such as airlines and steel companies and makes the key economic decisions. Individuals own some businesses.

Mixed Economies

In reality, few nations have a pure market economy or a pure command economy. Most nations have a mixed economy in which private ownership of property and individual decision making are combined with government intervention and regulations. A **mixed economy** is an economy that contains both private and public enterprises. A mixed economy combines elements of capitalism and socialism. In the United States, for example, the government provides things such as defense, education, and aid to those with lower incomes. These are characteristics of a command economy. Yet the United States is primarily a market economy. That means the market makes more of the decisions regarding the allocation of resources than the government. This is also true of Japan. France, Germany, and Sweden are also classified as market economies. However, many of their major industries, such as steel and health care, are owned by the government. In other words, their governments have more **control** of the resources than U.S. and Japanese governments. These economies are considered more socialistic because of greater governmental control of resources.

● **As You Read**

Think about the freedoms you enjoy by living as a citizen in a market economy.

Section 2.2

○ After You Read

Review Key Concepts
1. How does a market system decide what will be produced?
2. In a market system, what determines how many goods and services an individual can buy?
3. Some nations can produce more goods with fewer workers than other countries that have more workers. How can that be true?

Academic Skills
4. **English Language Arts** An economy is not only affected by the decisions that are made in the marketplace. Factors such as natural disasters, war, or political changes can also impact an economic system. Observe a news program, or read a newspaper, magazine, or Internet article on a current event. Write a one- or two-page paper on how the event has impacted a national economic system.

5. **English Language Arts** Choose a country with a different economic system than the U.S. system. Use reference materials such as encyclopedias, Internet sources, history books, and magazines to gather research on the economic systems of both countries. Then prepare a three-minute presentation comparing and contrasting the systems. Illustrate at least one or more of the points you make using a visual aid.

 Go to **connectED.mcgraw-hill.com** to check your answers.

Chapter 2 Review and Activities

Section 2.1 *Summary*	Section 2.2 *Summary*
Economic Resources Just as individuals have to deal with a lack of resources, so do societies. Resources are necessary to make what people want and need. A shortage of resources is called scarcity. Individuals and groups of individuals have to deal with the problem of scarcity. Nations do not have enough economic resources or factors of production to satisfy all of the wants and needs of their people. Factors of production that go into making goods and services include natural, labor, capital, and entrepreneurial resources.	***Economic Systems*** Because all nations must deal with the scarcity of economic resources, each must set up an economic system that determines what and how much will be produced, how items will be produced, and who will receive what is produced. There are two primary types of economic systems. A market economy focuses on individuals answering the three economic questions through the interaction of supply and demand. In a planned economy, the government makes those decisions. Each country has attributes of both.

Vocabulary Review

1. On a sheet of paper, use each of these key terms and academic vocabulary terms in a sentence.

Key Terms

		Academic Vocabulary
scarcity	economic systems	factors
factors of production	market economy	processed
natural resources	price	labor
labor resources	supply	individuals
capital resources	demand	relationship
entrepreneurial resources	equilibrium price	interact
entrepreneurship	command economy	observed
entrepreneur	mixed economy	control
economics		

Review Key Concepts

2. Explain how scarcity requires individuals and nations to make decisions about resources.

3. Describe the four factors of production.

4. Describe the three basic economic questions that each country must answer to make decisions about using their resources.

5. Contrast how a market economy and a command economy answer the three economic questions.

Critical Thinking

6. Why does a country need an economic system?

7. In the last 10 to 20 years, several nations have moved toward having a market economy with less emphasis on planned economies. Why do you think some nations choose to adopt a more market-based economy?

8. Explain the reason for the difference between capital and capital goods.

9. Why is the profit motive considered an incentive in a market system?

10. Are some natural resources more valuable than others? Explain.

11. Countries have different levels of scarcity of their economic resources or factors of production. Think of two countries with different levels of scarcity for the same item. How does that affect the economic choices the nations make?

12. A company produces a new toy that is in great demand. It raises its price because there is no competition. Supplies cannot keep up with demand, so the company raises its price again. Are such price increases allowed in a market system? Should the government control the price? What are other toy producers likely to do?

Write About It

13. Write a diary entry about a career you might be interested in pursuing. What capital resources would you need?

14. In a one-page essay, describe at least two situations in which competition has been beneficial to you.

15. Which factor of production do you believe is the most important in the production of goods and services? Write an e-mail to your teacher. Give reasons for your opinion.

16. Write a paper either supporting or rejecting the following statement: "The market system in America focuses too much on individual achievement and not enough on the needs of society."

17. How does recycling help bridge the gap between renewable and nonrenewable resources? Write two or more paragraphs explaining your answer.

18. Create a table that compares and contrasts the quality differences between machine-made products and handmade products.

19. Write two or more paragraphs discussing reasons that trade-offs between labor and capital resources might impact the supply and demand for a product.

Technology Applications

Web Page Design
20. Research a country that has recently moved from a command economy to a mixed or market economy. Prepare a Web page that includes a report on the transitional process. Describe the conditions that led to it. Discuss the rights and responsibilities of businesses, consumers, and the government before and afterward.

Business Ethics

Ethics and Economies
21. Economists study how society distributes scarce resources to produce goods and services. They conduct research, collect and analyze data, monitor economic trends, and develop forecasts. Do you think ethics should be considered when making economic decisions? Explain your answer.

Applying Academics to Business

English Language Arts

22. The main part of the word *capitalism* is *capital*, which has several meanings and can be used in different contexts. Research the original word in Latin and tell what it means. Then read its various definitions and write a few sentences to demonstrate the meanings of the English word. Finally, list synonyms and a few related words.

Mathematics

23. List five things you buy often, several places where you can buy them, and the price charged at each place. Find the range and median of the prices for each item, and write a ratio comparing the range to the median. How would a ratio for a product with a small range of prices differ from the ratio for a product with a large range of prices?

CONCEPT **Data Analysis and Probability** The range of a set of data is the difference between the greatest and smallest elements in the set. The mean is the average of the elements in the set, the median is the middle number— or the average of the middle two numbers—when the elements are listed from least to greatest, and the mode is the most frequently occurring number.

English Language Arts

24. Select a current economic event that you are familiar with from reading the newspaper or watching the news. Think about how the economic event impacts the lives of those directly involved and those who are related to the event in some way. Try to find information about the positive and negative economic impacts of the event. Write two or three paragraphs summarizing the economic event and its impacts.

Mathematics

25. Because of warmer-than-expected weather in the winter months, the demand for heating oil has decreased. Sketch a graph showing what a demand curve for heating oil might look like.

CONCEPT **Algebra/Graphing/Quantitative Relationships** Two-dimensional line graphs can be used to show how two changing values act relative to one another. In this case, as time progresses, demand for heating oil declines.

Active Learning

Community Survey

26. Develop a list of five goods or services. Use a local business directory to determine how many firms in the community offer those goods or services. Rank the goods or services from those with the most competition to those with the least competition.

Business in the Real World

Competition and Product Differentiation

27. Select an article from a recent business publication on how one business is trying to differentiate its products or services in order to attract more customers. Write a letter to your teacher about how each competitor differentiates its products from others in the market.

Real LIFE skills

ASSESSING YOUR WORKPLACE BASIC SKILLS

28. The skills and qualities essential for success in the workforce include basic skills (reading, writing, mathematics, listening, and speaking), thinking skills, and personal qualities. Create a table of these skills and qualities. Then use a 1–5 ranking scale to evaluate your proficiency at these skills. Write an essay that describes how you plan to improve your greatest weakness.

Business CAREERS

FIND YOUR DREAM JOB

29. Locate the Occupational Outlook Handbook Web site. Click on the "OOH Search/A-Z Index" link and enter the job title "customer service representative." Then write a one-page report about this type of occupation. Conclude your report with a list of things you could do now to prepare yourself to pursue the occupation.

Role Play

THE ADVANTAGES OF MARKET ECONOMIES

30. Situation You are an economist who consults politicians and other economists in a country that wants to move from a command economy to a market economy.

Activity Prepare and give a presentation on the differences between a command economy and a market economy.

Evaluation You will be evaluated on how well you meet the following performance indicators:

- Explain the characteristics of a market economy, including: profit; competition; private ownership; the ability of individuals to start businesses; freedom of the individual to make career, consumer, and business decisions.

- Explain the characteristics of a command economy.

- Prepare a logical outline of the talk with correct grammar and punctuation.

Standardized Test Practice

Directions Choose the letter of the best answer. Write the letter for the answer on a separate piece of paper.

1. In the sentence below, which underlined word or phrase contains a spelling error?

<u>Cheryl's</u> paper comparing <u>capitalism and socialism</u> was written <u>hurriedly,</u> but she <u>recieved</u> a high mark from the teacher.

A   Cheryl's   C   hurriedly,

B   capitalism and socialism   D   recieved

 TEST-TAKING TIP Study for tests over a few days or weeks, and continually review class material. Do not wait until the night before and try to learn everything at once.

Economic Activity in a Changing World

> **Chapter Objectives** After completing this chapter, you will be able to:

▶ **Section 3.1** *U.S. Economic History*
- **Describe** the four types of economic shifts the United States has experienced.
- **Describe** what is shown by GDP, unemployment rate, rate of inflation, and national debt.

▶ **Section 3.2** *The Business Cycle*
- **Explain** how individuals and the government influence the economy.
- **Describe** the four stages of the business cycle.

Ask AN EXPERT

Understanding Financial Risk

Q: I am a drummer in a band. I can't decide if I should buy a new drum set now, or wait until next year when we go on the road. Should I buy now, or wait until next year and hope prices don't go up?

A: Financial risk is always a factor when making major purchasing decisions. You have identified one risk—inflation. Prices may go up, but they also may come down. If you need a loan to buy the drum set, changing interest rates represent another risk. You also have liquidity risk. If the band breaks up, how long will it take you to sell your drums so you can pay off your loan? Some risks can be evaluated mathematically, others cannot.

Mathematics You can calculate the effects of price and interest rate fluctuation on purchases. For example, if a drum set costs $7,500, and the interest rate for one year is 7 percent, the total cost will be $(0.07 \times \$7,500) + \$7,500 = \$8,025$. Calculate the total cost with interest for each of the scenarios in the comparison chart and determine the least expensive option.

CONCEPT **Comparison Charts** A chart can help in comparing different scenarios of price and interest rates.

Price	Interest Rate
$7,500	7%
$7,450	8%
$8,200	5%

Ilene MacDonald/Alamy

● **Ups and Downs** A market economy has its ups and downs. **How is the business cycle similar to a roller-coaster ride?**

U.S. Economic History

Reading Guide

Before You Read

Think of some factors that affect the health of the U.S. economy.

Read to Learn

- Describe the four types of economic shifts that the United States has experienced.
- Describe what is shown by GDP, the unemployment rate, rate of inflation, and national debt.

The Main Idea

Throughout the years, the U.S. economic system has changed. Each change affected what was produced and how people were employed. To gauge the health of our economic system, we use a variety of economic indicators.

Key Concepts

- The Changing U.S. Economy
- Measuring Economic Activity

Vocabulary

Key Terms

gross domestic product (GDP)
standard of living
inflation
deflation
budget deficit
national debt
budget surplus

Academic Vocabulary

You will find these words in your reading and on your tests. Make sure you know their meanings.

shifts
emphasis
sum
period

Graphic Organizer

Use a timeline like this one to indicate the changes in the U.S. economy from the 1700s to the 2000s. Mark the timeline to designate the following eras: Agricultural, Industrial, Production of Services, and Information Technology.

| 1700 | 1800 | 1900 | 2000 |

 Go to **connectED.mcgraw-hill.com** to print out this graphic organizer.

The Changing U.S. Economy

Sometimes major **shifts** in certain growth areas can change the **emphasis** of the U.S. economy. The United States has experienced four major economic shifts.

During the early 1600s, the colonists bartered, or traded, goods and services. This created our service-based economy. In the 1700s, farming was a common way of life. This formed the agriculture-based economy. In the mid-1850s, the Industrial Revolution enabled the advent of big machines for producing goods. This started the industry-based economy. The 1900s saw the rapid movement of information, with the invention of the computer. This created the information-based economy. Computers have transformed the ways that goods and services are produced, delivered, and sold.

While we live in the information age, we also still rely upon aspects of the other types of economies. Agriculture, industry, services, and information all contribute to the health of the U.S. economy.

> ● **As You Read**
>
> What changes have you seen in the economy in your lifetime?

Business Case Study

Innovate for Good

Businesses think big to combine financial success with sustainability

Can businesses be responsible stewards of the planet while still remaining profitable and competitive?

Yes, says the World Economic Forum (WEF), which recently issued a report highlighting 16 companies that are doing exactly this. These "new sustainability champions" include companies from India, Brazil, Costa Rica, and other emerging markets. They represent industries including banking, fishing, solar energy, water technology—and even cement production, one of the largest contributors to global warming.

These companies combine superior financial performance with sustainable, innovative business practices. Shree Cement in India, for example, developed the world's most energy-efficient process for making cement. Chinese air-conditioning manufacturer Broad Group invented a device to measure air pollution that fits inside a cell phone.

These companies have three things in common. They use innovation to turn challenges into opportunities. They are guided by a vision for sustainability. And they work to change the world around them to improve the way business is done.

> **Active Learning**
>
> Brainstorm in small teams about businesses in your community that you have seen advertising themselves as "green" or "sustainable." Call one or more of these businesses and ask about their philosophy of sustainability, as well as about specifics of their practices. Brainstorm ways the business could use innovation to be even more sustainable. Present your ideas to the class.

Measuring Economic Activity

Baseball fans know that batting averages, strikeouts, RBIs, and ERAs are figures used to measure a player's performance. Figures are also used to measure economic performance. These figures are called *economic indicators*. They measure things such as how much a country is producing, whether its economy is growing, and how it compares to other countries.

Gross Domestic Product

One way of telling how well an economy is performing is to measure how many goods and services it produces. The total value of the goods and services produced in a country in a given year is called its **gross domestic product (GDP)**. GDP is one of the most important indicators of the status of an economy. To calculate the GDP, economists compute the **sum** of goods and services sold to businesses, consumers, the government, and other countries. The United States has a very high GDP compared to other countries.

Standard of Living

Another important measure of a country's economic health is its standard of living. The **standard of living** is the level of material comfort as measured by the goods and services that are available. The more goods and services produced per person, the higher the standard of living.

The United States has a high standard of living largely because of its productive workforce. The standard of living refers to the amount of goods and services people can buy with the money they have. In the free-enterprise system, the wealth created by businesses benefits the entire community because businesses pay taxes and provide jobs.

?ETHICS in Business

Environmental Awareness

■ **Critical Reading** Life is full of important decisions. Think about the kinds of decisions that you make as you read the question below.

You are a purchasing agent for a large furniture manufacturer. You have received several bids from lumber companies for a supply of teak, a very dense and decay-resistant type of wood. The lowest bid comes from a lumber company that has been known for not placing a strong emphasis on local environmental concerns, especially resource depletion, when it cuts down trees.

■ **Decision Making** How does the lumber company's reputation affect your decision? Explain your answer.

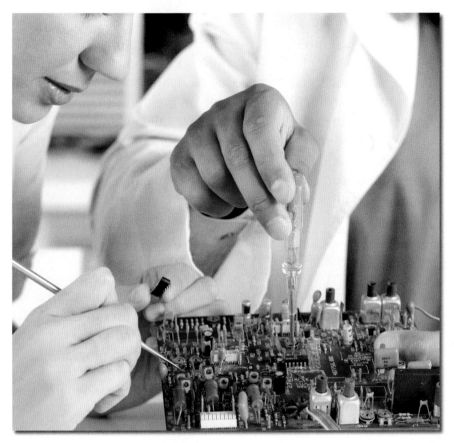

mediaphotos/Getty Images

● **A Changing Economy**
Our economy has been affected by many developments. The development of information technology has transformed the ways goods and services are produced. **What other changes have affected the U.S. economy?**

Unemployment Rate

The *unemployment rate* measures the number of people who are able and willing to work but cannot find work during a given **period**. Changes in the unemployment rate show whether an economy is picking up or slowing down.

✔ **Reading Check** **Identify** What does the unemployment rate measure?

Rate of Inflation

Another important measure of economic strength is the rate of inflation. **Inflation** is a general increase in the price of goods and services. With inflation, one's buying power decreases because it costs more to buy goods and services.

Inflation has many causes. It can occur after a war because scarce resources were transferred to the war effort. Inflation can be caused by increases in the costs of raw materials, expenses, and salaries. Inflation can also occur when the government allows too much money to circulate in the economy.

When the supply of goods is greater than demand, deflation can result. **Deflation** is a general decrease in the price of goods and services. When an economy produces more goods than people want, sellers have to lower prices and cut production. As a result, people have less money to buy goods, so the demand continues to go down.

Worker Shortage
In recent years, Japan has found that it does not have enough workers. Corporations have had to react by retaining their skilled laborers. Toyota Motor Corporation is preparing for a shrinking workforce by offering one-year contracts to top employees who turn 60. Japan's largest untapped source is its women. *What steps do you think Japan might take to ease its current labor shortage?*

National Debt

Countries can run up large debts. The main source of income for a government is taxes. Governments use tax money to pay for programs such as defense, education, and Social Security. When the government spends more on programs than it collects in taxes, the difference in the amount is called a **budget deficit**. To pay for the difference, governments borrow money from the public, banks, and even other countries. The total amount of money a government owes is its **national debt**. If the debt gets too large, a nation can become dependent on other nations or unable to borrow more money. This is the case in many developing nations.

Sometimes, a government's revenue can exceed its expenditures. When a government's revenue exceeds its expenditures during a one-year period, it has a **budget surplus**. The United States experienced several years of budget surpluses in the late 1990s. The government often uses a surplus to cut taxes, reduce the national debt, or increase spending for certain programs.

Section 3.1

After You Read

Review Key Concepts
1. When did the service-based economy begin?
2. What do economic indicators measure?
3. What is the difference between a budget surplus and a budget deficit?

Academic Skills
4. **Mathematics** Suppose a recent study shows the U.S. Gross Domestic Product (GDP) is $11.5 trillion. The study also shows that personal spending accounts for 70.4 percent of the total GDP. How much is personal spending in dollars?

CONCEPT Number and Operations: Percents
A percent is a ratio comparing a number to 100. It can also be represented as a fraction, with 100 as the denominator. To find a decimal equivalent, divide the percent by 100. Multiply that decimal by the total amount to determine the dollar amount that it represents.

 For math help, go to the Math Appendix.

 Go to **connectED.mcgraw-hill.com** to check your answers.

The Business Cycle

Reading Guide

● Before You Read

Think about the ups and downs local businesses experience in a market economy.

Read to Learn

- Describe the four stages of the business cycle.
- Explain how individuals and government influence the economy.

The Main Idea

In a market economy, there is an economic cycle, which includes four stages: prosperity, recession, depression, and recovery. These are also the four stages of the business cycle. In the last few decades, we have experienced the economic cycle a number of times.

Key Concept

- Guiding the Economy
- Four Stages of the Business Cycle

Vocabulary

Key Terms

business cycle   depression
prosperity   recovery
recession

Academic Vocabulary

You will find these words in your reading and on your tests. Make sure you know their meanings.

enormous   purchase
policy   decline

Graphic Organizer

On a figure like the one below, label each of the four boxes with the appropriate stage of the business cycle.

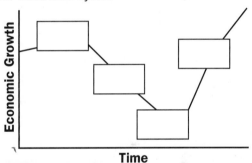

 Go to connectED.mcgraw-hill.com to print out this graphic organizer.

Guiding the Economy

The U.S. economy is shaped by a mix of public and private forces. Individuals have an **enormous** role on the market for goods and services. Congress and the President enact laws that impact fiscal **policy**. Whenever tax money is spent, it has an effect on the economy. These expenditures are often planned to guide the economy. The Federal Reserve, informally called "the Fed," is a government agency that guides the economy by regulating the amount of money in circulation, controlling interest rates, and controlling the amount of money loaned. State and local governments may also take steps to influence their local economies.

● **As You Read**

One country's economy can affect other countries. How does the economy of your community affect you and your family?

Four Stages of the Business Cycle

Economies go through ups and downs. This can happen for many reasons, including wars, foreign competition, changes in technology, and changes in consumer wants. Over long periods of time, these changes form patterns. For example, the U.S. economy went through slumps in the 1930s, the 1950s, the 1970s, and the early part of 2000. These slumps in economic activity with increased unemployment were followed by new waves of increased productivity and rises in GDP. The rise and fall of economic activity over time is called the **business cycle**. There are four stages of the business cycle—prosperity, recession, depression, and recovery. **Figure 3.1** illustrates the business cycle.

In a global economy, one country's economy can affect other trading partners. If a nation is in a period of economic expansion, it may **purchase** goods and services from other countries, promoting expansion in those countries.

✔ **Reading Check** **Identify** What are the four stages of the business cycle?

Figure 3.1 — *Business Cycle Model*

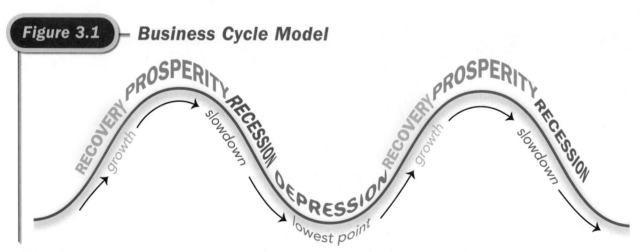

● **The Business Cycle** The repeated rise and fall of economic activity over time is called a business cycle. **Does every business cycle have all four of these stages?**

Prosperity

When unemployment is low, production of goods and services is high, new businesses open, and there is prosperity. **Prosperity** is a peak of economic activity. This condition spreads throughout the economy. Wages are usually higher, so workers have more income. There is a greater demand for goods to be produced. More people can buy houses, which creates more work for builders. People also want to buy more goods from other countries, which benefits those countries as well.

Recession

During a **recession**, economic activity slows down. Businesses produce less, so they need fewer workers. As the unemployment rate increases, people have less money to spend. Without a steady source of income, unemployed workers consume fewer goods and services. The general drop in the total production of goods and services makes GDP decline.

In a recession there are downturns in many industries. A downturn in one industry can affect others. For example, a recession in the auto-making industry can lead to a recession in businesses that make parts for cars. When this happens, it is called the ripple effect. Because of the ripple effect, downturns in major industries can bring on a recession.

● **As You Read**

When an economy enjoys prosperity, there is a greater demand for goods. What new technologies were developed in the last few decades as a result of good economic conditions?

Science/Tech TRENDS

Jobs in Your Future

Job opportunities result from the relationships between the population, the labor force, and the demand for goods and services. Population changes influence the demand for goods and services. When the population changes, the size and makeup of the labor force change as well.

The Bureau of Labor Statistics recently released a report stating that nearly all the 30 fastest-growing occupations between now and 2022 are related to health care and construction. These occupations include home health aides, industrial psychologists, supervisors, and trade workers.

WebQuest

Locate Web sites where you can research population trends between now and 10 years from now. Make some predictions about how the demand for goods and services will change over the next 10 years.

● **Different Scenes for Different Stages of the Business Cycle** When workers go on strike, they usually want more wages or benefits. **At what stage of the business cycle would this type of event most likely occur?**

"Depressionproof" During the Great Depression, millions of people lost their homes and livelihoods. However, a large percentage of middle-class Americans were able to keep their jobs. These people were in professions considered "depressionproof." *What professions do you think are more secure during a depression, and why?*

Depression

During a depression there is high unemployment and low production of goods and services. A **depression** is a deep recession that affects the entire economy and lasts for several years. It can be limited to one country but usually spreads to related countries. During a depression, many people are out of work, and fewer goods and services are produced. There is also a lot of unused manufacturing facilities. Fortunately, depressions are rare.

The stock market crash on October 29, 1929, or "Black Tuesday," marked the beginning of the Great Depression. Between 1929 and 1933, GDP fell from approximately $103 billion to $55 billion—a **decline** of nearly 50 percent. At the same time, the number of people out of work rose nearly 800 percent—from 1.6 million to 12.8 million. During the worst years of the Depression, one out of every four workers was jobless. Even workers who had jobs suffered. The average manufacturing wage, which had reached 55 cents an hour by 1929, plunged to five cents an hour by 1933.

Many banks across the country failed. The FDIC did not exist at the time, so depositors were not protected. To prevent panic withdrawals, the federal government declared a "bank holiday" in March 1933. Every bank in the country closed for several days, and many never reopened. The money supply fell by one-third. Currency was in such short supply that towns, counties, chambers of commerce, and other civic bodies resorted to printing their own money.

✔ Reading Check **Describe** What happens to the economy during a depression?

Andrew Resek/McGraw-Hill Education

Recovery

During a recovery, production starts to increase. A **recovery** is a rise in business activity after a recession or depression. People start going back to work and have money to purchase goods and services. The new demand for goods and services stimulates more production, and the GDP grows. Recovery leads back to prosperity as new businesses open and existing businesses increase productivity.

A recovery can take a long time or it can happen quickly. In 1939, the United States was only beginning to recover from the depression when World War II began. During the war, the United States recovered much faster because of the demand for war production.

During a recovery, some businesses innovate—meaning that they bring out new goods and services. These innovations can be different from what the businesses previously produced. They could also be different from what their competitors make. If the innovation is popular with consumers, sales increase dramatically, per unit costs decrease, and profitability increases. Businesses grow and economic activity soars.

Section 3.2

After You Read

Review Key Concepts
1. What is the stage that follows a recession or depression?
2. What is the difference between a recession and a depression?
3. Why may innovation play an important role in the recovery stage of the business cycle?

Academic Skills
4. **English Language Arts** The business cycle is often described using terms that describe how large bodies of water behave. Two of those terms are *ebb and flow* and *ripple effect.* Write a few sentences about each of these terms. Explain what they mean and why they are good metaphors for different aspects of the business cycle.

5. **English Language Arts** The words listed below are all synonyms, or closely related in meaning. They all can be used to describe negative movement in the business cycle. Notice that some of the words imply a more serious fall in the economy than others. Rewrite the list so that the words are, in your best judgment, ordered from least serious to most serious. Then write a few sentences explaining why you ordered the words as you did.

recession   slump   depression
decline   downturn

 Go to **connectED.mcgraw-hill.com** to check your answers.

Chapter 3 *Review and Activities*

Section 3.1 *Summary*	Section 3.2 *Summary*
U.S. Economic History Throughout the years, our economic system has evolved and changed. In colonial times, the United States had begun its service-based economy. The 1700s saw the rise of the agriculture-based economy. The Industrial Revolution in the l850s brought about the industrial economy, characterized by the large-scale manufacturing of goods. During the latter part of the 20th century, the information technology economy revolutionized the business world. To measure the health of our economic system, we use a variety of economic indicators, including GDP, unemployment rate, rate of inflation, and national debt.	**The Business Cycle** In a global economy, one country's economy can affect the economy of its other trading partners. The Fed adjusts monetary policies to try to level out the ups and downs of the economy. An economic cycle includes four stages: prosperity, recession, depression, and recovery. Prosperity is the peak of economic activity. Recession is a slowdown in economic activity. Depression is a deep recession that affects the entire economy and lasts for several years. A recovery is a rise in business activity after a recession or depression. Fortunately, the United States has not had a depression since the l930s.

Vocabulary Review

1. On a sheet of paper, use each of these key terms and academic vocabulary terms in a sentence.

Key Terms

gross domestic product (GDP)	budget surplus
standard of living	business cycle
inflation	prosperity
deflation	recession
budget deficit	depression
national debt	recovery

Academic Vocabulary

shifts	enormous
emphasis	policy
sum	purchase
period	decline

Review Key Concepts

2. Describe the four types of economic shifts the United States has experienced.

3. Describe what is shown by GDP, unemployment rate, rate of inflation, and national debt.

4. Explain how individuals and the government influences the economy.

5. Describe the four stages of the business cycle.

Critical Thinking

6. Would the cars made in this country by a foreign-owned company be included in GDP? Why or why not?

7. Which would be included in GDP: babysitting at home or working at a day-care center?

8. Why are people who are unemployed but not looking for work not included in the unemployment figures?

9. Why is inflation especially difficult for retired people?

10. Why might deflation be a bad thing?

11. Suppose you go to a store to buy a soda but notice the price is 20 cents higher than it was last week. Other prices are unchanged. Is this an example of inflation? Why or why not?

12. In which stage or stages of the business cycle would there be more personal bankruptcies? More business formations?

13. Explain why the standard of living is higher in the United States than in many other countries.

Write About It

14. Many economists believe that some unemployment is necessary because many of the unemployed are between jobs. Write an essay explaining why this might be true.

15. To pay for expenses, the federal government issues bonds. Many of these bonds are bought by foreign countries. Write a paragraph indicating whether you think this is good or bad for America.

16. Write a letter to your school counselor that explains how understanding the unemployment rate can be beneficial to you as you look for a job.

17. Assume the current inflation rate is 3 percent. Write an e-mail to your teacher explaining how that might help you decide where to put your savings.

18. Write a summary of the pros and cons of your starting a new business in the prosperous stage of the business cycle.

19. The unemployment rate in your community has increased considerably because of the closure of two firms. Write a letter to the editor of the newspaper explaining what steps you might take in your business as a result.

Technology Applications

Web Pages

20. You want to do business on the Internet. You know what kind of business you want to open. Use the Internet to research several businesses that might be considered your competition. Write a report that evaluates their Web sites. Print pages from each Web site and include them in your report.

Business Ethics

Dealing with Ethical Systems

21. You are the president of a biotechnology company that produces vaccines. A foreign government has asked to buy a vaccine to help stop a deadly infectious disease, but the negotiator expects a bribe. Should you look the other way so that you can get the vaccine to people who need it?

Applying Academics to Business

English Language Arts

22. Major novelists of the 1920s, a time of prosperity in the United States, and the 1930s, the time of the Great Depression, include John Steinbeck, William Faulkner, F. Scott Fitzgerald, Ernest Hemingway, and John Dos Passos. Find out more about their work and the work of other writers of the period. Make a bibliography of novels that portray everyday life during the 1920s and 1930s. Choose one to read and write a review of it to share with your classmates.

Mathematics

23. The Agriculture sector of the U.S. economy produces $\frac{1}{50}$ of the GDP while the Industry sector produces 18 percent. The rest is produced by the Service sector. What percent of GDP is contributed by the service sector?

CONCEPT **Number and Operations:**
Comparing Numbers After converting the two numbers $\frac{1}{50}$ and 18 percent so that they are either both percents or both fractions, they can be added together and then subtracted from the whole to find the part contributed by the service sector.

English Language Arts

24. The words Internet, interdependent, and international have the same prefix. Write a sentence in your own words telling what the prefix is and what it means. Give examples of other words that use the same prefix, and write sentences using them. Do the same for productivity and prosperity. Then check your work by looking in a dictionary or other resource.

Mathematics

25. Find unemployment statistics for the years 1933, 1944, 1955, 1966, 1977, 1988, 1999, and the most recent year for which statistics are available. Present the information in a bar graph. Write a few sentences discussing the reasons for the differences shown in the graph.

CONCEPT **Data Analysis and Probability:**
Bar Graphs Bar graphs are great for making multiple comparisons, showing frequencies, and displaying trends. They are sometimes confused with histograms, which are used to graphically show the distribution of a set of data. In this case, the bar graph will show how unemployment levels rose and fell with the cycles of the economy.

Active Learning

Track News Stories

26. During a two-week period, read the newspaper or watch the national news on television. Pick out three articles or report on three sequences of television news programming that relate to one of the topics discussed in this chapter, such as unemployment, inflation, deflation, and national debt. Write a report or give an oral presentation to the class on your findings.

Business in the Real World

Interview a Businessperson

27. Identify a businessperson in your community who has been in business for several years and experienced a number of business cycles. Interview the business owner to find out how his or her company performed during periods of recession and periods of prosperity. Then write a report summarizing the business owner's responses.

Real LIFE skills

ASSESSING YOUR SKILLS

28. These skills are needed by all employees: creative thinking, decision making, and problem solving. Give an example of how you have implemented each skill in the last month. Then indicate which skills you believe you are fairly good at doing. Recommend how you can become better at doing the skill or skills in which you need work.

 **Business CAREERS**

FIND YOUR DREAM JOB

29. Locate the Occupational Outlook Handbook Web site. Click on the "OOH Search/A-Z Index" link and enter the job title "economist." Then write a one-page report about this type of occupation. Conclude your report with a list of things you could do now to prepare yourself to pursue the occupation.

Role Play

ANALYZING ECONOMIC INDICATORS

30. Situation You are an intern for a federal bureau that collects and analyzes economic data. You have been asked to research recent economic indicators.

Activity Choose a sector of the economy to measure how well the economy is doing. Give a presentation to the bureau's economists. Sectors include housing construction, gross domestic product, and retail and food services.

Evaluation You will be evaluated on how well you meet the following performance indicators:

• Research an economic sector.

• Interpret economic data.

• Answer questions about your findings.

• Present clear and relevant information.

• Project your voice, and use correct grammar and English.

Standardized Test Practice

Directions Read the paragraph and answer the question that follows. Write the letter for the answer on a separate piece of paper.

Some reasons for unemployment represent more of a problem for the economy than others. For example, recently graduated students and those who are voluntarily looking for a new job are only temporarily unemployed. Some workers are seasonal workers and only unemployed during part of the year. However, those workers who have lost their jobs because the economy has slowed down may be out of work until the economy recovers.

1. Which best describes the way the paragraph is organized?

A sequence of events

B comparison

C statement and example

D cause and effect

 TEST-TAKING TIP When studying from a textbook, read the chapter summaries. They usually do a good job at summarizing important points.

Business Ethics and Social Responsibility

Chapter Objectives After completing this chapter, you will be able to:

▶ **Section 4.1** *Business Ethics*
- **Define** ethics and business ethics.
- **Describe** why ethical behavior is good for business.
- **List** the steps for dealing with an ethical dilemma.

▶ **Section 4.2** *Social Responsibility*
- **Define** what is meant by the social responsibility of business.

Ask

AN EXPERT

The Time Value of Money

Q: This past summer I worked as a carpenter. I saved close to $4,000. I'm thinking about buying a new computer with my savings. My father said that if I didn't spend the money, but let it sit in my savings account without touching it, I would be a millionaire when I retire. Could that be true?

A: Your father is teaching you the time value of money. Because of compounding interest, savings can grow substantially over time. That is why it is important to start saving and investing money early in your life.

Mathematics The balance of your account in the future is known as the *future value* of your starting principal. Calculate the future value of your $4,000 in 50 years at a 5% interest rate.

CONCEPT **Calculating Future Value** To find a formula for future value, write P for your starting principal, r for the rate of return expressed as a decimal, and n for the number of years in the future. (Assume that the interest rate is 5%, so r equals .05). Your balance will grow according to the following formula:

$$FV = P(1 + r)^n$$

Photo by Keith Weller, USDA-ARS

● **Duty-Bound** Businesses and customers both have ethical responsibilities. **What are some of your ethical responsibilities?**

Business Ethics

Reading Guide

Before You Read

Think about an example of an ethical business you have read or heard about and the reasons you consider it to be ethical.

Read to Learn

- Define ethics and business ethics.
- Describe why ethical behavior is good for business.
- List the steps for dealing with an ethical dilemma.

The Main Idea

Ethics are moral principles by which people conduct themselves personally, socially, and professionally. Business ethics are rules that guide the behavior of a business and its employees. Business ethics are generally based on moral principles. In business, good ethics is beneficial for long-term profitability and success.

Key Concepts

- The Nature of Ethics
- Ethics as Good Business
- Ethical Questions

Vocabulary

Key Terms

ethics
business ethics
code of ethics

sweatshop
conflict of interest

Academic Vocabulary

You will find these words in your reading and on your tests. Make sure you know their meanings.

principles
conduct

encounter
alternative

Graphic Organizer

Print or draw a graphic like the one below. In the left column, list three questions you need to ask when facing an ethical dilemma. In the right column, list the five steps to take to decide which choice to make.

Ethical Questions	Steps to Take
1.	1.
	2.
2.	3.
	4.
3.	5.

 Go to **connectED.mcgraw-hill.com** to print out this graphic organizer.

The Nature of Ethics

Ethics are moral **principles** by which people **conduct** themselves personally, socially, or professionally. For example, you do not cheat on a test or lie to friends or your family because of your personal honor and integrity. For the good of society, you may recycle to take care of the environment. **Business ethics** are rules based on moral principles about how businesses and employees ought to conduct themselves. Most businesses are committed to providing safe products, creating jobs, treating their employees fairly, protecting the environment, and being truthful about their financial situation.

The effects of unethical behavior by customers are not always obvious. However, to make up for problems caused by unethical behavior, businesses have to charge more for their products. As a result, customers have to pay more.

Different cultures, businesses, and industries have different ethical standards. For example, in some cultures, including the United States, excessive gift giving is considered bribery, which is unethical. Bribery occurs when gifts, money, or favors are offered to encourage a business deal. In other cultures, excessive gift giving is overlooked or considered ethical.

> ✔ **Reading Check** **Identify** What are three kinds of ethics?

● **As You Read**

Think about some businesses that you consider to be run ethically. In what ways are they ethical?

PhotoAlto/SuperStock

● **Business Ethics** Businesses have a set of moral principles that they follow. **In what ways can a business behave ethically toward its employees?**

Law and Ethics

Ethics involve a system of moral principles that govern the appropriate conduct for a person or group. Laws involve rules for conduct that may be used to punish violators. In business, people follow rules as well as a code of ethics. A **code of ethics** is a set of guidelines for maintaining ethics in the workplace. Most businesses follow their own code of ethics. **Figure 4.1** includes some findings about how employees feel about ethical behavior in their workplace.

Many unethical behaviors lead to the passage of legislation that makes those behaviors illegal. In the United States, bad working conditions are not only unethical, they are also illegal. On March 25, 1911, a fire at the Triangle Shirtwaist Factory Company in New York City killed 146 workers—mostly young female immigrants. The business's inadequate exit doors and fire escapes along with overcrowded conditions led to the deaths of the workers. This industrial tragedy brought about changes in laws governing conditions in sweatshops. A **sweatshop** is a shop or factory in which workers are employed for long hours at low wages and under unhealthy conditions.

The Occupational Safety and Health Administration (OSHA) is a division of the U.S. Department of Labor. OSHA sets and enforces work-related health and safety rules. Other agencies protect consumers, address discrimination in the workplace, and promote truthfulness in financial reporting.

Figure 4.1 — *Ethical Observations by Employees*

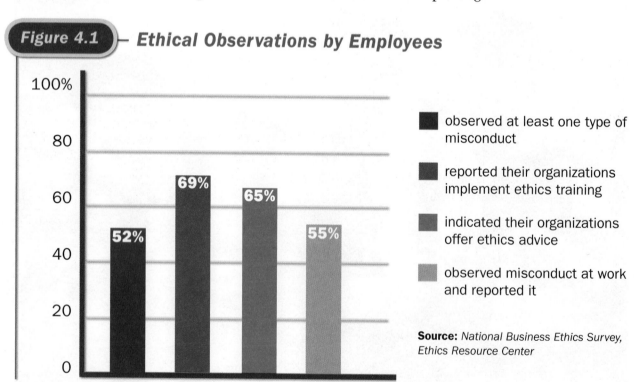

- observed at least one type of misconduct
- reported their organizations implement ethics training
- indicated their organizations offer ethics advice
- observed misconduct at work and reported it

Source: *National Business Ethics Survey, Ethics Resource Center*

● **A National Survey of Employees** These are some of the key findings of a recent National Business Ethics Survey. **Does American business seem to be becoming more or less concerned about ethical behavior?**

Ethics as Good Business

Most businesses police themselves with codes of ethics. Professionals such as doctors, lawyers, journalists, and teachers have their own codes of ethics. A code of ethics can cover issues such as employee behavior and environmental safety.

Unethical business practices include lying, offering merchandise known to be substandard, or treating customers or employees unfairly. If a business violates government regulations, the owner can be fined or go to jail. If an employee violates a company or professional code of ethics, the employee might be fired or lose his or her license. Not all unethical practices are covered by the law. Unethical business practices affect businesses indirectly.

Suppose you own an auto-body paint shop. To increase your profits, you charge top price and use the cheapest paint. One of your customers complains about the quality of the paint, but you do not care because she has already paid. What is one customer, right? The fact is that most businesses (especially small businesses) rely on repeat customers and word of mouth to get new customers. The amount you make in profits from one unhappy customer may not be worth the lost business.

Treating employees unethically can also backfire. Suppose you manage a small film distribution company. You hire Jaime fresh out of business school to run the office. You teach him how to use the computer system, how to deal with customers, and how the business works. You also pay him very little, make him do all your work, and treat him poorly. The first chance Jaime gets, he quits and ends up being hired by one of your competitors. You now have to retrain a new employee to take his place. Meanwhile, your competition now has a well-trained employee, who is much more efficient.

Conflicts of Interest

Another major ethical question that is generally not illegal relates to conflict of interest. A **conflict of interest** is a conflict between self-interest and professional obligation. Suppose that a manager of a small business hires his sister to do some work in the firm, but she is clearly unqualified to do the work. Giving the position to the sister will help out the family but will create morale problems with the other employees. It may also damage the business if her work does not get done. When making business decisions, employees have an ethical obligation to act in the best interest of the company.

International Business

Trade Barriers

Before a business can enter a foreign market, its managers must first recognize the barriers to trade that it faces. For example, a fast-food hamburger restaurant chain will face considerable barriers if it tries to expand into India, a place where beef is seldom eaten. A U.S. company wanting to market its products in Cuba will face prohibitions and regulations from the U.S. government. From cultural barriers to legal and political barriers, there are a lot of things a company needs to consider when looking at expanding into international markets.

Examples of Languages Across Cultures

Q: In Bahasa-Indonesian, how do you say: "Hello"?

A: Halo (pronounced: Hǎ-lōw)

What are some cultural differences that might create barriers to trade? How can they be overcome?

● As You Read

Think about how your school operates and the practices that could be included in a school code of ethics.

As You Read

Consider a conflict of interest you have encountered in your life. How did you resolve it?

Ethical Questions

When you **encounter** an ethical decision and must choose a course of action, ask yourself these important questions:

- Is it against the law? Does it violate company or professional policies?
- Even if everyone is doing it, how would I feel if someone did this to me?
- Am I sacrificing long-term benefits for short-term gains?

The Ethical Decision-Making Process

Here are some steps to take if you find yourself in an ethical dilemma:

1. Identify the ethical dilemma.
2. Discover **alternative** actions.
3. Decide who might be affected.
4. List the probable effects of the alternatives.
5. Select the best alternative.

Using this process will enable you to make a more informed ethical choice. Making an ethical decision involves more people than just you.

Section 4.1

After You Read

Review Key Concepts

1. What is the difference between personal and business ethics?
2. Describe some of the ways that unethical business practices can affect a business.
3. What is the relationship between illegal behaviors of business and unethical behaviors of business?

Academic Skills

4. Mathematics A large company decided it would give $\frac{1}{8}$ of its profits to charity. If the amount given was spread equally among five different charities, what fraction of the company's profits was given to each? What percent of the company's profits is this?

CONCEPT Number and Operations: Dividing Fractions To divide a fraction, invert the divisor and multiply.

 For math help, go to the Math Appendix.

 Go to **connectED.mcgraw-hill.com** to check your answers.

Social Responsibility

Reading Guide

● Before You Read

Think about some things a business can do to be socially responsible.

Read to Learn
- Define what is meant by the social responsibility of business.

The Main Idea

Social responsibility is the duty to do what is best for the good of society. Producing goods and services that are beneficial to society and providing jobs for people are not sufficient for a business to be considered socially responsible. They are expected to do more. Many businesses provide money for projects that benefit society.

Key Concept
- Business and Social Responsibility

Vocabulary

Key Term

social responsibility

Academic Vocabulary

You will find these words in your reading and on your tests. Make sure you know their meanings.

integrity   benefit
integral   sufficient

Graphic Organizer

In a figure like the one below, list four responsibilities of each business.

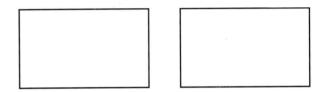

Business Responsibilities

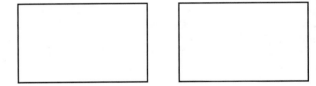

 Go to **connectED.mcgraw-hill.com** to print out this graphic organizer.

As You Read

Think about the damage that is done to the environment when people do not recycle.

Business and Social Responsibility

Business ethics focus on decisions considered good or bad, correct or incorrect. The social responsibility of business takes into consideration all that business does or does not do to solve the problems of society. **Social responsibility** is the duty to do what is best for the good of society. Businesses that follow ethical standards value **integrity** and honesty in employees. Ethics are an **integral** part of their business practices.

Some people believe that if a company produces goods that **benefit** society, it is fulfilling its social responsibility. However, many people and businesses do not think that is **sufficient**. They consider social responsibility to be more than that.

Some firms are very concerned about limiting the damage that they do to the environment. The *Los Angeles Times,* a daily newspaper with more than 1 million readers, uses recyclable paper and environmentally friendly soy-based ink. Automakers such as Honda and Toyota offer eco-cars, which reduce air pollution.

✔ Reading Check   Explain What ways can a business fulfill its social responsibilities?

Business Case Study

Reduce, Reuse, Repurpose

From parachutes to paint, this company diverts materials from landfills and has fun doing it

It takes imagination see a street-sweeping brush and think, "Rhinoceroses at the zoo would love to scratch their hides on that!" Damon Carson not only thought it, he made it happen.

Carson's Colorado company, repurposed MATERIALS, gives second life to discarded industrial supplies. Buyers benefit because they pay a lower price than they would for something new. The environment benefits because materials are diverted from landfills and from the energy-intensive process of recycling. When he's stumped about how to reuse materials, Carson crowd sources ideas through the company's e-newsletter, which has over 100,000 subscribers.

All kinds of things get reused: Wooden bleacher seats become shelves in a Nike store. A steamboat conveyor belt becomes a farm fence.

And expired Hawaiian cane sugar is just fine for a beekeeper to make sugar water for his bees.

Carson enjoys his socially responsible entrepreneurship. "I just love to come to work every day, because you never know what kinds of products or materials will come across your desk," he says.

Active Learning

Reusable materials are all around you! In small teams, explore your classroom and school and identify five items that could be repurposed at the end of their useful life. Be creative as you dream up new purposes for these items. Present your ideas to the class. Include the estimated combined weight of all the items you would be saving from the landfill, and how reuse of materials would be more environmentally friendly than sending them to be melted, chipped, or ground for recycling.

Responsibility to Customers

Customers are a business's first responsibility. Businesses should offer a good, safe product or service at a reasonable price. The Food and Drug Administration (FDA) is a federal government agency that protects consumers from dangerous or falsely advertised products. Most companies obey the government's rules.

Some companies do not act responsibly in the marketplace, especially when it comes to fair competition. Fair competition between businesses is necessary for the marketplace to operate effectively. It is a major component of a market economy. The market economy relies chiefly on market forces to allocate goods, services, and other resources, and to determine prices. Some companies use unethical tactics to eliminate competition. One of the most common means is to conspire with other companies to control the market for a product. Together, the companies can control the supply of a product and the prices they charge.

When companies restrict competition, consumers are affected. Consumers have fewer choices in what they can buy and how much they have to pay. When a company does not have to compete, its productivity decreases. This can backfire on a business. When the market changes or new markets open up, a company can find itself unprepared to compete. For example, in the 1940s, a handful of entertainment studios controlled the film industry. They kept control by owning most of the theaters. Smaller studios could make movies, but they could not get them shown anywhere. The government sued the big studios and forced them to sell their theaters. As a result, small studios were able to compete in the marketplace.

Earth-Friendly Products Many beauty-product companies include mission statements regarding the environment in their advertising and on their labels. Origins™, for one, promises to preserve the earth, animals, and the environment. *What products do you have at home that promise to be environmentally friendly?*

● **A Public Festival** People enjoy going to community and arts festivals. **How could a business demonstrate social responsibility by participating in an event like this?**

Carol M. Highsmith's America, Library of Congress, Prints & Photographs Division [LC-DIG-highsm- 04874]

Responsibility to Employees

Some businesses provide work experience for people with limited job skills. Many of these people are public assistance recipients. The purpose of such programs is to develop the skills and confidence levels necessary for success.

Volunteerism is another way businesses tackle societal problems. Some companies allow employees to take one or more paid days off during the year to work on community projects.

Businesses have a social responsibility to provide employees with safe working conditions, equal treatment, and fair pay. Less than 100 years ago, however, workers had few rights. Over the years the government has passed laws to protect workers from a range of issues, from child labor abuses to the rights of workers to organize. As the workplace has changed, the government has passed new laws. The Equal Pay Act (passed in 1964) requires that men and women be paid the same wages for doing equal work. More than 40 years later, however, the gap still exists. Another law, the Americans with Disabilities Act, bans discrimination against people with physical or mental disability. More than 50 million workers are likely to be covered by this law.

It is in a company's best interest to treat its workers fairly. Otherwise, it may suffer from low morale, poor production, and a high turnover rate.

Responsibility to Society

Businesses have responsibilities not only to customers and employees but also to society. One of the biggest social issues facing businesses today is environmental responsibility.

In 1970, the U.S. government created the Environmental Protection Agency (EPA), which enforces rules that protect the environment and control pollution.

✔ **Reading Check** **Identify** What is one of the biggest social issues facing businesses today?

● **As You Read**

Think about owning a business. What type of project would you like your employees to do to benefit your community?

Responsibility to Creditors and Owners

In the late 1990s and the early part of the 21st century, a number of major corporations reportedly kept inaccurate accounting records. Records showed that the firms had higher profits than they reported. Their behaviors were unethical and unlawful. Such behaviors are harmful to creditors (those who loan money) and outside shareholders (those who are owners but do not work in the business). Because of these behaviors, the federal government passed additional legislation. The Sarbanes-Oxley Act mandates truthful reporting and makes the CEO more accountable for the actions of the financial managers of a firm.

Section 4.2

◦ *After You Read*

Review Key Concepts
1. How is producing a good or service a way of being socially responsible?
2. What is the mission of the Food and Drug Administration?
3. What is one of the biggest social issues that businesses face today?

Academic Skills
4. **English Language Arts** Situations involving ethics and social responsibility are not found only in the business world. They come up in everyone's day-to-day life. Write a paragraph explaining an ethical decision made by you or someone you know. Explain what made it an ethical decision and the steps that were taken to make the final decision.

5. **English Language Arts** The terms below all relate to business ethics. Imagine that you are asked to explain these terms to a group of sixth-grade students who are just beginning to study how businesses work. Plan a talk designed to define each term. Give examples that might help a sixth grader understand the ideas.

code of ethics	conflict of interest
social responsibility	volunteerism

 Go to **connectED.mcgraw-hill.com** to check your answers.

Section 4.1 *Summary*

Business Ethics Ethics are the set of moral principles by which people conduct themselves personally, socially, and professionally. Business ethics are guidelines for how businesses should conduct themselves. Many unethical business practices are against the law. The guidelines that can be used when facing ethical dilemmas are similar to the steps of the problem-solving process. Good ethics can be beneficial for the long-run profitability and success of a business.

Section 4.2 *Summary*

Social Responsibility Social responsibility is the duty to do what is best for the good of society. In today's society, producing goods and services that are beneficial to society is not enough for a business to be considered socially responsible. Businesses must also be ethical and fair to consumers, workers, creditors, and society in general. Businesses also have a responsibility to the environment. In a corporation, management must be truthful about the financial health of the firm.

Vocabulary Review

1. On a sheet of paper, use each of these key terms and academic vocabulary terms in a sentence.

Key Terms	**Academic Vocabulary**
ethics	principles
business ethics	conduct
sweatshop	encounter
code of ethics	alternative
conflict of interest	integrity
social responsibility	integral
	benefit
	sufficient

Review Key Concepts

2. Define ethics and business ethics.

3. Describe why ethical behavior is good behavior for business.

4. Using the ethical decision-making process, list the steps for dealing with an ethical dilemma.

5. Define what is meant by the social responsibility of business.

Critical Thinking

6. Give an example of an unethical decision that is not illegal. Can a legal decision also be an unethical one?

7. Do you think the United States should trade with countries that have a poor human rights record? Why or why not?

8. Why do you think businesses with written codes of ethics and ethics programs for their employees have fewer ethical problems than other companies?

9. One study showed that young, inexperienced managers are twice as likely to feel pressured to compromise ethical standards as their older counterparts. Why do you think that is true?

10. Why do you think that some employees tell their managers about unethical behaviors of other workers? Do you think this is a good development?

11. Imagine that your manager says she cannot give you a raise but will allow some personal items in your travel expense report. What impression does that give you of her professional ethics?

12. Is ethical behavior always easy? Why or why not? What can a person do to make the best decision regarding an ethical dilemna?

Write About It

13. Some people believe that to solve social problems, money should come from government, not businesses. Write a letter to the editor of your local newspaper about your opinion of this stance.

14. Imagine that you discover your company is cheating the government out of thousands of dollars each year. Write a short essay about your options in this case.

15. In a paragraph or two, describe a situation in which you showed ethical behavior that resulted in some positive reactions from others.

16. Think of a business that you believe shows ethical behavior. Write a letter to the business owner about your observations.

17. Write an e-mail to your teacher discussing whether the drive to maximize profits is the reason some businesses are ethical and others are unethical.

18. Businesses have an ethical responsibility to their employees. Describe the type of ethics you would look for in an employer.

19. Write at least two paragraphs detailing ways that the government has helped working people.

Technology Applications

Internet

20. Using the Internet, select three codes of ethics from various professions (such as the medical, legal, educational, and accounting fields) or businesses. Compare and contrast the codes of ethics. Report your findings to the class.

Business Ethics

Making Ethical Decisions

21. What would you do if a friend at work was making about $100 worth of personal phone calls each month? Would your answer be different if the cost were $10 a month? Use the ethical decision-making process to determine what you should do.

Chapter 4 Review and Activities

Applying Academics to Business

English Language Arts

22. Each of the following sentences contains a grammatical mistake. Identify the errors, and rewrite the sentences to make them correct.

A. Businesses must concerned with environmental issues.

B. Most nonprofit organizations are social responsible.

Mathematics

23. Jimmy's company had a code of ethics that only allowed its sales representatives to accept gifts from clients if they cost less than $\frac{1}{8}$ of the employee's yearly bonus. The bonuses were equal to $\frac{1}{36}$ of the employee's total sales for the year. If Jimmy's total sales equaled $58,000, could he ethically accept a $250 TV from a client?

CONCEPT Number and Operations: **Multiplying Fractions** Multiply fractions by multiplying the numerators and then multiply the denominators. To find how much Jimmy's bonus will be, multiply $58,000 by $\frac{1}{36}$. Then multiply that product by $\frac{1}{8}$.

English Language Arts

24. Read the following phrases and note the underlined words. Write a sentence describing what they have in common and naming their part of speech.

decision-making process

short-term goals

Mathematics

25. A manufacturing company with 8 million shareholders normally pays a $2 dividend per share at year-end. Because of an unexpected $20 million windfall in profits, one member of the board of directors proposes raising the dividend by 40 percent and reserving $15 million for future environmental cleanup operations. Is there enough extra money to do both?

CONCEPT Problem Solving Solving word problems sometimes requires several mathematical steps. Read the situation described carefully in order to figure out what the steps should be. To better understand the problem, you might try restating the question: *Is $20 million greater than the additional dividend paid to shareholders plus the $15 million reserve?*

Active Learning

Dealing with a Dilemma

26. Ask a family member if he or she has ever been faced with an ethical issue at work. If so, find out what happened and how it was resolved. Ask that person to explain the steps in making an ethical decision. Write two paragraphs listing what you learned from your conversation.

Business in the Real World

Interview a Businessperson

27. Interview a manager of a business in the local community. Ask the manager if the business has a code of ethics and how it is enforced. What are some common violations of the code? Ask for at least three experiences in which ethical behavior was beneficial to the firm. Then prepare a report based on your findings.

Real LIFE skills

DEVELOP ETHICAL SKILLS

28. As a class, create a formal code of ethics for the classroom. Be sure to include the purpose of the code, the rules for classroom behavior, the steps for making ethical decisions, and the consequences of breaking the code. Use the code of ethics in the class for the remainder of the year. Revise as needed.

Cool Business CAREERS

FIND YOUR DREAM JOB

29. Locate the Occupational Outlook Handbook Web site. Click on the "OOH Search/A-Z Index" link and enter the job title "paralegals and legal assistants." Then write a one-page report about this type of occupation. Conclude your report with a list of things you could do now to prepare yourself to pursue the occupation.

Role Play

BUILDING ON A HISTORIC SITE

30. Situation Your firm wants to put up an apartment building on a site where the oldest building in town currently rests. The people in the area are very interested in historical preservation.

Activity When the initial planning for the apartment building was made, there was no idea that this property was historically significant. Prepare a report to the president of your firm with recommendations for the project.

Evaluation Your report will be evaluated on how well you meet the following performance indicators:

- Explain alternate courses of action.
- Explain the ethical implications of proceeding with the project.
- Describe the community's reaction to the project.
- Demonstrate an understanding of the ethical decision-making process.

Standardized Test Practice

Directions Choose the answer that is the most effective substitute for the underlined part of the sentence. If no substitution is necessary, choose "Leave as is."

1. **Consider your values and goals when determining the advantages and disadvantages of** <u>alternatives: you can</u> **use this information to compare and evaluate your choices.**

   A   alternatives, you can
   B   alternatives; you can
   C   alternatives. You can
   D   Leave as is

 TEST-TAKING TIP Budget your time. Make sure you have sufficient time to study so that you are well prepared for the test.

Keri Barney
Ken Hall
Jodene Jensen

Co-Founders, P.B.Loco Holdings

P.B.Loco Holdings is a company that produces gourmet peanut butter and has cafés, franchises, an online store, and other ventures.

Q & A

Describe your job responsibilities.

Jodene: Right now Keri handles the day-to-day operations and takes care of our production facility. Ken and I support our franchisees and handle the finances and the Web site.

Ken: For the first three months, the three of us actually made the peanut butter just so we would know how.

Keri: We have a daily meeting in the morning. We always have multiple task lists.

What skills are most important in your business?

Keri: Knowing how to wear different hats and deal with different people. I was a communications studies major in college; it is a nice skill to have for dealing with people. Basic business knowledge and analytical skills also help.

Ken: You have to assimilate a great deal of facts and make sure everything works together as far as your strategy goes.

Jodene: So much of what we do involves making decisions. Relationships with other people are also important.

What is your key to success?

Ken: When we have a new idea, we're able to implement it quickly.

Keri: We're constantly juggling things and staying in communication.

Jodene: There's almost a cult-like feeling about peanut butter, because people feel very nostalgic about it. We have a premium product.

What advice would you give students interested in starting a business?

Jodene: Learning how to juggle tasks is critical. It's important to do different things. So take a class, play a sport, and if you can, get a job.

Keri: Educate yourself in all aspects related to the business. And put in sweat equity, the hard work.

Ken: Keep an open mind. There's always something great if you use your imagination.

Critical Thinking
Why is it important to conduct market research before starting a business?

Some Qualifications of a Food Services Business Owner

Academic Skills and Abilities

Mathematics; verbal and written communication skills; general business management; creativity; interpersonal skills; multitasking, organizing, and planning skills.

Academic Skills Required to Complete Tasks at P.B.Loco			
Tasks	Math	Science	English Language Arts
Hold meetings			◆
Assign duties			◆
Develop recipes		◆	
Customer service	◆		◆
Contact vendors			◆
Schedule employees	◆		◆
Order supplies	◆		◆
Analyze financials	◆		◆

Education and Training

At least a high school diploma, with coursework in basic math and work experience within the food industry or other service-oriented field.

Career Path

Retail careers often begin with entry-level positions in established stores. Niche businesses, such as P.B.Loco, often spring from a personal hobby or interest.

Trends in the World of Business

The business world is constantly changing. To meet the challenges of the dynamic business environment, businesses and workers need to understand and react to trends.

Thematic Project Assignment

In this project, you will research trends that are affecting businesses and careers and write a report about them. These trends include the rise of globalization, the evolution of technology, and the increasing importance of cultural diversity.

Step 1 Brainstorm Skills You Need to Complete This Activity

Your success in business will depend on your skills. Preview the activity, then brainstorm a list of the skills you will need to use to complete the activity and describe how you will use them. Skills you might use include:

Academic Skills   reading, writing, math, and science skills

Basic Skills   speaking, listening, thinking, problem-solving, and interpersonal skills

Technology Skills   word processing, keyboarding, database, spreadsheet, presentation, telecommunications, and Internet skills

@ *SKILLS PREVIEW* Go to **connectED.mcgraw-hill.com** to download a graphic organizer you can use to brainstorm the skills you will use to complete the project.

Step 2 Choose a Business and a Career That Interest You

Think of a business that you find interesting. Then think of a career that interests you. As you investigate trends in business, you will research the effects of globalization, technology, and cultural diversity on the business and career of your choice.

Step 3 Build Background Knowledge

Preview the business trends you will research.

Business *Trends*

The globalization of the world's economies has increased competition for businesses and jobs. Globalization is the process by which the world economy is becoming a single interdependent system.

Globalization has been spurred by the evolution of technology. New technology has resulted in the growth of certain jobs and businesses and the decline of others.

Cultural diversity has become increasingly important to businesses. The blending of people with different skills and perspectives in the workplace can help businesses understand and react to an increasingly diverse population.

Step 4 Connect with Your Community

Interview an adult family member about how the business world has changed. Find out what the workplace was like when he or she first entered the workforce.

Step 5 Research Business Trends

Use library and Internet resources to research business trends. Use the Preview Project checklist as a guide to your research. Keep records of your sources of information.

Step 6 Develop a Report

Use word processing and other software to develop a two-page report that includes all of the information described in this checklist.

Business Trends

✔ Describe globalization and the factors that have promoted globalization.

✔ Describe the effect of globalization on businesses and the job market.

✔ Create a time line showing the technological innovations that have promoted globalization.

✔ Describe how technology has changed the global business environment.

✔ Explain how technological change has created new businesses and affected existing businesses and jobs.

✔ Describe how diversity creates an advantage for businesses.

✔ Use information from the U.S. Census Bureau to create a chart that compares the U.S. population today with projections for the population in 2050.

Self Connections

✔ Describe the results of your interview with an adult family member.

✔ Describe how technology, globalization, and diversity have affected the business and career in which you are interested.

✔ Explain what the investigation and its results mean to you.

Step 7 Evaluate Your Report

 RUBRIC Go to connectED.mcgraw-hill.com to download a rubric you can use to evaluate your final report.

Owning and Operating a Business

Courtesy of Seventh Generation

Seventh Generation makes environmentally safe household products such as dish soap and laundry detergent. At the end of this unit, you will learn about Seventh Generation® founder Jeffrey Hollender and how he achieved his success.

Decision Making What type of ownership would you use if you decided to open a company?

Unit 2   *Thematic Project Preview*

Entrepreneurship in a Global World After completing this unit, you will research to find out how entrepreneurs conduct business in a global economy.

Project Checklist As you read the chapters in this unit, use this checklist to prepare for the unit project.

- ✔ Think about how globalization affects entrepreneurs.
- ✔ Analyze how technology helps entrepreneurs build global businesses.
- ✔ Look for entrepreneurial businesses in your community that are working in the global marketplace.
- ✔ Discover how different entrepreneurial businesses can increase their market share through globalization.

Chapter 5

Entrepreneurship

Chapter Objectives After completing this chapter, you will be able to:

▶ **Section 5.1** *Rewards and Challenges of Entrepreneurship*
- **Define** entrepreneur and entrepreneurship.
- **List** at least five rewards of being an entrepreneur.
- **Identify** at least four challenges of being an entrepreneur.
- **Discuss** why entrepreneurs are important to the American economy.

▶ **Section 5.2** *The Business Plan*
- **Discuss** the initial steps in setting up a business.
- **Identify** the parts of a business plan.

Ask

AN EXPERT

The Value of a Long-Term Investment Strategy

Q: I have read that it is important for a new investor to invest for the long-term. What does this mean, why is this important, and how do I do it?

A: "Long-term" usually means five years or beyond. Investments meant for the long term, such as stocks, tend to fluctuate. Money designated for short-term events is best kept in safer havens, such as savings accounts. The risk of loss in the stock market diminishes with time, though.

Mathematics You are planning to save for 20 years of retirement. Just before you retire, your annual salary will be the equivalent of about $50,000 in today's dollars. You will need 70% to 80% of your pre-retirement income to maintain your lifestyle. Based on this rule, you would need a minimum of $35,000 for your first year of retirement. Replace the variables in the algebraic expression below and evaluate the expression to calculate how much money you will need to retire.

Evaluate xy if $x = 20$ and $y = \$35,000$

CONCEPT **Algebra: Variables and Expressions** Algebra is a language of symbols. A variable is a symbol, often a letter, used to represent a number. Algebraic expressions are combinations of variables, numbers, and at least one operation. Once the variables have been replaced, you can evaluate, or find the value of, the algebraic expression.

● **Realizing a Dream** The opening of a new business is a proud moment for entrepreneurs. What dreams might entrepreneurship turn into reality in your life?

Rewards and Challenges of Entrepreneurship

Reading Guide

Before You Read

Think about what it might take to become a successful entrepreneur.

Read to Learn

- Define entrepreneur and entrepreneurship.
- List at least five rewards of being an entrepreneur.
- Identify at least four challenges of being an entrepreneur.
- Discuss why entrepreneurs are important to the American economy.

The Main Idea

An entrepreneur is someone who recognizes a business opportunity and organizes, manages, and assumes the risks of starting a business. Entrepreneurs face many challenges. However, those who succeed see many rewards.

Key Concepts

- Entrepreneurship
- Rewards of Entrepreneurship
- Challenges of Entrepreneurship
- The Impact of Small Businesses

Vocabulary

Key Terms

small business
virtual business or dot-com company

Academic Vocabulary

You will find these words in your reading and on your tests. Make sure you know their meanings.

area
significant
research
estimate

Graphic Organizer

In a chart like the one below, list four rewards and four challenges of being an entrepreneur as you read.

Rewards	Challenges
1._____	1._____
2._____	2._____
3._____	3._____
4._____	4._____

 Go to **connectED.mcgraw-hill.com** to print out this graphic organizer.

Entrepreneurship

If you have ever thought about going into business for your-self, then you have thought about becoming an entrepreneur. An entrepreneur is a person who recognizes a business opportunity and organizes, manages, and assumes the risks of starting and operating a business. Entrepreneurship is the process of recognizing an opportunity, testing it in the market, and gathering the resources necessary to go into business.

Creating and running a business venture requires a variety of skills. A *venture* is a new business undertaking that involves risk. Even if you do not become an entrepreneur, the lessons you learn about entrepreneurship will help you in any job. Knowing more about business will also benefit you as a consumer.

● **As You Read**

Think about a business opportunity offering a service that could be improved. What type of service would you choose?

Personal Characteristics of Entrepreneurs

Most entrepreneurs have similar characteristics. The Small Business Administration (SBA) created a checklist to help people see if they have the recommended traits for a career in entrepreneurship. These traits include leadership, decision-making, self-discipline, planning, and people skills.

Figure 5.1 — *Twelve Characteristics of Successful Entrepreneurs*

Persistent	**Risk-taking**	**Self-confident**	**Restless**
Entrepreneurs are willing to work until a job is done, no matter how long it takes.	Entrepreneurs take risks, but they are not reckless.	Entrepreneurs believe in themselves.	Once entrepreneurs achieve their goals, they start looking for new challenges.
Goal-oriented	**Action-oriented**	**Responsible**	**Self-demanding**
Entrepreneurs set and achieve goals.	Entrepreneurs are doers instead of spectators. They take action.	Entrepreneurs take responsibility for their decisions and actions.	Entrepreneurs have high expectations.
Creative	**Independent**	**Inquisitive**	**Enthusiastic**
Entrepreneurs look for new ways to solve old problems.	Entrepreneurs want to make their own decisions.	Entrepreneurs conduct research and ask questions to solve problems.	Entrepreneurs are energetic and passionate about their pursuits.

● **Ranking the 12 Traits** Entrepreneurs plan for success by setting goals. **In what order would you rank the importance of these entrepreneurial characteristics?**

Small Businesses

The SBA is a U.S. government agency that protects the interests of small businesses. It defines a **small business** as an independently owned business that usually has the owner as its manager. A small business serves a limited geographic **area** and employs fewer than 500 people.

Internet Businesses

Many entrepreneurs open virtual businesses. A **virtual business** or **dot-com company** is a business that operates and advertises on the Internet. Many dot-com companies make shopping easier and more efficient for consumers. This shows how an entrepreneurial venture can make a **significant** improvement to what already exists.

Online businesses can attract a huge number of customers. Anyone with an Internet connection can purchase from them. Entrepreneurs on a budget can take advantage of the Internet for sales, marketing, and other purposes. Businesses can build their own low-cost Web sites. Social media and mobile technology have also revolutionized business as Facebook® and Twitter® are inexpensive ways to promote a small business and interact with customers.

Business Case Study

Finding Revenue Outside the Box

An advertising innovation becomes a standard business practice.

By thinking outside the box, entrepreneurs can tap into "nontraditional revenue" (NTR) to grow their businesses.

The term NTR comes from the media advertising industry. Originally, ad salespeople at radio and TV stations could only charge high rates for ads if a show's ratings were high. Sales were also limited by the number of ad minutes available on air. Salespeople got around this problem by organizing events like concerts and parades, attracting audiences with their stations' names. This earned NTR such as event admissions, beverage sales, and sponsorships.

Many kinds of businesses can generate NTR. If a bridal shop earns its traditional revenue from sales, for example, it could also earn nontraditional revenue by putting on a bridal show. The owner of a Web design firm could offer a coding seminar. A restaurant with extra space could rent out rooms for private events.

NTR makes use of a business's name recognition, staff expertise, facilities, or other unique assets to expand its niche.

> **Active Learning**
>
> Divide into small teams. Your teacher will assign each group a type of small business for your group to "own." Write three sources of revenue for your business that you consider standard or "traditional." Then, based on the unique assets of the business, brainstorm a list of NTR sources. Try to come up with at least five. Present your sources to the class.

Rewards of Entrepreneurship

People become entrepreneurs for a number of reasons besides making money. Being the boss, doing what they enjoy, and using their creativity are just a few.

Being the Boss

An important advantage of being a small-business owner is the ability to be in charge. In fact, this is the main reason people become entrepreneurs. Unlike people who run corporations and partnerships, entrepreneurs do not have to consult with others before making a decision.

Doing What You Enjoy

A business venture typically starts with an activity that the entrepreneur enjoys. Someone who enjoys cooking for others might start a catering business. Someone who likes to ride bikes might open a bike shop. The new business owner gets satisfaction from developing the enterprise.

Having the Opportunity to Be Creative

Most people who work for others follow procedures. Entrepreneurs make procedures. They are able to shape a business in ways employees cannot. This is especially true with daring or creative ideas. A business owner with a creative idea has the power to act on it.

Building an Enterprise

Many successful entrepreneurs work in a related business before starting their own company. People who decide to open a business must consider whether to buy an existing company or start a new one. They must **research** the viability of the venture and choose the form of business to start.

✔ Reading Check   **Identify** What are some reasons to become an entrepreneur?

Young Entrepreneurs More than ever, teens are starting businesses across the country. The SBA even offers a teen business link at its Web site. The link helps teens determine if their ideas have potential. The site also helps put them on a path toward entrepreneurship. *List reasons for teens to strike out on their own. Research entrepreneurs who started businesses while they were still students.*

● **As You Read**

Think about an activity you enjoy that would make a good business venture.

Sole Proprietorships, Partnerships, and Corporations Most U.S. businesses are *sole proprietorships,* which means they are owned and operated by one person. Another form of business is a partnership. A *partnership* is owned and run by two or more people. A *corporation* has many owners. Corporations are run by a chief executive officer, who answers to a board of directors.

Sole proprietors do not share their company's income and expenses, profits or losses. All responsibilities rest with the sole proprietor. The sole proprietor assumes all of the risks and reaps all of the benefits. You will learn more about the different types of business organizations in Chapter 6.

? ETHICS in Business

Facing Money Problems

- **Critical Reading** Life is full of important decisions that must be made. Think about the kinds of decisions that you make as you read the question below.

  You are an entrepreneur trying to build a new business. One of your most important clients is late paying your recent invoice because its computerized accounting system is down. You face a cash-flow problem. Since your client has not paid you, you cannot pay all of your bills. However, you could get by if you did not pay your rent for the month.

- **Decision Making** What are some ways of handling this situation so that you maintain relationships with your clients, landlord, and other vendors while acting ethically? Explain your answer.

Home-Based Businesses Some home-business experts say the best opportunities to start a home-based business stem from tasks employees do for their employer. *What tasks might an employee of an Internet bookstore perform as part of a home-based business?*

Other Reasons for Entrepreneurship

Entrepreneurs enjoy developing their own schedule. Many run home-based businesses, such as consultancies or editing, housekeeping, and bookkeeping services. They make an economic contribution to their community through investment and the creation of jobs. Entrepreneurs are rewarded for assuming risk.

 **Identify** Name some types of home-based businesses.

Challenges of Entrepreneurship

There are rewards to becoming an entrepreneur. There are also some challenges that business owners deal with in order to be successful.

Getting Funds to Start the Business

One of the biggest obstacles in starting a business is obtaining financing. Most people must borrow money to start their business. It is often difficult to get loans from financial institutions. They are concerned about whether the business would succeed and they would be repaid.

Being Fully Responsible for the Business

Business owners are responsible for more than just decision making. They must see that everything gets done—from sweeping the floors and paying the bills, to hiring employees and making repairs. Duties include handling financial records as well as training employees.

Other Challenges for Entrepreneurs

Entrepreneurs also face the challenge of feeling alone and insecure about making the right decisions. They work long hours, especially during start-up. They also face uncertain income levels and the risk of losing their investment if the business fails. About four out of five small businesses fail in their first five years. Most failures are due to inadequate financial planning and management, and a poor response to change.

● As You Read

Think about ways you could lose an investment in a new business. What can be done to help prevent this from happening?

The Impact of Small Businesses

More than 99 percent of U.S. firms are small businesses. Small businesses employ more than 52 percent of the U.S. workforce. A majority of them are one-person operations that generate more than half the nation's income. Small businesses are also the principal source of new jobs. Some **estimate** that two-thirds of all new jobs are generated by small businesses. The number of virtual businesses continues to increase. This allows more small businesses to enter the global marketplace and other economies.

Section 5.1

○ After You Read

Review Key Concepts

1. What are some characteristics of successful entrepreneurs?
2. What reward is the main reason most people become an entrepreneur?
3. Identify some of the challenges of entrepreneurship.

Academic Skills

4. **Mathematics** Rick is thinking about starting his own business. The start-up costs he has identified include $12,000 to lease an office, $25,000 for inventory, and $30,000 for the first year's payroll. For the first year, he projects that he would make a slight profit of $3,250. Would it be better to use the money to open the business or to invest the money in a savings bond with a first-year return of 5.99 percent?

CONCEPT **Problem Solving: Adapt Strategies** Read word problems carefully to make sure you know what you are being asked. It sometimes helps to restate the question in your own words. In this problem, you are asked to make a judgment about which is more valuable, $3,250 in profit from a new business or 5.99 percent of the sum of $12,000 + $25,000 + $30,000.

 For math help, go to the Math Appendix.

 Go to **connectED.mcgraw-hill.com** to check your answers.

The Business Plan

Reading Guide

● Before You Read

Think of some reasons for having a business plan before starting a business.

Read to Learn
- Describe how to prepare for your own business.
- Discuss the parts of a business plan.

The Main Idea

Once an entrepreneur discovers a good business opportunity, the next step is to do market research. Market research helps to determine whether there will be a demand for a new product or service. It can also uncover issues to address in a business plan.

Key Concepts
- Initial Steps in Setting up a Business
- Parts of a Business Plan

Vocabulary

Key Terms

business plan
executive summary
vision statement
mission statement

Academic Vocabulary

You will find these words in your reading and on your tests. Make sure you know their meanings.

section   established
concept   data

Graphic Organizer

Using a figure like the one below, fill in the parts of a business plan as you read.

 Go to **connectED.mcgraw-hill.com** to print out this graphic organizer.

Initial Steps in Setting up a Business

Before you decide to start a particular business, you need to see if there is a demand for your product or service. This requires doing market research. If your market research shows that your business has the potential to succeed, then develop a business plan. A **business plan** is a written description of a new business venture that describes all aspects of the business. It helps entrepreneurs focus on what they want to do, how they will do it, and what they expect to accomplish. The business plan is used by potential investors and financing agencies that new entrepreneurs go to for start-up funds.

Checklist for Starting a Venture

A checklist is a good way to organize your thinking when you begin planning your own business. Entrepreneurs should keep these questions and their answers in mind as they develop and write their business plan.

Here are some questions to consider:

- What will I produce?
- Who are my main competitors?
- Why is my product or service needed?
- How much will my product or service cost to produce?
- How many people will I need to run the business?
- What physical facilities will I need?
- What licenses, permits, or other legal documents do I need?
- How much money will I need to get started?

✔ **Reading Check**   **Identify** List some questions to consider before starting a business.

● **As You Read**

Think about how careful planning increases a new business's chances of success.

Parts of a Business Plan

A business plan must be well organized and easy to read. It must also follow a logical format. There are 16 essential parts of a business plan.

Executive Summary

The **executive summary** is a brief account of the key points contained in a business plan. It should be no more than two pages and should include the most important information from each section of the plan. It should open with a compelling story to persuade the reader that the business is going to succeed. Then it should support that statement with evidence gathered through market research.

● **Selling the Business Plan** Most lenders prefer to meet with entrepreneurs before giving them a loan based on a business plan. Why do they want to meet with the entrepreneur?

● *As You Read*

Prospective entrepreneurs must convince potential investors, such as banks, that they are capable of making their business a success. What qualifications do you have that could be presented in your business plan? How would you handle the gaps in experience you might have?

Management Team Plan

This section presents your qualifications and those of any partners you might have. You must describe your team's capabilities to execute your business concept. You should discuss how you will fill gaps in expertise. You may need to hire consultants, or form partnerships or advisory boards.

Company Description

The description of the firm provides an outline of the business. It helps investors understand the size, scope, and type of business you plan to start. It describes the business opportunity and explains why the venture will succeed.

Product and Service Plan

Describe the product or service you want to offer. The nature of your business should be clear. You should note the unique features of the product or service and possible spin-offs. Spin-offs are additional products and services that you might offer when the business is more established. They show that the venture has growth potential.

Vision and Mission Statements

The vision and mission statements section states the guiding principles by which a business functions. A **vision statement** establishes the scope and purpose of a company and reflects its values and beliefs. A **mission statement** expresses the specific aspirations of a company, the major goals it will try to reach.

Ingram Publishing

Industry Overview

This section presents your research of the industry. Every business operates within an industry. Think of your industry as companies that provide similar, complementary, or different products and services. Discuss trends and growth within the industry.

Market Analysis

This section presents research about your customer profile. The results help you determine your overall marketing and sales strategies. In addition, this section analyzes your customers and the competition. Include geographic, economic, and demographic data about the target market and business location.

Competitive Analysis

Indicate how the proposed business has an advantage over its competitors. You can gather information on competitors by viewing their Web sites; talking to their customers, vendors, suppliers, and employees; and attending trade shows. See if any articles have been written about them.

Marketing Plan

A marketing plan discusses how a company makes its customers aware of its products or services. It includes features such as the market niche, pricing, company image, marketing tactics, a media plan, a social media marketing plan, and a marketing budget.

Real World

Mission Statements
A mission statement should clearly express a company's main goals. Find an example of a good mission statement on the Internet. *What makes your example a good model?*

Science/Tech TRENDS

The Technology Sector
Digital technology has the ability to improve our personal and business lives in many ways. Technology is one of the fastest growing sectors of our economy. The increasing demand for consumer electronics, such as iPods and digital cameras, the popularity of cell phones, and the opening up of new markets around the world have fueled the impressive growth of this sector. For the individual investor, buying shares in a technology sector mutual fund is a way to capitalize on this growth. However, investing in a single sector of the economy carries with it greater risk than does a more diversified approach to investing.

Web Quest

Locate Web sites where you can find more information about technology sector mutual funds. List one or two mutual funds as examples. Then write a sentence or two describing their investment strategies, goals, and objectives.

Operational Plan

The operational plan includes the business processes that result in production and delivery of the product or service.

Organizational Plan

This part looks at the people who will run the firm as well as management's philosophy. The form of business organization that is chosen, such as a sole proprietorship, is also discussed.

Financial Plan

This section presents forecasts for the business. Data are usually shown in financial statements. The plan provides proof that the new business will be financially healthy.

Growth Plan

The growth plan looks at how the business will expand in the future. Investors and lenders like to know that a business has plans to grow and deal with growth.

Figure 5.2 — *Parts of a Business Plan*

● **Creating a Business Plan** There are several steps involved in creating a business plan. **Do you think one part of the business plan is more important than the others?**

Contingency Plan

The contingency plan looks at likely risks to the business, such as lower-than-expected sales and emergencies that might affect it. It then suggests a way to minimize risk.

Cover Page, Title Page, Table of Contents, and Supporting Documents

The cover page should include the company's name, address, phone number, Web site and e-mail addresses, and logo. The title page follows the cover page. It includes the company name; the names, titles, and addresses of the owners; the date the plan was submitted; and the name of its preparer. The table of contents details the components of the business plan. Supporting documents include exhibits and other information relevant to the business.

Section 5.2

After You Read

Review Key Concepts

1. Why is a business plan important?
2. Why should entrepreneurs carefully study their competitors before starting a business?
3. Why is a growth plan important to include in a business plan?

Academic Skills

4. **English Language Arts** With a partner or small group, brainstorm and write questions you can use to interview two or three entrepreneurs or small-business owners. Think of questions that will get the interviewees to tell how their lives changed as a result of starting or running a small business. Present the interview results to the class as part of a panel discussion. Compare and contrast the stories with information presented in the text.

5. **English Language Arts** You want to strengthen your entrepreneurial skills. Complete these steps to learn more about other entrepreneurs and yourself:

   - Reading: Go online or to the library and read articles and books about entrepreneurial activities.
   - Writing: Write about individuals you know who are entrepreneurs and the obstacles they had to overcome.
   - Watching: Find films about athletes, businesspeople, or others who achieved success.
   - Practice: Find case studies that involve goals, creativity, and risk taking.

 Go to **connectED.mcgraw-hill.com** to check your answers.

Section 5.1 Summary

Rewards and Challenges of Entrepreneurship An entrepreneur is a person who recognizes a business opportunity, tests it in the market, and gathers the resources necessary to start and operate a business. Entrepreneurs make or sell products or services to meet consumers' wants and needs. Some advantages of being an entrepreneur include being the boss, doing what you enjoy, having the opportunity to be creative, building an enterprise, and possibly making a substantial income. Challenges include getting start-up funds, risk of failure, and having an uncertain income. Small businesses are important to the U.S. economy because they provide goods and services, and jobs.

Section 5.2 Summary

The Business Plan Before you decide to start a particular business, you need to see if there is demand for your product or service. This requires doing market research. If research shows that you have a viable business, then develop a business plan. A business plan is a written description of a new business venture. It describes all aspects of the business. It also helps entrepreneurs to focus on exactly what they want to do, how they will do it, and what they expect to accomplish. The business plan is an essential tool to attract potential investors and financing agencies for start-up funds. It includes a description of the firm, market analysis, competitive analysis, and financial information.

Vocabulary Review

1. On a sheet of paper, use each of these key terms and academic vocabulary terms in a sentence.

Key Terms
small business
virtual business or dot-com company
business plan
executive summary
vision statement
mission statement

Academic Vocabulary

area	section
significant	concept
research	established
estimate	data

Review Key Concepts

2. Define entrepreneur and entrepreneurship.

3. Describe five rewards of being an entrepreneur.

4. Describe four challenges of being an entrepreneur.

5. Describe the reasons entrepreneurs are important to the American economy.

6. Describe how to prepare for your own business.

7. Discuss the parts of a business plan.

Critical Thinking

8. Many Internet businesses have started and failed. Why do you think some virtual businesses fail?

9. It is important that entrepreneurs be take-charge, self-directed people. Why do you think this is true?

10. What are some reasons the owner of a business usually puts in more hours at work than an employee?

11. Why is it important for small-business owners to keep good financial records?

12. The industry overview section of the business plans calls for the entrepreneur to analyze the trends of the industry in which the entrepreneurial venture falls. Why is this information an important part of the business plan?

13. Give reasons why some small businesses fail if they do not respond quickly to change. Why do you think it is difficult for small businesses to respond quickly to change?

14. Is there a difference between being self-disciplined and self-motivated? Explain.

15. Review the 12 characteristics of successful entrepreneurs. Think about the traits that you have. Why do you think you have these traits? How could they benefit you as an entrepreneur?

Write About It

16. Look for an opportunity that you think could be turned into a small business. Write a one-page essay outlining the nature of the opportunity and why you think it has potential.

17. Select three business opportunities to pursue in your community. Talk to someone who knows the business community in your area, such as the head of the chamber of commerce. Determine whether these are good ideas. Then write an e-mail to the business leader reviewing your discussion.

18. Visit a nearby library and select a book or article on the life of an entrepreneur. The entrepreneur could be living or deceased. Read the account, and write a report on his or her life, noting your subject's influences, obstacles, education, and experience with starting a business.

19. Go to the U.S. Census Bureau's Web site and research the latest survey of small business. Determine how many jobs are created and how much income is generated by small business. Write a 500-word report based on your findings. Discuss the importance of small businesses to economies.

Technology Applications

Internet

20. Use word-processing software to create a survey that can be sent to local small-business owners and entrepreneurs. Find out what technical skills they possess and will need in the future. As a class, compile the results using spreadsheet or database software.

Business Ethics

Making Ethical Decisions

21. For the grand opening of your hardware store, you issue flyers advertising lawn mowers for $150. However, you have only five mowers. Should you encourage customers to buy more expensive ones or issue rain checks for the advertised price?

Applying Academics to Business

English Language Arts

22. The ability to innovate is a key skill for a successful entrepreneur. What does it mean to be innovative? Write a sentence or two explaining what it means to be innovative. List synonyms, antonyms, and related words.

Mathematics

23. In one year, the combined purchasing power of minority groups in the United States was $1.3 trillion, or 20 percent of the country's purchasing power. It is estimated that, in 40 years, minority-group purchasing power will equal $4.3 trillion, or 32 percent of the total. By how much will the country's total purchasing power grow over 40 years?

CONCEPT **Numbers and Operations: Working With Large Numbers** Problems like this can be solved more easily by expressing large numbers using scientific notation. A number expressed in scientific notation is the product of a decimal between 1 and 10 and a power of 10. For example, $1,100 = 1.1 \times 10^3$.

English Language Arts

24. In one type of paragraph, a statement is followed by examples that support it. In another type, a cause is presented followed by a description of its effect. Write two paragraphs about the special skills an entrepreneur needs. Use a statement-and-example organization for one and cause-and-effect for the other.

Mathematics

25. The business plan for a large corporation called for 15.5 percent of annual profits to be reinvested in research and development (R & D) of new products. If this company shows $3.4 million in revenue and $2.8 million in expenses, how much would be invested in R & D?

CONCEPT **Number and Operations: Decimals and Percents** A percent can be converted to a decimal by moving the decimal point two places to the left and dropping the percent sign. To solve this problem, multiply profits (revenue less expenses) by 0.155.

Active Learning

Investigate Product Loyalties

26. Create an inventory of the products and services you and your family use that are produced or offered by small businesses. Categorize them by family member. Then interview each family member. Discover why he or she purchases the products or services from a small business. Make a report of your results. Share it with the class.

Business in the Real World

Research a Small-Business Idea

27. With a classmate, research the requirements for setting up a small business venture in your community. Investigate areas such as government regulations, financing, and the cost of leasing space and buying equipment. The local chamber of commerce might direct you in your research. Write a report on your findings.

Real LIFE skills

INCREASING YOUR ENTREPRENEURIAL SKILLS

28. Turn back to Figure 5.1 and assess how many entrepreneurial skills you have. Identify three characteristics that you think could be improved. Write a 250-word essay on how you could improve in those areas.

Business CAREERS

FIND YOUR DREAM JOB

29. Locate the Occupational Outlook Handbook Web site. Click on the "OOH Search/A-Z Index" link and enter the job title "operations research analyst." Then write a one-page report about this type of occupation. Conclude your report with a list of things you could do now to prepare yourself to pursue the occupation.

Role Play

SUBMITTING A BUSINESS PLAN

30. Situation You are seeking funds to start a new business venture. Along with a business plan, you must give an oral presentation to a banker to consider before loaning you the money.

Activity Create a presentation that focuses on various aspects of the business plan.

Evaluation You will be evaluated on how well you meet the following performance indicators:

- Describe the new business venture.
- Cover at least seven of the parts of a business plan.
- Use visuals when necessary.
- Make persuasive arguments.
- Use clear diction and correct grammar.

Standardized Test Practice

Directions Choose the letter of the best answer. Write the letter for the answer on a separate piece of paper.

1. Which word or phrase should be left out of the following sentence in order to change it from passive voice to active voice?

A <u>successful</u> owner <u>of a small business</u> <u>is one who</u> possesses <u>multiple</u> skills.

    A   successful
    B   of a small business
    C   is one who
    D   multiple

 TEST-TAKING TIP When answering multiple-choice questions, ask yourself if each option is true or false. This may help you find the best answer if you are unsure.

Business Ownership and Operations

> **Chapter Objectives** | After completing this chapter, you will be able to:

▶ **Section 6.1** *Types of Business Ownership*
- **Describe** the advantages and disadvantages of the three major forms of business organizations.
- **Describe** how cooperatives and nonprofits are like and unlike corporations and franchises.

▶ **Section 6.2** *Types and Functions of Businesses*
- **Differentiate** the six types of businesses.
- **Describe** the five functions of business.
- **Discuss** how the five functions of business relate to each other.

Ask AN EXPERT

The First Steps in Investing: Diversification

Q: What is "portfolio diversification," and how can it help me achieve my investment goals?

A: Diversification is spreading your money throughout a number of investments in order to reduce risk. You can diversify through asset allocation, investing in more than one type of investment, such as stocks, bonds, or cash. You can also diversify your holdings within an asset category. With stocks, for example, you might own 20 stocks scattered across different industries. In addition, you might consider owning stocks from countries outside the United States. Economies and markets are cyclical, and diversification helps you avoid the pitfalls of those cycles.

Mathematics Linda is investing for retirement 30 years from now. She wants 70% of her money in stocks, 20% in bonds, and the remaining 10% in a money market fund. Stocks now comprise 80% of her portfolio, so she needs to rebalance her portfolio. If her portfolio is worth $100,000, what percent of her stock holdings should she sell in order to rebalance?

CONCEPT **Finding Percents** Percent means "per hundred." To figure out what percent of a number, *a*, another number, *b*, is, divide *b* by *a*.

● **Meeting Diverse Needs** Businesses are of different types and sizes. Why do you think there is so much variation in the sizes and forms of businesses?

McGraw-Hill Education

Types of Business Ownership

Before You Read

Think about a business you would like to start, the form of organization you would use, and the type of business it would be.

Read to Learn

- Describe the advantages and disadvantages of the three major forms of business organizations.
- Describe how cooperatives and nonprofits are like and unlike corporations and franchises.

The Main Idea

Sole proprietorships, partnerships, and corporations are the most common forms of business organization. Cooperatives and nonprofits are other forms.

Key Concepts

- Organizing a Business
- Other Ways to Organize a Business

Vocabulary

Key Terms

sole proprietorship	limited liability
unlimited liability	cooperative
partnership	nonprofit organization
corporation	franchise

Academic Vocabulary

You will find these words in your reading and on your tests. Make sure you know their meanings.

sole	partners
income	regulates

Graphic Organizer

In boxes like the ones below, list the types of business organizations.

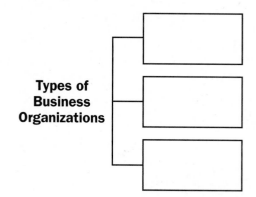

Types of Business Organizations

 Go to **connectED.mcgraw-hill.com** to print out this graphic organizer.

Organizing a Business

There are three main types of business organizations: sole proprietorships, partnerships, and corporations. As part of a business plan, entrepreneurs must decide which type best fits their situation and describe their choice and the reasons for it. During the life of a business, its form can change. These changes often occur when a business is growing.

Sole Proprietorships

About three-quarters of all businesses in the United States are sole proprietorships. A **sole proprietorship** is a business owned by one person. **Figure 6.1** includes the percentage of U.S. sole proprietorships, partnerships, and corporations.

Advantages of Owning a Sole Proprietorship Starting a sole proprietorship is easy to do. Depending on local laws, the sole proprietor might need only a license or a permit to start. Sole proprietors are in charge of their businesses. They can make all the decisions and run the companies as they see fit. As the sole owner, they can also keep all the profits. Finally, their income taxes are usually lower than a corporation's. Income from a sole proprietorship is taxed once. However, income from corporations can be taxed twice. A corporation pays taxes on the income it receives. Then a corporation's stockholders pay taxes on the income they receive as dividends on stock. A sole proprietor's personal tax rate is often lower than the corporate tax rate.

● **As You Read**

Suppose you decide to make and sell jewelry as a business. Why might you want to be the sole owner of the business?

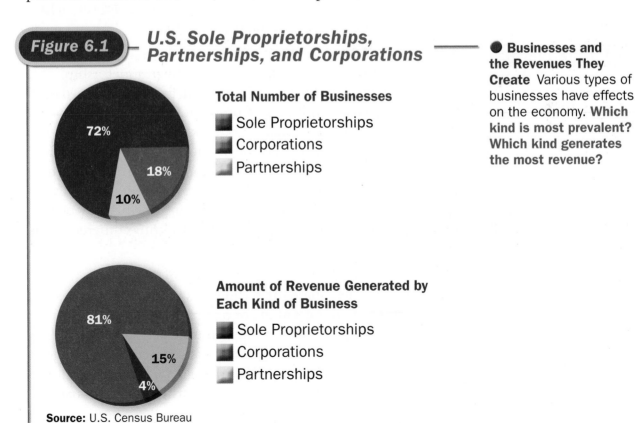

| Figure 6.1 | U.S. Sole Proprietorships, Partnerships, and Corporations |

Total Number of Businesses

- Sole Proprietorships
- Corporations
- Partnerships

72%
18%
10%

Amount of Revenue Generated by Each Kind of Business

- Sole Proprietorships
- Corporations
- Partnerships

81%
15%
4%

Source: U.S. Census Bureau

● **Businesses and the Revenues They Create** Various types of businesses have effects on the economy. **Which kind is most prevalent? Which kind generates the most revenue?**

Understanding Cultural Differences

The first time you travel for business internationally, you'll probably need help with things such as booking hotels, renting a car, managing the effects of jet lag, and understanding the cultural differences of the people at your destination. A whole information industry has developed around helping the international business traveler. Now, books, magazines, and Web sites are devoted to helping unravel the mysteries of other countries and cultures so that commerce can flourish.

Examples of Languages Across Cultures

Q: In Russian, how do you say: "Do you understand?"

A: Вам понятно? (pronounced: Văm pă-nyăt-nă?)

What kinds of information do you think a first-time international business traveler needs?

As You Read

Say you had a partner who made a bad business decision that caused your business to lose money. What steps could you take to correct the situation?

Disadvantages of Owning a Sole Proprietorship A major disadvantage of owning a sole proprietorship is that the owner has unlimited liability. **Unlimited liability** means the owner is responsible for the company's debts. If the owner has more debt than she or he receives in **income**, then the owner has to make up the difference.

Limited access to credit is another disadvantage. If the potential owner does not have much experience or money saved, lenders will be reluctant to offer credit. Many proprietorships fail because they run out of money. A third disadvantage is that the person in charge may not have all of the skills needed to run the business. For instance, the owner of a bakery might know everything about making cakes, but nothing about record keeping. A fourth disadvantage is that the sole proprietorship ends when the owner dies.

✔ **Reading Check** **Identify** What are four disadvantages of owning a sole proprietorship?

Partnerships

A **partnership** is a business owned by two or more people who share its risks and rewards. To start a partnership, you need a partnership agreement. This agreement is a contract that outlines the rights and responsibilities of each partner.

Advantages of Owning a Partnership There are several advantages of owning a partnership. As with a sole proprietorship, partnerships are easy to start. Potential **partners** might need only to obtain a license. Unlike a sole proprietorship, it is easier for partnerships to obtain capital. Also, each partner usually contributes money to start the business. Another advantage is that banks are often more willing to lend money to partnerships than to sole proprietorships. Partnerships are not dependent on a sole person. As with a sole proprietorship, the income of a partnership is taxed only once. Lastly, each partner brings different skills and talents to the business.

Disadvantages of Owning a Partnership One disadvantage is that all the partners share the business risks. Problems occur when partners do not get along or one of them decides to leave. In that case, the other owners must end the partnership and reorganize the business since the original partnership no longer exists. Partners also share unlimited legal and financial liability. If one partner makes a bad decision, all partners are responsible.

Corporations

A **corporation** is a company that is registered by a state and operates apart from its owners. To form a corporation, the owners must get a corporate charter from the state where their main office will be located. A corporate charter is a license to run a corporation. To raise money, the owners can sell stock, or shares in the company. The company also must have a board of directors, who will govern the corporation.

Advantages of Forming a Corporation A major advantage of a corporation is limited liability. **Limited liability** holds a firm's owners responsible for no more than the capital that they have invested in it. Another advantage is its ability to raise money when people buy stock. A third advantage is that the corporation does not end if an owner dies. If that happens, the deceased owner's shares are sold, and the business continues.

Disadvantages of Forming a Corporation Corporations face several disadvantages. They pay taxes on their income, and stockholders pay taxes on profits issued to them. That is called double taxation. There are some special types of corporations, such as S corporations and limited liability companies, which do not have double taxation. However, they have other restrictions. The government **regulates** corporations more than other types of businesses. Corporations are also difficult and costly to start.

● **Corporations and Big Business** Many corporations are big businesses that sell stock on the stock exchange to raise money. **Who governs a corporation?**

Other Ways to Organize a Business

There are other ways to organize a business venture.

A **cooperative** is an organization that is owned and operated by its members. When groups of businesses, such as small farms, pool their resources, they form a cooperative. The purpose is to save money on the purchase of certain goods and services. A cooperative can make marketing of goods and services more efficient and profitable. Juice maker Ocean Spray is a cooperative of cranberry growers.

A **nonprofit organization**, or nonprofit, is a type of organization that focuses on providing a service, but not to make a profit. Nonprofits must also register with the government. Because they do not make a profit, they do not pay taxes.

A **franchise** is a contractual agreement to use the name and sell the products or services of a company in a designated geographic area. Fast-food restaurant Taco Bell and cleaning service Merry Maids are two common franchises. To run a franchise, you have to invest money and pay franchise fees or a share of the profits. In return, the franchiser offers a well-known name and a business plan.

Section 6.1

After You Read

Review Key Concepts
1. What is the difference between a sole proprietorship and a partnership?
2. If a partner makes a bad decision, what responsibility do the other partners have?
3. Why are cooperatives formed?

Academic Skills
4. **Mathematics** Approximately 22% of businesses are corporations, 7% are partnerships, and the rest are sole proprietorships. In a sentence or two, describe how to construct a circle graph about the various forms of business ownership using this information.

CONCEPT **Data Analysis and Probability: Circle Graphs** A circle graph, also called a pie chart, uses wedge-shaped pieces to represent all the parts of the whole. If a part is 20% of the whole, then the wedge takes up 20% of the circle. In other words, the angle of the wedge is 20% of 360°.

 For math help, go to the Math Appendix.

 Go to **connectED.mcgraw-hill.com** to check your answers.

Types and Functions of Businesses

Reading Guide

● Before You Read

Think about the tasks that are performed by businesses to get goods and services to consumers.

Read to Learn
- Differentiate the six types of businesses.
- Describe the five functions of business.
- Discuss how the five functions of business relate to each other.

The Main Idea
There are many different types of businesses. The five functions of business are involved in every type of business.

Key Concepts
- Types of Businesses
- Functions of Business
- How the Functions of Business Are Interdependent

Vocabulary

Key Terms

producer	production
processor	procurement
manufacturer	marketing
intermediary	management
wholesaler	finance
retailer	accounting

Academic Vocabulary
You will find these words in your reading and on your tests. Make sure you know their meanings.

distributes	functions
tasks	involves

Graphic Organizer
In a box like the one below, arrange the six types of businesses in the order in which their tasks would be performed.

1.	**wholesaler**
2.	**processor**
3.	**manufacturer**
4.	**retailer**
5.	**producer**
6.	**intermediary**

 Go to **connectED.mcgraw-hill.com** to print out this graphic organizer.

Types of Businesses

As previously discussed, the business environment consists of many forms of organizations. There are many different types of businesses and various ways to classify them. One way is to group them by the kinds of activities they perform.

● **As You Read**

Think of a product you own. What kind of business made the product?

Producers

A **producer** is a business that gathers raw goods. Raw goods are materials gathered in their original state from natural resources such as land or water. Agriculture, mining, fishing, and forestry are some of the industries that produce raw goods.

Processors

A **processor** changes raw materials into more finished products. Processed goods are made from raw goods that require further processing. For example, sugar cane is turned into sugar, crude oil into gasoline, and iron ore into steel.

Manufacturers

A **manufacturer** is a business that makes finished products out of processed goods. Manufacturers turn raw or processed goods into finished goods. Goods are material products such as cars, CDs, and computers.

Business Case Study

Spotlight on Microfinancing: Tiny Loans, Change Lives

For only $25, you can fund a global entrepreneur's dreams

Entrepreneurs need money to get a new business off the ground. But what about entrepreneurs in remote or impoverished areas of the globe, who want to improve their lives but have no access to traditional banks? That's where the nonprofit organization Kiva comes in. Through a worldwide network of "microfinancers," Kiva gives aspiring entrepreneurs a chance to show the world what they want to do. You can invest in someone's dream for as little as $25.

Kiva's site has hundreds of profiles for campaigns you can help fund. Leroy from Belize seeks $750 for seedlings for his new cacao-farming business. Afida from Tanzania needs $475 to buy utensils and hire an employee for her restaurant.

Kiva connects them with microfinancers who give them a chance to get started.

As of late 2014, Kiva had enabled over $630 million in loans to entrepreneurs in 83 nations. The loan repayment rate was 98.8 percent. Over 1 million lenders had taken part in this tech-savvy effort to alleviate world poverty.

Active Learning

Go to Kiva's website, Kiva.org, and click the Lend tab. Read about the campaigns until you find one that interests you. Write a one-page report describing the entrepreneur, his or her country of origin, his or her business, and how the money will benefit his or her community. Explain whether you believe this business opportunity is a good investment, and why.

● **The Interdependence of Businesses** Many businesses rely on other businesses. **Which types of businesses might be involved in the manufacture of an automobile?**

Intermediaries and Wholesalers

An **intermediary** is a business that moves goods from one business to another. It buys goods, stores them, and then resells them. A **wholesaler** **distributes** goods. Wholesalers are also known as distributors. A clothing wholesaler, for example, may buy thousands of jackets from several manufacturers. The wholesaler then divides the large quantities into smaller ones and sells them to retailers.

Retailers and Service Businesses

A **retailer** purchases goods from a wholesaler and sells them to consumers, the final buyers of the goods. Service stations, record stores, and auto dealers are examples of retailers.

Service businesses perform **tasks** rather than provide goods. Some service businesses meet needs, such as medical clinics and law firms. Others provide conveniences, such as taxi companies and copy shops. Service businesses employ about three-quarters of the workforce and are rapidly increasing in numbers.

Functions of Business

There are five main **functions** involved in the operation of all types of businesses. They are production and procurement; marketing; management; finance; and accounting.

✔ **Reading Check** **Identify** What are the five main functions of business?

iStockphoto.com/RicAguiar

As You Read

Think about starting a surfboard business that sells boards you design and make. Would your business be involved in production or procurement?

Production and Procurement

Production is the process of creating, expanding, manufacturing, or improving goods and services. Most retailers procure goods from producers for resale. **Procurement** is the buying and reselling of goods that have already been produced. Wholesalers buy goods from producers to resell to retailers and other wholesalers.

Marketing

Marketing is the process of planning, pricing, promoting, selling, and distributing ideas, goods, and services. Marketing **involves** getting consumers to buy a product or service. Marketers make decisions based on market research of trends and consumer habits.

Management

Management is the process of achieving company goals by planning, organizing, leading, controlling, and evaluating the effective use of resources.

Finance and Accounting

Finance is the business or art of money management. It requires analyzing financial statements to make future decisions. **Accounting** involves maintaining and checking records, handling bills, and preparing financial reports for a business.

Science/Tech TRENDS

The History of Information Technology

The information technology (IT) practices of today have evolved and developed through several stages, each with the goal of solving the input, processing, output, and communication problems of the time. During the Premechanical Age, from 3000 BC to AD 1450, writing and alphabets developed, books and libraries were invented, and the first calculator, the abacus, came into popular use. The Mechanical Age, from 1450 to 1840, brought with it the first real computers. During the Electromechanical Age, from 1840 to 1940, the discovery of ways to harness electricity meant knowledge and information could be converted into electrical impulses. From 1940 to the present, the Electronic Age has the ongoing communications revolution in our homes and places of business.

Web Quest

Locate Web sites where you can find out more about the history of information technology. Write a few paragraphs about a person, invention, or time period that interests you.

How the Functions of Business Are Interdependent

The functional areas of business depend on each other. For example, say a furniture maker's sales have been decreasing. The accounting and finance departments have noted the drop in sales. If the products are too high-priced, then more efficient procedures will have to be implemented. This will involve management and production. A new marketing plan may be required. Accounting and finance will have to closely monitor the effects that new efforts have on profits.

Sometimes the functional areas conflict with each other. Suppose management wants to increase sales by 20 percent within three years. The production department suggests improving quality to attract more customers. However, changing the quality would add to costs. Meanwhile, the marketing department says the problem is that there is not enough marketing being done. It requests more funds for projects. Accounting then says neither plan is good since both would lower profits by raising costs. It suggests improving production efficiency. The final plan involves ideas from all functions of business. Companies benefit when all functional areas work together.

Real World

To Advertise or Not
Advertising is used to influence consumers to buy one product or service over another. *Do you think you could run a successful business without doing major advertising? Why or why not?*

Section 6.2

After You Read

Review Key Concepts
1. What is the difference between a producer and a processor?
2. Identify the five functions of business.
3. Give an example of how the accounting and finance functions can affect a business's marketing and production processes.

Academic Skills
4. **English Language Arts** Brainstorming is a technique you can try to come up with ideas to use in your writing. Imagine that you have written a book encouraging high school students to start their own part-time business. Work with a group to brainstorm titles for your book. Ask the group to think of titles that would be intriguing to high school students.

5. **English Language Arts** Write a three-sentence summary of the material in this section. Share it with four classmates, and ask them to either add a sentence containing something you missed, correct any errors they find, comment about how you could write a better summary, or compare their summary to yours. Then rewrite your summary, incorporating any ideas or corrections you feel are appropriate.

 Go to **connectED.mcgraw-hill.com** to check your answers.

Chapter 6 Review and Activities

Section 6.1 Summary

Types of Business Ownership Three primary forms of business ownership are sole proprietorships, partnerships, and corporations. A major advantage of sole proprietorships and partnerships is their ease of formation. One advantage corporations have over sole proprietorships and partnerships is limited liability. Limited liability means an owner cannot suffer a loss that is more than he or she invested. An advantage partnerships and corporations have over sole proprietorships is better access to capital. Nonprofits, cooperatives, and franchises are other forms of organizations.

Section 6.2 Summary

Types and Functions of Businesses There are different types of businesses. Most can be categorized as producers, processors, manufacturers, intermediaries, or retail or service businesses. There are five functions of business: production and procurement; marketing; management; finance; and accounting. These functions take place in every company. The functional areas are interdependent and must work together for the business to succeed. Sometimes the functional areas are in conflict with one another. Conflicts can be resolved by considering ideas from all functional areas.

Vocabulary Review

1. On a sheet of paper, use each of these key terms and academic vocabulary terms in a sentence.

Key Terms

sole proprietorship	franchise	production
unlimited liability	producer	procurement
partnership	processor	marketing
corporation	manufacturer	management
limited liability	intermediary	finance
cooperative	wholesaler	accounting
nonprofit organization	retailer	

Academic Vocabulary

sole	distributes
income	tasks
partners	functions
regulates	involves

Review Key Concepts

2. Describe the advantages and disadvantages of three major forms of business organizations.

3. Describe how cooperatives and nonprofits are like and unlike corporations and franchises.

4. Differentiate the six types of businesses.

5. Describe the five functions of business.

6. Discuss how the five functions of business relate to each other.

Critical Thinking

7. Why might two or more people decide to form a partnership instead of each forming a sole proprietorship?

8. Working as a team member is similar to being in a partnership. What are some advantages and disadvantages of working with others?

9. There are more sole proprietorships than partnerships or corporations in the United States. Why do you think so many businesses are organized as sole proprietorships?

10. Identify what happens during the production, processing, and delivery stages within each type of business responsible for the manufacturing and sale of a loaf of bread.

11. Explain how a producer, a processor, and a manufacturer are not involved in producing a service.

12. How can accountants in a firm provide an idea of the general financial health of the company?

13. Imagine that you and a friend have developed a new engine and would like to manufacture the engine and sell it to major automakers. What form of business organization would you select for your company? Why?

Write About It

14. Write an e-mail to a friend, explaining the reasons for the differences between the cost of manufacturing a product and its final sales price.

15. Interview a business partner. Ask why he or she entered into a partnership. What are the challenges of being in a partnership? Write a report based on the person's responses.

16. Form groups. Have each member interview someone who works in finance, marketing, production, human resources, management, or sales. Ask them about the responsibilities of their positions. How do their departments function within their companies? Write a report on your findings.

17. Look in reference books for information about what is included in the articles of incorporation. Write a one-page report about your findings.

18. Research the characteristics of an S corporation or a limited liability company. In two or more paragraphs, discuss how they are like and unlike a conventional corporation.

19. Interview the director of a nonprofit. Find out how its functions are similar to or different from a for-profit business. Prepare a one-page report on your findings.

Technology Applications

Creating a Database

20. Compile a database of at least 10 businesses from a phone book. Include fields for the name, address, telephone number, and the category of business. Find at least one business that is a producer, a processor, a manufacturer, an intermediary, and a retail or service business.

Business Ethics

Go Solo or Form a Partnership?

21. Imagine that you and a friend invent a new material for fixing leaky faucets. You would like to sell this new product. Your friend wants to be your partner. Since he worked with you on the new invention, should you form a partnership with him? Write a letter to your friend discussing your decision.

Applying Academics to Business

English Language Arts

22. List the words *producer, manufacturer, wholesaler,* and *retailer*. Underline the base word within each and circle the suffix. Write a definition for the suffix and list a few other words that use it in the same way. What other suffixes have a similar meaning? Give some examples.

Mathematics

23. The neighborhood bakery makes bread, cakes, cookies, and pies. At the end of the day, the prices of all the leftover products are reduced by 75%. If bread sells for 87¢ at the end of the day, what is its regular price?

   CONCEPT **Algebra: Equations** Using the information given in the problem, you can write an algebraic equation and find the solution. Let *x* stand for the regular price of the bread.

English Language Arts

24. The word *corporation* is related to other words in the English language that might not seem connected such as *corps,* as in *Marine Corps, corpulent* (meaning obese), and *corpus delicti* (meaning the facts that prove a crime was committed). Research the origins of these words, and explain why they are related.

Mathematics

25. Zack wanted to open a business having to do with his favorite sport, skiing. Since he lives in a warm climate, he decided to open an indoor ski park. The beginner's slope is 822 feet long and 65 yards wide. What is its area?

   CONCEPT **Geometry: Finding Areas** The areas of two-dimensional geometric figures can be found using various formulas. Area is measured in square units. In solving this problem, decide which units to use.

Active Learning

Learning from Working

26. Most nonprofit organizations provide charitable services to people and communities. They rely upon volunteers to conduct much of their business. Volunteer to work in a nonprofit organization. Find out what workers do, how they do it, how the nonprofit is set up, what people like about working there, how it is funded, and what challenges it faces. Write a one-page report about your findings. Present your report to the class.

Business in the Real World

Comparing Business Organizations

27. Invite local businesspeople from sole proprietorships, partnerships, and corporations to serve on a panel discussion in your class. If there is a cooperative in your community, have a representative from the organization attend. Ask the panel members about the advantages and disadvantages of their type of business ownership, how they got their start, and the qualities they feel are important for success. Be sure to thank them for their time.

Real LIFE skills

ASSESSING YOUR SKILLS

28. Successful business ownership requires several personal qualities. They include: responsibility, self-esteem, sociability, self-management, integrity, and honesty. In your own words, write definitions of these qualities and rate your possession of them from 1 to 5, with 5 being your strongest quality and 1 being your weakest. What can you do to develop the two qualities that you have ranked as the lowest?

Business CAREERS

FIND YOUR DREAM JOB

29. Locate the Occupational Outlook Handbook Web site. Click on the "OOH Search/A-Z Index" link and enter the job title "top executive." Then write a one-page report about this type of occupation. Conclude your report with a list of things you could do now to prepare yourself to pursue the occupation.

Role Play

FUNCTIONAL AREAS OF BUSINESS

30. Situation You are the sales manager of a company that makes bicycles. Your salespeople report that several bicycles have been returned because of a faulty brake.

Activity The president wants to know what you think should be done to correct the problem. You need to prepare a report for him that demonstrates what you think should be done. Your report should include the actions to take in the functional areas of the business.

Evaluation You will be evaluated on how well you meet the following performance indicators:

- Make valid recommendations for each department.
- Describe each department function.
- Understand how the five functions of business depend on each other.
- Prepare a written report.
- Speak clearly and use correct grammar.

Standardized Test Practice

Directions Choose the letter of the best answer. Write the letter for the answer on a separate piece of paper.

1. Which word or phrase best completes the sentence?

Many people _____ hard over the years to make the business a success.

A   work
B   will work
C   works
D   have worked

TEST-TAKING TIP When taking a test, work on a problem only until you get stuck. Think about it for a minute or two, and if nothing comes to mind, then move on to another problem.

Chapter 7

Business Management

Chapter Objectives After completing this chapter, you will be able to:

▶ **Section 7.1** *Management Functions*
- **Describe** the overall purpose of management.
- **Discuss** the four functions of management.

▶ **Section 7.2** *Management Structures*
- **Identify** the differences between management structures.
- **Name** six skills necessary for effective management.

Ask AN EXPERT

Establishing Investment Goals

Q: Next year I plan to attend college and major in food management. When I graduate, I want to open a restaurant. I know it takes a lot of money to get started, so my first restaurant will have to be small—maybe a take-out pizza shop. How can I start investing money now to meet my goal?

A: Identifying your goals is a good first step. However, an investment plan requires a specific, measurable goal. First, you need to determine how much money you will need to open your restaurant. Then you can develop a plan for how you will acquire the funds.

Mathematics To start, estimate the capital required to open the business. Create a list of all your initial expenses. Include items that you will need to purchase once, such as pizza ovens, pans, plates, and other service items. Then make another list of recurring costs, such as rent, ingredients, and paper products. Next to each expense, estimate how much that item will cost. If it is a recurring cost, estimate how much you will spend during the first year of operation.

CONCEPT **Estimation** To estimate your needs, round numbers to the nearest hundred or thousand. To round a number, look at the place to the right of the place to which you are rounding. If you are rounding to thousands, for example, look at the digit in the hundreds place. If the digit is 5 or greater, round up; if it is 4 or less, round down.

Chris Ryan/age fotostock

● **Communication Is Key** Effective managers have good communication and people skills. Why do you think effective managers need to be good communicators?

Management Functions

Reading Guide

● Before You Read

Think about the processes involved in managing a baseball team and how they might apply in business.

Read to Learn

- Describe the overall purpose of management.
- Discuss the four functions of management.

The Main Idea

The purpose of management is to set goals for the company and to help meet those goals as efficiently and effectively as possible. There are four functions of management: planning, organizing, leading, and controlling.

Key Concepts

- Introduction to Management
- The Four Functions of Management

Vocabulary

Key Terms

management
planning
organizing
organizational chart
top-level manager
middle manager
operational manager
leading
controlling

Academic Vocabulary

You will find these words in your reading and on your tests. Make sure you know their meanings.

focus
goals

teams
enforce

Graphic Organizer

In a figure like the one below, write examples of the types of positions that might be held by top-level managers, middle managers, and operational managers.

Top-Level Manager	Middle Manager	Operational Manager

 Go to **connectED.mcgraw-hill.com** to print out this graphic organizer.

Introduction to Management

Entrepreneurs who start and run businesses by themselves do not have to manage other people. They have to manage themselves. However, if the firm has employees, then some type of management plan is necessary. **Management** includes the processes or functions of planning, organizing, leading, and controlling.

For example, suppose you have created your own comic book and want to start a comic book company. Do you want to produce comic books and market them as well? Do you also want to produce cartoons, video games, and action figures based on your comic books? Because of the complexity of your business, you will need employees to help. Managers can help by supervising and directing employees.

Management helps businesses **focus** on setting and meeting **goals** efficiently and effectively so that a profit can be made. The word *management* also refers to the people who are in charge of running a business. Managers need a thorough understanding of business operations, which involve all the activities of a company. They develop the objectives for a firm or a department and then figure out how to meet those objectives through people, work processes, and equipment.

● **As You Read**

Think about all the things that are involved in managing your local grocery store.

The Four Functions of Management

Most managers carry out four different functions of management: planning, organizing, leading, and controlling. Some managers may primarily focus on one or two of them. These functions are indicated in the order in which they occur. Planning must be completed first, then organization can take place. Organization allows managers to lead and control employees and activities to get work done. Leading involves providing guidance to employees so they can fulfill their responsibilities effectively. Controlling involves measuring how the business performs to ensure that financial and operational goals are met.

A challenge for many managers, especially in small businesses, is dealing with multiple objectives, each at a different functional level. For example, suppose your company's manager discusses plans to produce a new comic book with the marketing and production **teams**. The manager directs the marketing team to research the national and global markets for comic books. The manager also tells the production team to prepare to produce the new product.

❓ETHICS in Business

A Conflict of Interest

■ **Critical Reading** Life is full of important decisions. Think about the kinds of decisions that you make as you read the question below.

You and your best friend, Jeremiah, were helping your little brother figure out how to make molded cars from melted crayons using a kit you gave him. You decide to sell the cars at a local toy shop. Jeremiah hears you talking with your business teacher about your new business idea, and he wants to be a partner.

■ **Decision Making** Since Jeremiah was involved in the initial experiment, do you have an obligation to make him a partner in your business venture? What about your little brother? Should he also own a piece of the new business? What are the advantages and disadvantages of a partnership? Explain your answer.

It is up to the manager to organize, analyze, and monitor the project to assure that the production process works efficiently and effectively. Communicating with employees at all times helps assure that objectives are met. **Figure 7.1** describes the four functions of management.

✔ Reading Check **Describe** What are the four functions of management?

Planning

Planning is the act or process of creating goals and objectives as well as the strategies to meet them. Planning also involves figuring out the resources that are needed and the standards that must be met.

Organizing and Staffing

Organizing is getting the resources arranged in an orderly and functional way to accomplish goals and objectives. A manager must organize people, work processes, and equipment so that the work is well coordinated. Managers also hire and train employees—and fire them when necessary. They are responsible for making sure employees have all the tools they need to do their jobs well.

Figure 7.1 — *Management Functions*

PLANNING	ORGANIZING
Setting objectives and making long- and short-term plans for meeting the objectives	Obtaining and coordinating resources so that a business's objectives can be met

LEADING	CONTROLLING
Influencing, guiding, and directing people under one's management to carry out their assigned tasks	Setting standards for work, evaluating performance, and solving problems that prevent certain tasks' completion

● **Management Functions** Managers carry out four different functions. **Which function involves coordinating resources?**

Levels of Management   Another important part of organizing is determining how different individuals in the firm relate to one another. An **organizational chart** shows how the firm is structured and who is in charge of whom.

A **top-level manager** is responsible for setting goals and planning for the future as well as leading and controlling the work of others. There is only one top-level manager at the Small Wonders Comic Book Company because it is a small business. In larger firms, top-level management can be composed of a chief executive officer (or CEO), a president, and at least one vice president.

A **middle manager** carries out the decisions of top management. Middle managers are often responsible for various departments in a business, such as the production, marketing, and accounting departments. Middle management is responsible for the organizing function as well as leading and controlling the work of others. Although middle managers do some planning, they are usually responsible for carrying out plans made by top management.

An **operational manager** is responsible for the daily operations of a business. Supervisors, office managers, and crew leaders are types of operational managers. Operational managers also do some planning and organizing. However, their main duties include overseeing workers and meeting deadlines (leading and controlling).

● **As You Read**

Many companies have eliminated middle managers to save money. Do you think this is a good business practice?

Leading

Good management also requires good leadership. There is more to leading than just giving orders. **Leading** means providing direction and vision. You have to create a vision of the company to inspire your employees. You need to set standards, such as deadlines and sales quotas, so your managers and workers know their goals. Leaders also have to delegate work, **enforce** policies, oversee time management, and provide feedback on employees' work. Resolving conflicts between workers is also a leadership task.

Blend Images/Alamy

● **Responsibilities of a Manager**
A manager has many different responsibilities. **What responsibility is this manager fulfilling?**

Good managers lead by example. This is especially important when leading a team. Showing respect to others, honesty, loyalty, courtesy, and a strong work ethic can have a positive effect on employees. Managers who show motivation, initiative, cooperation, and punctuality demonstrate to employees the importance of each person's contribution.

✔ Reading Check **Analyze** Why is there more to leading than giving orders?

Controlling

Controlling the operation means keeping the company on track and making sure goals are met. Managers keep track of the budget, the schedule, and the quality of the products or services they provide. They also monitor their employees and review their performance according to standards. Taking corrective action when goals are not met is another management task.

Controlling also involves monitoring customer satisfaction. Your marketing manager can measure the success of your comic book by studying sales figures and reviews. You might find out your comic book sold well in certain parts of the country but sold poorly in others. If your comic book is more popular with adults than children, you might want to develop a new marketing plan.

Section 7.1

After You Read

Review Key Concepts
1. What is management?
2. What are three levels of management?
3. Which of the three levels is most involved in the day-to-day supervision of employees?

Academic Skills
4. **Mathematics** You are a delivery manager at Blue Bag, a wholesale bakery. The bakery employs two drivers and owns two trucks. Each truck can deliver up to 175 crates of bread per day. The bakery has standing orders for 340 crates a day, but a new supermarket is opening up, and you expect orders to increase 225%. If you hire two more drivers, you can run two shifts. Will it be enough? Write a paragraph explaining how you found your answer.

CONCEPT **Problem Solving: Reflect on the Problem-Solving Process** Solving complex word problems such as this requires thinking through different scenarios, writing equations to match those scenarios, solving those equations, and comparing the results.

 For math help, go to the Math Appendix.

 Go to **connectED.mcgraw-hill.com** to check your answers.

Management Structures

Reading Guide

● Before You Read

Think about the characteristics you would need to be an effective manager.

Read to Learn
- Identify the differences between management structures.
- Name six skills necessary for effective management.

The Main Idea
Businesses have many different management structures that they can adopt. People who are interested in management should pay attention to the skills and knowledge needed to be an effective manager.

Key Concepts
- Managerial Structures
- Is a Manager's Job for You?

Vocabulary

Key Terms

line authority
line and staff authority
centralized organization
decentralized organization
departmentalization
entry-level job

Academic Vocabulary
You will find these words in your reading and on your tests. Make sure you know their meanings.

structure   evident
authority   sector

Graphic Organizer
In a figure like the one below, list the qualities you need to be a good manager as you read.

Skills Needed by Managers

 Go to **connectED.mcgraw-hill.com** to print out this graphic organizer.

Managerial Structures

There are several ways to organize a management **structure**. **Line authority** is an organizational structure in which managers on one level are in charge of those beneath them. An advantage of the line authority structure is that **authority** is clearly defined. Each employee knows to whom she or he reports. A disadvantage to line authority is that the managers have few specialists who help with their responsibilities.

A **line and staff authority** organizational chart shows the direct line of authority (indicated by solid lines) as well as staff who advise the line personnel (indicated by dotted lines). **Figure 7.2** shows a line and staff organizational chart. The line and staff authority structure enables managers to get advice. However, a disadvantage is that it can lead to overstaffing, which can be costly.

Some firms have a **centralized organization** that puts authority in one place—with top management. This helps managers throughout the firm to be consistent in decision making.

Figure 7.2 – **Line and Staff Authority Organization Chart**

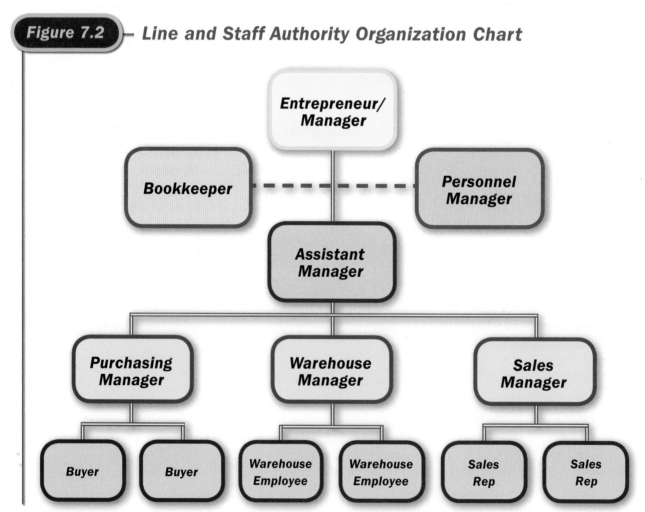

● **Solid and Dotted Lines** A line and staff organizational chart shows different roles of staff with different types of lines. **What is the difference between the personnel linked by solid lines and staff positions linked by dotted lines?**

Decentralized organization gives authority to a number of different managers. Decentralized organizations are often **evident** in international businesses. Some U.S. managers working in foreign countries have more decision-making power because they know their markets well.

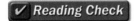 **Contrast** What is the advantage and the disadvantage of line authority?

Formal Structure

Formal structures are usually departmentalized. **Departmentalization** divides responsibility among specific units, or departments. Departments can be organized many different ways, such as by geographical location, function, customer groups, and product.

Informal Structure

Smaller businesses can be run informally. If a business does not need a big marketing or distribution network, it does not need a lot of managers. Employees can be more flexible and share duties. For example, partners can work on projects alone or together. The informal structure often works well for them.

Employee Input
Forward-looking companies are on a new track to encourage worker participation, new ways of thinking, and a move away from a formal structure. *How is this good for business?*

● As You Read

Think about an informal business you have seen or read about. Do you think this type of business can be successful?

Science/Tech TRENDS

Decision Science

Solving highly complex business problems requires a manager to be an effective decision maker. Effective decision makers seek input from many sources and gather varied data to inform their thinking about business problems. Since the 1940s, the field of decision science, also known as management science or success science, has developed new ways to use mathematics and the scientific method to make decisions. Business managers faced with the need to analyze mounds of data and choose among risky alternatives can hire decision scientists to help them. These consultants offer data analysis services, education in mathematical concepts, and data analysis tools and techniques.

Web Quest

Decision science evolved from game theory, which deals largely with how individuals interact with one another in an effort to win. Locate Web sites where you can research more about how game theory and decision science have developed since the 1940s. Write a paragraph or two describing how an understanding of game theory and decision science could help a person make complex business decisions.

Is a Manager's Job for You?

Most managers begin their career in an entry-level job. An **entry-level job** is a beginner-level position. New employees who gain experience and show certain qualities can be promoted to higher positions, including management.

Skills Needed by Managers

Managers are usually task-oriented. This means that they can handle many tasks at the same time. They have to plan their time and decide which tasks are most important. They also must keep accurate business records. A manager often has to work under pressure and solve many small problems. Good problem-solving and time-management skills are a must. Every manager must communicate well. Most of a manager's day is spent interacting with other people. This involves listening, an important part of communication. Managers need human relations skills, or skills in dealing with people. All managers must have some knowledge about the technical aspects of their business.

Business Case Study

What Makes a Good Boss?

Effective managers rely on collaboration and trust

Managers are accountable for the performance of their teams. Effective managers ensure performance by motivating their employees and giving them what they need to be productive.

The modern workplace is more open to manager-employee collaboration than in the past. A top-down attitude is giving way to a team environment in which everyone feels invested in a company's success. Employees' motivation rises when they feel their contributions are valued and their managers provide them with adequate resources and support.

Workplace experts encourage managers to treat employees like responsible adults. Many organizations are rethinking counter-productive policies such as strict dress codes, performance reviews focused mainly on criticism,

three-strikes-style discipline, and unneeded monitoring of how work time is spent.

Trust is a two-way street, according to consultant Liz Ryan in an article for *Forbes* magazine: "Trust people to rise to the occasion, and the vast majority of them will do it."

Active Learning

Do you currently work at a job, or have you been employed in the past? Write a short essay describing the management style of your workplace. Was it a collaborative, trusting environment? What would you have done differently if you worked in management? Why? If you have not been employed yet, write about an example from home or school where you were trusted with a responsibility and rose to the occasion

Managers, especially top-level managers, must be able to understand how various parts of the company relate to the whole business. This includes knowing how economic conditions and competition can affect the business. Higher-level managers have to know what is happening in the world and in their sector of the business world. Otherwise, they will have trouble conceptualizing and solving problems that the company faces.

Advantages of Being a Manager

Managers usually earn more money than employees in non-management jobs. People become managers because they have the ability to lead. Managers who are good leaders are respected. Being a respected manager builds prestige. Managers have more influence and authority than other employees because they plan, organize, direct, and control company resources. They also have greater control over their time.

Disadvantages of Being a Manager

There are several disadvantages to being a manager. Managers are often blamed when things go wrong, even if they did not cause the problem. Their mistakes can be very costly to a company so they are under a lot of pressure to make the right decisions.

● **As You Read**

Think about an opportunity to manage a local restaurant. Would you want to take on the responsibility? Why or why not?

Section 7.2

After You Read

Review Key Concepts

1. What is an advantage of a line and staff authority organization structure over a line authority organization?
2. Why do some businesses use a decentralized organization?
3. What are some characteristics of an effective manager?

Academic Skills

4. **English Language Arts** Work with a partner to role play two business situations involving a manager and an employee. If possible, choose a partner who has a different cultural background from your own. Each of you should take the role of manager in one of the situations you choose. List the management responsibilities and skills that you and your partner think are important for handling the situations you examined.

5. **English Language Arts** In which kind of organization would you like to work? Should it have a formal or informal structure? Write a short description of the ideal business environment for you. Then imagine starting a garden design and maintenance business. Decide what jobs you will need to hire people to fill. Create an organizational chart for your company.

 Go to **connectED.mcgraw-hill.com** to check your answers.

Section 7.1 *Summary*

Management Functions Management includes the processes or functions of planning, organizing, leading, and controlling. Most managers carry out all four of the functions. However, some spend more time on some of the functions than others. There are generally three levels of management: top-level, middle, and operational. Top-level managers usually spend more time on planning than operational managers. Middle managers spend more time organizing. They also lead and control the work of others. Operational managers generally spend more time on leading and controlling than do top-level managers.

Section 7.2 *Summary*

Management Structures There are several different management structures, including line authority; line and staff authority; centralized or decentralized authority; and formal or informal authority. Each has its own advantages and disadvantages. A business should adopt the structure that makes it operate at its best to maximize profits. Successful managers are task-oriented and able to work under pressure. Many people aspire to become managers because of advantages such as increased income, prestige, and the ability to make things happen. Disadvantages of being a manager include stress and accepting responsibility for other people's mistakes.

Vocabulary Review

1. On a sheet of paper, use each of these key terms and academic vocabulary terms in a sentence.

Key Terms

management
planning
organizing
organizational chart
top-level manager
middle manager
operational manager
leading

controlling
line authority
line and staff authority
centralized organization
decentralized organization
departmentalization
entry-level job

Academic Vocabulary

focus
goals
teams
enforce
structure
authority
evident
sector

Review Key Concepts

2. Describe the overall purpose of management.

3. Discuss the four functions of management.

4. Identify the differences between management structures.

5. Name six skills necessary for effective management.

6. Some people believe that the planning function is the most important one for a manager. Why might that be true?

7. Suppose top-level management decides how to produce and market a new product. Do you think the plans might change during the organizing, leading, and controlling stages?

8. Since companies are using fewer middle managers, how have the jobs of top-level management and operational managers changed?

9. Why do you think it is a good idea for workers to have more decision-making duties and provide input to managers?

10. Give reasons for working within either a formal or an informal business structure.

11. Describe the qualities of a manager for whom you would like to work someday.

12. One problem with line and staff authority as compared to line authority is that some line and staff managers tend to overanalyze a problem. Why might that happen?

13. Why might a manager decide to change an informally structured organization into a formally structured one?

14. In what ways are an entrepreneur and a manager alike? In what ways are they different? Write an e-mail to your teacher on your thoughts.

15. Imagine you are in charge of the next school dance. In one page, indicate some tasks that you would complete in each function of management.

16. What are reasons some managers are hired from within a company? Why are some hired from outside a company? Write two or more paragraphs explaining your answers.

17. Research the requirements for a management major at a local two- or four-year college. Determine the types of courses that students must take. In a one-page article, describe the required courses in the program.

18. One requirement of a good manager is effective communication skills. Write a short essay about the importance of communication to managers. Be sure to include listening skills.

19. Managers generally receive more pay than the workers they manage. Write two or more paragraphs indicating why you believe this is fair or unfair.

Organization Chart

20. Work in small groups. Imagine you are starting a greeting card company. Decide what functions your team members will perform. Consider each person's talents and interests. Will your company be structured formally or informally? Make a chart using presentation software to show how you organized your company. Present your chart to the class.

Managerial Decision Making

21. You are an operations manager for a ceramics manufacturer. The president's son is assigned to work for you, but after two weeks, you notice that he spends a lot of time on the Internet, does little work, and does not get along with other workers. If you do nothing, then production will be affected. What should you do?

Applying Academics to Business

English Language Arts

22. Hyphens and dashes are used in several situations. Look through this textbook and note two examples of each of the following: a dash separating parts of a sentence; a hyphen separating syllables in a word that turns a line; hyphenated adjectives; and hyphenated proper nouns.

Mathematics

23. Fran, a merchandising manager for Blue Bag, is planning her department's yearly budget. She earns $500 a week and is in charge of three employees, each earning $350 a week. The business pays FICA (Federal Insurance Contributions Act) taxes of 8.15% on employee earnings to cover the cost of Social Security. Write an equation Fran could use to figure how much her department needs to budget to pay salaries and FICA taxes for the year.

CONCEPT **Algebra: Writing Equations** Simplify your equation by multiplying the total of the departmental salaries by a percent, greater than 100, that represents total salaries increased by the percent for FICA taxes.

English Language Arts

24. Copy the following paragraph onto a piece of paper and add the correct punctuation: Successful managers are able to carry out varied tasks perform under pressure communicate effectively relate to people and grasp and use information. Managers have prestige influence and power however they usually experience a lot of pressure too.

Mathematics

25. Fred tracked the number of days members of his department were absent. For the second quarter, the results were: 5, 3, 5, 6, 9, 13, 15, 12, 8, 7, 5, 7, and 5. What are the range, mean, median, and mode of the data?

CONCEPT **Data Analysis and Probability: Measures of Central Tendency** For any given set of data, the range is the difference between the greatest and least value; the mean is the average; the median is the middle value when all values are ordered from least to greatest; and the mode is the most frequently occurring value.

Active Learning

Workplace Organization

26. Ask a family member how his or her workplace is organized. How is the management structured? Is the company divided into different divisions? How many employees are there in each division, if any? Does the company operate in more than one location? Create a poster summarizing your findings.

Business in the Real World

Managers as Leaders

27. Interview a business manager to find out how he or she uses leadership skills and resources on the job. Ask about job duties, delegating, what the manager most likes about his or her job, and what his or her greatest challenges are. Then ask how much time is spent on each of the four functional areas of management. Use this information to write a report of 250 words of more.

Real LIFE skills

EVALUATING MANAGEMENT SKILLS

28. Review the six different traits necessary for effective management. These traits include technical and conceptual skills. Choose a successful entrepreneur, and research how she or he became successful. Identify the traits that helped this businessperson reach his or her goals. Write at least a one-page report on your findings.

Cool Business CAREERS

FIND YOUR DREAM JOB

29. Locate the Occupational Outlook Handbook Web site. Click on the "OOH Search/A-Z Index" link and enter the job title "medical and health services manager." Then write a one-page report about this type of occupation. Conclude your report with a list of things you could do now to prepare yourself to pursue this occupation.

Role Play

INTERVIEWING FOR A MANAGEMENT JOB

30. Situation Last summer you planned and implemented an educational trip for 30 young people for three weeks. Now you are interviewing for a summer job managing a recreational program for 8- to 10-year-olds in your community. You would be developing this program on your own.

Activity Discuss the experiences you have that show the skills and background needed for the job.

Evaluation You will be evaluated on how well you meet the following performance indicators:

- Mention how you used the four functional areas of management.
- Demonstrate how you have at least five of the management skills mentioned in the chapter.
- Make concise and clear statements while showing self-confidence.
- Use correct grammar.

Standardized Test Practice

Directions Choose the letter of the best answer. Write the letter for the answer on a separate piece of paper.

1. Which could be added to 4 to get an integer x that is less than -2?

   A   any integer greater than -3

   B   any integer less than 0

   C   any integer less than -6

   D   any integer greater than -6

 TEST-TAKING TIP You can improve your score on multiple-choice items by covering the options while you read the question and try to answer it. Then select the option that most closely matches your answer.

Chapter 8

Leadership in Management

Chapter Objectives After completing this chapter, you will be able to:

▶ **Section 8.1** *Leadership Qualities*
- **Define** leadership.
- **Describe** the qualities of a leader.
- **Name** at least three ways in which an individual can develop leadership skills.

▶ **Section 8.2** *Leadership Styles*
- **Identify** and describe the autocratic, democratic, and free-rein leadership styles.
- **Describe** the self-managed team approach and the two ways in which such an approach is organized.

Ask

AN EXPERT

Getting Professional Help with Investing

Q: I have just inherited some money and need help making investment decisions. What kinds of professional services are available to new investors?

A: The service that is best for you depends partly on how much time and effort you want to spend tending to your investments. Certified financial planners can help you look at the larger picture, identify goals, and structure a portfolio. Stockbrokers can help you buy and sell individual stocks. You'll want to investigate credentials and experience, and get recommendations from other clients before choosing. Investment help is also available from publications such as Standard & Poor's *The Outlook*. Finally, investment clubs are a great way for like-minded people to share their investing experiences. You might consider joining one.

Mathematics Mary Ann hired a certified financial planner to help her invest $100,000 she inherited. When she asked the CFP how he would be paid, he said his fee would be 2% of the amount under management plus a half-percent commission on any stock purchase. Mary Ann chose to invest $60,000 in stocks and the rest in other types of investments. Write an equation that shows what she paid her financial planner (*p*) for his services.

CONCEPT **Choosing Operations** Solving most real-world problems requires several steps. Read carefully to make sure you understand which operations to use.

Comstock Images/SuperStock

● **Captain of the Team** All kinds of groups need leaders. **Why do you think it is good to have a leader?**

Leadership Qualities

Reading Guide

Before You Read

Think about the essential qualities that make someone an effective leader.

Read to Learn

- Define leadership.
- Describe the qualities of a leader.
- Name at least three ways in which an individual can develop leadership skills.

The Main Idea

Leaders develop a vision for the organization that they are leading. They move employees and their organization toward that vision. The qualities of leaders include motivation, confidence, communication skills, and integrity.

Key Concepts

- Managing and Leading Others
- Developing Leadership Skills

Vocabulary

Key Terms

leadership
initiative
human relations
integrity

Academic Vocabulary

You will find these words in your reading and on your tests. Make sure you know their meanings.

vision   conflict
trends   techniques

Graphic Organizer

List and define the qualities of a good leader in a figure like the one below.

```
┌──────────────┐      ┌──────────────┐
│              │      │              │
│              │      │              │
└──────────────┘      └──────────────┘

        Leadership

┌──────────────┐      ┌──────────────┐
│              │      │              │
│              │      │              │
└──────────────┘      └──────────────┘
```

 Go to **connectED.mcgraw-hill.com** to print out this graphic organizer.

Managing and Leading Others

Leadership means taking a company and its employees in a direction based upon a **vision**. Leaders see the big picture and never lose sight of their goal. Good leaders manage others by inspiring them.

There is more to leadership than just being in charge. In today's world, true leaders know their business and the capabilities of their employees, analyze current **trends**, and steer their business on the right course. Some people who are managers are not leaders. They may focus on specific tasks to make sure work gets done, but they may not be visionaries or inspire others.

Good leadership is needed not only in the business world but also in areas such as nonprofits, education, and sports. For example, a football team depends on its quarterback to call the signals and direct the offensive play. The quarterback has to think quickly and counts on his teammates to follow through after a decision is made. Ideally, the person in charge of a business or business team is also a leader.

Leaders also make sure that the basic operations of an organization are running smoothly. That could involve making sure office duties get done; handling records management; and planning, organizing, and running meetings. Being a good leader takes several qualities. Motivation, confidence, communication skills, and integrity are among them.

● **As You Read**

Think about some people you know who are managers.

✔ **Reading Check** **Identify** What does leadership involve in today's world?

International Business

Total Quality Management

After World War II, Japan had a reputation for producing poorly made products. In order to bring about change, Japanese business leaders hired Dr. W. Edwards Deming, an American management consultant. Deming promised that if they followed his directions, they could achieve the desired outcome in five years. The system he implemented came to be known as TQM—total quality management. Deming is now known as the father of the Japanese postwar industrial revival. For his efforts, he was awarded the Second Order of the Sacred Treasure by Emperor Hirohito in 1960.

Examples of Languages Across Cultures

Q: In Japanese, how do you say: "Happy birthday?"

A: お誕生日おめでとう！ (pronounced: Ōtăn-jō-bā ōmādātō!)

Deming believed in the right to have pride in your workmanship. Why do you think pride in workmanship is important in improving quality?

Motivation

Motivation has three different components. One involves inspiring others. Good leaders have the ability to motivate others to meet goals. Some do this by inspiring them with their energy, enthusiasm, and charisma as well as their personal efforts.

Another component is initiative. **Initiative** is the ability to act and make decisions without the help or advice of others. People with initiative do not wait to be told what to do. Initiative is an important quality of entrepreneurs and good leaders. Generally, it involves taking risks.

Most important, motivation means having a goal, whether it is to create the best video game or to make the best skateboard. A true leader is motivated by a vision and uses it to inspire others. Activist and theologian Dr. Martin Luther King, Jr. delivered many powerful speeches during the civil rights movement. In his famous "I Have a Dream" speech, he painted a vivid picture of a future in which all people were treated equally. One year later Congress passed the Civil Rights Act of 1964.

✔ **Reading Check** **Explain** What are the three components of motivation?

Confidence

Leaders also need self-confidence. Being self-confident means knowing what to do and taking action. Self-assurance makes others feel confident in their leader's abilities. The more others are convinced that their leader knows what to do, the more confidence they will have in him or her.

A confident leader is also decisive. Suppose you run a student magazine. The latest issue has come back from the printer with a big mistake on the cover. You could sell it as it is, remove the covers, or send it back to the printer. You could get advice from your workers, but you need to make the final decision. If your decision turns out to be wrong, you must take responsibility for it. People have confidence in a leader who is willing to make decisions and learn from them.

Communication Skills

Being able to communicate and discuss employee issues helps leaders deal effectively with different situations. A leader must be good at human relations. **Human relations** is the study of how people interact in the workplace and how communication can be improved. Most large companies have a human relations department, which handles employee hiring, records, and problems. To deal with some human relations problems, leaders have to apply conflict resolution **techniques.**

Good communication also involves mentoring. A *mentor* is a trusted counselor or guide. Mentors usually have more experience than the people they counsel. They should also be good listeners. Leaders need to listen to people to be informed about what they are doing, and what their strengths and weaknesses are. As mentors, leaders can better understand employees and their needs. This is especially important when working with teams and trying to increase productivity. Leaders must also communicate the types of behavior that are considered acceptable at the organization. **Figure 8.1** asks you to evaluate your communication skills.

Integrity

Integrity is an adherence to a code of ethical values such as honesty, loyalty, and fairness. Integrity is the most highly valued quality in a leader. Leaders need to set a good example and follow standards. If they are willing to sacrifice the quality of their product to make a bigger profit, people are not going to have much faith in their vision.

 **Reading Check** **Explain** What is the difference between initiative and integrity?

Figure 8.1 — *How Good Are Your Communication Skills?*

Communication Skills
1. People usually understand what I am saying.
2. I find it easy to see things from someone else's point of view.
3. I listen actively to keep my mind from drifting.
4. When I am wrong, I am not afraid to admit it.
5. I rarely jump to conclusions.
6. I try to put myself in the other person's shoes when we are talking.
7. It helps me understand if people tell me that they disagree with me.
8. When I work with others, I try to do my fair share of the work.

● **The Importance of Good Communication Skills** Evaluate your communication skills. **Do these traits apply to you?**

Developing Leadership Skills

Some people say leaders are born and not made. However, while some people have natural leadership abilities, others can develop them over time. A person with charisma, such as a star athlete or a popular person in class, is often mistaken for a natural born leader. Charisma alone, however, does not make somebody a good leader.

To manage activities successfully, you must draw on a specific set of skills. These include human relations, communication, networking, problem solving, and decision-making skills.

Leadership qualities are learned through knowledge and experience. Skills can be developed in a number of ways, such as

- through reading books, watching videos, and taking courses on leadership.
- by working with someone who has leadership ability and studying what he or she does.
- by joining a club, a team, a drama group, or a community organization.
- by taking initiative at school, at work, or in club activities.

Section 8.1

After You Read

Review Key Concepts

1. Why are some managers not leaders?
2. What are the three motivational qualities that leaders have?
3. How can leadership skills be developed?

Academic Skills

4. **Mathematics** Your manager at the Burger Barn wants each employee to sell $350 worth of hamburgers and fries during his or her shift. Yesterday, your sales totaled $330. Today, your sales total $440. Determine the percentage you achieved above or below the goal for yesterday and today.

CONCEPT **Problem Solving: Make a Plan**
Many problems require more than one step to solve. Think through your approach, and make a plan before you choose the operations to use.

 For math help, go to the Math Appendix.

 Go to **connectED.mcgraw-hill.com** to check your answers.

Leadership Styles

Reading Guide

● Before You Read

Think about the difference in leadership styles between a football coach and a doctor.

Read to Learn

- Identify and describe the autocratic, democratic, and free-rein leadership styles.
- Describe the self-managed team approach and the two ways in which such an approach is organized.

The Main Idea

Leaders differ in the leadership styles that they use. Autocratic, democratic, and free-rein leadership are common styles. The leadership style that should be used depends on the work to be done and the type of worker being managed.

Key Concepts

- Types of Leadership
- Leadership in Teams

Vocabulary

Key Terms

autocratic leadership
democratic leadership
free-rein leadership
delegating
self-managed teams

Academic Vocabulary

You will find these words in your reading and on your tests. Make sure you know their meanings.

inclined   approach
role   theory

Graphic Organizer

As you read, write notes about the three types of leadership styles in a figure like the one below.

AUTOCRATIC	DEMOCRATIC	FREE-REIN

 Go to **connectED.mcgraw-hill.com** to print out this graphic organizer.

● **As You Read**

There are some situations in which autocratic leadership is necessary. What situations can you think of in which it would be necessary to rule in an autocratic manner?

Types of Leadership

Different leaders have different styles. Some rule with strict discipline while others leave employees alone to do their work. Many leaders use more than one style. There are three basic styles of leadership: autocratic, democratic, and free-rein.

Autocratic Leadership

An **autocratic leadership** style is one in which one person runs everything and makes all decisions without consulting others. When autocratic leaders give orders, they expect them to be obeyed without question. Autocratic leaders assume others must have decisions made for them and that workers have to be watched all the time. A major problem that autocratic leaders face is that many people do not like to work for them.

Autocratic leadership is useful in situations in which it is important to obey orders without question. Firefighters, combat troops, and police officers have autocratic leadership.

Business Case Study

Communicate the Right Way

**Texting at work is actually OK!
(Well, sometimes.)**

Texts. IMs. Emails. Phone calls. Snail mail. Tweets. What is the right way to communicate at work?

Each workplace has its own norms for communication. At some companies, social media and texting are acceptable ways to communicate. At others, email, interoffice mail, and phone calls are considered more appropriate.

The rules of business communication also shift as new technologies emerge. Today the traditional phone call can seem intrusive, especially for workers in open offices without privacy. Postal ("snail") mail is used less and less, though it remains great for getting across a personal touch. A handwritten card of thanks to a client, for example, will make a lasting positive impression.

Email is the most common form of business communication, especially for sharing information

that is complex or will need to be retrieved later. For people with established working relationships, instant messaging or texting can be useful for simple questions requiring a quick reply. But be careful: the fewer characters you use, the greater the risk that your tone or content will be misunderstood!

Active Learning

Imagine you're at work, preparing to send the following four messages: 1. A holiday greeting to a vendor; 2. A confirmation to a coworker of a meeting time; 3. A PDF of a document to your manager; 4. An inquiry about a client's business hours. Write out these messages in one column. Make another column with the following communication types: a. email, b. text/instant messaging, c. postal mail, d. phone call. Match the messages and the most effective ways of communicating each.

Democratic Leadership

Democratic leadership is a style in which managers work with employees to make decisions. Everyone meets, discusses a situation, and listens to each other's opinions. New ideas are encouraged in such workplace environments. Democratic leaders still make the final decisions, but they might explain their reasons for making them. A democratic leader assumes that people have ideas and are **inclined** to contribute.

✔ Reading Check **Contrast** How do the leadership styles of an autocratic leader and a democratic leader differ?

Free-Rein Leadership

Free-rein leadership requires the leader to set goals for managers and employees and then leave them alone to get the job done. This style places the most trust and confidence in workers. Another name for this type of leadership style is *hands-off leadership.* Free-rein leaders deal with broader decision making. They have to be available to answer questions and resolve problems.

Giving managers and employees the power to run things and make decisions is called **delegating**. There are several reasons for a leader to delegate:

- The managers do not have time to do everything.
- The managers can focus on more important work.
- Employees have more ownership of the production process.
- Employees have a chance to develop their own potential.

Science/Tech**TRENDS**

Contamination Crisis

In 1996, Odwalla Inc., a producer of fresh-fruit beverages, faced a crisis. Its apple juice had caused an outbreak of *E. coli*. One child died. Odwalla executives ordered an immediate recall of all products containing apple or carrot juice, costing the company about $6.5 million. The next step was to tackle the problem of contamination. Odwalla used unpasteurized juice because it tasted best. They moved quickly to introduce a process called "flash pasteurization" to destroy bacteria, while leaving the best flavored juice possible.

Locate Web sites where you can find out more about flash pasteurization. Write a few paragraphs explaining how decisive leadership and good science helped a company survive a crisis.

As You Read

Think of a task that you have had to delegate. Why did you make that choice?

There are also reasons not to delegate. Shifting responsibility because of laziness or a lack of interest or self-confidence is not good leadership. Choosing the right people to delegate power to is a test of your leadership skills. Hiring workers who are experienced, reliable, and knowledgeable leads to success.

Leadership in Teams

Thirty to forty years ago, autocratic leadership was the main style used in most U.S. businesses. As companies learned the value of giving workers more power, they started using a more democratic or free-rein style. Today, the trend is to go even further. Many companies have been putting workers in self-managed teams. **Self-managed teams** are work groups that supervise themselves. With these teams, the manager's role is replaced by the team leader's role.

Self-Managed Teams

The use of the self-managed team approach started in Japan and came to the United States in the 1980s. U.S. companies had emphasized people working as individuals on separate jobs. Japanese companies had stressed people working in teams and making decisions as a group. The Japanese method was such a success that American companies also started using it.

In a self-managed team, the leader is a team player rather than a boss. A team leader makes decisions with the team rather than alone. This person learns a range of jobs instead of just one. The team usually works on a single project, such as designing a video game. This way the project is more goal-oriented rather than task-oriented.

✔ **Reading Check** **Explain** What is the position of the leader in a self-managed team?

● **Problem Solving** When groups brainstorm, more ideas can develop. **What is the leadership style that is apparent here?**

skynesher/Getty Images

The Organization of Self-Managed Teams

Self-managed teams are organized in two ways: (1) the team selects one team leader, or (2) each team member employs specialized skills, but there is no team leader.

The first type of self-managed team appoints a team leader. A team leader is not so much a manager as a team captain. If you are a team leader, your job is not to give orders but to motivate your team and get the members to work toward a shared goal. Team members usually evaluate each other's performance.

The **theory** behind self-managed teams is that the whole is greater than the sum of its parts. Self-managed teams have many advantages:

- They are more goal-oriented than task-oriented.
- Team members have a chance to learn each other's job and obtain new skills.
- Team members learn to participate and cooperate.
- Self-managed teams learn to solve their own problems.

The disadvantage of self-managed teams is that some people do not have the skills and initiative to work together productively.

Section 8.2

After You Read

Review Key Concepts

1. In which situations is an autocratic style of leadership useful?
2. Why should a manager delegate authority?
3. Name a similarity and a difference between free-rein management and self-managed teams.

Academic Skills

4. **English Language Arts** Locate and read articles about effective leadership styles. Become familiar with the characteristics of different leadership styles. Then write an essay. In the first paragraph, explain the range of possible styles a leader might exhibit. In the second paragraph, compare and contrast two or three of the styles identifying both positive and negative aspects. In the final paragraph, discuss which style fits your personality best.

5. **English Language Arts** Your company has developed a new video game for girls aged 11 to 14. You are the team leader assigned to develop a marketing campaign. The team includes an art director, a market researcher, and a copywriter. Write a memo to your team explaining the goals of the project. Think about the leadership qualities and approaches you wish to exhibit and incorporate them into your memo. Read your memo to the class.

 Go to **connectED.mcgraw-hill.com** to check your answers.

Section 8.1 *Summary*

Leadership Qualities A leader has a vision for the firm and inspires others to work toward that vision. Being a manager is not necessarily the same as being a leader. Many managers tell people what to do and make sure they do it. However, managers who lack a vision and do not inspire others are not leaders. In today's world, true leaders know their business and the capabilities of their employees. They analyze trends to steer their business on the right course. They also make sure that the basic operations run smoothly. Good leadership traits include motivation, confidence, integrity, and communication skills.

Section 8.2 *Summary*

Leadership Styles The three basic styles of leadership are autocratic, democratic, and free-rein. An autocratic leader is one who runs everything and makes all of the decisions. A democratic leader is one who seeks input from his or her employees before making decisions. A free-rein leader sets goals and permits employees to work alone to get their jobs done. Today's leadership trend is toward self-managed teams. Self-managed teams govern themselves. They determine how to produce their business's goods and services using the expertise of individual team members. Many of today's leaders use a combination of leadership styles.

Vocabulary Review

1. On a sheet of paper, use each of these key terms and academic vocabulary terms in a sentence.

Key Terms

leadership	democratic leadership
initiative	free-rein leadership
human relations	delegating
integrity	self-managed teams
autocratic leadership	

Academic Vocabulary

vision	inclined
trends	role
conflict	approach
technique	theory

Review Key Concepts

2. Define leadership.

3. Describe the qualities of a leader.

4. Name at least three ways in which an individual can develop leadership skills.

5. Identify and describe the autocratic, democratic, and free-rein leadership styles.

6. Describe the self-managed team approach and the two ways in which such an approach is organized.

Critical Thinking

7. Good leadership is needed in the business world as well as in areas such as government, nonprofits, education, and sports. Why do all institutions need leaders?

8. Why is it essential that a leader have integrity?

9. Why are professionals such as engineers and doctors usually managed with a free-rein style rather than an autocratic management style?

10. Imagine that you have five employees—a bookkeeper with years of experience, two college students who have worked with you for six months, and two high school students who started last week. What leadership style(s) will you use with each of your employees?

11. What are some instances in which self-managed teams will not work?

12. Why do managers who use leadership styles that empower employees have to think differently than those who use the autocratic style?

13. What traits must workers have if self-managed teams are to operate efficiently and effectively?

14. Explain how a leader can use different leadership styles.

Write About It

15. Working on a team project requires you to exercise different skills than you would use if you did the assignment alone. Write an essay about the pros and cons you have experienced working on a team for a project.

16. Find an article in a current issue of a business magazine that focuses on the experiences of a CEO. In a one-page report, describe the characteristics you believe he or she possesses that make this person a leader.

17. Michael Eisner, former CEO of Disney, said business leaders must be willing to take intelligent risks. He also said they must encourage failure, because "you will not get success without it." Write a one-page essay either agreeing or disagreeing with his statement.

18. Leaders often have different ways of inspiring the people who work for them. Write a brief essay discussing reasons why leaders delegate.

19. In a one-page report, indicate three important communication skills that you believe a good leader should have. Share them with a group of other people. List the communication skills that your group believes are most important.

Technology Applications

Technological Leadership

20. Technology offers many tools that help leaders be more effective, from telephones to computers to software that helps track employee performance. Research five ways leaders can use technology tools to help them be more effective. Write a one-page article about the benefits and costs associated with using these tools.

Business Ethics

When a Leader Wants Your Help

21. Imagine your manager has been asked to speak at a national trade show and tells you to write the speech. Later, she is asked to write a book on the topic. Her name will be on the cover. Would it be appropriate for her to ask you to write the book? In two or more paragraphs, discuss some of the ethical issues involved.

Applying Academics to Business

English Language Arts

22. Read the following list of two-word phrases. Think about their meanings. Use a dictionary to learn more about them. Then cross out the phrase that does not belong with the others, and add another phrase that does belong.

free-rein   high-handed
carte blanche   laissez-faire

Mathematics

23. Imagine that you need to train an employee to manage purchasing. It takes $10\frac{1}{2}$ hours a week, and the employee needs to work on it two days a week. Your staff has the following work hours:

- Maya: 8:00 A.M. to 1:00 P.M., Monday, Wednesday, and Friday
- Susan: 9:15 A.M. to 3:00 P.M., Monday through Friday, with an hour lunch
- Kyle: 11:30 A.M. to 5:30 P.M., Monday through Friday, with a half-hour lunch

Who would be the best choice? How many hours a week will this person have available to work on other tasks?

CONCEPT **Measurement: Time** Think about elapsed time when calculating duration.

English Language Arts

24. Your work team at Tropic Aquaria has been assigned to plan and write a pamphlet describing how to run successful teams. In a small group, create a pamphlet with helpful tips and guidelines.

Mathematics

25. You are in charge of finding storage facilities for your company's surplus inventory. The inventory is stored on pallets and has a total volume of 2,690 cubic feet. You find a storage site with an area that fits your needs. If the floor measures 23 feet by 13 feet, how high would the ceiling have to be to accommodate your inventory?

CONCEPT **Geometry: Volume** The volume of a three-dimensional geometric figure is measured in cubic units. You can memorize the formulas for finding the volumes of various figures, or you can look them up in a math glossary. To find the volume of a rectangular solid, multiply length by width by height.

Active Learning

Attend a Student Council Meeting

26. At a student council meeting, notice how each council member communicates. In a one-page article for your school newspaper, identify the person who demonstrated leadership qualities and how he or she did so at the meeting. Indicate other people's reactions to the council member's leadership styles.

Business in the Real World

Observe a Manager

27. Observe the activities of a manager for a one-week period. What leadership styles does the manager use? Are employees organized into teams? If so, how effective do you think they are? Present your findings in a two-page report. (Note: If you are not employed, observe the activities of a teacher for one week.)

Real LIFE skills

DEVELOPING LEADERSHIP SKILLS

28. Interview a leader in a business or your community. Ask how he or she developed leadership skills. Indicate what the biggest challenge in developing the skills was and how she or he met that challenge. In a thank-you letter to the leader, indicate what you learned from him or her.

 **Business CAREERS**

FIND YOUR DREAM JOB

29. Locate the Occupational Outlook Handbook Web site. Click on the "OOH Search/A-Z Index" link and enter the job title "education administrator." Then write a one-page report about this type of occupation. Conclude your report with a list of things you can do now to prepare yourself to pursue the occupation.

Role Play

CHOOSING A MANAGEMENT STYLE

30. Situation You are the CEO of a new automaker. The board of directors wants you to indicate the best management style to use.

Activity You are to give a presentation describing the management style that you believe should be used in your company. You expect questions from the board.

Evaluation You will be evaluated on how well you meet the following performance indicators:

- Understand the characteristics of the management style that you are promoting.
- Discuss the advantages and disadvantages of the style. Indicate how the business can deal with the disadvantages.
- Answer the board's questions effectively.
- Project your voice and provide concise explanations.

Standardized Test Practice

Directions Choose the letter of the best answer. Write the letter for the answer on a separate piece of paper.

1. $3\frac{1}{2} \div 1\frac{1}{3} =$

   A $\frac{8}{12}$ B $\frac{1}{4}$ C $2\frac{5}{8}$ D $3\frac{3}{8}$

 TEST-TAKING TIP Find a regular place to study where you can focus without much outside interference. Make sure that you have all the necessary materials before you begin studying.

Chapter 9

Technology and Business

Chapter Objectives After completing this chapter, you will be able to:

▶ **Section 9.1** *The History of Technology*
- **Describe** how technological inventions have an effect on business.
- **Give** examples of how technology has changed jobs in business.

▶ **Section 9.2** *E-Commerce*
- **Explain** why doing business on the Internet has become a major factor in many industries.

Ask
AN EXPERT

Researching Stocks

Q: I'm thinking about buying stock in a company my father used to work for. It's a well-known company with a long history of paying dividends. Is there any kind of research I can do to help me figure out if this stock will continue to do well in the future?

A: There are many different ways to evaluate a stock. *Fundamental analysis* involves looking at the company behind a stock to see if it's in good financial shape. *Technical analysis* involves looking at charts and graphs to figure out where a stock may go next. However, you shouldn't rely on just one measure to assess a stock. Most successful investors evaluate a potential investment in a number of different ways.

Mathematics As part of his research into a stock he was considering, George found a graph showing the S&P 500 Price Index for 12 months beginning December 2001. The index reached a high of 1170 in mid-December, fell almost 10% by February, and climbed back to its high by March. It declined steadily to about 800 in early July, jumped 150 points by August 1, and hit its low, 770, toward the end of October. The index then rose steadily to over 900 by the end of November. Sketch George's graph.

CONCEPT **Graphing** Line graphs have an *x*-axis and a *y*-axis. The *x*-axis is most often used to represent time.

Marc Romanelli/Blend Images LLC

● **On the Go** Technological devices make it possible for people to take their work, entertainment, and communication with them wherever they go. **What technological device do you rely on most? Why?**

The History of Technology

Reading Guide

Before You Read
Think about how technology has changed the way you do your work and communicate with others.

Read to Learn
- Describe how technological inventions have an effect on business.
- Give examples of how technology has changed jobs in business.

The Main Idea
Technology has changed the way people do business. Technological inventions have created new products, new markets, and new jobs.

Key Concepts
- Technology Influences Business
- Technology and the E-Workforce

Vocabulary
Key Terms
- e-workforce
- e-commerce
- digital workflow

Academic Vocabulary

You will find these words in your reading and on your tests. Make sure you know their meanings.
- technology
- edit
- images
- authors

Graphic Organizer
As you read the section, list 10 important technological innovations on a figure like the one below.

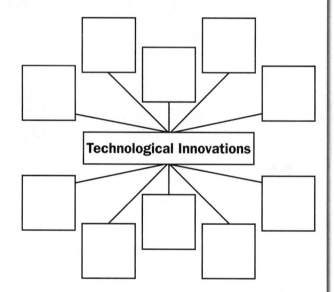

Technological Innovations

 Go to **connectED.mcgraw-hill.com** to print out this graphic organizer.

Technology Influences Business

Technology refers to the tools and machines that people have invented to make life easier. Inventions such as the radio and television entertain and inform us. The telegraph and then the telephone made it easier to communicate with one another. Trains, cars, and airplanes made it easier to travel. When computers were invented, they changed the way business was conducted.

Perhaps the most common technology staple in businesses today is the computer. Computers electronically store thousands of files, which saves time, labor, and space. Scanners read the prices of products and record sales instantly, making business move much faster. Accounting and bookkeeping software programs help organize, plan, and control business operations. The film industry uses digital technology to **edit** film as well as enhance colorful **images** and create animated scenes.

● **As You Read**

Think about how a large business, such as Home Depot, would have operated before computers. What problems might it have encountered?

Business Case Study

Changing the World through Technology

When disruption is a good thing.

In the technology world, reputations and fortunes are made through "disruptive innovation." A disruptive innovation is something that few people anticipated—the smartphone, for example—but that ends up changing markets, and the world.

Even brilliant people make spectacularly wrong predictions. In 2004, for example, Microsoft founder Bill Gates said the problem of spam email would be solved within two years. But that doesn't stop tech observers from speculating about the next big disruptive change.

In 2014, Citi Research published a list of 10 disruptive innovations on the horizon. These include 4-D printing (imagine a flat printout of a medical device assembling itself once implanted in the body), Bitcoin digital currency, precision agriculture (to feed a growing world population), electric vehicles, and immunotherapy (training the body to recognize cancer cells and attack them before they can spread).

Some of these innovations will change our lives. Others will be forgotten. The tough part is predicting which will be which.

Active Learning

Interview an adult who grew up before the 1990s. Ask them how they communicated, researched information, and accessed news and entertainment before the Internet. Write a short essay about how this innovation changed the life of your interview subject.

The Impact of Telephones

Even the simplest invention can have a huge impact on business. Before the telephone was invented, people had to communicate face-to-face or in writing. A letter could take several days to travel from the writer to the reader. The telephone made it possible for people to communicate instantly even if they were hundreds of miles away. Telephone companies sprang up, and people were hired as phone operators. Manufacturers began producing telephones and all the related equipment and supplies needed for telephone services.

Telephones were so useful that making them became a big business. Companies specialized in making them. Machinists were needed to make parts. There was a constant demand to produce new and more efficient tools. In time, cordless phones, cell phones, and radio telephones became useful tools for business and consumers.

Since the invention of the telephone, countless new inventions have changed the way we live, work, and do business. Some of the technologies we use today were made possible by the invention of the telephone. Cell phones are not just phones—they are small computers. Aside from talking on a cell phone, you can send and receive e-mail and text messages, take photographs, view video, and access and use the Internet on a smart phone. Fax machines use telephone lines to send images. Mobile phones of all types help businesses to communicate at all times. Without mobile phones and fax machines, doing business would be more difficult.

✔ **Reading Check** **Contrast** How did life before the telephone compare to life after its invention?

ETHICS in Business

Employment Contracts

- **Critical Reading** Life is full of important decisions. Think about the kinds of decisions that you make as you read the question below.

After graduating from college and getting an advanced degree, you accepted a great job. The only problem is that you had to sign an employee agreement with serious restrictions on what work you could do if you left the company. You have now been at your job for three years and have been promoted several times. However, a new opportunity has come up with another company that competes with yours in a small area of the market. You want to do what is right by your current employer, but you really want this new job.

- **Decision Making** How does the agreement you signed with your current employer affect your decision? What options could you explore?

Modern Technology

In the past 60 years, electronic devices have revolutionized business and society. Today, the economies of many countries, such as Japan and Taiwan, are based on manufacturing electronics. Business and consumers constantly demand smaller, faster, cheaper, and more powerful electronic devices.

Computers were first used only by the military. Now the computer is an important business tool, electronically storing thousands of files, saving time and space. The computer has created a boom in nearly all industries. Personal digital assistants, or PDAs, are handheld devices. They let users send e-mail, list contacts, and access the Internet.

● **Technology Careers**
Computers and the Internet have created new careers and a demand for workers, such as software writers, online writers, and Web page designers. **What type of person do you think would be a good software writer?**

Technology and the E-Workforce

Visualize an office worker typing a report on a computer. Another is sitting at his desk and talking to a customer while placing an order on his computer. A few rows down, another is printing photos to use in a sales presentation. This is a portrait of today's electronic workforce, or e-workforce.

The **e-workforce** consists of people who work with computers while doing business. According to the Bureau of Labor Statistics, more than 77 million workers use computers daily. Electronic commerce, or **e-commerce**, which uses the Internet to do business, means businesses can reach customers directly anywhere in the world.

✔ **Reading Check** **Explain** What is the difference between e-commerce and the e-workforce?

Employment

Technology has created a boom in many industries. New markets have opened for products such as printers, fax machines, video games, and cell phones. New products are constantly being invented, developed, and manufactured. Innovation means more jobs and more people learning new skills. Technology allows people to work easier and faster.

Mapping Locations
Some companies use Web-based mapping software to find the right location for their business. Starbucks uses software to determine factors such as how many offices are located near a site and the amount of foot traffic around a block. *What other types of businesses can you list that might benefit from mapping tools?*

Digital Workflow A **digital workflow** links all the steps in a process digitally. For example, digital workflow has greatly influenced the publishing and printing industries. **Authors**, editors, marketing, manufacturing, and archiving departments can work together at a seamless electronic pace. People now have easier access to a broad range of information. Library catalogs and encyclopedias are available in digital format. Information is at your fingertips in an instant.

Paper workflow, sending information in paper form, requires workers to exchange many pages of paper. By switching to a digital format, less paper is involved.

● **As You Read**

Think about the digital workflow processes involved in creating your favorite magazine.

Technology Centers The high-tech industry can be found in practically any city, but especially in technology centers such as California's Silicon Valley; New York's Silicon Alley; Oregon's Silicon Forest; and Austin, Texas's Silicon Hill.

New Jobs One important tool of the high-tech industry is the Internet. The Internet has created a demand for software writers, online writers, social media producers, and Web-page designers. Companies are now able to post job opportunities on their Web sites, and Internet job on Web sites, such as Monster.com and Indeed.com.

Section 9.1

○ *After You Read*

Review Key Concepts
1. What are some examples of inventions that have had a major impact on business?
2. How is digital workflow different from paper workflow?
3. What are four examples of new jobs that have been created by the Internet?

Academic Skills
4. **Mathematics** Suppose you run a business that develops Web sites for e-commerce. You charge a flat fee of $2,700 to create the Web site. One of your clients also pays you a $15 bonus for every seven people who visit the site. How many people need to visit the Web site in order for you to match your fee for creating the Web site? Write an equation and solve it.

 CONCEPT Algebra: Equations As you read a word problem, think through what you know and do not know. Assign an unknown to stand for a value you want to find. In this problem, let x equal the number of people who need to visit the site.

Math For math help, go to the Math Appendix.

 Go to **connectED.mcgraw-hill.com** to check your answers.

E-Commerce

Reading Guide

Before You Read

Think about the products and services that you have shopped for and purchased online.

Read to Learn

- Explain why doing business on the Internet has become a major factor in many industries.

The Main Idea

Businesses offer all types of goods and services online. Consumers can research almost any product or service from their home. They can buy just about anything online.

Key Concept

- The Importance of Virtual Business

Vocabulary

Key Terms

start-up
e-tail
multi-channel retailer
brick-and-mortar
clicks-and-mortar
e-ticket

Academic Vocabulary

You will find these words in your reading and on your tests. Make sure you know their meanings.

transports   rely
methods   fee

Graphic Organizer

In a graphic like the one shown, describe each type of business indicated as you read.

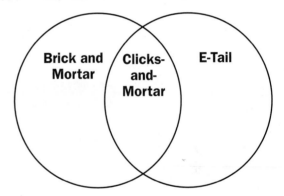

Brick and Mortar — Clicks-and-Mortar — E-Tail

 Go to **connectED.mcgraw-hill.com** to print out this graphic organizer.

The Importance of Virtual Business

The ease of doing business via the Internet has created a boom in new online businesses. This type of business is called a virtual business. Many entrepreneurs have developed businesses that they can operate from their homes. The Internet makes it possible to communicate online with customers and clients around the world via e-mail, Web sites, Facebook®, Twitter®, and other channels of communication. Some Internet businesses are start-ups. A **start-up** is a newly formed business that is usually small.

Technology **transports** your mind to new places in the world. If you do not have a muffin shop in your town but still want to purchase muffin mix and hot chocolate, you can order these products from companies doing business online. **Figure 9.1** shows you what consumers buy most online.

As You Read

Think about a virtual business you would like to start. What advantage would your business offer over a traditional type of store?

The Basics of E-Commerce

Everyone hooked up to the Internet is a potential customer. This has not only changed the way products are sold. It has also changed the way business activities are conducted. E-tail and e-tickets are two examples of e-commerce.

✔ **Reading Check** **Identify** What are two examples of e-commerce?

● **Top Consumer Purchases** People shop on the Internet for these types of purchases. **What do you think are reasons for buying these products online?**

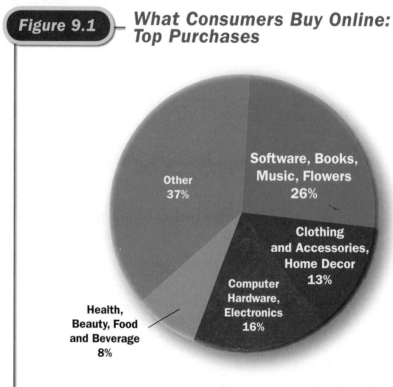

Figure 9.1 — **What Consumers Buy Online: Top Purchases**

Other 37%

Software, Books, Music, Flowers 26%

Clothing and Accessories, Home Decor 13%

Computer Hardware, Electronics 16%

Health, Beauty, Food and Beverage 8%

Source: *Statistic Brain*

E-Tail **E-tail** is electronic retail. E-tailers sell products over the Internet through e-commerce. For instance, J. Crew sells clothing and accessories in stores, by mail, and online. This type of company is called a **multi-channel retailer**. It uses several **methods** to sell products. Businesses often call their stores and warehouses **brick-and-mortar**, referring to the actual buildings. Grocery stores such as Kroger are brick-and-mortar companies. Businesses that also use the Internet are called **clicks-and-mortar** operations. Bookstore chain Barnes & Noble is a clicks-and-mortar company.

E-commerce makes it easier to send catalogs of e-tailers' products to consumers. This is especially useful for companies that do a lot of mail-order business, such as Land's End. Putting catalogs on the Internet rather than shipping them by mail saves a lot of money in printing and mailing costs.

How does e-tail benefit you as a consumer? Here are the advantages:

- **Convenience** You can shop at home without going to a store. You can shop 24 hours a day, seven days a week. Your purchase can be delivered to your door.

As You Read

Think of some brick-and-mortar businesses that also do business online.

• **Choices** The number of companies selling products online gives you more choices and makes comparing items easier. Web sites such as Shopping.com and ZDNet.com allow consumers to compare products and prices. Some online companies allow you to download music and computer games or preview movie trailers. This helps consumers make decisions about purchases.

There are some disadvantages to e-tail. They include:

• **Buying Power** It is easy to overspend online. If you are not careful, you can also order things by mistake.
• **Additional Charges** Since most products bought online are delivered by mail or express delivery services, you have to pay shipping charges and sometimes taxes. The exchange and return policies may be more strict than those of a bricks-and-mortar store.
• **Immediacy** While shopping online is convenient, you still have to wait for most products to be delivered. Most online companies promise speedy delivery, but delivery times vary.
• **Relying on Observation** It is hard to know for sure whether you like a sofa unless you see it and try it. The same can be said for clothes, CDs, or books. Online buying requires you to **rely** on pictures and descriptions instead of actually touching things yourself. In some ways, your decisions about what to buy can be easier. In others, they can be harder because you cannot examine the product before buying it.

✔ Reading Check   **Identify** What are some disadvantages to e-tail?

● **E-Tickets** A traveler can buy e-tickets online. **What other e-tickets are available?**

E-Tickets Businesses find that customers want to buy more goods and services online. Using their computers, people can now purchase an **e-ticket**, or electronic ticket. More than 70 percent of travelers in the United States shop for airline tickets online. E-tickets are also available for concerts, museums, movies, and amusement parks.

Some people find purchasing an e-ticket is easier and cheaper than visiting an actual store. For example, a travel agency may charge you a $25 **fee** for handling your airline ticket. If you buy a ticket from an online travel agency, you may be charged only $1. Many customers search online for the least expensive e-tickets. Browsing the Internet gives them time to compare offers and prices.

E-ticket holders can print their boarding passes online, use self-service check-in, and avoid some of the lines in crowded terminals. However, if an airline loses your e-ticket in its computer system, you might be required to buy another ticket.

● **As You Read**

Think about the kinds of problems that could arise from buying a ticket online.

Section 9.2

○ *After You Read*

Review Key Concepts
1. How have virtual businesses changed the business world?
2. How is an e-tailer different from other businesses?
3. What are two advantages and two disadvantages to buying products and services via e-tail for you as a consumer?

Academic Skills
4. **English Language Arts** If you spend any time surfing the Internet, you are familiar with banner ads. These small rectangular advertisements appear on all sorts of Web pages. If you click on them, your Internet browser will take you to the advertiser's Web site. Imagine that you have just set up a Web site for your sportswear catalog company. Your target market includes four distinct groups: boys and girls ages 11 to 18, and men and women in the 18-to-35 age range. Write four banner ads designed to appeal to each group.

5. **English Language Arts** A topic sentence is the most important sentence in a paragraph. It tells what the paragraph is mostly about. Topic sentences often appear at the beginning of a paragraph, but sometimes they are found in the middle or at the end of a paragraph. Skim through the paragraphs in this section, and find an example of a paragraph with a topic sentence at the beginning and an example of one occurring at the middle or end. Then write a sentence that indicates what the paragraphs are about, based on each topic sentence you selected.

 Go to **connectED.mcgraw-hill.com** to check your answers.

Section 9.1 *Summary*

The History of Technology Technology has changed the business world through tools and machines that make life easier. Inventions such as the radio and television entertain and inform us. Trains, cars, and airplanes make it easier to travel. The telephone makes it possible for people around the world to have instant communication. With computers and the Internet, workers are able to do business around the world and reach customers directly. Technology has created new markets for many products. Files flow digitally, placing information at your fingertips instantly. Part of the effect of technology has been to build new technology centers for high-tech companies. Those companies have created new types of jobs for people working with high-tech products.

Section 9.2 *Summary*

E-Commerce E-commerce has changed the way we do business. Virtual businesses operate through the Internet. Technology has created a boom in online businesses, providing new employment opportunities and ways for people to make purchases. Many brick-and-mortar stores have become clicks-and-mortar businesses, adding Web sites so customers can shop online. Online shopping is a way of life for many consumers. They go to an e-tailer's Web site and shop any time of the day or night. E-tickets can be used for traveling, concerts, museums, and amusement parks. Advantages of e-commerce are convenience and the availability of choices. Disadvantages are that you can easily overspend, and you must rely on pictures and descriptions.

Vocabulary Review

1. On a sheet of paper, use each of these key terms and academic vocabulary terms in a sentence.

Key Terms

e-workforce
e-commerce
digital workflow
start-up
e-tail

multi-channel
 retailer
brick-and-mortar
clicks-and-mortar
e-ticket

Academic Vocabulary

technology
edit
images
authors

transports
methods
rely
fee

Review Key Concepts

2. Describe how technological inventions have an effect on business.

3. Give examples of how technology has changed jobs in business.

4. Explain why doing business on the Internet has become a major factor in many industries.

5. Imagine your life without technology. What difference do you think you would notice in your communications?

6. Devices for downloading and storing information and music have grown in popularity. What other devices do you think may be developed in the future?

7. Online children and teens watch more TV, see more movies, and read more magazines and books than offline children and teens. What do you conclude from these facts?

8. Internet job services make it possible for people to find jobs and companies to find employees. How could you benefit by using an Internet job service?

9. In a "smart" kitchen, a refrigerator can keep track of food stored in it and remind you when you need to shop. What other technology might be possible for a smart kitchen?

10. How might a brick-and-mortar company be encouraged to or discouraged from engaging in e-commerce?

11. Smartphones combine a phone with a PDA, calendar, address book, note pad, Internet access, built-in camera, and display screen for reading documents. What other capabilities might they have someday?

12. A number of companies have become very successful as Internet service providers (ISPs). Write an e-mail to your teacher that explores reasons ISPs are an important part of business.

13. Write a one-page story describing life in the business world without computers.

14. Why do you think the telephone had such an influence on business? Write two or more paragraphs on the subject.

15. Describe how you think the average workplace has been changed by technology.

16. Write an article on online shopping for your school newspaper. Describe the differences between shopping with a paper catalog and shopping online.

17. Using the decision-making process, write a one-page essay describing the process you would go through in choosing a product online.

18. Your friend has never bought anything on the Internet, but would like to buy the same DVD player you just bought online. In an e-mail to him, list the reasons why you would or would not advise him to use e-tail.

19. In two or more paragraphs, write about a disadvantage to e-tail that you think is most important to you.

Spreadsheet

20. Choose a product such as a book, an electronic device, or a game. Check the prices of the product online, researching several companies to find what they would charge for that product. Then create a spreadsheet to compare the companies and their prices. Finally, prepare a graph that shows the companies and their prices.

Online Shopping Safety

21. Identity theft is a big concern in online shopping. If a hacker gains access to your credit card information, you may find yourself a victim of it. However, you might want to buy online and pay for your purchases with your credit card. What guidelines would you advise online shoppers to follow to prevent problems?

Applying Academics to Business

English Language Arts

22. The following terms have become a common part of the English language. Find out more about these terms using a dictionary or other resource. List them in the order in which you think they first appeared in the English language. Ask family members to do the same, and compare the results.

instant replay	nanotube
TV	beatnik
Silicon Valley	in-line skate

Mathematics

23. Jason's Web business jumps in sales, and he needs to hire more people to keep up. He hires 8 people to fill the extra orders and pays them $11 per hour. Four of them work 4 hours a day for 10 days, and the other four work 6 hours a day for 10 days. Jason does some quick mental arithmetic and concludes that he owes these workers about $4,000. Describe how he might have used mental math to estimate his cost.

CONCEPT **Numbers and Operations: Mental Math** Using basic multiplication facts and rounding can help you make mental computations.

English Language Arts

24. A simple sentence contains a subject and a verb to express a complete thought. A compound sentence contains two independent clauses joined by *for, and, nor, but, or, yet,* or *so.* A complex sentence has an independent clause joined by one or more dependent clauses. Write examples of each type of sentence on the topic of technology's impact on business.

Mathematics

25. Shannon charges clients a regular rate for the first 40 hours she spends working during a week and twice that rate for overtime. Last week, she spent 56 hours working for one client and was paid $1,152. Write an equation using x to represent her regular rate. Solve for x.

CONCEPT **Algebra: Writing Equations** Read word problems carefully to understand how mathematical ideas connect and build on one another. Use symbols in equations to stand for the numbers you are trying to find.

Active Learning

Clicks-and-Mortar Businesses

26. Team up with a classmate, and list 10 businesses in your community. Select businesses that sell to consumers or businesses that sell to other businesses. Then research which of those businesses have online sites to offer their products and services. Prepare a report of at least two pages indicating which local businesses are also e-tail businesses.

Business in the Real World

Investigate E-Tailing

27. Interview a businessperson in your community about e-tailing. Does the businessperson sell products or services online? Why or why not? Ask him or her to list questions to ask when considering becoming an e-tailer. Write a report of at least one page on your findings. Be prepared to share your information with your class.

Real LIFE skills

INTERNET SKILLS

28. Efficient use of technology is important in our fast-paced business world. Many people waste a great deal of time browsing the Internet because they get sidetracked and spend time looking for information that does not meet their needs. Write a one-page report about how to seek information on the Internet quickly and effectively. Include tips on how to avoid getting distracted and wasting time.

Cool Business CAREERS

FIND YOUR DREAM JOB

29. Locate the Occupational Outlook Handbook Web site. Click on the "OOH Search/A-Z Index" link and enter the job title "computer scientists and database administrators." Write a one-page report about this occupation. Conclude your report with a list of things you could do now to prepare yourself to pursue the occupation.

Role Play

CLICKS-AND-MORTAR COMPANIES

30. Situation You are an employee of a clicks-and-mortar company. Your manager has asked you to prepare a presentation about your company for a group of high school students who are coming for a field trip.

Activity Prepare an outline of the major points of your presentation to the high school students. Then make the presentation to your class.

Evaluation You will be evaluated on how well you meet the following performance indicators:

- Explain what a clicks-and-mortar company is.
- Describe how this company is different from a brick-and-mortar company.
- Describe how customers can buy from your company.
- Prepare a written outline.
- Speak clearly and use correct grammar.

Standardized Test Practice

Directions Choose the letter of the best answer. Write the letter for the answer on a separate piece of paper.

1. If the formula for converting from Celsius to Fahrenheit is $F = \frac{9}{5}C + 32$, what is the formula for converting from Fahrenheit to Celsius?

   A $C = \frac{5}{9}(F - 32)$ B $C = \frac{5}{9}(F + 32)$ C $C = 32 - \frac{9}{5}F$ D $C = \frac{9}{5}(F - 32)$

TEST-TAKING TIP Study for tests over a few days or weeks, and continually review class material. Do not wait until the night before to try to learn everything.

Jeffrey Hollender

President/Chief Inspired Protagonist, Seventh Generation

Seventh Generation is the leading brand of environmentally safe household products in the United States. Since 1988, consumer purchases of his products have saved more than 240,000 trees, more than 1 million gallons of petroleum, 92 million gallons of water, and almost 230,000 pounds of greenhouse gases—the kind that contribute to global warming.

Q & A

Describe your job responsibilities.

Jeffrey: I manage a small team of senior managers and see my role as providing overall vision and leadership. Outside the company, I have three roles: building relationships with shareholders, public speaking, and participating in interviews.

What skills are most important in your business?

Jeffrey: You need to be clear about what you know and what you don't know so that you can find talented people who complement you. I look for an alignment of values instead of just skills when hiring new employees, especially management.

What is your key to success?

Jeffrey: Being clear about my purpose. I know who I am and what I want to do. Developing ecologically-safe products through Seventh Generation is related to my personal purpose in life: being authentic, having a positive impact on the world, and being socially just. Other keys are having a good business plan, identifying the need or product I'll fulfill or create, and knowing how much capital is needed to help grow the company until it becomes self-sustaining.

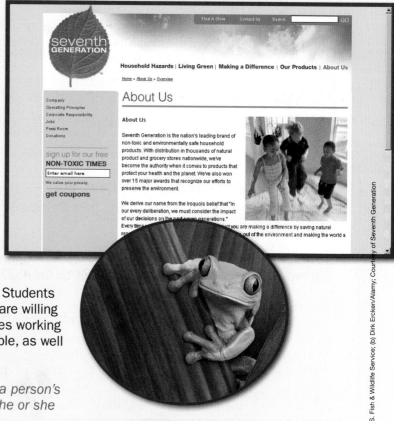

What advice would you give students interested in starting a business?

Jeffrey: Know what you're getting into. Students also need to ask themselves if they are willing to do all that is required. This includes working long hours, and managing other people, as well as doing very basic tasks.

Critical Thinking

What role does a person's belief system play in the type of company he or she develops and its products and services?

Some Qualifications of a Manufacturing Company Owner

Academic Skills and Abilities

Biology, chemistry; marketing; interpersonal skills; general business management skills; verbal and written communication skills; multitasking, organizing, and planning skills

Academic Skills Required to Complete Tasks at Seventh Generation			
Tasks	**Math**	**Science**	**English Language Arts**
Hold meetings			◆
Assign duties			◆
Develop new products		◆	◆
Assess products' market performance	◆		◆
Customer service			◆
Schedule employees	◆		◆
Order supplies and equipment	◆		◆
Analyze financials	◆		◆

Education and Training

Most owners and managers need a four-year college degree in addition to experience in the industry. As in other highly technical industries, top managerial positions often are held by those with substantial technical experience.

Career Path

Owners and managers can advance without additional formal training outside the workplace, although competition is keen. In general, advancement into the highest management ranks depends on one's experience and proven ability to handle responsibility in several functional areas. Among larger, multinational firms, international experience is important for career advancement.

Entrepreneurship in a Global World

Globalization and technology are creating a worldwide marketplace. Smart entrepreneurs recognize the opportunities in a worldwide marketplace and adjust to doing business at a global level.

Thematic Project Assignment

In this project you will conduct an interview and create a presentation about entrepreneurship in a global world. Your interview may be in person, on the phone, or through e-mail.

Step 1 Brainstorm Skills You Need to Complete this Activity

Your success in interviewing an entrepreneur will depend on your skills. Preview the activity. Then brainstorm a list of the skills you will need to use to complete the activity and describe how you will use them. Skills you might use include:

Academic Skills   reading, writing, social studies

Basic Skills   speaking, listening, thinking, and interpersonal skills

Technology Skills   word processing, keyboarding, presentation, telecommunications, and Internet skills

 SKILLS PREVIEW Go to connectED.mcgraw-hill.com to download a graphic organizer you can use to brainstorm the skills you will use to complete the project.

Step 2 Choose a Business and a Career That Interest You

Think of an entrepreneurial business that you find interesting. Then think of a career in this entrepreneurial business that interests you. As you investigate how entrepreneurs work in the global marketplace, you will research the effects of globalization and technology on the business and career of your choice.

Step 3 Build Background Knowledge

Preview entrepreneurship in a global economy.

Young **Entrepreneurs** Enter a **Global** Marketplace

The whole world is now the marketplace for young entrepreneurs. Anyone with a computer and Internet connection can enter the international marketplace almost overnight. Entrepreneurs are no longer confined to their local communities, or even to the United States. Now they can open their virtual doors to the world.

Globalization, the development of an increasingly integrated global economy, was brought on in large part by the growth of technology. The Internet allows entrepreneurs to build their businesses on an international stage, confined only by the capabilities of their technology.

Step 4 Connect with Your Community

Interview two adults in your community about inconveniences they experience during the course of a day. Then think about what goods or services an entrepreneur could create or import to lessen or eliminate these inconveniences. Could these goods or services be exported to other countries?

Step 5 Research Entrepreneurship in a Global Economy

Interview a local entrepreneur to find out about entrepreneurship in a global economy. Then prepare your presentation. Use the project research checklist as a guide to help you develop your interview questions and prepare your presentation.

Step 6 Develop Your Presentation

Use presentation software to develop a 5-minute presentation that includes all of the information described in the checklist.

Entrepreneurship in a Global Economy

✔ Create a chart that illustrates the countries in which the entrepreneur you interviewed conducts business. Use the chart in your presentation.

✔ Explain how technology helped this company become global.

✔ Explain how the economy in the United States and in other countries helps or hinders the company's success.

✔ Explain the rewards and risks this company has experienced in the global marketplace.

✔ Give examples of how this company is socially responsible.

Self Connections

✔ Describe the results of your research with a family member or other adult.

✔ Describe how the entrepreneur you interviewed influenced the business and career in which you are interested.

✔ Explain what the investigation and its results mean to you.

Step 7 Evaluate Your Presentation

 RUBRIC Go to connectED.mcgraw-hill.com to download a rubric you can use to evaluate your final report.

159

Influences on Business

Real-World Business and Career Profile

Jenzabar provides e-learning products, services, and Web-based software to colleges and universities. At the end of this unit, you will learn about Jenzabar® founder Ling Chai and how she achieved her success.

Decision Making What decisions do you think will be most important for you to make as you enter the business world?

Unit 3 — *Thematic Project Preview*

Community Outreach and Service Learning
After completing this unit, you will research how businesses come together for the good of the community, and how students and volunteers can help.

Project Checklist As you read the chapters in this unit, use this checklist to prepare for the unit project.

✔ Think about how a business can help a community.

✔ Look for ways you and your friends might volunteer to help with a community project that a local business is sponsoring.

✔ Reflect on how a business benefits by helping the community.

✔ Consider how you benefit by volunteering to help a business with a community project.

Chapter 10

Business in a Global Economy

Chapter Objectives After completing this chapter, you will be able to:

▶ **Section 10.1** *The Global Marketplace*
- **Explain** why the world has become a global economy.
- **Explain** why people and countries specialize in producing goods and services.

▶ **Section 10.2** *Global Competition*
- **Describe** free trade.
- **Indicate** who benefits and who does not benefit from free trade.

Ask | **AN EXPERT** **Evaluating Investment Alternatives**

Q: I know that diversifying my portfolio is a key to building wealth, but how do I evaluate which investment alternatives are right for me?

A: Start by determining how much risk you are willing to accept. Take a risk tolerance test available online or from an investment advisor. Then you can decide if you need an aggressive portfolio (for example, 75 percent stocks, 20 percent bonds, and 5 percent money market funds), a moderate portfolio (60 percent stocks, 30 percent bonds, and 10 percent money markets), or a conservative portfolio (40 percent stocks, 45 percent bonds, and 15 percent money markets).

Mathematics You have chosen a conservative investment strategy, and your portfolio has grown to $23,000. According to your recent account statement, you have $4,600 in money market funds. You realize that you need to reallocate some of these funds to stocks and bonds in order to maintain a conservative approach. Write an equation you can solve to find how much of the $4,600 you need to reallocate so that only 15% of your money will be in money markets.

CONCEPT **Writing Equations** An equation is a mathematical sentence that states that two expressions are equal. The two expressions in an equation are always separated by an equal sign. When solving for a variable in an equation, you must perform the same operations on both sides of the equation in order for the mathematical sentence to remain true.

● **International Markets** Trade between nations is an important part of today's world. Why do you think international trade has grown in recent years?

F1online digitale Bildagentur GmbH/Alamy

The Global Marketplace

Reading Guide

Before You Read

Think about how international trade might affect your life and the ways you contribute to global trade.

Read to Learn

- Explain why the world has become a global economy.
- Explain why people and countries specialize in producing goods and services.

The Main Idea

International trade has increased because more countries specialize and offer their goods and services to other countries. Also, the value of one nation's currency in relation to other currencies affects what it buys and sells to other nations.

Key Concepts

- The Global Economy
- International Trade

Vocabulary

Key Terms

global economy
international trade
multinational
  corporation
trade
imports
exports
balance of trade
comparative advantage
exchange rate

@ Go to **connectED.mcgraw-hill.com** to print out this graphic organizer.

Academic Vocabulary

You will find these words in your reading and on your tests. Make sure you know their meanings.

specific   sustains
professionals   vehicles

Graphic Organizer

In a graphic like the one below, list items mentioned in the section that are either imported into the United States or exported from the United States.

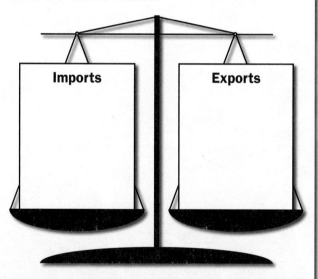

Imports   Exports

The Global Economy

The **global economy** is the interconnected economies of the nations of the world. We live in a global economy fueled by international trade. **International trade** involves the exchange of goods and services between nations. The development of the global economy is often referred to as globalization.

A **multinational corporation** is a company that does business in many countries and has facilities and offices around the world. Sony is a multinational corporation.

International Trade

Trade has several meanings. It can be a specific area of business or industry, such as the book trade. It can refer to a skilled occupation, such as auto mechanics. It can also refer to the people who work in a specific area of business or industry, such as construction workers. This chapter looks at trade as the activity of buying and selling goods and services in domestic or international markets. Trading goods and services allows countries to meet their individual wants and needs as well as to help their own economy.

✔ **Reading Check** **Explain** What are some meanings of the word *trade?*

Types of Trade

Domestic trade is the production, purchase, and sale of goods and services within a country. *World trade* is the exchange of goods and services across international boundaries. In many cases, a country cannot produce a desired good because it does not have a suitable climate or the necessary raw materials. In other cases, businesses in one country may produce better products or services at cheaper prices than businesses in other countries. As a result, world trade takes place.

Since the 1970s, world trade has increased considerably. Better transportation and telecommunications, along with a decrease in trade barriers, enables more world trade. These changes also help many countries' economies to grow.

Imports and Exports The United States buys pepper from India, bananas from Honduras, coffee from Colombia, and automobiles from Japan. These products are called imports. **Imports** are goods and services that one country buys from another country. The United States also sells wheat and airplanes to

International Business

Devaluing Currency
In a global economy, countries need to closely monitor the exchange rates of their currencies. For example, when the value of the U.S. dollar goes up compared to the European euro, it is said to have a favorable exchange rate. With a favorable rate, Americans can buy more European products with their currency. However, it also means that American products become more expensive for Europeans to buy.

Examples of Languages Across Cultures

Q: In Dutch, how do you say: "What time is it?"

A: Hoe laat is het?
(pronounced: Who lǎwt ǐss hět?)

Why might countries with a favorable exchange rate choose to devalue their currency?

countries such as Australia and Russia. These products are called exports. **Exports** are goods and services that one country sells to another country.

Countries can also invest in other nations by opening businesses there. They import and export the services of **professionals**, such as doctors and engineers. One country's exports are another country's imports. **Figure 10.1** shows the major imports and exports of the United States.

✔ Reading Check **Contrast** What is the difference between an import and an export?

Balance of Trade

When a country exports more than it imports, it has a trade surplus. When a country imports more than it exports, it has a trade deficit. A **balance of trade** is the difference in value between a country's imports and exports over a period of time.

A country can have a trade deficit with one country and a trade surplus with another. For instance, the United States has a favorable balance with Australia. That means it takes in more money from sales to Australia than Australia takes in from sales to the United States. The United States has an unfavorable balance with France, which means the United States takes in less money from sales to France than France takes in from sales to the United States.

Figure 10.1 — *Major Imports and Exports of the United States*

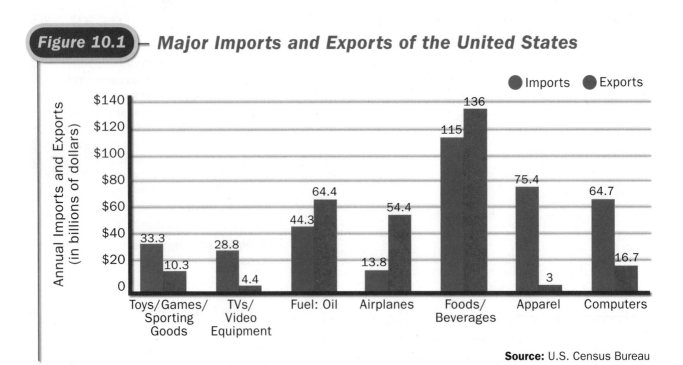

Source: U.S. Census Bureau

● **Major Imports and Exports of the United States** Look at the graph to see a comparison of products the United States imports and exports. **Name the products that the United States exports more than it imports.**

● **Currency exchange**
Financial institutions fulfill many different functions. **What does an exchange rate specify?**

Specialization

To *specialize* means to focus on a particular activity, area, or product. Specialization builds and **sustains** a market economy. Countries specialize in producing certain goods and services. Many take advantage of their specialties by trading them with other countries in the global marketplace. Similarly, individuals specialize by concentrating their activities in a particular area or field, such as carpentry, medicine, or office administration. Each worker's income buys goods and services that others have specialized in producing.

Using Resources to Specialize

Countries also specialize and trade some of the items that they produce in order to obtain other countries' goods and services. For example, the United States, Japan, and Germany are the world's top automobile producers. They have the technology, factories, and labor forces needed to produce lots of **vehicles**. Therefore, these countries have a comparative advantage in producing vehicles. A **comparative advantage** is the ability of a country or company to produce a particular good more efficiently than another country or company. Money gained from auto sales to other countries is then used to buy items that other countries produce. This helps to improve the standard of living for each country.

Currency

Countries have to pay for products and services with currency. Currency is another name for money. Just as different countries use different languages, they also use different currencies. Mexico uses pesos, Japan uses yen, and India uses rupees. Some countries use the same name for their currency. The United States, Canada, and Australia all call their currency dollars.

> ● **As You Read**
>
> Think about how a comparative advantage might help a country to compete in a global marketplace.

To trade with another country, businesses and countries must convert their money into that nation's currency. To do that, their currency is exchanged on the *foreign exchange market*. The foreign exchange market is mostly made up of banks where different currencies are exchanged.

Exchange Rates Each country's currency has a value that is different from those of other countries. The price at which one currency can buy another currency is called the **exchange rate**. For example, one American dollar is worth a certain number of Mexican pesos or Japanese yen. Exchange rates change from day to day and from country to country. The amount a country's currency is worth depends on the number of other countries that want to buy its products.

Prices Companies follow the change in exchange rates to find the best prices for products. When the value of a country's currency goes up compared to another country's, it appreciates, or goes up in value. A country with an appreciated exchange rate can buy more of the other country's products. When it goes down, the currency depreciates, or goes down in value. For example, if the U.S. dollar goes up compared to the euro, it will take fewer dollars to buy French cheese or Italian furniture. It also means U.S. goods will cost more because it will take more euros to buy them.

Section 10.1

After You Read

Review Key Concepts

1. What is the global economy?
2. What is the difference between domestic trade and international trade?
3. Why would a country want its currency to appreciate?

Academic Skills

4. **Mathematics** Next week you will take an exciting biking trip in Thailand. You have saved $850 for the trip. When your plane lands in Bangkok, you will convert your U.S. dollars to Thai baht. The service charge for exchanging currency is a flat rate of 185 baht. Using the exchange rate below, how many baht will the clerk give you?

   1 U.S. dollar = 39.22 Thai baht

 CONCEPT **Problem Solving** Solving some word problems requires more than one step. Read carefully so you can represent the problem in mathematical terms.

Math For math help, go to the Math Appendix.

 Go to **connectED.mcgraw-hill.com** to check your answers.

Global Competition

Reading Guide

● Before You Read

Think about some of the products you use that came from other countries.

Read to Learn

- Describe free trade.
- Indicate who benefits and who does not benefit from free trade.

The Main Idea

Protectionism is the practice of putting limits on foreign trade to protect businesses at home. However, protectionism decreases competition and generally increases the prices that consumers pay for goods and services. More nations are moving toward free trade.

Key Concept

- Protectionism and Free Trade

Vocabulary

Key Terms

protectionism
tariff
quota
embargo
free trade

 Go to **connectED.mcgraw-hill.com** to print out this graphic organizer.

Academic Vocabulary

You will find these words in your reading and on your tests. Make sure you know their meanings.

disputes   cooperate
restrict   controversy

Graphic Organizer

In boxes like the ones below, write notes about trade barriers. In the left box, write notes about tariffs. In the middle box, write notes about quotas. In the right box, write notes about embargoes.

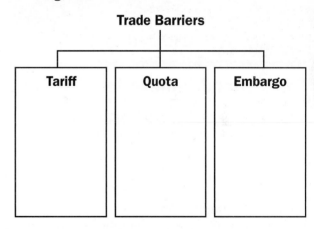

Trade Barriers

Tariff	Quota	Embargo

Protectionism and Free Trade

In the global marketplace, countries benefit from buying one another's products. Countries compete by making the same products. The United States, Japan, and Germany all specialize in making cars and are major competitors in that market. China, the Ukraine, and the United States are major producers of steel.

Global competition often leads to trade **disputes**, which occur when nations put barriers on trading particular items with another country. For example, suppose the United States decides that no Chinese-made steel can be imported into the country. The Chinese may respond by not allowing any more U.S. cars to be imported into China. At the heart of most trade disputes is whether there should be limits on trade or whether trade should be unrestricted. Protectionism and free trade are two opposing points of view involved in trade disputes.

✔ **Reading Check** **Analyze** What is at the heart of most trade disputes?

Business Case Study

Switzerland, Innovation Capital of the World

Swiss teens join the workforce as early as age 15, but their education continues

What is the world's most innovative country? Every year, the Global Innovation Index (GII) offers an answer. The GII studies many factors that support innovation, such as education, infrastructure, regulations, and youth creativity.

In 2014, Switzerland claimed the top spot in the GII for the fourth consecutive year. Switzerland is noted for its strong investment in information and communication technologies, as well as an education-apprenticeship system that grooms innovators from a young age.

In Switzerland's apprenticeship system, teens can elect to begin vocational training in one of hundreds of careers at age 15 or 16. At the end of two to four years of work-study, they test for a diploma that entitles them to work full-time in their chosen field or attend university for an advanced degree. By age 18 or 19, Swiss young adults already have years of entry-level work experience and are ready to move on in their careers.

Active Learning

Would a work-study apprenticeship appeal to you? Write a short essay explaining why or why not. Reflect on the pros and cons of taking an entry-level job at age 15 or 16, versus staying in school full time.

Protectionism

Protectionism is the practice of the government putting limits on foreign trade to protect businesses at home. Many companies want to sell what they produce at home. They often want to keep out foreign competitors. For example, rice farming and auto production are two major contributors to the Japanese economy. To limit competition from other countries, Japan practices protectionism in these segments. Some countries also do not want to share what they produce with other countries. Reasons to **restrict** trade include the following:

- Foreign competition can lower the demand for products made at home.
- Companies at home need to be protected from unfair foreign competition.
- Industries that make products related to national defense (such as satellites, aircraft, and weapons) need to be protected.
- The use of cheap labor in other countries can lower wages or threaten jobs at home.
- A country can become too dependent on another country for important products such as oil, steel, or grain.
- Other countries might not have the same environmental or human rights standards.

Science/Tech TRENDS

Motoring Technology

Automobiles have been an important part of our lives for more than 100 years. Today's cars are actually designed to have human characteristics. For example, an Australian invention helps drivers read road signs. Cameras mounted in various parts of the car send pictures of what is ahead to a computer. Software is then used to detect road signs by recognizing their shapes: rectangles, diamonds, octagons, or circles. Once a sign is detected, the image is compared to a list of signs stored in the computer's memory. If it recognizes a stop sign, the computer checks to determine if the car is slowing down.

Web Quest

Locate Web sites where you can find examples of other futuristic technology applications you may soon find on your car. Search to learn more about alternative fuel sources for cars and how they might help us reduce the dependency on oil. Write a paragraph or two describing the car of the future.

Trade Barriers To limit competition from other countries, governments develop *trade barriers*. For example, the United States and Brazil both produce sugar, but Brazil can sell it for less than the United States can. The U.S. government can protect U.S. sugar producers in three different ways: with a tariff, a quota, or an embargo.

A **tariff** is a tax placed on imports to increase their price in the domestic market. By placing a tax on sugar from Brazil, the United States can make it more expensive than American sugar. A **quota** is a limit placed on the quantities of a product that can be imported. If the United States allows only a small amount of Brazilian sugar into the country, most Americans have to buy American sugar. An **embargo** is a ban on the import or export of a product. Embargoes are rare and usually are used against another country for political or military reasons.

Free Trade

Economic or foreign policy often determines which countries trade with each other. **Free trade** occurs when there are few or no limits on trade between countries. Supporters of free trade think all countries should be free to compete anywhere in the world without restrictions. Free trade offers several benefits:

- It opens up new markets in other countries. There are more than 298 million people in the United States, but more than 6 billion worldwide.
- It creates new jobs, especially in areas related to global trade, such as shipping, banking, and communications.
- Competition forces businesses to be more efficient and productive.
- Consumers have more choices in the variety, prices, and quality of products.
- It promotes cultural understanding and encourages countries to **cooperate** with each other.
- It helps countries raise their standard of living.

Trade Alliances As the world economy becomes more global, many countries are moving toward a free trade system. To reduce limits on trade, nations form *trade alliances*. In a trade alliance, several countries merge their economies into one huge market. For example, NAFTA (North American Free Trade Agreement) combined the economies of the United States, Canada, and Mexico. As a result, it is easier for the United States to buy oil from Mexico and to sell its cars there.

Free trade is good in general, but it is not without problems. Some people opposed NAFTA because they feared some workers would be displaced when trade barriers were lowered. Opponents predicted that some high-paid U.S. jobs would be lost to Mexico.

That did happen in areas where Americans and Mexicans were competing. Those in favor of NAFTA predicted that trade among all three nations would increase dramatically, stimulating growth and bringing a wider variety of lower-cost goods to consumers. Indeed, that has occurred since the passage of NAFTA.

Despite the early **controversy** over NAFTA, the alliance has resulted in various business projects between the three countries.

Some of the major trade alliances in the world today are:

- **North American Free Trade Agreement (NAFTA):** United States, Canada, and Mexico
- **European Union (EU):** Austria, Belgium, Cyprus, Czech Republic, Denmark, Estonia, Finland, France, Germany, Greece, Hungary, Ireland, Italy, Latvia, Lithuania, Luxembourg, Malta, the Netherlands, Poland, Portugal, Slovakia, Slovenia, Spain, Sweden, and the United Kingdom
- **Association of Southeast Asian Nations (ASEAN):** Brunei, Cambodia, Indonesia, Laos, Malaysia, Myanmar, Philippines, Singapore, Thailand, and Vietnam

Real World

DR-CAFTA
The Dominican Republic-Central America Free Trade Agreement (DR-CAFTA) encompasses Costa Rica, El Salvador, Guatemala, Honduras, Nicaragua, the Dominican Republic, and the United States. The goal of the agreement is the creation of a free trade zone, similar to NAFTA. *What advantages and disadvantages do you think DR-CAFTA has?*

Section 10.2

After You Read

Review Key Concepts
1. Give three reasons for protectionism.
2. Give three reasons for free trade.
3. What are some of the major trade alliances in the world today?

Academic Skills
4. **English Language Arts** In order to better understand the challenges and opportunities of selling products in global markets, interview three local business owners who export goods overseas. Write a series of questions that will help you understand these businesses and how the products or services were chosen, whether they have changed in response to consumer demands or currency values, and how the business owner keeps in touch with international customers. Present your findings to the class.

5. **English Language Arts** Today's global marketplace means that business people need to have a working knowledge in more than one language. Identify two languages other than English that would be of special benefit to a global businessperson. Write two or more paragraphs that identify the languages, and explain why you chose them. Join in a discussion with your class to compare your answers.

 Go to **connectED.mcgraw-hill.com** to check your answers.

Section 10.1 *Summary*

The Global Marketplace Domestic trade is the production, purchase, and sale of goods and services within a country. Countries do not produce everything their citizens want or need and must trade with other countries. World trade is the exchange of goods and services across international boundaries. Most nations produce items in which they specialize, thus gaining a comparative advantage. A comparative advantage allows countries to trade their specialty with other countries for other things that they want or need. Items purchased across borders are bought in the currency used by the country that produced them. Foreign exchange markets allow one country's currency to be converted into another country's currency.

Section 10.2 *Summary*

Global Competition Global competition often leads to trade disputes, which occur when nations enact barriers to trade. Three common trade barriers are tariffs, quotas, and embargoes. Countries use trade barriers, or protectionism, to protect business from world competition. One reason for protectionism is that outside competition can lower the demand for domestically made products. Free trade opens up new markets, creates jobs, increases consumer choices, and promotes international cooperation. Major trade alliances that have promoted free trade include NAFTA, the EU, and ASEAN. Free trade is good in general, but it is not without problems. Some workers get displaced after an alliance is formed. However, alliances often lead to lower-cost goods.

Vocabulary Review

1. On a sheet of paper, use each of these key terms and academic vocabulary terms in a sentence.

Key Terms

global economy	exchange rate
international trade	balance of trade
multinational corporation	protectionism
trade	tariff
imports	quota
exports	embargo
comparative advantage	free trade

Academic Vocabulary

specific	disputes
professionals	restrict
sustains	cooperate
vehicles	controversy

Review Key Concepts

2. Explain why the world has become a global economy.

3. Explain why people and countries specialize in producing goods and services.

4. Describe free trade.

5. Indicate who benefits and who does not benefit from free trade.

Critical Thinking

6. Why does free trade generally increase people's standards of living?

7. Why would a nation choose not to produce everything its citizens want?

8. If the dollar decreases in value in relation to the euro, what is the probable effect that this will have on exports to Europe?

9. If the dollar increases in value in relation to the British pound, what is the probable effect on imports from Britain?

10. Why is an embargo a stronger measure against free trade than tariffs?

11. Protectionism may help certain segments of the economy but may hurt consumers. Why might this be so?

12. If the exchange rate is fixed between the U.S. dollar and the Chinese yuan, America imports more from China than vice versa. If the exchange rate can be determined by the market, what should happen to the relative value of the dollar?

13. Should companies making items for national defense be protected by trade barriers?

Write About It

14. List the countries where 10 items of clothing from your closet were made. Write a one-page essay on why you think they were not all made in the United States.

15. Write an editorial explaining and defending your opinion on the following statement: "It is unpatriotic to buy foreign-made goods."

16. Research the three major exports for another country. Write an argument for why it may have a comparative advantage in those areas.

17. Find an article about the increasing foreign competition that American businesses are facing. Summarize the article.

18. Compare the value of two currencies over five days. Write a one-page report about what happened and why the change occurred.

19. Research the U.S. balance of trade. Is there a trade deficit or a surplus? Write an e-mail to your teacher explaining imbalances between imports and exports and giving reasons for the imbalances.

Technology Applications

Presentation Software

20. As the world economy becomes more global, many countries decide to form trade alliances or to join an existing alliance. Research a trade alliance discussed in this chapter. Make a presentation about the countries involved, the alliance's history, and the impact the alliance has on the world.

Business Ethics

Cultural Differences

21. Imagine you work as a sales manager for a U.S. firm. You have been assigned a new account in Spain. Your Spanish host, the new client, expects you to attend soccer matches with him. Should your company pay for this expense? Write a one-page essay on the matter.

Applying Academics to Business

English Language Arts

22. Research and write a list of synonyms for each of the following terms from the chapter. Write a sentence about two of the words, telling how their meanings are alike and different.

tariff   protectionism
embargo   quota

Mathematics

23. NAFTA created a total market of more than 410 million people: 30 million live in Canada, more than 300 million live in the United States, and 100 million live in Mexico. What type of graph could best be used to represent this data? Why?

CONCEPT **Types of Graphs** A graph or chart is used to present facts in visual form. It is a drawing that displays the relative sizes of numerical quantities. A graph is one of the easiest ways to compare numbers.

English Language Arts

24. Read the following terms from the chapter. Organize the terms using one of them as the heading under which the others are listed as examples.

embargo   protectionism
limit   quota

Mathematics

25. The value of the dollar affects the values of other currencies. Morgan tracked the values of the U.S. dollar and the Mexican peso over one year to see if she could find a relationship. What kind of graph could best be used to represent her data? Why?

CONCEPT **Types of Graphs** Graphs can be used to illustrate many types of data and are not limited to the simpler types, such as line, bar, and circle. They should be used to make facts clearer and more understandable.

Active Learning

International Products

26. Think of three different items that you and your family use that were made in another country. List the items and where each one was made. Research the type of trade relationship each country has with the United States. Find out if similar items are made in the United States. If not, explain why not. If there are, why do you buy the international product? Write a one-page report on your findings.

Business in the Real World

Chart Exchange Rates

27. Choose a country and research its currency and the current rate of exchange. As a class, create a chart that combines the countries, their currencies, and the exchange rates each student has chosen. Make a list of questions about how the bank processes currency exchanges. Then invite someone who deals with currency exchanges at a financial institution to speak to the class.

Real LIFE skills

PREPARING TO WORK ABROAD

28. With two classmates, find an individual to interview who has worked in another country. Ask about the cultural differences between working in another country and in the United States. Ask for suggestions on dealing with that culture. As a class, make a chart with the subjects' names. Compare their overseas job titles, types of work performed, the countries where they worked, and tips for preparing for work abroad.

Business CAREERS

FIND YOUR DREAM JOB

29. Locate the Occupational Outlook Handbook Web site. Click on the "OOH Search/A-Z Index" link and enter the job title "cost estimator." Then write a one-page report about this type of occupation. Conclude your report with a list of things you could do now to prepare yourself to pursue the occupation.

Role Play

EXAMINING FREE TRADE

30. Situation Imagine that you are an economics expert for another country that is highly protectionist, with a lot of tariffs and quotas on global products. This protectionism keeps many of its major industries secure from global competition. However, the country lacks products and services that its citizens want and need.

Activity Take one of two sides—either continue the protectionist strategies or move toward free trade. Make a persuasive argument for your position.

Evaluation You will be evaluated on how well you meet the following performance indicators:

- Define protectionism and free trade.
- State all of the possible reasons for either position in a clear way.
- Use proper English grammar.
- Speak clearly.

Standardized Test Practice

Directions Choose the letter of the best answer. Write the letter for the answer on a separate piece of paper.

1. How many kilometers is 2,300,000 meters?

A   less than 300 kilometers

B   between 300 and 2,000 kilometers

C   between 2,000 and 3,000 kilometers

D   more than 3,000 kilometers

TEST-TAKING TIP When taking a test, if you have time at the end, check your answers and solutions. Did you answer each part of every question? Did you answer the questions asked? Do your answers look reasonable? Do your calculations check out?

Chapter 11

The Role of Government in Our Economy

Chapter Objectives After completing this chapter, you will be able to:

▶ **Section 11.1** *Government as Regulator*
- **Name** four ways in which government regulates business.

▶ **Section 11.2** *Government as Provider*
- **Name** five aspects of the government's role in society.
- **Name** three items that the national government provides and three items that local governments provide.
- **Explain** how government can stimulate or restrict economic activities.

Ask AN EXPERT

Types of Investments

Q: I think I understand the differences between stocks and bonds, but what are mutual funds and REITS? What about options and futures contracts?

A: Stocks represent equity, or ownership, in a company. Bonds represent debt. When you buy bonds, it's as if you are the bank, and you're lending money to the company. Shares of mutual funds, bond funds, and REITS are securities that sell like stocks; you can buy them on an exchange. A mutual fund is a pool of money invested by an expert manager in a variety of stocks with a specific investment goal in mind. Bond funds and REITs are similar. Bond funds are invested in bonds, and REITs are invested in real estate. Options and futures contracts offer sophisticated investors ways to gamble on future changes in the prices of securities or offset risks in their existing portfolios.

Mathematics Frank and his wife Mara have separate investment accounts. Frank's account has $7,680 invested in stocks and $2,560 in bonds. Mara's total investment in stocks and bonds is $4,000 split in the same proportion as her husband's. Write and solve a proportion to calculate how much Mara has invested in bonds.

CONCEPT **Proportions** A proportion is an equation with equivalent ratios on each side. When one of the four numbers in a proportion is unknown, the proportion may be solved by using cross products to find the unknown number. Question marks or letters are frequently used in place of the unknown number.

Kent Steffens/Getty Images

● **Government Roles** Governments play important roles in our economy. **How is the federal government's role different from that of a state government?**

Government as Regulator

Reading Guide

Before You Read
Think about some government regulations that affect what you do.

Read to Learn
- Name four ways in which government regulates business.

The Main Idea
Our government's role is to foster success in the economy. One way it does this is by creating rules and regulations that organizations and consumers must follow. Laws cover aspects of the economy. They protect competition. They protect business agreements and creative properties. They are also used to regulate the production process.

Key Concept
- How the Government Regulates Business

Vocabulary

Key Terms

interstate commerce
intrastate commerce
monopoly
oligopoly
trust
antitrust laws

contract
breach of contract
copyright
patent
trademark

Academic Vocabulary
You will find these words in your reading and on your tests. Make sure you know their meanings.

federal
enables

symbol
registered

Graphic Organizer
In a figure like the one below, write notes about government's role in the economy.

Protecting Competition	Protecting Business Agreements
Protecting Creative Properties	Regulating the Production Process

 Go to **connectED.mcgraw-hill.com** to print out this graphic organizer.

How Government Regulates Business

One of government's roles is to foster economic success. It also tries to aid in the quality of life of its citizens. In a market economy, a country's economic health depends on businesses doing well. In some cases, government helps people so that they are not abused by businesses. To fulfill these duties, local, state, and national governments pass laws to protect and regulate business.

There are three levels of government: **federal**, state, and local. The federal government runs the country. State governments run their state. Local governments run counties, townships, cities, and towns. The federal government oversees interstate commerce. **Interstate commerce** is business that takes place between states. State governments oversee intrastate commerce. **Intrastate commerce** is business that takes place within states.

Laws govern the workings of the economy. These laws regulate the production process and protect competition, business agreements, and creative properties.

Companies that break the law can be fined, sued, or forced to close. People who do not follow the rules also face penalties.

Business Case Study

Exposing Unethical Business Practices

This nonprofit upholds business ethics and resolves business-consumer complaints

If you get ripped off by an unscrupulous business, a friend might tell you, "Call the BBB!"

The BBB, or Better Business Bureau, was founded in 1912 to protect the public from companies peddling worthless "medicines." The BBB collects and provides reviews of businesses and steps in to help resolve disputes between businesses and customers. Today this nonprofit organization has over 100 local chapters across the U.S. and Canada.

The BBB is funded by dues paid by its 400,000-plus member businesses. The members agree to conduct business by the BBB Code of Business Practices. In turn, they can promote themselves as BBB members, which symbolizes their commitment to ethics and customer service.

If you do need to call the Better Business Bureau, chances are you'll have a happy outcome. The BBB claims a 70 percent success rate in resolving business-customer disputes.

Active Learning

The Better Business Bureau encourages voluntary self-regulation by businesses to serve customers fairly and ethically. Visit the BBB's site, bib.org, enter your zip code to access your local chapter's page, and read "Mission and Vision" (accessed through the "Get to Know Us" drop-down menu). Write a brief report explaining how the BBB's system encourages good business practices and explaining whether you think the system is likely to be effective.

Protecting Competition

A **monopoly** occurs when a company controls an industry or is the only one to offer a product or service. An **oligopoly** occurs when a small number of companies control an industry. Monopolies are problematic for several reasons. One is that monopolies do not compete with other firms. This **enables** them to charge any price they want for products or services. Also, quality may not be their biggest concern. Both monopolies and oligopolies limit choice.

Companies can also form a monopoly by establishing a trust. A **trust** is a group of companies that band together to form a monopoly and cut out competition. The U.S. government passed antitrust laws to promote competition. **Antitrust laws** allow the federal government to break up monopolies, regulate them, or take control of them. These laws have not always stopped firms from competing unfairly. The government formed the Federal Trade Commission (FTC) to enforce antitrust laws. For example, in the 1940s, the government sued a group of studios for trying to take over the film industry. The FTC also regulates interstate trade. It keeps competition between U.S. businesses free and fair. Its job includes setting standards for honest advertising.

Protecting Business Agreements

One of the most basic ways government protects business is by enforcing contracts. A **contract** is a legally enforceable agreement between two or more parties. It can be written, verbal, or even formed over a handshake. A rental agreement, a car-repair order, and the warranty on a CD player are all types of contracts.

?ETHICS in Business

Out of State Advertising

- **Critical Reading** Life is full of important decisions. Think about the kinds of decisions that you make as you read the question.

  You own a clothing shop in a state that has a low sales tax on consumer goods; neighboring states have higher sales taxes. When an in-state customer buys clothing, you add the state tax. When an out-of-state customer buys clothing at your shop, you don't add any tax. The customer is supposed to report the purchase and pay the appropriate tax to his or her state government. Many out-of-staters from nearby towns shop at your store, and you don't know if they pay the tax they're supposed to pay.

- **Decision Making** Knowing that some people don't pay their state sales taxes, is it appropriate for you to advertise your shop in nearby out-of-state towns? Explain your answer.

Breach of contract occurs when one party fails to live up to the terms of a contract. It is easier to prove a breach of contract occurred if there is a written contract. For example, suppose you are in a band that plays at a coffeehouse, and the manager refuses to pay you. It can be very difficult to prove that the manager agreed to pay if the agreement is not written in a contract.

Protecting Creative Properties

Laws also protect the right to own creative properties. Creative properties, items such as inventions and art, can be protected with a copyright, a patent, or a trademark.

Copyrights A **copyright** gives artists the legal right to own their creations. Copyrights protect photographs, music, paintings, books, plays, and other written material. Today, a person creating an original work automatically holds the copyright to it. An artist who also registers it with the U.S. Copyright Office in Washington, D.C., gains additional legal protection. If you own the copyright to a story you wrote, others who want to use it must get your permission beforehand. A copyright usually lasts until 70 years after the owner's death.

Patents A **patent** is a legal grant for the sole right to own an invention. The federal government grants patents. No one can copy a patented product or process without permission for 20 years after the inventor filed his or her application with the U.S. Patent and Trademark Office.

● **As You Read**

Think about works of art you have seen or heard that are protected by copyright laws.

● **Government as Watchdog** Federal laws limit the amount of waste factories can discharge into the environment. **Why does the government work to curb pollution?**

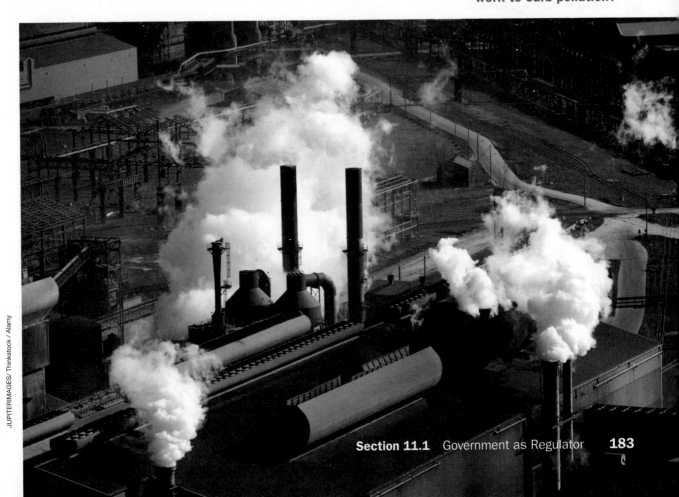

JUPITERIMAGES/ Thinkstock / Alamy

Trademarks A **trademark** is a name, a **symbol**, or a characteristic that identifies a product. It is also **registered** with the government. Only the owner of the trademark can legally use it. Well-known trademarks include Frito-Lay's *Doritos*®, Kellogg's *Rice Krispies Treats*®, and *Visa*®. Trademarks are protected from being copied if they are registered appropriately.

> ✔ **Reading Check** **Contrast** What is the difference between a copyright and a patent?

Regulating the Production Process

The government also steers economic activity by regulating the production process. It tries to stop companies from polluting by enacting laws. Some laws limit the amount of waste that factories can discharge into the environment. Worker protection laws impose safety requirements and work procedures and regulate the minimum wage. Organized labor, or labor unions, often help to report violations of worker protection regulations.

The Food and Drug Administration (FDA) regulates the manufacture and sale of drugs in the United States. Local and state governments regulate production processes, too.

Section 11.1

After You Read

Review Key Concepts
1. What is the difference between interstate and intrastate commerce?
2. What are the ways that the government can deal with a monopoly?
3. What kinds of property are protected by copyrights?

Academic Skills
4. **Mathematics** You are an event coordinator. You work from 8:30 A.M. to 5:00 P.M. from your office in Philadelphia. Tomorrow you need to place phone calls to an acrobatic team in New York, a specialty caterer in California, a display designer in Hawaii, and a magician in Colorado. The companies are open from 9:00 A.M. to 5:00 P.M., and the employees take lunch from noon to 1:00 P.M. Taking into account time zone differences, make a list of the times you might call each vendor.

CONCEPT **Working with Time** The United States is spread across six time zones. From east to west they are: eastern, central, mountain, Pacific, Alaska, and Hawaii-Aleutian. Philadelphia is in the eastern time zone. The time is an hour earlier in each time zone as you go from east to west.

 For math help, go to the Math Appendix.

 Go to **connectED.mcgraw-hill.com** to check your answers.

Government as Provider

Reading Guide

● Before You Read

Think about some of the items that the government provides you or your community.

Read to Learn

- Name five aspects of the government's role in society.
- Name three items that the national government provides and three items that local governments provide.
- Explain how government can stimulate or restrict economic activities.

The Main Idea

The different levels of government do more than regulate business activities. One of their main roles is to provide goods and services. These are provided using tax money collected from people and organizations.

Key Concepts

- Government's Role in Society
- How Government Is Funded
- How Government Allocates Resources

Vocabulary

Key Terms

revenue
privatization
subsidies

tax
tax incentive

Academic Vocabulary

You will find these words in your reading and on your tests. Make sure you know their meanings.

incentives
welfare

ensure
allocate

Graphic Organizer

In a box like the one below, list and describe five aspects of the government's role in society.

1.	
2.	
3.	
4.	
5.	

 Go to **connectED.mcgraw-hill.com** to print out this graphic organizer.

Government's Role in Society

The role of government in business is not limited to law making. Government also plays a big role in society. It provides key services to the public. It also gives **incentives** to businesses and people. Other services include providing jobs and distributing income. These activities occur at every level of government.

● As You Read

Think about the goods and services government provides and those that you buy directly from businesses.

Providing Goods and Services

Government is the largest provider of services in the country. Businesses offer goods and services to people to make a profit. However, government provides services to the public as a whole for the good of society.

Highways, bridges, water treatment plants, and national defense are examples of public goods and services. *Public goods and services* are items provided by government and paid for using tax money. They are different from private goods and services. *Private goods and services* are items that consumers purchase directly from businesses. They include CDs, clothing, food, and housekeeping services.

Other services promote social **welfare**. Government provides parks, libraries, museums, and swimming pools. These facilities improve people's quality of life. The cost of providing all these services is high. Governments pay for them with revenues they receive. **Revenue** is the income that governments get from all sources. That includes taxes and fees that consumers sometimes must pay to use certain public goods and services. Revenue is also money that comes into a business from the sale of goods and services.

In some cases, a business may provide a public good or service. **Privatization** occurs when a business offers a public good or service. The government body that pays for it oversees the business. For example, most cafés in government buildings are run by private businesses, not the government.

Aiding Citizens Through Transfer Payments

People's well-being is another concern of government. To improve their quality of life, the federal government provides transfer payments. A *transfer payment* is a government expense that is provided to help people. These payments **ensure** that people have money when they need it. Unemployment, Social Security, and veterans' benefits are forms of transfer payments.

Providing Employment

The government is the largest employer in the United States. More than 3 million people work for the federal government. State and local governments also employ millions of people. Mayors, firefighters, and the U.S. president are all public workers.

Consuming Goods and Services

Government is also the largest consumer of goods and services. It has to buy computers, furniture, and supplies for schools and government offices. To maintain the military, it has to buy uniforms, food, ships, aircraft, and weapons. Government buys most of its equipment directly from businesses or has equipment specially made. It also hires businesses to build aircraft, courthouses, schools, and roads.

Supporting Business

The government is involved in many activities that support business. The Small Business Administration (SBA) is a U.S. agency that encourages the development of small businesses. The SBA offers loans and advice to people who want to open small businesses.

The U.S. government helps some businesses compete internationally by providing subsidies. **Subsidies** are monetary grants given to producers or consumers to encourage certain behaviors. They are usually given to firms that are considered to benefit the public. Agriculture and steel are two industries that have historically received subsidies.

Government Jobs
The U.S. federal government's official job Web site lists federal jobs and provides general employee information. The Web site also helps applicants create résumés. *How do you think the government can aid firms with its job Web site?*

Science/Tech TRENDS

Commercial Space Travel

The space shuttle looks like an airplane because it has to travel through Earth's atmosphere just like an airplane. However, the space industry has not developed in the same way that the aviation industry developed over the course of the 20th century. Aviation was largely developed by inventors and entrepreneurs, although government and the military played important roles. In the case of the space industry, however, governments in the United States, Europe, and Japan established monopolies to open the space frontier on behalf of the public. Today, with growing interest in commercial space travel, the role of government in the space industry is changing. The innovations that come from public sector space travel research help scientists and create new opportunities for business.

WebQuest

Locate Web sites where you can find information on commercial space travel. What will it take to fly adventurers and commuters to the edge of space? Give a talk to your class about the future of commercial space travel. Use presentation software and include pictures taken from a spacecraft or space telescope.

● **As You Read**

Think of a government good or service that does not directly benefit you. Do you think it is fair for you to share the tax burden for something you do not use?

How Government Is Funded

A **tax** is an amount of money people and businesses pay governments to help run the nation, state, county, city, or town. For some goods, such as gasoline, taxes are included in the purchase price. If you have a job, income taxes are deducted from your wages. Your income tax revenue helps pay for public goods and services and provide money for transfer payments.

The purpose of taxes is to pay for public goods and services by spreading the cost among many people. **Figure 11.1** provides a glimpse of the amount of time it takes for taxpayers in some states to work to pay their taxes. However, some people may not receive direct benefits from all the taxes they pay. For instance, some people may never need to call a fire department. However, the fire department is important to everyone in a community.

Each level of government collects taxes for different kinds of services. For example, federal income tax pays for national highways and defense. State taxes pay for state police and motor vehicle departments. Local taxes pay for streets and parks. All three levels of government pay for public education.

✔ **Reading Check** **Analyze** Why are taxes necessary?

Figure 11.1 – *Working to Pay Taxes*

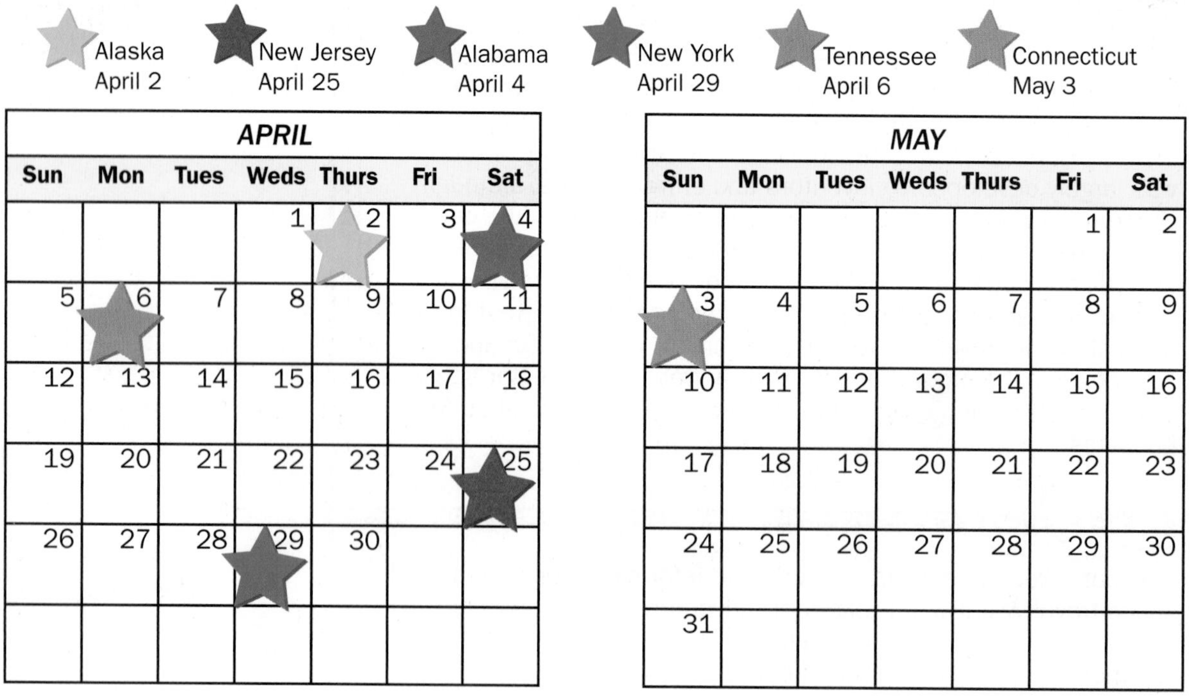

★ Alaska April 2 ★ New Jersey April 25 ★ Alabama April 4 ★ New York April 29 ★ Tennessee April 6 ★ Connecticut May 3

APRIL						
Sun	Mon	Tues	Weds	Thurs	Fri	Sat
			1	★2	3	★4
5	★6	7	8	9	10	11
12	13	14	15	16	17	18
19	20	21	22	23	24	★25
26	27	28	★29	30		

MAY						
Sun	Mon	Tues	Weds	Thurs	Fri	Sat
					1	2
★3	4	5	6	7	8	9
10	11	12	13	14	15	16
17	18	19	20	21	22	23
24	25	26	27	28	29	30
31						

Source: Tax Foundation

● **Tax Freedom Day** Tax Freedom Day is the first day of the year when the average person has earned enough to pay all of his or her annual federal, state, and local taxes. **Why does it take residents of Connecticut longer to pay all of their taxes?**

Providing Incentives

The government provides many incentives to businesses and consumers. A **tax incentive** is a temporary reduction or elimination of a tax that is meant to encourage or discourage an activity. A *tax break* is a special tax benefit given to promote specific economic or social objectives. Tax deductions for mortgage interest and property tax expenses encourage home ownership.

Government also tries to discourage certain behaviors. For example, taxes on cigarettes have increased dramatically. The reasoning is that some people may stop smoking if they decide it is too expensive to smoke.

● **As You Read**

Think about the tax incentives your town or city might give to local businesses. Do you think it is fair for some businesses to receive tax incentives?

How Government Allocates Resources

Governments **allocate** resources by deciding the best ways to spend tax revenues. They determine which projects are priorities for funding. For example, the government may decide to pay more for projects in rural areas than projects in urban ones. Such a decision can help the economies in rural areas.

Government spending also affects the distribution of income. For example, people who receive transfer payments such as unemployment pay can see their income rise or fall if the government raises or lowers the amount of their payments.

Section 11.2

○ After You Read

Review Key Concepts
1. What are some services that the government provides for the public?
2. How is government funded?
3. How does the government allocate resources?

Academic Skills

4. **English Language Arts** In a group of three or four, brainstorm a list of ways to make a business more competitive. Consider topics such as innovation, pricing, marketing, and customer service. Also brainstorm a list of reasons businesses lose their competitive edge. Use your list for a presentation about the advantages and disadvantages of government regulation of business.

5. **English Language Arts** The U.S. Department of Labor publishes various major economic indicators including the unemployment rate, the consumer price index, the producer price index, and the employment cost index. Choose one of these and find out more about it. Write a paragraph explaining what it is and why it is valuable to people in business and government.

 Go to **connectED.mcgraw-hill.com** to check your answers.

Section 11.1 *Summary*

Government as Regulator There are three levels of government: federal, state, and local. The federal government runs the country. A state government runs each state. Local governments run counties, cities, towns, and townships. Each level of government oversees a different level of business. One of government's roles is to foster success in our market economy. It does this by enacting laws for organizations and people to follow. Laws protect competition, business agreements, and creative rights. They also help the government to regulate the production process. In some cases, government must approve an item before it can be produced.

Section 11.2 *Summary*

Government as Provider Government is the largest provider of services in the country. It provides goods and services that are not easy for consumers to buy on their own and for the good of society. Individuals cannot buy highways, bridges, or national defense. These public goods and services are provided by the government and paid for with tax revenues. Government provides incentives to businesses to encourage or discourage certain activities. Since governments do not have unlimited resources, they must choose how their limited resources should be used. Their decisions can affect the economic health of an area.

Vocabulary Review

1. On a sheet of paper, use each of these key terms and academic vocabulary terms in a sentence.

Key Terms

interstate commerce
intrastate commerce
monopoly
oligopoly
trust
antitrust laws
contract
breach of contract

copyright
patent
trademark
revenue
privatization
subsidies
tax
tax incentive

Academic Vocabulary

federal
enables
symbol
registered

incentives
welfare
ensure
allocate

Review Key Concepts

2. Name four ways in which government regulates business.

3. Name five aspects of the government's role in society.

4. Name three items that the national government provides and three items that local governments provide.

5. Explain how governments can stimulate or restrict economic activities.

Critical Thinking

6. Why does our government want businesses to succeed?

7. How is competition a form of consumer protection?

8. Suppose a business is required by U.S. law to install pollution-control equipment. Who ultimately pays for the cost of the equipment and in what way?

9. Do you think patent protection can lead to monopolies over a patented good? Is that a good or a bad thing?

10. How do people in a democracy acknowledge their social wants so that the government can help satisfy them?

11. Why are many public goods and services being offered through privatization?

12. Are transfer payments good for society? Why or why not?

13. Imagine that you run a coffee shop in an area where there is a military base. The government decides to close the military operation. Will that have an effect on your coffee shop? Explain.

Write About It

14. Attend a city council or county board meeting in your area. Write a one-page article describing what took place. What decisions were made that might affect you and your community? Be sure to include residents' comments.

15. Write a one-page essay discussing whether you believe the federal government looks out for the well-being of all people in the country.

16. Make a list of people in your community who help pay for the cost of public goods and services but do not directly use them. In two or more paragraphs, state why you think it is right for them to contribute to the cost of these services.

17. In two or more paragraphs, discuss your opinion of high taxes on cigarettes.

18. Write a one-page letter to the mayor of your city or town expressing a problem that you would like solved. Indicate why the problem should be addressed.

19. In at least one page, argue for or against the value of government giving tax incentives to business.

Technology Applications

Internet Research

20. Research three laws that the government has created to protect individuals. Include one law in each of the following categories: environmental protection, consumer protection, and employee protection. Investigate the costs and benefits of the laws to citizens as well as their effects on business. Prepare a presentation about the role of the legal system in business and how these laws impact society.

Business Ethics

Should You "Bid" This Project Farewell?

21. Suppose you own a small business that makes nuts and bolts for machines. You would like to compete for a bid to make nuts and bolts for the U.S. military. You could submit a low bid to beat your competitors' proposals. However, you know that your costs will be higher than what is shown on your bid. Is this ethical? Explain your answer.

Applying Academics to Business

English Language Arts

22. Use a dictionary or other resource to find out more about the prefixes in the following word pairs. Write a phrase or sentence giving the meanings of the prefixes and list other words that use them.

monopoly   *oligopoly*
interstate   *intrastate*

Mathematics

23. You recently moved to a city with a lower sales tax. The sales tax where you used to live was 5.75%, and the new tax rate is a quarter percent less. Explain two different ways you could calculate how much less you would pay for a $12 CD in your new city than your old, and then solve the problem.

CONCEPT **Percents** A percent is a ratio that compares a number to 100. A percent can be converted to a decimal by dividing the percent number by 100.

English Language Arts

24. Copyrights, patents, and trademarks protect creative properties. This legal protection extends to *trade dress* and *trade secrets*. Research the meanings of these terms, and write a sentence or two explaining each.

Mathematics

25. You work for a lumber yard and a customer orders 25 pieces of plywood cut to 60 cm × 90 cm. You must cut them from larger sheets that measure 4 ft. by 8 ft. What is the fewest number of sheets of plywood you need to fill the customer's order?

CONCEPT **Geometry and Measurement** You can convert metric and U.S. customary measurements using tables found in math books, reference books, and other online resources. For example, use the formulas 1 in. = 2.54 cm, and 12 in. = 1 ft. Then use the problem-solving strategy "draw a diagram" to solve the problem.

Active Learning

Analyze Student Government

26. Write a report about your school's student government. What is its role in the school? How are officials chosen? How does your school's government look out for students' common welfare? What kind of rules and regulations does it enact, and how are they enforced? How is the government funded? How are spending decisions made?

Business in the Real World

Workplace Safety

27. Form a group and choose a local business owner or manager to interview. Ask how he or she works to avoid work-related accidents. Which rules regarding job safety apply most in this type of business? Compare your findings with those of other groups. Then as a class, list the safety rules that were discussed.

Real LIFE skills

DEVELOPING SKILLS IN BUSINESS LAW

28. Interview someone involved in the legal field. Possible contacts include lawyers, judges, legal assistants, teachers, or job counselors. Ask the professional about career opportunities in business law. What kinds of skills are important in this field? How can you develop them? Write a report of at least one page. Share your findings with the class.

 Business CAREERS

FIND YOUR DREAM JOB

29. Locate the Occupational Outlook Handbook Web site. Click on the "OOH Search/A-Z Index" link and enter the job category of "state and local government, excluding education and hospitals." Then write a one-page report about this area of occupation. Conclude your report with a list of things you could do now to prepare yourself to pursue this occupation.

Role Play

A CASE FOR OR AGAINST PUBLIC GOODS OR SERVICES

30. Situation Imagine that you are a lawyer who is asked to justify a position on a public good or service to the mayor.

Activity Choose an existing public good or service in your community. Prepare an argument explaining why it should either continue to be provided as a public good or service or should instead be provided by the private sector.

Evaluation You will be evaluated on how well you meet the following performance indicators:

- Demonstrate an understanding of the difference between private and public goods and services.
- Give reasons why the good or service should be provided in the public or private sector.
- Deliver your presentation in a logical sequence.
- Use correct grammar and project your voice.

Standardized Test Practice

Directions Choose the letter of the best answer. Write the letter for the answer on a separate piece of paper.

1. Which word is spelled correctly and completes the sentence?

A Supreme Court decision about antitrust laws sets an important _____.

A   president
B   presedent
C   precedant
D   precedent

 TEST-TAKING TIP Taking tests can be stressful. Stay relaxed. If you begin to get nervous, take a few deep breaths slowly to relax yourself. Then get back to work.

Chapter 12

Money and Financial Institutions

Chapter Objectives | After completing this chapter, you will be able to:

▶ ## Section 12.1 *Money and Banking*
- **Describe** the functions and characteristics of money.
- **Discuss** three main functions of a bank.

▶ ## Section 12.2 *Types of Financial Institutions*
- **Compare and contrast** three types of banks that are found in our economy.
- **Explain** the major functions of the Federal Reserve System in the U.S. economy.

Ask ## AN EXPERT | **Statistical Analysis**

Q: What are statistics, and how do they help analysts predict which investments will be good over the long term?

A: One minute a stock is up. The next it may be down. Values can fluctuate from day to day and minute to minute. Financial analysts must consider a wide variety of data every day to forecast market trends. One of their most powerful tools is a branch of mathematics called statistics. Using statistics, analysts use powerful computers to "crunch" numbers. The results allow analysts to predict trends. One way stocks are evaluated uses weighted averages to compare companies. You can use a simple averaging technique to see one way statistics help analysts.

Mathematics Cynthia picked five stocks yesterday. Their closing prices were $17.09, $13.80, $2.81, $26.16, and $8.08. Today their closing prices, respectively, are $17.22, $13.93, $2.84, $23.43, and $7.79. Average the values for each day, and compare them for a broader view of what is happening in the overall market.

CONCEPT **Average (Mean):** The average, or mean, is a single number used to represent a group of numbers. The average of two or more numbers is the sum of the numbers divided by the number of items added. The formula for each day's mean stock price is:

$$\frac{Stock_1 + Stock_2 + Stock_3 + Stock_4 + Stock_5}{5}$$

Financial Institutions Banks are intermediaries that help with the flow of money between borrowers and lenders. **What other financial institutions serve as intermediaries between lenders and borrowers?**

Money and Banking

Reading Guide

● Before You Read

Think about how bartering, or trading goods or services, might work in your life.

Read to Learn

- Describe the functions and characteristics of money.
- Discuss three main functions of a bank.

The Main Idea

Money functions as a standard of value, a medium of exchange or payment, and a store of value. Most countries create and circulate their own money. Banks are in the business of handling money.

Key Concepts

- The Purpose of Money
- The Functions of Banks

Vocabulary

Key Terms

money
monetary system
financial institution
bank account
deposit
withdrawal
interest

electronic funds
  transfer (EFT)
direct deposit
collateral
mortgage
safe-deposit box

Academic Vocabulary

You will find these words in your reading and on your tests. Make sure you know their meanings.

acquire   primary
stable   secure

Graphic Organizer

As you read, write notes about the functions of money in a box like the one below.

The Functions of Money	
Medium of Exchange	
Standard of Value	
Store of Value	

 Go to **connectED.mcgraw-hill.com** to print out this graphic organizer.

The Purpose of Money

Money enables people and businesses to buy and sell goods and services more easily around the world. **Money** is a standard of value and a means of exchange or payment. It can be anything that people accept as a standard for payment. In the past, people used shells, stones, corn, parrot feathers, and even gopher tails for money. Modern society uses coins, currency, checks, and debit cards as part of the **monetary system**. Goods and services are directly exchanged using money. The seller of the goods or services can then take the money and exchange it for other goods and services.

✔ Reading Check **Identify** What kinds of money does modern society use?

The Functions of Money

Whether you buy a soda or sell a corporation, money changes hands. Without money, people would be forced to *barter,* or trade goods or services directly for other goods or services. Bartering can be a difficult method of exchange. Suppose you have grown a bushel of tomatoes. You would like to trade the tomatoes for new sneakers. In the barter system, you would have to find someone willing to accept tomatoes for sneakers. You would also have a hard time figuring out the value of the sneakers in relation to the tomatoes. You might have to make several trades to **acquire** something the sneaker owner would accept.

Money has three basic functions:

- It is a *medium of exchange.* A medium of exchange is anything that is generally accepted as a measure of value and of wealth. In a system that uses money, buyers and sellers agree to exchange money.

● **What Is Money?**
Money is most commonly considered to be coins, currency, and checking accounts. **What are some other ways that people and businesses can pay for goods and services?**

D. Hurst/Alamy

- Money functions as a *standard of value*. A standard is a way to measure the weight, amount, size, or value of something. Money provides a means of measuring the value of goods and services.
- Money functions as a *store of value*. That means it holds its value over time and can be stored or saved. Money that is saved can build wealth.

Characteristics of Money

Paper money and coins are common forms of money. For money to carry out its functions, it must have these characteristics. Money must be *stable* in value. Money that is **stable** has little if any change in value. To be used as money, an item must be *scarce*. If the supply of an item is overly plentiful, it loses its value and cannot serve as money or a store of value since it would have little worth. People would lose faith in its value as a medium of exchange.

Money must be *accepted*. People have to be willing to take money in exchange for goods and services. It should be *divisible* into parts. Money also has to be *portable* and *durable*. Finally, it must be hard to counterfeit. To *counterfeit* means to make a copy of something in order to defraud or deceive people.

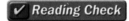 **Reading Check** **Explain** What are the characteristics of money?

The Functions of Banks

A **financial institution** is a firm that manages money. Banks are the main types of financial institutions. Banks offer a variety of financial services. They help other businesses and consumers manage their money. **Figure 12.1** shows how banks and customers interact.

Storing Money

One of the main services banks provide is storing money in bank accounts. To *store* money means to place or leave it for preservation or later use. A **bank account** is a record of the amount of money a customer has deposited into or withdrawn from a bank. The money put in a bank account is called a **deposit**. The money taken out is called a **withdrawal**. Keeping your money in a bank prevents you from losing it, spending it, or having it stolen easily.

The two main types of bank accounts are checking accounts and savings accounts. Checking accounts are used for storing money in the short term. Banks usually charge a fee for checking accounts. Savings accounts are used for storing money over a longer period of time. An advantage of a savings account is that it earns more interest than most checking accounts. **Interest** is a rate that the bank pays customers for keeping their money.

● **As You Read**

Think about some ways you protect your money. Do you believe that having your money in a bank is the best way to keep from spending it?

Transferring Money

Banks use checks and electronic funds transfers to move money. Checks are primarily used to transfer money from one party to another. **Electronic funds transfer (EFT)** allows money to be transferred from one bank account to another through a network of computers. **Direct deposit** is the electronic transfer of a payment directly from the payer's bank account to that of the party being paid. Many employers issue payroll checks this way.

Lending Money

Lending money is the **primary** way banks generate profits. The money you deposit in a bank makes it possible for the bank to lend money to other customers. Just as banks pay customers interest on their savings, customers pay interest on the money they borrow from banks. Banks then use the interest they earned to pay interest on customers' savings accounts. Most bank loans require some form of collateral. **Collateral** is property or goods pledged by a borrower to use as security against a loan if it is not repaid.

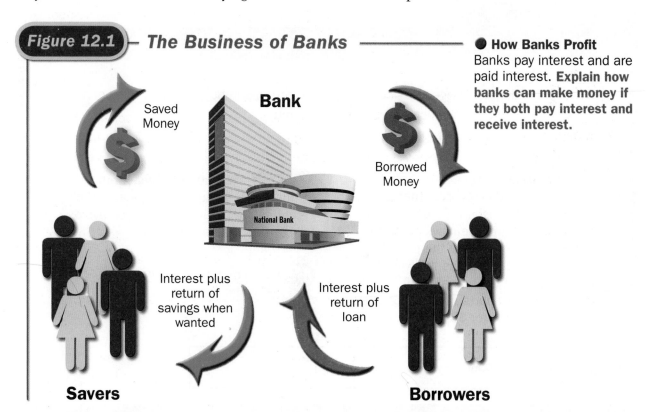

Figure 12.1 — **The Business of Banks**

Saved Money

Bank

National Bank

Borrowed Money

Interest plus return of savings when wanted

Interest plus return of loan

Savers

Borrowers

● **How Banks Profit**
Banks pay interest and are paid interest. **Explain how banks can make money if they both pay interest and receive interest.**

As You Read
Think about whether you would be willing to use collateral to borrow money.

There are four main types of loans that banks offer to businesses and individuals:

- A *mortgage loan* is a loan used to buy real estate, such as a house or an office building. A **mortgage** is an agreement in which a borrower gives a lender the right to take the property if the loan is not repaid.
- A *commercial loan* is a loan made to businesses to buy supplies and equipment.
- An *individual loan* is a loan made to an individual to pay for personal items, such as a car, home repairs, or a vacation.
- A *line of credit* is a credit arrangement in which a financial institution agrees to lend a specific amount of money to be used at any time for any purpose.

Other Financial Services

Banks also offer other services. Many provide financial advice on managing and investing money. Banks not only store money, they can also store valuable items, such as jewelry and birth certificates, in a safe-deposit box. A **safe-deposit box** is a **secure** box in a bank's vault used for the safe storage of a customer's valuables. As another service, many banks offer debit cards and credit cards, such as MasterCard® or Visa®. Banks also have trust departments that manage money for individuals and organizations.

Section 12.1

After You Read

Review Key Concepts

1. What is a major advantage of using money over bartering in buying goods and services?
2. What are at least five characteristics that money must have?
3. What are four types of loans that a bank makes?

Academic Skills

4. **Mathematics** Imagine that the U.S. Mint has issued a new coin that is worth $1 and weighs 0.5 ounce. Find the total weight of the new coins you would need to purchase the following items with cash. Express the weights using the most appropriate unit: a pizza for $16, a new sports car for $32,000, and a new condo for $96,000.

CONCEPT Weights and Measures
Choosing the best unit of measure to express a quantity can help you avoid excessively large numbers.

 For math help, go to the Math Appendix.

 Go to **connectED.mcgraw-hill.com** to check your answers.

Types of Financial Institutions

Reading Guide

● Before You Read

Think about the different banking services you and your family use every day.

Read to Learn

- Compare and contrast three types of banks that are found in our economy.
- Explain the major functions of the Federal Reserve System in the U.S. economy.

The Main Idea

There are three types of institutions that operate as banks. They are commercial banks, savings and loan associations, and credit unions. A Federal Reserve Bank is a banker's bank. The Federal Reserve System manages the banking system and controls the money supply.

Key Concepts

- Financial Institutions
- The Federal Reserve System

Vocabulary

Key Terms

commercial banks
savings and loan
  associations
credit unions
mortgage companies

finance companies
insurance companies
brokerage firms
Federal Reserve System
reserves

Academic Vocabulary

You will find these words in your reading and on your tests. Make sure you know their meanings.

granted
bonds

monitors
flexible

Graphic Organizer

As you read, write notes about the types of financial organizations on a figure like the one below.

Types of Financial Institutions	
Commercial Bank	
Savings and Loan	
Credit Union	
Mortgage Company	
Finance Company	
Insurance Company	
Brokerage	

 Go **connectED.mcgraw-hill.com** to print out this graphic organizer.

Financial Institutions

Banks operate on state, national, and international levels. There are strict rules for starting one because banks handle large amounts of money. To open a federal or a state bank in the United States, the owners have to meet special requirements. They must also apply for a charter from the federal or state government. The owners need to prove they have enough capital to start a bank. In the United States, there are three main types of banks. They are commercial banks, savings and loan associations, and credit unions.

✔ **Reading Check** **Explain** What are some of the rules for starting a bank?

Commercial Banks

Most of the banks in the United States are commercial banks. **Commercial banks** offer the entire range of banking services, such as checking and savings accounts, loans, and financial advice. They are often called *full-service banks*. Commercial banks serve individuals and businesses. They are authorized to conduct business through a charter, or license, that is **granted** by either the federal government or a state government. To make a profit, commercial banks charge more interest on the money that they lend than the interest they pay on savings accounts.

Science/TechTRENDS

Digital Cash
Star Trek fans may recall that members of the Federation abolished money a long time ago. Perhaps they were able to create a moneyless society because they had invented a replicator machine that allowed them to make copies of everything from food to cars to clothing and homes. That is not possible in our world, but some communities are experimenting with digital cash to replace bills and coins. For example, New Haven, Connecticut, became one of the first cities to use the new "smart card" payment system for parking and retail. The card can be bought and loaded with $100, used to pay for parking meter fees, lattes at a coffee shop, and books at bookstores. When the value on the card runs low, it can be refilled.

Web **Quest**

Locate Web sites where you can find out more about smart card technology. How do smart cards work? Where are they being used? What are the advantages and disadvantages of using them?

Savings and Loan Associations

Savings and loan associations are financial institutions that hold customers' funds in interest-bearing accounts and invest mainly in mortgage loans. Savings and loans were originally set up to offer savings accounts and home mortgage loans. Their purpose was to encourage people to save money and make it easier to buy a home or start a business. To do this, they charged lower interest rates on loans and paid higher interest on savings accounts than banks.

In 1982, the government passed new regulations allowing them to charge higher interest rates and offer more services. In the late 1980s, about 20 percent of savings and loan associations failed. In response, new regulations were passed. The services offered by savings and loan associations today are very similar to the services offered by commercial banks and credit unions.

✔ Reading Check **Define** What is a savings and loan association?

Business Case Study

Goodbye to the Bank Branch

Online banks edge out the competition through cost savings.

Twenty years ago, paying bills online was a bold new option for bank customers. Today, a majority of bank customers use the Web to do banking tasks. In fact, many new banks—including Ally Bank, American Express Bank, and Simple—don't bother with physical branches at all.

Because branches cost money to build and run, online banks can offer higher interest rates and lower fees than traditional banks. They also provide 24-7 service through their websites or apps. Customers can withdraw cash through a network of ATMs and deposit checks by submitting a photo.

Is your information secure with an online bank? Financial analysts say generally yes. Online and traditional banks store financial data in a similar way. Just make sure to use a secure Internet connection to minimize the risk of your information being intercepted, advice that is true for all financial transactions.

While many people still prefer face-to-face service, even traditional banks are cutting costs and responding to competition by closing local branches. It could be that before long, everyone banks online.

Active Learning

Imagine that you are trying to decide where to open a bank account. Think of a traditional bank in your community and go to its website. Research the features and fees of the bank's personal checking accounts, ATM locations, and certificates of deposit (CDs). Next, look up the same information for one of the online banks listed in this feature. Compare and contrast the two banks' offerings and write a short explanation of which appeals to you more, and why.

As You Read

Credit unions offer a variety of services to their members. Do you think it would be better for you to open an account at a credit union or a bank?

Credit Unions

Credit unions are not-for-profit banks set up by organizations for their employees to use. Credit union customers are also called members. Credit unions offer members credit cards, checking accounts, low-interest loans, and high interest savings accounts. Many of them also pay interest on checking accounts.

Other Financial Institutions

There are other financial institutions that offer some of the same services as banks. **Mortgage companies** provide loans specifically for buying a home or business. **Finance companies** offer short-term loans to businesses and consumers, but at much higher interest rates than banks charge. **Insurance companies** not only provide protection against problems such as fire and theft, but they also offer loans to businesses and consumers. **Brokerage firms** that sell stocks and **bonds** may also offer a wide range of financial services to their customers.

The Federal Reserve System

The **Federal Reserve System** (or Federal Reserve) is the central bank of the United States. Also known as "The Fed," the Federal Reserve is the banker's bank. It **monitors** the money supply. **Figure 12.2** shows a map of the 12 Federal Reserve Districts.

Figure 12.2 — *The Federal Reserve System*

● **The Federal Reserve System** The Federal Reserve System is based in Washington, D.C., and has 12 districts. **In which Federal Reserve District is your community?**

Congress set up the Federal Reserve System in 1913. Its mission is to provide the United States with a safe, **flexible**, and stable monetary and financial system. The Federal Reserve System consists of 12 regional Federal Reserve Banks and 25 branch banks. It also has about 5,000 member banks. The Federal Reserve is run by the Board of Governors. It supervises the 12 district banks and regulates activity of the member banks. The Federal Reserve has six functions:

1. **Clearing Checks** Funds are transferred from one bank to another when someone writes or deposits a check.
2. **Acting as the Federal Government's Fiscal Agent** The Federal Reserve distributes money to Federal Reserve member banks and commercial banks. It also tracks the deposits and holds a checking account for the U.S. Treasury.
3. **Supervising Member Banks** The Fed regulates banks that are members of the Federal Reserve System.
4. **Regulating the Money Supply** The primary responsibility of the Federal Reserve is to determine the amount of money in circulation and either increase or decrease it.
5. **Setting Reserve Requirements** Member banks must keep a certain percentage of deposits as reserves. **Reserves** are funds set aside for emergencies, such as a rush of withdrawals.
6. **Supplying Paper Currency** The Federal Reserve is responsible for printing and maintaining U.S. paper currency.

The Federal Reserve One of the Federal Reserve's main duties is to monitor the inflation rate. Inflation is a general increase in the cost of goods and services. *When the inflation rate is high, why is it important for the Federal Reserve to take action?*

Section 12.2

After You Read

Review Key Concepts
1. How is a credit union different from a commercial bank?
2. List the seven types of financial institutions discussed in the section.
3. What is the mission of the Federal Reserve?

Academic Skills
4. **English Language Arts** Banks operate on several levels from local to international. We use the word *federal* to describe some banks. Write a definition for the word *federal* and use it in a sentence. List some synonyms and antonyms for *federal.*

5. **English Language Arts** Interview family members about their experience with banks. Ask them to describe how their experience of banking has changed over the years. Is banking more customer-friendly today? How has technology changed banking? Write a paragraph summarizing your findings.

 Go to **connectED.mcgraw-hill.com** to check your answers.

Section 12.1 *Summary*

Money and Banking Money functions as a medium of exchange, a standard of value, and a store of value. It enables people and businesses to buy and sell goods and services more easily. For money to carry out its functions, it must have several characteristics. It must be scarce, acceptable, portable, divisible, durable, and hard to counterfeit. Financial institutions such as banks manage money. They store, transfer, and lend it. The products and services banks offer help other businesses and consumers manage their money.

Section 12.2 *Summary*

Types of Financial Institutions The three main types of banks are commercial banks, savings and loan associations, and credit unions. Mortgage, finance, and insurance companies offer some of the same services as banks. The Federal Reserve is the central bank of the United States. It provides the country with a safe, flexible, and stable monetary and financial system. It consists of 12 regional Federal Reserve Banks, 25 branch banks, and about 5,000 member banks. The Federal Reserve's most important function is regulating the money supply.

Vocabulary Review

1. On a sheet of paper, use each of these key terms and academic vocabulary terms in a sentence.

Key Terms

money
monetary system
financial institution
bank account
deposit
withdrawal
interest
electronic funds transfer
   (EFT)
direct deposit
collateral

mortgage
safe-deposit box
commercial banks
savings and loan associations
credit unions
mortgage companies
finance companies
insurance companies
brokerage firms
Federal Reserve System
reserves

Academic Vocabulary

acquire
stable
primary
secure
granted
bonds
monitors
flexible

Review Key Concepts

2. Describe the functions and characteristics of money.

3. Discuss three main functions of a bank.

4. Compare and contrast three types of banks that are found in our economy.

5. Explain the major functions of the Federal Reserve System in the U.S. economy.

Critical Thinking

6. Why do you think banks pay interest on deposits left in savings accounts?

7. Credit cards can be used to make purchases. However, credit cards are not considered money. Why do you think this is so?

8. Why do you think coins have been a more desirable form of money than paper currency throughout history?

9. How can the reserve requirement for banks be used to slow the economy's growth?

10. What do you think would happen if all the depositors of a bank requested their deposits at the same time? What is done to keep this from happening?

11. The British pound cannot be used in most U.S. stores to buy goods and services. Why do you think this is so?

12. Loans with collateral generally have a lower interest rate than loans without collateral. Why?

13. Is it unfair to require banks and savings and loans to pay federal income taxes on their income but not credit unions, which do not have to pay taxes because they are nonprofit organizations? Explain your answer.

Write About It

14. Research a bank to see which kinds of trust services are available. Find out how their trust accounts differ from their other accounts. Write a 250-word article about trust services offered by that bank.

15. Visit or contact a bank. Find out about its interest rates and the terms on its checking and savings accounts. Write a report comparing the accounts.

16. How has the Internet affected competition in the area of financial services? Write at least two paragraphs explaining your response.

17. Research the history of U.S. currency. Create a timeline with explanations for the development of money from colonial times to the present.

18. Go online to research the history of counterfeiting. Then write a two-page report on your findings. Include strategies that are being used to combat it.

19. Observe the recent activities or decisions of the Federal Reserve Board. Then write a two-page essay on your findings. Be sure to discuss the effects its decisions have on the economy.

Technology Applications

Access Cards and Digital Cash
20. Although cash and checks are still commonly used, various access cards are becoming more popular. Gift cards are examples of access cards. Digital cash refers to buying goods and services with funds that are transferred from one account to another through computers. Research access cards and digital cash. Write an essay on your findings. Include whether you think cash and checks will soon be outdated.

Business Ethics

Banks as Citizens of the Community
21. When Hurricane Katrina hit Louisiana, it caused a break in the levee system. Most of New Orleans was flooded. The coasts of Mississippi and Alabama also suffered heavy damage that caused a humanitarian crisis on a vast scale. Hurricane Katrina was one of the most costly natural disasters in U.S. history. In situations such as this, what is the responsibility of banks? What ethical issues do they face?

Applying Academics to Business

English Language Arts

22. Collect various types of advertisements for financial institutions. Include a commercial bank, a savings and loan, and a mortgage company or credit union. Based on the ads you collect, chart the different services offered. Write a paragraph or two comparing and contrasting the institutions.

Mathematics

23. Pauline needs to get a $5,000 loan to buy a car. Her bank offers a loan at 6% simple interest, which she will pay back in three years. If she takes this loan, how much interest will she pay?

> **CONCEPT** **Simple Interest** The formula for finding simple interest is $I = prt$, where I is the amount of the interest, p is the principal, r is the interest rate, and t is time.

English Language Arts

24. As a noun, the word *interest* has several meanings. It can also be used as a verb. Look at the definition of *interest* in at least two different dictionaries. Then write four sentences using the word or one of its forms to illustrate four of its meanings. One of your sentences should use it as a verb.

Mathematics

25. Heather uses an ATM three times a week. She spends a week out of town for work every fifth week, and has to use an ATM that charges her $1.50 in service fees each time she uses it. How many weeks does she spend out of town each year? How much will she spend on service fees in a year?

> **CONCEPT** **Multiplying Fractions** To multiply a fraction by a whole number, multiply the whole number by the numerator of the fraction and then divide by the denominator.

Active Learning

Research the Federal Reserve

26. Write a letter to the Federal Reserve Bank in your area. Ask for information about the Federal Reserve System. Find out how the branch fulfills the Federal Reserve mission. Request information about the member banks in your area. Share the information you receive with your classmates.

Business in the Real World

Interview a Loan Officer

27. Interview a business loan officer at a local bank about business loans. Ask about the size of a typical loan and the percentage of loans backed by collateral. Find out why some business loans have no collateral. Also, ask about the length of a typical loan. Why are some loans not repaid? Share what you find with the rest of the class.

Real LIFE skills

SKILLS NEEDED IN BANKING

28. Research the training and qualifications that are required to be a bank teller. Get this information from banks' Web sites, bank employees, the Occupational Outlook Handbook, or other sources. Write a one-page report that includes this information. Indicate if you think you would be interested in preparing for this position.

Business CAREERS

FIND YOUR DREAM JOB

29. Locate the Occupational Outlook Handbook Web site. Click on the "OOH Search/A-Z Index" link and enter the job category "loan counselors and officers." Then write a one-page report about this area of occupation. Conclude your report with a list of things you could do now to prepare yourself to pursue the occupation.

Role Play

CURRENCY FOR AN ISLAND ECONOMY

30. Situation Imagine that you live on an island that has few modern conveniences. You and your neighbors want to figure out something you can use for currency.

Activity Make a presentation about items you would consider using as currency and why.

Evaluation You will be evaluated on how well you meet the following performance indicators:

- Know the characteristics of money.
- Accurately relate the characteristics of money to the characteristics of the items that are suggested as currency.
- Use correct grammar.
- Organize your presentation in a logical way.

Standardized Test Practice

Directions Choose the letter of the best answer. Write the letter for the answer on a separate piece of paper.

1. Which sentence contains an error in the use of commas?

A   All over the world, paper money and coins are common forms of money.

B   Without money, buying and selling is difficult.

C   With money, however transactions become easy.

D   As a standard of value, money makes it possible to set a fixed value on a product.

TEST-TAKING TIP Even though the first answer choice you make is often correct, do not be afraid to change an answer if you change your mind after thinking about it.

Ling Chai

Founder, President, and COO, Jenzabar

Jenzabar offers Web-based software and e-learning products and services to colleges and universities. Its founder, Ling Chai, is also known for her leadership role in the Tiananmen Square democracy movement, which landed her on the Chinese government's most wanted list. She has been nominated for the Nobel Peace Prize twice.

Q & A

Describe your job responsibilities.

Ling: I am involved in almost every aspect of the business, with a particular focus on the company's product development and product marketing.

What skills are most important in your business?

Ling: A solid academic, technology, and business background, which is particularly key to my type of business and marketplace. In becoming a manager, it is essential to develop and maintain people skills, knowing what it takes to create and motivate a team. Defining culture is the key to managing a company—in our case a service-oriented, customer-centric culture.

What is your key to success?

Ling: Success comes through hard work and dedication to an idea. Persistence has been a key attribute for me, and certainly a little luck helps, too.

What advice would you give students interested in starting a business?

Ling: Most important is a solid educational background. Go for it, and follow your heart. Do something that makes you want to wake up and go do it every day, because you'll need that attitude to support the hard work and persistence necessary to be successful.

How has your experience in China, especially Tiananmen Square protests, shaped who you are today?

Ling: My leadership in Tiananmen Square protests helped shape the democracy movement in terms of organizing people in a disorderly situation, and developing an action plan. There are similarities between leading a political movement and running a business. Both deal with managing people, developing a mission, handling situations and issues as they emerge, and maintaining a direction.

Critical Thinking

Why is it important to maintain a balance of education, experience, and networking while developing and running a business?

Some Qualifications of the Owner of a Software Development Company

Academic Skills and Abilities

Computer science; mathematics; information systems; computer programming; interpersonal skills; general business management; verbal and written communication skills; multitasking, organizing, and planning skills

Academic Skills Required to Complete Tasks at Jenzabar			
Tasks	**Math**	**Science**	**English Language Arts**
Hold meetings			◆
Assign duties			◆
Develop new products	◆	◆	◆
Assess marketplace opportunities	◆	◆	◆
Customer service			◆
Schedule employees	◆		◆
Order supplies and equipment	◆		◆
Analyze financials	◆		◆

Education and Training

Occupations in the software publishing industry require varying levels of education. The level of education and type of training required depend on the employer's needs, which often change due to changes in technology and business conditions. Another factor driving employers' needs is the time frame within which a project must be completed.

Career Path

Computer software engineers need a broad knowledge of and experience with computer systems and technologies. Usual degree concentrations for applications software engineers are computer science or software engineering; for systems software engineers, usual concentrations are computer science or computer information systems. Graduate degrees are preferred for some of the more complex software engineering jobs.

Community Outreach and Service Learning

Community outreach and service learning are smart business practices. Community outreach is good public relations. It helps keep the community strong and healthy, brings in new customers to a business, and helps mentor young people through service learning.

Thematic Project Assignment

In this project you will research and then write a news story, with pictures, about a business that is working on a community project. Include information about student volunteers for the project and how they acquire knowledge while working in service to the community.

Step 1 — Brainstorm Skills You Need to Complete This Activity

Your success in researching and writing a news feature story will depend on your skills. Preview the activity. Then brainstorm a list of the skills you will need to use to complete the activity and describe how you will use them. Skills you might use include:

Academic Skills   reading, writing, art/photography
Basic Skills   speaking, listening, thinking, and interpersonal skills
Technology Skills   word processing, keyboarding, presentation, and Internet skills

@ *SKILLS PREVIEW* Go to **connectED.mcgraw-hill.com** to download a graphic organizer you can use to brainstorm the skills you will use to complete the project.

Step 2 — Choose a Business and a Career That Interest You

Use your local newspaper, business magazines, and the Internet to find news stories about businesses that interest you that are helping communities. Make sure they offer a career in which you are interested and are using student volunteers with the project.

Step 3 — Build Background Knowledge

Preview the stories and look for the who, what, when, where, and why in each story.

Local Business Helps Clean Up Community Park

Young volunteers from local schools helped Montgomery Hardware clean up downtown Community Park and build new playground equipment. Organized by Montgomery Hardware, the Saturday event brought out 44 students. Montgomery Hardware donated tools and supplies. The students, who were supervised by members of the carpenter's union, did the work.

"It was a whole team effort," states Edwin Hubble, president of Montgomery Hardware. "Students were mentored by carpenters, so they have a step-up when wanting to get jobs in the industry."

Step 4 — Connect with Your Community

Interview a local business owner about the company's involvement in community projects. Find out how the owner benefited. Ask if he or she had student volunteers and how the volunteers benefited.

Step 5   Research Community Outreach

Use library and Internet resources to research community outreach. Use the checklist as a guide to your research. Keep records of your sources of information.

Step 6   Develop a News Feature Story

Use word processing or page design software to write a 350- to 400-word newspaper feature story, with photos. Use your imagination to create the "facts" for your story. Stage your friends for the photos. Include all the information described in this checklist.

News Feature

✔ Use the stories you have already read as models for your story.

✔ Write a draft of your story. Include the who, what, when, where, why, and how.

    Who: Who is the story about? What is the name of the business? Who are the student volunteers? Who had the idea?

    What: What is the community project? What is the company philosophy about community outreach?

    When: When did the business and students get together to tackle the project? When did they first meet? How did the business find student volunteers?

    Where: Where did the project take place?

    Why: Why did the business decide to take on this community project?

    How: How did the company benefit? How did the student volunteers benefit?

✔ Stage your friends for the photos. Have a few friends dress in clothing appropriate for your story and do things that illustrate the story. For example, if your story is about cleaning up a park, have your friends wear outdoor clothing and plant flowers or rake leaves.

Self Connections

✔ Describe the results of your research to a family member or other adult.

✔ Describe how businesses you are interested in benefit by helping the community, and how volunteers acquire knowledge while servicing the community.

✔ Explain what the investigation and its results mean to you.

Step 7   Evaluate Your News Story

 RUBRIC Go to **connectED.mcgraw-hill.com** to download a rubric you can use to evaluate your final report.

Expeditiontrips.com is an Internet-based company that specializes in trips on small cruise ships to remote locations such as Alaska and Antarctica. At the end of this unit, you will learn about Expeditiontrips.com co-founder Kristy Royce and how she achieved her success.

Decision Making If you were about to start an online travel business, how would you market it?

Frank Krahmer/Getty Images

Unit 4 | *Thematic Project Preview*

Marketing in a Global Economy After completing this unit, you will develop marketing strategies for a marketing product and/or service in a foreign market.

Project Checklist As you read the chapters in this unit, use this checklist to prepare for the unit project.

- ✔ Think about how a country's geography and culture affect the marketplace.
- ✔ Think about how a country's economy and government affect the marketplace.
- ✔ Consider the types of goods and services that are needed and wanted in a country.
- ✔ Think about how our wants and needs are affected by the region and culture of a community.

Marketing in Today's World

Chapter Objectives After completing this chapter, you will be able to:

▶ **Section 13.1** *Marketing Essentials*
- **Define** marketing.
- **Identify** the functions of marketing.
- **List** the elements of the marketing mix.

▶ **Section 13.2** *Market Research and Product Development*
- **Describe** the kinds of market research a company may use.
- **Identify** the steps in developing a new product.

Ask AN EXPERT   Industry Surveys

Q: Lately, I've been buying all of my clothes at a couple of online outlet Web sites. I think they're great, and I'll bet that companies like these are poised for big growth. Is there a way for me to find out more about this type of business so I can consider investing?

A: Your local library is a good place to start. Most libraries carry *The Value Line Investment Survey,* a weekly publication providing data on 1,700 stocks. Standard & Poor's also publishes *The Outlook,* a weekly investment advisory newsletter; *Stock Guide,* with key data on more than 11,000 securities; *Industry Surveys,* which provides in-depth analyses of 53 different industries; and *Stock Reports,* which covers about 2,000 companies.

Mathematics Which type of graph would be best to show the fluctuation in the price of a stock over time? Why? Describe a graphing technique that you could use to predict the short-term movement in the price of a stock.

CONCEPT **Graphs** Different types of graphs include bar graphs, line graphs, circle graphs, scatter plots, and stem-and-leaf plots. They are used for different purposes. For example, circle graphs show how the parts of a whole relate in size to each other and to the whole.

Ingram Publishing

● **Marketing Business** Businesses provide
a wide array of products and services in
stores, online, and through catalogs. **How do
businesses attract buyers?**

Chapter 13 Marketing in Today's World **217**

Marketing Essentials

Reading Guide

Before You Read

Think about the role marketing plays in your life and how it affects your buying decisions.

Read to Learn
- Define marketing.
- Identify the functions of marketing.
- List the elements of the marketing mix.

The Main Idea
To sell their products or services, businesses engage in marketing activities. They find and analyze potential customers and then try to meet their wants and needs.

Key Concepts
- The Basics of Marketing
- The Functions of Marketing
- The Marketing Mix

Vocabulary

Key Terms
- market
- marketing
- relationship marketing
- marketing mix
- channel of distribution
- direct distribution
- indirect distribution
- break-even point

Academic Vocabulary

You will find these words in your reading and on your tests. Make sure you know their meanings.
- genders
- physical
- located
- aware

Graphic Organizer

As you read, write the four parts of the marketing mix in a graphic like the one below.

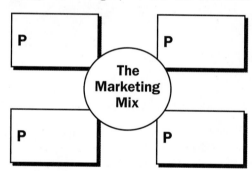

P P

The Marketing Mix

P P

 Go to **connectED.mcgraw-hill.com** to print out this graphic organizer.

The Basics of Marketing

Marketing a CD requires a different strategy than marketing diamond earrings. Each item appeals to people of different ages, genders, and income ranges. Every holiday season more gadgets, toys, and clothes hit stores. The companies that make these and other items do research before developing and selling them. To market a product successfully, a company has to understand what people want to buy and why they want to buy it.

It all comes down to knowing your market. From a marketing viewpoint, a **market** is a group of customers who share common wants and needs. These people have the ability to purchase the product or service. In the global marketplace, many countries can make up a market for a product. **Marketing** is the process of creating, promoting, and presenting a product or service to meet the wants and needs of consumers, wherever they are.

Marketing involves a number of stages, from studying what people want to buy to designing a product's packaging. For example, you might be part of the $15 billion market for recorded music and music video purchases. Businesses want you to buy their products, so they perform detailed research to find and analyze potential customers in their market. Knowing what groups of people want and need helps companies decide how and what to sell.

The Functions of Marketing

There are seven functions of marketing. These functions define all the aspects that are part of marketing.

1. *Distribution* is the process of getting goods and services to customers. The process includes purchasing, stock handling, inventory control, and **physical** distribution. Goods are usually transported by trucks, trains, airplanes, and ships. Distribution also involves the systems that track products so they can be **located** at any time.
2. *Financing* is getting the money that is necessary for setting up and running a business. Finance also includes protecting investments through risk management.
3. *Marketing information management* is gathering and analyzing information about consumers, trends, and competitors' products. Making informed decisions requires good research and development.

As You Read

Think about the "hot" new product that appealed to you this year. Was there a marketing strategy that influenced your decision to want the product?

?ETHICS in Business

Marketing Questions

■ **Critical Reading** Life is full of important decisions. Think about the kinds of decisions that you make as you read the question below.

Imagine that you have just gotten a job working for a toy company as a marketing director specializing in action figures for boys ages 7 to 12. In planning a special promotion, a team member under your direction suggests a contest. Children would fill out a questionnaire about their preferences and have a chance to win a chest full of toys and games. You can then use the information compiled from the questionnaires to design an action figure children will want.

■ **Decision Making** To prepare for your new assignment, you do some research into ethical marketing to children and understand that you have a special responsibility in communicating with children. What are some guidelines you would use in designing a promotional contest for children? Explain your answer.

4. *Pricing* is deciding how much to charge for a product or service so the business can make a profit.
5. *Product/service management* is obtaining, developing, maintaining, and improving a product or product mix in response to market opportunities.
6. *Promotion* is any effort to inform, persuade, or remind potential customers about a business's products or services.
7. *Selling* is providing customers with the goods and services they choose to buy. A popular trend today is using relationship marketing. Companies use **relationship marketing** to build and maintain relationships with their customers.

✔ **Reading Check** **Identify** What are the seven functions of marketing?

Business Case Study

Getting Social With Marketing

Social media marketing can be highly effective—if done right.

For today's businesses, marketing on social media is a must. But on which platforms? How often? Using what kinds of content? Moreover, how can businesses know whether social media marketing is working? Today's savvy marketers pursue two proven strategies:

Content Marketing. Social media users don't like to feel like they're being sold. Content marketing uses creative storytelling to grab people's attention and entice them to like, comment, and share. Blog posts, videos, interesting links, and inspiring photos are popular kinds of content marketing material. Businesses that publish useful, engaging content build trust and reputation.

Nimble Strategy. New social media platforms are always emerging, while others fade. Heard of Friendster? (Your teacher might know.) Social media-savvy businesses make decisions based on clear goals, joining relevant new platforms and leaving others that are not providing solid ROI (return on investment).

According to the most recent annual survey by Social Media Examiner, 92 percent of businesses say the main benefit to social marketing is exposure—getting more people to learn about their brand. The key is getting that exposure to make an impact.

Active Learning

Select a large brand you like. Visit its website and find which social media platforms it uses—such as Facebook, Twitter, Instagram, Pinterest, or YouTube. Visit these platforms and see what kinds of content the brand posts. Make a chart with the following columns: Platform; Types of Content; Frequency; Is the Content Successful? Choose three platforms and fill out the columns for each.

The Marketing Mix

The **marketing mix** consists of four basic marketing strategies: product, place, price, and promotion, collectively known as the *four Ps*. In recent years, many people have begun to include a fifth P for people because the success of a marketing mix depends on people: good employees and customers.

Product

First, marketing is used to find out if there is a demand for a product. Then marketing predicts how to make the product appeal to consumers. Packaging is a major part of marketing. It includes the design, color, size, and brand name of a product.

Place

Marketers have to decide how and where customers will buy their goods and services. For example, a company is more likely to sell snowshoes in Maine than in Texas because of the snowy weather in Maine. Then marketers have to consider in *what kind of location* to sell their product. Does the product need to be in a large department store or a boutique?

To make place decisions, marketers select the right channel of distribution. A **channel of distribution** is a pathway to direct products to consumers. **Direct distribution** occurs when goods or services are sold from the producer directly to the customer. **Indirect distribution** involves one or more intermediaries. Distribution decisions affect the price of products. The cost of distributing a product has to be added to its price.

● **As You Read**

Imagine that you have designed a new line of sunglasses for teens. Think about a particular location you would choose to sell your sunglasses.

● **Product Strategies**
Businesses make product strategy decisions when developing new products for their markets. **Do you think this product will appeal to consumers? Why?**

danlefeb/Getty Images

Channel Members It takes an intermediary to move a product from the manufacturer to the final user. As discussed in Chapter 6, intermediaries can include distributors, wholesalers, or retailers. Even the Internet can be considered an intermediary. It allows people and businesses to interact with each other.

Price

To determine the price of a product, a marketer considers three questions: (1) How much are customers willing to pay? (2) Is the price competitive with other products? and (3) Can the company make a profit? Marketers must find the break-even point. The **break-even point** is the point at which total revenues, or sales, equal total costs and expenses of developing and offering a product or service.

Promotion

Promotion involves making customers **aware** of a product. The most familiar form of promotion is advertising, which will be covered in Chapter 14. Automakers spend billions of dollars each year on ads. There are, however, many other ways companies can promote a product. One way is to offer discounts in the form of coupons, rebates, and sales. They can also give away items.

Section 13.1

After You Read

Review Key Concepts

1. Define marketing.
2. What are the seven functions of marketing?
3. What four elements are in the marketing mix? What is sometimes considered a fifth element?

Academic Skills

4. **Mathematics** You are manager of the sweatshirt department at Trends, a clothing manufacturer. Trends plans to produce 25,000 sweatshirts. The sweatshirts will be sold to stores for $16 each. The cost of manufacturing and marketing each sweatshirt is $10. How many sweatshirts need to be sold for the company to break even? Write an equation using *x* for the unknown that could be used to solve this problem.

 Writing Equations The unknown quantity in this problem is the number of sweatshirts that, when sold at $16 apiece, equals the manufacturing cost of all the sweatshirts.

For math help, go to the Math Appendix.

 Go to **connectED.mcgraw-hill.com** to check your answers.

Market Research and Product Development

Reading Guide

Before You Read

Think about how businesses decide when to market new products and when to discontinue old products.

Read to Learn

- Describe the kinds of market research a company may use.
- Identify the steps in developing a new product.

The Main Idea

Businesses must know their markets to provide products that will sell. They do market research to collect information and then develop products that will meet their customers' wants and needs.

Key Concepts

- Market Research
- The Seven Steps of Product Development

Vocabulary

Key Terms

market research
marketing concept
demographics
target marketing
market segmentation
test-market

Academic Vocabulary

You will find these words in your reading and on your tests. Make sure you know their meanings.

surveys   strategy
potential   crucial

Graphic Organizer

In a graphic organizer like the one below, list the seven steps of product development as you read.

1.	
2.	
3.	
4.	
5.	
6.	
7.	

 Go to **connectED.mcgraw-hill.com** to print out this graphic organizer.

Market Research

Market research helps businesses make decisions. **Market research** is the gathering and analysis of information on the size, location, and makeup of a market.

Market researchers ask shoppers to answer questions or give an opinion about new foods, or watch a new commercial. This helps businesses discover consumers' wants and needs. Market research helps companies to produce and market products and services that attract customers. This is known as the marketing concept. The **marketing concept** involves determining the wants and needs of customers and providing them more efficiently and effectively than competitors.

✔ Reading Check | **Identify** What is market research?

Information About Consumers

Before a product is put on the market, marketers gather information about the people who make up the market. They analyze and label their markets by demographics. **Demographics** are facts about the population. These facts include age, gender, location, and income. This information comes from **surveys**, sales figures for current products, databases, and the census.

Science/Tech TRENDS

Flat-Screen TVs

Liquid crystal displays (LCDs) are used in all kinds of devices used every day—from laptop computers to cell phones to microwave ovens. LCDs have helped manufacturers transform the bulky, boxy TV into a slim screen that can hang on a wall. LCDs offer an environmental advantage over the cathode ray TV tube they replace because they draw much less power and are therefore more energy-efficient. LCDs also have some advantages over Plasma technology when it comes to TV screens. Just what are liquid crystals? The term "liquid crystal" sounds like a contradiction. We think of a crystal as a solid material such as quartz, usually as hard as rock, and a liquid is obviously different. How could any material combine qualities of the two?

WebQuest

Locate Web sites where you can find out more about LCDs and how they work. List the products in which they are used. Make a chart to compare the advantages and disadvantages of LCDs versus plasma displays in flat-screen TVs. Write a report about how flat-screen TVs with LCDs are being marketed. What do advertisers say about these new products?

After studying a market, firms can aim their product or service at a group of **potential** customers. **Target marketing** helps companies focus on the people most likely to buy their goods or services. Once marketers know the demographics of a market, companies can make products to fit that group. **Market segmentation** is the division of a market for a product into groups of customers who have the same needs and traits. **Figure 13.1** shows different ways businesses can reach customers.

● **As You Read**

Think about the target markets to which a marketer might seek to sell a new computer football game.

The Seven Steps of Product Development

New products energize the marketplace. Companies take seven steps in developing a new product. You could use these to develop a car, dish soap, a book, or even clothing.

Step 1: Generate Ideas

It usually takes more than one person to come up with new ideas. Workers often get together to think of new products. This is called *brainstorming*. People from a company's development department, the market research staff, and even outside market researchers may be involved. Collaboration is key in this step.

Step 2: Screen Ideas

Once the team puts together a list of ideas for a product, the team must evaluate each idea. How do these ideas fit the company's mission and **strategy**? Does the new product compete with one of the company's existing products? Consumers can identify what they liked or disliked about the concept. Their responses are **crucial** as to whether the company continues with a proposed product.

Figure 13.1 — *Conducting Market Research*

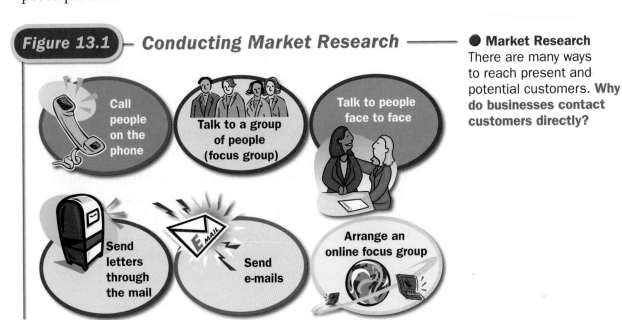

● **Market Research**
There are many ways to reach present and potential customers. **Why do businesses contact customers directly?**

● **Concept Cars** Car makers develop concept cars, or prototypes, to introduce new cars to the buying public. **In the seven steps of product development, which step does this photograph illustrate?**

● **As You Read**

Think about why it is important to develop a business plan before you develop a product.

Step 3: Develop a Business Plan

Once the creative ideas pass the screening process, one or two of the ideas are developed into a business plan. The written proposal provides a look at the market. This includes estimated sales, costs, profit potential, market trends, and competing products.

Step 4: Develop the Product

If the company's decision makers are in favor of the product, a *prototype* will be made. A prototype is a model of the actual product. It is used to see what the new product will look like. It also tests how it can be made. If any aspects of the prototype need to be changed, now is the time to make changes. A company might experience delays in finalizing the product as it is tested.

Step 5: Test-Market the Product

Once the product is fully developed, it should be test-marketed. To **test-market** a product means to offer it in a limited market for a limited time. The goal is to collect customers' responses to see if the product is likely to be a success. Testing may give a competitor time to produce a similar product. Then both products may enter the market at the same time, and the first firm loses its competitive advantage.

pagadesign/Getty Images

Step 6: Introduce the Product

When the product has passed the market test, it is ready for the marketplace. A publicity campaign introduces the product. The costs of launching a new product are often high. The company has a short time in the market before competitors start to develop similar products. This is especially true after a new product becomes successful.

Step 7: Evaluate Customer Acceptance

Once the product is introduced, marketers track customers and their responses to it. Their reports answer key questions that can be used in the company's research and development plans. Who are the best customers? What new products are they buying? How often do customers buy the new product? If customers like the new product, the company will continue to produce it. If not enough customers like it, it may not be on the market long.

Product Failures
Not all products that are test-marketed succeed. After Ford® introduced the Edsel in 1958, the car failed to meet sales expectations. Marketing experts say Ford did not understand U.S. consumers. *Compile a list of other commercial flops. Explain why they were not accepted.*

Section 13.2

After You Read

Review Key Concepts

1. What are some tools used by market researchers?
2. What are the seven steps of product development?
3. How can a company know if its new product is succeeding?

Academic Skills

4. **English Language Arts** Find advertisements in magazines and newspapers that appeal to different demographic categories. For example, look for ads for products that teens, parents with young children, and retirees would be especially interested in buying. Mount the ads on poster board and write captions for them. Prepare a five-minute talk about the demographic groups represented, telling why the ads are well-designed for their target demographic. Discuss the ads' headlines, visual imagery, and the words used in the ad copy.

5. **English Language Arts** During the next week, save all of the advertising and promotional material that comes in the mail for you and your family. Create categories based on the types of products and services offered. Organize the material accordingly, and prepare a brief questionnaire to give to your family members. Try to find out whether they would buy any of the goods or services based on the advertising material. Which advertisements do the best job of marketing their product or service? Write a summary of your findings.

 Go to **connectED.mcgraw-hill.com** to check your answers.

Section 13.1 *Summary*

Marketing Essentials To market a product successfully, a company has to understand what people want to buy and why they want to buy it. Marketing is the process of creating, promoting, and presenting a product to meet the wants and needs of consumers. Marketing research studies how to promote, sell, and distribute a product or service. It helps companies determine who will buy the product or service and how much it should cost. Marketing research includes studying the marketing mix. The marketing mix consists of four marketing strategies: product, place, price, and promotion, or the *four Ps.* Some people also include a fifth P—for people.

Section 13.2 *Summary*

Market Research and Product Development Market research is the gathering and analysis of information on the size, location, and makeup of a product market. It helps companies make decisions based on demographics, which include age, gender, location, and income. Marketers use surveys, sales figures for current products, databases, and the census to gather this information. Companies generate ideas, screen the ideas, and develop a business plan. They also create the product, do test-marketing, introduce the new product, and evaluate customer acceptance. Their goal is to come up with a product that people would like to buy.

Vocabulary Review

1. On a sheet of paper, use each of these key terms and academic vocabulary terms in a sentence.

Key Terms

market
marketing
relationship marketing
marketing mix
channel of distribution
direct distribution
indirect distribution

break-even point
market research
marketing concept
demographics
target marketing
market segmentation
test-market

Academic Vocabulary

genders   survey
physical   potential
located   strategy
aware   crucial

Review Key Concepts

2. Define marketing.

3. Identify the functions of marketing.

4. List the elements of the marketing mix.

5. Describe the kinds of market research a company may use.

6. Identify the steps in developing a new product.

Critical Thinking

7. The basics of marketing apply to more than just products and services. If you want a job, you must market yourself to your potential employer. What questions would you research before applying for the job?

8. Compare and contrast the target markets for a music CD and diamond earrings.

9. If you planned to develop and market a sit-down restaurant that offered inexpensive meals, who would be your target market? Explain your answer.

10. Why is pricing such an important part of the marketing mix?

11. Why do you think many consumers now shop on the Internet? What types of products do you think they probably buy online?

12. Companies use many kinds of promotions to attract customers besides advertising. Which types of promotions work best at persuading you to buy?

13. What types of organizations can you list that have a limited role in marketing their products or services? Why do you think those businesses do not engage in more marketing?

Write About It

14. Write a one-page story about what you think the business world would be like without marketing.

15. Imagine that you are part of a team that is developing a new cereal. List the features you would promote for it and its packaging. Write an e-mail to your teacher on how each feature would help the promotion succeed.

16. Write at least one page about the target market for a new cereal. What group or groups would you recommend your company target in marketing the product?

17. Research different trucking companies. List their names, and then write at least two paragraphs about their role in marketing products.

18. Note three products that are marketed to a highly segmented market. Write two paragraphs about each of your choices. Include reasons why these items would be for a segmented market.

19. List at least five items you have purchased recently. Write a page about where each product was produced, where you bought it, and how you think it was brought to the market.

Technology Applications

Spreadsheets and Bar Graphs
20. Survey as many people as you can in your class. Ask them to name their favorite flavor of ice cream. Summarize your data in a spreadsheet. Make a bar graph of their favorites. If you were an ice cream vendor, how would this information be useful to your marketing plan?

Business Ethics

Marketing to Children
21. You have been working on developing a new snack food. Your team has identified small children as the target market. You know this snack food is not very healthful. However, market research shows that the new snack food would very likely sell well. What should you do?

Applying Academics to Business

English Language Arts

22. *Advertising, publicity, promotion,* and *marketing* are listed in a thesaurus as synonyms. However, the words have slightly different meanings. Write a few sentences clarifying the meanings of these words and explaining the relationships among them.

Mathematics

23. Market research shows that people prefer rectangular boxes over cylinders. If a company switches from cylinders with a volume of 528 cubic inches to rectangular boxes with a base measuring 8″ × 11″, how tall would the boxes need to be to have the same volume?

CONCEPT **Finding Volume** The volumes of a three-dimensional solid can be found using a formula. For a rectangle, use $V = lwh$ where V is volume, l is length, w is width, and h is height.

English Language Arts

24. The words *media, bacteria, strata,* and *phenomena* have something in common. They are all plurals. List the singular forms of these words and research their histories using a dictionary, an online source, or other reference material.

Mathematics

25. In a market research study, Acme Corporation showed that every 3¢ increase in the price charged for its widgets lost the company $\frac{1}{2}$ of 1% of its customer base to its competition. If its customer base is 2.3×10^5 people, how many customers would the company lose if it raised the price 6¢?

CONCEPT **Scientific Notation** To express a number in scientific notation in standard form, look at the exponent. Move the decimal point in the base number that many places to the right.

Active Learning

Design a New Product

26. Packaging must be as appealing as possible to catch the attention of customers. Pair up with a classmate and design a box for a new snack food called Twirls. This new item is nutritious, tastes like your favorite candy, is low-fat, and would be a good after-school snack. Develop a theme for your box and choose colors that will catch the attention of buyers. Design a logo and write a slogan. Share your ideas with the class.

Business in the Real World

Decision Making for Marketing

27. Interview at least two people about what they consider when shopping. Ask questions about the marketing mix: product, place, price, and promotion. Which part of the marketing mix do they consider to be the main factor when making buying decisions? Prepare a written report of your findings. Give an oral presentation to the class about the considerations your subjects considered most important.

Real LIFE • skills

WISE BUYING

28. Critics of marketing sometimes say that products would cost less if consumers did not have to pay for marketing. Others say that, without marketing, we would not know about all of the products available, and there would be less competition. Write guidelines for shoppers to follow so that they can take advantage of the benefits that marketing provides.

 Business CAREERS

FIND YOUR DREAM JOB

29. Locate the Occupational Outlook Handbook Web site. Click on the "OOH Search/A-Z Index" link and enter the job category "market and survey researchers." Then write a one-page report about this type of occupation. Conclude your report with a list of things you could do now to prepare yourself to pursue the occupation.

Role Play

MARKETING A PRODUCT

30. Situation You have been asked to give a short speech to your class about the steps a company must follow to market a new running shoe.

Activity Prepare an outline of the points you will include in your presentation on the importance of marketing.

Evaluation You will be evaluated on how well you meet the following performance indicators:

- Define and discuss marketing research.
- Describe the different ways to gather market research.
- Discuss the marketing mix involved in marketing a new running shoe.
- Give reasons why marketing is so important to the success of a product.
- Prepare a written outline of the points in your speech.
- Speak clearly and use correct grammar.

Standardized Test Practice

Directions Choose the letter of the best answer. Write the letter for the answer on a separate piece of paper.

1. By 2000, Skillful Marketing Inc. had collected 1,245,850 names of people who vacation in Mexico for its marketing database. By 2006, the database had grown to 1,594,688. What was the percentage increase in names from 2000 to 2006?

  A   1.28%

  B   21.87%

  C   28%

  D   78%

 TEST-TAKING TIP Concentration can reduce anxiety when you are taking a test. Do not worry about whether you should have studied more. Pay close attention to one question at a time.

Chapter 14

Advertising

Chapter Objectives After completing this chapter, you will be able to:

▶ **Section 14.1** *Advertising Media*
- **Define** advertising.
- **List** types of media that businesses use to reach potential customers.

▶ **Section 14.2** *Media Measurement and Rates*
- **List** the components of media measurement.
- **Identify** how advertising costs are measured.
- **Describe** how media rates are determined.

Ask

AN EXPERT

Industry Classifications

Q: What are industry classifications?

A: Companies that make different types of products often face different challenges in the global economy. To make comparisons easier, analysts use industry classifications to divide the economy into a number of different economic sectors. These sectors are further subdivided into industry groups, industries, and sub-industries. Subdivisions make it easier to compare companies within and across industries.

Mathematics You are interested in two competitors in the information sector of the economy and research their financial histories to find out if one company is better than another. McLain Publishing has a gross profit of 20%, and Fisher Press has a gross profit of 17%. Graphs showing financial histories of the companies suggest that Fisher's gross profit has been steady over the years and that McLain's has fluctuated between 16% and 24%. What conclusions can you draw from this information?

CONCEPT **Interpreting Data** Since the two companies are in the same business, you can assume that the company with better fundamentals is a better company. When looking at gross profit (revenues minus cost of goods sold) keep in mind that the lower gross profit is as a percentage of sales, the more profitably the company can manufacture its products.

● **Target Marketing** Businesses advertise in media that will reach their intended market. **How is this an example of target marketing?**

OnlyUSuperStock

Advertising Media

Reading Guide

Before You Read

Think about the types of media businesses can choose from to advertise their products and services.

Read to Learn
- Define advertising.
- List types of media that businesses use to reach potential customers.

The Main Idea

Businesses must find ways to reach potential customers. Advertising is one type of promotion that can be used to reach local, regional, national, or even worldwide markets.

Key Concepts
- Why Companies Advertise
- Types of Media

Vocabulary

Key Terms

advertising
mass media
infomercial
direct-mail advertising
pop-up ads
banner ads
webcast

 Go to **connectED.mcgraw-hill.com** to print out this graphic organizer.

Academic Vocabulary

You will find these words in your reading and on your tests. Make sure you know their meanings.

media   unique
communicate   transit

Graphic Organizer

As you read, list the types of advertising media, and add notes about each in a chart like the one below.

Types of Media	Notes

Why Companies Advertise

Advertising is the public promotion of something such as a product, service, business, or event, to attract or increase interest in it. Advertisements, or ads, are everywhere. The average person sees hundreds of ads every day. They are on the Internet, in magazines and movie theaters, and on TV and the street.

Advertisers use humor, creativity, style, and originality to create an image for their products and services. They try to get consumers' attention. Using catchy advertising slogans is one way companies get customers to remember them (see **Figure 14.1**).

● **As You Read**

Think about an item you recently purchased. What image do you feel was attached to the product? Did it influence your purchase?

Types of Media

A *medium* is a channel or system of communication. For example, television is a medium. **Media** are the members of the mass media. **Mass media** are channels of communication, such as television, radio, and newspapers. Advertisements are delivered to consumers through mass media. The type of medium an advertiser uses depends on the market it wants to reach. *Print media* use words and pictures to **communicate**. Print media include newspapers, magazines, signs, and billboards.

Newspapers

Newspapers are the main advertising medium in the United States. Newspapers allow advertisers to target people within a certain area. However, newspaper ads have a short life. Most people throw newspapers away after they read them.

Figure 14.1 — *Catchy Slogans*

Just do it®

When It Rains, It Pours®

The Breakfast of Champions®

The Pause that Refreshes®

Where's the Beef?®

Good to the Last Drop®

The milk chocolate melts in your mouth — not in your hands®

We bring good things to life®

Source: *Advertising Age Magazine*

● **How Many Do You Know?** Some advertising slogans have become so well known that people all over the country recognize them. *Advertising Age* magazine judged these slogans to be some of the best. How many of the products or services can you name?

Magazines

Most magazines are national and appear every week (such as *Time*) or every month (such as *Seventeen*). People from all over the country see national magazine ads. Many magazines offer regional editions for different parts of the country. Special-interest magazines such as *Sports Illustrated* make it possible to reach target markets on a large scale.

Magazine ads have a longer life than newspaper ads. People take their time when reading magazines. Some even save them.

Television

Television advertising combines sounds, images, and motion. TV ads can be informative, entertaining, or creative. Most TV ads are 30 seconds long. A **unique** type of TV ad is the infomercial. An **infomercial** is a 30-minute commercial.

TV ads can be shown on national, local, or cable stations. TV advertisers can reach a wide audience. They can also reach target markets by showing ads during certain types of shows.

Ads for TV can be expensive to produce and run. The more popular a show is, the more it costs to air an ad during that show. **Figure 14.2** illustrates the amount of money some corporations spend to advertise their products.

Figure 14.2 — *Big Spenders*

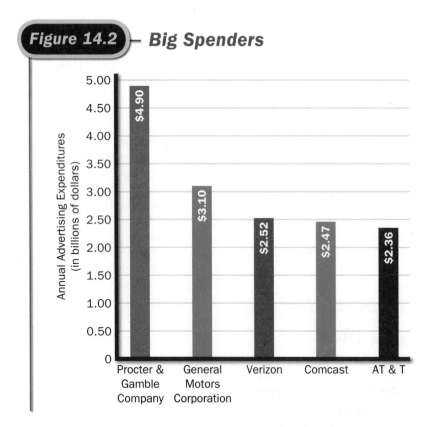

Source: *Advertising Age*

● **Big Spenders** This chart shows ten companies who spent the most on advertising in a recent year. General Motors Corporation, for example, spent about $3.10 billion on advertising. **Think about advertisements for these five companies. In what media have you seen their ads?**

Direct-Mail Advertising

Direct-mail advertising is the biggest advertising medium after television and newspapers. **Direct-mail advertising** consists of ads sent by mail to people's homes and businesses. Direct mail allows advertisers to reach a specific target market.

Direct-mail advertisers contact consumers in a variety of ways. They use letters, flyers, postcards, and catalogs. They often include coupons or free samples. The cost of sending ads through the mail can be high. Direct mail is often referred to as "junk mail." People who receive direct-mail advertising often throw it out without ever looking at it.

Directory Advertising

Directory advertising appears mostly in phone books. It is especially useful for local advertisers. They can display an ad under a heading for the type of product or service they offer and list their phone number and address. The cost of a directory ad is usually low. A disadvantage of directory ads is that they have to compete with other similar ads.

Radio Advertising

Radio ads can reach a wide audience. However, they may not be as effective as TV or magazine ads because they cannot use images. They use music, dialogue, and sound effects to get a listener's attention.

As You Read

Think about the junk mail your household gets. If few people actually respond to this mail, why do you think advertisers keep sending it?

Online Media

Two types of online ads are pop-up and banner ads. **Pop-up ads** appear in a new browser window on a Web page. **Banner ads** are displayed across the top or bottom of a Web page.

Another way to advertise online is through webcasting. A **webcast** is a broadcast on the Internet. It often consists of a live broadcast made using a Web camera, or cam.

Many businesses also use social media as a means to promote and advertise. Social media creates interest by engaging customers and clients online. A number of sites, besides company blogs, allow businesses, customers, and clients to interact. Some channels include Facebook®, Twitter®, Google+, and LinkedIn®, as well as image sites such as Instagram®, Tumbler®, and Pinterest®.

✔ **Reading Check**   **Identify** Name two kinds of online ads.

Other Types of Media

Billboards provide the most common form of *outdoor advertising.* Most billboards are large and placed near highways where they are very visible.

Transit advertising usually consists of posters placed on the sides of buses, in subway stations, inside trains, and at airports.

Section 14.1

After You Read

Review Key Concepts

1. Why do companies advertise?
2. What are some types of media used by businesses to advertise?
3. What advantages do print and cyber ads share?

Academic Skills

4. **Mathematics** The top rate paid one year for a 30-second TV ad during the Super Bowl was 6% greater than the previous year's top rate. If the new top rate paid was $2.4 million, what was the top rate paid the previous year?

CONCEPT   **Working with Percents** In this problem, $2.4 million represents 106% of the previous year's rate. Percents can be converted easily to decimals by moving the decimal point two places to the left.

  For math help, go to the Math Appendix.

  Go to **connectED.mcgraw-hill.com** to check your answers.

Media Measurement and Rates

Reading Guide

Before You Read

Think about how companies make plans to advertise and determine the cost of an advertisement.

Read to Learn

- List the components of media measurement.
- Identify how advertising costs are measured.
- Describe how media rates are determined.

The Main Idea

Businesses need to reach as many targeted customers as possible. Many companies do this by advertising. It is important to calculate ad costs and measure media effectiveness to best reach a potential audience.

Key Concepts

- Media Planning
- Media Measurement
- Media Rates

Vocabulary

Key Terms

media planning   impression
advertising agency   frequency
ad campaign   cost per thousand (CPM)
audience   prime time

Academic Vocabulary

You will find these words in your reading and on your tests. Make sure you know their meanings.

medium   prime
display   network

Graphic Organizer

As you read, write notes about media planning questions in a figure like the one below.

Media Planning Questions

1.	?
2.	?
3.	?

 Go to **connectED.mcgraw-hill.com** to print out this graphic organizer.

As You Read

Think about the different images that some companies convey in their ads.

Media Planning

Media planning is the process of selecting advertising media and deciding the time and space in which the ads should appear. To create a media plan and select the right **medium** to use, advertisers address three basic questions:

1. Can the medium present the product or service and the appropriate business image?
2. Can the desired customers be targeted with the medium?
3. Will the medium get the desired response rate?

Effective media planning can help a business project the desired image to the target market.

Advertising Agencies

Many businesses develop advertising by hiring advertising agencies. An **advertising agency** is a business that specializes in developing ads and ad campaigns for its clients. An **ad campaign** is a series of ad messages that share a single idea and theme. Ad agencies vary in size—from small agencies that serve regional markets to large international firms.

Science/Tech TRENDS

Sensory Branding

Some of the world's most recognizable brands from the 20th century are Ivory® soap, Gerber® baby food, Coca-Cola®, and McDonald's®. These brands mean something to most people and have managed to become part of our everyday lives. How are companies creating the brands of the future? Marketing and branding guru Martin Lindstom is encouraging today's marketing professionals to appeal to all the senses, not just sight and sound. He says that touch and smell are the future when it comes to creating a brand identity. For example, chemists develop special scents, and aestheticians design sound and tactile elements. These create a deeper emotional connection to the brand. Singapore Airlines used a patented smell called Stefan Floridian Waters throughout its airplanes to differentiate its brand from others. They even put it on flight attendants' uniforms and on the hot towels they gave passengers.

WebQuest

Locate Web sites where you can find out more about how marketers are appealing to all the senses when establishing brand identity. Give some specific examples, and explain how appealing to all the senses can help influence people's attitudes, preferences, and purchasing behavior.

Media Measurement

Media planners are concerned with the correct medium to use and its costs. They are also concerned with how to measure an ad's overall effectiveness. An effective ad will help raise a firm's sales.

To understand media measurement, you need to become familiar with several key terms. First, the number of homes or people exposed to an ad is called the **audience**. A single exposure to an advertising message is called an **impression**. **Frequency** is the number of times an audience sees or hears an ad. **Cost per thousand (CPM)** is the media cost of exposing 1,000 readers or viewers to an advertising impression. (The "M" in CPM comes from the word *mille,* which is Latin for "thousand.")

Media Audiences

TV audience measurement is based on diaries and viewer data collected by Nielsen Media Research®. The Nielsen organization takes a sample of TV viewers in more than 200 markets. Arbitron Inc.® uses listener diaries to measure radio audiences in more than 260 markets. Online audiences are measured through online tracking services such as Google Analytics, surveys, and computer software tracking systems.

Knowing the potential audience, how frequently your ad will be seen, and its CPM can tell you if the rates charged by various media are right for your ad budget.

● **Successful Ads** The purpose of advertising is to attract attention and transmit a message. **What catches your attention in this ad?**

 **Analyze** Why do advertisers rely on media measurement?

Media Rates

To reach customers, advertising uses a set format that is defined in terms of time (a 60-second TV or radio ad) or space (a half-page newspaper ad). Media costs vary greatly, not just with type of media but also with geographic location and audience.

A *media rate* or *advertising rate* is the amount of money it costs to **display** or broadcast an ad. It is separate from the amount it costs to make an ad. Ad rates are determined by several factors: the size of the ad, the number of people it reaches, how often it appears, when it appears, and where it is placed.

Lars Niki

Print Media Ad Rates

Ad rates for newspapers and magazines are based on circulation, or the number of people who buy them, and audience, the number of readers per issue. An advertiser usually pays a rate for every 1,000 people (CPM) a newspaper or magazine reaches.

The size of the ad also affects the cost. Newspaper and magazine ads are sold by the inch on a page. A column inch is an area that is one column wide by one inch deep. If a newspaper quotes a column inch rate, multiply the number of inches by the number of columns. This gives you the total number of column inches. Then multiply the total column inches by the rate. For example, if the rate for a column inch is $17, then an ad that measures four inches long by three columns wide will cost $204 ($17 × 4 inches × 3 columns = $204).

Magazine rates are based on circulation, the type of readership, and production techniques. *Premium position* refers to ad placement. Ads placed in **prime** positions, such as on the back cover or the inside of the first page, are more expensive to buy.

Business Case Study

Ratings Aren't Just for TV

A new system tracks all forms of entertainment to see what's getting watched

For over 60 years the Nielsen Company had one business: measuring TV ratings. Working with representative households, it tracked how many people watched specific shows, then calculated which were the most popular. The higher a show's ratings, the more advertisers had to pay for air time.

Today new forms of online content—videos, podcasts, games, blogs, and music—attract millions of viewers who would once have been glued to the TV. To respond, in late 2014 Nielsen expanded its ratings system to measure all kinds of digital content, in addition to TV.

The new system combines Nielsen's audience tools with analytics data from tech company Adobe. Now all kinds of digital content will be ranked together. As advertisers and networks see it, there's no longer any difference between a video, a podcast, and a blog. If it's popular, advertisers want to buy in.

> **Active Learning**
>
> How much time do you spend online? What do you read or watch? Calculate your own ratings. For two days, keep track of what you look at online. You don't have to reveal exact content, but note the form of content, such as web videos, TV shows, movies, blogs, podcasts, music, social media, fan fiction, and online games. Also note the amount of time you spend looking at each, and what ads were placed in or around this content. Compare your own ratings with those of other students in a small group and present your combined findings to the class

Broadcast Media Ad Rates

The cost of TV and radio ads depends on the size of the audience, the reach of the station, and the time of day an ad is broadcast. **Prime time** is the time period when the **network** TV or radio audience is the largest. TV audiences are usually largest between 7 P.M. and 11 P.M., when most viewers are at home. For radio, prime time on weekdays is during the morning or afternoon hours, also called drive times.

Internet Ad Rates

The cost of Internet advertising is based on the type, size, and format of ads. Types include banner ads, rich-media enhanced banner ads, and pop-up ads. The length of time an ad runs also affects the price. Like newspaper and magazine ads, Internet advertisers pay a certain amount for every 1,000 people who get the ad. Rates vary based on the volume of monthly page views.

Paid search ads are Internet ads that online advertisers bid on for search engine queries. The advertiser pays a fee to the search engine whenever someone clicks on the ad. The advertiser that bids the highest for a particular keyword has its ad show up first on the list of ads next to the search results.

● **As You Read**

Think about the different costs for magazine ads. Why would it cost more to place an ad on the back of a magazine than on the inside?

Section 14.2

○ **After You Read**

Review Key Concepts
1. What are the three basic questions advertisers must address in media planning?
2. Name the four components of media measurement.
3. Define media rate or advertising rate.

Academic Skills
4. **English Language Arts** Work with a partner to create a radio ad for a product you both like and think would interest other people your age. Write a 30-second script and use music or other sound effects to enhance the ad. Use words and music that will have special appeal to your audience. If possible, record the ad and play it for your class. Join in a discussion with your classmates about the ad's effectiveness.

5. **English Language Arts** Which type of text structure best describes these sentences: Transit advertising is most common in urban areas where public transportation is widely used. For this reason, it is useful for advertising things such as concerts, public events, and local TV. compare and contrast, cause and effect, or statement and example? Write a few sentences of your own that use the same type of structure.

Go to **connectED.mcgraw-hill.com** to check your answers.

Section 14.1 *Summary*

Advertising Media Businesses use advertisements, or ads, to promote their products and services. Ads are everywhere—in movie theaters, on the street, and on the Internet. They are placed in print media, which includes newspapers, magazines, and direct mail. Commercials run on TV and radio. Businesses try to build an image for their products and services through their ads. Companies often use humor in ads to leave a lasting impression with consumers. They carefully select the types of advertising and media they will use to reach their target market.

Section 14.2 *Summary*

Media Measurement and Rates Media planning is the process of selecting advertising media and deciding when and where ads should appear to meet the marketing objective. A media plan helps advertisers present an interesting message and project the desired business image to the target market. It is important to calculate costs and measure media effectiveness to best reach an audience. Ad rates vary according to the medium in which the ad appears and how long it runs. Other factors include size, length of time, and the type of ad used.

Vocabulary Review

1. On a sheet of paper, use each of these key terms and academic vocabulary terms in a sentence.

Key Terms

advertising	advertising agency
mass media	ad campaign
infomercial	audience
direct-mail advertising	impression
pop-up ads	frequency
banner ads	cost per thousand (CPM)
webcast	prime time
media planning	

Academic Vocabulary

media	medium
communicate	display
unique	prime
transit	network

Review Key Concepts

2. Define advertising.

3. List the types of media that businesses use to reach potential customers.

4. List the components of media measurement.

5. Identify how advertising costs are measured.

6. Describe how media rates are determined.

7. Think about your favorite magazine. When you read it, do you glance at the ads, or do you read them carefully? Explain your answer.

8. What products or services are advertised in your favorite magazine? Why would you purchase any of those products or services?

9. Do you think advertising on network TV will be done less or more often in the future? Why?

10. When people record a TV show, they are likely to skip the ads when they watch the show later. What do you think this means to TV advertisers?

11 Many companies advertise their goods and services on the Internet. They also sell space on their Web sites to advertisers. However, the response rates to online ads are low. Why do you think more advertisers are using online ads even if the response rates are low?

12. Why do you think a TV producer would sign a contract with an ad agency?

13. What impact do you think the increasing popularity of cable TV will have on advertising?

14. What are some ways to promote a business besides advertising? Write a brief essay offering some examples.

15. Write one page describing an ad from a magazine. Name the product advertised, and list some product descriptions from the ad. Decide if the ad is well designed.

16. In two or more paragraphs, describe the purposes of the following characters used in ads: the Energizer Bunny® (Energizer® batteries); and Tony the Tiger (Kellogg's Frosted Flakes®).

17. Look at a newspaper, and review its ads. Write a one-page description of three ads that appear. Compare and contrast their effectiveness.

18. What will be the effect on online advertising if people use software to block pop-up ads? Write at least two paragraphs on your response.

19. Companies pay more to advertise their products and services during special events, such as the *Academy Awards* or the Olympics. Why do you think advertisers are willing to pay up to $1.9 million for a 30-second ad? Write a brief summary of your thoughts.

Word-Processing Software

20. Select one of the following advertising agencies to research: Ogilvy & Mather; McCann Worldgroup; TBWA Worldwide; Leo Burnett Worldwide; BBDO Worldwide; Agency.com; J. Walter Thompson Company; or Saatchi & Saatchi. Write a two-page report about the ad agency's services. Include some of its clients and the types of ads it helped create.

Ethical Advertising

21. Companies must disclose all information necessary for a customer to make a safe and informed decision. If a company promotes a food product as a "diet product," what types of information do you think it should provide in order to be ethical in its advertising? What would you consider to be unethical? Write at least two paragraphs on your responses.

Applying Academics to Business

English Language Arts

22. List businesses that advertise on TV, radio, and billboards. Are there any types of businesses that advertise using all three media? Do large, multinational corporations seem to use one type more than others? Which is used by smaller, more local businesses? Write a one-page paper explaining what you have learned.

Mathematics

23. Of a company's $140 million in sales, 56% was credited to TV ads, $\frac{1}{4}$ to magazine ads, and 10% to radio. The rest of the business came from direct mail. What percent of the total revenue was generated by direct mail?

CONCEPT **Fractions, Decimals, and Percents** Fractions, decimals, and percents are similar in that they are all used to represent part of a whole. To solve this problem, start by converting the fractions and percents to decimals.

English Language Arts

24. List the words below on a sheet of paper. Four of them have something in common. Cross out the word that does not belong. Add a fifth word from the chapter that does belong. Write a sentence or two explaining your choices.

update	lifespan	infomercial
billboard	webcast	

Mathematics

25. Assume that Production costs for a 30-second TV commercial are $420,000. Airtime costs $\frac{1}{3}$ of that each time the ad runs. Write an equation to find the total cost of creating the commercial and then running it 12 times. Write a sentence or two explaining the steps to take to find the solution.

CONCEPT **Order of Operations** Equations are solved by first performing any operations within parentheses, then exponents, multiplication and division from left to right, and finally addition and subtraction from left to right.

Active Learning

Describe TV Ads

26. Ads sometimes convey their message by showing people using a product in their everyday life. Others present a fantasy. Some ads use a song or jingle to help people remember the product or service. Others give information. Watch three popular TV shows. List the products that are advertised during those shows. For each product, describe the approach of the ad.

Business in the Real World

Small Business Advertising

27. Interview a person who has a service business that is seasonal, such as a lawn mowing or snow removal company. Ask the business owner if he or she advertises. If so, how? Are there highs and lows in the owner's business? If so, does the owner offer other services in the off-season in order to have a steady income? How does advertising affect the business's budget?

SUITABLE ADVERTISING

28. Advertisers use different types of appeals to reach their potential customers. Write a short report describing the types of appeals that are successful in persuading teens to buy products. If you could advise advertisers on marketing to teens, what advice would you give them? What can advertisers do that will convince teens to buy their products?

Business CAREERS

FIND YOUR DREAM JOB

29. Locate the Occupational Outlook Handbook Web site. Click on the "OOH Search/A–Z Index" link and enter "advertising, marketing, promotions, public relations, and sales managers." Then write a one-page report about this field. Conclude your report with a list of things you could do now to prepare yourself to pursue the occupation.

Role Play

A COMMUNITY PROJECT

30. Situation A *sponsor* is a person or organization that provides money to help fund an event as a form of advertising. Plan a presentation to convince a local firm to sponsor a community activity in your neighborhood.

Activity Outline the points you would make to the company about the advertising value of its sponsorship.

Evaluation You will be evaluated on how well you meet the following performance indicators:

- Explain the purpose of the community activity, its audience, and potential attendance figures.
- Outline several points about how the sponsorship is valuable to the community and how it can build a good image of the company.
- Identify what the company would do as the sponsor.
- Prepare a written outline of the points you will make in your presentation.

Standardized Test Practice

Directions Choose the letter of the best answer. Write the letter for the answer on a separate piece of paper.

1 Which are dependent events?

   A   flipping a coin, and then flipping it again

   B   taking a marble out of a bag, then taking another marble out of the bag

   C   spinning a spinner, then moving your piece that many spaces

   D   tossing a number cube, then tossing another number cube

TEST-TAKING TIP Just before taking a test, try to avoid talking about it with other students. Test anxiety can be contagious.

Kristy Royce

Vice President/Founder, Expeditiontrips.com

This Internet-based adventure travel company focuses on expeditions. They specialize in trips on small cruise ships to remote locations. The company was founded by Ashton Palmer and Kristy Royce. This interview is with Kristy Royce.

Q & A

Describe your job responsibilities.

Kristy: My main job responsibilities are marketing, managing our Web site, public relations, and coordinating all in-house documents. On a typical work day, I work with our site manager to update site text, coordinate an e-mail blast, update our search engine marketing, speak with an intern about site submissions, and then edit text for trip documents.

What skills are most important in your business?

Kristy: Our business is the travel business, so the most important quality is to truly love travel. From there, great communication skills: you must be able to express yourself to others and describe a travel experience both verbally and in writing. You also need to be organized, pay attention to details, and prioritize tasks.

What is your key to success?

Kristy: Our key to success was finding a unique niche that we could fill better than anybody else. I would also say treating our clients extremely well is key to our success. If there is a problem, we fix it, no questions asked.

What advice would you give students interested in starting a business?

Kristy: Get an education in the field that interests you. This can be university, trade school, or work, but it is important to have an understanding of the field before you start. Everything you do prior to starting your business will help you once you start. If you fail, get up and try again.

Another very important thing is to do something that you truly love. Starting a business is very hard work, so it helps to believe in what you are doing and believe that it is an important service. In addition, you must fill a need for a service. Other people need to want whatever it is that you offer or your business will never get off the ground.

Critical Thinking   *What are the pros and cons of running a Web-based business?*

Some Qualifications of an e-Travel Business

Academic Skills and Abilities

Geography; geology; meteorology; computer skills; foreign languages; world history; interpersonal skills; general business management skills; verbal and written communication skills; multitasking, organizing, and planning skills

Tasks	Math	Science	English Language Arts
Hold meetings			◆
Assign duties			◆
Develop itineraries	◆	◆	◆
Plan routes to minimize distance traveled and optimize weather conditions	◆	◆	
Customer service			◆
Schedule employees	◆		◆
Order supplies and equipment	◆		◆
Analyze financials	◆		◆

Academic Skills Required to Complete Tasks at Expeditiontrips.com

Education and Training

A few colleges offer bachelor's or master's degrees in travel and tourism. A college education is sometimes desired to establish a background in fields such as computer science, geography, communication, foreign languages, and world history. Courses in accounting and business management are also important for those who expect to manage or start a travel agency.

Career Path

Personal travel experience or experience as an airline reservation agent is an asset. As the Internet has become an important tool for making travel arrangements, more travel agencies are using Web sites to provide services to clients. This trend has increased the importance of computer skills in the occupation.

Preparing for a Career
Self-Assessment Checklist
Use this self-assessment checklist to help determine ways you can make your career path more satisfying.

✔ Have confidence in your own abilities and talents.

✔ Keep an open mind about careers that seem difficult or require a lot of education or training.

✔ Base career decisions on your interests, not on a high salary or others' expectations.

✔ Consider ways you can make your values a part of your career.

✔ Define clear goals.

✔ Stay informed of changes in the global business environment.

✔ Expect the best of yourself and others.

✔ Keep an open mind so that you may learn from others.

✔ Maintain a positive outlook so that you are able to see alternatives instead of obstacles.

Marketing in a Global Economy

Today's marketing executives base marketing strategies on global needs. Marketing researchers gather information on consumers in foreign countries, study that information, and report their findings. The research findings become the basis for marketing strategies.

Thematic Project Assignment

In this project you will prepare a market research report that recommends marketing strategies that could be implemented by an American company marketing its goods or services in another country. You will need to research factors that should be considered in the country, study that information, and then write a two-page report.

Step 1   Brainstorm Skills You Need to Complete This Activity

Your success in writing a marketing report will depend on your skills. Preview the activity. Then brainstorm a list of the skills you will need to use to complete the activity and describe how you will use them. Skills you might use include:

Academic Skills   reading, writing, social studies, geography, and researching

Basic Skills   speaking, listening, thinking, and interpersonal skills

Technology Skills   word processing, keyboarding, telecommunications, and Internet skills

@   **SKILLS PREVIEW** Go to **connectED.mcgraw-hill.com** to download a graphic organizer you can use to brainstorm the skills you will use to complete the project.

Step 2   Choose a Business and Career That Interest You

Think of a business that you find interesting. Then think of a career related to that business. As you conduct research on marketing in a global economy, consider how it affects the business and career in which you are interested.

Step 3   Build Background Knowledge

Preview information on marketing in a global economy.

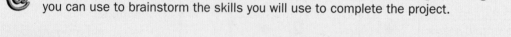

Marketing *Internationally*

Conducting business internationally can be very different from doing business in the United States. There are language barriers, international trade laws, and political, economical, cultural, and technological factors that affect international business. Marketers working on the global stage must be willing to put the time and effort into being savvy about the country in which they want to conduct business.

Businesses must study the characteristics of a country and find ways to target consumers with similar needs and wants. Then businesses must adapt their products to each country where they do business.

Step 4 Connect with Your Community

Conduct a local market survey by interviewing three business owners in your community to ask in which countries they market their goods or services. Ask how they market differently in this country and in other markets.

Step 5 Research Marketing in a Global Economy

Use library and Internet resources to research factors that should be considered when marketing another country. Use the checklist as a guide to your research. Keep records of your sources of information.

Step 6 Prepare a Report

Use word processing and other software to develop a two-page market research report that includes all of the information described in this project research checklist.

Marketing in a Global Economy

✔ Describe how a U.S. company can learn about the needs of the consumers in another country.

✔ Describe how the language barrier affects trade with this country.

✔ Describe how the political, economical, cultural, and technological factors affect doing business with this country.

✔ Explain how the climate affects the types of goods and services that could be marketed in this country.

Self Connections

✔ Describe the results of your research to a family member or other adult.

✔ Describe how marketing in a global economy affects the business and career in which you are interested.

✔ Explain what the investigation and its results mean to you.

Step 7 Evaluate Your Report

 Rubric Go to **connectED.mcgraw-hill.com** to download a rubric you can use to evaluate your final report.

Human Resources

ALIENWARE

brillenstimmer

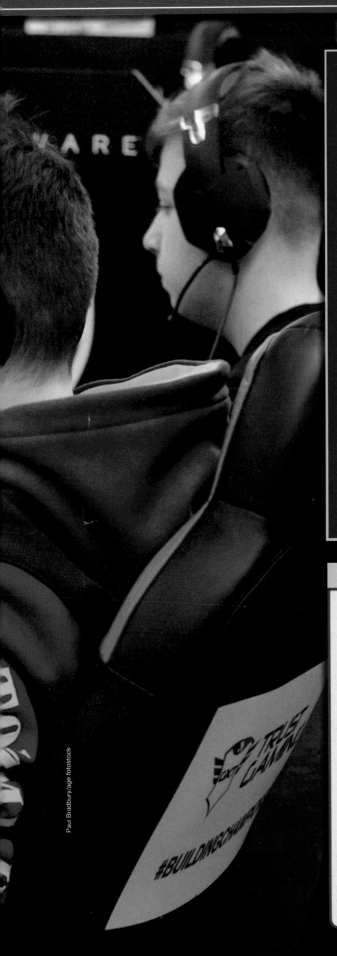

Paul Bradbury/age fotostock

Real-World Business and Career Profile

Preview

Alienware makes customized computers that are assembled specifically for high performance for gamers. At the end of this unit, you will learn about the Alienware co-founders Nelson Gonzalez and Alex Aguila and how they achieved their success.

Decision Making Why do you think it is so important for companies to make good decisions about selecting employees?

Unit 5 — *Thematic Project Preview*

Cultural Diversity in the Business World After completing this unit, you will understand how cultural diversity affects today's businesses.

Project Checklist As you read the chapters in this unit, use this checklist to prepare for the unit project.

- ✔ Think about the rich cultural heritage of different students in your school, including exchange students.
- ✔ Consider how the Internet, television, and movies expose you to people of different cultures.
- ✔ Think about how globalization is creating a more culturally diverse workforce.
- ✔ Consider how businesses benefit from a multinational workforce.

Chapter 15

Human Resources Management

Chapter Objectives After completing this chapter, you will be able to:

▶ **Section 15.1** *Employees: The Key to Success*
- **Define** human resources management.
- **Describe** how a company attracts and rewards good employees.
- **Discuss** what a human resources manager should consider about job applicants.

▶ **Section 15.2** *Developing and Retaining Employees*
- **Identify** responsibilities of human resources managers after they have hired a new employee.
- **Describe** how the status of employees changes.

Ask

AN EXPERT

Earnings and the P/E Ratio

Q: I've heard a lot about P/E ratio. For what purposes do investors use P/E ratio?

A: The Price/Earnings ratio is a popular indicator used to judge whether a stock is a good value. The P/E ratio compares the company's share price to its per-share earnings. A P/E of 15, for example, indicates that investors are willing to pay $15 for every dollar of yearly earnings the company generates. Investors use the P/E ratio to compare companies in the same industry. In general, a high P/E suggests that investors expect higher earnings growth in the future compared to companies with a lower P/E.

Mathematics Imagine that a company's stock is trading at $40. If it announces $2 in earnings per share, what is the company's P/E ratio?

CONCEPT **Using Ratios** The P/E ratio is a useful way to look at the relationship between a stock's price and its underlying value. You can compare the P/E ratio of one company to another, across different sectors and industries. You can also compare similar companies to get a better idea of challenges in an industry.

Blend Images/DreamPictures/Getty Images

● **Managing Human Resources** Businesses must be careful to select the best workers for job openings. **Why do you think it is important to choose good employees?**

Employees: The Key to Success

Reading Guide

● Before You Read

Think about the steps a business must take to find the right person for a job.

Read to Learn

- Define human resources management.
- Describe how a company attracts and rewards good employees.
- Discuss what a human resources manager should consider about job applicants.

The Main Idea

A human resources manager finds new employees for a company. Human resources staff members assist new workers through training and evaluations.

Key Concepts

- Human Resources
- Meeting Staffing Needs
- Considering Job Applicants

Vocabulary

Key Terms

human resources
human resources
  management
job description
compensation
wage

salary
benefits
recruitment
background check
reference

Academic Vocabulary

You will find these words in your reading and on your tests. Make sure you know their meanings.

temporary
fund

summary
comments

Graphic Organizer

List and write notes about the steps needed to select the right candidate for a job in a figure like the one below.

STEP	NOTES
1.	
2.	
3.	
4.	

 Go to **connectED.mcgraw-hill.com** to print out this graphic organizer.

Human Resources

Pioneer automaker Henry Ford once said, "You can take my factories, burn up my buildings, but give me my people and I'll build the business right back again." **Human resources** are the people employed in a business, commonly referred to as personnel. Employees provide the skills, knowledge, labor, and experience needed to make a business productive.

Managing human resources is not the same as supervising workers. **Human resources management** is the process of finding, selecting, training, and evaluating employees. The first step in this process is finding the right person for a job.

● **As You Read**

Do you think automaker Henry Ford was right in believing that his employees were more important than his factories or equipment?

Meeting Staffing Needs

Most businesses have specific staffing needs. These needs are usually handled by a human resources manager. When filling a job, human resources managers begin by writing a job description.

Writing a Job Description

A **job description** is a detailed outline of the duties, qualifications, and conditions required to do a specific job (see **Figure 15.1** on page 258). For example, the job description for a graphic artist position could say the job involves being creative, meeting deadlines, and using a computer. The job might also require a certain level of experience and education. It could be part-time, full-time, permanent, or **temporary**.

✔ **Reading Check** **Analyze** Why is a job description essential when trying to fill a job?

❓ETHICS in Business

Psychological Testing

■ **Critical Reading** Life is full of important decisions. Think about the kinds of decisions that you make as you read the question below.

Imagine you own a retail store. You are looking for a cashier and want to make sure you hire someone who won't be likely to steal from you. You know that the federal government has banned the use of lie detectors for most employment situations, but that you can ask a prospective employee to take a psychological test. These exams can predict an individual's tendency to steal by matching his or her answers to those of known thieves. Questions may be obvious ("How often do you tell the truth?") or obscure ("How often do you make your bed?").

■ **Decision Making** Do you think it is appropriate to decide whether a person will steal based on the results of a psychological test? Explain the possible consequences of your decision.

Figure 15.1 — *Job Description*

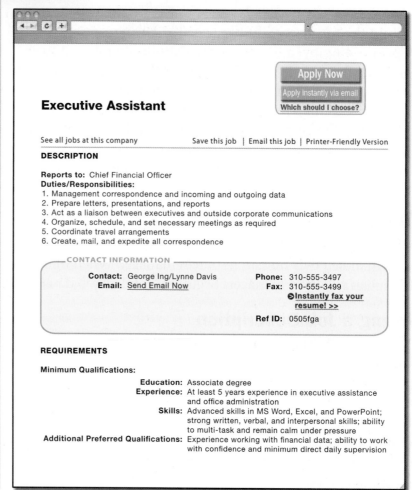

Executive Assistant

Apply Now
Apply Instantly via email
Which should I choose?

See all jobs at this company | Save this job | Email this job | Printer-Friendly Version

DESCRIPTION

Reports to: Chief Financial Officer
Duties/Responsibilities:
1. Management correspondence and incoming and outgoing data
2. Prepare letters, presentations, and reports
3. Act as a liaison between executives and outside corporate communications
4. Organize, schedule, and set necessary meetings as required
5. Coordinate travel arrangements
6. Create, mail, and expedite all correspondence

— CONTACT INFORMATION —

Contact: George Ing/Lynne Davis
Email: Send Email Now

Phone: 310-555-3497
Fax: 310-555-3499
⊙**Instantly fax your resume! >>**

Ref ID: 0505fga

REQUIREMENTS

Minimum Qualifications:

Education: Associate degree
Experience: At least 5 years experience in executive assistance and office administration
Skills: Advanced skills in MS Word, Excel, and PowerPoint; strong written, verbal, and interpersonal skills; ability to multi-task and remain calm under pressure
Additional Preferred Qualifications: Experience working with financial data; ability to work with confidence and minimum direct daily supervision

Pay and Benefits

To attract and keep good employees, businesses must offer competitive compensation. **Compensation** is pay and benefits. Pay can be in the form of a wage or a salary. A **wage** is an amount of money paid to an employee on an hourly basis. A **salary** is a fixed amount of pay for each week, month, or year. **Benefits** are extra compensation that workers receive such as health and life insurance, sick leave, holiday pay, and retirement plans. Retirement plans provide employees with money after working at a company for a certain number of years.

Some companies offer pension plans. A *pension plan* is a retirement plan that is funded at least in part by an employer. Some also offer profit-sharing plans. A *profit-sharing plan* makes an annual contribution to an employee's retirement **fund** when the company makes a profit. Another type of retirement plan is a 401(k). With a *401(k)*, employees set aside a percentage of funds from each paycheck to go into their 401(k) investment account. Many employers match a percentage of an employee's contribution to a 401(k).

Job Recruitment

Human resources managers often work as recruiters. Recruitment means actively looking for qualified people to fill a job. **Figure 15.2** illustrates qualities needed to succeed in all types of jobs. Most recruiters first consider filling a new job with someone who already works for the company. If no one is qualified, interested, or available, then the manager recruits outside the company. One way to recruit people is by placing ads in newspapers and magazines, at schools, or on the Internet. Employment agencies, referrals from employees, and job fairs are also ways to find qualified workers.

Considering Job Applicants

After recruiting job applicants, a human resources manager has to decide which one to hire. There are four steps to selecting the right person or *candidate* for the job. First, the recruiter must review each candidate's application and/or résumé. An *application* is a form companies give to potential employees to complete. It lists their work experience, education, skills, and references. Many applicants also submit a résumé. A *résumé* is a worker's **summary** of academic and work history. Reviewing the application and résumé leads to the screening step. *Screening* is a system of selecting suitable people for a job. Recruiters review applications to see which people meet their minimum qualifications. Only those who do will be considered further.

The next step is for the human resources manager to interview qualified candidates. An *interview* is a meeting in which a recruiter asks an applicant questions to see if the applicant is right for a job. It allows a company to get more details about a

Hiring Older Workers More businesses are hiring people of retirement age. Companies such as Home Depot® have joined with the American Association of Retired Persons, or the AARP, in a commitment to hire older workers. *What advantages can older workers bring to a company?*

Figure 15.2 — *Workplace Skills*

RESPONSIBILITY

initiative

dependability

punctuality

professional dress

POSITIVE ATTITUDE

SELF-RESPECT

Integrity

RESPECT FOR OTHERS

● **What Qualities Are Needed?** Here are a number of personal and interpersonal skills that are important to demonstrate in the workplace. **How can you demonstrate these skills?**

potential employee. It shows the interviewer how the applicant communicates. Interviews also allow applicants to find out more about a company. They help applicants to see if the company is a good place to work. Many companies test job candidates as part of the interview process. *Testing* helps companies make sure that job candidates have the right skills and character for a job.

Background Checks and References

The human resources manager's final step before hiring a new employee is to check the applicant's background and references. A **background check** is the process of verifying certain information provided by a job applicant. This includes information about past and present jobs and education. Some background checks also include a review of a job applicant's financial history.

A **reference** is someone who **comments** on a job applicant's character and qualifications for a job. The statement itself is also known as a reference. References give recruiters a better idea of the kind of person the job applicant is.

It is important to be truthful on job applications and résumés, and in interviews. Failing to do so can prevent you from being hired. If it is discovered that you gave false information that led to your being offered a job, you could be fired.

Section 15.1

After You Read

Review Key Concepts

1. What are human resources?
2. What do human resources managers do to help businesses meet staffing needs?
3. What are the four steps to selecting the right person for a job?

Academic Skills

4. **Mathematics** Your manager at a landscaping company tells you that he wants you to stock up on gasoline for the mowing equipment for the next week. Each of the four mowers you maintain will use $1\frac{1}{2}$ gallons each day, Monday through Saturday. Gasoline costs $3.50 per gallon. Explain how you might use mental math to figure out how many gallons you need and how much the gasoline will cost.

CONCEPT **Mental Math** Begin by converting the fraction to a decimal. Then use addition and multiplication to determine the total number of gallons needed. Use multiplication again to calculate the total cost of the gasoline.

 For math help, go to the Math Appendix.

 Go to **connectED.mcgraw-hill.com** to check your answers.

Developing and Retaining Employees

Reading Guide

Before You Read

Think about some steps a company must take to develop good employees.

Read to Learn

- Identify responsibilities of human resources managers after they have hired a new employee.
- Describe how the status of employees changes.

The Main Idea

After employees are hired, a company has to develop their skills. New employees receive orientation, training, and evaluations. These processes help them become more valuable to a company.

Key Concepts

- Developing Employees
- Changes in Employee Status

Vocabulary

Key Terms

orientation	promotion
on-the-job training	transfer
group training	separation
performance appraisal	turnover

Academic Vocabulary

You will find these words in your reading and on your tests. Make sure you know their meanings.

demonstates	complement
relaxed	technical

Graphic Organizer

As you read, describe employee experiences on a figure like the one below.

Experience	Description
Orientation	
On-the-Job Training	
Performance Appraisal	

 Go to **connectED.mcgraw-hill.com** to print out this graphic organizer.

Developing Employees

Even people with work experience need to adjust to new jobs. They may have to learn new skills and need to keep track of how they are doing on the job. To develop as employees, they need to be oriented, trained, and evaluated. Human resources staff members assist in developing employees.

Orientation

Orientation is the process of helping new employees adjust to a company. New hires are usually taken on a tour of the building and introduced to other employees. They might also attend a group orientation session and watch a video about the company. Most new employees receive a manual that offers information on matters such as the company's organization, procedures, and safety rules. They also need to read about the company's code of ethics and policies. These documents give details about the company's goals and appropriate employee behavior.

Business Case Study

The Telecommuting Boom

When done right, "work from home" does not mean "hardly working."

Telecommuting is growing in popularity. The number of hours spent working away from a central work site, such as at home or in a client's office, grew 80 percent in the U.S. between 2005 and 2012. As of 2016, there are nearly 4 million telecommuters.

Telecommuting isn't a good match for every job. But telecommuting programs can be extremely effective when:

Employees are self-starters. Workers who complete assignments well and on time are a good match for telecommuting, because they have a strong work ethic and sense of personal accountability.

Technology is in place for efficiency. Technology, such as email, instant messaging, and project-management software, is vital for communication among a distributed team. Most large employers provide full-time teleworkers with the tools they need to get work done.

Results count more than just showing up. Telecommuting works best where managers value set specific performance goals and focus on results. The measure of telecommuters' success is productivity, not the number of hours spent working.

A well-run telecommuting system greatly expands the hiring pool for a job. The best candidate could live virtually anywhere, even thousands of miles away!

Active Learning

Select a field that interests you and write a one-page essay in which you make the case for or against telecommuting instead of coming to a work site each day. Explain, with examples, how telecommuting would increase or decrease your productivity. Give specific examples.

● **Workplace Skills**
It is important to start developing workplace skills now. **How can you develop skills that will be valuable to you on the job?**

Training

New employees usually need some training for the specific job they were hired to do. **On-the-job training** involves learning a new job by actually doing it. It is usually done under the guidance of a supervisor, who **demonstrates** different tasks.

Many companies offer ways for employees to learn new skills in a more **relaxed** way and to share ideas with others. **Group training** involves teaching several employees in a class. An instructor or manager might teach a group of employees how to use a new software program at the same time.

Job rotation moves employees to different tasks or departments to help them gain experience. Sometimes if workers are absent or on leave, others have to handle their tasks. Job rotation also prevents boredom and increases morale. *Morale* is the general level of confidence or enthusiasm felt by a person or group of people.

Developing Soft Skills *Soft skills* refer to personality traits and personal abilities such as social skills, language skills, personal habits, and friendliness. Soft skills **complement** hard skills, which are the **technical** requirements of a job.

You can begin to develop soft skills now. Dress professionally and be organized. Be punctual, dependable, and take initiative and responsibility for tasks. Integrity, a positive attitude, and respect for yourself and others are important workplace characteristics. Try to improve your problem-solving, decision-making, and reasoning skills by thinking through issues. Evaluate yourself, and identify areas you can improve now.

> ● **As You Read**
>
> Think about working in a company that offers the opportunity to do a variety of different tasks.

As You Read

Think about the types of evaluations you have received.

Evaluating Employees

A **performance appraisal** is an evaluation of how well an employee is doing a job. Employees are evaluated periodically. The evaluation might consist of an employee and his or her manager discussing the employee's strengths and weaknesses. During an evaluation, managers usually offer suggestions for improvement. Employees can also note their own progress.

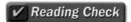 **Reading Check** **Analyze** Why are performance appraisals valuable to both the employer and the employee?

Changes in Employee Status

Human resources managers keep track of changes in the status of employees. For example, an employee might be promoted to a different position, transferred to another department, or fired. As a result, the worker might need to be reoriented, retrained, or replaced.

Promotion

A **promotion** gives an employee a higher-level job with more authority, responsibility, and pay. Most promotions are merit-based and encourage performance. If an employee is doing a great job, she or he might be promoted. Promotions are also given on the basis of seniority. *Seniority* is the status given to an employee based on rank or length of service.

Transfer

A **transfer** is a move to another job within a company, usually at the same level and pay. Employees might be transferred because another department needs them or their job in their present department has been eliminated. They might also be transferred if the company moves or opens a new office.

Separation

Separation is leaving a company for any reason. A voluntary separation occurs when an employee resigns or retires. When an employee voluntarily leaves, an *exit interview* is given to pinpoint why the employee is leaving.

Involuntary separations include layoffs and terminations. A worker may be fired or *terminated* if he or she breaks rules, becomes unable to perform at the expected level, or cannot get along with others. If the company needs to *downsize,* employees might be laid off. A *layoff* occurs when there is not enough work for all employees.

Turnover It costs companies a lot of money to search for, hire, and train new employees. Therefore, businesses are concerned with keeping turnover low. **Turnover** is the number of employees who leave an organization and are replaced over time. Careful hiring decisions and sufficient training increase chances for success with new employees.

Section 15.2

After You Read

Review Key Concepts
1. How can a company help a new employee to develop?
2. What are three ways in which new employees can be trained?
3. What are some changes in status an employee might experience?

Academic Skills
4. **English Language Arts** Work in groups of three or four to plan, write, and illustrate a handbook for new students entering your school. Include a map of the school, behavior expectations, and information about sports and clubs.

5. **English Language Arts** Apprenticeship is one form of on-the-job training that has existed for hundreds of years. Write a 250-word paper on the history of apprenticeship. Include information about the current status of such programs.

 Go to **connectED.mcgraw-hill.com** to check your answers.

Section 15.1 Summary

Employees: The Key to Success
Human resources are the people employed in a business. Employees are also referred to as personnel. They provide the skills, knowledge, labor, and experience needed to make a business productive. Human resources managers work as recruiters. Recruiters try to find the right person for a job. They also help people develop as employees so they can do their jobs well. Human resources managers begin the recruitment process by writing a job description. The job description is included in ads for the job.

Section 15.2 Summary

Developing and Retaining Employees
New employees need to be oriented, trained, and evaluated. Human resources staff members assist with all the activities for developing employees. New employees usually need training to learn the specific job they were hired to do. This includes on-the-job training and job rotation. Once they have been on a job for a while, new employees must be evaluated. A performance appraisal is used to determine whether an employee should get a raise, a promotion, or more training.

Vocabulary Review

1. On a sheet of paper, use each of these key terms and academic vocabulary terms in a sentence.

Key Terms		Academic Vocabulary
human resources	reference	temporary
human resources management	orientation	fund
job description	on-the-job training	summary
compensation	group training	comments
wage	performance appraisal	demonstrates
salary	promotion	relaxed
benefits	transfer	complement
recruitment	separation	technical
background check	turnover	

Review Key Concepts

2. Define human resources management.

3. Describe how a company attracts and rewards good employees.

4. Discuss what a human resources manager should consider about job applicants.

5. Identify responsibilities of human resources managers after they have hired a new employee.

6. Describe how the status of an employee can change.

7. What do you think are the most important skills that you can work on now for success in a job in the future?

8. A job description tells potential employees about the types of duties that need to be performed. Why do you think job descriptions often indicate that the employee will "perform other duties as assigned"?

9. Why would a business list a new position as temporary but intend to have an employee in the position permanently?

10. Think about some different types of jobs in your community. What types of jobs are available for workers on a salary basis?

11. Most job interviews are structured the same for all candidates. Why do you think recruiters might ask the same questions of all applicants, instead of letting applicants decide what to emphasize?

12. Who would you list as references for a job application? Why would you select those people?

13. What changes do you think will occur in the workplace because of a rise in the number of younger workers (aged 16 to 34) and older workers (aged 55 and older)?

14. Read the job announcements in a local newspaper. In a one-page report, list the requirements or duties and responsibilities of five jobs.

15. Assume that you are a recruiter for a restaurant and need to fill a part-time job for a food server. In at least two paragraphs, write a job description for a newspaper ad.

16. In at least one page, describe the type of training that would best help you learn to do a new job entering and processing data using a computer.

17. Research a job that you would like to have someday. Use various resources for your research, including newspaper ads, the Internet, and career guides. Write two or more paragraphs about it.

18. Survey five people about their jobs. Ask them to state their job title and duties. How did they find the job they have? How long did it take to get a job with the company? How do they feel about their job? Write a two-page report summarizing their comments.

19. Write at least two paragraphs summarizing information from the yellow pages about employment agencies in your area.

Presentation Software
20. As recruiters, human resources managers try to bring in qualified workers to fill openings. Their efforts help assure that companies hire the best people for their jobs. Use graphic presentation software to prepare slides outlining the steps human resources managers take to fill a position. Then give a presentation to your class.

Hiring Decisions
21. You have just been put on the employment screening committee for an all-male law firm. There are two finalists being considered for a position: a man and a woman. They are equally qualified. What guidelines do you think your committee should follow in selecting the right person for the job? Should gender be a factor?

Applying Academics to Business

English Language Arts

22. Parallel construction is a balance of two or more similar words, phrases, or clauses. Rewrite the following sentence to solve problems with parallel construction:

Human resources management is the process of finding, selecting, to train, and to evaluate employees.

Mathematics

23. As a human resources professional for a local biomedical company, you want to offer good research workers a competitive salary. You survey similar companies in your area and find out that medical researchers are paid:

Company A: $60,100
Company B: $45,900
Company C: $64,000

What is the mean of this data? What is the median?

CONCEPT **Data Analysis** The mean of a set of data is the average. The median is the middle number when the data is arrayed in order from least to greatest.

English Language Arts

24. Write a job description for a task you perform. Make a list of the duties and responsibilities that consists of at least four phrases or complete sentences using parallel construction.

Mathematics

25. As manager of an aircraft parts department, you need to increase prices by 17%. Customers who buy in volume will get an 8% discount. A replacement engine mount used to cost $67. To find the new price for a high-volume customer, use the following method:

17% − 8% = 9%
$67 × 9% = $6.03
$67 + $6.03 = $73.03

You calculate the price to be $72.12. What mistake was made?

CONCEPT **Working with Percents** A discount is an amount off a selling price, often determined by multiplying the selling price by a given percent.

Active Learning

Developing Job Skills

26. Survey family, friends, or others about their work experience. Ask these questions: How did you acquire the skills and knowledge for your job? What type of training did you receive? How long was it? Is it ongoing? What type of training do you think you might need in the future? Prepare a two-page report about your findings. Present your report to your class.

Business in the Real World

Dealing with Personnel Problems

27. Ashley was hired as a Web designer. When she began work, her work was excellent, and she worked well with others. Lately, Ashley's work has slipped. She has been late to work and has been having arguments with her co-workers. What should her supervisor do to solve the problem? What would happen if her supervisor did nothing? In two or more paragraphs, discuss the supervisor's options.

INTERVIEW QUESTIONS

28. A job applicant cannot be asked the following questions during an interview: What nationality are you? Are you married? What are your day-care arrangements? What religious meetings or holidays do you observe? Write at least two paragraphs, explaining why these questions are considered inappropriate for a job interview.

Business CAREERS

FIND YOUR DREAM JOB

29. Locate the Occupational Outlook Handbook Web site. Click on the "OOH Search/A-Z Index" link and enter the job category "human resources, training, and labor relations managers and specialists." Then write a one-page report about this field. Conclude your report with a list of things you could do now to prepare yourself to pursue the occupation.

Role Play

RESOLVING CONFLICTS

30. Situation As the human resources manager of a department store, you must resolve a conflict between two members of the sales staff. Both are good at their jobs and well-liked by customers and others.

Activity Have a one-on-one talk with each of the two salespeople to determine possible solutions to resolve the conflict. Choose the best solution and present it to the employees' supervisor.

Evaluation You will be evaluated on how well you meet the following performance indicators:

• Allow both co-workers to explain their view of the situation.

• Identify the source of the conflict.

• Explain your perception of the problem and possible solution for it.

• Develop a solution to the problem.

• Speak clearly and use correct grammar.

Standardized Test Practice

Directions Choose the letter of the best answer. Write the letter for the answer on a separate piece of paper.

1. For which of these situations would you need an exact number?

A   estimating the number of people who will attend a company picnic

B   determining how many round trips your car can make on a full tank of gas

C   ordering copies of a new employee benefits manual for present and future employees

D   calculating deductions for taxes and health insurance from an employee's payroll check

TEST-TAKING TIP When answering essay questions, make sure that you support generalizations with evidence. Back up your ideas with names, dates, and places. A short essay question should be answered with accurate explanations backed up by facts.

Chapter 16

Culture and Diversity in Business

Chapter Objectives After completing this chapter, you will be able to:

▶ **Section 16.1 Culture in Business**
- **Describe** the effect of culture on doing business globally.
- **Describe** how corporate cultures differ among businesses.

▶ **Section 16.2 Diversity in the Workplace**
- **Identify** ways in which cultural diversity has an impact on business.

Ask

AN EXPERT

The Balance Sheet

Q: What is a balance sheet, and what should I look in it for when researching a stock?

A: A balance sheet is a statement of the total assets and liabilities of a company at a particular time, usually the last date of an accounting period. Using a company's balance sheet, you can find the current ratio, a comparison of current assets (assets that can be converted into cash in less than a year), and current liabilities (money owed that is due within a year) to assess liquidity. You can compare debt to shareholder's equity to see how leveraged the company is, or how much it owes. For conservative investors, a strong balance sheet is a must. If a company has little or no debt, it tends to be conservatively managed. If it has more cash and assets that can be turned into cash within a year than current liabilities and long-term debt, it is financially sound and should be able to weather financial storms. Companies publish their balance sheets in their financial reports.

Mathematics The balance sheet for Monique's Boutique showed current assets including accounts receivable of $3,560 and cash of $5,600. Current liabilities were accounts payable of $4,500. What is the current ratio?

CONCEPT **Current Ratio** To compute the current ratio, divide current assets by current liabilities. A ratio of 2:1 or higher is considered favorable by creditors. It indicates that a business is able to pay its debts.

John A Rizzo/Pixtal/SuperStock

● **Shared Values** Many companies promote a strong corporate culture. **Why might it be important for employees in a company to share values, beliefs, and goals?**

Culture in Business

Reading Guide

Before You Read

Think about what makes up a company's culture and how different cultures can impact a business.

Read to Learn

- Describe the effect of culture on doing business globally.
- Describe how corporate cultures differ among businesses.

The Main Idea

A company's culture is its shared values, beliefs, and goals that affect the way its management and employees interact. It also impacts the way it works with people in other countries with which it does business.

Key Concepts

- Culture in a Global Economy
- Corporate Culture

Vocabulary

Key Terms

culture
business etiquette
corporate culture
hierarchy
bureaucracy

Academic Vocabulary

You will find these words in your reading and on your tests. Make sure you know their meanings.

distinct
ethnic
region
tradition

Graphic Organizer

List some attributes of a formal culture and an informal culture in a figure like the one below.

Corporate Culture

Formal	Informal

 Go to **connectED.mcgraw-hill.com** to print out this graphic organizer.

Culture in a Global Economy

The word "culture" can have several different meanings. In general, **culture** is the beliefs, customs, and attitudes of a **distinct** group of people. A group's culture is often considered in terms of its dress, food, language, and art. It can also be considered in terms of a group's history, geography, and religious beliefs. Culture can refer to an entire country or **ethnic** group. It can also refer to a specific social group or institution.

The global economy creates a diverse culture for business. As companies trade worldwide, they must be aware of different cultural and business practices. Each country has its own rules for etiquette, business customs, and personal interaction. Properly approaching people from various cultures can give them a better impression of you.

In business, culture has two important meanings. In the broad sense, it refers to the customs of other countries with which companies do business. A *custom* is a practice followed by people of a particular group or **region**. Business culture refers to the standards of a particular company. Companies that conduct business in other countries must be aware of differences in laws, currencies, eating habits, and even systems of measurement. Failure to understand the culture of a country with which you do business can ruin a deal or lead to a marketing disaster.

● **As You Read**

Think about the benefits of understanding other cultures.

✔ **Reading Check**   **Identify**   What factors make up a group's culture?

Don Mason/Getty Images

● **Work Environment**
Different work environments reflect various types of corporate culture. **How would you describe the culture of this workplace?**

Today you can find a McDonald's® restaurant on every continent except Antarctica. Appealing to local tastes in some markets is an important way McDonald's has grown globally. In Brazil, you can order a "Quiche de Queijo," a cheese pie. Norwegians can order a "McLaks," a grilled salmon sandwich with dill sauce; and when you're in Hong Kong, you can try the Red Bean Pie. Because personal service is so important to customers in the Middle East and Southeast Asia, McDonald's even delivers there.

Examples of Languages Across Cultures

Q: In Bahasa-Indonesian, how do you say: "Goodbye"?
A: Selamat tinggal (pronounced: Slă-mă̆t tēng-gŭll)

If you could add a local twist to a fast-food menu or restaurant in your area, what would it be?

Marketing Abroad

To market products successfully in another country, companies must research the country's languages, customs, and tastes. For example, when Pillsbury® translated "Jolly Green Giant" into Arabic, the phrase became "Intimidating Green Ogre." Soft-drink maker Coca-Cola changes the amount of carbonation and sugar in its products to suit the tastes of different countries.

Doing Business Abroad

> **As You Read**
>
> Think about marketing goods in other countries. What are some obstacles you might face?

Companies doing business in other countries must be aware of cultural differences that affect the workplace. When the Walt Disney Company opened Euro Disney, French workers objected to certain practices that were typical at Disney's U.S. theme parks. As a result, 3,000 workers quit.

Business Etiquette

Business etiquette is conduct that is considered socially acceptable in business. It differs from country to country. For example, in the United States, receiving a gift from a potential business partner could be seen as a bribe. In Japan, it is customary to give gifts, and there are many rituals involved. Before doing business in India, it is customary to have tea. In Mexico, throwing documents on a table during a meeting is considered an insult.

Many companies avoid cultural problems by hiring local managers in other countries. Some also prepare their own managers to live and work abroad. As more companies trade globally, there is an increased demand for people who have studied other languages and cultures.

Corporate Culture

A company's **corporate culture** is its shared values, beliefs, and goals. It can be defined formally through a company code of ethics, a written manual, and the orientation process. It can also be defined informally through dress codes, work habits, and social activities. The culture at McDonald's, for example, stresses customer service and family values. Employees are expected to be clean-cut and greet each customer with a smile. FedEx Office®, Ben & Jerry's®, and Patagonia® stress worker satisfaction and concern for the environment.

A company's founder can influence its culture. For instance, William Hewlett of computer-maker Hewlett-Packard stressed a "people first" culture. Region and **tradition** can also play big parts. A banker at a Wall Street firm in New York may be expected to wear a suit and tie. At a high-tech company in California's Silicon Valley, workers might wear T-shirts and shorts to work.

 **Reading Check** **Contrast** What other differences might you encounter if you worked at a Wall Street firm or a Silicon Valley company?

Business | Case Study

International Etiquette

Successful global trade requires cultural fluency

As global commerce expands, so do the opportunities for cross-cultural interactions. First impressions can be crucial. You can avoid causing unintended confusion or offense by doing some cultural homework before an initial meeting.

Today's businesspeople need basic competence in the customs of other cultures. This competence includes sensitivity to language, gestures, gender roles, facial expressions, dress and appearance, and communication styles. For example, did you know that in Korea, business cards are presented with both hands? Or that in Germany, being even a few minutes late to a meeting is considered unprofessional?

When a meeting takes place, a reserved and respectful approach is best. Take your cues from the body language of the people you're meeting. Earning the trust of people with whom you do business is a critical part of the business itself.

Active Learning

Imagine that the company you work for is about to receive a group of executives from abroad to negotiate an important business deal. You have been asked to use online resources to compile a dossier (report) on the etiquette and business culture of your visitors' native country. Pick from among these nations: Brazil, China, Japan, Saudi Arabia, Turkey. Create a one- or two-page report with illustrations that covers topics such as appropriate greetings, gestures, personal space, and differences in interactions between different genders.

As You Read

Think about working at a company with a formal culture. Why do some companies prefer this type of organization?

Formal Culture

A company's culture affects the way it is organized and does business. A formal business culture may have a strict **hierarchy**, or chain of command. A hierarchy usually has one person at the top who makes all the decisions. There might be several levels of management below. This is known as a **bureaucracy**. In formal cultures, making changes or passing down decisions can be complicated. Job titles are indicators of power and status within a company. Dress codes and work hours are strictly enforced.

Informal Culture

At a company with an informal culture, employees are encouraged to make decisions on their own. They are allowed to dress casually and have more flexible work hours. In some cases they can even work at home. Job titles are not as important as creativity and teamwork. At computer memory maker Kingston Technology®, the founders sit in cubicles so they can interact with employees and be available to them. Few companies have a culture that is entirely formal or informal. Within one company there are often different cultures.

Section 16.1

After You Read

Review Key Concepts

1. Why should businesses involved in global trade be aware of cultural differences?
2. How is a company's corporate culture defined?
3. What are some characteristics of a formal corporate culture?

Academic Skills

4. **Mathematics** Monica was traveling to England and France on business. She flew from London to Paris and wanted to exchange some U.S. dollars (USD) and British pounds (GBP) into euros (EUR). She went to the exchange bank and saw this sign:

Currency	Sell	Buy
GBP	1.46990 EUR	0.68032 EUR
USD	0.83399 EUR	1.19962 EUR

Compare the values of a single dollar, euro, and pound by writing an expression that orders them from least to greatest.

CONCEPT Inequalities Use the symbol $>$ to mean *greater than* and $<$ to mean *less than*.

 For math help, go to the Math Appendix.

 Go to **connectED.mcgraw-hill.com** to check your answers.

Diversity in the Workplace

Reading Guide

Before You Read

Think about how cultural diversity can help a company become successful.

Read to Learn

- Identify ways in which cultural diversity has an impact on business.

The Main Idea

Companies are more aware of the growing spending power of different consumer groups. Human resources managers find ways to draw on the strengths of culturally diverse workers.

Key Concept

- Cultural Diversity

Vocabulary

Key Terms

diversity
stereotype
baby boom generation

discrimination
ageism

Academic Vocabulary

You will find these words in your reading and on your tests. Make sure you know their meanings.

diverse
assignments

prohibits
accommodation

Graphic Organizer

As you read, list the benefits of diversity in a figure like the one below.

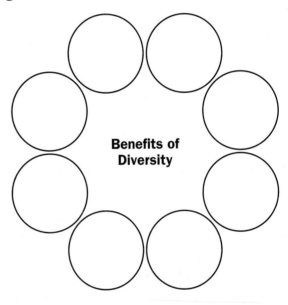

Benefits of Diversity

 Go to **connectED.mcgraw-hill.com** to print out this graphic organizer.

Cultural Diversity

Companies tend to thrive when they have **diversity**, a variety of employees with different backgrounds and identities. People are **diverse** in terms of age, gender, ethnicity, and individual needs. They also differ in terms of education, marital status, income, and religious beliefs. Diversity in the workplace means differences in skills, work habits, and approaches to tasks. People with the same **assignments** will carry them out in different ways.

Some people stereotype others who are different from them. To **stereotype** people is to identify them by a single trait or as a member of a certain group rather than as individuals. In fact, no two people are alike. Your success on the job will depend on how well you work with and for people who are different from you.

✔ **Reading Check** **Identify** What are some ways in which people are diverse?

● **As You Read**

Think about the growth of the U.S. population. What effects do you think that the increasingly diverse population will have on business in the future?

The Impact of Diversity on Business

The U.S. population is becoming more ethnically diverse. Each year, more than 1 million people come to the United States from all over the world. As total population grows, the percentages of people with African, Asian, and Hispanic or Latino

Science/Tech**TRENDS**

Adaptive Technologies

Hiring people with physical disabilities and accommodating their special workplace needs is easier than ever, thanks to the development of adaptive technologies. For example, voice recognition software transforms the human voice using a computer input device that can replace the mouse and keyboard, and improves the productivity of people with movement problems. Unique authoring tools now enable Web designers to incorporate sign language into their Web sites to assist those with hearing impairment. Improvements in videoconferencing technologies are making telecommuting a reality for many who couldn't enter the workplace any other way. Fully incorporating employees with these kinds of special needs increases workplace diversity and impacts corporate culture.

Locate Web sites where you can find out more about adaptive technologies and how they help people and companies reach their potential. Research the stories of individuals who use adaptive technologies in their daily work lives. Write a few paragraphs about how adaptive technologies are changing the diversity of the workplace.

tage also grow. The fastest growing groups in the country are people of Hispanic and Asian origins.

The population is also living longer. More workers aged 65 and over are working past retirement age. The growth rate for women in the labor force is expected to rise at a slightly faster rate than for men. Workers aged 25 to 54 are the largest share of the workforce. (See **Figure 16.1**.)

Changes in the Workplace As the population becomes more diverse, so does the workplace. There are greater numbers of women, Asians, Hispanics, and African Americans in management positions. Many workers from various cultures meet people of different ages, ethnic backgrounds, and abilities.

Changes in the Marketplace A more diverse population also means a more diverse marketplace. With more jobs, women and ethnic groups have more spending power and a larger share of the market. Companies target several market segments. For example, many companies run ads in both English and Spanish. The 76 million babies born in the United States between 1946 and 1964 are called the **baby boom generation**. Many members of this generation are reaching retirement age and developing specific needs.

Those born between the early 1980s and the early 2000s are known as the *millennial generation*. At about 80 million in the U.S., they have been called "echo boomers" and are considered the first generation to grow up with technologies such as computers and cell phones.

● **As You Read**

Think about some of your favorite TV commercials. What groups were targeted in these ads?

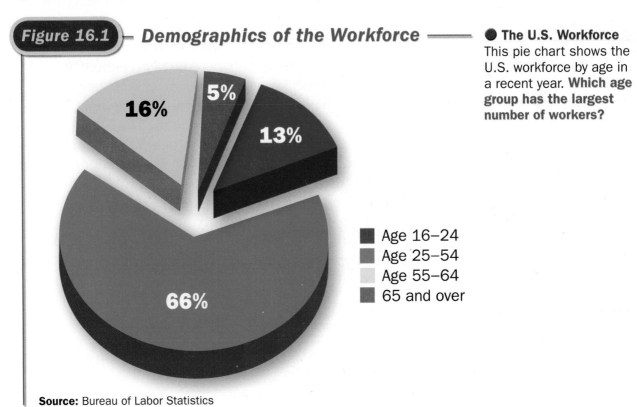

Figure 16.1 — **Demographics of the Workforce**

5%
16%
13%
66%

■ Age 16–24
■ Age 25–54
■ Age 55–64
■ 65 and over

● **The U.S. Workforce**
This pie chart shows the U.S. workforce by age in a recent year. **Which age group has the largest number of workers?**

Source: Bureau of Labor Statistics

● **A Diverse Workplace** The blending of people with different skills and perspectives into the workplace can help businesses understand and react to an increasingly diverse population. **How does a diverse workforce aid a business in serving a diverse market?**

Managing Diversity

Human resources managers oversee diversity. They seek ways to make the company inclusive by hiring people of different characteristics, backgrounds, and ethnicities. This diversity leads to a more realistic world view, which can lead to a competitive advantage. Employee diversity is an asset in dealing with clients and customers of various cultures. Diversity management programs try to draw on the strength of a company's melting pot.

Laws Against Discrimination **Discrimination** is unfair treatment of a person or group, usually because of prejudiced attitudes about race, ethnicity, age, religion, or gender. Many laws have been passed to prevent discrimination. For example, in the past, workers over the age of 40 were often fired or denied jobs in favor of younger workers. This form of discrimination is called **ageism**. To protect older workers, the U.S. government passed the Age Discrimination in Employment Act. It **prohibits** discrimination against workers because of their age.

The Equal Employment Opportunity Act was passed to strengthen laws that protect workers from discrimination based on race, ethnicity, religion, or gender. Workers with specific needs often could not work because buildings lacked proper access or equipment. In 1990, the Americans with Disabilities Act (ADA) was passed. ADA prohibits discrimination against qualified people who have disabilities. Employers must make a reasonable **accommodation** for a qualified person with a disability. Examples of *reasonable accommodation* include adjusting buildings so that people in wheelchairs can move around them.

Seeking All Qualified Workers
Many companies state that they are equal opportunity employers in their employment ads. Some also stress that women and people with disabilities are encouraged to apply for jobs. *Why do you think companies do this?*

280   **Chapter 16**   Culture and Diversity in Business

Diversity Programs Most codes of ethics have rules against discrimination. These codes, however, are not always enough to prevent personnel problems. Some employees still have trouble working with people who are different from them. Companies offer diversity training programs to promote tolerance among workers. Diversity training breaks down stereotypes. Managers must avoid stereotyping. They must create a work environment in which prejudice is not tolerated and diversity is welcomed and respected. They must promote a corporate culture that values diversity.

Benefits of Diversity Businesses that promote diversity in the workplace have discovered many benefits:

- A diverse workforce offers a broader range of ideas and points of view.
- Greater diversity in the workplace helps a company better understand and serve diverse markets.
- Diversity improves morale among employees and strengthens their commitment to company goals.
- Companies that value diversity have increased productivity and efficiency, lower turnover rates, less absenteeism, and fewer legal costs from employee complaints. Diversity training also helps reduce conflicts among workers.

Section 16.2

After You Read

Review Key Concepts
1. In what ways are people diverse?
2. What are two laws about discrimination?
3. What are some benefits of diversity in the workforce?

Academic Skills
4. **English Language Arts** Think ahead to the time when you will be 60 years old. Create a poster that visually describes what you will be doing. Will you be working? Will you be retired? What activities will you do? What products and services will you buy? How will you provide for yourself financially? Display your poster in the classroom.

5. **English Language Arts** Spend some time observing others at a distance. Note any repeated rituals you see, such as saying hello or goodbye. What gestures or other body language tells you how people are feeling? Write a short essay about your observations, and discuss them with others.

 Go to **connectED.mcgraw-hill.com** to check your answers.

<table>
<tr><th>Section 16.1 Summary</th><th>Section 16.2 Summary</th></tr>
<tr><td>

Culture in Business Culture is the beliefs, customs, and attitudes of a distinct group of people. It can refer to an entire country or ethnic group as well as to a specific social group or institution. As companies trade globally, they must be aware of different cultural and business practices and etiquette. Each country has its own rules for etiquette, business customs, and personal interaction. Companies that are culturally aware are better able to market products globally. Cultural differences are also present in the workplace. Just as each country has its own culture, each corporation has its own culture. A company's corporate culture is its shared values, beliefs, and goals.

</td><td>

Diversity in the Workplace Companies tend to thrive when they have diversity. Diversity is a variety of employees with different backgrounds and identities. People can be diverse in many ways, including age, gender, ethnicity, skills, work habits, and approaches to tasks. The U.S. population has become more ethnically diverse and is getting older and living longer. These changes affect business. Diversity in the workplace helps a company better understand and serve diverse markets. Human resources managers oversee diversity. They seek ways to make companies more inclusive by hiring different types of people. They also make sure their companies follow employment laws.

</td></tr>
</table>

Vocabulary Review

1. On a sheet of paper, use each of these key terms and academic vocabulary terms in a sentence.

Key Terms

culture	diversity
business etiquette	stereotype
corporate culture	baby boom generation
hierarchy	discrimination
bureaucracy	ageism

Academic Vocabulary

distinct	diverse
ethnic	assignments
region	prohibits
tradition	accommodation

Review Key Concepts

2. Describe the effect of culture on doing business globally.

3. Describe how corporate cultures differ among businesses.

4. Identify ways in which cultural diversity has an impact on business.

Critical Thinking

5. What cultural differences would you experience working in another country?

6. How could you prepare to fit into the culture of another country?

7. What would you do if you moved to another country and were expected to follow business practices that you considered unethical?

8. What aspects of your classroom's culture shape how you work, act, and deal with problems?

9. List some ways the management of a company can foster acceptance of diversity among workers.

10. What changes in the business world do you think are the result of our population being more diverse?

11. What changes do you think will help to eliminate discrimination?

12. If you had an opportunity to become an exchange student in another country, what would you do to learn about the culture there?

13. What types of businesses are likely to have an informal corporate culture?

Write About It

14. Research several definitions and statements on diversity. Summarize what you learned in a brief report.

15. Corporate culture has been described as "the personality of a company." Imagine that you own your own business. Write two or more paragraphs describing the business and its corporate culture.

16. A glass ceiling is an unofficial but real barrier to advancement and is usually due to discrimination. Is this fair? Write an e-mail to your teacher explaining your answer.

17. List five words or phrases that you would use to describe the culture of a company in which you would enjoy working. Is it "formal" or "informal"?

18. Describe the qualities that would make you a good employee for a company that takes pride in its diverse staff. Write a one-page essay describing your attributes as they relate to diversity.

19. Research the Americans with Disabilities Act. Write a two-page article for your school newspaper on ways businesses can accommodate people with disabilities.

Technology Applications

Spreadsheet Software

20. Use these figures about the education of U.S. residents to prepare a spreadsheet comparing the groups. Completed Grades K–9: 3.41%; Completed Grades 9–11, No Diploma: 7.48%; High School Graduate: 31.42%; Some College, No Degree: 27.37%; College: Associate's Degree: 8.10%; College: Bachelor's Degree: 15.12%; College: Graduate Degree: 7.10%

Business Ethics

Foreign Customs

21. Imagine you and a co-worker are experts in your field. One of you is female and the other is male. Your company wants to send you both to negotiate a business deal in a country whose society discriminates against women. Women who do business there must arrange for men to handle direct negotiations with its businessmen. How would you handle this situation?

Applying Academics to Business

English Language Arts

22. Research two of the following words. How are they broken into syllables? How are they pronounced? What is their origin? What is their meaning in the context of culture and diversity in business? Do they have other meanings in different contexts? What are some synonyms and antonyms? Write a few sentences about each of the two words you choose.

hierarchy   stereotype   ageism
culture   discrimination

Mathematics

23. The Americans with Disabilities Act has opened the way for people with disabilities to join the mainstream of American life. Today, the Department of Justice estimates that people with disabilities as a group have discretionary spending power of about $175 billion a year. Write $175 billion in standard form and scientific notation.

> **CONCEPT**   **Scientific Notation**   A number written in scientific notation is written as the product of a number between 1 and 10 and a power of 10.

English Language Arts

24. Write a paragraph about a local company, predicting the type of corporate culture it has. Then contact the business and find out about its corporate culture. Ask for examples of how the company's corporate culture is formal or informal. Then write another paragraph that describes the company's corporate culture and explains how your prediction of it differed from or was similar to the company's description of it.

Mathematics

25. The Department of Justice estimates that Americans with disabilities have discretionary spending power that is twice that of the teenage market and four times that of 8- to 12-year-olds. If so, what fraction of the spending power of people with disabilities is the combined spending power of 8- to 12-year-olds and teenagers?

> **CONCEPT**   **Inverse Operations**
> Multiplication and division are inverse operations. In other words, if you know that x is 2 times y, you can find y by dividing x by 2. Dividing a number by 2 is the same as multiplying it by $\frac{1}{2}$.

Active Learning

Balancing Work and Family

26. Some companies promote a corporate culture that encourages a balance between work and personal life. Work in groups and choose one of the following companies: Intel®, Zappos.com, Google, Inc., and Amazon. com®. Visit the career pages of the company's Web site. Create a brief presentation about the services the company provides its workers.

Business in the Real World

Employee Survey

27. Survey a group of workers about the culture of their companies. Consider asking these and other questions: Does your company have a formal or an informal culture? Do members of your work group have different ethnic backgrounds, age groups, and genders? Write a two-page report of your findings.

Real LIFE skills

INTERPERSONAL SKILLS

28. Interpersonal skills include the qualities that make diversity work. They include the ability to accept other people, to appreciate their differences, and to work well with them. Prepare an outline listing the qualities and skills that workers should develop that will enable them to work well with people of all types of backgrounds.

Business CAREERS

FIND YOUR DREAM JOB

29. Locate the Occupational Outlook Handbook Web site. Click on the "OOH Search/A-Z Index" link and enter the job category "interpreters and translators." Then write a one-page report about this area of occupation. Conclude your report with a list of things you could do now to prepare yourself to pursue the occupation.

Role Play

HOW CUSTOMS ARE DIFFERENT

30. Situation You have been asked to present a skit that illustrates acceptable and unacceptable business behavior in another country. You will present your skit to your class with the help of one or more of your classmates.

Activity Choose a country to research and illustrate its business customs.

Evaluation You will be evaluated on how well you meet the following performance indicators:

- Describe the business situation you will illustrate.
- Demonstrate an awareness of the customs of the country you chose.
- Give examples of behaviors that are acceptable and unacceptable in that country.
- Describe why each behavior that you presented is acceptable or unacceptable.
- Present your skit to your classmates.

Standardized Test Practice

Directions Choose the letter of the best answer. Write the letter for the answer on a separate piece of paper.

1. Which rule can be used to determine the *nth* term in the pattern below?

2, 5, 10, 17, 26...

A $2n + 1$
B $n^2 + 1$
C $n^2 - 1$
D $n^3 + 1$

TEST-TAKING TIP When taking a test, do not use a mechanical pencil, ink pen, or correction fluid. Use a soft lead No. 2 pencil to mark your answers, and make changes with a good eraser.

Nelson Gonzalez

CEO, Chairman, and Co-Founder, Alienware

Nelson Gonzalez and Alex Aguila started Alienware, a Miami-based company that makes customized computers for gamers. The company assembles machines specifically for performance, using only parts that gamers need.

Q & A

Describe your job responsibilities.

Nelson: When I get to the office, the first thing I do is check our sales numbers. I then meet with Alex Aguila and we speak about operational issues. Our Web site is the portal to the world. I am constantly looking at it and making suggestions in terms of design, functionality, and performance. I also do news searches for Alienware and I find out what news we've generated that day. We have a very customer-centric culture here and I believe in the importance of giving our customers a great experience. We are always in a state of change. It's my job to reinforce a culture of change and have our people embrace it and thrive on it.

What is your key to success?

Nelson: My parents emigrated from Cuba, and I came from a very modest background. I had a lot of ambition to be successful, and not just in making money, I wanted to make a difference in the work I did and products I made.

What skills are most important in your business?

Nelson: The first thing that needs to take place is the identification of a niche. I identified the opportunity because I was my own customer. Having a solid understanding of finance and accounting is essential. You also need to have a certain level of technical/engineering aptitude to feel comfortable in a high-tech business environment.

What advice would you give students interested in starting a business?

Nelson:

- Believe in the product or service you are going to offer. Passion drives success.
- It's OK to fail, but it's not OK if you never gave it a shot.
- Seek advice from experienced entrepreneurs.
- Embrace change and always be willing to entertain new ways of doing things.

Critical Thinking
How does the type of product or service dictate how a business operates?

Some Qualifications of the Owner of a Computer Hardware Development Company

Academic Skills and Abilities

Computer science; physics; mathematics; engineering; interpersonal skills; general business management abilities; verbal and written communication skills; multitasking, organizing, and planning skills

Academic Skills Required to Complete Tasks at Alienware			
Tasks	Math	Science	English Language Arts
Hold meetings			◆
Assign duties			◆
Design new products	◆	◆	◆
Assess marketplace opportunities	◆	◆	◆
Customer service			◆
Schedule employees	◆		◆
Order supplies and equipment	◆		◆
Analyze financials	◆		◆

Education and Training

Occupations in computer hardware engineering need a bachelor's degree in engineering for almost all entry-level engineering jobs. College graduates with a degree in a physical science or mathematics occasionally may qualify for some engineering jobs, especially in specialties that are in demand. Engineers should be creative, inquisitive, analytical, and detail-oriented. They should be able to work as part of a team.

Career Path

Computer engineering graduates usually work under the supervision of experienced engineers. As new engineers gain experience, they are assigned more difficult projects with greater independence to develop designs, solve problems, and make decisions. Engineers may advance to become technical specialists or to supervise a staff or team of engineers and technicians. Some may become engineering managers or enter other managerial or sales jobs.

Unit 5 — Thematic Project

Cultural Diversity in the Business World

Globalization has increased cultural diversity in the workplace. Smart business managers utilize the talents, backgrounds, and knowledge of every member of the workforce.

Thematic Project Assignment

In this project you will prepare an international instruction booklet. Your booklet will be used to educate businesses about different cultures.

Step 1 Brainstorm Skills You Need to Complete This Activity

Your success in writing an international instruction booklet will depend on your skills. Preview the activity. Then brainstorm a list of the skills you will need to use to complete the activity and describe how you will use them. Skills you might use include:

Academic Skills   reading, writing, social studies, geography, and researching

Basic Skills   speaking, listening, thinking, and interpersonal skills

Technology Skills   word processing, keyboarding, telecommunications, and Internet skills

@ SKILLS PREVIEW Go to connectED.mcgraw-hill.com to download a graphic organizer you can use to brainstorm the skills you will use to complete the project.

Step 2 Choose a Business and a Career That Interest You

Think of a business that you find interesting. Then think of a career related to the business that interests you. As you investigate cultural diversity in the business world, you will research the effects of cultural diversity on the business and career of your choice.

Step 3 Build Background Knowledge

Preview cultural diversity in the business world.

Diversity in the Workplace

The modern-day global economy that is creating a diverse culture for business also is creating a diverse culture in the workplace. Just as businesses that trade internationally have become aware of a country's customs and business practices, businesses in the United States must be aware of the diversity within their own borders.

Employees must understand their coworkers' cultures in order to create successful and harmonious working relations. Failure to understand the diverse cultural differences among coworkers can lead to dissatisfaction and disharmony in the workplace.

Step 4 Connect with Your Community

Interview an adult you know who works in a cultural diverse workplace. Find out how his or her company does or does not take advantage of the employee's diversity.

Step 5 Research Cultural Diversity in the Business World

Use library and Internet resources to research cultural diversity in the business world. Use the checklist as a guide to your research. Keep records of your sources of information.

Step 6 Develop a Booklet

Use word processing and other software to develop an international instruction booklet that educates others about different cultures and includes all the following information:

Cultural Diversity in the Business World

✔ Choose a country that does business with the business of your choice.

✔ Explain the type of government this country has and the ways that the government affects the people.

✔ Explain the language spoken in the country and any language taboos.

✔ Explain any customs of the country that would be helpful for Americans to understand.

✔ Create a pictorial that illustrates foods, traditions, and holidays that are associated with this country.

✔ Use the information from the U.S. Census Bureau to create a pie chart that illustrates the number of American citizens who were born in another country and the country of their birth.

Self Connections

✔ Describe the results of your research to a family member or other adult.

✔ Describe how cultural diversity in the business world affects the business and career in which you are interested.

✔ Explain what the investigation and its results mean to you.

Step 7 Evaluate Your Report

 RUBRIC Go to connectED.mcgraw-hill.com to download a rubric you can use to evaluate your final report.

Unit 6

Financial and Technological Resources

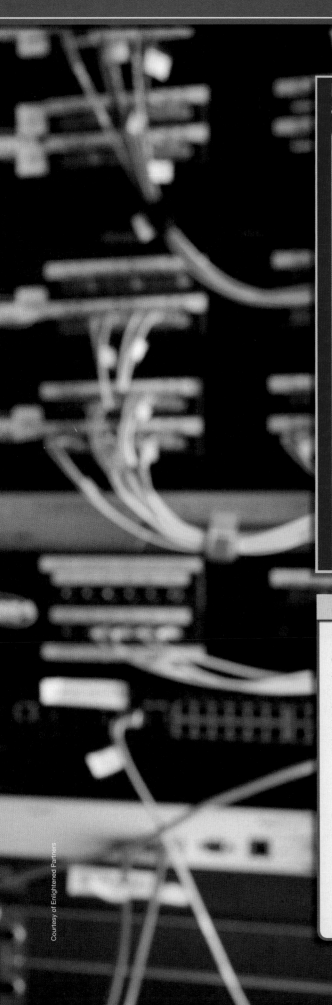

Courtesy of Enlightened Partners

Enlightened Inc. offers consulting services and assistance in planning the use of information technology. At the end of this unit, you will learn about Antwanye Ford and Andre Rogers, the founders of Enlightened Inc., and how they achieved their success.

Decision Making Why do you think wise use of financial and technological resources is important to a company?

Unit 6   *Thematic Project Preview*

Technology's Effect on Global Business After completing this unit, you will research ways technology is affecting global business.

Project Checklist As you read the chapters in this unit, use this checklist to prepare for the unit project.

- ✔ Think about technology's effect on globalization.
- ✔ Think about how the Internet has enabled small businesses to conduct e-commerce.
- ✔ Think about how advances in telecommunications have made worldwide communication accessible to businesses.
- ✔ Think about how technology connects you to your friends in a virtual world.

Chapter 17

Managing Business Finances

> **Chapter Objectives**   After completing this chapter, you will be able to:

▶ Section 17.1 *Financial Management*
- **Identify** the six reasons for creating a financial plan.
- **Explain** what a budget is and how it is used.

▶ Section 17.2 *Accounting*
- **Explain** the purpose of accounting.
- **Describe** how property rights are measured.
- **Define** the three components of the accounting equation.
- **Describe** the three main financial statements used by businesses.

Ask

AN EXPERT

Venture Capital

Q: I want to expand my small bookstore. How do I find money to grow my business?

A: There are two ways to get the money you need: go into debt or raise equity capital. It can be difficult for a small business to raise equity capital, so ask yourself if you can get by on loans. Lenders like small businesses such as yours, especially if you have a track record of success and can offer some collateral, such as equity in your home. If you are thinking about raising equity capital, consider how much you need, how fast you think you can grow your business, and how much ownership in your business you are willing to give up. Equity investors are usually looking for high growth and high returns over a short period of time, say four to five years. Many small businesses look for angel investors, who are wealthy individuals willing to back an ongoing business in return for big payoffs down the road. Venture capitalists often look for larger companies requiring millions of dollars in investments.

Mathematics   Portia borrowed $51,750 for five years at 6% interest. She is paying the loan back at the rate of $1,000 per month. How much interest will she pay in all?

CONCEPT   **Calculating Interest**   To calculate interest you will pay on a loan when you are making the same payment every month, multiply the payment amount by the number of payments, then subtract the amount of the original loan.

● **Managing Money** All businesses use accounting and record keeping to manage finances. **Why do you think it is important for businesses to keep track of their money?**

Purestock/Superstock

Financial Management

Reading Guide

● Before You Read

Consider how a financial plan helps the entrepreneur or business manager.

Read to Learn

- Identify the six reasons for creating a financial plan.
- Explain what a budget is and how it is used.

The Main Idea

A financial plan outlines the essential financial facts about a new business or venture. Businesspeople use a financial plan to help them make decisions about the future. This plan shows the amount of money a business will need to start and operate. It also explains how the business will acquire money to expand.

Key Concepts

- The Purpose of the Financial Plan
- Budgets

Vocabulary

Key Terms

financial plan
capital
financial forecast
budget

Academic Vocabulary

You will find these words in your reading and on your tests. Make sure you know their meanings.

project   require
expand   predict

Graphic Organizer

In a figure like the one below, list the six items an effective financial plan identifies, describes, or explains.

An Effective Financial Plan
1.
2.
3.
4.
5.
6.

 Go to **connectED.mcgraw-hill.com** to print out this graphic organizer.

The Purpose of the Financial Plan

When starting a new business or **project** at an existing firm, managers must determine if it is likely to be financially viable. A **financial plan** is a set of documents that outline the essential financial facts about the new venture. It is a road map that can be used to guide a company into the future. A financial plan can also be used to attract investors. Lenders and investors provide money to businesses with sound financial plans. An effective financial plan

- identifies the assets that need to be purchased.
- describes the amount of money a business needs to start and operate.
- describes the expenses the business will incur and explains how a business will cover its expenses.
- describes how the business will document and report financial records.
- forecasts finances to project future profitability.
- explains how the business will acquire money to grow or **expand**.

✔ **Reading Check** **Explain** How is a financial plan like a road map?

Business Case Study

Locating the Exit Sign

A good financial plan gets you both into, and out of, your business

You've created your business financial plan and are ready to open: space rented, employees hired, equipment purchased, sales projections set. But does your plan also include an exit strategy?

It might sound strange to plan for the end of a business before it even starts. But whether you hope to pass down your business, sell it, or close it, planning ahead for the end of your involvement will save you time and money later. Common business exit strategies include buyout (transfer to a family member or sale of shares to a co-owner), merger with another company, and sale. You will also need to think about what to do if the business fails or you become ill, or die. What assets will be sold, and how? What will happen to commitments you have made on behalf of the business?

Your business will be more attractive to a potential buyer if it's in working order, with organized financial records and solid contingency plans. Of course, these are good strategies to follow even if you don't intend to sell!

Active Learning

Divide into small groups. Each group consists of partners in a hypothetical business currently valued at an amount given by your teacher (each group's business will have a different value). One person represents a partner who holds 45 percent of the shares, the largest of the ownership group, but who wants to cash out and leave the business. The other partners have equal shares. Working together with the numbers you are given, calculate how much money each remaining partner must come up with to buy out the exiting partner and end up with equal ownership shares. The first team to answer correctly wins!

?ETHICS in Business

Recognizing Bribes

- **Critical Reading** Life is full of important decisions. Think about the kinds of decisions you make as you read the question below.

  You work as the purchasing agent for a small chain of restaurants. One of your duties is deciding where to purchase supplies, staples, and food items, such as coffee. A coffee purveyor you have bought from in the past sends you a free case of coffee beans just as you are making the purchasing decision about which coffee supplier to use for the next quarter. The coffee came with a message thanking you for purchasing from him in the past and suggesting that you try some of their new coffee blends.

- **Decision Making** Would you consider the case of coffee a bribe? Explain how you would make the determination.

● As You Read

Think about the start-up expenses you would have if you wanted to start a graphic arts business from home.

Identifying Business Assets

A financial plan identifies the assets needed for the business or project. Cash, equipment, buildings, supplies, inventory, and land are examples of assets. Business owners and managers must make purchasing decisions carefully. They should research their options before buying business assets. They can analyze and compare the price of each item. The information obtained might show that buying used items instead of new ones, or renting them, would be best.

Determining Needed Capital

A financial plan estimates the amount of capital the business will need. **Capital** is money supplied by investors, banks, or owners of a business. *Start-up capital* is the money used to pay for the various assets and expenses of a new venture or business. A new business has no track record to prove that it will survive. For that reason, it may have a hard time attracting investors. Major sources of start-up capital for entrepreneurs are personal resources—friends, family, and others. These resources can include savings, loans, and investments.

Describing Start-Up and Operating Expenses

A new business or venture has start-up expenses and operating expenses. Start-up expenses often **require** a large amount of cash. Start-up expenses include the cost of business assets as well as remodeling costs, security deposits, advertising, insurance, supplies, and legal permits and licenses. Operating expenses include payroll, rent, utility bills, delivery charges, and bank fees.

Describing Financial Records Management

A financial plan explains how a business will manage its records. It describes who will maintain the financial records and why. Some business owners maintain their own records. Others hire professionals for that purpose. A financial plan also describes any legal agreements that influence the way records are kept. For an existing business that is starting a new venture, the person who maintains the accounting records would probably keep the records regarding the new project. There are different types of accounting software available to businesses.

Forecasting Future Finances

A financial plan includes financial forecasts. A **financial forecast** is an estimate of a business's financial outlook for each of the next few years. The forecast should consider business conditions in the future, including changes in the economy. A financial forecast might show that a new business or venture will not make money in the first year. It is best to be conservative when preparing financial forecasts. Keep estimates for income low and estimates for expenses high.

● **Financing Expansion** This business is expanding its space. **What types of financial materials does a business need to submit to creditors to get the money to finance a building expansion?**

Pixtal/AGE Fotostock

Describing Growth Financing

Every company needs to grow in order to remain competitive. Planned growth can be very rewarding. Unplanned growth can be chaotic. Investors and lenders want to know that a business has thoughtfully developed strategies to finance controlled growth. The financial plan should explain the company's plans for financial growth.

Budgets

Financial statements indicate the financial condition of a firm in a past period. However, a budget helps guide its future. A **budget** is a plan specifying how money will be used or spent during a particular period. Budgeting helps business owners **predict** how much money the business will need. It also helps to control spending. To avoid financial problems, business owners and financial managers sometimes need to compare the business's budget to its actual income and expenses.

There are three main types of budgets. A start-up budget is a plan for your income and expenses from the time you start a business to estimated time it will make a profit. A cash budget is a plan for the actual money the business owner spends on a daily, weekly, or monthly basis. An operating budget is a plan for the amount expected to be spent and earned over a given period of time, usually six months or a year.

Section 17.1

After You Read

Review Key Concepts
1. What is the purpose of the financial plan?
2. What does an effective financial plan do?
3. Why do business owners use a budget?

Academic Skills
4. **Mathematics** When big companies create financial statements, they often shorten large numbers by omitting zeroes and adding a caption such as "all numbers in billions." Another way is to use scientific notation. What is 55 billion (55,000,000,000) expressed in scientific notation?

CONCEPT **Scientific Notation** In scientific notation, a number is expressed as the product of two factors. One is a number between one and ten, and the other is a power of 10.

 For math help, go to the Math Appendix.

 Go to **connectED.mcgraw-hill.com** to check your answers.

Accounting

Reading Guide

Before You Read

Think about the reasons companies create and maintain financial records.

Read to Learn

- Explain the purpose of accounting.
- Describe how property rights are measured.
- Define the three components of the accounting equation.
- Describe the three main financial statements used by businesses.

The Main Idea

Accounting provides financial information about an organization. It also helps guide business decisions regarding operations and finances. Balance sheets, income statements, and statements of cash flows show the financial position of a business.

Key Concepts

- Accounting for Business
- Property Ownership and Control
- Financial Statements

 Go to **connectED.mcgraw-hill.com** to print out this graphic organizer.

Vocabulary

Key Terms

accounting	liabilities
generally accepted accounting principles (GAAP)	accounts payable
	owner's equity
	accounting equation
property	financial statements
assets	income statement
current assets	balance sheet
accounts receivable	cash flows
fixed assets	statement of
equity	cash flows

Academic Vocabulary

You will find these words in your reading and on your tests. Make sure you know their meanings.

converted	release
generate	formulas

Graphic Organizer

On a figure like the one below, define the components of the accounting equation.

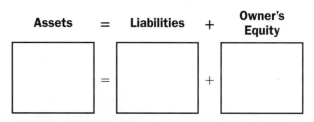

Assets = Liabilities + Owner's Equity

Accounting for Business

Operating a business costs money. Imagine that you are planning to open a restaurant someday. You will need to buy or rent a building, equipment, and furniture. You will need to hire employees. You will also need to buy food and supplies. Before and after your business opens, you will need to keep track of the money that you spend and receive. This aspect of business is called accounting.

Accounting is the systematic process of recording and reporting the financial position of a person or an organization. The accounting system is designed to collect, record, and report financial transactions that affect the operation of a business. Small businesses usually hire an independent accountant. An *accountant* maintains and reviews business records. However, many larger companies hire accounting firms to manage or audit their financial records. An *audit* is a review of accounting records and procedures. The biggest accounting firms are known as the "Big Four." PricewaterhouseCoopers®, Deloitte Touche Tohmatsu®, Ernst & Young®, and KPMG® are accounting firms that operate worldwide.

Accounting Software There are software categories for all levels of accounting, from home use to high-end corporate use. *Do you think people who are not accountants can produce accurate financial records by using accounting software?*

Science/Tech TRENDS

EDI

Short for electronic data interchange, EDI is a convenient way for businesses and others to transfer large amounts of data using the Internet. EDI is poised to revolutionize the health-care industry because of the Health Insurance Portability and Accountability Act (HIPAA), which was passed by Congress in 1996. HIPAA requires that health-care providers, insurance companies, and others use EDI to simplify and reduce the high cost of administering health care. Those costs are huge: An average of 26¢ of each health-care dollar is spent on administrative overhead, including such tasks as enrolling individuals in health plans, paying health insurance premiums, checking eligibility, obtaining authorization to refer patients to specialists, processing claims, and notifying providers about the payment of claims. Since EDI offers a standard format for trading partners to use, it allows partners to exchange information and transact business in a fast and cost-effective way.

WebQuest

Locate Web sites where you can research different applications of EDI. Write a paragraph about the advantages and disadvantages of EDI in at least two different applications.

Because it is so vital to the communication of financial information, accounting is often called the "language of business." This is because it is a way of communicating how well a business is doing. Just as a foreign language has different words and meanings, accounting has its own terminology.

Everyone involved in a business should understand some of the basics of accounting. A business manager, an employee of a firm, or an investor can use this information to gauge the health of the firm that they are working for or in which they want to invest.

Rules for Accountants

All accountants use the same set of rules, called **generally accepted accounting principles,** or **GAAP** (pronounced *gap*), to prepare reports. These rules provide a way to communicate financial information to others. *Financial reports* are summarized information about the financial status of a business. Each company sets up an accounting system according to its specific needs, but all businesses follow GAAP.

 **Identify** What is an accounting system designed to do?

Property Ownership and Control

The right to own property is basic to a free enterprise system. **Property** is anything of value that is owned or controlled. When you own an item of property, you have a legal right or financial claim to it. Businesses also own and control property. One of the purposes of accounting is to provide financial information about property and rights to it. In accounting, property and financial claims are measured in dollar amounts. Dollar amounts measure both the cost of the property and the *property rights,* or *financial claims* to the property.

Financial Claims in Accounting

Assets are property and other items of value owned by a business. They are either current or fixed. **Current assets** are assets that are either used up or **converted** to cash during the normal cycle of the business. The normal cycle is usually one year. Cash, supplies, merchandise, and accounts receivable are all current assets. **Accounts receivable** is the total amount of money owed to a business. It represents money to be received in payments after goods or services are sold on credit. **Fixed assets** are items of value that will be held for more than one year. These include equipment and buildings. The accounting term for the financial claims to all assets is equity. **Equity** is the present value of an asset less all claims against it.

When people or businesses buy property and agree to pay for it later, they are buying on *credit.* The business or person selling the property is called the *creditor.* **Liabilities** are creditors' claims to the assets of a business. They are the debts of a company. Liabilities are measured by the amount of money a business owes its creditors. They include accounts payable. **Accounts payable** represents the short-term liabilities that a business owes to creditors. **Owner's equity** is an owner's claim to the assets of the business. It is also referred to as the owner's *capital* in the business. It is measured by the dollar amount of the owner's claims to the total assets of the business.

The Accounting Equation

The accounting equation ensures that all accounting records will be correct. The **accounting equation** is a rule that states that assets must always equal the sum of liabilities and owner's equity. As a result, both sides of the equation must always balance. The accounting equation is expressed as follows:

Assets = Liabilities + Owner's Equity

The assets side of the equation shows the value of everything that the business owns or possesses. The other side shows the rights to those assets. Liabilities are the rights that creditors have to the assets. Owner's equity shows the rights that the owner has to the assets. For example, if a company's assets are worth $100,000 and liabilities against those assets are $40,000 (the amount owed creditors), then the owner has $60,000 in rights to the assets that the business possesses.

✔ Reading Check **Explain** What is the accounting equation?

Financial Statements

The accounting system is designed to **generate** financial statements and reports. **Financial statements** are documents that summarize the changes resulting from business transactions that occur during an accounting period. An *accounting period* is the period of time reflected by an accounting report.

Financial statements provide information that business owners use to make financial decisions. Even small sole proprietorships might prepare financial statements, but these documents are usually for the owner's use only. However, the federal government requires corporations to **release** their financial records to the public. Stockholders, employees, banks, and investment companies use financial statements to learn about the financial condition of a business. They can compare recent statements with earlier ones and evaluate the business's growth or decline. The main financial statements used are income statements, balance sheets, and statements of cash flows.

Income Statement

At the end of an accounting period, you want to know how much money your business made or lost. You will want to know your total revenue in sales and where the money went. This information is reported on the income statement. The **income statement** is a report of the revenue, expenses, and *net income* or *net loss* over an accounting period. It is sometimes called a *profit and loss statement*. If a restaurant's total revenue, or earnings, is greater than its total expenses, it has a net income. If expenses are greater than revenue, then it has a net loss. Managers use income statements to see if revenues have increased or decreased from one period to another.

Income statements for different types of business operations vary in content. A service business would have sales, expenses, and net income. A merchandising business would also include the cost of merchandise purchased for resale. **Figure 17.1** shows an income statement.

Figure 17.1 — *Income Statement Using Peachtree Accounting Software*

<Standard> Income/Budgets

Close Save Options Print Setup E-mail Preview Design Find Excel PDF Help

Bellwether Garden Supply
Income Statement
For the Three Months Ending March 31, 20--

	Current Month Actual	Current Month Budget	Year to Date Actual	Year to Date Budget
Revenues				
Sales	$ 175.00 $	0.00 $	175.00 $	0.00
Sales - Aviary	5,628.01	14,583.33	50,153.16	43,749.99
Sales - Books	149.75	5,000.00	7,293.10	15,000.00
Sales - Ceramics	0.00	0.00	0.00	0.00
Sales - Equipment	15,139.29	18,000.00	57,492.78	54,000.00
Sales - Food/Fert	1,006.96	1,000.00	5,204.15	3,000.00
Sales - Furniture	15,000.00	5,000.00	15,000.00	15,000.00
Sales - Hand Tools	729.67	1,500.00	7,058.12	4,500.00
Sales - Landscape Services	7,469.43	6,000.00	16,977.53	18,000.00
Sales - Miscellaneous	0.00	0.00	45.00	0.00
Sales - Nursery	31,200.48	25,000.00	65,042.56	75,000.00
Sales - Pots	5,905.08	500.00	9,469.51	1,500.00
Sales - Seeds	1,457.43	100.00	8,661.39	300.00
Sales - Soil	655.02	2,500.00	9,082.55	7,500.00
Sales - Statuary	0.00	0.00	0.00	0.00
Sales - Topiary	0.00	0.00	0.00	0.00
Interest Income	0.00	0.00	0.00	0.00
Other Income	0.00	0.00	25,500.00	10,000.00
Finance Charge Income	0.00	0.00	0.00	0.00
Sales Returns and Allowances	0.00	0.00	0.00	0.00
Sales Discounts	(122.22)	0.00	(132.12)	0.00
Total Revenues	84,393.90	79,183.33	277,022.73	247,549.99

● **Financial Information** Up-to-date financial information can provide a snapshot of how well a company is doing. **What do the total revenue figures tell you about this company?**

Balance Sheet

A **balance sheet** is a report of the balances in all assets, liability, and owner's equity accounts at the end of an accounting period. It is like a photograph of a business's finances at a specific moment. The balance sheet applies the accounting equation. When added up, the two sides of the equation are equal, or in balance. Managers and investors look at the balance sheet to determine if liabilities (claims against the assets) are increasing too much. The balance sheet can also indicate if there is too much cash available. Too much cash can mean that money is not being used efficiently. **Figure 17.2** shows a balance sheet.

Statement of Cash Flows

The income statement and balance sheet show important financial information. However, neither shows the cash position of a business during an accounting period. **Cash flows** are the money that is available to a business at any given time. The **statement of cash flows** is a financial report that shows incoming and outgoing money during an accounting period (often a month, quarter, or year).

Personal Finance
You use accounting every day. At home, your family manages income, expenses, and cash flows. *What types of income and expenses would your personal financial statement show? How do you handle your cash flow?*

Figure 17.2 — *Balance Sheet*

The Starting Line Sports Gear Comparative Balance Sheet December 31, Current Year and Previous Year				
	Current Year	**Previous Year**	**Increase (Decrease) Current over Previous**	
			Dollars	**Percent**
Assets				
Cash in Bank	$ 15,179.00	$ 10,135.28	$ 5,043.72	49.76 %
Accounts Receivable	10,404.00	8,220.00	2,184.00	26.57
Merchandise Inventory	81,385.00	84,921.00	(3,536.00)	(4.16)
Supplies	1,839.00	1,587.00	252.00	15.88
Prepaid Insurance	1,375.00	0.00	1,375.00	—
Delivery Equipment	19,831.00	12,462.00	7,369.00	59.13
Office Equipment	9,825.00	5,854.00	3,971.00	67.83
Store Equipment	5,200.00	3,500.00	1,700.00	48.57
Total Assets	$ 145,038.00	$ 126,679.28	$ 18,358.72	14.49 %
Liabilities				
Accounts Payable	$ 13,850.00	$ 28,113.14	$ (14,263.14)	(50.73)%

● **Computerized Accounting** Accounting programs such as QuickBooks can generate financial statements. **Which financial statement is shown here?**

One reason that a cash flow statement is very important is that firms can run out of cash even when they make a profit. In today's world, most things are sold on credit. Credit sales are considered revenue to the firm. Businesses that do not receive credit payments from customers right away may not have cash available to pay bills. Cash flow is very important, especially for a business that wants to borrow money. Lenders and investors expect business loan applicants to be able to show a consistently positive cash flow. This gives lenders more assurance that the loan will be repaid.

● **As You Read**

Think about how it is possible for a business to run out of cash even though it is making a profit.

Computerized Accounting

Today, most companies use computer programs to simplify their accounting procedures. Computer spreadsheets are important tools for organizing and analyzing such data. A spreadsheet is made up of rows and columns. The columns are identified by letters, and the rows are identified by numbers. As you create a spreadsheet, you enter numbers, labels, and **formulas** into cells. Cells are the small boxes within a spreadsheet. Microsoft Excel is a spreadsheet application that is commonly used in business. Accounting software such as Peachtree Accounting and Quick-Books are programs that help people and businesses manage their finances.

Section 17.2

○ **After You Read**

Review Key Concepts
1. How does accounting help a business?
2. Discuss property ownership and control. How are they related to the accounting equation?
3. What are the three main financial statements used in business?

Academic Skills

4. **English Language Arts** Research the three different financial software programs mentioned in the text. Find what is available. Then write a recommendation in the form of a business memo about which would best suit a small business. Compare and contrast the software products.

5. **English Language Arts** *Liability, asset, gross profit, net profit, depreciation,* and *fiscal year* are all terms used by accountants. Find out what these words mean, and create an accounting glossary with definitions and examples of the terms used in sentences. You might want to expand the list of terms and work with others in a team to create a larger glossary.

 Go to **connectED.mcgraw-hill.com** to check your answers.

<table>
<tr><td>

Section 17.1 *Summary*

Financial Management A financial plan outlines the financial projections about a new firm or venture. Businesses use financial plans to make decisions about the future. Financial plans include the amount of money a business will need to start and operate. They also include financial forecasts. A forecast estimates the financial outlook for a business over the next few years. Financial planning also involves budgeting. A budget is a plan that specifies how money will be used or spent during a particular period.

</td><td>

Section 17.2 *Summary*

Accounting An accounting system collects, records, and reports financial transactions that affect the operation of a business. Accountants follow a uniform set of rules. These rules provide a consistent way to share financial information. The accounting equation is the basis of accounting. It equates assets to liabilities plus owner's equity. Key documents include the balance sheet, the income statement, and the statement of cash flows.

</td></tr>
</table>

Vocabulary Review

1. On a sheet of paper, use each of these key terms and academic vocabulary terms in a sentence.

Key Terms

		Academic Vocabulary
financial plan	fixed assets	project
capital	equity	expand
financial forecast	liabilities	require
budget	accounts payable	predict
accounting	owner's equity	converted
generally accepted accounting principles (GAAP)	accounting equation	generate
	financial statements	release
property	income statement	formulas
assets	balance sheet	
current assets	cash flows	
accounts receivable	statement of cash flows	

Review Key Concepts

2. Identify the six reasons for creating a financial plan.

3. Explain what a budget is and how it is used.

4. Explain the purpose of accounting.

5. Describe how property rights are measured.

6. Define the three components of the accounting equation.

7. Describe the three main financial statements used by businesses.

8. Why do you think an entrepreneur might realize that he or she could not secure any investors after developing a financial plan?

9. A budget helps businesses determine how money will be spent in a given period. Will a business fail if it does not meet its budget?

10. How can having and extending credit on purchases be both good and bad for business?

11. Why do you think the federal government gets involved in the way businesses create and manage their finances?

12. If a business buys $4,000 worth of new equipment on credit, which inputs to the accounting equation are affected? Is the accounting equation still in balance?

13. It is important to use financial statements on a regular basis. What might happen to a business that analyzes its finances just twice a year?

14. Why does the income statement provide an incomplete picture of a business?

15. What are some reasons a company might not have enough cash reserves?

16. Choose a well-known corporation and research its most current income statement. Write a one-page report describing the income statement. Indicate the accounting period(s) covered.

17. Amy Sullivan has hired you to handle the accounting for her pet-grooming business. Based on the following totals, calculate the assets, liabilities, and owner's equity for the shop: cash: $200; grooming equipment: $300; accounts receivable: $500; accounts payable: $900; owner's equity: $100. Prepare a report, giving your opinion of the financial condition of the shop.

18. Accounting standards differ from country to country. Several groups are developing international accounting standards. Write a 200-word essay on the effect these standards might have on business.

19. As an investor in a certain company, would you like to see the accounts receivable on the balance sheet increase, decrease, or stay the same from one year to another? What should the company do to reach that point? Write a letter of two or more paragraphs to a financial manager supporting your answer.

Automated Accounting Programs

20. Investigate different accounting software programs and the types of financial documents that can be created using them. Can these programs be used by individuals, businesses, or both? Are they for small or large businesses, or can any business or organization use them? Write a report on your findings.

Confidentiality

21. Imagine that you were recently hired as the accountant for a well-known music group and have access to personal information. Your friends ask you for details about the band members, such as the amount of money they make and where they live. Your friends say they will not give anyone this information. What should you do?

Applying Academics to Business

English Language Arts

22. *Funds, capital, wealth, currency,* and *cash* are all words having to do with money. Research the meanings of the words and use each in a sentence so that someone unfamiliar with the words could infer their meanings from the context.

Mathematics

23. Three accounting supervisors in a large corporation earn different salaries based on their experience and time on the job. The median base salary is $76,948, with a range of $64,494 to $91,617. Write an inequality comparing the mean and the median.

> **CONCEPT** **Data Analysis: Mean, Median, and Range** The range of a set of data is the difference between the greatest and least number, the median is the number in the middle when all are listed in order from least to greatest, and the mean is the average.

English Language Arts

24. The topic sentence of a paragraph sometimes appears at the beginning. Sometimes it appears in the middle or at the end, and sometimes it is not directly stated in the paragraph, but must be inferred. Take notes from one of the sections by identifying and jotting down the key words and phrases from the topic sentences of each paragraph.

Mathematics

25. Tran, an entrepreneur, wants his computer business to earn $42,000 in profits. His research shows that the average net profit for his type of business is 15%. If Tran's business earns the average net profit percentage, how much revenue must be generated to deliver that net profit?

> **CONCEPT** **Working with Percents** If you know that a number, x, is a certain percent of an unknown, y, divide x by the percent to find y.

Active Learning

Financial Statements

26. Prepare a personal balance sheet. Price your assets at the cost that you paid for them. Next, use spreadsheet software, such as Excel, to prepare a personal budget for the next six months. Then write a one-page report on your financial goals for the future. Lastly, create separate folders for your balance sheet, personal budget, and goals.

Business in the Real World

Interview a Financial Manager

27. In groups of three or four, interview a financial manager or an accountant for a business. Ask about the business's long-term plans; the way financial forecasting is done and used; the software used for financial management of the firm; and the most common financial mistakes businesses make. As a group, prepare a written report on the interview.

Real LIFE *skills*

PERSONAL QUALITIES OF ACCOUNTANTS

28. General skills and abilities needed by accountants include the following: aptitude in math; ability to analyze, compare, and interpret data; communication skills; people skills; and a high level of integrity. Write at least two paragraphs indicating whether you have the interests and abilities necessary to pursue this type of career. Discuss ways you think you might overcome any weaknesses.

Business CAREERS

FIND YOUR DREAM JOB

29. Locate the Occupational Outlook Handbook Web site. Click on the "OOH Search/A-Z Index" link and enter the job category "accountants and auditors." Then write a one-page report about this area of occupation. Conclude your report with a list of things you could do now to prepare yourself to pursue the occupation.

Role Play

THE ACCOUNTING DEPARTMENT'S FUNCTION

30. Situation You are an accountant at a movie studio. Your manager asks you for reasons why the company needs such a large accounting department. She wonders if it would cost less to pay an outside accounting firm to perform the same services.

Activity You are called upon to justify the importance of the accounting department's function to the business.

Evaluation You will be evaluated on how well you meet the following performance indicators:

- Demonstrate a knowledge of business operations.
- Demonstrate knowledge of the important contributions that accounting makes to the health of the business.
- Organize comments in a logical way.
- Project your voice well and make good eye contact.

Standardized Test Practice

Directions Choose the letter of the best answer. Write the letter for the answer on a separate piece of paper.

1. Which sentence best develops the topic sentence below?

Effective financial managers deserve to earn a high salary.

A   They spend all their time thinking about numbers.

B   Some live lavishly and have lots of expenses.

C   They make even more for their clients.

D   Every financial manager deserves to do well financially.

TEST-TAKING TIP When taking a test, always read the directions before you work on a section. Failing to read directions can cause you to completely misinterpret what the test is asking you to do.

Technology in the Workplace

Chapter Objectives After completing this chapter, you will be able to:

▶ **Section 18.1** *Information Technology*
- **Describe** the role of information technology in business.
- **Identify** ways that technology has changed the workplace.

▶ **Section 18.2** *Internet Basics*
- **Describe** the Internet and its components.
- **Identify** tools for managing threats when using the Internet.

Ask AN EXPERT

Fundamental Research

Q: What do I look for when researching a company whose stock interests me?

A: Since stock represents ownership in a company, the best way to gauge a stock's appeal is to research the fundamentals of the business—the company's basic financial condition. You might look at aspects such as gross margin to see how profitably a company is able to manufacture its products; at earnings and the price to earnings ratio to see how much of a premium other investors are willing to pay for a company's future earnings; and at the company's history of paying dividends to tell whether the company has been stable or growing over time. All the information you'll need to perform fundamental analysis on a publicly traded company is available to the public.

Mathematics If a company has a gross margin of 20%, what is the cost of manufacturing its products?

CONCEPT **Gross Margin** Gross margin is profit divided by net sales. It is usually expressed as a percentage.

● **Telecommuting to Work** Technology makes it possible to move the worker from the workplace to the home. **What technologies could allow you to do work at home?**

LWA/Dann Tardif/Blend Images LLC

Information Technology

Reading Guide

Before You Read

Think about ways information technology is used for business and personal reasons.

Read to Learn
- Describe the role of information technology in business.
- Identify ways that technology has changed the workplace.

The Main Idea

People want instant access to information. At home and at work, they use hardware and software to create, store, and communicate information. Information technology allows people to access information from anywhere.

Key Concepts
- The Role of Information Technology
- How Technology Has Changed the Workplace

Vocabulary

Key Terms

information technology (IT)
telecommunications
telecommuting
wearable computer
computer-aided design (CAD)
virtual reality

Academic Vocabulary

You will find these words in your reading and on your tests. Make sure you know their meanings.

transmit   simulate
automatic   visual

Graphic Organizer

In a figure like the one below, list the advantages of telecommuting in the left column and the advantages of working in an office in the right column.

Advantages of Telecommuting	Advantages of Working in an Office

 Go to **connectED.mcgraw-hill.com** to print out this graphic organizer.

The Role of Information Technology

People depend on getting information quickly and easily. **Information technology (IT)** uses computing, electronics, and telecommunications to process and distribute information in digital and other forms. **Telecommunications** is the transmission of information over communication lines. This covers many technologies, including telephones and computer networks.

Computers are an important part of information technology. So are telephones, fax machines, personal digital assistants (PDAs), and other handheld devices. MP3 players digitally store music for listening anywhere. Wireless technology (wireless fidelity, or WiFi) lets people with a wireless-enabled computer or PDA connect to the Internet. Buildings wired for WiFi can transfer information from one part of a computer system to another. Computers used to design and make new products have improved the manufacturing process. Millions of employees work from home. IT makes these innovations possible.

● **As You Read**

Think about changes in technology that have taken place at your school in the last decade.

✔ Reading Check **Identify** What are some forms of information technology?

How Technology Has Changed the Workplace

New technology makes it possible to do tasks in different ways. When computers were first used in business, they were too big and heavy to take from the office. Today, mobile computers are light enough to take anywhere. *Electronic mail,* or e-mail, allows workers to communicate with others electronically. Wearable computers, manufacturing technology, and specialized software allow more work flexibility. Wireless phones, broadband access, and voice technology also let the workspace become mobile. For example, Capital One Financial Corp. replaces traditional offices and cubicles with mobile work areas and a casual environment. At hospitals, nurses can use a wireless computer to enter information about patients from anywhere in the facility. Through *WiFi,* the information is sent to a database available to the doctors, technicians, and others who need it.

fotostorm/Getty Images

● **Internet Tools** Technological innovation has changed the way people and businesses interact. **How can a business use technology to improve sales?**

Telecommuting

Telecommuting is a work arrangement that replaces a daily commute with telecommunications. Co-workers communicate with each other from off site using various technologies. This allows employees flexibility in where and when they work. Telecommuting has offered job possibilities for those who would otherwise be unemployed, such as stay-at-home moms, people with physical disabilities, and those who live in remote locations. It has also increased the opportunities for people to work internationally.

Examples of Languages Across Cultures

Q: In Korean, how do you say: "May I speak with _____, please?"

A: 제가 _____ 씨와 좀 얘기 나눌 수 있을까요?
(pronounced:
J-gă _____ sē-wă yĕ-ghēē năw-nool-soo ĭss-sool-gă-yō?)

What jobs might be best suited to telecommuting? What opportunities has telecommuting brought to international business?

Telecommuting

Telecommuting is an arrangement that allows employees to work at home while communicating with the workplace by phone, fax, or modem. Telecommuting has advantages. It decreases traffic in busy areas since workers spend less time traveling. It allows for flexible work hours. Companies also find that the quality of work often improves for telecommuters. Many employees are absent less often than when they worked full-time at the office.

Telecommuting also has disadvantages. Some employees dislike the lack of contact with other workers. Many miss the social part of the office. Some also find that they get distracted at home and cannot get their work done. For employers, a major problem is supervising an employee at a remote site. Telecommuters must have computers and other equipment to do their work. In many cases, this adds to company expenses. **Figure 18.1** shows that younger people use computers more frequently than older people.

Wearable Computers

Ever more portable computers are being developed by the IT industry. One goal is to make more wearable computers. A **wearable computer** is a small portable computer designed to be used while it is worn on the body. Some can be worn as wristbands; others work as headsets or clip onto a belt or backpack. For example, portable music players may be able to understand and record speech by workers who need to take dictation.

Open-Source Systems An *operating system* is the basic set of programs and utilities that make your computer run. Users can modify and redistribute open-source operating systems such as Linux®. *What are some issues that computer users should consider before using open-source systems?*

Technology in Manufacturing

Computers have also made a difference in the way products are designed and made. **Computer-aided design (CAD)** is software for designing products with a computer. With CAD, engineers can design without paper. They can change designs quickly and easily. By using CAD and computer-aided manufacturing (CAM) programs together, companies can custom-design and make products.

Most manufacturing plants are partly automated. Robots and computer-controlled machine tools do much of the work. They can do many of the hard or monotonous jobs that were done by people in the past, freeing workers to direct the robots and machine tools. Workers usually receive technical training to do these jobs.

Electronic Information Transfer

Electronic information transfer allows tasks to be done quicker. For example, many companies electronically transfer paychecks to employees' bank accounts. A national sales manager uses electronic mail to **transmit** sales figures to regional managers. Consumers use electronic information transfer, too. They can use an **automatic** teller machine (ATM) or their own computer to transfer funds from one bank account to another.

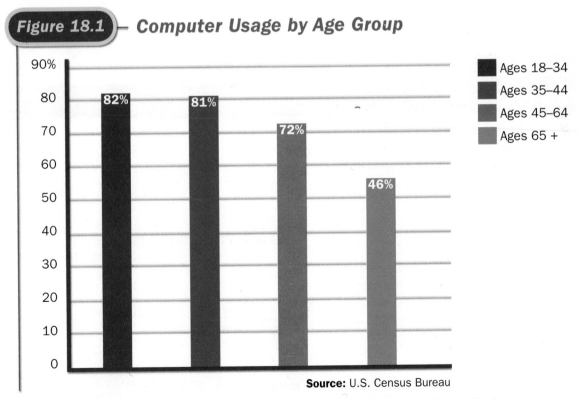

Figure 18.1 — *Computer Usage by Age Group*

Ages 18–34
Ages 35–44
Ages 45–64
Ages 65 +

82%
81%
72%
46%

Source: U.S. Census Bureau

● **Tools for Everyone** This chart shows the percentages of people in the United States who used computers in a recent year. **What changes do you predict will happen over the next several years in these figures?**

Virtual Training

Virtual training allows people to **simulate** a real situation using a computer. For instance, a computer-run flight simulation program allows pilots to learn how to fly aircraft. Pilots enter a room equipped with cockpit controls and a video screen, and practice flying the "aircraft." The screen shows them the results of their actions. The entire room is movable, with its motion controlled by a computer. In this case, virtual training offers pilots a safe way to learn to fly. Schools use computer-based science labs. Students try different science experiments using a computer. Menus allow them to choose chemicals to combine and tell them the amounts to use. Experiments done on computers are safe, with no danger involved if students make mistakes.

Virtual reality is also used in training. **Virtual reality** is an artificial, three-dimensional **visual** world created by a computer. In a *virtual world,* the computer re-creates places and actions that seem real. Users wear special goggles and fiber-optic gloves called data gloves. They enter and move about, and interact with objects as if inside the virtual world. The data gloves are the input devices, relaying movements of the user's hand to the computer. The senses of sight, sound, motion, and touch give the illusion of real objects or places. For example, in medical training, computers allow surgeons to practice procedures without real patients.

Section 18.1

After You Read

Review Key Concepts

1. What are some forms of information technology?
2. How has technology, especially mobile technology, changed the workplace?
3. What are some of the pros and cons of telecommuting?

Academic Skills

4. **Mathematics** At a Silicon Valley computer networking company, 17,000 people, or 47% of its workforce, telecommute for part or all of the workday. Write a sentence or two describing how you could determine the number of employees who do not telecommute.

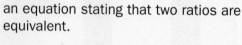 **CONCEPT** **Proportions** A proportion is an equation stating that two ratios are equivalent.

 For math help, go to the Math Appendix.

 Go to **connectED.mcgraw-hill.com** to check your answers.

Internet Basics

Reading Guide

Before You Read

Think about how the Internet and its components are used to access and communicate information.

Read to Learn

- Describe the Internet and its components.
- Identify tools for managing threats when using the Internet.

The Main Idea

The Internet has changed the way business is done. However, it poses risks to the information that is stored on computers. Companies and people must protect their computers from threats.

Key Concepts

- The Internet
- Managing Technology Threats

Vocabulary

Key Terms

Internet
World Wide Web
Web browser
search engine
intranet
extranet
hacker
cookies
virus

Academic Vocabulary

You will find these words in your reading and on your tests. Make sure you know their meanings.

guidelines   reject
authorized   insert

Graphic Organizer

In a figure like the one below, define intranet in the left circle and extranet in the right circle. Write notes about similarities among intranets and extranets in the area where the two circles overlap.

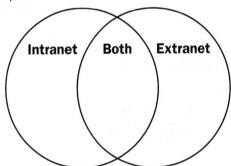

Intranet   Both   Extranet

 Go to **connectED.mcgraw-hill.com** to print out this graphic organizer.

The Internet

The **Internet** is a global computer network. It connects many computer networks, allowing information to flow freely around the world. People access the Internet through their telephone lines or digital subscriber line (DSL) service, which provides a high-speed connection. Other high-speed connections can be established over cable or Ethernet connections. These connections are possible through modems, devices used to send data from one computer to another.

✔ Reading Check **Explain** What is the Internet?

The World Wide Web

The World Wide Web is part of the Internet. The **World Wide Web** (or simply the Web) is a system for accessing, changing, and downloading a large set of hypertext-linked documents and other files located on computers connected through the Internet. *Hypertext* is a computer language that allows Internet users to access stored images, text, and other files. It enables direct links to related text, images, sound, and other data.

Business Case Study

The Future Is in the Cloud

Cloud computing saves money and enhances collaboration

Have you heard of cloud computing? It means accessing software and files from "the cloud"—computers that are linked together through the Internet. Today, most business software is based on cloud computing; just think of Gmail or Dropbox.

Before cloud computing, companies relied on software installed on employees' computers. They also stored files on-site on their own servers or on physical media such as hard drives or DVD-ROMs.

Today's cloud software and storage services are typically offered by subscription. Businesses or individual users pay a fee to use the service as long as it is needed. The software company is responsible for keeping the software up-to-date and for backing up files so they are not lost. Cloud software applications can also improve collaboration, because they enable team members in any location to work together on shared files and projects. Cloud computing saves businesses an average of 24 percent annually, according to a recent poll.

The downside of cloud computing is that businesses lose hands-on control of their software and files. That's why experts recommend that businesses keep local copies of important data.

Active Learning

You likely use cloud applications for all kinds of computing—storing data, sharing files, communicating with friends and family. You might even use a cloud app for composing reports and other schoolwork. Research your own IT use to make a list of all the cloud apps that you use. Do online research if you're unsure whether a particular app is cloud-based. Share your list with the class.

Science/Tech**TRENDS**

Ergonomics

Ergonomics is the understanding of how the interaction of humans and other elements in a system or setting affects people's health. The study of ergonomics goes back to the 1700s, when Italian physician Bernardino Ramazzinni published "De Morbis Artificum (Diseases of Workers)." During World War II, ergonomics was first used in the design of products to reduce workplace medical issues. At that time, ergonomically designed cockpit controls were invented and greatly reduced the sort of pilot error that led to plane crashes. In the time since WWII, the study of ergonomics has grown a great deal. With so many people using computers today, new health challenges have surfaced. It is the task of the designers to create technological tools that not only accomplish their purpose but also keep us healthy.

Web**Quest**

Locate Web sites where you can research the different ways that ergonomics can be applied in the design of products. Look at examples of things in various fields. Write a few paragraphs about how items are designed ergonomically and the health concerns they are intended to affect.

Who Sets Standards for the Internet? The Internet is not owned or controlled by any one person or country. The World Wide Web Consortium (W3C) is an international association in which member organizations, a full-time staff, and the public work together to develop Web standards. The group oversees research and sets standards and **guidelines** for many areas of the Internet. More than 500 organizations from around the world are members of W3C.

The Web connects sources of information. However, there are too many Web sites for people to visit. To access the information they need, computer users use Web browsers and search engines.

A **Web browser** is a program used for displaying and viewing pages on the Web. The inclusion of design, graphics, and sound on the Web makes it more enjoyable to *surf,* or search for information. Browsers include Mozilla Firefox®, Google Chrome®, and Microsoft Internet Explorer®. A **search engine** is a computer program that can produce a list of documents related to a given topic. Users find information that they need by giving the search engine a key word. The search engine then sifts through countless Web pages and creates a list of documents related to the key word. Some search engines are Yahoo!®, Google®, and Bing®.

Collaboration Software Many businesspeople find they can communicate better with their customers and employees using collaboration software. WebEx™, Microsoft's Live Meeting®, and IBM Lotus Sametime® are some types of this software. *What do you think are some advantages of collaboration software?*

Intranets and Extranets

Unlike the Internet, an intranet is closed to access by the public. An **intranet** is a computer network used by an organization. It works like the Internet, but its access is restricted to **authorized** users. A company might keep its employee directory and code of ethics on an intranet. An **extranet** is an extension of the intranet of a company or organization. It gives authorized users controlled access to the intranet. This semi-private network allows more than one company to access the same information. With an extranet, companies can share information and collaborate.

✔ **Reading Check** **Contrast** What is the difference between an intranet and an extranet?

Managing Technology Threats

Privacy and security risks are threats to users of computer technology. A **hacker** is a person who illegally gains access to and sometimes tampers with information in a computer system. Internet users are especially open to security risks. To avoid privacy and security threats, do not click on pop-up ads unless you know and trust the company. These ads may not be secure.

Privacy Issues

Companies use software tools to track computer users online. Many Web sites that users visit send cookies to their computer. **Cookies** are bits of information about a computer user that are stored on that computer's hard drive. The information is accessed by a server when the user revisits a Web site. Users who visit online stores can have their personal information stored even if they do not buy anything. Some computer users see cookies as a convenience. Others see them as an invasion of privacy. Those who do not want companies to store and use their personal information must **reject** or delete cookies.

As You Read

Think about how cookies affect you when you surf the Internet.

● **Computer Protection** As more companies' computer networks are connected to the Internet, the need for computer security has become increasingly important. **What types of protection are available?**

iStockphoto.com/GodfriedEdelman

Protection for Data A computer **virus** is a program that can **insert** copies of itself into a computer without the user's knowledge, often damaging stored data. Viruses are a problem for computer users. They may do little harm, or they may destroy computer files. A worm is a special virus that invades a computer network and multiplies itself as it spreads throughout the network. Security programs such as anti-virus software protect against different types of viruses. New viruses are created every day, so updates of anti-virus software must be installed regularly.

Spyware is software that tracks what a user does on the Internet. Users can download free software or buy special software to prevent spyware. Some software packages offer several kinds of protection.

Software packages can protect users from other types of security threats. A *firewall* is computer software that prevents unauthorized access to system software or data on a user's computer. It acts as a security wall between your computer and the Internet. Firewalls can also reduce spam. *Spam* is unwanted e-mail.

A security breach occurs when someone manages to obtain unauthorized access to your system. Finding and fixing the security breach can be time-consuming and costly.

Section 18.2

After You Read

Review Key Concepts
1. How would you describe the Internet and the World Wide Web?
2. How does a search engine work?
3. How can a computer user protect against spam, viruses, worms, and spyware?

Academic Skills
4. **English Language Arts** Choose a type of technology that is important to business such as cell phones, telecommuting, WiFi, wearable computers, or expert systems. Research the technology so that you can describe how it is used in a business setting, the solutions it offers, and how you think it will develop in the future. Present a brief oral presentation or write a three- or four-paragraph paper about your topic.

5. **English Language Arts** Imagine that the company you work for has grown, and your manager has decided to switch from an older system of independent computers to one in which each worker's computer is linked to a network with Internet access. Write a list of the advantages a network offers and the precautions to take to keep company information secure.

 Go to **connectED.mcgraw-hill.com** to check your answers.

Section 18.1 *Summary*

Information Technology Information technology (IT) has changed the way business is done. Computers are an important part of IT. So are telephones, fax machines, PDAs, and other handheld devices. Wireless technology lets people with a wireless-enabled computer or PDA connect to the Internet. E-mail lets them communicate with others electronically. Wearable computers help workers to become more mobile. All of these technologies enable business to be done more quickly and easily. Telecommuting can help employees decrease their travel time. Virtual training lets people simulate real situations using a computer to help them learn new tasks.

Section 18.2 *Summary*

Internet Basics The Internet connects many computer networks. It allows information to flow freely around the world. The World Wide Web is part of the Internet. The Web consists of stored files and images. A Web browser is a program that displays Web pages. Users find information they need by giving key words to a search engine, which produces a list of Web pages related to the key words. Some companies use intranets and extranets as ways of communicating with their employees. Computers can be threatened by privacy and security risks. Security programs such as anti-virus software protect against threats.

Vocabulary Review

1. On a sheet of paper, use each of these key terms and academic vocabulary terms in a sentence.

Key Terms		Academic Vocabulary
information technology (IT)	Web browser	transmit
telecommunications	search engine	automatic
telecommuting	intranet	simulate
wearable computer	extranet	visual
computer-aided design (CAD)	hacker	guidelines
virtual reality	cookies	authorized
Internet	virus	reject
World Wide Web		insert

Review Key Concepts

2. Describe the role of information technology in business.

3. Identify ways that technology has changed the workplace.

4. Describe the Internet and its components.

5. Identify tools for managing threats when using the Internet.

Critical Thinking

6. Wireless technology, which makes it possible to transfer information without cables, is less secure than wired technology. What risks do people take when they use wireless technology?

7. What are some reasons why a company might encourage an employee to telecommute?

8. How is the workforce affected by technical advances developed for manufacturing processes?

9. The electronic transfer of information has replaced much of the paper used in offices. What are some benefits of using less paper in the office?

10. Virtual reality is used by business for training. What is another way that virtual reality is used?

11. What kinds of technology are involved in tracking an online order?

12. Computer users can delete cookies from their machines. When do you think you would delete cookies?

13. Suppose you are hired to work in an office that uses the latest technology related to its business. How would you prepare to use new technology?

Write About It

14. With mobile technology, workers can be in touch with their workplace all the time. Write an e-mail to your teacher about the pros and cons of mobile technology.

15. Research the work of a computer software engineer. Write a one-page report that describes this career.

16. Look up future trends in technology that will affect the workplace. Write a 500-word article for your school newspaper on the impact some of these trends may have on the business world.

17. People who work with computers in business are often referred to as knowledge workers. Write at least two paragraphs describing the relationship between computers and knowledge in business.

18. Telephones are often used in customer service. Write a skit that involves using the telephone to resolve a customer complaint. Present your skit in class.

19. Research the different types of electronic communications that businesses use, including videoconferencing and telephone conferencing. Write a one-page report on your findings.

Technology Applications

Research Security Software

20. Using the Internet, research companies that provide security software packages. Use the information you collect to develop a database of software information. Include prices and facts about the types of security risks each company's products address.

Business Ethics

Ethical Computer Use

21. Explain why the following statements about the ethical use of computers are true. (1) Computer users should respect the privacy of other users' computer files. (2) You do not have a right to share software with your friends. (3) It is your responsibility to secure your computer. (4) Information on a Web site does not always belong to the Web site owner.

Chapter 18 Review and Activities

Applying Academics to Business

English Language Arts

22. As new technologies come into use, new words are added to the English language to describe them. Below are several terms that have come into common usage in recent years. Write a definition for each, and tell something about its origin.

blog   dodgy   domain   hot spot

Mathematics

23. An executive at a large telecommunications company claimed that $1.9 billion in operating expenses could be saved if the company merged with a competitor. What is the place value of the 9 in 1.9 billion? Write your answer in two ways.

CONCEPT **Place Value** In the base 10 number system we use most often, each place in a number has a value that is a power of 10. The value of a number in the ones place is 10^0; the value of a number in the tens place is 10^1; the value of a number in the hundreds place is 10^2, and so on.

English Language Arts

24. An appositive describes words or phrases that refer to the same person or thing and have the same relationship to other parts of the sentence. Combine each pair of sentences below by using an appositive. Use commas correctly.

Microsoft Internet Explorer is a program that makes it easier to search for information on the Internet. Microsoft Internet Explorer is a Web browser.

Expert systems are applications that store the kind of knowledge that humans use. Expert systems are used in many businesses.

Mathematics

25. A cell tower has an effective range of between 0.5 mile and 5 miles. What is the minimum and maximum coverage area for the cell tower?

CONCEPT **Area** The range represents the radius and is the distance from the center of a circle to any point on the circle. To find the minimum and maximum areas, find the area of the circles. The area of a circle can be found using the formula $A = \pi r^2$.

Active Learning

Create a Computer-Use Policy

26. Many companies develop a policy on the personal use of computers at work. Rules that restrict workers from visiting certain Web sites or downloading software help to protect computer networks from security risks. Pair up with a classmate. Imagine that you are the co-owners of a small delivery service. Write a policy on employees' use of computers at work. Be sure to consider telecommuters.

Business in the Real World

Technology's Effect on Business

27. Interview a small-business owner in your community to learn how technology affects his or her business. What changes have been made because of information technology? What additional expenses were incurred? Is the Internet used for business? If so, how? After the interview, prepare a summary of your results, and share it with your class.

Real LIFE skills

TELECOMMUTING HABITS AND SKILLS

28. Some employees choose to telecommute. Telecommuters usually work at home at least one day a week. Create a list of habits and skills that you think are important to a technical writer who telecommutes. Include the personal characteristics and technical skills that would be important for someone who works at home. Be prepared to share your list in class.

 **Business CAREERS**

FIND YOUR DREAM JOB

29. Locate the Occupational Outlook Handbook Web site. Click on the "OOH Search/A-Z Index" link and enter the job title "computer systems analysts." Then write a one-page report about this type of occupation. Conclude your report with a list of things you could do now to prepare yourself to pursue the occupation.

Role Play

USING THE INTERNET SAFELY

30. Situation You have been asked to give a short presentation to a group of consumers about proper procedures for shopping online. Most of your audience members have not used the Internet for online shopping.

Activity Prepare an outline of your presentation, stressing ways to use the Internet. Give your audience some "do's and don'ts" about Internet use.

Evaluation You will be evaluated on how well you meet the following performance indicators:

- Explain the advantages and disadvantages of shopping online.
- Explain concepts such as security software, a secure Web site, a Web site shopping cart, cookies, and online payment.
- List at least three guidelines to follow when shopping online.
- Prepare a written outline of your presentation.

Standardized Test Practice

Directions Choose the letter of the best answer. Write the letter for the answer on a separate piece of paper.

1. Which is a synonym for *virtual*?

   A   secondary

   B   actual

   C   precise

   D   near

 TEST-TAKING TIP Real learning occurs through studying that takes place over a period of time. Relate the information you are learning to what you already know, and you will be better able to understand and retain it. Plan more than one review session.

Chapter 19

Computer Basics

Chapter Objectives After completing this chapter, you will be able to:

▶ **Section 19.1** *Computer Hardware*
- **Describe** some ways that people use computers.
- **Identify** the parts of a computer system.

▶ **Section 19.2** *Computer Software*
- **List** some types of software.

Ask AN EXPERT

Stock Buying Strategies

Q: What are some strategies I can use to acquire stocks if I'm investing for the long term?

A: There are many different stock strategies floating around out there. Value investing involves purchasing stocks considered undervalued by one or more fundamental measures. Growth investing focuses on companies that have quickly increased their earnings or revenues. Market-timing investors aggressively buy and sell based on their prediction of whether a stock will go up or down. For example, daytraders buy and sell with all activity occurring within a single day. But for a long-term investor, a strategy such as dollar cost averaging makes the most sense. You invest a fixed amount of money in the same stock or stocks on a regular basis. In this way you establish a position in a stock over a long, steady period of time. During that time, the stock price is likely to fluctuate, and you can take advantage of periods of weakness by buying more shares for the same amount of money.

Mathematics You are investing $180 each month in stock in the McKay Brick Company. The stock sells for $6 in January, and drops to $5 in February and $4 in March. How many shares do you buy over the three months?

CONCEPT **Dollar Cost Averaging** Since you are spending a fixed amount each month, the number of shares you can buy varies with the price.

● **Computer Applications** Businesses use many different types of software applications. **What software applications do you use on your computer that a business might also use?**

Computer Hardware

Reading Guide

Before You Read

Think about the ways you use computer systems for your personal use.

Read to Learn

- Describe some ways that people use computers.
- Identify the parts of a computer system.

The Main Idea

Each day, businesses and individuals use computers to perform different tasks. Desktop computers, laptops, tablet PCs, and handheld devices allow many tasks to be done easily and quickly. Hardware enables a computer system to function properly.

Key Concepts

- The Importance of Computers
- Parts of a Computer System

Vocabulary

Key Terms

computer
ergonomics
e-learning
hardware
random access memory (RAM)

Academic Vocabulary

You will find these words in your reading and on your tests. Make sure you know their meanings.

linked   element
quotes   random

Graphic Organizer

In a figure like the one below, list four components of a computer's hardware system.

Hardware

1. _____
2. _____
3. _____
4. _____

 Go to **connectED.mcgraw-hill.com** to print out this graphic organizer.

The Importance of Computers

People depend on computers to handle all kinds of tasks. When a person pays a bill online, buys gasoline, or withdraws money from a bank, computers handle the transactions. Computers also handle different tasks in the workplace. Businesses of all sizes use computers to collect data and keep track of records. Laptops and tablet PCs allow people to work outside the office. Handheld devices track appointments, telephone numbers, and other data. Most businesses consider computers to be essential.

Computers for Business

A **computer** is an electronic device that accepts, processes, stores, and outputs data at high speeds, based on programmed instructions. A *personal computer,* or PC, is a small computer that is intended to be used by one person. A *desktop computer* is a personal computer that is small enough to fit in an individual workspace. PCs and desktop computers are generally the same. Dell and Hewlett-Packard are two of the world's top PC makers. Apple is also a leading computer maker. Its Macintosh systems are personal computers, too. However, they are usually called "Macs" rather than PCs.

In most companies, computers are **linked** through either a central mainframe computer or a network. A *mainframe* is a fast, powerful computer with a large storage capacity. It can accommodate several users at the same time. Linking workstations allows users to share files, data, and printers, send e-mails, and access the Internet.

Computers in Marketing Nielsen Media Research® is the top media researcher in the United States. It is best known for its TV ratings. Nielsen uses small computers to gather data from 10,000 TV meters placed in U.S. homes. They record the viewing activities of participants and transmit these records nightly to Nielsen. *Why are computers important in this type of research?*

ThinkStock/SuperStock

● **Digital Security** Biometric devices such as this fingerprint reader can be used to limit access to computers and data. **How can these devices save time, too?**

?ETHICS in Business

Intellectual Property

- **Critical Reading** Life is full of important decisions. Think about the kinds of decisions that you make as you read the question below.

  You work in the human resources department of a large computer company. The company is developing a new software platform, but the developers are having problems working out the bugs, and the project is behind schedule. Your manager asked you to contact a friend who works in the information technology department of a competitor to see if she would be interested in joining your company. You find out that she is working on a secret project that's very similar and would surely be able to help you solve your problems.

- **Decision Making** Is it appropriate to hire a competitor's employee who can help you solve a problem even if it means she will use your competitor's company secrets to do it? Explain your answer.

• As You Read

Think about special computers and how they might affect your work. If you worked in a graphic arts studio, what type of computer do you think you would need?

The Computer Workstation A well-organized computer workstation is important for both business and home use. **Ergonomics** are design factors for the workplace that are intended to maximize productivity by minimizing a worker's discomfort. Well-designed workstations can help workers reduce stress and avoid straining their eyes, neck, shoulders, and wrists. They also help to increase efficiency.

To create a safe and comfortable computer workstation:

- Place the tools you need most close to you.
- Place your monitor at or just below eye level and at arm's length.
- Keep your wrists straight when you type.
- Use a chair that is adjustable, and keep it at a height that suits you.
- Position your chair so that it supports your lower back.
- Keep your feet flat on the floor or on a footrest.

Computers as Learning Tools Businesses also use computers to provide workers with the information, tools, and training they need to do their job. **E-learning**, or electronic learning, is the process of learning online. For instance, a large insurance company uses a Web-based system to train new employees to handle **quotes** and claims. Some training companies specialize in online education and tutorials for workers. Training with simulation software lets employees practice new tasks at their own pace. With e-learning, workers can be trained in an efficient and cost-effective way.

Parts of a Computer System

A computer system includes three main parts: hardware, software, and data. The physical components of a computer system are the **hardware**. Computer systems include at least four hardware **elements**: a microprocessor; memory; input and output devices; and data storage devices. Computers control data made up of characters, sound, graphics, and numbers. Here is a closer look at the parts of the system.

> ✔ **Reading Check** **Identify** What are the three main parts of a computer system?

Microprocessors

A *microprocessor* is a small computer chip. It is the brain of a computer. It is also called the central processing unit (CPU), or microchip. A microprocessor receives instructions and carries them out at extremely high speeds. Each chip contains millions of circuits for data storage. A circuit is an electrical device that provides a path for the flow of electricity. Devices such as calculators, PDAs, electronic toys, and mobile phones also use computer chips.

Memory

Memory is hardware that stores information for instant retrieval and processing. It can be thought of as a kind of scratch pad. The computer uses its **random access memory (RAM)** to hold all the data and instructions required during operations. When a computer is using information, it stores it in **random** access memory. As long as your computer is on, the information remains in this temporary memory so that the computer can use it quickly. As soon as you turn off the computer, RAM loses information. For that reason, data storage devices are a very important part of a computer.

Real World

Fast Times Intel® Corp. is the world's leading developer of microprocessors. It makes chips that can handle billions of instructions per second. Still, the company strives to make its chips even faster and more powerful to meet market demands. *Why do chip makers seek ways to make their products faster and more powerful?*

sot/Getty Images

● **Portable Hardware**
Laptop computers contain several hardware devices in a single product. **Where are the input devices on this computer? Where are the output devices?**

As You Read

Think about some input and output devices in your home or school and ways that you use them.

Input and Output Devices

An *input device* is hardware that is used for entering data into a machine, such as a computer. Input devices include keyboards, computer mice, touchpads, joysticks, and scanners. An *output device* is hardware that is used for producing results from a machine. Output devices include computer monitors, printers, fax machines, and speakers.

Data Storage Devices

There are a variety of devices for storing large amounts of data. *Data storage devices*—which include hard drives, CD-ROM drives, and DVD drives—save information for later use. Portable storage devices are also popular because they can easily be moved from one machine to another. Disks, flash drives, portable hard drives, and DVDs are widely used for portable storage. Data storage helps to protect important information. Data storage is measured in

- kilobytes (1,024 bytes),
- megabytes (1,024 kilobytes),
- gigabytes (1,024 megabytes), and
- terabytes (1,024 gigabytes).

Section 19.1

After You Read

Review Key Concepts

1. What are some ways that people use computers at work?
2. What are the parts of a computer system?
3. Name five data storage devices.

Academic Skills

4. **Mathematics** *Kilo-, mega-, giga-, tera-,* and *peta-* are prefixes used to note the quantity of something, such as a bit in computing. Sometimes called *prefix multipliers*, these prefixes can denote powers of 10. For example, bits per second is a measurement used to express the transmission rate of data. 1 kbps (1 kilobit per second) is 1×10^3 bits per second. Express 10^3, 10^4, and 10^5 as numbers in standard form.

 CONCEPT **Exponents** An exponent tells how many times the base number is multiplied by itself.

Math For math help, go to the Math Appendix.

 Go to **connectED.mcgraw-hill.com** to check your answers.

Computer Software

Reading Guide

Before You Read

Think about the different types of software that businesses and people use.

Read to Learn

• List some types of software.

The Main Idea

Without software, a computer is just a collection of parts. Software tells a computer what to do. Programs such as word-processing and spreadsheet applications allow the creation of documents for business and personal use.

Key Concept

• Software Programs

Vocabulary

Key Terms

software
operating system
word processing
spreadsheet

database management
presentation program
desktop publishing

 Go to **connectED.mcgraw-hill.com** to print out this graphic organizer.

Academic Vocabulary

You will find these words in your reading and on your tests. Make sure you know their meanings.

creating
incorporate

schedules
facilitate

Graphic Organizer

In a figure like the one below, list and describe 10 different types of software.

Software	Purpose
1.	
2.	
3.	
4.	
5.	
6.	
7.	
8.	
9.	
10.	

Software Programs

Computers are just machines. They cannot do anything without instruction from people. **Software** is a computer program that contains a set of instructions that tells a computer what to do. Software is also referred to as a program or an application. Some software programs tell a computer how to calculate numbers or arrange words.

Operating Systems

An **operating system** is software that controls the operation of a computer and directs the processing of programs. It maintains files, runs software applications, and handles devices such as a computer mouse and printer. The most widely used operating system is Microsoft Windows®. Windows-based PCs are used in most businesses and perform many tasks, such as **creating** word processing documents, presentations, and spreadsheets. Apple uses its own operating system, called OS X. Newer Macs can also run using the Windows operating system. Macs are often used to create graphic designs and illustrations.

Business Case Study

Smartphones for Science

Open-source software uses phone photos to advance botany.

Picture a scientist out in the field and you might imagine her carrying all kinds of specialized, expensive equipment. Using new software, however, a scientist might need nothing more than her phone to do cutting-edge research.

To study crops and ecosystems, botanists calculate a measurement called "specific leaf area." They measure the leaf cover in a space to see how crops, trees, and other plants grow in their environment. New software, called Easy Leaf Area, uses smartphone photos to make the process easier, faster, and less destructive to plants. The software scans researchers' photos, separates out the area of leaves, then analyzes the data.

Botanist Hsien Ming Easlon, who helped develop Easy Leaf Area, hopes the software will allow botanists to do better, more efficient research. He also sees potential for applying the tool to other types of study. Smartphones, he says, have "great potential to replace many single-purpose devices for scientific data collection."

Active Learning

Easy Leaf Area is a freely downloadable, editable type of software known as open source. Do online research to learn more about open-source software and how it differs from proprietary software. Write a one-page summary of your findings, including examples of both open-source and proprietary software.

334   Chapter 19   Computer Basics

Office Suites

A *suite* is a collection of integrated application programs or software applications that works as a single program. In a suite, each program can **incorporate** data from the others, eliminating the need to re-enter or transfer data. An office suite usually includes word-processing, spreadsheet, database management, presentation, and communications software. Microsoft Office®, Corel® WordPerfect Office®, and Google Docs are office suites.

✔ Reading Check **Define** What is a suite?

Application Programs Application programs handle different tasks. Each type of application program performs a specific function for the user. **Word processing** is the writing, editing, and production of documents, such as letters and reports, through the use of a computer program. Word-processing software, such as Microsoft Word, is used to create, edit, and print documents. A **spreadsheet** program is a computerized worksheet for entering and charting data. Sales figures, quantities, prices, and production costs can be listed and compared with a spreadsheet.

Science/Tech**TRENDS**

Heads-Up Display

A Heads-Up display, or HUD as it is commonly known, is any display that doesn't alter the user's view when it displays data. HUD was first used in military aircraft but can now be seen in a wide variety of applications. Many games include HUDs. One example is the speedometers and instrument panels on the screen in racing games. The two types of HUD are fixed and helmet-mounted. The fixed type would typically be mounted to a surface such as an aircraft's airframe. The helmet-mounted display moves with the user's head. The user must wear a helmet or other headgear that is secured to the head. Two characteristics of any HUD are that the image is transparent, and the information is projected with its focus at infinity, which allows users to change their focus of attention between the data and the outside world without having to refocus their eyes.

Web Quest

Locate Web sites where you can research different applications of Heads-Up displays. Look for ways HUD has helped the industries in which they are used. Write a few paragraphs describing what you find.

A **database management** program is used to store data organized especially for rapid search and retrieval. With database software, lists can be updated, changed, or rearranged. A **presentation program** includes software for creating slide shows for presentations. Data from word-processing documents and spreadsheets can be put into graphs, charts, or figures as part of a presentation.

Desktop publishing software is used to produce publications such as reports, newsletters, and magazines. A user can write, design, and lay out documents on a computer like a professional publisher. Users can create high-quality publications with art and illustrations. Desktop publishing software can be a part of an office suite. Adobe® InDesign® is a desktop publishing software package. The illustration below shows some of the options available in Microsoft Office Publisher, which is also used for desktop publishing.

There are many other types of software that businesses depend on in their day-to-day operations. *Accounting software* helps people keep accurate records and prepare reports. Intuit® QuickBooks® is a well-known accounting program. *Communications software* allows access to databases, accounts, schedules, and other shared files. It makes it possible for computers to communicate or transfer files. With communications software, users can receive faxes and voice mail directly on their computer. Microsoft Outlook® is a communications program. *Speech recognition software* allows a user to enter text and give commands to the computer by speaking into a microphone. Philips® SpeechExec Pro® is a speech recognition program.

● **Software Options**
Many software programs come with preformatted templates for you to customize. **What software templates have you used?**

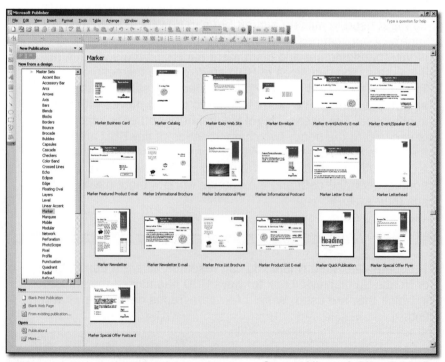

Source: Microsoft Office Publisher

Groupware

Groupware is project management software. It provides tools for groups of users on a computer network to plan, develop, and complete a project. Team members on the same network can use groupware to track costs, schedules, and tasks for a project.

There are three categories of groupware: communication tools, conferencing tools, and collaborative management (or coordination) tools. Communication tools send messages, files, data, or documents between people. Examples include e-mail, faxing, voice mail, and Web publishing. Conferencing tools also **facilitate** the sharing of information, but in a more interactive way. Internet forums, chat rooms, and videoconferencing are conferencing tools. Collaborative management tools facilitate and manage group activities. They include electronic calendars (or time management software) and project management software.

Web Site Development Programs

The Internet plays an important part in many businesses' ability to reach consumers around the world. Web pages make it possible for companies to market their goods and services globally. Web site development programs allow users to choose from several templates or designs, or to customize their site according to their needs. Adobe Dreamweaver® and Microsoft WebMatrix® are Web site development programs.

Section 19.2

After You Read

Review Key Concepts
1. What is software?
2. Name three types of software programs and their purposes.
3. What kind of software is useful for managing team projects?

Academic Skills

4. **English Language Arts** Locate and read a review of a software program commonly used in or designed for use in business. Write a one-paragraph summary of the review. Explain what the software is designed to do, describe its positive and negative characteristics, and tell whether the reviewer recommends the software.

5. **English Language Arts** Work in groups of four. Choose a category of software. List four to six popular software programs that fit within the category you have chosen. Use software to create a chart showing cost, features, benefits, and the availability of each program.

 Go to **connectED.mcgraw-hill.com** to check your answers.

Section 19.1 *Summary*	Section 19.2 *Summary*
Computer Hardware People and businesses depend on computers to handle all kinds of tasks. Computers record data and keep track of records. Businesses also use them to provide workers with the information, tools, and training they need to do their jobs. Many people use a personal computer at home and at work, where they may be part of a network. A computer system includes three main parts: hardware, software, and data. Its physical components make up the hardware. The four hardware elements found in each computer system—a processor; memory; input and output devices; and storage devices—enable a computer to function as needed.	**Computer Software** A computer needs instructions to perform tasks. Software tells it what to do. There are many different types of software. An operating system is software that controls the operation of a computer. It maintains files, runs software applications, and handles devices such as computer mice and printers. Application programs handle specific task-oriented functions. Word-processing software is used to create, edit, and print documents. Spreadsheet software is an electronic worksheet for entering and charting data. These and other forms of software allow users to do certain tasks easily and quickly.

Vocabulary Review

1. On a sheet of paper, use each of these key terms and academic vocabulary terms in a sentence.

Key Terms

computer
ergonomics
e-learning
hardware
random access memory
   (RAM)
software

operating system
word processing
spreadsheet
database management
presentation program
desktop publishing

Academic Vocabulary

linked   creating
quotes   incorporate
elements   schedules
random   facilitate

Review Key Concepts

2. Describe some ways that people use computers.

3. Identify the parts of a computer system.

4. List some types of software.

Critical Thinking

5. If you leave high school with very few computer skills, what problems might you face in the future?

6. What advice would you give users about protecting information on their computer?

7. A *chat room* is a form of groupware that lets computer users communicate instantly. What are some advantages and disadvantages of using chat rooms?

8. What can companies that make computer hardware and other items do to improve ergonomics?

9. Why is a microprocessor called the "brain of a computer"?

10. Describe the ways e-learning helps business. Do you think e-learning will become more or less popular in the future? Explain your answer.

11. Some people list four components of computer systems: hardware, software, data, and *people.* Why do you think it is important to include people as part of the system?

12. What types of businesses can you think of that do not use computers or that use them infrequently?

13. Discuss some ways to make sure both the classroom and computer equipment are safe.

Write About It

14. With two classmates, research ways to avoid computer problems. Use software to prepare a demonstration presentation on tips for keeping your computer running smoothly.

15. Ask family members and friends about the ways they use computers and the types of software they use. Write a report of at least one page about your findings.

16. Interview someone who works with your school's computer system. Ask him or her about the types of problems that occur and how they are addressed. Write a one-page article based on your interview.

17. Technology usually improves an old invention. In two or more paragraphs, describe how the PC improved on the typewriter.

18. List ways in which business software may be used. Include the types of documents that can be created using software.

19. Research speech recognition software. How does it work? Why do businesses use it? What type of equipment is needed to use speech recognition? Write a one-page report on your findings.

Technology Applications

Software Programs

20. Go to a computer lab or use your own computer to research database, spreadsheet, presentation, scheduling, and integrated software packages. Use tutorials, online help, or information from the software maker to find out how each can be used to enhance communications. Then write a report of at least one page on your findings.

Business Ethics

Using Computers Ethically

21. Ethics are the principles and standards we use to decide how to act. Your behavior while using a computer is also guided by ethics. Team up with a classmate. Develop a list of at least three ethical situations and problems associated with computers. Then list possible reactions to these issues and problems.

Applying Academics to Business

English Language Arts

22. Biometric devices identify people by physical traits such as fingerprints, voices, and faces. Separate the word *biometric* into its prefix and base word. Write a definition of each part and list other words in which they appear. Then write a definition for the word *biometrics*.

Mathematics

23. The relationship between the width and height of a computer screen is 4:3. How could you use the Pythagorean theorem to figure out the length of the diagonal of a screen that is 15 inches in height?

CONCEPT **Geometry** The Pythagorean Theorem states that the square of the hypotenuse of a right triangle equals the sum of the squares of the lengths of the other two sides: $a^2 + b^2 = c^2$.

English Language Arts

24. Compound words are words made up of two or more parts, each of which can stand alone as a word. Compound words can often mean something very different from the meaning the two words would have if they were used separately. Skim the chapter, and list as many compound words as you can. Alphabetize your list.

Mathematics

25. Clarice bought a 128 MB memory chip and a 256 MB memory chip to upgrade the memory in her computer. List the factors of 128 and 256, and explain why 128 has an even number of factors and 256 has an odd number of factors.

CONCEPT **Factoring** Factors are the numbers you multiply to get another number.

Active Learning

Hold a Tech Fair

26. Work in small groups. Set up booths in your classroom for a tech fair. Each group should bring in a technology item or a picture of one. Categorize the hardware as an input, output, or storage device, or as other computer hardware. Decide ahead of time which device each group should bring. Be prepared to demonstrate or explain the item and answer questions about it. Afterward, write a short essay on what you learned about the different items.

Business in the Real World

Technology Product Development

27. Form groups. Go online to research a company that makes hardware or software. Contact the company for more information. Ask how it learns about ways that consumers use its products. How does it decide if something should be changed or discontinued? What does the company do when another company offers a new technology that is successful? Write a report on your findings. Present your report to the class.

Real LIFE skills

DEVELOPING KEYBOARDING SKILLS

28. Open a Microsoft Word file that contains a previous assignment. Click "Help" on the menu bar. Go to "Keyboard shortcuts for Word" and find the quick reference link. Practice using the shortcuts listed by retyping the first paragraph from your assignment. Include the following in a printout: Make the letters of the first word bold and italic; decrease the font size of the second word to 9 points; and increase the font size of the third word to 16 points.

Business CAREERS

FIND YOUR DREAM JOB

29. Locate the Occupational Outlook Handbook Web site. Click on the "OOH Search/A-Z Index" link and enter the job title "computer programmer." Then write a one-page report about this type of occupation. Conclude your report with a list of things you could do now to prepare yourself to pursue the occupation.

Role Play

USING SOFTWARE FEATURES

30. **Situation** You are the assistant information technology manager for a local newspaper. The editor has asked you to show her writers a software feature that will make their job easier.

Activity Plan and demonstrate how to use the feature. If necessary, use online help, tutorials, or manuals for the software.

Evaluation You will be evaluated on how well you meet the following performance indicators:

- Explain ways in which the feature can be used.
- Present the feature in steps that your audience can follow easily.
- Answer questions from your audience about the feature and how to use it.
- Prepare a written outline of the points of your presentation.
- Speak clearly and use correct grammar.

Standardized Test Practice

Directions Choose the letter of the best answer. Write the letter for the answer on a separate piece of paper.

1. **The hypotenuse of a triangle measures 20 mm. Which could be the lengths of the legs?**

   A   6 mm and 8 mm
   B   9 mm and 16 mm
   C   12 mm and 16 mm
   D   13 mm and 14 mm

TEST-TAKING TIP Make sure you do not read too much into test questions. Avoid imagining detailed scenarios in which the answer could be true. In most cases, "trick questions" are not as difficult as you think.

Antwanye Ford

President/CEO/Co-Founder, Enlightened Inc.

Andre Rogers

CFO/Co-Founder, Enlightened Inc.

Enlightened Inc. is an information technology consulting firm based in Washington, D.C. Friends and founders Antwanye Ford, Andre Rogers, and Thomas Spann met at George Washington University.

Q & A

Describe your job responsibilities.

Antwanye: As the President of the company, I am responsible for the general direction and vision of the company. This is done by establishing the corporate goals and objectives, and ensuring we have the necessary people in place to achieve those goals.

Andre: I am in charge of two main areas, all financial and administrative duties, and all technical projects. My daily duties include ensuring that projects are done on time and on budget, while making certain that the customer receives more than they expect.

What skills are most important in your business?

Antwanye: Passion, vision, belief in yourself, a thick skin, an ability to deal with failure, self-motivation, and persistence. Interpersonal and academic skills are also essential.

Andre: The most important aspect of being an entrepreneur is passion. There will be some things that a person would be natural at doing, while others would be a stretch. But drive and passion will allow a person to do both.

What is your key to success?

Antwanye: I believe that you must see what others cannot see, and see it as if it already exists.

Andre: Relationships have been key to obtaining customers. Delivering high-quality services and exceeding customers' expectations have allowed us to retain several of our customers for years.

What advice would you give students interested in starting a business?

Antwanye: You need to find something you have passion for beyond what money you might make.

Andre: If it is your passion, then do it! Don't let anything stop you. Learn as much as you can about your passion. Value your relationships. Find a mentor—no one knows everything.

Critical Thinking *Why is being known for a product or service—developing a brand identity—important to a company?*

Some Qualifications to be the Owner of an Information Technology Consulting Company

Academic Skills and Abilities

Computer science; mathematics; information systems; computer programming; interpersonal skills; general business management skills; verbal and written communication skills; multitasking, organizing, and planning skills

Academic Skills Required to Complete Tasks at Enlightened Inc.			
Tasks	**Math**	**Science**	**English Language Arts**
Hold meetings			◆
Assign duties			◆
Monitor developments in technology	◆	◆	◆
Assess marketplace opportunities	◆	◆	◆
Customer service	◆	◆	◆
Schedule employees	◆		◆
Order supplies and equipment	◆		◆
Analyze financials	◆		◆

Education and Training

Despite employers' preference for those with technical degrees, people with degrees in a variety of majors find employment in information technology. The level of education and the type of training that employers require depend on their needs. One factor affecting these needs is changes in technology.

Career Path

Computer scientists employed in private industry may advance into managerial or project leadership positions. Database administrators may advance into managerial positions on the basis of their experience managing data and enforcing security. Computer specialists with work experience and considerable expertise in a particular subject or a certain application may find lucrative opportunities as independent consultants or may choose to start their own computer consulting firms.

Preparing for a Career
Self-Assessment Checklist
Use this self-assessment checklist to help determine ways you can build your professionalism.

✔ Be informed about careers. Search the newspaper and the Internet for available jobs in your field of interest.

✔ Take advantage of resources available through teachers or your school's guidance counselor.

✔ Create a résumé that highlights your professional and personal strengths.

✔ Write a cover letter that advertises your best qualities.

✔ Utilize all your contacts for networking, including friends and family members.

✔ Prepare for interviews by researching the company and by dressing professionally.

✔ Have confidence in yourself and in your abilities.

✔ Be personable, professional, organized, and ready to take advantage of good opportunities.

Technology's Effect on Global Business

Improvements in technology have had an enormous impact on international trade. Information exchange that once took days or weeks now takes place in seconds with development of the Internet, fax machines, e-mail, and telecommunication advances.

Thematic Project Assignment

In this project you will conduct research and design a Web page that illustrates technology's effect on global business. Technology includes the Internet, fax machines, teleconferencing, digital TV, Web conferencing, and other technology used in international business.

Step 1 Brainstorm Skills You Need to Complete This Activity

Your success in designing your Web site depends on your skills. Preview the activity. Then brainstorm a list of the skills you will need to use to complete the activity and describe how you will use them. Skills you might use include:

Academic Skills	reading, writing, social studies
Basic Skills	speaking, listening, thinking, and interpersonal skills
Technology Skills	word processing, keyboarding, presentation, telecommunications, and Internet skills

@ *SKILLS PREVIEW* Go to connectED.mcgraw-hill.com to download a graphic organizer you can use to brainstorm the skills you will use to complete the project.

Step 2 Choose a Business and a Career That Interest You

Think of a business that you find interesting. Then think of a career related to the business that interests you. As you investigate technology's effects on global business, you will research the effects of technology on the business and career of your choice.

Step 3 Build Background Knowledge

Preview technology's effects on the global business that you will research.

Technology's Influence on Global Business

The 21st century has seen technology revolutionize global business. Today, the economies of many countries are based on international trade. E-commerce, or electronic commerce, has made it possible for businesses to directly reach customers anywhere in the world.

For example, the Internet allows a business in India to sell goods to a student in New Mexico. Telecommunications allows for corporate meetings to take place via TV screens with managers being in different parts of the world. Fax machines allow for contracts to be delivered, signed, and returned in a matter of minutes instead of days or weeks.

Step 4 Connect with Your Community

Interview an older family member about the advances in technology in his or her life-time. Find out what computers were like when he or she first entered the workplace. Ask how he or she communicated with other workers or companies.

Step 5 Research Technology's Effects on Global Business

Use library and Internet resources to research technology's effects on global business. Use the project research checklist as a guide to your research. Keep records of your sources of information.

Step 6 Develop a Web Site

Use word processing and other software to develop a Web site that includes all of the information described in the project checklist.

Technology's Effects on Global Business

✔ Write a summary that explains the effects of technology on global business. Include information that explains how technology helps companies become global.

✔ Make a list of the newest trends and products in technology that are used in business. Identify how the new products and developments impact the way global business is conducted.

✔ Explain how businesspeople can keep up with new developments in technology.

✔ Create a time line that illustrates technological advances in the last 50 years.

✔ Prepare a map of the world and illustrate it with graphics to show how the world is connected through technology.

✔ Use the Internet to find an article on a new technology that is being used in international business. Write a summary of the article. Include your source.

Self Connections

✔ Discuss the results of your research with a family member or other adult.

✔ Describe how technology effects the business and career in which you are interested.

✔ Explain what the investigation and its results mean to you.

Step 7 Evaluate Your Presentation

 RUBRIC Go to connectED.mcgraw-hill.com to download a rubric you can use to evaluate your final report.

Courtesy of Rachel Muir

Girlstart runs after-school programs, Saturday camps, and summer camps to empower girls in mathematics, science, and technology. At the end of this unit, you will learn about Girlstart® founder Rachel Muir and how she achieved her success.

Decision Making Have you started making decisions about the career you will pursue?

Unit 7 | *Thematic Project Preview*

Lifelong Learning After completing this unit, you will research to find out how lifelong learning will help you in your career throughout your life.

Project Checklist As you read the chapters in this unit, use this checklist to prepare for the unit project.

- ✔ Think about how changes in the world are affecting the job opportunities in the career of your choice.
- ✔ Think about how lifelong learning will increase job opportunities in adult education.
- ✔ Look for opportunities for adult learning experiences in your community and in different career choices.
- ✔ Consider how lifelong learning will affect your future.

Chapter 20

Career Planning

Chapter Objectives   After completing this chapter, you will be able to:

▶ Section 20.1 *Preparing for a Career*

- **Discuss** the importance of career planning.
- **Define** at least five attributes you should know about yourself when analyzing careers.
- **Describe** how work is changing.

▶ Section 20.2 *Developing a Career Plan*

- **Name** four sources where you can learn about careers.
- **Describe** some aspects of the working world that may affect a worker.
- **Define** short-, medium-, and long-term goals.
- **Identify** the three lists needed to make a career plan.

Ask AN EXPERT

Developing a Retirement Plan: IRAs

Q: How do I plan for my retirement?

A: While planning for retirement is something everyone should do, an alarming number of people never get around to opening even one retirement account. According to the Employee Benefit Research Institute (EBRI), 24 percent of workers with an annual income between $35,000 and $74,999 do not have a retirement account. IRAs, individual retirement accounts, are an extremely popular way to save for retirement. There are many kinds of IRAs, including the traditional IRA, which is tax-deductible, and the Roth IRA, which is nondeductible. It's important to start investing early. Be sure to allocate your assets appropriately, and don't touch what you've already put in! Many people borrow against what they've saved, promising themselves they'll replace the money later, but they never get around to doing so. Finally, it's a good idea to choose one or more beneficiaries for your investments.

Mathematics   How much will a Roth IRA be worth in 5 years if you invest $3,000 now? Assume a 20% future tax rate and 10 percent annual earnings.

CONCEPT   **Multiplying by a Decimal** To multiply by a decimal, count the total number of decimal places in the two numbers you are multiplying. Place the decimal point in the product by counting that number of places from the right.

● **Learning from Experience** One of the best ways to learn about occupations is to experience the work firsthand and talk to people about their jobs. **What lessons do you think you could learn from a more experienced worker?**

Echo/Getty Images

Preparing for a Career

Reading Guide

Before You Read

Think about the types of work that interest you and ways you can start preparing for a career.

Read to Learn

- Discuss the importance of career planning.
- Define at least five attributes you should know about yourself when analyzing careers.
- Describe how work is changing.

The Main Idea

Choosing a career is one of the most important decisions that you will make. Career planning can help put you on the right path. It involves considering your interests and skills.

Key Concepts

- Making Decisions About Work
- Self-Awareness
- How Work Is Changing

Vocabulary

Key Terms

full-time job	values
job	skill
occupation	ability
career	aptitude
interests	personality

Academic Vocabulary

You will find these words in your reading and on your tests. Make sure you know their meanings.

pursuing	via
overseas	adaptable

Graphic Organizer

In a graphic like the one shown, note five things you need to know about yourself before you begin career planning.

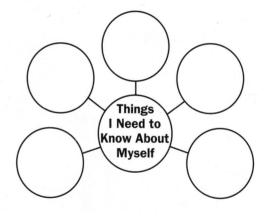

Things I Need to Know About Myself

 Go to **connectED.mcgraw-hill.com** to print out this graphic organizer.

Making Decisions About Work

Choosing a career is an important decision that everyone must make. The decision will affect the rest of your life. It will affect the amount of money you will earn. It will also affect the amount of satisfaction you will get from your work and life. A **full-time job** requires at least 40 hours of work every week. Most full-time workers spend 2,000 hours working each year. That is time you will want to spend doing something you enjoy.

Jobs and Careers

Work is essential to almost everyone's economic and social well-being. It includes jobs, occupations, and careers. A **job** or **occupation** is work that people engage in to earn pay. A **career** is a work history of one or more jobs in the same or related fields of interest. Each occupation in a career builds on interest, knowledge, training, and experience from the other jobs.

Pursuing a career requires career planning. *Career planning* consists of assessing your potential, analyzing your options, and preparing for the future. That preparation could include education or training as well as developing specialized skills or abilities.

✔ **Reading Check** **Contrast** What is the difference between a job and a career?

● **As You Read**
Think about some jobs you might like to do.

Self-Awareness

Before you start thinking about careers, you should note what interests you. Knowing yourself is a key part of your journey into the working world. Who are you? What do you value most? Answering these and other questions can help steer you down the right career path.

ColorBlind Images/Blend Images LLC

● **Careers in Aviation** Carefully consider the unique characteristics of the careers in which you are interested. **What is the work environment for people who work in commercial aviation?**

● **As You Read**

Your talents and hobbies are also part of your interests. Think about a particular talent you have or a hobby you like to do. How could you use this in a particular job or career?

Your Interests

Your **interests** are your favorite activities. They could lead to a career that you would enjoy. Make a list of your interests. What are your favorite things to do? What school subjects do you enjoy? Which types of books do you read, and what TV shows and films do you watch? You might see patterns in your list of interests. Things that you enjoy doing may involve working with people, information, technology, or all three.

Most people who enjoy working with others have a friendly demeanor. If you are interested in working with people, then you might enjoy being a salesperson or a nurse. However, several careers deal with information. Jobs that require handling information usually involve reading or doing research. Maybe you enjoy visiting libraries or learning about history. If so, then you might like being a detective or a lawyer. Many people interested in technology enjoy making or fixing things. If this sounds like you, then you might find reward in being a video producer or an electrician.

Business Case Study

Developing a Career Plan

To make meaningful decisions about your career, think long-term

Can you guess how long the average U.S. worker holds a single job? Only 4.4 years. Few workers spend decades in the same role, or even in the same company. In fact, the average American worker holds 11 jobs throughout his or her adult life.

Despite this trend, studies show most workers stick with the first career area they choose—and that many later regret that choice. To find the right career match, you need to understand your preferences, values, and personality traits. For example, are you an introvert who prefers to work alone, or an extrovert who enjoys talking through tasks with others? A personality quiz can help you decide. Do you like to take charge or take direction? Experiment or follow clear rules? A work-preference questionnaire can offer insight.

You will change jobs as you grow and change, but researchers say that job preferences are remarkably stable over time. What you like to do today, you will probably still enjoy in 20 years' time.

Active Learning

What factors do you think will be most important to you in a career? Pick your top five from the following: Status; Income; Power; Geographic location; Working inside/outside; Working alone/with people; Helping people/animals; Flexibility; Each day the same/different; Prestige; Creativity. For each of your chosen factors, write a brief explanation of why it is important for your career. If you are not sure, ask trusted adults for input, and work with your teacher to select online personality and career quizzes that can help you determine your preferences.

Your Values

Values are what you believe to be important. They are the beliefs and ideas by which you live. Your values help you to make all kinds of decisions—from choosing friends to choosing a career. Your *work values* are the aspects of work that are important to you. Understanding your work values will help you select a career that suits you.

Your Skills, Abilities, Aptitudes, and Personality

Once you have some idea of your interests and values, you should consider your skills, abilities, aptitudes, and personality. A **skill** is proficiency for performing a task that is developed through training and experience. An **ability** is a natural or acquired skill or talent. Besides basic skills such as reading and writing, you may have a special ability to learn languages or to play a sport. An **aptitude** is your potential for learning a skill. Having an aptitude is like having a knack for something.

Personality is the set of characteristics that make someone special. It is the sum total of your feelings, actions, habits, and thoughts. If someone asked you to describe your personality, what would you say? You might start naming some of your characteristics. What are some of the first words that come to mind?

✔ Reading Check **Explain** What are values?

Online Self-Assessment
Online firms such as Monster.com® and CareerBuilder.com™ help match employers with employees. They also offer job seekers self-assessment services to help them decide which careers will bring them the most satisfaction and success. *How do you think you could benefit from using online self-assessment services?*

International Business

Offshore Outsourcing

Offshore outsourcing is the term used when jobs are transferred to countries overseas. In the past, outsourcing was a way to reduce costs, primarily with blue-collar jobs. More recently, there has been a growing shift in the number of white-collar jobs being outsourced, such as software development and medical and financial services jobs. This has raised a debate over how outsourcing will affect the U.S. unemployment rate and overall economy. Some argue that this trend will lead to decreased U.S. wages. Others claim that the United States has an edge with its innovation. They argue that this innovation will continue creating high-paying positions and that the recent increase in white-collar outsourcing is insignificant.

Examples of Languages Across Cultures

Q: In German, how do you say: "It's nice to meet you"?
A: **Es hat mich sehr gefreut, Sie kennenzulernen.** (pronounced: Ěs hŭtt mēkh zǎĭr ghě-froyt, zēē kěn-něn-tsŏŏ-lǎĭr-něn.)

Do you think outsourcing is good or bad for American workers? Explain your answer.

How Work Is Changing

The world of work is constantly changing. Some businesses fail, while new ones start. Certain workers are no longer needed. Others are in demand. The way people work is also changing. As previously discussed, technology enables work to be performed more quickly, easily, and in more cost-effective ways.

The working world is no longer limited by U.S. borders. The global economy continues to grow. People around the world want many goods and services that U.S. businesses sell. More U.S. companies are opening offices abroad, and **overseas** firms are operating within the United States. Companies do business **via** e-commerce. These changes create more job opportunities for workers.

Adapting to Change

Today's workers must be **adaptable** and willing to learn new technologies and ways of working. Every day you should work to improve your basic skills, develop thinking skills, and build personal skills. You will use these skills in all kinds of work later. They will help you adjust to new technologies and to change. They will also help you to compete with others in the working world.

Shifting Careers
Some baby boomers will have begun and ended their career at one company. However, studies show that the generations that follow the baby boom generation will have between five and nine different careers during their lifetime. *Why do you think this change has occurred?*

Section 20.1

After You Read

Review Key Concepts
1. What is the difference between a job and a career?
2. What is the difference between an aptitude and an ability?
3. Discuss some ways that work is changing.

Academic Skills
4. **Mathematics** George got his dream job after graduating from college. He became a construction manager, helping to build commercial buildings. His starting salary was $40,000. He will receive a 3% raise in six months and, if he does well, another 5% raise at the end of the year. Will he then be earning more, less, or equal to $42,923, the average salary offered to new graduates for this job according to the *Occupational Outlook Handbook*?

CONCEPT **Percents** A percent increase in a number can be found by multiplying the number by the sum of 100% and the percent increase.

 For math help, go to the Math Appendix.

 Go to **connectED.mcgraw-hill.com** to check your answers.

Developing a Career Plan

Reading Guide

Before You Read

Think about ways to get information about careers to help you make plans about your future.

Read to Learn

- Name four sources where you can learn about careers.
- Describe some aspects of the working world that may affect a worker.
- Define short-, medium-, and long-term goals.
- Identify the three lists needed to make a career plan.

The Main Idea

After you identify potential careers, you should research them. The information you gather will enable you to pinpoint the right career for you.

Key Concepts

- Finding Information on Careers
- Understanding the Working World
- Setting Goals
- Making a Career Plan

 Go to **connectED.mcgraw-hill.com** to print out this graphic organizer.

Vocabulary

Key Terms

networking
job shadowing
internship

volunteerism
entry-level job
outsourcing

Academic Vocabulary

You will find these words in your reading and on your tests. Make sure you know their meanings.

series
internal

challenging
ultimate

Graphic Organizer

In each box of a graphic like the one shown, note the preparation you will need to develop a career.

Graduation Plan	Education and Training Plan	Experience Plan

Finding Information on Careers

After you identify potential careers, it is time to do some research. The information you gather will enable you to pinpoint the right career and develop a career plan. There are many sources of job information. **Figure 20.1** offers a list of relevant skills and qualities to investigate when doing career research.

✔ **Reading Check** **Explain** Why is it important to research careers?

Written Sources

There is a lot of written information about careers at libraries and on the Internet. Also, the *Occupational Outlook Handbook* (OOH) describes hundreds of jobs. It lists the fastest-growing fields and gives addresses of places to write for more information.

Career Counselors

A *career counselor* is someone who is trained to provide information and guidance on choosing a career. A career counselor can also help you learn more about your interests and abilities. Most school counselors can provide career counseling.

Networks

Another way to get information is by networking. **Networking** is the practice of building informal relationships with people whose friendship could bring advantages such as job or business opportunities.

Figure 20.1 – *Skills for Success*

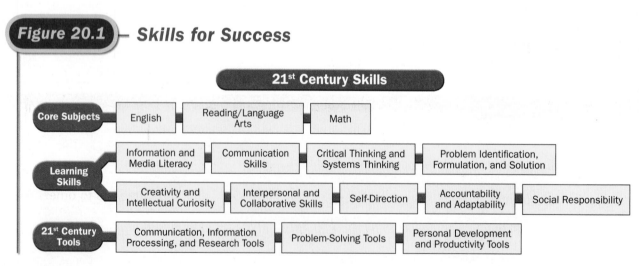

● **Workplace Skills** To succeed in the 21st century job market, all workers need information, communication and media literacy skills, thinking and problem-solving skills, and interpersonal and self-directional skills. **Why do you think creativity and intellectual curiosity are important?**

Work

The best way to learn about a career is to work. New workers often benefit from **job shadowing**, which involves following another worker on the job for a few days. Internships are another option. An **internship** is a temporary paid or unpaid position that involves direct work experience in a career field. You might also consider **volunteerism**, or working without pay.

Understanding the Working World

There are some general aspects about the working world that you should know. They may affect you at some point during your career.

The Career Ladder

Most occupations have career ladders. A *career ladder* is a **series** of different jobs within a career. You might start with an **entry-level job**, which is suitable for a worker who is new to a job, field, or subject. From there you might be promoted to a higher level job with more responsibilities. Continually improving your skills will help you to succeed by climbing a career ladder.

Outsourcing

While U.S. companies face global competition for sales, some U.S. workers face global competition for jobs. Many U.S. firms outsource work to other countries. **Outsourcing** is using outside sources to do tasks traditionally handled by **internal** staff. It is usually done to cut costs.

The Role of Supply and Demand

Many people think that supply and demand affect only the prices they pay for goods and services. However, supply and demand also affect the job market. If there are more qualified people than there are openings for a job, then it will be difficult for a worker to get the position. People who have special skills, talents, or knowledge are also highly sought after for jobs. The more demand there is for a worker's set of skills, the easier it will be for him or her to get a job.

● **Supply and Demand** The supply of workers relative to the demand for workers affects job opportunities in an area. **Does this business have a demand for workers? How can you tell?**

Regrouping After Job Loss In recent years, some U.S. companies have moved parts of their operations to other countries in order to cut production costs. As a result, many U.S. workers have lost their jobs. *In a situation such as this, what can a worker do after losing a job?*

John Lund/Sam Diephuis/Blend Images LLC

Job Stress and Healthy Careers

Many otherwise exciting jobs can also be quite stressful. Police officers and air traffic controllers have some of the more stressful jobs. Studies have found that a machine-controlled pace can also lead to job stress. Working alone at a monotonous job can be stressful. Over time, job stress can lead to serious health concerns. High blood pressure and heart attacks are extreme examples of how a job with high stress levels can affect the human body. Research into what a healthy career looks like has begun, but stress researchers hope to offer solutions that will enhance both productivity and worker health.

Web Quest

Locate Web sites where you can research what makes a healthy career. Look for ways researchers can gauge stress levels in people and the ways they determine the stress levels of different jobs. Write a paragraph about what you find.

As You Read

Make sure your goals are realistic. Aim high, but aim at what is possible.

Setting Goals

Before you reach your career goal, you must first set and reach other goals. Goals can be short-, medium-, or long-term. A *short-term* goal is something you might start and reach quickly. A *medium-term goal* is usually more **challenging** and takes longer to achieve. A *long-term goal* may take a long time to reach. Short- and medium-term goals can help you achieve a long-term goal. When setting goals, be as specific about each one as you can. Specific goals are easier to aim for and achieve.

Making a Career Plan

As you can see, making a career plan takes effort. You can create one now for one of your career choices. It is a good way to prepare for future career decisions.

Plot Your Career Course

Now that you have seen the process of career planning, get started with your own career. First, write your **ultimate** goal at the top of a sheet of paper. Then use library and Internet resources to research and make three lists. Your teacher, school counselor, and family can also help.

Graduation Plan In the first list, identify and select current courses, activities, and experiences that are related to your career goal. This list could lead to a specific career choice.

Education and Training Plan In the second list, detail the education or training you will need after high school. Be specific. List and explain your education and training alternatives, including courses you might take, and certificates or degrees you must earn.

Experience Plan In the third list, note experiences that will lead to your specific career choice. Include internships and volunteer, part-time, and temporary jobs.

Set Your Goals Once your lists are complete, determine whether each of the items listed is a short-, medium-, or long-term goal. Chart your goals in the order in which they will happen. Think about when you might start and complete each one. What can you do now? What will you do one, three, or five years from now? How long will it take to reach your ultimate goal?

Achieving Your Goals

The more specific and realistic your goals are, the more likely you are to achieve them. However, your goals and the time you spend on them may change over time. If you are not reaching your goals, do not lose motivation. Find out why you are stuck. As you review and revise your goals, you must also renew your motivation. The most important thing is to have a plan that gets you moving toward your ultimate career goal.

Employment Agencies Adecco is the world's largest employment agency. Each day, the Swiss company helps more than 700,000 people find work. Its services include temporary staffing, permanent placement, project assistance, and outsourcing. The firm also trains workers to meet local needs. *How can an employment agency help you as you enter the workforce?*

Section 20.2

After You Read

Review Key Concepts
1. Identify some sources to use for career research.
2. What are some ways to gain work experience?
3. What are short-, medium-, and long-term goals, and how do they relate to a career plan?

Academic Skills
4. **English Language Arts** Work in a small group with other students to produce a print advertisement, radio ad, or television spot designed to recruit applicants with certain aptitudes and skills to a specific position. For example, you might recruit recent law school graduates for positions.

5. **English Language Arts** Find a partner and write a role play about a job interview. Perform your role play for the class and conduct a discussion about it.

 Go to **connectED.mcgraw-hill.com** to check your answers.

Section 20.1 *Summary*

Preparing for a Career Choosing a career is one of the most important decisions that you will make. While a job is work that people do for pay, a career usually builds on interest, knowledge, training, and experience from one or more jobs. Career planning can help you determine the right path to take. It involves considering factors such as your interests and skills. Other aspects to consider are changes that have affected the working world, such as the growth of the global economy and e-commerce. These and other changes create more job opportunities for workers.

Section 20.2 *Summary*

Developing a Career Plan After you identify potential careers, you should research them. Research sources include libraries, the Internet, networks, and work. New workers can learn more about careers through job shadowing, internships, and volunteering. They should also be aware of aspects of the working world that might affect them, such as career ladders and outsourcing. Setting short-, medium-, and long-term goals can give you direction. The more specific and realistic your goals are, the more likely you will achieve them and reach your ultimate career goal.

Vocabulary Review

1. On a sheet of paper, use each of these key terms and academic vocabulary terms in a sentence.

Key Terms

full-time job	aptitude
job	personality
occupation	networking
career	job shadowing
interests	internship
values	volunteerism
skill	entry-level job
ability	outsourcing

Academic Vocabulary

pursuing	series
overseas	internal
via	challenging
adaptable	ultimate

Review Key Concepts

2. Discuss the importance of career planning.

3. Define at least five attributes you should know about yourself when analyzing careers.

4. Describe how work is changing.

5. Name four sources where you can learn about careers.

6. Describe some aspects of the working world that may affect a worker.

7. Define short-, medium-, and long-term goals.

8. Identify the three lists needed to make a career plan.

Critical Thinking

9. How can your strengths and weaknesses affect your job objectives, career choice, personal development, and life goals?

10. Suppose you have developed a plan for a career that has a good outlook. If the outlook became negative by the time you were ready to pursue the career, what would you do?

11. A *profession* such as law or medicine usually requires a high level of education. A *trade* such as mechanics requires a high level of manual or technical skills. Which one would you most likely pursue? Explain your answer.

12. Besides the resources mentioned, what other resources could you use to find information about careers?

13. Why might it be helpful to research information about careers in other countries?

14. Think about your personality. Write a list of words that describe you, such as outgoing, energetic, caring, loyal, quiet, serious, confident, friendly, creative, or shy. What potential business careers might fit your personality?

Write About It

15. Research the impact new technologies and global competition have on U.S. jobs. How do changes in technology and global competition affect workers? Write a one-page report on your findings.

16. Select two careers—one in business and the other in a different field that interests you. Research the careers. Use different techniques, such as job shadowing, volunteering, watching videos, or doing interviews. Write a review of each career.

17. Talk to a guidance counselor about your interests and skills. Develop a plan for personal growth and skill development. Write a thank-you letter to your counselor reviewing your plan.

18. Research types of self-assessment tools. See if there are any specific tools offered for people seeking business careers. Then write a two-page report summarizing your findings.

19. A *mentor* acts as an advocate, offering advice as a trusted counselor or guide. In two or more paragraphs, discuss how a mentor can help you prepare for a career.

Technology Applications

Spreadsheets and Written Reports

20. Create a spreadsheet listing your interests, values, skills, aptitudes, and personality traits. Identify and research two potential business careers—one in the United States and one in another country. Compare and contrast the careers. Choose one. Write a report assessing your skills and the education or training you might need for the chosen career.

Business Ethics

Job Shadowing

21. Imagine you just started an internship at a large phone company. You spend the first day job shadowing a longtime employee. During a tour of the office, you are given access to confidential information about the company's customers. Is this right or wrong? Explain your answer.

Applying Academics to Business

English Language Arts

22. Write an e-mail or letter introducing yourself to someone working in a career that interests you. Describe why you are interested in the career and request an information interview. Include a list of at least six questions for the person.

Mathematics

23. Using the *Occupational Outlook Handbook,* research the median annual salaries for five or six different careers that interest you. Consider careers suchs as architect, fire fighter, flight attendant, teacher, lawyer, or salesperson. Make a bar graph to compare the data you have gathered.

CONCEPT **Graphs** A bar graph is a chart that uses either horizontal or vertical bars to show comparisons among categories. One axis of the chart shows the specific categories being compared, and the other axis represents a discrete value.

English Language Arts

24. Others can often see strengths in a person that the person himself or herself does not recognize. Pair up with another student you know fairly well. Each of you should list four or five strengths of your partner, and then exchange the lists and discuss them. Write a sentence or two telling what you learned about yourself from the experience.

Mathematics

25. The average earnings of a real estate agent in a medium-sized midwestern city have been growing at a rate of 1.5% per year for several years. If the average earnings were $35,670 last year, what are they likely to be next year?

CONCEPT **Word Problems** Read carefully to make sure you understand the question. To solve this problem, ask yourself how many time periods are in question. Round to the nearest dollar.

Active Learning

Diagram Career Paths

26. Interview a family member or a friend of the family about his or her career ladder. Create a diagram that shows the jobs the interviewee has had. Then connect the skills, experience, education, and leadership roles that led to advanced positions on the ladder. Write a brief report about the interview, and share your work with the class.

Business in the Real World

School-to-Work Programs

27. Create a chart of the programs in your school and community that link school to work. Ask your guidance counselor and teachers to help you. Include names, addresses, and telephone numbers of people to contact. Then, as a class, compile all the charts, and prepare a document that can be shared with the rest of your school.

Real LIFE skills

ANALYZE ENTRY-LEVEL JOB SKILLS

28. Interview the personnel manager of a large firm or the person who hires employees for a small firm. Determine the qualities that the manager looks for in an entry-level employee. Ask about the noted strengths and weaknesses of today's applicants. Then prepare a brief report of your findings. Share it with the class.

 Business CAREERS

FIND YOUR DREAM JOB

29. Locate the Occupational Outlook Handbook Web site. Click on the "OOH Search/A-Z Index" link and enter the job title "architects, except landscape and naval." Then write a one-page report about this type of occupation. Conclude your report with a list of things you could do now to prepare yourself to pursue the occupation.

Role Play

CREATING A CAREER PLAN

30. Situation Imagine you are a career counselor for a state employment agency. A nearby high school asks you to talk to students about developing a career plan.

Activity Develop a presentation on the steps of a career plan.

Evaluation You will be evaluated on how well you meet the following performance indicators:

- Convey the importance of career planning.
- Outline the steps to complete a career plan.
- Give a well-organized presentation.
- Answer questions about planning a career.
- Project your voice, and use correct English and grammar.

Standardized Test Practice

Directions Choose the letter of the best answer. Write the letter for the answer on a separate piece of paper.

1. Given the following set of data, which is greatest?

{1, 3, 4, 5, 5, 7, 8, 8, 8, 9, 10, 10}

A mean
B median
C mode
D the mean and median are equal

 TEST-TAKING TIP Look for key words in test directions and questions such as *choose, describe, explain, compare, identify, similar, except, not,* and *but.*

Getting a Job

Chapter Objectives After completing this chapter, you will be able to:

▶ **Section 21.1** *Qualifying for a Job*
- **Discuss** the importance of understanding employers' wants and needs.
- **Describe** some of the qualifications employers seek in employees.

▶ **Section 21.2** *Getting the Job You Want*
- **Discuss** the parts of a résumé.
- **Describe** the elements involved in the application process.
- **Discuss** how employers and job candidates both benefit from a job interview.

Ask

AN EXPERT

Getting a Job: Employee Stock Options

Q: A prospective employer has offered me stock options. How do I know if they are valuable?

A: Options are contracts that permit their holders to either buy or sell a stock at a pre-set price during a specified length of time. Options that allow investors to purchase stock are known as call options, while those that allow investors to sell stock are called put options. When a stock's current price makes an option's strike price attractive, the option is said to be "in the money." For example, if you're holding a call option with a strike price of $30, and the stock is currently trading at $35, your option is "in the money."

Mathematics A *Wall Street Journal* options listing reads: IBM Oct 90 Call at $2.00. This means that you could purchase an IBM call option for $2 that will expire in October for a strike price of $90 a share. If you decide to buy 100 shares because the stock is currently in the money, how much will you spend if you also must pay a $75 commission?

CONCEPT **Order of Operations** To solve a complex equation, it is important to write the equation correctly, and solve it in the correct order. This is called the order of operations. First, simplify within parentheses, and then evaluate any exponents. Then multiply and divide from left to right, and add and subtract from left to right.

● **Extracurricular Activities** Employers prefer applicants who are involved in activities, such as sports and student government, as well as their school classes. **What extracurricular activities do you like the most?**

Images-USA/Alamy

Qualifying for a Job

Reading Guide

Before You Read

Think about the skills you have that will help you stand out when pursuing a job.

Read to Learn

- Discuss the importance of understanding employers' wants and needs.
- Describe some of the qualifications employers seek in employees.

The Main Idea

Businesses and nonprofits provide different products and services. They need all kinds of workers to perform various tasks. You need to know what employers look for in an employee.

Key Concepts

- Finding a Job
- Your Qualifications and Skills

Vocabulary

Key Terms

qualifications
employability skills
body language
extracurricular activities

Academic Vocabulary

You will find these words in your reading and on your tests. Make sure you know their meanings.

administrator
accessing
seek
attitude

Graphic Organizer

In a table like the one below, list five qualifications employers look for in an employee, and describe what those qualifications mean to you.

Employment Qualifications	Description

 Go to **connectED.mcgraw-hill.com** to print out this graphic organizer.

Finding a Job

Once you have an idea of what you want to do, you can take the next step and start your job search. As you search for a job, you will learn more about the various qualities employers look for in employees.

Knowing What Employers Want and Need

Businesses and nonprofits provide different products and services. They need all kinds of workers to perform different tasks. For example, a hospital needs doctors, nurses, cooks, janitors, supervisors, and an **administrator** who oversees operations. A department store needs retail buyers, sales associates, stock clerks, assistant managers, and a store manager who supervises everything. Each of these jobs carries tasks and a certain level of responsibility. Each also requires a different level and type of skills. You need to know what employers want and need in an employee.

Your Qualifications and Skills

Different jobs require different **qualifications**, or the education, skills, and work experience needed to do a particular job. What is important for one job might be less important for another. Employers look for more than job qualifications. They also look for employability skills. **Employability skills** are basic skills that you need to get a job, keep a job, and do well at a job.

✔ Reading Check | **Define** What are employability skills?

Work Permits Most people under the age of 16 must obtain a work permit to have a job. In some states the age requirement is 18. A work permit is a legal document that allows a minor to hold a job. It shows the number of hours a minor can work and the kinds of jobs that can be held. *Why do you think the government requires work permits for minors?*

?ETHICS in Business

Applying for a Job

■ **Critical Reading** Life is full of important decisions. Think about the kinds of decisions that you make as you read the question below.

You are in the process of applying for a position at a large accounting firm. In a discussion with a friend who also applied for the position, you learn that applicants with more experience than you are being hired.

■ **Decision Making** Would learning about the applicants with more experience make you change your application, résumé, cover letter, or answers in an interview to make yourself look more qualified? Explain your answer.

Figure 21.1 – *Median Earnings of Full-Time Workers*

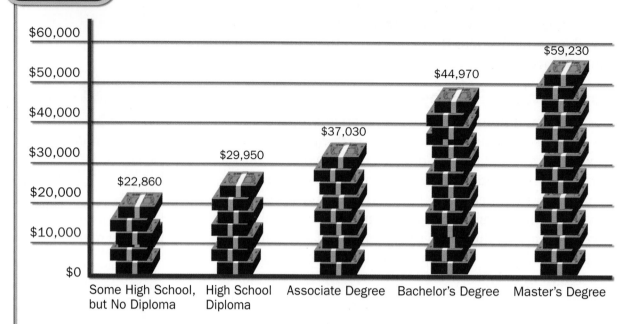

Source: U.S. Census Bureau, Bureau of Labor Statistics

● **Education and Earnings** One of the many advantages of education is that it increases your earnings potential. **What is the difference in the annual earnings of a high school dropout and a high school graduate?**

Level of Education

For most jobs, employers want applicants to have at least a high school diploma. High school dropouts have fewer job opportunities, especially if they have no previous work experience. The more skills and education a worker has, the wider the job market will be for him or her. **Figure 21.1** illustrates the median income for workers based on their level of education.

● **As You Read**

Think about what it would be like to work at a TV studio. What skills do you think you would need?

Basic Skills

Almost all jobs require basic skills. Employees must be able to read well enough to function in their job. They should be able to do simple mathematical problems. They must also be able to communicate with others. Basic computer skills, such as entering or accessing data, are necessary. Many jobs also require basic work-related skills. For instance, a warehouse worker may need to know how to operate a forklift or specific machinery.

Work Experience

Experienced workers have proven skills and a familiarity with a job. They need less training to do a new job. That is why many employers want workers who have some work experience. It is important to get some kind of experience. Most jobs that require skills and experience pay more than those that do not.

Character and Personality

Skills are important, but employers also **seek** certain character traits in potential employees. Employers value hard work, honesty, dependability, and an ability to finish tasks. They also look for a good **attitude** toward work, a desire to do the job well, and the ability to work with others. Workers who can follow instructions as well as take initiative are also wanted. Sometimes, having strong character and personality traits can make up for weaknesses in other areas, such as experience. An employer can learn about these traits in several ways. In addition many employers do background research on job candidates that includes viewing soical media sites, such as Facebook®. It is important to always present yourself in the best light online and in person.

Body Language Body language often says more about you than spoken or written words. Your **body language**, or nonverbal communication, includes your posture, eye contact, facial expressions, and gestures. They can either add to or detract from the impression you make. For example, if you fidget during interviews, you may appear to lack interest in the job.

Business Case Study

Job Tips from the Pros

Follow this simple advice to stand out during the hiring process

Human resources professionals are in the business of picking, and retaining, the best workers. What advice would they give to aspiring job seekers? *Business Insider* gathered their top tips, which include:

Focus and act fast. Keep a short, manageable list of potential employers and apply quickly when a new job posting appears. Early responders have an advantage.

Tailor your résumé and build your network. Edit your résumé with each application to include keywords from the job description. Referrals by employees go to the top of the pile, so seek out these referrals whenever possible.

Come to the interview prepared. Plan your day around the interview, not the other way around.

Be enthusiastic. Ask the interviewer smart questions that don't have answers you could have googled. And last, don't hide gaps in your employment—non-job experiences are relevant and might even make you stand out!

Active Learning

Volunteer and extracurricular activities teach important job skills such as teamwork, time management, and responsibility. Make a list of such activities in which you have taken part. Write brief descriptions of how your experiences helped you grow and prepared you for paid work experiences. Workshop your answers with another student until you feel you would be confident describing them in a job-interview situation.

School Performance Employers might check school records to see how a potential employee performs. Good grades show motivation and a willingness to apply oneself to a task. Some employers check attendance records. Even if you do not have the best grades, good attendance and punctuality indicate that you are reliable and will show up for work on time.

Extracurricular Activities **Extracurricular activities** are activities that you do besides schoolwork. They indicate extra effort and interests on your part, as well as possible leadership ability. For example, taking part in team sports shows an ability to work in a group. Volunteer work shows commitment and responsibility. Your efforts in and out of school create a record that future employers may want to see.

Your Overall Impression Think of a personnel director with three piles of job applications. One pile is labeled "Yes." One is labeled "Maybe." One is labeled "No." Your goal is to get your application into the "Yes" pile. Consider the way you present yourself. Your writing, problem solving, creative thinking, and reasoning skills will show. Employers will be influenced by the way you dress and whether you are well-groomed. They will also notice if you use slang or anything other than standard English. A good first impression increases your chances of getting hired.

Section 21.1

After You Read

Review Key Concepts
1. Why is it important to know what employers look for in an employee?
2. What are employability skills?
3. What are some of the qualifications that employers consider for potential new employees?

Academic Skills
4. **Mathematics** Mike got a job offer from Loom Inc. He would earn $25,000 a year plus benefits. The value of the premiums the company pays to the insurance company is $\frac{3}{5}$ of 10% of his base salary. How much are the premiums for a year?

CONCEPT **Numbers and Operations: Fractions, Decimals, and Percents**
Fractions, percents, and decimals are three ways to express numbers between 0 and 1. You can convert one to another. To solve this problem, convert "$\frac{3}{5}$ of 10%" to a decimal, and multiply by $25,000.

 For math help, go to the Math Appendix.

 Go to **connectED.mcgraw-hill.com** to check your answers.

Getting the Job You Want

Reading Guide

● Before You Read

Think about some ways that potential employers can get more information about job applicants.

Read to Learn
- Discuss the parts of a résumé.
- Describe the elements involved in the application process.
- Discuss how employers and job candidates both benefit from a job interview.

The Main Idea
One of the first steps in finding a job is to prepare a résumé. A résumé tells an employer what a worker has to offer. Cover letters, job applications, and interviews also provide information about potential employees.

Key Concepts
- Beginning Your Job Search
- Contacting Potential Employers
- Interviewing for Jobs

Vocabulary
Key Terms
> résumé
> chronological résumé
> job objective
> cover letter
> job interview

Academic Vocabulary
You will find these words in your reading and on your tests. Make sure you know their meanings.

assess	transferable
achievements	objective

Graphic Organizer
In a figure like the one below, note five sources you can use to find a job.

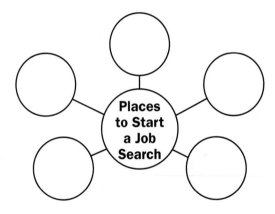

Places to Start a Job Search

 Go to **connectED.mcgraw-hill.com** to print out this graphic organizer.

● As You Read

Think about jobs you might like most and might be able to do best.

Beginning Your Job Search

Before you begin looking for a job, you need to discover which jobs you would like most and would be able to do best. You should avoid limiting your search to one type of job. **Assess** the job market objectively. Some jobs require little or no experience. Other jobs require work experience. Still others might require certain skills.

Preparing Your Résumé

One of the first steps in finding a job is to prepare a résumé. A **résumé** is a summary of your skills, education, and work experience. It tells an employer what you can offer as a worker. Its purpose is to persuade potential employers to interview you. Some people also list their hobbies on their résumé to provide an indication of their personal interests and other work-related qualifications.

Your résumé gives an employer his or her first impression of you. If it is disorganized and full of mistakes, your chances of getting an interview will be slim. Check your grammar and spelling before submitting your résumé. Make sure it is neat and that the information in it is correct. Try to limit it to one page.

There are different types of résumés. The most common type is the chronological résumé. A **chronological résumé** lists your **achievements** in time order. It has five parts: the heading, the job objective, a skills summary, work experience, and education. **Figure 21.2** shows an example of a chronological résumé.

Science/Tech**TRENDS**

Becoming an Astronaut

Many young people want to be astronauts someday. What does it take to become an astronaut? While there is no real step-by-step way to ensure employment as an astronaut, there are some things you can do that will put you on the right path. A bachelor's degree in science or mathematics is the first step toward a career in space travel. Extracurricular activities such as participating in your school's science club can also help you reach your goal of becoming an astronaut. An understanding of the physical challenges of space travel is also important.

WebQuest

Locate someone would become an astronaut. Look for examples of how astronauts can be affected by space travel. Write a few paragraphs describing what steps you would take to become an astronaut.

Figure 21.2 – *Résumé*

24 Mill Creek Road
Sunnyville, FL 32300

Phone (850) 555-0123
TPhilips@school.edu

Teri Philips

Job Objective

Full-time administrative position in law office.

Skills Summary

- Dependable, responsible, and hard-working.
- Strong interpersonal and communication skills.
- Maintain confidentiality working with legal documents.
- Knowledge of word-processing and database software.
- Bilingual in English and Spanish.
- Typing speed: 70 wpm.

Work Experience

Jan. 2011–present, O'Malley Law Firm, Bremerton, FL
Administrative Assistant (part-time)
- Perform essential administrative tasks such as scheduling, filing, managing correspondence, and answering phones.
- Transcribe case files and notes.

Feb. 2009–Dec. 2010, Sunnyville Museum, Sunnyville, FL
Staff Assistant (part-time)
- Performed administrative and managerial duties such as handling phone calls, assisting at museum events, filing, and answering questions from visitors.
- Coordinated projects for exhibits.

Nov. 2008–Feb. 2011, Community Law Center, Morgantown, FL
Volunteer Staff Assistant (part-time)
- Assist lawyers in providing free legal services to community residents.
- Perform administrative tasks such as typing documents and corresponding with clients.

Education

2009, Morgantown High School, Morgantown, FL
High School Diploma
- Course work in criminal justice and introduction to law.
- Participation in statewide Law Honors Project.
- Three semesters of computer applications courses.

● **Market Yourself** A résumé is a tool you can use to market yourself to prospective employers. It tells who you are, what you want to do, what you have done, and what you can do. **What are some things you should emphasize on your résumé?**

● **Perfect Attendance**
Employers value employees who understand the importance of attendance and punctuality. **Why is it important that all participants in a meeting are on time?**

The Parts of a Résumé The first part of the résumé is the heading. The heading contains your name and contact information. Include your street address, city, state, zip code, home phone number, and e-mail address. The second part, the **job objective**, is a statement about the type of job you want. The third part, the skills summary, includes job-specific skills such as keyboarding, computer use, and **transferable** skills. The fourth part, the work experience section, lists the jobs you have done. The fifth part, the education section, shows your secondary and postsecondary education. List the name and location of each school, and the date you finished or the date you will finish.

 **Reading Check** **Identify** What are the essential parts of a résumé?

Looking for Openings A *job lead* is information about a job opening. Job leads can come from several sources, including a network of people who could help you. Some of them might also give you a *referral*, or a recommendation to an employer or another job lead. *What are some other ways you can find out about job openings?*

Contacting Potential Employers

Once you have prepared a résumé and found interesting job openings, you can tailor your résumé to each job. Then start to apply for the jobs. The process of applying for a job can include submitting a cover letter, filling out a job application, taking an employment test, and being interviewed.

Cover Letter

You should always include a cover letter with your résumé. A **cover letter** tells the employer about you and why you are applying for a job. It can also be used to inquire about possible job openings. As with your résumé, your cover letter also needs to make a good impression. It should be formatted and error-free. **Figure 21.3** shows an example of a cover letter.

Figure 21.3 — *Cover Letter*

Teri Philips
24 Mill Creek Road
Sunnyville, FL 32300
Phone: (850) 555-0123   TPhilips@school.edu

October 30, 20--

Thomas L. Warren
T.L. Warren & Associates
300 Commerce Center Plaza
Miami, FL 33109

Dear Mr. Warren:

Peter Cortez suggested I write to you about a full-time administrative position at your law firm.

I have three years of experience working in an office environment. My experience includes volunteer work for a nonprofit organization that provides free legal services to community residents. I have handled incoming and outgoing phone calls, and typed and distributed documents. Please see my enclosed résumé to learn more about my background.

I am dependable, efficient, and personable. I pay attention to detail, have excellent communication and organizational skills, and enjoy working with people.

If there are job opportunities at your law firm for which I might be qualified, I would appreciate an interview to discuss what makes me a good match for your company.

Sincerely,

Teri Philips

Teri Philips

Enclosure

● **Introduce Yourself** A cover letter introduces you to a prospective employer. It should be tailored to the position of interest to you. **What should accompany the cover letter?**

The Job Application

A job application form is a printed sheet with blank spaces that you fill in to apply for a job. The person who applies for a job is called a job applicant. Like your résumé, an application form presents you to a potential employer. It is easier to fill out if you have a résumé and a list of available references.

Employment Testing

When you apply for a job, you might be asked to take a test to see if you have the required skills. For example, truck drivers must take a driving test before being hired. Jobs for government or law enforcement may require drug and lie-detector testing.

Interviewing for Jobs

After you have found a job opening, filled out an application, and sent your cover letter and résumé, an employer may call you for a interview. A **job interview** is a formal face-to-face discussion between an employer and a potential employee. Employers use interviews to make hiring decisions. It is important to do well in an interview.

Interviews are also helpful to job candidates. They provide a chance to see if you really want the job. They also allow you to see whether you and the employer are a good match. You can do well in an interview if you prepare. Research the company. Prepare answers to common interview questions. Think of questions to ask the interviewer. Practice your interview skills.

● **The Job Interview**
The job interview is an important part of the job search process. Suppose this is an interview for a management trainee position. **Is the person being interviewed dressed appropriately?**

©Chris Ryan/OJO Images/age fotostock

Job Interview Tips

Before you go on a job interview, keep these things in mind:

- *Do some homework.* Find out about the job.
- *Be on time.* Otherwise, you may be considered disrespectful.
- *Wear appropriate clothes.* Dress neatly and in a style appropriate for the job you are seeking.
- *Put your best foot forward.* Shake the interviewer's hand. Be courteous. Be aware of your body language.
- *Ask questions about the job.* You need to find out if it is right for you.
- *Ask about the next step.* After the interview, say, "I am very interested in this job. What is the next step?"
- *Do not expect an answer right away.* The employer will need time to decide who to hire.

Follow up after the interview by calling or writing a letter thanking the interviewer. In the letter, restate your **objective** and describe how your skills and experiences are well-suited to the job. This shows your interest in the job and allows you to add anything you forgot to mention. Learn from each experience, and work on your weaknesses. Doing so will increase your chances of getting the job you want.

Accepting a Job Offer Job offers often come over the phone. However, writing a letter of acceptance is an appropriate way to begin a professional relationship. An acceptance letter states when the new employee expects to start work, what position he or she will be filling, the agreed-upon wage, and other known terms of employment. *Why would you want to accept a job offer in writing?*

Section 21.2

After You Read

Review Key Concepts

1. What is a résumé? What is its purpose?
2. Explain what is usually involved in the process of applying for a job.
3. How can an employer and a job applicant both benefit from a job interview?

Academic Skills

4. **English Language Arts** Read the employment want ads in your local newspaper for a week. Write three paragraphs about the kinds of jobs advertised in your area, the salary ranges for those jobs, the benefits available, and the qualifications or work experience required.

5. **English Language Arts** Working in a group of three, participate in mock job interviews for a grocery store clerk, lifeguard, and newspaper delivery person. Have group members take turns role-playing the interviewer, job applicant, and observer. The observer should provide written feedback to the interviewer and job applicant.

 Go to **connectED.mcgraw-hill.com** to check your answers.

Chapter 21 Review and Activities

Section 21.1 *Summary*

Qualifying for a Job Within an organization, each job carries a certain level of responsibility and tasks to be done. Jobs also require different levels and types of skills. As a worker, you need to know the qualifications employers look for in an employee. Skills are important, but employers also seek certain character traits in potential employees. Employers value hard work, honesty, dependability, and an ability to finish tasks. They also look for good personality traits in workers.

Section 21.2 *Summary*

Getting the Job You Want Before you begin looking for a job, you should discover which jobs you would like most and would be able to do best. One of the first steps in finding a job is to prepare a résumé, which tells an employer about your qualifications. Its purpose is to persuade potential employers to interview you. The process of applying for a job can include submitting a cover letter, filling out a job application, taking an employment test, and being interviewed.

Vocabulary Review

1. On a sheet of paper, use each of these key terms and academic vocabulary terms in a sentence.

Key Terms	Academic Vocabulary
qualifications	administrator
employability skills	accessing
body language	seek
extracurricular activities	attitude
résumé	assess
chronological résumé	achievements
job objective	transferable
cover letter	objective
job interview	

Review Key Concepts

2. Discuss the importance of understanding employers' wants and needs.

3. Describe some of the qualifications employers seek in employees.

4. Discuss the parts of a résumé.

5. Describe the elements involved in the application process.

6. Discuss how employers and job candidates both benefit from a job interview.

7. Why is it important to find out as much as possible about a position before being offered the job?

8. How does your personality affect your relationships with your coworkers?

9. What are some ways to ensure that your résumé is correct before sending it to an employer?

10. Why is a referral considered to be better than a job lead?

11. Imagine you just received a college degree in accounting. You interview for two jobs: an entry-level job at a large accounting firm and a lead accountant position at a small grocery store. Which job would you prefer? Explain your answer.

12. Why might an employer want to know whether an applicant for an entry-level job has developed leadership skills while in high school or college?

13. Indicate how you affect your own employability as a student today.

14. *Productivity* is the rate at which a company or worker produces goods or services. What traits enhance a worker's productivity? What traits hinder it?

15. Suppose you would like to get a summer job. Write a letter inquiring about possible job opportunities at a company where you would like to work.

16. A personnel assistant contacts you about your letter of inquiry. He says the company will have several summer jobs for which you might qualify. Prepare a résumé and a cover letter for a specific summer job at the company.

17. Imagine you have been interviewed for an office job at a company that makes machines. You would do a variety of tasks. You would receive a good salary. However, you would work in a very noisy area. Consider your likes and dislikes about the job. Write a thank-you letter to the interviewer.

18. Get a job application. You might get one from a teacher, a school career center, a business, a library, an employment agency, or the Internet. Complete the form. List the items that are on the application form that are not covered in your résumé.

19. Imagine that you have been offered the job you wanted. Write a letter of acceptance to the employer.

Word-Processing Software

20. Analyze the job market. The Internet, newspaper want ads, and job boards are all sources of current information. Which fields seem to have the most job openings? Which ones have the fewest? What types of entrepreneurial opportunities are available? What seems to be the current outlook for the types of jobs that interest you? Write a one-page report on your conclusions. Include information on job duties and requirements, pay, and benefits.

Stretching the Truth

21. Suppose you completed $3\frac{1}{2}$ years of college but did not graduate. You see an ad for a job that you really want, but the job description states that you must have a college degree. You meet all the other requirements and feel that you would be perfect for the job. If you state that you received a college degree, you will increase your chances of being interviewed and subsequently hired. What should you do?

Chapter 21 Review and Activities

Applying Academics to Business

English Language Arts

22. Résumés usually include an employment objective. Write three different employment objectives for different types of jobs. Make your objectives brief and to the point, and use the active voice.

Mathematics

23. Imagine that you have two job offers. The first pays $2,000 a month and requires a 48-mile round-trip commute. The second is closer to home and you could easily walk or ride a bike to work, but it pays only $1,920 a month. You will be working five days a week. Taking into account the current price of gas and a car that gets 20 miles per gallon, how much will the commute to the first job cost? Which job will benefit you more?

CONCEPT **Algebra: Solving for the Unknown** One of the steps in solving this problem is to write and solve a proportion: mileage / one gallon = 48 / x gallons. The letter x represents the unknown quantity—number of gallons used per trip. Plug in the known quantities, and solve for the unknown.

English Language Arts

24. Linda read the following list of responsibilities and accomplishments at a former job on an applicant's resume. Rewrite the list using parallel construction.

- presented a session on teamwork at new-employee training session
- management training program graduate
- figuring out weekly schedules for part-time employees

Mathematics

25. Franklin works as a cashier. A customer bought four dozen eggs at $1.60 a dozen, and a carton of yogurt for 80¢ to the checkout counter. The customer also had a promotional coupon worth 10% off on any purchase. When the customer tried to pay with a $5 bill, Franklin told him it was not enough, so the customer put back the yogurt. Did he then have enough for the eggs? Explain how you would figure out if he had enough to buy the eggs.

CONCEPT **Problem Solving** When thinking through an approach to solving a problem, disregard extraneous information.

Active Learning

Mock Interview

26. Break into groups of three. Select an interviewer, a job candidate, and an observer. Participate in a mock interview for a job as a cook, bus driver, or cashier. After 10 minutes, the observer should provide feedback. Repeat until everyone has been in each role.

Business in the Real World

Job Applications

27. Most job applications require a lot of personal information. Look at an employment application to determine the information needed to complete it. Then create a spreadsheet or word-processing document listing the information you would need to provide.

Real LIFE skills

PREPARING FOR AN INTERVIEW

28. Interview two relatives or family friends who work. Ask how they prepare for job interviews. What types of questions have they been asked? How did they respond? What advice would they give on preparing for an interview? Summarize your findings in a report. Note similarities and differences in their statements. Present it to the class.

Cool Business CAREERS

FIND YOUR DREAM JOB

29. Locate the Occupational Outlook Handbook Web site. Click on the "OOH Search/A-Z Index" link and look up the job title "teacher" (preschool, kindergarten, elementary, middle, and secondary). Then write a one-page report about this type of occupation. Conclude your report with a list of things you could do now to prepare yourself to pursue the occupation.

Role Play

KNOWING WHAT COMPANIES WANT

30. Situation Imagine that you are a recruiter for a large corporation. You have been asked to participate in a community job fair.

Activity With other students acting as job candidates, make a presentation on the types of jobs at your company and the requirements for them.

Evaluation You will be evaluated on how well you meet the following performance indicators:

- Research the types of jobs that are available at your chosen corporation.
- Indicate the qualifications your company requires.
- Discuss job openings and how résumés are handled.
- Answer questions from the job candidates.
- Organize your thoughts.
- Project your voice, make eye contact, and use correct grammar.

Standardized Test Practice

Directions Choose the letter of the best answer. Write the letter for the answer on a separate piece of paper.

1. Which underlined word in the paragraph below uses the apostrophe incorrectly?

Businesses often post job <u>notice's</u> on bulletin boards in supermarkets or in shopping malls. You can also call a <u>company's</u> personnel office to see if they have jobs open. You might find help-wanted signs in <u>businesses'</u> windows. Sometimes you can find a job by walking into a local business and asking if <u>they're</u> hiring.

    A   notice's
    B   company's
    C   businesses'
    D   they're

TEST-TAKING TIP Read and consider all of the answer choices before you choose the one that best responds to the question. Examine each choice and think about how it differs from the others.

Rachel Muir

Fearless Leader/Founder/Executive Director, Girlstart

Girlstart is a nonprofit organization that aims to empower girls in mathematics, science, and technology. It teaches girls the fun part of academic achievement and runs after-school programs for underserved schools, free Saturday camps, and summer camps.

Q & A

Describe your job responsibilities.

Rachel: I lead my staff, helping them achieve results, solve problems, prioritize our goals and support my board. I make sure that I am proud of everything that leaves this office, be it a brochure, a T-shirt, or an intern going to lead a program.

What skills are most important in your business?

Rachel: Bravery, generosity, compassion, thoughtfulness, creativity, passion, ambition, confidence, thirst for knowledge, respectfulness, admiration, gratitude, and inclusiveness are ones that come to mind.

What is your key to success?

Rachel: My three key skills for success are ambition, communication, and creativity. I believed in my idea to create Girlstart, and this determination to succeed helped me get through the tough times. Being an effective communicator is vital. It helps me solve problems, apply for grants, give presentations, and work with staff and volunteers. Creativity means being open to new ideas, and to also accept that I don't have to have all the answers. My job is to find the people who do.

Your Web site mentions that you weren't good at math, hence your idea to create Girlstart. What steps did you take to improve your math?

Rachel: A friend taught me how to build Web sites, and I took programming and accounting classes. If you can get over your lack of confidence and believe that you can totally do this, you will succeed. Don't be limited by what you don't know. Turn your weakness into your strength by identifying it and making changes. Never give up on your idea. If you love what you do, you will work as hard as it takes to be successful.

What advice would you give students interested in starting a business?

Rachel: You will never know until you try! Be afraid, and do it anyway. Thank others every step of the way in every inventive way that you can, and be patient with yourself and those around you.

Critical Thinking   *Why is identifying a target market vital to shaping an organization?*

Some Qualifications Needed to be a Director of an Educational Camp

Academic Skills and Abilities

Computer science; mathematics; student literacy training; teaching skills; interpersonal skills; general business management skills; verbal and written communication skills; multitasking, organizing, and planning skills

Academic Skills Required to Complete Tasks at Girlstart			
Tasks	Math	Science	English Language Arts
Hold meetings			◆
Assign duties			◆
Develop curricula	◆	◆	◆
Assess student achievement	◆	◆	◆
Customer service			◆
Schedule employees	◆		◆
Order supplies and equipment	◆		◆
Analyze financials	◆		◆

Education and Training

The minimum educational requirement is a bachelor's degree, usually in education, but a master's or higher degree is preferable. State licensing is necessary for instructional coordinators in public school systems, although specific requirements vary by state. In some states, a teaching license is needed, while in others an education administrator license is needed as well as training in curriculum development and instruction, or in the specific field for which the director is responsible, such as mathematics or science.

Career Path

To successfully empower students, directors must have a good understanding of how to teach specific groups of students, in addition to expertise in developing educational materials. As a result, many people become instructional coordinators after working for several years as teachers. Work experience in an education administrator position, such as principal or assistant principal, can also be beneficial.

Lifelong Learning

Regardless of the career choice, lifelong learning will most likely play a factor in the future of today's students. Changes in technology, globalization, and greater competition among qualified job candidates are creating the need for continuing adult education. At the same time, adult education is an emerging new industry.

Thematic Project Assignment

In this project you will design and write a brochure that describes the benefits of lifelong learning for adults and the types of careers available in adult education.

Step 1   Brainstorm Skills You Need to Complete This Activity

Your success in designing and writing a brochure will depend on your skills. Preview the activity, then brainstorm a list of the skills you will need to use to complete the activity and describe how you will use them. Skills you might use include:

Academic Skills   reading, writing, designing/art/photography

Basic Skills   speaking, listening, and thinking

Technology Skills   word processing, keyboarding, design and photo programming, and Internet skills

@   **SKILLS PREVIEW** Go to **connectED.mcgraw-hill.com** to download a graphic organizer you can use to brainstorm the skills you will use to complete the project.

Step 2   Choose a Business and a Career That Interest You

Make a list of businesses that interest you. Add to the list any careers within this business that interest you. Think about the lifelong learning you might need in these careers. Then think of adult education courses that might help people in these businesses and careers. For example, if you are interested in overseeing an assembly line in a large factory, you might need lifelong education in robotics or other technology. Some careers in adult education might include teaching robotics, being an administrator at a school that teaches robotics, or writing manuals for the classes.

Step 3   Build Background Knowledge

Preview information on lifelong learning.

Lifelong **Learning**

Thousands of adults return to college every year or engage in training within their companies. Some take classes for self-development or personal interest. Most, however, return to the classroom to keep up with the demands of their jobs, learn a new skill, or gain a new qualification or certification.

New career opportunities in adult education are not to be overlooked by anyone interested in education. As with traditional education, many jobs require advanced degrees, but not all. On-the-job experience counts when teaching adults.

Step 4   Connect with Your Community

Interview two adults in your community who have returned to college, taken a course at a community education center, or been involved in training at the workplace. Ask them about why they went back to school and what their experience was like. Ask them how they benefited. Then think about the people who were involved in their education, such as enrollment counselors, financial aid assistants, and instructors.

Step 5   Research Lifelong Learning

Use library and Internet resources to research lifelong learning. Keep records of your sources of information. Then prepare a brochure. Use the checklist as a guide to help you.

Step 6   Develop Your Brochure

Use design, photo, and other software to develop a three-fold brochure that includes all of the information described in the project checklist.

Lifelong Learning

✔ Make a list of the main points and supporting details on the benefits of lifelong learning.

✔ Use the main points to write headings and subheadings. Include information on the benefits of lifelong learning, how lifelong learning is becoming a major trend as more adults participate, and how this trend is creating more career opportunities associated with adult education.

✔ Write the supporting details under each heading and subheading.

✔ Use computer software to add graphic designs to your brochure.

✔ Edit and proofread your brochure to make sure everything is correct.

✔ Print the brochure and fold it into three panels.

Self Connections

✔ Discuss the results of your research with the adults you interviewed.

✔ Describe how the adults you interviewed benefited by lifelong learning.

✔ Explain what the investigation and its results mean to you.

Step 7   Evaluate Your Presentation

 RUBRIC Go to connectED. mcgraw-hill.com to download a rubric you can use to evaluate your final report.

New Leaf Paper makes environmentally friendly recycled paper that is 100 percent post-consumer, processed, and chlorine-free paper. At the end of this unit, you will learn about New Leaf Paper co-founder Jeff Mendelsohn and how he achieved his success.

Decision Making Do you think it is important to buy goods and services that do not harm the environment?

Unit 8 | *Thematic Project Preview*

How the Consumer Movement Affects Business

After completing this unit, you will research to find how the consumer movement affects business and your life and career.

Project Checklist As you read the chapters in this unit, use this checklist to prepare for the unit project.

- ✔ Think about what the consumer movement is, and how the consumer movement affects the way business is conducted.
- ✔ Think about how the Internet has given voice to the consumer movement.
- ✔ Consider how the consumer movement affects you as a consumer.
- ✔ Consider how the consumer movement could affect your future job and career.

U.S. Fish & Wildlife Service/John & Karen Hollingsworth

Chapter 22

Making Consumer Decisions

> **Chapter Objectives**   After completing this chapter, you will be able to:

▶ **Section 22.1** *Consumer Choices*

- **Identify** four decisions that consumers make when they buy goods and services.
- **Compare** brand-name and generic products.
- **Identify** choices that consumers must make about when to buy.
- **List** several choices that consumers have when selecting a store to make purchases.
- **Describe** tools that consumers can use to compare prices for goods and services.

▶ **Section 22.2** *How to Be a Smart Consumer*

- **Identify** types of information that can be helpful to a consumer in making wise shopping decisions.

Ask

AN EXPERT

Making Consumer Decisions: Buying Bonds

Q: Can bonds help protect me against inflation?

A: Bonds are basically IOUs between a borrower and a lender. Governments and corporations borrow billions of dollars a year from investors, and bonds are a common way for them to do so. Like a savings account, the initial amount borrowed is called the principal, while the lender is generally paid in the form of interest. There are two main types of bonds: those issued by the government and those issued by private companies. If you are concerned about inflation, there are two kinds of U.S. government securities, the Treasury Inflation Protected Securities (TIPS) and the Series I Savings Bond (or I Bond), that are guaranteed to rise more rapidly than inflation. This is because their rates of return are directly tied to a common measure of inflation—the CPI-U, or Consumer Price Index for All Urban Consumers.

Mathematics The interest rate on an I Bond has two parts: a 30-year fixed rate and an inflation rate that changes every six months. The composite earning rate is the fixed rate plus the semiannual inflation rate. Determine the interest on a $5,000 I Bond over a six month period in which the fixed rate is 2% and the inflation rate is 0.28%.

CONCEPT **Percents Less Than 1** Percents less than 1 represent values less than $\frac{1}{100}$. In other words, 0.1% is one-tenth of one percent, which can also be represented in decimal form as 0.001, or in fraction form as $\frac{1}{1,000}$.

Image Source/Alamy

● **Conserving and Recycling** It is important for businesses and people to conserve and recycle. **What can young people do to promote a healthy environment?**

Consumer Choices

Reading Guide

● Before You Read

Think about some decisions you will have to make about some goods or services you are planning to buy.

Read to Learn

- Identify four decisions that consumers make when they buy goods and services.
- Compare brand-name and generic products.
- Identify choices that consumers must make about when to buy.
- List several choices that consumers have when selecting a store to make purchases.
- Describe tools that consumers can use to compare prices for goods and services.

The Main Idea

Consumers must make many buying decisions. They must decide what, when, and where to buy goods and services, and how much to pay for them.

Key Concepts

- Buying Goods and Services
- Deciding What to Buy
- Deciding When to Buy
- Deciding Where to Buy
- Deciding How Much to Pay

 Go to **connectED.mcgraw-hill.com** to print out this graphic organizer.

Vocabulary

Key Terms

consumer   generic products
brand name   comparison shopping

Academic Vocabulary

You will find these words in your reading and on your tests. Make sure you know their meanings.

disposes   version
priority   bulk

Graphic Organizer

In boxes like those on the figure below, list four decisions a consumer must make before buying goods or services.

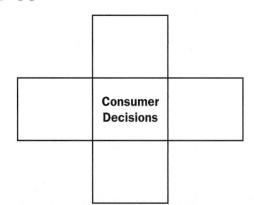

Consumer Decisions

Buying Goods and Services

When shopping, making choices is not always easy. A **consumer** (a person who selects, purchases, uses, and **disposes** of goods and services) is faced with many buying options. Making consumer decisions involves determining what is most important to you.

If you had unlimited money, you could buy whatever you wanted. However, no one has unlimited funds. They have to budget their money to satisfy their wants and needs. A *budget* is a plan that specifies how resources—particularly money—will be allocated or spent during a particular period.

Consumers must make many decisions about buying goods and services. They must decide what, when, and where to buy, and how much to pay.

✔ Reading Check **Define** What is a budget?

Business Case Study

Buying Based on the Box

Product packaging affects consumer decisions.

What sways you to buy one product rather than another? Research shows that fully one third of consumers' buying decisions is based on something most of us take for granted: packaging.

Distinctive packaging helps you find what you want while scanning store shelves. But it also appeals to your subconscious mind. Packaging with a distinctive appearance and iconic logo—think of Starbucks, Apple, or Nike—triggers feelings and memories connected to your past experiences with these brands.

Appealing packaging has several features. It evokes the brand's personality. Images and type are clear and easy to understand at a glance. Colors are carefully chosen to evoke the right feelings. Starbucks green, for example, suggests freshness and health, while Coca-Cola red implies energy and excitement.

Just how seductive is packaging? Almost 40% of consumers said they would share a product photo with friends on Facebook if the packaging was "attractive or gift-like."

Active Learning

Divide into small groups. Brainstorm about different brands (companies) and products you like. Make a list of these brands and products and concentrate on the packaging. Talk about your intellectual and emotional reaction to the packaging. What about it attracts you? Does it remind you of past experiences? Share with the class your favorite example of packaging, along with the reasons for your choice.

● **As You Read**

Think of some items on which you would not mind spending a little more money for the brand-name version and some things that are fine as generic items.

Deciding What to Buy

Consumers must first decide what product they want to buy. Usually they decide what is a top **priority** for them. Then they can choose to buy either a brand-name product or a generic product. A **brand name** is the trade name for a product or service produced by a particular company. Familiar brand names include Nike®, Kellogg's®, and Pepsi®. Buyers often associate quality with brand names.

Generic products are plainly labeled, unadvertised products that are sold at lower prices than brand-name goods. Many brand-name medicines and grocery items have a generic **version**. Despite the difference in cost, they may be equal in quality to some brand-name products. **Figure 22.1** illustrates a comparative graph for making a buying decision.

Deciding When to Buy

Prices for many items change during different times of the year. Postponing or planning a purchase can sometimes save you money. For example, you would probably save more money if you bought an air conditioner in the winter instead of in the summer. There is less demand for air conditioners during cold months, which means prices for them are lower then.

Stores often run special promotions during and after holidays, just before a school year begins, and at the end of a season. There are often more choices when products are first available. However, you may find better prices if you wait until the items go on sale.

Figure 22.1 — *Making Consumer Decisions*

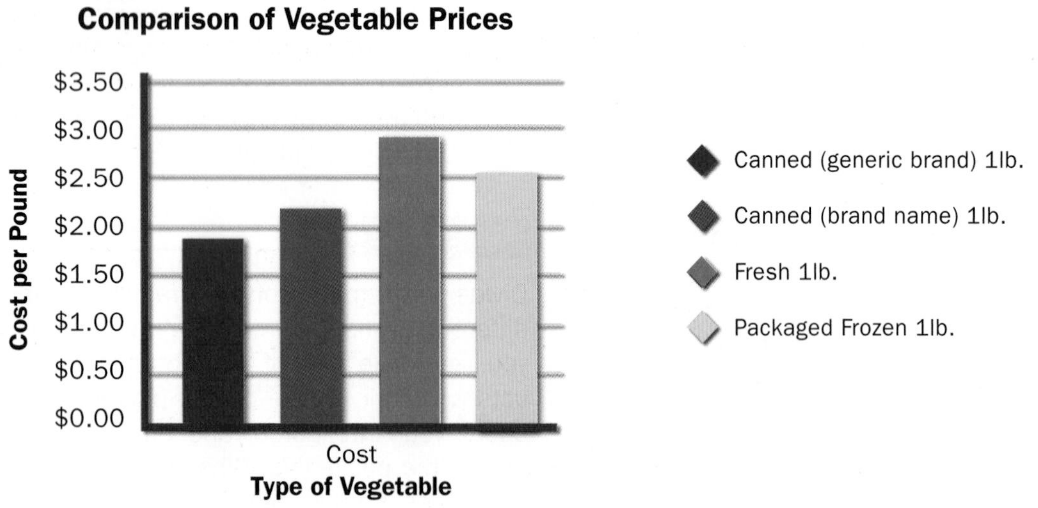

Comparison of Vegetable Prices

◆ Canned (generic brand) 1lb.

◆ Canned (brand name) 1lb.

◆ Fresh 1lb.

◆ Packaged Frozen 1lb.

Source: http://retailtrafficmag.com/mag/retail_america_shops

● **Your Choices at the Supermarket** Generic brands usually cost less than brand-name products. Food products may come fresh, frozen, or canned. **Which would you choose from these different vegetable products?**

Deciding Where to Buy

Along with choosing what to buy, consumers have to decide where to shop. There are three factors that affect a consumer's decision on where to shop: the kinds of goods and services sold, prices, and convenience.

Department Stores

Department stores sell a wide variety of goods. Because they offer name brands and customer service, their prices may be higher than other types of stores. Most sell many lines of products, such as furniture, clothing, and shoes.

Discount Stores

Discount stores also sell a variety of goods. However, discount stores generally offer lower prices. They can sell for less because they offer fewer services and keep large quantities of goods. They include Wal-Mart® and Kmart®.

Off-Price and Outlet Stores

These types of stores carry well-known brand names at bargain prices. They offer big discounts because the items they sell may have flaws, may be out of season, or may be discontinued merchandise. Examples are T.J. Maxx®, Marshalls®, and Ross® Stores.

Limited-Line Retailers

Limited-line retailers, or specialty stores, sell an assortment of goods in one product line or a few related lines. They often have a variety of items and high levels of service and expertise. Foot Locker®, PetSmart®, and Ace Hardware® are specialty stores.

Superstores

Superstores are like supermarkets but sell items such as books, hardware, sporting goods, and clothing as well as groceries. Like supermarkets, they are also self-serve. Kroger®, Walmart®, and Safeway® operate superstores.

Convenience Stores

As their name implies, convenience stores provide easy access to products that consumers often buy as necessities or impulse items. They offer limited lines of products, mostly grocery items. The world's largest chain of convenience stores is run by 7-Eleven®.

● **As You Read**

Think about an item you are planning to purchase. Do you think you could save money if you waited to buy it?

International Business

Adapting to New Cultures

Wal-Mart is one of the leading U.S. retailers. In December 2005, it acquired 545 stores in South America and Japan. Walmart purchased the Sonae retail company's operations in Brazil, which will add a variety of new retail formats to Walmart's already diverse catalog. Walmart Canada is in the process of expanding its stores to include fresh food and a wider selection of products. All of the stores will keep the basic "feel" of the stores in America while offering products that are more fitting to the country in which they are sold.

Examples of Languages Across Cultures

Q: In Brazilian Portuguese, how do you say: "What time should I arrive?"

A: **A que horas devo chegar?**
(pronounced: Ăh kā ōr-dăs dāy-voo shā-găr?)

Why is it important for a company to adapt to new cultures? What types of changes does a company need to adopt when entering a foreign market?

Unit Prices Some products come in many different sizes, making it hard to determine the best buy. In this situation, look at the unit price. The *unit price* is the cost of an item divided by a standard unit of measurement, such as an ounce. Suppose a store offers two brands of milk. Brand A is 10 ounces and costs $2. Brand B is 15 ounces and costs $2.85. *Which brand offers the lowest unit price?*

Warehouse Stores

Warehouse stores are typically about the size of a football field. They carry a huge selection of food and nonfood items at low prices and in **bulk** quantities. Some require customers to become members to get buying privileges and discounts. They include Costco and Sam's Club.

Shopping at Home

Consumers can shop at home through the Internet, TV channels, and catalogs. Some companies such as Service Merchandise sell items only on the Internet. Others offer catalog and online services. Some retail stores, such as Crate & Barrel and Eddie Bauer, also mail catalogs.

Deciding How Much to Pay

Comparison shopping is an important factor in buying products or services. **Comparison shopping** is comparing the prices and the characteristics of competing brands or stores. It is most important for major purchases because the difference in cost can be significant. Some people think the most expensive item is always the best product. However, sometimes the least expensive item or the one in the middle might be the best buy for the money.

Section 22.1

After You Read

Review Key Concepts
1. What are four decisions that consumers must make when they buy goods and services?
2. Compare brand-name and generic products.
3. Identify choices that consumers must make when they buy.

Academic Skills
4. **Mathematics** Paper towels come in two sizes, regular and jumbo. A regular roll costs 89¢ and contains 80 sheets, each 11×9 inches. A jumbo roll costs $1.37 and contains 146 sheets, each also 11×9 inches. What is the difference in the cost per square foot of the two sizes?

CONCEPT **Finding Areas** The formula for finding the area of a rectangle is $A = l \times w$. To convert square inches into square feet, divide the number of square inches in the roll by 12×12, the number of square inches in one square foot.

Math For math help, go to the Math Appendix.

 Go to **connectED.mcgraw-hill.com** to check your answers.

How to Be a Smart Consumer

Before You Read

Think about what you can do to make the best buying decisions.

Read to Learn

- Identify types of information that can be helpful to a consumer in making wise shopping decisions.

The Main Idea

To get the most value for your shopping dollar, you can collect information to make an informed decision when you shop. You should plan ahead so that you can make the best choices and get the best buys.

Key Concept

- Preparing to Shop

Vocabulary

Key Terms

promotional sale
clearance sale
loss leaders
impulse buying
warranty

Academic Vocabulary

You will find these words in your reading and on your tests. Make sure you know their meanings.

convince   label
publications   document

Graphic Organizer

In a figure like the one below, list the steps you need to take when you prepare to shop.

Preparing to Shop

 Go to **connectED.mcgraw-hill.com** to print out this graphic organizer.

Preparing to Shop

Consumers have to decide what a bargain is to them. You can become a smart consumer by planning in advance. Before making a purchase, a smart consumer should

- study advertisements.
- read consumer publications.
- shop at sales.
- use shopping lists.
- resist pressure and gimmicks.
- read labels and warranties.

✔ Reading Check **Identify** What should a smart consumer do before purchasing a product or service?

● As You Read

Think about some recent ads that have attracted your attention. Why did they appeal to you?

Study Advertisements

To be a wise consumer, you must learn how to read ads for information that will be helpful. Most ads are one of two types. *Rational advertising* attempts to **convince** consumers with facts and information. It tries to persuade buyers to choose a specific product because it is the best one for their purposes. *Emotional advertising* appeals to people's feelings. For example, it might suggest that if consumers buy a particular car, they will be popular.

When you look at advertising, decide whether it provides useful information. An ad that simply says, "The best buy in town!" will not necessarily help you become a smarter consumer. However, an ad that says, "6 oz. Sparkle-Plenty Toothpaste, $1.99," might be very helpful. If you know that this toothpaste is good and usually sells for $2.79 for 6 ounces, then you will know that the sale is a good buy.

● Advertisers Provide Information
Advertisers help you make shopping choices. **What types of advertising inserts are provided to consumers?**

Figure 22.2 — *Shopping Choices*

Selection	Convenience	Price
Always in stock	Convenient location	Good value for the price
Have what I want	Good service	High quality
Unique merchandise	Products easily accessible	Low or fair prices

Source: http://retailtrafficmag.com/mag/retail_america_shops

● **What Consumers Want** There are many things that are important to consumers when they shop. **What do you consider to be the most important reason for choosing a particular store?**

Read Consumer Publications

Publications such as *Consumer Reports* and *Consumers' Research Magazine* give detailed information about goods that have been tested and rated. If you need to buy an expensive item, you can begin comparison shopping by studying what these magazines say about the competing brands.

Consumer magazines examine and rate products ranging from bottled iced teas to travel agencies. Many specialty magazines, such as those for photographers or hikers, rate equipment such as cameras or hiking boots. Libraries and online services are good places to find these **publications**.

Shop at Sales

Stores often use sales to attract customers. A **promotional sale** is one that offers a special buy on a new product or a product that is in season. It is usually held at a time when consumer purchases are down, such as after holidays. A **clearance sale** is a sale to clear out goods that are going out of season or are no longer profitable. These sales often make room for new merchandise. Clearance sales often mark the end of a season. Many businesses also hold other sales throughout the year.

During a sale, look for products that are advertised as selling at a loss or below cost. **Loss leaders** are advertised products that sell at a loss to bring customers into a store. Even though a store does not make money on them, their low prices are intended to attract more customers. Store managers hope consumers will buy other items along with loss leaders. **Figure 22.2** shows why consumers shop at certain stores.

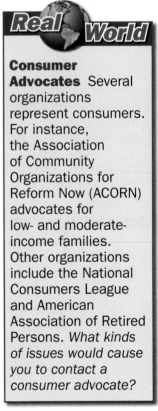

Real World

Consumer Advocates Several organizations represent consumers. For instance, the Association of Community Organizations for Reform Now (ACORN) advocates for low- and moderate-income families. Other organizations include the National Consumers League and American Association of Retired Persons. *What kinds of issues would cause you to contact a consumer advocate?*

As You Read

Stores are in business to make a profit. Think about the reasons a store would sell a product at a loss.

Use Shopping Lists

Impulse buying is the act of making unplanned purchases. Impulse buying can ruin a consumer's budget and result in buying items that are not needed. To cut down on unplanned buying, use a shopping list. It might keep you from making unnecessary shopping trips because you forgot something you need. It can also save you money, because you can decide in advance what to buy and how much to spend.

Resist Pressure and Gimmicks

Some salespeople use high-pressure tactics to get consumers to buy their goods and services. They can be very persuasive. You should always ask yourself if what the salesperson is saying is true, if you need the product or service, and if you can afford it.

Sales gimmicks, such as ads for prizes or "super-low prices," are meant to grab consumers' attention and get them into a store to buy something. For example, you might get a notice in the mail that says you have won a prize. However, after reading closely, you realize you will not get the prize unless you buy something. Always examine any deal that seems too good to be true.

✔ **Reading Check** **Analyze** Why do some consumers make impulse purchases?

Read Labels and Warranties

Before buying a product, read its **label**. You might find information on it that will lead you to decide not to buy the product. For instance, before buying fruit juice, read the food label for the contents. What you thought was 100 percent fruit juice could mainly be corn syrup and water.

Many items come with a warranty. A **warranty** is a written guarantee from the manufacturer or distributor that states the conditions under which the product can be returned, replaced, or repaired. It is a legal **document** that states the rights and responsibilities of the consumer and the store or manufacturer. Federal law requires sellers of products that cost more than $15 (and that have a warranty) to make the warranty available to customers before a purchase. It is often printed on the package.

Warranties are divided into two basic types: implied and express. *Implied warranties* are unwritten guarantees that cover certain aspects of a product or its use. An implied warranty of mechantability guarantees that a product is fit for its intended use. *Express warranties*, which are usually written, come in two forms. *Full warranties* state that the seller will repair or replace a product that does not work, usually free of charge, or give a refund. Full warranties are usually good for a stated time period, such as 90 days or one year. *Limited warranties* cover only certain parts of a product. They may require the buyer to pay a portion of the repair costs.

Section 22.2

After You Read

Review Key Concepts

1. What can you do before shopping that can help you make a wise choice?
2. Describe promotional sales and clearance sales.
3. What types of protection do a full warranty and a limited warranty provide to consumers?

Academic Skills

4. **English Language Arts** List products that you would buy at a store that is convenient to you. Then list products for which you shop around at several stores even if you have to travel to get to them. Write a paragraph comparing the lists.

5. **English Language Arts** With a partner, create a poster to advise students about ways to be a smart shopper and to avoid getting "taken in" by ads and promotions. Use some of this chapter's key words in your poster.

 Go to **connectED.mcgraw-hill.com** to check your answers.

Section 22.1 Summary

Consumer Choices Making shopping decisions is not always easy, especially when there are many options available. Most people have limited funds. As consumers, they have to budget their money to satisfy their wants and needs. Consumers must decide what, when, and where to buy goods and services as well as how much to pay for them. They must also decide whether to buy generic or brand-name items. The best buy depends on what is important to the individual consumer.

Section 22.2 Summary

How to Be a Smart Consumer You can become a smart consumer by planning in advance. Smart consumers study advertisements, read consumer publications, and shop at sales. They also use shopping lists, resist pressure and gimmicks to buy goods and services, and read labels and warranties. Many consumers turn to consumer magazines when researching products and services. Planning helps them to avoid impulse buying and allows consumers to get the best warranty.

Vocabulary Review

1. On a sheet of paper, use each of these key terms and academic vocabulary terms in a sentence.

Key Terms
consumer
brand name
generic products
comparison shopping
promotional sale
clearance sale
loss leaders
impulse buying
warranty

Academic Vocabulary
disposes
priority
version
bulk
convince
publications
label
document

Review Key Concepts

2. Identify four decisions that consumers make when they buy goods and services.

3. Compare brand-name and generic products.

4. Identify choices that consumers must make about when to buy.

5. List several choices that consumers have when selecting a store to make purchases.

6. Describe tools that consumers can use to compare prices for goods and services.

7. Identify types of information that can be helpful to a consumer in making wise shopping decisions.

Critical Thinking

8. What time(s) of the year would be best for department stores to offer sales because of a decrease in consumer purchases?

9. Some specialty stores set higher prices and still find a niche with shoppers. What factors do you think make them successful?

10. What types of products do you think consumers should consider buying in large quantities to save money?

11. Think about three items you have bought recently. Where did you buy each one? Did you comparison shop before you made the purchases? Why or why not?

12. In many stores, racks by the checkout counter have a wide range of "convenience goods" on display. These goods include candy, magazines, batteries, and chewing gum. Why do you think they are placed here?

13. Warehouse stores offer a wide variety of items. Why do you think consumers and small businesses choose to shop at them?

14. Do you think consumers can make informed decisions without advertising?

Write About It

15. Choose an ad from your local newspaper for a department store where you like to shop. Write two or more paragraphs describing the products that are featured in the ad. Include your ideas about why these products are being featured at this time of year.

16. Use your local phone book and prepare a list of 10 stores in your shopping community. Classify each store as one of the types of stores you have read about in this chapter.

17. Choose a store in one of the categories discussed in this chapter. Visit the store's Web site and research the types of information it offers to consumers. Write two or more paragraphs on your findings.

18. Go to a library and find an issue of a consumer magazine such as *Consumer Reports* or *Consumers Digest*. Write a short summary of the magazine features.

19. Visit a Web site for a large company that sells appliances, electronic equipment, or computers. Search for information on warranties. Summarize what you find in a brief report.

Technology Applications

Database Software

20. Research the stores that offer an item you want to buy. Use database software to create a database of the stores. Include names, addresses, telephone numbers, Web site addresses, prices, and any other information to use in comparison shopping. Use the information to determine the best place to buy the item.

Business Ethics

The Ethics of Advertising

21. A store in your neighborhood announces it will hold a sale. You know that the store raised prices before the sale was announced, but everything was later discounted for the sale. Is this ethical? What can consumers do in response?

Applying Academics to Business

English Language Arts

22. Ads use writing that is designed to persuade. Choose a product you like and use often. Write both a rational and an emotional ad for it. Include an attention-grabbing headline and two or three sentences describing features of the product. Present your ads to the class and lead a discussion about their differences.

Mathematics

23. The computer you bought includes a one-year service warranty. The cost of servicing computers averages about $45 in parts and labor per service. If the retail price of the computer was $750, about what percentage of that price covers the cost of the warranty?

CONCEPT **Problem Solving** It is often helpful to restate the problem in your own words before solving. In this case you are asked to express the cost of the warranty as a percent of the cost "per computer."

English Language Arts

24. Sort the words below to make a list of eight two-word phrases about making consumer decisions.

generic	brand
clearance	discount
comparison	name
buying	unit
leader	shopping
product	price
store	impulse
sale	loss

Mathematics

25. Go through a coupon mailer or flyer for a local grocery store. List the face value for at least 20 coupons. Find the mean and median of the data.

CONCEPT **Data Analysis** The mean of a set of numbers is their average; the median is the middle number, or the average of the two middle numbers, when the data are listed from least to greatest.

Active Learning

Wise-Shopping Presentation

26. Prepare a short presentation for your class on wise-shopping tips for buying an electronic device of your choice. Include some ideas in your presentation for making the best choices when preparing for a shopping trip and during shopping. Include information about the best places to shop in your community for the product you chose. Present your ideas to the class.

Business in the Real World

Generic Brands

27. Visit a grocery store or supermarket. Choose five items that are available as generic products. Record their prices. Then find brand-name versions of those items and record their prices. Calculate the unit prices of the 10 items. Prepare a chart showing the unit price of each item and the amount a shopper could save by buying the generic products.

Real LIFE skills

CONSUMER ISSUES AND DECISION MAKING

28. Sometimes the government or a business that produces a good or a service makes a decision about a consumer issue that greatly affects consumers' finances. Research a consumer issue, and determine the financial implications for consumers. What might consumers do in response to this action?

Business CAREERS

FIND YOUR DREAM JOB

29. Locate the Occupational Outlook Handbook Web site. Click on the "OOH Search/A-Z Index" link and enter the job title "sales representative" (wholesale and manufacturing). Then write a one-page report about this type of occupation. Conclude your report with a list of things you could do now to prepare yourself to pursue the occupation.

Role Play

SHOPPING FOR A NEW COMPUTER

30. Situation With two or three of your classmates, discuss the points you need to consider in deciding to buy a new computer.

Activity Plan a short skit that your group will present to your class, demonstrating the questions you would ask before you make your decision.

Evaluation You will be evaluated on how well you meet the following performance indicators:

- Describe some different types of computers from which you could choose.
- Outline at least five questions your group will discuss.
- Identify the best choice.
- Prepare a written outline of the points in your skit.

Standardized Test Practice

Directions Choose the letter of the best answer. Write the letter for the answer on a separate piece of paper.

1. What is 559,607 rounded to the nearest hundred thousand?

   A   500,000

   B   560,000

   C   559,600

   D   600,000

TEST-TAKING TIP When answering an essay question on a test, focus on one main idea per paragraph. Do not write long introductions and conclusions. Spend most of your time answering the question asked.

Chapter 23

Consumer Rights and Responsibilities

Chapter Objectives After completing this chapter, you will be able to:

▶ **Section 23.1** *Consumer Rights*
- **Describe** seven protections that are included in the Consumer Bill of Rights.

▶ **Section 23.2** *Consumer Responsibilities*
- **Describe** the responsibilities of consumers.

Ask

AN EXPERT

Taxes and Investing

Q: What responsibilities do I have for paying taxes on my investment earnings?

A: Everyone is required to pay taxes on investments. The amount of taxes you owe on an investment is dependent on how much your investment grew, how long you held the investment, and on your tax bracket. Your tax bracket is the amount at which your regular income is taxed. It is important to figure taxes into your calculations when comparing your investment choices. The difference they can make is startling. In fact, the tax advantage afforded to long-term capital gains is another big reason why long-term investing approaches work so well.

Mathematics John and Esperanza both fall in the 35% tax bracket. John decides to make a single $10,000 investment at the beginning of the year and hold it into the next year. Esperanza moves her $10,000 from stock to stock throughout the year. John's investment doubles to $20,000, while Esperanza's increases by 125% to $22,500. However, because John's investment qualifies as a long-term investment, he owes only $1,500 in taxes. Esperanza owes the full 35%, $5,250, because she bought and sold multiple times. At what rate was John taxed?

CONCEPT **Use a Variable to Represent a Percent** Just as a variable can represent an integer, it can also represent a decimal or percent. Just as you would solve any other algebraic expression, isolate the variable on one side to determine its value.

● **Knowledge Is Power** Consumers can learn about ingredients by reading the labels on food products. **Do you compare the labels of food products before deciding which product to buy?**

Onoky/SuperStock

Consumer Rights

Reading Guide

Before You Read

Think about the importance of your rights as a consumer and the ways those rights can impact your life.

Read to Learn

- Describe seven protections that are included in the Consumer Bill of Rights.

The Main Idea

Consumers are protected by the Consumer Bill of Rights. The bill states that consumers have the right to be informed, the right to choose, the right to safety, the right to be heard, the right to have problems corrected, the right to consumer education, and the right to service.

Key Concept

- The Consumer Bill of Rights

Vocabulary

Key Terms

consumer rights
consumer movement
product liability
bait and switch

Academic Vocabulary

You will find these words in your reading and on your tests. Make sure you know their meanings.

accurate
devices
resolved
scenario

Graphic Organizer

List the benefits of each of the seven basic consumer rights in a figure like the one below.

Consumer Right	Benefit of that Right
The Right to Be Informed	
The Right to Choose	
The Right to Safety	
The Right to Be Heard	
The Right to Have Problems Corrected	
The Right to Consumer Education	
The Right to Service	

 Go to **connectED.mcgraw-hill.com** to print out this graphic organizer.

The Consumer Bill of Rights

● **As You Read**

Think about your rights as a consumer. Have you ever observed your consumer protection rights when dealing with a defective product you purchased?

Imagine that you just bought an MP3 player. The first time you play it, you do not hear a sound. The good news is that you have rights as a consumer. These rights protect you when a product is defective.

In 1962, President John F. Kennedy outlined what he called the Consumer Bill of Rights. The bill stated that every person has four basic **consumer rights**—the right to be informed, the right to choose, the right to safety, and the right to be heard. These rights received a lot of attention from the **consumer movement**, a movement to pass laws protecting consumers from unfair and unsafe business practices. Over the years, three other rights were added: the right to have problems corrected, the right to consumer education, and the right to service.

The Right to Be Informed

As a consumer, you have a right to receive **accurate** information. Consumers can make wise decisions only if they have the information they need. Businesses are required to provide certain details about their products. For example, drug companies must list the complete contents of every medicine. Clothing manufacturers must list the fibers used in materials. Packaged foods must show all ingredients, with the main one listed first. Companies provide this information through product labeling.

The Right to Choose

Because the United States has a market economy, its consumers can choose from a wide variety of goods and services. Businesses compete with each other to sell their products to consumers. They offer new products, lower prices, higher quality, or improved services to get you to choose their products. Competition provides choices. A lack of it hurts consumers.

?ETHICS in Business

Product Safety

■ **Critical Reading** Life is full of important decisions. Think about the kinds of decisions that you make as you read the question below.

A product your company makes has a slight design flaw. You are the only one who knows about the problem, and the chances of it causing someone harm are negligible. The warning label that was printed, although thorough, does not address the design flaw. To reprint the warning labels would put this product over budget.

■ **Decision Making** Would you have the warning labels reprinted? Explain your answer.

The federal government has the power to keep markets competitive. It can use antitrust laws to break up monopolies or keep them from forming. Sometimes it will prevent a large company from buying a smaller one if the purchase would lead to control of a market.

✔ **Reading Check** **Explain** What type of economy gives its citizens the right to choose from a wide variety of goods and services?

The Right to Safety

You have a right to products that are safe to use. **Product liability** is the legal responsibility that manufacturers have to make a safe product. For example, tools and appliances must include safety **devices** for your protection. Federal laws ensure that clothing, food, toys, and other items will not harm consumers. The U.S. Consumer Product Safety Commission enforces product-safety standards.

Business Case Study

Your Right to Safety

Companies can end up paying millions when their products threaten health

When products harm consumers, lawsuits can force manufacturers to pay damages—sometimes in the millions—to those who have been harmed. Here are just three such cases that made headlines:

Exploding cans: Blitz, the U.S.'s largest producer of gas cans, went bankrupt in 2012 because of dozens of liability lawsuits that cost the company $60 million in legal fees. The lawsuits alleged that the cans failed to prevent the gas inside from catching fire.

Too-hot coffee: In this famous case, a woman sued McDonald's after suffering serious burns from spilled coffee. Her lawyers argued that McDonald's coffee was dangerously hot, and that the company had ignored hundreds of similar complaints. A jury awarded her $2,860,000 in damages and expenses.

Bad ignitions: In 2014 General Motors recalled 26 million vehicles for repairs and created a $400 million compensation fund after admitting

that they produced faulty ignition switches. The switches could shut off engines while cars were in motion, disable power steering, and prevent air bags from inflating. The bad switches are linked to at least 13 deaths. Several lawsuits were filed, including a $10 billion class action suit, a type of action in which multiple plaintiffs join together.

Many business organizations argue that lawsuits like these are ridiculous and driven by simple greed. Consumer advocates counter that legal action is necessary to keep companies honest and to help injured victims.

Active Learning

Laws protecting consumer safety are a relatively recent development in U.S. history. The U.S. Consumer Product Safety Act (CPSA) and the Consumer Product Safety Improvement Act (CPSIA) are the main federal laws governing product safety. Do research online and write a one-page report that describes what these laws do to product consumers. If your state has additional laws, summarize these as well.

The Right to Be Heard

Consumers who have complaints about products or services have a right to be heard. Suppose you buy a bike helmet from a sporting goods store. After wearing the helmet a few times, you find that the chinstrap keeps coming loose. You have the right to let the store know you are not satisfied with the helmet. Businesses rely on customer satisfaction. The purpose of the customer service department is to listen to the concerns of customers.

The Right to Have Problems Corrected

Sometimes products do not work properly after they are purchased. Usually if a customer takes a defective item back to a store with a receipt, the business will replace it or issue a refund. If a business cannot or will not correct a problem, consumers can write to the manufacturer to find out how to get the matter **resolved**. If the manufacturer will not help, a government agency might be your next step. **Figure 23.1** asks you to match each **scenario** with the appropriate consumer right.

Real World

Consumer Resources
Consumer.gov is an online resource for consumer information from the federal government. It is designed so that consumers can locate information by category—such as food, health, product safety, money, and transportation. *How might this consumer resource be useful to you?*

Figure 23.1 — *Know Your Consumer Rights*

Consumer Issue	Consumer Right
1. An automaker recalls its new model after some of its seat belts fail to keep children safe.	Right to be heard
2. A restaurant asks you to fill out a comment card after eating your meal.	Right to choose
3. An advertisement for a new TV informs the consumer about the total cost and interest rate.	Right to service
4. An electronics store displays three competing brands of computers from which to choose.	Right to safety
5. A shoe store replaces your new shoes after you discover a problem with the soles.	Right to be informed
6. *Consumer Reports* educates consumers who are researching different models of cameras.	Right to have problems corrected
7. You pay an auto-repair service to rebuild your car's engine.	Right to consumer education

● **Consumer Rights** The Consumer Bill of Rights states that every person has the right to be informed, to choose, to be safe, to be heard, to have problems corrected, to receive consumer education, and to receive service. **Can you match the consumer issue with the appropriate consumer right?**

The Right to Consumer Education

Consumers have the right to learn how a market system works. You should know how to get the best value and satisfaction for your money. When you decide to buy an item, you should know that different stores might charge different prices. You should know how to comparison shop to find the best buy. Check the information required by law on labels, and read fact sheets about products.

The Bait-and-Switch Tactic There are always some businesses that do not operate in the best interests of the consumer. Some might try a tactic known as bait and switch. **Bait and switch** is a sales tactic in which buyers are tempted by an advertised bargain but are then persuaded to buy a more expensive item instead.

The Right to Service

Customers have a right to be treated in a respectful and courteous manner. You have the right to expect prompt delivery of goods or services that meet the standard of quality a business claims. You also have the right to be served without discrimination on the basis of your race, gender, income, or age. These rights apply wherever you are being served.

Section 23.1

After You Read

Review Key Concepts

1. What are four basic consumer rights provided by the 1962 Consumer Bill of Rights?
2. What three consumer rights have been added to the Consumer Bill of Rights since 1962?
3. How does the bait-and-switch tactic work? Why is it unfair to consumers?

Academic Skills

4. **Mathematics** Today you found the tablecloth you wanted to buy on sale for the bargain price of $20. At other stores the same tablecloth costs $23. Write an expression that could be used to determine the percent discount of the bargain tablecloth.

CONCEPT **Percent Discount** Percent discount is a ratio of the difference in price divided by the original price. To convert a decimal to a percent, multiply by 100 by moving the decimal point two places to the right.

 For math help, go to the Math Appendix.

 Go to **connectED.mcgraw-hill.com** to check your answers.

Consumer Responsibilities

● Before You Read

Think about your responsibilities as a consumer and the ways those responsibilities can impact businesses.

Read to Learn

- Describe the responsibilities of consumers.

The Main Idea

Along with your consumer rights, you have responsibilities. You must use information provided to you, choose carefully, use products safely, and learn consumer skills. It is your responsibility to speak out and seek a remedy when problems occur.

Key Concept

- Your Responsibilities as a Consumer

Vocabulary

Key Terms

pollution   recycling
conservation   boycott

Academic Vocabulary

You will find these words in your reading and on your tests. Make sure you know their meanings.

adjust   contact
manuals   adequate

Graphic Organizer

In a table like the one shown, list examples of each of the six responsibilities of consumers.

Consumer Responsibility	Example
The Responsibility to Be Informed	
The Responsibility to Choose Carefully	
The Responsibility to Use Products Safely	
The Responsibility to Speak Out	
The Responsibility to Seek a Remedy	
The Responsibility to Learn Consumer Skills	

 Go to **connectED.mcgraw-hill.com** to print out this graphic organizer.

Your Responsibilities as a Consumer

Along with rights come responsibilities. As a consumer, you have the responsibility to educate yourself. If information about a product is available, you have the responsibility to read that information and to use the product the way it is intended.

The Responsibility to Be Informed

Responsible consumers know what they are buying. When you shop for food, read the labels for nutritional facts. Product labels can tell you how much salt, sugar, fat, or protein a product contains. When you shop for clothes, read the labels to find out what materials they contain. The labels will also indicate how the clothes should be cleaned.

Before making a major purchase, you should always do some homework. Some consumers read the fact sheets from the U.S. Consumer Product Safety Commission. The fact sheets tell how a product is rated on safety, performance, and value. There is also lots of information on the Internet. Read consumer magazines such as *Consumer Reports* and *Consumers' Research Magazine*, which evaluate and rate products. Most consumer organizations and manufacturers have Web sites. **Figure 23.2** shows the Web site for J.D. Power and Associates®, a leading market research and consumer information firm.

✔ **Reading Check** **Contrast** How do product labels and fact sheets from the U.S. Consumer Product Safety Commission differ?

● **Stay Informed** It is your responsibility to learn about products before buying them. **How are these people taking responsibility as consumers?**

Juice Images/Alamy

The Responsibility to Choose Carefully

Responsible consumers make comparisons to find the best product or service at the best price. Which electronics company offers the best guarantee? Which cars have the best record for reliability? Which computer will best fit your budget and your needs? It pays to take time to make comparisons. You can examine the options and prices and then make an educated choice.

Choices That Affect the Environment Many consumer choices can affect the environment. Some vehicles emit more exhaust than others. Some materials, such as certain plastics, cannot be recycled and do not decompose easily. Illegal dumping can harm natural habitats. All of these things contribute to **pollution**, the contamination of air, water, and land. Pollution is caused by waste from products as well as the ways we use them. People and businesses must help to reduce it by making choices that are good for the environment.

Conserving Resources As the population grows, the demand for resources increases. **Conservation** is the process of preserving, protecting, and planning the management of resources. For example, as more people move into an area, the demand for water rises. Some areas may experience water shortages. Consumers should be aware of the limited supplies of certain resources and adjust their consumption accordingly.

● **As You Read**

Think about ways consumers can reduce pollution.

Science/Tech TRENDS

Eco-Friendly Packaging

If something is biodegradable, living organisms can break it down into simpler structures. This reduces the length of time it affects the environment. Packaging producers have increased research into the chemicals they use, looking for materials that can be broken down faster. A majority of packaging material is made of some form of ordinary plastic. While many plastics can be recycled, they are not biodegradable. This leaves it up to voluntary recycle programs to reduce the environmental impact.

WebQuest

Locate Web sites where you can research how packaging manufacturers are trying to lessen the environmental impact of their products. Write a paragraph describing what companies are doing in this area.

Recycling Part of conservation is learning to avoid waste. Consumers can help by reducing, reusing, and recycling materials in their daily lives. **Recycling** involves collecting products for processing so that they can be used again. Many cities have programs to collect products made of paper, plastic, metal, and glass for recycling.

✔ Reading Check **Define** What is recycling?

● **As You Read**

Think about a product you bought that was defective. What did you do to speak out about the defective product?

The Responsibility to Use Products Safely

Consumers must follow the instructions provided in product **manuals** or other materials on the safe use of products. For example, a consumer must read the label of a cold remedy to find out its recommended dosage. If you know a product is unsafe, first contact the seller or producer about it. If no action is taken by the company, **contact** a consumer protection agency.

The Responsibility to Speak Out

Responsible consumers can help improve the policies and products of the businesses where they shop. They can let a company know if they are dissatisfied with its products or policies. Consumers also have a responsibility to report unfair, unsafe, and illegal business practices. This helps to protect other consumers from problems. If you object to a company's policies or products, you could organize a **boycott**, a refusal to buy its goods or services. Boycotting is usually a last resort for consumers who have not received an **adequate** response from a company.

The Responsibility to Seek a Remedy

Part of being a good consumer is getting the best value for your money. You have a responsibility to seek a remedy for a defective product. If you plan to exchange an item or get a refund, you must take back the item, the receipt, and any warranties or guarantees that came with it. If the store cannot solve the problem to your satisfaction, you should contact the manufacturer or a consumer organization for help.

The Responsibility to Learn Consumer Skills

Find information to help you make consumer decisions. It is a bit overwhelming to think of researching every purchase before it is made. However, there are several ways to develop your consumer skills:

- Read information on labels and packages.
- Compare prices at different stores, and look for sales.
- Pay attention to the media to become aware of illegal practices.
- Read consumer information publications.
- Attend classes or workshops on consumer issues and problems.

Many purchases that you make will not require any research. Still, remember that the more informed you are about products and services, the better your consumer decisions will be.

Section 23.2

After You Read

Review Key Concepts

1. Where can you find information before making a major purchase?
2. Identify three steps you can take as a consumer to conserve resources.
3. If you object to a company's practices, what can you do as a consumer?

Academic Skills

4. **English Language Arts** Work together with one or two other students to create a bulletin-board display called "Consumers Speak Out!" Collect newspaper and magazine articles from consumer publications that illustrate how consumers have influenced businesses to change their policies or improve their products.

5. **English Language Arts** Write a 250-word report on how government regulations, such as those related to automobile safety, food and drug labeling, and secondhand smoke in stores and restaurants, have affected the safety of consumers.

 Go to **connectED.mcgraw-hill.com** to check your answers.

Section 23.1 *Summary*

Consumer Rights The U.S. Consumer Bill of Rights states that every person has seven basic consumer rights. The first four are the right to be informed, the right to choose, the right to safety, and the right to be heard. Since the bill was developed in 1962, three other rights have been added to it: the right to have problems corrected, the right to consumer education, and the right to service. As a consumer, you are protected if you buy a defective product or receive poor service. However, it is up to you to make sure that your rights are observed.

Section 23.2 *Summary*

Consumer Responsibilities Along with rights come responsibilities. It is your responsibility to educate yourself before making consumer decisions. If you plan to make a major purchase, you can read and investigate your choices so that you can make a wise decision. Comparison shop by reading consumer magazines, checking companies' Web sites, and visiting different stores. Reducing pollution, conserving resources, and recycling are also responsibilities. If you take your consumer responsibilities seriously, you can get the best value for your money.

Vocabulary Review

1. On a sheet of paper, use each of these key terms and academic vocabulary terms in a sentence.

Key Terms	Academic Vocabulary
consumer rights	accurate
consumer movement	devices
product liability	resolved
bait and switch	scenario
pollution	adjust
conservation	manuals
recycling	contact
boycott	adequate

Review Key Concepts

2. Describe four protections for consumers that are included in the Consumer Bill of Rights.

3. Describe the responsibilities of consumers.

4. After the Consumer Bill of Rights was developed, the consumer movement was a strong force for consumer protection. Why do you think the consumer movement became so strong at that time?

5. In what ways do you think that consumers may not exercise their right to be heard?

6. Where can people go for help in making consumer decisions?

7. When might a loss leader (product sold below cost) become a bait and switch?

8. What do you think causes poor customer service?

9. Check the label on an item of clothing. How would you suggest the manufacturer improve the label?

10. How does it help consumers to have information about a single serving on food labels?

11. What do you think would justify a consumer boycott of a store or company?

12. What do you think is the most important thing that consumers can do to protect their interests when they buy goods and services?

13. Write two or more paragraphs about why you think auto-repair complaints have led the list of consumer concerns for several years.

14. List several reasons why you think large companies often have entire departments devoted to consumer affairs.

15. List an item you recently bought that you are not satisfied with now. Write a short essay about actions you could take to resolve the matter.

16. Research the proper ways to dispose of items such as old clothes and used oil. Then write an essay on your findings.

17. Choose a company and write a short paper on the consumer information it provides. How can consumers remedy a problem with the company's product or service?

18. Find out about environmental issues in your community. List three pollution problems and discuss ways consumers can help solve them.

19. Research different consumer scams. Use the Internet, newspaper articles, and other materials. Write a news article on ways to avoid them.

Spreadsheet Software

20. Study a label for canned or packaged food. Answer these questions: What is the serving size? How many servings are there per can or package? How many calories per serving? How many calories per can or package? What vitamins and minerals does the food provide? Develop a spreadsheet of your findings. Share your results with the class.

Consumer Ethics Policy

21. Consumers have rights and responsibilities. Ethical behavior is one of the most important consumer responsibilities. Write a policy that offers general ethical guidelines and lists specific ways consumers should act when they shop. Discuss your policy with your classmates.

Applying Academics to Business

English Language Arts

22. Research the etymology, or history, of the word *boycott*. How and why did it come into use? What are some important ways boycotts have been used over the years? Write two or three paragraphs about what you discover.

Mathematics

23. Francine has nine cousins. By coincidence, they are all getting married this year. Francine decides to buy each one an engraved silver pitcher as a wedding gift. She finds that the pitcher she wants to buy costs $130. However, if she buys 10, she will get a 10% discount. What is the difference in cost for 9 pitchers versus 10?

CONCEPT **Percent Discount** Percent discount is a ratio of the difference in price divided by the original price. To find a discounted price, multiply the original price by the discount and subtract the product from the original price.

English Language Arts

24. Manufacturers sometimes recall products that have been discovered to be unsafe. Consumer magazines and Web sites post recall notices. Become familiar with at least three recalls of related products in a category such as infant products or electrical components. Describe the reasons for the recalls and the procedures for resolving the problem.

Mathematics

25. VidMania sells DVDs for $14.98 each. In January, the store sold 208 DVDs. The manager wanted to compute the total sales of DVDs for the month. If you were to estimate the answer using mental math, what would be an appropriate estimate?

CONCEPT **Mental Math** Simplifying numbers and computation by rounding and estimating makes it possible to solve problems in your head.

Active Learning

Environmental Awareness

26. Work in a team of two or three to develop a survey about awareness of environmental issues. Survey local businesspeople and consumers. Possible questions to include: Which items do you recycle? How do you dispose of hazardous materials? Then prepare a report of your findings.

Business in the Real World

Consumer Information

27. Visit one or more stores in your community that sell large appliances or electronic equipment. Ask for brochures, pamphlets, or warranty information they may provide to customers. Based on the information you receive, from which company would you most likely make a purchase? Write a brief report on your findings and response.

DEVELOP COMPARISON SHOPPING SKILLS

28. Think of a product that you plan to purchase soon. Then comparison shop. What are different companies' return policies? Which offers the best guarantee? Which offers the best value? Are there any customer reviews to consider? Prepare a report of your findings.

COOL Business CAREERS

FIND YOUR DREAM JOB

29. Locate the Occupational Outlook Handbook Web site. Click on the "OOH Search/A-Z Index" link and enter the job category "public relations specialists." Then write a one-page report about this area of occupation. Conclude your report with a list of things you could do now to prepare yourself to pursue the occupation.

Role Play

PRACTICE CUSTOMER SERVICE SKILLS

30. Situation You are a clothing store manager. The store's return policy states that customers without a receipt may exchange a returned item. A sales associate asks you to talk to a customer, who wants to return an item without a receipt.

Activity With two partners, prepare and perform a skit on how you would handle the customer.

Evaluation You will be evaluated on how well you meet the following performance indicators:

- Listen to both the sales associate and the customer.
- Explain the store's policy on returns.
- Describe what you can do to resolve the matter.
- Speak confidently, courteously, and tactfully.

Standardized Test Practice

Directions Choose the letter of the best answer. Write the letter for the answer on a separate piece of paper.

1. Which sentence contains two independent clauses?

A   When one company controls the market, it has a monopoly.

B   In 1962, President Kennedy signed the Consumer Bill of Rights.

C   The population has stayed the same, but consumer demand has increased.

D   Part of conservation is learning to avoid waste.

 TEST-TAKING TIP Take tests seriously. Schools use them to measure and then improve education. Tests can tell schools that they need to strengthen courses or change teaching techniques. Other tests are used to compare students by schools, school districts, or cities. All tests determine how well you are doing.

Chapter 24

Protecting Consumers

Chapter Objectives After completing this chapter, you will be able to:

▶ **Section 24.1** *Consumer Organizations and Agencies*
- **Explain** the steps consumers can take to find solutions to consumer problems.
- **List** nongovernmental consumer organizations that advocate for consumers.
- **List** some federal and state agencies that provide consumer information and protection.

▶ **Section 24.2** *Consumer Protection Laws*
- **Describe** ways that consumers are protected by laws related to the marketplace.
- **List** ways that the business community assists with consumer protection.

Ask

AN EXPERT

Protecting Consumers: Protecting Investors

Q: The U.S. government regulates the credit industry. How does it regulate the securities industry?

A: After both the crashes of 1929 and 1987, the government passed laws to protect against future crashes. The Securities Act of 1933 was designed to better regulate the market. In addition, the Securities and Exchange Commission was created in 1934 to ensure that the trading of securities is done properly. To this end, the SEC requires people intimately involved with a company to regularly disclose their stock holdings, as well as their intentions to buy or sell additional shares.

Mathematics The table below shows how devastating the stock market crash was to the economy. Read the table and write out the full amount that each number in the table represents.

Year	GNP*
1929	101.4
1931	84.3
1933	68.3
2004	12,151.00

* In billions of dollars

CONCEPT **Expressing Large Numbers** Sometimes, for simplicity sake, large numbers are abbreviated. To avoid placing zeros on the end of each number in a table, the numbers may be shortened, and a note will let you know how they were shortened.

● **Consumer Information** Advertisements provide information to consumers. **What types of information would you want to know before buying a dishwasher?**

Consumer Organizations and Agencies

Reading Guide

Before You Read

Think about some public and private organizations or agencies that provide protection to consumers.

Read to Learn

- Explain the steps consumers can take to find solutions to consumer problems.
- List nongovernmental consumer organizations that advocate for consumers.
- List some federal and state agencies that provide consumer information and protection.

The Main Idea

Many public and private organizations work on behalf of consumers. Federal, state, and local agencies provide information and enforce laws that protect consumers. Consumer advocates work to protect, inform, and defend consumers.

Key Concepts

- Nongovernmental Consumer Organizations
- Government Consumer Organizations

Vocabulary

Key Terms

consumer advocates
grade labels
recall
legal monopoly
licenses

Academic Vocabulary

You will find these words in your reading and on your tests. Make sure you know their meanings.

behalf
panels
supplements
assurance

Graphic Organizer

In a figure like the one below, describe the consumer protection roles of the governmental agencies as you read the section.

Agencies that Protect Consumers	Agency Function
Federal Trade Commission	
Department of Agriculture	
Food and Drug Administration	
National Highway Traffic Safety Administration	
Consumer Product Safety Commission	
State Public Utilities Commissions	
State Insurance Commissions	
State Licensing Agencies	

 Go to **connectED.mcgraw-hill.com** to print out this graphic organizer.

Finding Solutions to Consumer Problems

At some point, you may have trouble with a product or service. There are things you can do to resolve the matter yourself. When faced with a purchasing problem, review your receipts and warranties. Contact the seller and explain the problem. Take your receipts. If the seller does not resolve the situation, take the problem to a higher level. Contact the seller's customer service department and then its headquarters. Consumer organizations may be able to help. If you do not get the results you want, you might decide to file a claim in small claims court.

Nongovernmental Consumer Organizations

There are many organizations that work on **behalf** of consumers. Groups and individuals who work to protect, inform, and defend consumers are called **consumer advocates**. Many consumer advocates are private, nonprofit groups. Some test products and report their findings. Many work to promote consumer protection laws.

The Consumer Federation of America

The Consumer Federation of America (CFA) works to inform the public and government about consumer issues. It works with public officials to promote policies that benefit consumers and to ensure a fair and balanced debate about issues that are important to consumers. It studies federal laws that affect consumers and lets its members know so they can help to support legislation to help the public.

The National Consumers League

The National Consumers League is the nation's oldest nonprofit consumer group with membership open to anyone. It provides government agencies, businesses, and other organizations with the consumer's point of view. One of its services is a national fraud information center. It also monitors the Internet to alert consumers to fraud.

Consumers Union

Consumers Union is a nonprofit organization that publishes the magazine *Consumer Reports*. Researchers with Consumers Union test products and report their findings in the magazine. The magazine does not advertise products or allow its findings to be used in ads. Consumers Union also testifies before government agencies on consumer concerns.

Testing for Safety
Many products around your home probably are labeled "UL Listed." This is the certification by Underwriters Laboratories, a testing facility that develops standards and test procedures for materials, tools, and equipment. Underwriters Laboratories chiefly deals with product safety and utility. *What other types of products can you think of that are tested for safety?*

● **As You Read**

Consumer Reports does not accept advertising. Why do you think it has this policy?

International Business

Import Regulations

Foreign companies wanting to sell their products in the United States are subject to a wide range of regulations. Beyond homeland security issues, there are many other things to consider. Some regulations are concerned with health and foreign foodstuffs. Others have to do with political differences between the United States and the countries from which the imports originate.

Examples of Languages Across Cultures

Q: In Arabic, how do you say: "My name is _____"?

A: إسمي...

(pronounced:
_____ iss-mē.)

What regulations does the United States impose on foreign companies? What is the basis for these regulations?

Major Appliance Consumer Action Program

Some industries have consumer assistance **panels**. The Major Appliance Consumer Action Program (MACAP) helps consumers solve problems with large appliances, such as washers, stoves, and freezers. Most major appliance dealers are members of MACAP.

The Media

Internet sites, radio, TV stations, and newspapers advocate for consumers. They often have a *consumer reporter* who reports on issues that are important to consumers, such as product safety, testing, and shopping. The reporter might feature one consumer's problem with a local business and visit the business to try to resolve the problem.

Government Consumer Organizations

In the United States, each state has a consumer affairs division. In some states, the attorney general's office handles consumer affairs.

Many state and federal agencies have been set up to protect consumers. They publish materials to help consumers with their buying decisions and problems. They also enforce laws. The Federal Citizen Information Center is a good source for consumer information.

The Federal Trade Commission

The Federal Trade Commission (FTC) enforces federal antitrust and consumer protection laws by investigating complaints against companies. It seeks to ensure that the nation's markets function competitively by eliminating unfair or deceptive practices.

U.S. Department of Agriculture

The U.S. Department of Agriculture (USDA) inspects foods and grades them. **Grade labels** indicate the level of quality of foods. For example, meat might be graded as "prime" or "choice." Consumers can use the grades as a guide in choosing what to buy.

✔ **Reading Check** **Analyze** Why is it important for the government to inspect foods such as meats?

The Food and Drug Administration

The Food and Drug Administration (FDA) regulates the labeling and safety of food, drugs, cosmetics, dietary **supplements**, and medical devices sold in the United States. The FDA tests and approves all drugs before they can be offered to consumers. It also reviews products that are already on the market.

The National Highway Traffic Safety Administration

The National Highway Traffic Safety Administration is part of the U.S. Department of Transportation. This agency sets and enforces safety standards for motor vehicles. The administration can require an automaker to issue a recall of the automaker's vehicles. A **recall** is an order to take back and repair or replace a product that has defective parts. **Figure 24.1** shows a government Web site where consumers can find information about recalls.

The Consumer Product Safety Commission

The U.S. Consumer Product Safety Commission is a federal government agency that oversees the safety of products such as toys, cribs, power tools, electronics, and furniture. The commission has contributed significantly to a 30 percent decline in the rate of deaths and injuries associated with consumer products over the last 30 years.

Figure 24.1 — **Finding Information About Recalls** —

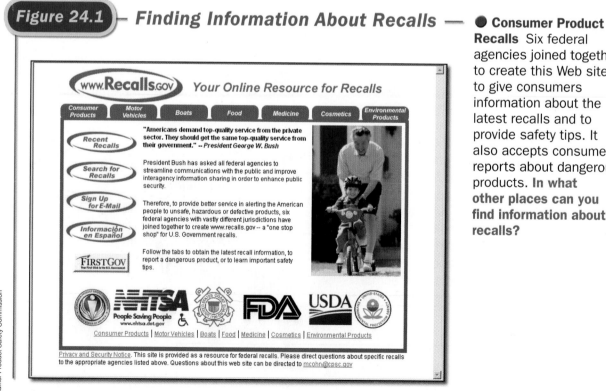

● **Consumer Product Recalls** Six federal agencies joined together to create this Web site to give consumers information about the latest recalls and to provide safety tips. It also accepts consumer reports about dangerous products. **In what other places can you find information about recalls?**

State Public Utilities Commissions

State public utilities commissions regulate the rates charged by electric, gas, and water companies. In some areas, they also regulate local telephone services. They protect consumers from unfair pricing. They do this because public utilities are legal monopolies. A **legal monopoly** is a company that is allowed to operate without competition.

State Insurance Commissions

State insurance commissions are the state government bodies responsible for regulating the activities of insurers and health plans. They control and approve insurance rates. Most have procedures for handling consumer complaints.

State Licensing Agencies

State licensing agencies issue **licenses**, or legal permits to conduct business. A license provides **assurance** to consumers that the license holder is qualified to do a service. Doctors, teachers, roofers, hair stylists, architects, and even professional wrestlers are required to have a license.

Section 24.1

After You Read

Review Key Concepts

1. In what ways do nongovernmental consumer organizations assist consumers?
2. What are some government agencies that help to protect consumers?
3. What is a recall?

Academic Skills

4. **Mathematics** The Better Business Bureau is a nonprofit organization that supports consumers. The 112 BBBs in the United States handle 100 million questions a year. One third of these are questions about retail businesses, one third are about home improvement companies, and one fourth are about service firms. The remaining portion of questions the BBB receives concerns other types of businesses. Draw a pie chart of this data. Record the actual number of consumer questions in each category on your chart.

CONCEPT **Data Analysis** Pie charts are an effective way to represent the parts that make up a whole.

 For math help, go to the Math Appendix.

 Go to **connectED.mcgraw-hill.com** to check your answers.

Consumer Protection Laws

Reading Guide

● Before You Read

Think about the ways government protects consumers and how shopping would be different without its involvement.

Read to Learn

- Describe ways that consumers are protected by laws related to the marketplace.
- List ways that the business community assists with consumer protection.

The Main Idea

A number of laws have been passed at all levels of government to protect consumers. Businesses and consumer organizations help resolve problems when consumers find a product or service to be unsatisfactory.

Key Concepts

- Laws That Protect Consumers
- How the Business Community Protects Consumers

Vocabulary

Key Terms

price discrimination
warranty
express warranty
full warranty
limited warranty
Better Business Bureau (BBB)

Academic Vocabulary

You will find these words in your reading and on your tests. Make sure you know their meanings.

justify   reveal
guarantee   community

Graphic Organizer

On a figure like the one below, write notes about how different warranties protect consumers.

Express Warranty	Full Warranty	Limited Warranty

 Go to **connectED.mcgraw-hill.com** to print out this graphic organizer.

Laws that Protect Consumers

The U.S. government allows businesses to compete in the marketplace with relative freedom. However, many laws have been enacted to regulate and restrict business practices. These key trade laws were created to preserve competition. They also help to protect consumers.

Manufacturers of products for the public must become familiar with consumer protection laws. This helps them to avoid possible recalls of their products and potential lawsuits. Most trade laws are designed to protect the consumer. These laws protect against dishonest sellers, unreasonable credit terms, unsafe products, and mislabeling of products.

✔ **Reading Check** **Explain** Why has the U.S. government enacted consumer protection laws?

Price Discrimination Laws

Price discrimination is the act of charging more than one price for the same product or service in different markets or to different customers. The Clayton Act of 1914 and the Robinson-Patman Act of 1936 are aimed at prohibiting price discrimination. Businesses must **justify** giving one customer a lower price than another. Fair pricing means businesses must be fair to all customers when setting prices.

Science/Tech TRENDS

Safety Belts

Safety belts save approximately 13,000 lives in this country every year. According to the National Highway Traffic Safety Administration (NHTSA), an estimated 5,500 more lives could be saved each year in the United States if just 90 percent of passengers and drivers used them. Yet only 68 percent of Americans wear safety belts. When they were first invented (Edward Claghorn was the first to obtain a U.S patent for the seat belt in 1885) they were simple leather straps fastened over the operator's lap. As the technology behind cars develops, so does the technology that produces safety belts. Today, the safety belt is a system of interdependent parts and space age fabrics.

WebQuest

Locate Web sites where you can research how safety belts do their job and the latest technologies used in safety belt systems. Write a few sentences about how new technologies have increased safety.

The Fair Packaging and Labeling Act

The Fair Packaging and Labeling Act requires that manufacturers' labels truthfully list all ingredients and raw materials used in production. Labels must include the name and place of business of the manufacturer, packer, or distributor. The act also requires the size, weight, and contents of a product to be included on the label.

The Uniform Commercial Code

The Uniform Commercial Code (UCC) is a group of laws that regulate commercial business transactions. The UCC protects the economic interests of buyers and sellers in contracts. It also regulates sales warranties. A **warranty** is a promise or **guarantee** given to a customer that a product will meet certain standards. A business may also be protected by disclaimers that describe exceptions or exclusions from a warranty. A common disclaimer limits a customer's recovery to a refund of the purchase price.

Under the UCC, a seller may make several warranties:

- An **express warranty** is a warranty that is explicitly stated, in writing or verbally. It specifies the conditions under which the product can be returned, replaced, or repaired.
- A **full warranty** is a guarantee about the quality of goods or services. With a full warranty, a purchase found to be defective within the warranty period will be repaired or replaced at no cost to the purchaser.
- A **limited warranty** covers only certain parts of the product or requires the customer to bear some of the expense in case repairs are needed.

● **Consumer Information** Advertisements provide information to consumers. **What types of information would you want to know before buying a laptop computer?**

● **As You Read**

Look at the different types of information on the labels of some products you have at home or school.

Consumer Credit Protection Act

The Consumer Credit Protection Act requires those who give credit to **reveal** all the terms and conditions of their credit agreements. This law applies to anything purchased over a period of time greater than four months. Finance charges must be expressed as an annual rate so that the consumer has a clear estimate of the cost of credit. Truth-in-lending laws are enforced by the Federal Trade Commission (FTC).

Truth-in-Advertising Laws

The Federal Trade Commission Act protects consumers from false and misleading advertising with truth-in-advertising laws. Under these laws, advertising must be truthful and nondeceptive, and advertisers must have evidence to back up their claims.

How Businesses Protect Consumers

The business **community** protects consumers by providing information. Labels, brochures, manuals, and online details are some of the ways that businesses educate consumers about their products and services.

The Better Business Bureau

The **Better Business Bureau (BBB)** is a nonprofit organization that collects information on local businesses and handles complaints. It also shares information about problems that consumers have had and distributes consumer publications. It does not enforce laws or recommend one business over another.

Business Case Study

Banks Improve Their Image

Happy customers tell a friend.
Unhappy customers tell two!

During the Great Recession, bank fees became a major issue for financially stressed customers. Anger grew about ever-higher fees for basic services such as teller transactions, checking accounts, and ATM withdrawals.

Attitudes toward banks have since improved. In fact, J.D. Power's 2014 banking survey revealed that customer satisfaction was at an all-time high. Banks' efforts to better explain fees contributed to their improved image. Only 16 percent of the 2014 survey respondents reported having a complaint, compared with 24 percent in 2010. The biggest banks, which received the most criticism during the recession, made the biggest gains in customer satisfaction.

It is in a business's best interest to promptly resolve customer complaints. One study showed that customers tell 4 to 6 people on average when a complaint is resolved by the business to their satisfaction—but when it isn't, they tell 9 to 15 people. Dissatisfaction has a multiplier effect!

Active Learning

Pick three financial institutions that do business in your community: a large bank, a local or regional bank, and a community credit union. Go online to find each bank's policy for resolving customer complaints. If this information is difficult to locate online, email or call a branch to request it. Write a brief report outlining these policies, noting how they are similar or different. Note which of the three institutions you think would most likely resolve a complaint promptly and effectively.

Customer Service Representatives

Many businesses have a customer service department. A customer service representative can answer questions or help resolve problems. Product packages often list the address, telephone number, or Web site to use to contact a customer service representative.

Advertising

Advertising can be a good source of consumer information. Although businesses use ads to promote their products, they also use them to tell consumers as much about their products as possible. Ads tell you not only a product's cost, but also the features it offers. You can use ads to compare products and services.

Magazines

Some commercial magazines are good sources of consumer information. They include articles or guides to help you make choices. *Good Housekeeping* features consumer information and endorses products with a "seal of approval." Specialty magazines on items such as cars and travel also provide information on related products.

Section 24.2

After You Read

Review Key Concepts
1. How do price discrimination laws protect consumers?
2. How is a full warranty different from a limited warranty?
3. What is the role of a customer service representative in consumer protection?

Academic Skills
4. **English Language Arts** Study an issue of *Consumer Reports* or *Consumers' Research Magazine.* List the types of products that are reported. Write a summary of the kinds of information provided about each product and indicate how you might find more information about the products.

5. **English Language Arts** Prepare a presentation showing how to file a complaint about a product or service. Choose a product or service that a family member has found unsatisfactory. Include a description of how to approach the business, a sample letter describing the problem and a possible solution, and the name of a private or government advocate or agency that might help you with the complaint.

 Go to **connectED.mcgraw-hill.com** to check your answers.

Section 24.1 *Summary*	Section 24.2 *Summary*
Consumer Organizations and Agencies All consumers encounter purchasing problems at some point. Fortunately, there are ways that you can resolve issues yourself. Consumer advocate groups work to protect, inform, and defend consumers. Many organizations are nonprofit associations that monitor consumer information and work to prevent unfair treatment of consumers. In addition, government agencies and organizations enforce consumer protection laws and provide consumer information.	**Consumer Protection Laws** Many laws have been passed to protect consumers, and government agencies enforce those laws. In addition, the business community provides information and services for consumer protection. Businesses may have a customer service department to assist consumers. Also, the Better Business Bureau works to resolve problems that consumers have with local businesses. These are some of the available sources that help consumers make good choices when they shop.

Vocabulary Review

1. On a sheet of paper, use each of these key terms and academic vocabulary terms in a sentence.

Key Terms

consumer advocates	warranty
grade labels	express warranty
recall	full warranty
legal monopoly	limited warranty
licenses	Better Business Bureau
price discrimination	(BBB)

Academic Vocabulary

behalf	justify
panels	guarantee
supplements	reveal
assurance	community

Review Key Concepts

2. Explain the steps consumers can take to find solutions to consumer problems.

3. List nongovernmental consumer organizations that advocate for consumers.

4. List some federal and state agencies that provide consumer information and protection.

5. Describe ways that consumers are protected by laws related to the marketplace.

6. List ways that the business community assists with consumer protection.

Critical Thinking

7. Some people argue that government should not be so involved in consumer protection. What are some arguments for and against this opinion?

8. What advice would you give a friend who purchased a movie on DVD that has a flaw that prevents him from viewing all of it?

9. Some people say consumers can make wise buying choices and do not need all of the protections that are provided. Others say consumer affairs offices and government agencies play a necessary role. Choose a partner and debate this topic.

10. What should people do if their credit card is stolen?

11. U.S. companies that furnish utilities such as water, gas, and electricity must get governmental approval before adjusting their rates. Do you think these businesses should be more or less regulated?

12. Why do you think some merchandise breaks soon after buying it?

13. Some products have grade labels, which indicate the quality of the product. Do you think most consumers pay attention to these labels?

Write About It

14. Write two or more paragraphs about ways older consumers can protect themselves from sellers who are not fair and honest.

15. Research the Federal Citizen Information Center. Write a brief summary about the types of information the center offers.

16. State governments protect consumers by requiring licenses for some professions. Write an essay of two or more paragraphs for or against the requirement of licenses.

17. Write an e-mail to your teacher about ways consumers can protect themselves when dealing with an offer that sounds too good to be true.

18. Research information from the FTC about how to solve the problem of unordered merchandise. Write a one-page summary of your findings.

19. Note the specific claims, incentives, or time limits made in an ad in the newspaper. Write a letter to the seller, supplier, or vendor to verify the information in the ad.

Technology Applications

Presentation Software
20. Using presentation software, prepare a slide show on consumer protection. Include at least six slides, with information such as resources for consumers, agencies that provide consumer protection, and advice on protection against scams, fraud, and other consumer problems.

Business Ethics

The Ethics of Advertising
21. Many packaged-food producers now provide single-serving versions of their most popular products. These items often come in smaller packages and use the same brand name as the original products. Their ads usually declare that they taste like the originals. However, some items may contain different ingredients, which can affect their look and taste. Is this ethical? Why or why not?

Applying Academics to Business

English Language Arts

22. Watch or listen to a consumer news program. Write a paragraph or two about a specific consumer complaint that is discussed, how it was resolved, and whether you would purchase the same product from the store in question.

Mathematics

23. In order to strengthen its domestic automobile industry, a country places a 7.5% tariff on all imported cars. If one foreign car company has brought 4,000 cars at $19,000 each into the country, how much will the company pay in tariffs? Write a sentence or two telling how you will solve this problem, and then solve it.

CONCEPT **Problem Solving** Think about which operations you will use to solve the problem.

English Language Arts

24. Sometimes new products fail in the marketplace in spite of careful market research done before the product launch. For example, New Coke with a slightly different flavor, and NutraSweet Simple Pleasure ice cream, made with a fat substitute, both seemed like sure bets. Research a product that did not sell as expected and write a paragraph summarizing your findings.

Mathematics

25. Contact one of the public utilities in your area. Find out what the rates are for the utility service. Also, find out the last time the rates were changed and calculate the percent decrease or increase.

CONCEPT **Percents** To calculate percent increase or decrease, find the difference between the two costs and divide by the original cost.

Active Learning

Researching Purchasing Decisions

26. Suppose you need a new digital camera. You are unaware of the latest trends in digital cameras. However, you need one that is versatile. You have about $200 to spend. Do research. Use various sources of information, such as consumer publications, company Web sites, store visits, or consumer groups. Write a report on your findings and purchasing decision.

Business in the Real World

Small Claims Court

27. Sometimes a business might refuse to satisfy a customer. In that case, the customer can take the company to small claims court. In the United States, *small claims court* settles cases involving relatively small amounts of money. Determine the small claims court limit amount in your area. Use library materials or the Internet in your research. Obtain information about filing a case. Then write a brief summary of your findings.

Real LIFE skills

PRACTICE PROBLEM SOLVING

28. Work in teams of four or five students. Choose a product that someone has found unsatisfactory. Prepare a short presentation showing how to file a complaint about it. Be sure to include a description of how to approach the business where the product was purchased, a sample letter describing the problem and a solution, and a consumer agency that might help.

Business CAREERS

FIND YOUR DREAM JOB

29. Locate the Occupational Outlook Handbook Web site. Click on the "OOH Search/A-Z Index" link and enter the job title "science technician." Then write a one-page report about this type of occupation. Conclude your report with a list of things you could do now to prepare yourself to pursue the occupation.

Role Play

WHAT SHOULD YOU DO?

30. Situation You are deciding an appropriate response to resolve a consumer complaint about a product you bought. The product had a 30-day limited warranty and broke on the 31st day after you bought it.

Activity With a classmate, outline the choices you have and the action you will take to resolve your complaint.

Evaluation You will be evaluated on how well you meet the following performance indicators:

- Choose a product for this project, and describe the problem clearly.
- Outline at least two alternative actions you could take.
- Describe how you will contact the seller, consumer agencies, or other organizations about the problem.
- Prepare an outline of steps you will take to resolve your problem.

Standardized Test Practice

Directions Choose the letter of the best answer. Write the letter for the answer on a separate piece of paper.

1. What percent of 13 is 39?

   A   3%

   B   30%

   C   33.33%

   D   300%

TEST-TAKING TIP When you sit down to take a math test, jot down on your scrap paper important equations or formulas that you are trying to remember. This way, you will not worry about forgetting them during the test.

Jeff Mendelsohn

Founder/President, New Leaf Paper

Jeff Mendelsohn co-founded this recycled–paper company with the belief that environmental responsibility and good business go hand in hand, and that people will prefer green paper when given the choice. A few years ago, the company teamed up with the Canadian publisher of the *Harry Potter* series to print an installment on 100 percent post-consumer, processed, and chlorine-free paper.

Q & A

Describe your job responsibilities.

Jeff: I focus on creating awareness about environmentally responsible paper in the marketplace. I also work on developing new, environmentally leading printing papers, and help with sales to large customers.

What skills are most important in your business?

Jeff: New Leaf Paper employs a very diverse group of people, but all share a commitment to our mission. Salespeople have great people skills. They are self-motivated, and have strong passion for what we do. Customer service people are level headed, have strong math and computer skills, and enjoy helping others. Managers are multitalented, they listen well, they are highly reliable, and focus on our goals. Our staff comes from a variety of educational backgrounds. Most performed very well in school because we choose people who are deeply engaged in their activities and care about the quality of their work.

What is your key to success?

Jeff: Our greatest strength is our mission statement. It very concisely sums up our main value proposition and clearly links our business success to our environmental goals.

What advice would you give students interested in starting a business?

Jeff: Be an independent thinker and be truly committed to what you do. Beyond that, it is really important, and rewarding, to truly know yourself, what you enjoy, and what your strengths and weaknesses are. With this self-awareness, you are more likely to hire people that excel at things you struggle with, and give them the authority to do their jobs.

Critical Thinking *How does writing a mission statement help an entrepreneur decide which product or service his or her company will provide?*

Ingram Publishing

Some Qualifications Needed to be the Owner of a Paper Manufacturing Company

Academic Skills and Abilities

Chemistry; biology; physics; mathematics; interpersonal skills; general business management skills; verbal and written communication skills; multitasking, organizing, and planning skills

Academic Skills Required to Complete Tasks at New Leaf Paper			
Tasks	Math	Science	English Language Arts
Hold meetings			◆
Assign duties			◆
Develop new products	◆	◆	◆
Assess marketplace opportunities	◆	◆	◆
Ensure quality control	◆	◆	◆
Customer service			◆
Schedule employees	◆		◆
Order supplies and equipment	◆		◆
Analyze financials	◆		◆

Education and Training

Many engineering and natural science managers begin their careers as scientists, such as chemists, biologists, geologists, or mathematicians. Some who work in applied research or other areas have a bachelor's or master's degree, or a doctorate. Science managers must be specialists in the work they supervise. Graduate programs allow scientists to augment their undergraduate training with instruction in other fields, such as management or computer technology.

Career Path

Engineering and natural sciences managers may advance to progressively higher leadership positions within their discipline. Some may become managers in nontechnical areas, such as marketing, human resources, or sales. Most begin their careers as engineers after completing a bachelor's degree in the field.

Preparing for a Career
Self-Assessment Checklist

Use this self-assessment checklist to help determine ways you can display your commitment to your work.

✔ Expand your boundaries beyond your job description.

✔ Earn the respect of your peers first; respect from higher-ups will follow.

✔ Take risks.

✔ Be ready to make mistakes.

✔ Use intuition and creativity when solving problems and developing new ideas.

✔ Set short-, medium-, and long-term goals that are aligned with your company's overall mission.

✔ In meetings, listen actively and offer suggestions.

✔ Bring a willingness to work hard to your career, even on your worst day.

How the Consumer Movement Affects Business

The Internet has put consumers around the world in contact with one another. People are taking an active role in speaking out for good business practices and against businesses and products that are harmful to consumers, the environment, and the world. Consumers want to buy from businesses that are socially responsible. These businesses often succeed.

Thematic Project Assignment

In this project you will work with other students to design and create a bulletin board display that describes how the consumer movement affects business.

Step 1 — Brainstorm Skills You Need to Complete This Activity

Your success in designing and creating a bulletin board will depend on the skills you and your team members possess. Preview the activity, then brainstorm a list of the skills you will need to use to complete the activity and describe how you will use them. Skills you might use include:

Academic Skills   reading, writing, designing/art/photography
Basic Skills   speaking, listening, thinking, and interpersonal skills
Technology Skills word processing, keyboarding, design and photo programs, and Internet skills

 SKILLS PREVIEW Go to **connectED.mcgraw-hill.com** to download a graphic organizer you can use to brainstorm the skills you will use to complete the project.

Step 2 — Choose a Business and a Career That Interest Your Team

Make a list of businesses that interest your team. Add to the list any careers within this business that interest your team. Then think about how the consumer movement affects these businesses. Think about how you are affected as a consumer and also how you might be affected in your future career.

Step 3 — Build Background Knowledge

Preview information on how consumers affect business.

Consumers Affecting *How* **Business** *Is Conducted*

Consumers are not sitting still these days when it comes to what they like and do not like, what works and what does not work. They are coming together and speaking out in loud group voices. Businesses better listen. With the Internet connecting the world, someone in Idaho might know about a fuel-efficient vehicle being engineered in Japan almost as quickly as it could be in Detroit.

Consumers are speaking out where it hurts businesses the most—in the marketplace. This is what consumers are saying: *Build us better, more efficient products. Be more earth-friendly and socially responsible. Listen or we will take our business elsewhere. Elsewhere these days includes the whole world.*

Step 4 Connect with Your Community

Individually interview two adults in your community. Interview one adult who is active in a consumer movement or has taken action as a consumer. Interview another adult to learn how consumers affect the person's job or business. Bring your findings about these people's experiences to the team to use as stories for the bulletin board.

Step 5 Research How the Consumer Movement Affects Business

Use library and Internet resources to research how the consumer movement affects business. Keep records of your sources of information. Then work with your team to prepare your bulletin board. Use the project research checklist as a guide.

Step 6 Develop Your Bulletin Board

Use magazine cutouts, computer graphics, photographs, and other art supplies to create a bulletin board that includes all of the information described in the project checklist.

How the Consumer Movement Affects Business

- ✔ Assign tasks to team members. You will need researchers, writers, editors, and artists.
- ✔ Decide as a team on one type of consumer movement, such as efficient fuel for vehicles or socially responsible companies.
- ✔ Researchers can use library and Internet sources to find information on consumer movements and their effects on business. Look for information on how the businesses are changing because consumers are becoming active.
- ✔ Writers should write short paragraphs of information and picture captions.
- ✔ Editors should edit and proofread the information and captions.
- ✔ Artists should design and arrange the bulletin board.

Self Connections

- ✔ Individually discuss the results of your research with the adults you interviewed.
- ✔ Describe how the adult you interviewed spoke out as a consumer and how the other adult changed the way business was conducted.
- ✔ Explain what the investigation and its results mean to you.

Step 7 Evaluate Your Presentation

 RUBRIC Go to connectED.mcgraw-hill.com to download a rubric you can use to evaluate your final report.

Credit

Geomagic makes 3-D geometric modeling software that allows manufacturers such as Toyota® and Fisher-Price® to customize individualized products at the same cost as with mass manufacturing. At the end of this unit, you will learn more about Geomagic® founder Ping Fu and how she achieved her success.

Decision Making How do you plan to use credit in the future?

Unit 9   *Thematic Project Preview*

Making Credit Decisions After completing this unit, you will research ways credit decisions can affect your life and career.

Project Checklist As you read the chapters in this unit, use this checklist to prepare for the unit project.

- ✔ Think about how to obtain credit.
- ✔ Analyze how to use credit wisely.
- ✔ Determine how unwise choices can affect your credit.
- ✔ Consider the types of jobs and careers in the credit industry.

The Basics of Credit

Chapter Objectives After completing this chapter, you will be able to:

▶ **Section 25.1** *Credit Essentials*
- **Define** credit and indicate three factors that affect the interest that is paid.
- **Name** different groups in our economy who use credit.
- **Identify** three advantages and disadvantages of using credit.

▶ **Section 25.2** *Types of Credit*
- **Name** the places where you can get credit, and list the three different types of credit cards.

Ask

AN EXPERT

The Basics of Credit: The Advantages of Debt

Q: When is it worth going into debt for better liquidity?

A: Liquidity is simply the ease with which an asset can be bought, sold, or turned into cash. For example, suppose you need to buy a car. You have $20,000 saved that you could use to buy the car outright. However, after a little investigating, you realize that putting $10,000 toward the car, borrowing the remaining $10,000 for the car, and investing $10,000 in stocks might actually be a more profitable approach. If the interest rate on the loan is lower than the rate of increase on the stocks, going into some debt might be a good idea. Furthermore, since stocks can be more easily liquidated than a car, they allow you to access your money more quickly in case of an emergency.

Mathematics You've decided to buy that car. You're trying to choose whether to spend all of your savings on the car or to pay for part of the cost of the car now, take out a loan to pay the rest, and invest the rest of your savings. The interest rate on the loan will be 9.25% while the rate of increase on the investment is likely to be about 13.5%. What is the difference between these two rates?

CONCEPT **Subtracting Decimals** When subtracting decimals, write the numbers vertically, lining up the numbers by place value (the decimal points will also be lined up). If necessary, add zeros as place holders in the decimal places that do not have values, then subtract as you usually would. Do not forget to place a decimal point in the correct place in your answer.

BananaStock/SuperStock

● **The Importance of Good Credit** Paying your bills on time and keeping your total debt low will improve your credit rating. **What does a good credit rating tell lenders?**

Credit Essentials

Reading Guide

Before You Read

Think about the skills you need to obtain credit and to use it wisely.

Read to Learn

- Define credit and indicate three factors that affect the interest that is paid.
- Name different groups in our economy who use credit.
- Identify three advantages and disadvantages of using credit.

The Main Idea

Credit allows borrowers to purchase items that they otherwise could not afford. Consumers, businesses, and governments all borrow money. There are advantages and disadvantages to using credit.

Key Concepts

- Credit: The Promise to Pay
- Who Uses Credit?
- The Pros and Cons of Using Credit

Vocabulary

Key Terms

credit
creditor
debtor
interest
consumer credit
commercial credit
credit rating

Academic Vocabulary

You will find these words in your reading and on your tests. Make sure you know their meanings.

military
contributes
constantly
committed

Graphic Organizer

In a graphic such as the one shown, list some advantages of using credit in the PROS column and some disadvantages in the CONS column as you read.

PROS	CONS

 Go to **connectED.mcgraw-hill.com** to print out this graphic organizer.

Credit: The Promise to Pay

Buying an item now and paying for it later can be an easy and convenient way to make a purchase. Consumers use credit to buy all kinds of goods and services. **Credit** is an agreement to obtain money, goods, or services now in exchange for a promise to pay in the future. When buying on credit, you are delaying the payment for an item.

A **creditor** lends money or provides credit. A **debtor** borrows money or uses credit. Credit is based on the creditor's confidence that the debtor can and will repay the debt. Creditors charge a fee for using their money, which is called **interest**. The amount of interest to be paid is based on three factors. One is the interest rate, which is a percentage of the total amount borrowed. Interest rates vary from one provider to the next. Another factor is the length of time of the loan. The longer you take to pay it off, the more interest you will have to pay. The other factor is the amount of the loan. The larger the amount, the more interest that will be charged.

✔ **Reading Check**   **Identify** On what three factors is the amount of interest based?

Who Uses Credit?

Many people use credit. To a great extent it has replaced money as a means of making purchases. Credit is used practically everywhere. Many people use credit to pay for CDs, meals at restaurants, or even higher education.

The type of credit used by people for personal reasons is called **consumer credit**. Businesses often use credit for the same reasons that consumers do. Manufacturers borrow money to buy

● **As You Read**

Think about purchases you have seen people make using credit.

?ETHICS in Business

Credit Cards

■ **Critical Reading** Life is full of important decisions. Think about the kinds of decisions that you make as you read the question below.

You work in the promotions department of a credit card company. The company instructs you to set up a booth on college campuses in an attempt to get incoming freshmen to sign up for a card. You are told to offer a pre-approved line of credit with a higher-than-average interest rate. Your manager also recommends giving a bunch of free promotional gifts to attract students to your booth.

■ **Decision Making** Would the fact that the majority of people you will be soliciting have limited, if any, disposable income affect your actions? Explain your answer.

raw materials, new machinery, factories, or trucks. Some borrow money to buy goods that they later resell. Credit used by businesses is called **commercial credit**. When businesses borrow money, however, they often pass along the cost of interest to consumers by charging higher prices.

The federal government uses credit to pay for many of the services and programs it provides to its citizens. For example, during World War II, the federal government used credit to finance **military** spending. State and local governments use credit to pay for things such as highways, public housing, stadiums, and water systems.

The Pros and Cons of Using Credit

Credit is so common in today's society that most people choose to use it. To use credit effectively, the consumer must know its advantages and disadvantages.

Advantages of Credit

An important advantage of credit is that it is convenient. You can shop and travel without carrying large amounts of cash. Instead of saving for an expensive item, such as a car, you can buy the car on credit and use it right away. Credit is especially useful in an emergency. If your car breaks down and you do not have cash to fix it, you can use credit.

● **Credit Ratings** Credit scores are used for much more than financing decisions. Many employers check applicants' credit reports before making hiring decisions. **What could negatively affect your credit rating?**

TARIK KIZILKAYA/Getty Images

Figure 25.1 – *Annual Percentage Rate for Monthly Payments*

Finance Charge per $100 Borrowed at Various Interest Rates					
Number of Monthly Payments	7.0%	7.5%	8.0%	8.5%	9.0%
6	$2.05	$2.20	$2.35	$2.49	$2.64
12	$3.83	$4.11	$4.39	$4.66	$4.94
18	$5.63	$6.04	$6.45	$6.86	$7.28
24	$7.45	$8.00	$8.55	$9.09	$9.64
30	$9.30	$9.98	$10.66	$11.35	$12.04

● **Finding the Finance Charge** If you borrow money and do not pay it back right away, you will probably have to pay a finance charge. **What is the finance charge that you would pay if you borrowed $100 for 18 months at an APR of 9 percent?**

Buying on credit enables people to establish a credit rating. A **credit rating** is a measure of a person's ability and willingness to pay debts on time. A good credit rating tells other lenders that you are a responsible borrower and a good credit risk. Credit also helps consumers keep track of their spending. Whenever you buy something on credit, it goes on your credit card bill so you have a record of your expenses.

Finally, credit **contributes** to the growth of our economy. Credit allows consumers to buy more goods and services. Since so many consumers make credit purchases, businesses must hire more workers and produce more goods to keep up with the demand.

 **Analyze** What factors contribute to a good credit rating?

Disadvantages of Credit

Since credit is so convenient to use, it can also be easy to mis-use. With credit, it is tempting for people to buy things that they cannot afford or do not need. Advertisements and salespeople **constantly** urge consumers to buy more things. You might find it hard to resist sales or offers for more credit. Easy purchasing power should not encourage unnecessary purchases.

Items also cost more when you use credit instead of cash because of the interest. The more items you charge and the longer you take to pay off credit card debt, the more you pay in interest. Another disadvantage is that using credit means that you have **committed** some of your future income since the debt must be repaid. **Figure 25.1** shows the way total interest payments increase with higher interest rates and longer payment terms.

Credit Card Debt
The average American household carries a credit card balance of $7,100. *What do you think are some problems with carrying debt on your credit card?*

As credit card bills pile up, you might have trouble paying them. After a while, you may reach your *credit limit,* the point where you cannot charge any more. Late or missed payments lower your credit rating, which can make it difficult to get credit in the future. Always remember when you use credit that it is not money you own, it is money you owe.

Factors to Consider Before Using Credit Imagine that you have conducted research on the Internet regarding the possibility of financing (or getting money for) a used vehicle. Before you decide to finance a major purchase by using credit, you should consider the following points:

- Do you have the cash you need for the down payment?
- Do you want to use your savings instead of credit?
- Can you afford the item?
- Could you use the credit in some better way?
- Could you put off buying the item for a while?
- What are the costs of using credit?

As previously mentioned, one of the main factors to consider is that when you buy something on credit, you agree to pay a fee that a creditor may add to the purchase price. If you do not pay your credit card bill in full every month, you will be charged interest on the unpaid balance. Interest essentially increases the original price of the item you purchased.

Section 25.1

⌐ After You Read

Review Key Concepts
1. What is credit?
2. What is the difference between commercial and consumer credit?
3. Why is it important to have a good credit rating?

Academic Skills
4. **Mathematics** You have an unpaid balance of $100 on a credit card and plan to pay off the balance in 12 months. Your credit card company charges you 9% interest per year. You transfer the balance to a card that charges only 7% per year and plan to pay off the balance in 6 months. Use the table in **Figure 25.1** to calculate the difference in the total charge for interest.

CONCEPT Reading Tables To read a table, first locate the headings for the row and column requested. Reading across the row and down the column will let you compare data.

 For math help, go to the Math Appendix.

 Go to **connectED.mcgraw-hill.com** to check your answers.

Types of Credit

Before You Read

Think about the different types of credit that are available and the places where you can get it.

Read to Learn

- Name the places where you can get credit, and list the three different types of credit cards.

The Main Idea

There are many different types of credit plans, including charge accounts, credit cards, single payment loans, installment loans, and mortgage loans. There are also many different sources for credit.

Key Concept

- Sources of Credit

Vocabulary

Key Terms

charge account   collateral
installment loans

Academic Vocabulary

You will find these words in your reading and on your tests. Make sure you know their meanings.

available   range
annual   options

Graphic Organizer

In a table like the one below, write definitions for the different sources of credit.

Sources of Credit	Definitions
Charge account	
Credit card	
Banks/financial institutions	
Seller-provided credit	
Consumer finance company	
Payroll advance service	

 Go to **connectED.mcgraw-hill.com** to print out this graphic organizer.

Sources of Credit

Credit is **available** from many different sources. These sources provide different types of loans for varying lengths of time. Loans can be short-term (one year or less), medium-term (one to five years), or long-term (more than five years). The risk a creditor takes in lending money or selling on credit is the most important factor in determining the cost of credit.

Charge Accounts

A **charge account** is credit provided by a store or company for customers to buy its products. Customers who have charge accounts at a store can use their credit to buy now and pay later. When the bill arrives in the mail, the customer can pay part of the total amount owed or the entire amount.

Credit Cards

Credit cards are like charge accounts, but some can be used in many different places. Those issued by banks, for example, can be used in different stores, including companies that sell

Business Case Study

What's So New About Credit?

Innovative businesses use technology to reinvent an age-old practice

The concept of credit goes back thousands of years. But today's tech innovators are revolutionizing how loans are issued and paid.

The annual PYMNTS.com Innovator Project recognizes the most trail-blazing innovations in the payments industry, drawing over 600 submissions in 15 categories. In 2014, the Best Credit Innovation category produced three winners, each with a clever spin on credit:

Credit Karma is a free tool that enables consumers to track all of their loans and accounts in one place and monitor their own credit score.

Lending Club crowdsources credit by bringing individual lenders and borrowers together online. Lenders earn interest, and borrowers get lower rates than they would from a bank.

Klarna makes online payments fast and easy. Customers enter only their zip code and email address to make a purchase, and Klarna later collects the funds from the buyer and pays the seller.

> **Active Learning**
>
> With a partner or small group, do online research about one of the above credit innovators. Visit its website, learn in detail how its innovation works, and read reviews of the service. Gather your information to produce a short report about the service, including a prediction of whether it will succeed in the long term. Present your findings to the class.

on the Internet. Some of the cards have **annual** fees, which can **range** from $25 to $80. Credit card companies earn money from the interest they charge as well as from annual fees and penalties.

There are three basic types of credit cards: single-purpose, multipurpose, and travel and entertainment.

Single-Purpose Cards Single-purpose cards can be used to buy goods or services only at the business that issued the card. Each month cardholders receive a statement listing all the purchases they made in the last 30 days. They can pay part of the amount owed or the entire amount. Interest is charged on the unpaid balance. Credit cards issued by oil companies and department stores, such as Chevron® and Macy's®, are examples of single-purpose credit cards.

Multipurpose Cards Multipurpose cards are also called bank credit cards because banks issue them. Multipurpose cards work the way single-purpose cards do. Consumers can pay them off or pay only part of the bill, with interest due on the unpaid balance. These cards may be used at many different stores, restaurants, and other businesses all over the world. MasterCard and VISA are multipurpose cards.

Travel and Entertainment Cards These cards work a little differently than the others. Holders of travel and entertainment cards must pay the full amount due each month. Cards such as American Express® and Diners Club® are examples. They are accepted

Science/Tech**TRENDS**

Smart Cards

More and more credit cards around the world have computer chips embedded in the plastic. The information in the chip can be read when waved in front of a special reader. Smart cards first became popular in Europe and Asia as stored-value cards. They could be purchased to pay for calls in phone booths or fees on toll roads. Increasingly, chips are showing up in credit cards everywhere. The chips can hold more than 100 times as much information as the magnetic strip on a standard card, which increases security for consumers using them. MasterCard, Visa, and American Express each offer a version of these smart cards.

Web *Quest*

Locate Web sites where you can find out more about smart cards. What are some of the positives and negatives associated with their use?

worldwide for expenses connected with travel, business, and entertainment, such as restaurant and hotel bills, car rentals, and airline tickets. They often have an annual fee, which is higher than the fee for a multipurpose card.

Banks and Other Financial Institutions

Financial institutions such as banks, savings and loans, and credit unions offer many types of loans. However, they tend to place many demands on the borrower, which can make it more difficult to get a loan. For example, these financial institutions only want to lend money to people with good credit ratings. Many credit unions only lend money to credit union members and employees in a certain business or field (such as a teachers credit union).

Single-Payment Loan As the name suggests, the debtor pays back this type of loan in one payment, including interest (at the end of the loan period). Many farmers secure single-payment loans in the spring to pay for their seed and fertilizer. They pay back the loan in the fall, after they harvest their crops.

Installment Loan Student loans, car loans, and home improvement loans are types of **installment loans**, or loans repaid in regular payments over a period of time. The debtor receives the loan money for a certain period, such as two years. Over that period, the debtor makes equal monthly payments, which cover the loan and interest.

Mortgage Loan A mortgage loan is a form of an installment loan, only it is written for a long period, such as 15 to 30 years. It is used to purchase real estate, such as a home. Over the period of the loan, the debtor makes monthly payments. The home serves as **collateral**, which is something of value the bank can take if a borrower does not make the required loan payments.

✔ **Reading Check** **Analyze** What type of collateral does the bank receive when you take out a mortgage loan?

● **As You Read**

Think about a bank or some other financial institution where you could go to get a loan to open a computer repair business.

● **Installment Loans**
A mortgage loan to buy a house is an installment loan most often written for a period of 30 years. **Why is the house collateral?**

©Terry Vine/Blend Images LLC

452 **Chapter 25**

Seller-Provided Credit

Many stores provide credit for their customers. Clothing, furniture, and appliance stores as well as car dealerships are among those that offer credit to customers.

Consumer Finance Companies

Consumer finance companies specialize in loans to people who might not be able to get credit elsewhere. Loans from consumer finance companies cost more because there is greater risk involved.

Other Types of Loans

For people who have difficulty getting a loan, there are other options, although they are the most costly. *Payday advance services* offer short-term loans until payday. However, they charge high fees and interest. A *pawnshop* loan is based on the value of something you own that is left with a pawnbroker as security against money borrowed. You can later buy back your item. "Borrow until payday" loans are short-term, usually for 5 to 14 days. The cost of this kind of loan is especially high.

● **As You Read**

Think about high-interest loans that some companies offer. What reasons might a person have to seek a payday advance or pawnshop loan?

Section 25.2

○ After You Read

Review Key Concepts
1. Discuss the different sources of credit.
2. How is a multipurpose credit card different from a travel and entertainment card?
3. Which types of loans usually cost the most?

Academic Skills

4. **English Language Arts** Work with three or four other students to research the kinds of consumer credit used in at least two countries. Are there banks there? Are there places where you cannot use credit cards? Prepare a group presentation to present your findings.

5. **English Language Arts** Tina found a coat she liked at a department store, but it cost $20 more than she had. She did not have any credit cards and decided to leave. As she approached the exit, an employee offered her instant credit if she would apply for a store credit card. Tina signed up for the card and charged the coat. Write a sentence or two explaining various ways in which the store will benefit from extending credit to Tina.

 Go to **connectED.mcgraw-hill.com** to check your answers.

Section 25.1 *Summary*

Credit Essentials Credit is an agreement to get money, goods, or services now by promising to pay later. Creditors charge a fee (interest) for using their money. Consumers, businesses, and the government use credit extensively. Consumers find that credit is convenient, useful in an emergency, and helps to establish a credit rating and to keep track of one's spending. It also contributes to the growth of the economy. However, it costs more to buy items on credit, commits future income, can lead to overspending, and if handled improperly, may lower your credit rating.

Section 25.2 *Summary*

Types of Credit There are many different types of credit, including charge accounts, credit cards, single-payment loans, installment loans, mortgage loans, seller-provided credit, pawnshop loans, and "borrow until payday" loans. Loans are given by banks, credit unions, and savings and loan associations. Other financial firms specialize in specific loans (such as credit cards), and businesses that sell goods and services also offer credit. Businesses such as consumer finance companies offer loans to people who have difficulty obtaining one. However, these loans are usually costly.

Vocabulary Review

1. On a sheet of paper, use each of these key terms and academic vocabulary terms in a sentence.

Key Terms		Academic Vocabulary	
credit	commercial credit	military	available
creditor	credit rating	contributes	annual
debtor	charge account	constantly	range
interest	installment loans	committed	options
consumer credit	collateral		

Review Key Concepts

2. Define credit and indicate three factors that affect the interest that is paid.

3. Name different groups in our economy who use credit.

4. Identify three advantages and disadvantages of using credit.

5. Name the places where you can get credit, and list the three different types of credit cards.

Critical Thinking

6. Describe two situations in which cash is more convenient than credit. Then describe two situations in which credit is better to use than cash.

7. Why is it important to take care of your credit rating?

8. Why do credit card companies try so hard to persuade you to use their card?

9. If people use credit, does that mean they have money problems? Explain.

10. How do businesses use credit to help sell their products?

11. Imagine that you have a good credit rating and you want to buy a new car. Which would be the best place to get a loan for it, a bank, a consumer finance company, or a pawn shop?

12. Some people use a credit card and never pay any interest. How can that be?

13. Suppose you would like to pay for a course to improve your job skills, a new computer, and a new TV. You do not have enough cash, so you consider taking out a loan to buy at least one of them. Which one would be the best use of credit? Which would be the least wise use of it?

Write About It

14. Write at least two paragraphs either for or against this statement: "People should be charged the same interest rate, regardless of their credit rating."

15. Your friend wants to buy a ring for $400 using a credit card. He would pay 2% of the price each month, which would be $8. He would have to make payments for 95 months. Calculate the total cost of the purchase with interest. Write a letter to him about your opinion of the deal.

16. Write a short essay on whether you think it is fair or unfair for people to have to pay so much in interest on payday loans.

17. Research credit cards that offer rewards. Describe in writing the nature of the rewards you can get if you use them.

18. Write an e-mail to your teacher discussing how you will start to develop your credit rating.

19. Write a paragraph either agreeing or disagreeing with the following statement: "Businesses that charge high interest rates should be banned from the marketplace."

Technology Applications

Spreadsheet Software

20. Research interest rates and credit lines for multipurpose credit cards. Find examples of at least four and compare their rates, repayment terms, and the application process for each card. Do the companies charge an annual fee? How much are penalties for being over a credit limit or making a late payment? Develop a spreadsheet with your findings. Highlight the cells that show your choice for the best credit card to use.

Business Ethics

Borrowing from an Employer

21. You have an emergency, and you ask your employer for a loan. She gives you $100. You sign a form indicating that you received the loan and will start repaying it next month. However, you quit the job the following week. Your former manager calls and asks whether you are going to pay back the loan. You indicate that since you are a minor, the contract is voidable, meaning that you do not have to abide by it. Is it a good idea to avoid the contract?

Chapter 25 Review and Activities

Applying Academics to Business

English Language Arts
22. What is the difference in the meanings of the words *debt* and *debit?* List some synonyms and antonyms for each and use each in a sentence.

Mathematics
23. The Fair Isaac Corporation® (FICO) rates consumer credit worthiness according to a scale that ranges from 350 to 900 points. A good score is often considered to be 600 or greater. Banks or other companies may not give credit to those with scores below 600. List whether the following people are likely to receive credit.

Name	Credit Score
Sam	300
Jill	590
Tina	480
Guillermo	600

CONCEPT **Reading a Chart** Read down the column and across the row to the right to find information in a chart.

English Language Arts
24. Find newspaper and magazine articles and advertisements that demonstrate uses of credit by consumers, businesses, and governments. Write a paragraph explaining who benefits most from these examples of credit.

Mathematics
25. Research credit and the cost of credit from a variety of institutions, such as those listed below. Convert the rates to decimals, and use a number line to rank them in order from the lowest interest rate to the highest.

- consumer finance company
- revolving charge account
- travel and entertainment credit card
- credit union
- commercial bank

CONCEPT **Number Line** Positive decimals closer to zero on a number line are less than decimals closer to 1.

Active Learning

Analyze Advertisements
26. During the next two weeks, save all the advertisements and junk mail that try to persuade you and your family to apply for a credit card. Keep a log of the promotional offers. Conduct a mini-survey among your family and friends, and find out whether they would choose one of the cards based on the advertising material that has been sent to your home.

Business in the Real World

Comparing Credit Cards
27. Obtain a credit card application from two different retail stores or gas stations. Form groups. Compare the applications, listing similarities and differences. Be sure to examine the interest rates and repayment procedures. Then create a table using word-processing or spreadsheet software. Discuss your findings with the class.

ADVICE ON USING CREDIT

28. Interview a consumer credit counselor or a financial adviser at a bank, asking the following questions:

a. What are the major consumer credit problems and their causes?

b. What is their advice for using credit?

c. Is a person's credit rating very important? Why or why not?

COOL Business CAREERS

FIND YOUR DREAM JOB

29. Locate the Occupational Outlook Handbook Web site. Click on the "OOH Search/A-Z Index" link and enter the job category "bill and account collectors." Then write a one-page report about this area of occupation. Conclude your report with a list of things you could do now to prepare yourself to pursue the occupation.

Role Play

SHOP AROUND FOR A CAR

30. Situation You are a consumer advocate for a local news station. You are asked to prepare a news segment advising consumers on buying a car.

Activity Prepare a presentation that advocates that people shop around for credit when buying a car.

Evaluation You will be evaluated on how well you meet the following performance indicators:

• Show how consumers can save by reviewing different car loans.

• Answer questions from the newscaster(s) and/or consumers about buying a car.

• Use credit terminology correctly.

• Organize ideas in a logical sequence.

• Project your voice, and use correct English.

Standardized Test Practice

Directions Choose the letter of the best answer. Write the letter for the answer on a separate piece of paper.

1. $15\frac{1}{2}\%$ of [   ] = **\$403**

   A   \$6,246.5

   B   \$60.45

   C   \$26.00

   D   \$2,600

 TEST-TAKING TIP To control the stress of test taking, approach exams with a positive attitude. View the exam as an opportunity to show how much you have studied and to receive a reward for the studying you have done.

How to Get and Keep Credit

After completing this chapter, you will be able to:

▶ **Section 26.1** *Applying for Credit*
- **Explain** how you can develop a credit history.
- **Name** five factors to think about when deciding which credit card to secure.
- **Define** the three factors that creditors consider when granting a person credit.

▶ **Section 26.2** *Maintaining Credit*
- **Explain** one major difference between credit cards, installment loans, and mortgages.
- **Indicate** at least three ways to maintain a good credit rating.

Ask AN EXPERT

How to Get and Keep Credit: Inflation Risk

Q: How can I tell if a variable rate loan is right for me?

A: When you take out a loan or use a credit card, your interest rate will be either fixed or variable. With fixed rate plans, the interest rate does not change throughout the period of the debt. Interest rates change with variable rate plans, which may use such indices as the prime rate, the one-, three-, or six-month Treasury Bill rate, or the Federal Reserve discount rate to determine the rate to use. While a fixed rate may be a couple of percentage points higher than a variable rate at a given time, you have the advantage of knowing what the rate will be. Variable rates increase or decrease your finance charges. Fixed rates can be changed by the lender, on future purchases made on credit cards, for example, although the Truth in Lending Act requires the lender to provide 15 days' notice before changing the rate.

Mathematics You are trying to decide between a credit card that has an APR (annual percentage rate) of 18% and no annual fee, and a card that has an APR of 14% and an annual fee of $20. What would your average monthly balance need to be for the second plan to cost less in fees and interest?

CONCEPT **Using Variables to Solve an Inequality** A variable is a placeholder for an unknown value. Write an inequality inputting all of the values that you know and using a variable, such as x, to fill in for the value that you are trying to find.

John Lund/Drew Kelly/Blend Images LLC

● **Responsibility** Before creditors will give you a loan, they will want to make sure that you can manage your credit responsibly. **How do creditors gauge whether a credit applicant is responsible?**

Applying for Credit

Reading Guide

Before You Read

Consider what you know about using credit and how you might use a credit card.

Read to Learn

- Explain how you can develop a credit history.
- Name five factors to think about when deciding which credit card to secure.
- Define the three factors that creditors consider when granting a person credit.

The Main Idea

Developing a credit history is important. The first step will be choosing a credit card and applying for it. Before deciding to issue credit to a consumer, a creditor looks at the applicant's capacity, character, and capital.

Key Concepts

- Developing a Credit History
- Selecting a Credit Card
- Applying for a Credit Card

Vocabulary

Key Terms

annual percentage rate (APR)
cash advance
cosigner
grace period
credit limit

Academic Vocabulary

You will find these words in your reading and on your tests. Make sure you know their meanings.

impact   submit
anticipate   minimum

Graphic Organizer

In a figure like the one below, list and describe the three Cs of credit.

The Three Cs of Credit

 Go to **connectED.mcgraw-hill.com** to print out this graphic organizer.

Developing a Credit History

Credit can have a major **impact** on a consumer's life. If a consumer uses credit responsibly, it can make life easier in a number of ways. If the consumer uses credit irresponsibly, his or her ability to make future purchases will be harmed. To develop a credit history, you will need to apply for credit, be approved for it, use it, and then make payments to the creditor.

How do you prove to others that you can handle credit responsibly? First, develop a credit history. Most people start by getting a credit card in their own name (if they are 18 years of age or older) or getting one with an adult family member. Before getting a credit card, though, it is important to understand how credit cards work.

● As You Read

Think about ways you might use credit in the future.

Selecting a Credit Card

There are several things to consider when choosing a credit card. The five main factors to consider are the interest rate, extra fees, whether the interest rate will change, whether a cosigner is needed, and whether there is a grace period. Some other questions to ask are:

- What will the cost of credit be?
- Who will accept the card?
- What is the credit limit?
- Will I be able to use the card to get cash?

The Cost of Credit

Credit cards allow people to purchase goods and services without using cash. They enable consumers to make major purchases that might otherwise take years of saving. They also provide security during emergencies. Consumers usually need a credit card to rent a car or to place a reservation for a hotel room. However, for all of their conveniences, credit cards come with a cost.

Interest Rates To gauge the cost of credit, first look at the annual percentage rate. The **annual percentage rate (APR)** determines the cost of credit on a yearly basis. For example, an APR of 18 percent means that for every $100 you owe, you pay $18 per year ($100 × .18) or $1.50 per month. It is important to note if the interest rate will change on a credit card. In many cases, a credit card might offer a low introductory rate such as 3 percent. After a few months, the rate could jump to 20 percent.

International Business

International Monetary Fund
The International Monetary Fund (IMF) is an organization of 184 nations that monitors the global financial system. In the 1930s, a majority of industrial countries began trying to defend their economies with tougher restrictions on imports. Some countries abolished foreign imports entirely, while others devalued their currency in an attempt to defend their economies. These practices eventually proved detrimental to the economies they were trying to protect, and their demise showed the need for a global financial monitoring organization.

Examples of Languages Across Cultures

Q: In Finnish, how do you say: "How do you say _____?"
A: **Kuinka sanotaan** (pronounced: Koo-ink-ă să-nō-tăăn)

Find out more about the IMF and how it was founded. What are the purposes of the IMF, and how have they changed since its creation?

Fees Credit card companies charge different fees for different services. Some charge an annual fee. There is usually a fee for a cash advance. A **cash advance** is a loan given in cash by a credit card company in **anticipation** of the borrower's being able to repay it. A late- or missed-payment fee is charged when a payment is missed or is not made on time. Another fee is charged if the card holder is over the credit limit.

✔ Reading Check **Explain** What is the best way to gauge the cost of credit?

Other Considerations

There are other matters to consider before you will be able to get a credit card. One is that you may need a cosigner. A **cosigner** is someone who agrees to be responsible for a debt if the main applicant does not repay it. Another thing to consider is whether there is a grace period for payments. A **grace period** is an amount of time allowed to repay a debt without having to pay interest charges. There is also a grace period to make a late payment before a penalty is charged.

Business Case Study

Out With the Swipe, In With the Chip

U.S. consumers will soon manage their money through microchips.

For U.S. consumers, the "swipe-and-sign" method of credit card transactions will soon be a thing of the past. Much of the rest of the world has already switched from magnetic-strip cards to ones with an embedded microchip. The chip includes a personal identification number and other security information. This new system is known as EMV® (short for Europay, MasterCard®, Visa®) and resists fraud better than the older system. In fact, the United States' long reliance on magnetic-strip cards is a primary reason why half of the world's credit card fraud is committed here.

EMV technology will soon appear in portable formats other than cards. You might soon be using a microchip attached to your phone for mobile purchases, or carrying a credit fob on your keychain.

Active Learning

Do you use a credit or debit card? If you do, write a one-page essay describing the kind of cards you have and how you use them. Do you make most of your purchases with them, or do you use cash? Are the cards in your name? Describe the rules you and your parent or guardian have established for use of the cards. If you do not use a credit or debit card, describe in your essay the advantages and disadvantages of using cash, or other non-card forms of payment. Do you believe you would spend more or less if you had a credit/debit card? Why?

● **A Promise Made**
Americans buy a lot of things with credit cards. **What promises are made when making a credit purchase?**

Applying for a Credit Card

To secure a credit card, a consumer has to fill out an application form and **submit** it to the credit card company. The form asks for information about where the applicant lives and works, and what other credit the applicant has received. It also asks questions about an applicant's income and savings.

Creditworthiness: The Three Cs

Before creditors give a consumer a charge or credit account, they want to make sure the consumer is worth the risk. They consider the applicant's capacity, character, and capital, commonly referred to as the "three Cs of credit."

✔ Reading Check **Identify** What are the three Cs of credit?

Capacity is the applicant's ability to repay the loan. To determine an applicant's capacity to pay, creditors will verify the applicant's employment and income. If the applicant already has a lot of debt in relation to his or her level of income, lenders will be less willing to extend more credit. An applicant's *character* shows whether he or she has proven to be trustworthy in repaying debts. They will ask for credit references or check with credit bureaus, businesses that provide information about consumers' creditworthiness to companies or banks. They may ask for personal or professional references, and they may check to see if the applicant has a criminal record. An applicant's *capital* is the amount of money the applicant has beyond his or her debts. It includes savings and investments. Creditors want to know if an applicant has capital that can be used as collateral.

Credit Ratings A credit rating, or credit score, is a measure of a person's ability and willingness to pay debts on time. These ratings come from Fair Isaac Corporation (FICO). The company's FICO scores, which measure credit risk, are the most widely used credit scores in the world. *Why do you think credit issuers rely on FICO scores?*

Pixtal/AGE Fotostock

As You Read

Think about the capital you have that would qualify you for a loan. What are some of your assets?

Credit Limits

Creditors also consider capacity, character, and capital when determining the amount of a card holder's credit limit. A **credit limit** is the maximum amount a card holder can charge on a credit card. If a person pays his or her bills on time, most creditors will raise the person's credit limit.

Making the Minimum Payment

Credit card companies usually send card holders a monthly statement of their charges, the balance they owe, and the minimum amount due. If a consumer owes $2,000 on a credit card, he or she might have a minimum payment of $50 to make each month. Many people make the **minimum** payment due each month. However, consumers who pay more than the minimum amount will pay less in interest and will pay off their debt more quickly. When a consumer signs a credit card application, the application is a legal contract. The minimum payment is in the contract. If the consumer does not make at least the minimum payment, the consumer is not meeting his or her legal obligation.

Section 26.1

After You Read

Review Key Concepts

1. How can a consumer develop a credit history?
2. What is an annual percentage rate? Why is it important?
3. What are the three Cs of credit?

Academic Skills

4. **Mathematics** Mary Ellen bought some furniture on credit. Her total came to $1,036.29 and she qualified for interest-free financing. She made a down payment of $36.29 and agreed to pay $50 twice a month until the $1,000 balance was paid. As an alternative option, the store sent her a payment book. She could choose to use the 24 monthly payment coupons and pay the amount of $49.92. What are the differences in the two payment options?

CONCEPT **Interest Rate** To determine the rate of interest given a sequence of payments, add up the payments, subtract the principal, and divide the difference by the principal.

 For math help, go to the Math Appendix.

 Go to **connectED.mcgraw-hill.com** to check your answers.

Maintaining Credit

Reading Guide

Before You Read

Think about the ways that you could use credit wisely.

Read to Learn

- Explain one major difference between credit cards, installment loans, and mortgages.
- Indicate at least three ways to maintain a good credit rating.

The Main Idea

There are several similarities between credit cards, installment loans, and mortgages. There are also differences. Keeping a good credit rating is important if the consumer is interested in getting loans at a reasonable cost.

Key Concepts

- Understanding Loans and Mortgages
- Keeping a Healthy Credit Record

Vocabulary

Key Terms

variable rate
fixed rate
down payment
principal
finance charge
secured loan
unsecured loan
garnishment of wages
repossess

Academic Vocabulary

You will find these words in your reading and on your tests. Make sure you know their meanings.

similar   maintain
portion   obtain

Graphic Organizer

In a table like the one below, name and give examples of the five factors that affect your credit score.

Factors Affecting Your Credit Score	Example

 Go to **connectED.mcgraw-hill.com** to print out this graphic organizer.

Understanding Loans and Mortgages

Many of the principles of owning and using a credit card also apply to other types of credit. Loans and mortgages are **similar** to credit cards. They also allow consumers to borrow money that will be paid back with interest. Their requirements are similar to those of a credit card. However, there are some differences between credit cards and other forms of credit.

How Installment Loans and Mortgages Work

A *loan* is money lent by one party to another at interest. Most loans require collateral and are paid back in installments. Similarly, a *mortgage* is a loan agreement secured by property. This property is usually the item that the mortgage is for, such as a home. Installment loans and mortgages are written for a specific period of time. Many installment loans on appliances are written for three years. Installment loans for cars are often for five years. Mortgages are generally written for 15, 20, or 30 years.

With installment loans and mortgages, the interest rate is the same for the period of the loan except when the loan has a variable rate. A **variable rate** is an interest rate that fluctuates or changes over the life of the loan. A change in the rate causes changes in either the payments or the length of the term of the loan. With a **fixed rate**, the interest rate always remains the same.

● **Dream Home** Mr. and Mrs. Morgan are going to take out a loan to buy land and build their dream home. **What type of loan should they pursue?**

Ariel Skelley/Blend Images LLC

When purchasing an appliance, automobile, or home with an installment or mortgage loan, the applicant usually has to make a down payment. A **down payment** is a **portion** of the total cost that is paid when a product or service is purchased. The **principal** is the amount of borrowed money that is still owed and on which interest is based. On a *simple interest* loan, interest is based on the original principal alone.

According to the Truth in Lending Law, the lender must provide the borrower with the APR and all the finance charges of the loan. The **finance charge** is the total amount it costs the borrower to have the lender finance the loan. It includes the interest and any other charges, such as the application fee.

Secured and Unsecured Loans

When you receive an installment loan or mortgage, you must sign a written agreement to repay the loan within a certain period of time. If the loan is backed by collateral, it is called a **secured loan**. A loan that is not backed by collateral is called an **unsecured loan**. Because of the increased risk, the interest rate of an unsecured loan is often higher than that of a secured loan. A loan on a car or boat is secured. Mortgages are secured. Credit card debt is unsecured.

> **As You Read**
>
> Think about the impact a down payment can have on debt. Why would you want to offer a down payment on an item such as a car or a house?

✔ **Reading Check** **Contrast** What is the difference between a secured loan and an unsecured loan?

Credit Score Credit bureaus take several factors into consideration when assigning your credit score. **Which of these factors do you think is most important? Why?**

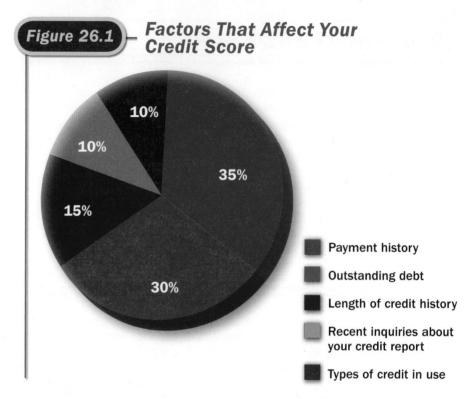

Figure 26.1 — *Factors That Affect Your Credit Score*

10%
10%
35%
15%
30%

- Payment history
- Outstanding debt
- Length of credit history
- Recent inquiries about your credit report
- Types of credit in use

Keeping a Healthy Credit Record

Someday you might want to get a loan for a major expense, such as a house or business. You also might want to increase your credit limit or apply for a credit card. To continue using credit or to get new credit, you need to **maintain** a good credit rating or score. To get the best credit rating, you need to pay your bills on time. If not, your credit rating will decrease, which will make it more difficult to **obtain** additional credit. Consumers with low credit ratings are usually given higher interest rates and more restrictions. **Figure 26.1** shows the factors credit bureaus consider when determining credit scores.

✔ **Reading Check** **Analyze** Is it possible to get credit if you have a bad credit rating?

Staying Within Your Income Limits

You need to know the amount of credit you can afford to have. Experts say consumers should not use more than 20 percent of their income for credit payments. Suppose your first full-time job pays $2,000 a month. After taxes, you bring home $1,500. You have two monthly loan payments—$120 for a student loan and $160 for a car payment. You want to buy a new entertainment system that would cost you $50 a month for three years. Can you afford it? No. Twenty percent of your income is $300. Your total payments each month would be $330, which is 22 percent of your take-home pay.

Signs of Credit Trouble

Here are some signs of credit problems.

- You cannot make monthly loan payments and minimum monthly payments on your credit cards.
- You receive second and third payment-due notices from creditors.
- You get calls from bill collectors.
- Your wages are being garnished. Credit card companies can obtain a court order to take all or part of a debtor's paycheck if he or she stops making payments. This is called **garnishment of wages**.
- The creditor takes back the item you purchased on credit. If that item was offered as collateral and you stopped making payments for it, the creditor has the legal right to **repossess** or take back the item.

There are a number of procedures you can follow to help you get out of financial trouble. Those procedures are discussed in Chapter 27.

Section 26.2

After You Read

Review Key Concepts

1. Which type of loan usually carries a lower interest rate—a secured or an unsecured loan? Why?
2. What is the maximum percentage of your income that you should allocate to credit payments?
3. What is garnishment of wages?

Academic Skills

4. **English Language Arts** The word *debt* comes from the Latin word *debitum* meaning "something owed." Research and describe the origin of the word *credit* and list some related words.

5. **English Language Arts** Imagine that you have decided to attend a special summer camp related to one of your interests (for example, music, sports, government, or debating). The camp experience promises to be very valuable to you, but it will cost $1,000 for the two-week program. Write an e-mail to your teacher explaining whether this would be a good use of credit.

 Go to **connectED.mcgraw-hill.com** to check your answers.

Section 26.1 *Summary*

Applying for Credit It is important to develop a credit history. Most people do this by applying for a credit card, being approved for it, using it to make purchases, and making payments on time. When looking for a credit card, there are many factors to consider, such as the APR, fees, and the grace period. When deciding whether an applicant should be granted credit, the creditor looks at the individual's capacity, character, and capital. After being approved for credit, the consumer is given a credit limit. The consumer must repay a minimum amount each month. It is wise to pay more than the minimum payment, though.

Section 26.2 *Summary*

Maintaining Credit There are several similarities and differences between credit cards, installment loans, and mortgages. Installment loans and mortgages are secured. Unlike unsecured loans, secured loans are backed by collateral and usually offer lower interest rates. Credit cards are unsecured. Installment loans and mortgages last for a fixed number of years. A fixed-rate loan requires the same payment each month. The interest rate on a variable-rate loan can be raised. To maintain a good credit rating, consumers must avoid using more credit than they can afford. They must also make payments on time.

Vocabulary Review

1. On a sheet of paper, use each of these key terms and academic vocabulary terms in a sentence.

Key Terms

annual percentage rate (APR)
cash advance
cosigner
grace period
credit limit
variable rate
fixed rate

down payment
principal
finance charge
secured loan
unsecured loan
garnishment of wages
repossess

Academic Vocabulary

impact
anticipate
submit
minimum

similar
portion
maintain
obtain

Review Key Concepts

2. Explain how you can develop a credit history.

3. Name five factors to think about when deciding which credit card to secure.

4. Define the three factors that creditors consider when granting a person credit.

5. Explain one major difference between credit cards, installment loans, and mortgages.

6. Indicate at least three ways to maintain a good credit rating.

Critical Thinking

7. When someone uses credit to buy a product or service, is he or she actually paying for the item?

8. Why would most credit card companies encourage consumers to make the minimum payment on a credit card balance instead of paying the full amount owed?

9. When you cosign on a loan, you agree to take responsibility for a debt if the primary credit applicant fails to pay it. Would you be willing to cosign a loan for a friend or family member? Why or why not?

10. A credit limit is a maximum amount of credit a lender will extend. Why do companies set credit limits on credit cards?

11. Do you think a debt should be repaid as soon as possible? Why or why not?

12. When is it possible to use a credit card and avoid paying interest?

13. Do you think most creditors want to repossess an item, such as a car, when the debtor cannot pay for it?

14. What criteria do you believe are most important in choosing a credit card? Explain your answer.

Write About It

15. Most credit card applications ask applicants to indicate the amount of time they have spent at their present residence and job. In two or more paragraphs indicate why you think companies want this information.

16. Many people who have a poor credit rating have a hard time getting a loan, an apartment, and a job. Is this fair or unfair? Write a brief essay discussing your opinions.

17. Some people use multipurpose credit cards for most of their everyday purchases. In at least two paragraphs, discuss why you think people use credit cards instead of cash or checks.

18. When people and companies do not pay their debts, businesses raise the prices of their goods and services. Write a brief e-mail to your teacher indicating whether that is fair. If you feel that is unfair, explain how would you change the practice.

19. For a fee, a credit bureau will provide potential creditors with a consumer's credit report. Use the Internet to find out more about the firms that provide credit scores. Then write a one-page report on your findings.

Technology Applications

Online Mortgage Calculators

20. Find the current annual interest rate offered on a 30-year fixed-rate mortgage for $100,000. Then use an online mortgage calculator to figure the amount of a monthly payment and the total amount of interest that will be paid over 30 years.

Business Ethics

Credit Applications

21. Suppose you have a job that pays you $15,000 a year. You receive a credit application in the mail stating that you have been pre-approved for $3,000 in credit, but that you must make at least $18,000 a year to receive the card. What should you do?

Chapter 26 Review and Activities

Applying Academics to Business

English Language Arts

22. Rewrite the following sentence using correct punctuation and capitalization.

before you apply to first national bank for a loan figure out the costs to make sure you can afford it

Mathematics

23. Your credit card has a limit of $3,000. You have charged goods totaling $\frac{2}{3}$ that amount. Your yearly APR is 12%. What is the finance charge one month?

CONCEPT **Finance Charges** The monthly finance charge rate is $\frac{1}{12}$ the annual rate.

English Language Arts

24. Write two or three sentences from this chapter that explain a cause-and-effect relationship. Then write two or three cause-and-effect sentences of your own about a different topic.

Mathematics

25. Total expenses for a year at college will be $9,000. You plan to pay $2,600 from your savings and finance the rest at a 5% simple interest. If you make 12 equal payments in one year, how much is each?

CONCEPT **Problem Solving** Computing the answer to some problems takes several steps.

Active Learning

Study Credit Habits

26. Choose a current article on the debt levels of college students, or interview someone at a local college or bank who is an expert on this topic. Find out the average debt load of college students, reasons for their debt, and how the students deal with it. Write a report of your findings. Then form groups and discuss your reports in class.

Business in the Real World

Credit Counselors

27. Research the career of a credit counselor. Find out what the job entails, the skills and formal education credit counselors should have, and the salary range for an entry-level counselor. Investigate the certification offered by the National Foundation for Credit Counseling. Write a one-page paper on your findings.

Real LIFE skills

LEARNING ABOUT LOAN APPLICANTS

28. Interview a loan officer at a bank regarding what he or she looks for in a credit applicant and why the loan officer looks for those qualities. Ask for the primary reasons people are not approved for a loan and the percent of loans that are not repaid. What action does the bank usually take when a loan is not repaid? Report your findings in writing or orally to the class.

 Business CAREERS

FIND YOUR DREAM JOB

29. Locate the Occupational Outlook Handbook Web site. Click on the "OOH Search/A-Z Index" link and enter the job category "credit authorizers, checkers, and clerks." Then write a one-page report about these types of occupations. Conclude your report with a list of things you could do now to prepare yourself to pursue the occupation.

Role Play

APPLYING FOR A CREDIT CARD

30. Situation You would like to apply for a credit card to use for most of your purchases. You must consider the different credit card options that are available.

Activity Research different types of credit cards from at least three financial institutions. Then present your creditworthiness to the institution you feel best suits your financial needs.

Evaluation You will be evaluated on how well you meet the following performance indicators:

- Demonstrate an understanding of the three Cs of credit.
- Evaluate the credit requirements of the financial institution that best suits your needs.
- Discuss the importance of maintaining a good credit score.
- Project your voice and use correct grammar.
- Answer questions about credit.

Standardized Test Practice

Directions Choose the letter of the best answer. Write the letter for the answer on a separate piece of paper.

1. A person's "safe debt load" is often defined as $\frac{1}{3}$ of a person's after-tax income less expenses. If Devon's after-tax income is $23,930, and his expenses are $4,800 for housing, $4,900 for food, $1,280 for transportation, and $950 for clothes, what is Devon's safe debt load?

   A $3,000
   B $4,000
   C $6,000
   D $12,000

 TEST-TAKING TIP If you do not know the answer to a question, make a note and move to the next question. Come back to it later, after you have answered the rest of the questions.

Chapter 27

Credit and the Law

Chapter Objectives After completing this chapter, you will be able to:

▷ **Section 27.1** *Credit Laws*
- **Discuss** state and federal regulation of credit.
- **Describe** federal laws that protect consumers.

▷ **Section 27.2** *Solving Credit Issues*
- **Identify** sources of credit fraud and precautions that can prevent it.
- **Discuss** ways to repair credit problems.

Ask

AN EXPERT

Bulls, Bears, and Crashes

Q: How does the stock market fluctuate?

A: Various terms are used to describe fluctuations in the stock market. A bull market is a prolonged period of increasing stock prices. While there's not a true definition of a bull market, it's generally thought of as a time when major stock indices increase by 20% or more. The opposite is a bear market, and as people who have been through a number of market cycles can tell you, for every bull there will be a bear around the corner. A bear market is generally referred to as a decline of 20% from peak to trough. However, it is always a time when stock prices decline over a long period. A stock market crash is perhaps the most dramatic occurrence an investor will experience. Generally, it's a quick and severe downward movement in stock prices, often occurring in a compressed time period so as to magnify the decline's impact. Crashes generally refer to declines of at least 15–20% over a short period.

Mathematics Suppose you are analyzing a graph of stock prices during a bear market in the 1970s. You would like to estimate the difference in stock prices between the worst quarter and the highest quarter. The actual numbers are as follows:

> Worst quarter: Fourth quarter of 1974 = $73.46 a share
> Highest quarter: First quarter of 1973 = $114.81 a share
> Estimate the difference between these numbers in whole dollars.

CONCEPT **Estimation by Rounding** If the digit to the right of the place to which you are rounding is 5 or higher, round up. If it is lower than 5, round down.

Purestock/SuperStock

● **Protecting Your Rights** The government regulates the credit industry to protect consumers. **What would you do if you had a complaint about credit?**

Credit Laws

Reading Guide

● Before You Read

Think about the role governments play in helping consumers deal with credit.

Read to Learn

- Discuss state and federal regulation of credit.
- Describe federal laws that protect consumers.

The Main Idea

Federal and state governments both provide assistance and protection to consumers who use credit. Laws indicate the rights and responsibilities of consumers as debtors and of businesses as creditors.

Key Concepts

- State and Federal Regulation of Credit
- Federal Credit Laws

Vocabulary

Key Terms

usury law   collection agent
credit report

Academic Vocabulary

You will find these words in your reading and on your tests. Make sure you know their meanings.

comprehensive   error
plus   remove

Graphic Organizer

In a figure like the one below, write the names of the federal laws that regulate fair credit in the left column and the purpose of the laws in the right column.

Federal Law	Purpose
1.	
2.	
3.	
4.	
5.	

 Go to **connectED.mcgraw-hill.com** to print out this graphic organizer.

State and Federal Regulation of Credit

To protect consumers, both federal and state governments control and regulate the credit industry. Most states have set a maximum on the interest rates that may be charged for certain types of credit. A law restricting the amount of interest that can be charged for credit is called a **usury law**.

The Federal Trade Commission (FTC) is the U.S. agency that enforces credit laws and helps consumers with credit problems and complaints. Many city and local governments also have consumer credit protection agencies. Several states have banking or consumer protection departments that deal with credit issues. **Figure 27.1** shows a page of consumer information from the FTC's Web site.

 **Reading Check**   **Identify** What is the federal agency that enforces credit laws and helps consumers with credit problems?

Federal Credit Laws

A number of federal laws help inform consumers about the costs of credit and set rules concerning the credit application process, credit history information, privacy, and debt collection.

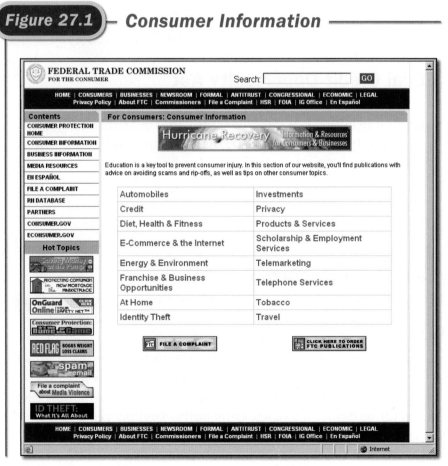

Figure 27.1 — *Consumer Information*

● **Preventing Consumer Injury** The Federal Trade Commission offers many tips to help consumers. **What is the role of the Federal Trade Commission in regulating credit?**

Federal Trade Commission

Information Collection

■ **Critical Reading** Life is full of important decisions. Think about the kinds of decisions you make as you read the question.

You are the owner of a small business that has been open for one year. You have only been dealing in cash sales since you opened, but are now looking into credit card machines to make things more convenient for your customers. You have researched a number of providers and have narrowed it down to two. One company charges slightly more than the other for its service, but the majority of customers use credit cards issued by the second company.

■ **Decision Making** Would learning that the lower cost provider offers a discount for giving it detailed information about the purchases your customers make affect your decision? Explain your answer.

Consumer Credit Protection Act

To make comparing credit costs easier, Congress passed the Consumer Credit Protection Act. The Consumer Credit Protection Act (also called the Truth in Lending Act) is a federal law that requires creditors to inform consumers about the costs and terms of credit. The law provides other protections. If your credit card is lost or stolen and someone else uses it, your payment for any unauthorized purchases will be limited to $50. Also, companies are not allowed to send a credit card to a consumer who did not request it.

The law states that advertisements for credit must communicate a fair and reasonably **comprehensive** indication of the nature and true cost of the credit. Ads must note the number of payments, the payment amount, and the period of payments if the amount of the down payment is given. The law requires that lenders inform borrowers regarding

- the cost of credit, or the total finance charge that includes the total interest **plus** required fees.
- the annual percentage rate (APR) so the borrower can compare interest rates.
- the credit terms and conditions. For instance, what happens if a payment is late?

Equal Credit Opportunity Act

The Equal Credit Opportunity Act is a federal law stating that credit applications can be judged only on the basis of financial responsibility. No person can be denied credit on the basis of marital status, gender, age, ethnicity, religion, or receipt of public assistance. The law allows only three reasons for denying credit: low income, large debts, and a poor payment record. A person who is denied credit must be given a written statement listing reasons for the denial.

Fair Credit Reporting Act

Each consumer with credit has a credit report. A **credit report**, also considered a credit history, is a record of an individual's past borrowing and repayments. It includes information about late payments and bankruptcy. You have the right to know what is in your credit report. The Fair Credit Reporting Act is a federal law that allows individuals to examine and correct information used by credit reporting agencies. Only authorized people and businesses can see your credit report. Lenders rely heavily on credit reports when they consider loan applications.

In the United States, most credit report information is collected and kept by three credit bureaus: Experian®, Equifax®, and TransUnion®. The credit bureaus are required to provide each consumer a free copy of his or her credit report upon request each year. Consumers should order their credit report and check it annually for mistakes. If a consumer finds an **error** on a credit report, then he or she shoud take steps to **remove** it. This involves writing the credit bureaus that are reporting the incorrect information. **Figure 27.2** shows what to do if you are denied credit.

OCC The Office of the Comptroller of the Currency (OCC) charters, regulates, and supervises national banks that issue credit cards, such as Bank of America. *Can you think of any other regulatory agencies that are like the OCC?*

✔ Reading Check **Analyze** What can you do if information on your credit report is incorrect?

Figure 27.2 — *What to Do if You Are Denied Credit*

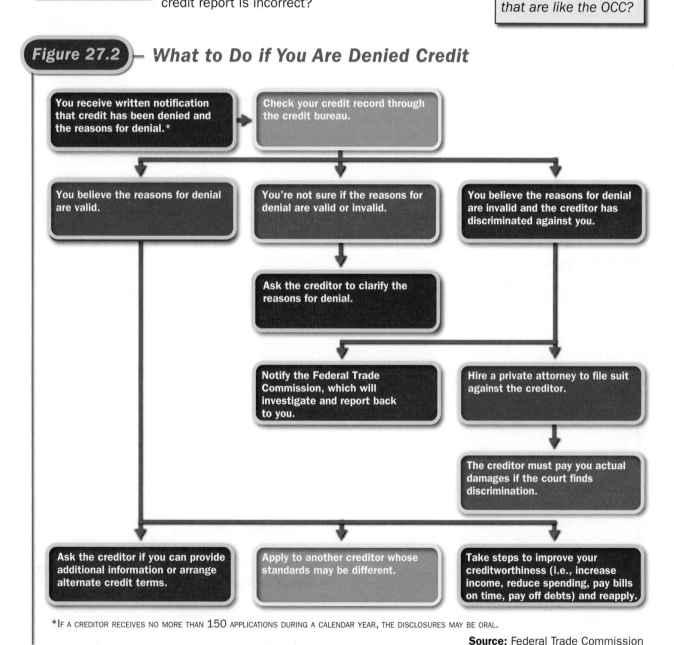

You receive written notification that credit has been denied and the reasons for denial.*

Check your credit record through the credit bureau.

You believe the reasons for denial are valid.

You're not sure if the reasons for denial are valid or invalid.

You believe the reasons for denial are invalid and the creditor has discriminated against you.

Ask the creditor to clarify the reasons for denial.

Notify the Federal Trade Commission, which will investigate and report back to you.

Hire a private attorney to file suit against the creditor.

The creditor must pay you actual damages if the court finds discrimination.

Ask the creditor if you can provide additional information or arrange alternate credit terms.

Apply to another creditor whose standards may be different.

Take steps to improve your creditworthiness (i.e., increase income, reduce spending, pay bills on time, pay off debts) and reapply.

*IF A CREDITOR RECEIVES NO MORE THAN 150 APPLICATIONS DURING A CALENDAR YEAR, THE DISCLOSURES MAY BE ORAL.

Source: Federal Trade Commission

● **Applying for Credit** People can be denied credit because of information in their credit report. **How can a consumer get a copy of his or her credit report?**

Fair Credit Billing Act

The Fair Credit Billing Act is a federal law that requires creditors to correct billing mistakes that are brought to their attention. The law also requires that consumers be informed of the steps they need to take to get an error corrected. To do this, the consumer must notify the creditor in writing. The creditor must either correct the error or explain in writing why the account is correct. If the creditor made the mistake, the consumer does not have to pay any finance charge on the incorrect amount. If there was no error, the consumer usually must pay interest plus the fee for any late payments.

The Fair Credit Billing Act also permits consumers to stop a credit payment for an item that is damaged or defective. Before stopping payment, however, consumers must attempt to resolve the problem with the company that sold it.

Fair Debt Collection Practices Act

The Fair Debt Collection Practices Act (FDCPA) is a federal law that serves to regulate collection agencies. The purpose of the FDCPA is to prevent deception, harassment, and other unfair debt collection practices by collection agents. A **collection agent** is a person or business that collects payments for overdue bills. The FDCPA requires that collection agents respect debtors' privacy and identify themselves to debtors when they call.

Section 27.1

○ After You Read

Review Key Concepts

1. Identify some government laws that protect consumers.
2. What three things are creditors required to tell consumers under the Consumer Credit Protection Act?
3. What are the only three reasons a person can be denied credit according to the Equal Credit Opportunity Act?

Academic Skills

4. **Mathematics** The Equal Credit Opportunity Act requires that all credit applicants be informed of whether their application has been accepted or rejected within 30 days. If you submitted your application for credit on February 1 in a year that is not a leap year, what is the deadline for the response?

CONCEPT **Adding Calendar Dates** Since the number of days in a month varies, it is often helpful to look at a calendar when adding calendar dates.

 For math help, go to the Math Appendix.

 Go to **connectED.mcgraw-hill.com** to check your answers.

Solving Credit Issues

Reading Guide

● Before You Read

Think about some actions you would take if you developed credit problems.

Read to Learn

- Identify sources of credit fraud and precautions that can prevent it.
- Discuss ways to repair credit problems.

The Main Idea

The main credit problems that consumers face are credit card and identity theft, and overuse of credit. There are specific steps to take to resolve each issue.

Key Concept

- Preventing Credit Fraud

Vocabulary

Key Terms

identity theft   consolidation loan
credit counselor   bankruptcy

Academic Vocabulary

You will find these words in your reading and on your tests. Make sure you know their meanings.

pose   overall
restore   instances

Graphic Organizer

In a figure like the one below, write notes about the things people can do to prevent identity theft.

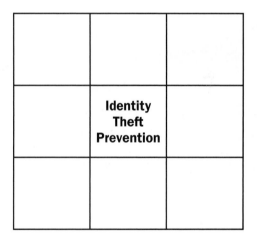

	Identity Theft Prevention	

 Go to **connectED.mcgraw-hill.com** to print out this graphic organizer.

As You Read

Have you ever lost something of value or had it stolen? What steps did you take to get it back?

Preventing Credit Fraud

Credit card theft, the misuse of credit information, and identity theft are increasing problems. Fortunately, there are ways to deal with them.

Dealing with Credit Card and Identity Theft

The first step a consumer should take when he or she gets a credit or ATM card is to write down the card issuer's phone number and other contact information. The information should be kept in a separate place from the card. This makes it easier to contact the company quickly if the card is lost or stolen.

A stolen credit card can lead to identity theft. **Identity theft** occurs when someone steals another person's financial information with the intention of committing fraud under that person's identity. People who commit identity theft often steal someone's

Business Case Study

Protecting Your Identity

Four simple tips to minimize your risk of identity theft

Identity theft is on the rise. In 2013 over 13 million people had their personal information stolen and used without their permission. These simple precautions can help you avoid becoming a victim.

1. **Send Securely.** Sensitive information can be captured by hackers who monitor Internet activity over insecure connections. Don't use public Wi-Fi connections to transmit personal or financial information. When you do send private data, make sure the website address begins with "https," not "http." The "s" means the connection is secure. Your information is encrypted so that only the intended recipient can open and access it.

2. **Protect your computer.** Keep your electronic devices protected from viruses, malware, and spyware by regularly updating your Internet security software.

3. **Guard your paper.** Protect all paperwork with personal information. For example, shred bank statements and credit card offers before recycling them.

4. **Monitor your money.** Keep a close eye on your accounts and report any charges or withdrawals you did not make. Take advantage of free credit reports. A sudden decline in your score could be a sign of trouble. You can never be too careful!

Active Learning

Break into small groups. Within your group, survey how frequently students shop or bank online, and how often they reveal things such as their name, birth date, Social Security number, and city of residence. Create a specific scenario in which your personal or financial information is obtained and used illegally, then decide as a group what to do if this happens. Share your scenario and plan with the rest of the class.

credit cards and Social Security numbers. They can **pose** as the person to get loans or more credit cards or to make purchases. People who discover that their identity has been stolen should take the following steps:

- **Contact the Credit Bureaus** The credit bureau will flag the file with a fraud alert that will prevent new accounts from being opened without permission.
- **Contact the Creditors** Creditors should be informed about fraudulent activities immediately by phone and in writing.
- **File a Police Report** A copy of a police report is important, in case creditors need proof of the crime.

Consumers can protect their identities by being careful with the way they handle their credit and ATM cards, checks, and Social Security number. Experts advise these precautions:

- Shred personal papers that contain your account numbers and Social Security number.
- Be careful when giving out your personal information.
- Watch what salespeople do with your credit or ATM card when you give it to them.
- Make sure your card is returned to you after purchases.
- Carry your checkbook, Social Security, ATM, and credit cards with you only when you expect to use them.
- When you make purchases online, read privacy policies and use a secure browser.
- Review your monthly bank and credit card statements for unauthorized purchases.

● **As You Read**

Think about some items that have your personal information on them, but that you always carry with you.

✔ **Reading Check** **Explain** What can you do to protect your identity from being stolen?

Repairing Credit Problems

Many consumers charge too many of their purchases and later realize that they cannot afford the monthly payments. To fix the problem, they have a few options to consider.

Contacting Creditors

The first thing a consumer should do is contact the creditor. Consumers can often work out a new payment plan to lower payments. They will still owe the original balances, plus more interest since it will take longer to repay the debts.

Talking to a Credit Counselor

Consumers who are unable to work out their credit problems should talk to a credit counselor. A **credit counselor** helps people work out a plan for getting out of debt. They also assist consumers with managing their money.

There are several different types of credit counseling services. Many credit counseling services charge a fee to "clean up" a poor credit report. However, they are seldom able to restore good credit to someone whose bad credit score is otherwise correct. Accurate reports of missed payments or bankruptcy cannot legally be removed from a person's credit report. If a consumer's credit rating has been unfairly damaged by inaccurate information, he or she can work with a credit bureau to correct the errors without the help of a counseling service.

Combining Debts

Another possible solution is a consolidation loan. A **consolidation loan** combines a consumer's debts into one loan with lower payments. If the interest rate on a consolidation loan is better overall, then a consolidation loan is a good idea. However, in some instances, the interest rate could be higher if the debtor has a poor credit history. Another problem is that some people begin to make charges again after they pay off their cards.

Filing Bankruptcy

The last resort is to declare bankruptcy. **Bankruptcy** is a legal process in which a borrower is relieved of debts after showing an inability to pay. One kind of bankruptcy involves selling most of the debtor's assets and passing the proceeds to the creditors. The debts are forgiven even though the creditors may not be paid in full. If the reorganizational form of bankruptcy is chosen, the debtor, the creditor, and a court-appointed trustee develop a plan to repay the debt on an installment basis. The debtor gets to keep more assets with this form.

People should avoid bankruptcy because it gives a debtor a bad credit record that can last for 10 years. This can make it difficult to obtain a home or car loan, buy major appliances, or get other forms of credit. People who have declared bankruptcy are charged higher interest rates because they are considered higher risks.

Bankruptcy Laws
In the United States, changes to bankruptcy laws have made it more difficult for debtors to declare bankruptcy. Before they can file, all debtors must get credit counseling. The declaration process also requires counseling on budgeting and debt management. *Do you think these laws are fair to debtors?*

Section 27.2

After You Read

Review Key Concepts
1. What are some credit problems that a debtor might face?
2. List some precautions to take to avoid identity theft.
3. What effect does declaring bankruptcy have?

Academic Skills
4. **English Language Arts** Write a brief summary explaining the content covered in this chapter. Then write a question about a concept that is either unclear to you or that you would like to know more about. Trade summaries and questions with a partner and write an answer to his or her question.

5. **English Language Arts** Zarina was recently denied a loan at a bank because her credit report included a statement about her non-payment of rent due to a lack of repairs that her landlord was obligated to make. On her behalf, draft a letter to the bank explaining the situation and requesting that her loan be approved.

 Go to **connectED.mcgraw-hill.com** to check your answers.

Section 27.1 Summary

Credit Laws In the United States, federal and state governments have passed several laws to help consumers avoid or handle credit problems. The Federal Trade Commission is the primary federal agency that enforces federal credit laws. Laws that protect consumers include the Consumer Credit Protection Act, the Equal Credit Opportunity Act, the Fair Credit Reporting Act, the Fair Credit Billing Act, and the Fair Debt Collection Practices Act. Several states have banking or consumer-protection departments that deal with credit issues.

Section 27.2 Summary

Solving Credit Problems The main credit problems consumers face are credit card and identity theft, and overuse of credit. Identity theft occurs when someone steals another person's financial information with the intention of committing fraud under that person's identity. It should be reported immediately to the proper authorities. When someone has overused credit and cannot repay it, the first step is to try to work out a new payment plan with the creditor. Credit counseling, debt consolidation, and bankruptcy are other possible solutions.

Vocabulary Review

1. On a sheet of paper, use each of these key terms and academic vocabulary terms in a sentence.

Key Terms
usury law
credit report
collection agent
identity theft
credit counselor
consolidation loan
bankruptcy

Academic Vocabulary
comprehensive	pose
plus	restore
error	overall
remove	instances

Review Key Concepts

2. Discuss state and federal regulation of credit.
3. Describe federal laws that protect consumers.
4. Identify sources of credit fraud and precautions that can prevent it.
5. Discuss ways to repair credit problems.

Critical Thinking

6. How can a truth-in-lending disclosure help protect consumers from credit problems?

7. People can now get free copies of their credit reports. Why do you think this change has occurred?

8. Why would a consumer need to use the Fair Credit Billing Act to stop a payment?

9. Why is it best to request changes of incorrect information in your credit report by letter rather than by phone?

10. What should a person do to correct errors on a credit report?

11. Some creditors will lower payments or interest, or even waive fees for debtors. Why do you think they are willing to make these changes?

12. Why would the Equal Credit Opportunity Act allow credit to be denied if a person has a poor credit record?

Write About It

13. Research the common ways identity theft occurs. Write a one-page paper on what you find.

14. Research credit counseling services. Write a one-page article for your school newspaper comparing and contrasting the services offered by two companies.

15. Research Chapter 7 and Chapter 13 bankruptcy. Write a report of at least 250 words discussing your findings.

16. In two or more paragraphs, describe how you could convince a credit manager that you are a good credit risk.

17. Write several reasons you might prefer using a credit card instead of cash, debit cards, or checks.

18. Write an essay about what you should do if your ATM card is stolen.

19. Research the process of filing and resolving a dispute at one of the three credit bureaus. Write a one-page report on your findings.

Technology Applications

Search the FTC's Web Site

20. The main mission of the Federal Trade Commission (FTC) is to promote consumer protection and the elimination and prevention of anticompetitive business practices. Explore the FTC's Web site. What major topics are found on consumer protection? Write a one- to two-page report summarizing your findings. Then give a brief presentation to the class.

Business Ethics

Making Credit Payments

21. Suppose you have had a difficult month financially. A couple of emergencies depleted your savings. However, you have two payments to make. One is for an installment loan on an appliance, for which you have two payments left. The other is for a credit card balance that has a minimum payment due. You can afford to make only one of the payments. What should you do?

Applying Academics to Business

English Language Arts

22. Paragraphs can be structured in various ways. For example, a paragraph may present a sequence of events or be organized around a statement followed by examples. Copy an example of each of these types of paragraph from this chapter. Then write a paragraph explaining the causes and effects of bankruptcy.

Mathematics

23. States regulate the maximum annual interest rate that may be charged for credit cards. The maximum in Connecticut is 19.8%; in New Jersey, it is 30%. Marika maintained a credit card balance of $750 for a year, paying only finance charges. If she lived in Connecticut, how much would she pay in finance charges? How much would finance charges be if she lived in New Jersey?

CONCEPT **Percents and Decimals** To change a percent to a decimal, drop the percent sign and divide by 100 by moving the decimal point two places to the left.

English Language Arts

24. Using the local telephone book, compile a list of all the agencies that provide consumer credit counseling and protection in your community. Organize the list according to whether they operate at the local, state, or federal level.

Mathematics

25. The total number of personal bankruptcies rose overall over a five-year period. Records indicate that there were 1.4 million bankruptcies filed in U.S. courts at the beginning of the period. Five years later, there were 1.6 million filed. What is the percent increase in bankruptcies filed over the five-year period?

CONCEPT **Percent Increase** Percent increase is a ratio of the net change over time divided by the original value.

Active Learning

Consumer Awareness of Credit Laws

26. Interview family members about their knowledge of credit protection laws. Ask them specifically about the Truth in Lending Act, the Equal Credit Opportunity Act, and the Fair Debt Collection Practices Act. Ask them if they think the three reasons for denying credit under the Equal Credit Opportunity Act are fair. Would they add any others? Why or why not? Write a report about their responses.

Business in the Real World

Multipurpose Credit Cards

27. Interview a business owner who has a store that accepts multipurpose credit cards, such as Visa and MasterCard. Ask about dealing with the credit card companies. What are the requirements to be able to accept these cards from customers? What are the associated costs and billing procedures? Ask whether all multipurpose credit card companies work the same way. Summarize your findings and share them with the class.

Real LIFE skills

Being Informed About Credit

28. Work with an adult family member to order a free copy of his or her credit report from one of the three U.S. credit bureaus. Then review the credit report. Is everything correct? Do any mistakes need to be corrected? Report what you did to get the credit report and the kind of information it presents.

Cool Business CAREERS

Find Your Dream Job

29. Locate the Occupational Outlook Handbook Web site. Click on the "OOH Search/A-Z Index" link and enter the job category "financial analysts and personal financial advisors." Then write a one-page report about these types of occupations. Conclude your report with a list of things you could do now to prepare yourself to pursue the occupation.

Role Play

Advocate for or Against a Usury Law

30. Situation The state legislature is having a session on whether it should implement a new usury law to restrict the interest rates that can be charged.

Activity Choose between being a consumer advocate who wants a usury law or a member of the banking industry who does not want a usury law. Give a presentation to the state legislature.

Evaluation You will be evaluated on how well you meet the following performance indicators:

- Explain how usury laws work.
- Consumer advocate: Give reasons why a new usury law would benefit debtors and creditors.
- Bank industry representative: Give reasons there should be less regulation of interest rates.
- Project your voice and use correct grammar.

Standardized Test Practice

Directions Choose the letter of the best answer. Write the letter for the answer on a separate piece of paper.

1. **William is making interest-only payments each month on a debt he owes to a credit card company. The interest rate he pays is 18% per year, and he pays $12. Which could be used to compute the principal?**

   A $12 \div (.18 \div 12)$

   B $12 \times (.18 \div 12)$

   C $12 \div 0.18$

   D 12×0.18

TEST-TAKING TIP If each item on a test is worth the same number of points, do not spend too much time on questions that are confusing.

Ping Fu

Chairperson/President/CEO, Geomagic

Geomagic makes 3-D geometric modeling software for manufacturers, such as Toyota® and Fisher-Price®. The North Carolina company was co-founded by Ping Fu, who grew up in China during the Cultural Revolution. Her company allows large-scale customization of individualized products at the same cost as mass manufacturing.

Q & A

Describe your job responsibilities.

Ping: The majority of my work involves talking to and corresponding with our headquarters and offices around the world. I believe strongly in empowering people. My job is to clear obstacles and provide directions that help them meet and exceed their goals.

What skills are most important in your business?

Ping: Geomagic is a technology-driven company, so an understanding of technical matters is important. The ability to understand how technology can be applied and used to make good products and services that people want to buy is vital. A person must also have the vision and be willing to take risks to change a long-entrenched way of doing business.

What is your key to success?

Ping: Great people—I can't make the company successful by myself. I need people to help me, and it's this desire to work for the company and make a positive contribution to society at large that makes Geomagic successful. I look at business in terms of contribution, rather than success.

What advice would you give students interested in starting a business?

Ping: First, think about why you want to start a business and try to imagine what success looks like, not how much money you can make. Then try to write a business plan that will deliver the success that you imagined. You will learn a lot by writing a business plan. If you find writing a business plan is difficult, just remember, running a business is at least ten times harder. Second, maintain a balanced life, with time for outside interests, friends, and family. Respect, motivate, and love the people who work for you and with you, and they will consider themselves partners in the company's success.

Critical Thinking

How is launching and running a company like or unlike being a parent?

Some Qualifications Needed to be the Owner of a Computer-Aided Design Company

Academic Skills and Abilities

Computer science; mathematics; information systems; computer programming; interpersonal skills; general business management skills; verbal and written communication skills; organizing and planning skills

Academic Skills Required to Complete Tasks at Geomagic			
Tasks	**Math**	**Science**	**English Language Arts**
Hold meetings			◆
Assign duties			◆
Determine client requirements	◆	◆	◆
Use CAD to visualize products	◆	◆	◆
Customer service			◆
Schedule employees	◆		◆
Remain technically up-to-date	◆	◆	◆
Analyze financials	◆		◆

Education and Training

Occupations in the computer-aided design (CAD) require a bachelor's degree in industrial design, architecture, or engineering. However, a master's degree or higher is preferred. Creativity and technical knowledge are crucial, as is a strong sense of the esthetic—an eye for color and detail and a sense of balance and proportion. Designers must understand the technical aspects of how products function. Despite the advancement of CAD, sketching ability remains an important advantage.

Career Path

Commercial and industrial designers usually receive on-the-job training and normally need 1 to 3 years of training before they can advance to higher-level positions. Experienced designers in large firms may advance to chief designer, design department head, or other supervisory positions. Some experienced designers open their own design firms.

Making Credit Decisions

Credit used wisely is a helpful way to buy large products, such as a vehicle or house. Smart consumers only use credit to buy things they need, not things they want.

Thematic Project Assignment

In this project you will write and give a speech that describes how to obtain credit and use it wisely. In your speech you also should discuss the misuse of credit and the consequences of using credit unwisely.

Step 1 — Brainstorm Skills You Need to Complete This Activity

Your success in writing and delivering a speech will depend on your skills. Preview the activity, then brainstorm a list of the skills you will need to use to complete the activity and describe how you will use them. Skills you might use include:

Academic Skills   reading, writing, and interpersonal skills

Basic Skills   speaking, listening, and thinking

Technology Skills   word processing and keyboarding

 SKILLS PREVIEW Go to **connectED.mcgraw-hill.com** to download a graphic organizer you can use to brainstorm the skills you will use to complete the project.

Step 2 — Choose a Purchase You Would Someday Like to Make

Think about the cost of the item you want to buy. Is it a vehicle? A DVD player? A sound system? Then think of how you will pay for the item on credit, and how this can help you or hurt you.

Step 3 — Build Background Knowledge

Preview information on making credit decisions.

Buying on Credit

Most consumers buy on credit, which can work for them or against them. Credit cards come in handy when you want to buy a new CD or even a player for it. Using credit cards too much gets young people into trouble. When many young people get their first taste of credit, they feel free to buy all those things that they could not afford before. That is a mistake. Having a credit card does not mean you suddenly have more money.

Protect your credit by using credit cards and making sure you pay them each month when they become due. Pay more than the minimum payment. Someday you will want to use credit for a large purchase, such as a car. Using a credit card wisely will help you get credit for large purchases. Misusing credit will keep you from getting more credit in the future.

Step 4 Connect with Your Community

Interview two adults in your community about their experiences with credit. Ask the adults what steps they take to help them obtain and then maintain credit. Think about how important it is to maintain a good credit history.

Step 5 Research How to Obtain Credit

Use library and Internet resources to research how you can obtain credit and what you need to do to maintain good credit. Also, research what happens when people misuse credit. Use the checklist as a guide to your research. Keep records of your sources of information.

Step 6 Develop Your Oral Presentation

Use word-processing software to develop a short speech that includes all of the information described in the project checklist.

Making Credit Decisions

✔ Make a list of main ideas and supporting details that you want to cover in your speech. Then give your speech to your class.

✔ Have three main points in your speech: (1) how to obtain credit, (2) how to maintain good credit, and (3) what happens if you misuse credit.

✔ Write an introduction for your speech by opening with one of the following: (1) an interesting idea about credit, (2) a fact, such as how many people use credit cards, or (3) a story about how you have or someone you know has used credit.

✔ Include details that support your three main points.

✔ Create a chart that illustrates what a monthly payment will be on a $1,000 loan at 12.99% interest. Use this chart to show how to maintain good credit as well as what happens if you do not make the payment each month.

✔ Wrap up your speech with one of the following: (1) an interesting idea about credit, (2) a fact, such as how many people use credit cards, or (3) a story about how you have or someone you know has used credit.

✔ Practice your speech at least five or six times in front of an adult. Ask him or her to help you make your speech better.

Self Connections

✔ Discuss the results of your research with the adults you interviewed.

✔ Describe how the adults obtain and use credit.

✔ Explain what the investigation and its results mean to you.

Step 7 Evaluate Your Presentation

 RUBRIC Go to connectED.mcgraw-hill.com to download a rubric you can use to evaluate your final report.

Integrated Management Services Engineers (IMS) offers civil engineering services that range from constructing buildings to digging ditches to aviation engineering. At the end of this unit, you will learn about IMS founders John Calhoun and Rod Hill and how they achieved their success.

Decision Making What steps can you take now to begin planning your career in a global economy?

Unit 10 — Thematic Project Preview

Building a Financial Future After completing this unit, you will research ways that building a financial future is important to your life.

Project Checklist As you read the chapters in this unit, use this checklist to prepare for the unit project.

- ✔ Think about the financial future you want to build.
- ✔ Think about ways you could build a financial future.
- ✔ Look for people and institutions in your community that will help you build a financial future.
- ✔ Think about the types of jobs and careers in the financial industry.

Managing Personal Finances

Chapter Objectives After completing this chapter, you will be able to:

▶ **Section 28.1** *Personal Financial Planning*
- **Explain** the steps involved in the financial planning process.
- **Identify** sources of financial information.
- **Discuss** sources of risk.
- **Discuss** the consequences of choices.

▶ **Section 28.2** *Money Management*
- **Discuss** the importance of budgeting.
- **List** the steps for preparing a budget.

Ask

AN EXPERT   **Understanding Hedge Funds**

Q: What are my options if I'm able to take a big risk?

A: Hedge funds are private investment funds for wealthy individuals and institutional investors. By law you must have an annual income exceeding $250,000 and invest-able assets of around $1 million to participate in the world of hedge funds. This is mainly because hedge funds are limited partnerships that operate like unregulated mutual funds, and therefore carry substantial risk. Hedge funds use a variety of investment strategies, some of which are more conservative, employing little or no leverage, while others carry more risk, using leverage and derivatives. The term *leverage* means that for a given amount of money, an investor can control an asset worth a larger amount.

Mathematics Ten years ago Mateo made a valuable long-term investment. He spent $2,000 on 100 shares of XYZ stock. His 100 shares are now worth $5,500. What is the percent increase on his investment?

CONCEPT **Percents Greater Than 100** Percents greater than 100 represent values greater than 1. For example, if the cost of an object is 250 percent of another, it is 2.5 or $2\frac{1}{2}$ times the cost.

● **Financial Planning** Money management is the process of planning how to get the most from your income. **How can financial planning help you to have the opportunity to enjoy the luxuries of life, such as entertainment?**

Blend Images - JGI/Jamie Grill/Getty Images

Chapter 28 Managing Personal Finances **497**

Personal Financial Planning

Before You Read

Think about some ways you manage your money now and your plans to manage money in the future.

Read to Learn

- Explain the steps involved in the financial planning process.
- Identify sources of financial information.
- Discuss sources of risk.
- Discuss the consequences of choices.

The Main Idea

Financial planning provides a solid foundation for making financial decisions. It involves looking at your financial position and setting goals.

Key Concepts

- Making Financial Decisions
- Sources of Financial Information
- Understanding Risk
- Consequences of Choices

Vocabulary

Key Terms

personal financial planning
goals
opportunity cost

 Go to **connectED.mcgraw-hill.com** to print out this graphic organizer.

Academic Vocabulary

You will find these words in your reading and on your tests. Make sure you know their meanings.

sources   revise
achieve   resources

Graphic Organizer

In a figure like the one below, list the six financial planning steps.

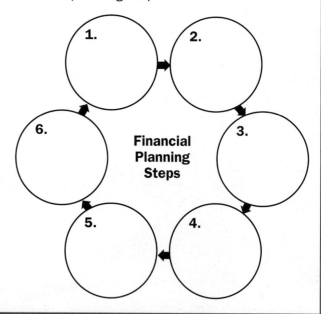

Making Financial Decisions

Personal finance refers to all the things in your life that involve money. **Personal financial planning** means spending, saving, and investing your money so you can enjoy the kind of life you want, along with financial security. Everyone has different financial goals. **Goals** are the things you want to accomplish. Getting a college education, buying a car, and starting a business are some examples of goals. Planning your personal finances is important because it will help you reach your goals. The financial planning process has six steps.

> **✔ Reading Check** **Define** What is personal financial planning?

Step 1: Determine Your Financial Situation

Once you have determined your financial situation, you will be able to start planning. First, make a list of your savings, monthly income (money you receive, such as job earnings, an allowance, tips, gifts, and interest on bank accounts), monthly expenses (money you spend), and debts (money you owe to others). A good way to estimate your expenses is to keep a careful record of every amount you spend for one month.

Step 2: Develop Your Financial Goals

To develop clear financial goals, you will need to think about your attitude toward money. Is it more important to you to spend your money now or to save for the future? What are your wants and needs? Would you rather get a job right after high school or continue your education?

● As You Read

Think about how your wants and needs affect your financial goals.

● **A Beginning Step** Planning your personal finances will help you reach your goals. **What is the first step in personal financial planning?**

Purestock/SuperStock

Step 3: Identify Possible Courses of Action

It is important to consider your options before making a decision. Generally, you will have several possible courses of action.

Step 4: Evaluate Your Alternatives

When you evaluate your alternatives, use the sources of financial information that are available. Look at where you are in your life, your present financial situation, and your personal values. Consider the consequences and risks of each decision you make. Your financial goals will help you determine the best option.

Step 5: Implement a Financial Plan of Action

A plan of action is a list of ways to achieve your financial goals. If your goal is to increase your savings, a plan of action could be to cut back on spending. If you want to increase your income, you could get a part-time job or work more hours at your present job.

Step 6: Review and Revise Your Plan

As you get older, your finances and needs will change. That means your financial plan will have to change, too. You should reevaluate and revise it every year.

Business Case Study

Wanted: Financial Planners

With longer retirements ahead, skilled money managers are in high demand

Personal financial planning is big business. Jobs in financial advising will grow by 27 percent through 2022, according to the U.S. Bureau of Labor Statistics. That's more than double the national average.

Why the growth? Workers in previous decades often received pensions from their employer. These guaranteed a steady retirement income until death, making planning relatively simple. Today, more workers are responsible for their own retirement savings. Life expectancy has also grown, which means more years of retirement to fund. These two factors are fuelling demand for professional help with financial planning.

Today's workers must carefully manage their money from a relatively young age. A tight job market, stagnating income, and rising health and education costs make careful, realistic money management crucial to the dream of a long, vibrant retirement.

Professionals with financial knowledge and good judgment, as well as a personable, collaborative work style, will be in demand for this growing job field.

> **Active Learning**
>
> Find out more about the financial planning field. Look up "Personal Financial Advisors" in the U.S. Bureau of Labor Statistics' online *Occupational Outlook Handbook*. After visiting the website and researching the job, write a short description of what you imagine to be a typical working day for a personal financial planner. At the end of your description, explain whether you think this job would suit your values, interests, and aptitudes

Sources of Financial Information

When making financial decisions, the Internet is a good place to get information on social and economic conditions. Most corporations put facts about their company and financial situation on their Web site. They will also mail information that is requested. Magazines such as *Bloomberg Businessweek, Time,* and *U.S. News & World Report* and newspapers such as *The Wall Street Journal, The New York Times,* and *Financial Times* can also help.

Understanding Risk

When you make a financial decision, you also accept certain risk. Some types of financial risk include:

- **Inflation Risk** Inflation is a general increase in the cost of goods and services. If you wait to buy an item you want, you risk the possibility that the price will increase.
- **Interest Rate Risk** Interest rates rise and fall, which may affect the cost of borrowing or the profits you earn when you save or invest.
- **Income Risk** Your income may rise or fall. You could lose your job due to unexpected health problems, family ussues or other reasons. You could also find a better job or get a raise.
- **Personal Risk** Some choices increase risk. Driving for eight hours on icy mountain roads instead of traveling by airplane may not be worth the money you would save.
- **Liquidity Risk** You may have to withdraw your savings or investments. Liquidity is the ability to convert your financial **resources** into cash easily without a loss in value.

An important part of financial planning is understanding which risks you can afford to take and which ones you cannot. If you decide a course of action is too risky, you might decide to choose an alternative. In some cases, insurance is available to limit your exposure to risk. Diversification of your assets is another way to minimize risk.

✔ Reading Check **Identify** List some types of financial risks.

Consequences of Choices

An **opportunity cost**, sometimes called a tradeoff, is what you give up when you make one choice instead of another. Suppose you want to become a full-time college student. You would like to work full time, but your work hours would conflict with your class schedule. If you choose to pursue your education, you will give up the opportunity to work full time, at least for a while. The opportunity cost of going to college is working at the full-time job. However, choosing between the alternatives involves more than just knowing what you forgo. It also involves knowing what you gain.

Section 28.1

⊙ *After You Read*

Review Key Concepts

1. What are some examples of long-range financial goals that consumers may have?
2. List the steps of the financial planning process.
3. Name some types of financial risk.

Academic Skills

4. **Mathematics** The average U.S. family spends about 16% of its income on housing and 12% on household expenses. If a family's monthly income is $3,125, how much does it spend on housing and household expenses?

CONCEPT The Distributive Property The Distributive Property states that $a \times c + b \times c = (a + b)c$. You can multiply each percent by the monthly income then add the products, or you can add the percents and multiply their sum by the monthly income.

 For math help, go to the Math Appendix.

 Go to **connectED.mcgraw-hill.com** to check your answers.

Money Management

a

Before You Read

Think about some steps you can take now in managing your money so that you can get the most from your income.

Read to Learn

- Discuss the importance of budgeting.
- List the steps for preparing a budget.

The Main Idea

Meeting your financial goals requires you to know your income and expenses. A budget can enable you to track your spending and make choices about your money.

Key Concepts

- The Importance of Budgeting
- Preparing a Budget

Vocabulary

Key Terms

money management	expense
budget	fixed expenses
income	variable expenses
gross pay	budget variance
deductions	surplus
net pay	deficit

 Go to **connectED.mcgraw-hill.com** to print out this graphic organizer.

Academic Vocabulary

You will find these words in your reading and on your tests. Make sure you know their meanings.

utilize	intermediate
hence	major

Graphic Organizer

In a figure like the one below, list the seven steps for preparing a budget.

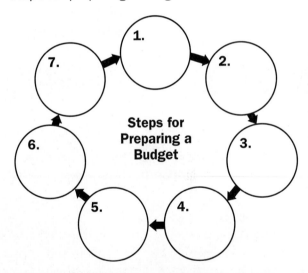

Steps for Preparing a Budget

Everyone Budgets
Families, corporations, and even governments set budgets. The budget of a government is similar to your budget, setting up the intended income and expenses for the year. Nearly all large businesses re-forecast their budgets on a quarterly basis. In the future, annual budgets may be replaced with monthly or rolling forecasts. *What does it mean if a company comes close to delivering its budgeted figures?*

The Importance of Budgeting

Money management is necessary for consumers, businesses, and governments. **Money management** is a method of planning to get the most from one's money. Like consumers, businesses and governments must figure out how to **utilize** their income to pay for things they want or need. Income is a limited resource for everyone. Most people want more goods and services than they have money to buy. A budget helps them to set financial priorities. **Figure 28.1** shows average U.S. household expenses.

A **budget** is a plan for using your income in a way that best meets your wants and needs. It includes a record of your expected income, your planned expenses, and your planned savings over a certain period of time. **Hence**, a good budget helps people set priorities for spending and saving and tracks their money.

✔ **Reading Check** **Analyze** Why is income a limited resource for everyone?

Preparing a Budget

Planning a budget is a seven-step process: Set your goals; estimate your income; budget for unexpected expenses and savings; budget for fixed expenses; budget for variable expenses; record what you spend; and review spending and saving patterns.

Figure 28.1 — *Average Household Expenses*

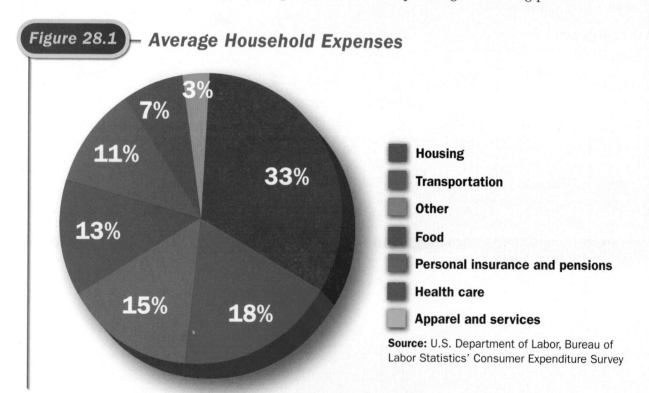

- Housing
- Transportation
- Other
- Food
- Personal insurance and pensions
- Health care
- Apparel and services

Source: U.S. Department of Labor, Bureau of Labor Statistics' Consumer Expenditure Survey

● **The Cost of Living** This graph shows how an average household in the United States spends its money. **If a family earns $3,000 a month, how much money (on average) would that family spend on housing?**

Step 1: Set Your Financial Goals

As you prepare to set your financial goals, you should consider several questions: What do I want to accomplish in the next month? The next year? The next five years? What is important to me? Are my goals practical? A budget should help you decide which goals you can meet with the amount of money you have. You might find it helpful to separate them into short-term, **intermediate**, and long-term goals.

Step 2: Estimate Your Income

Once you have set your goals, you can begin working on a budget. Start by recording your estimated income for the next month. Your **income** is the actual amount of money you earn or receive during a given period. Include all sources of income that you know you will receive, such as take-home pay and income on investments.

Pay and Deductions Your **gross pay** is the total amount of money you earned for a specific time. Your gross pay is reduced by various **deductions**, or amounts that are taken out of your pay before you receive your paycheck. Deductions include items such as taxes, insurance premiums, retirement contributions, and union dues. Your take-home pay, or **net pay**, is your gross pay minus deductions.

Real World

Withholding Full-time workers pay several kinds of taxes. *Withholding* is income tax withheld from an employee's wages and paid directly to the government by the employer. It is a form of deduction from pay. The funds are applied to the worker's federal, state, and local income taxes as well as his or her contribution to Social Security and Medicare. Self-employed people pay their taxes directly to the government. *Why do you think taxes are withheld from workers' paychecks?*

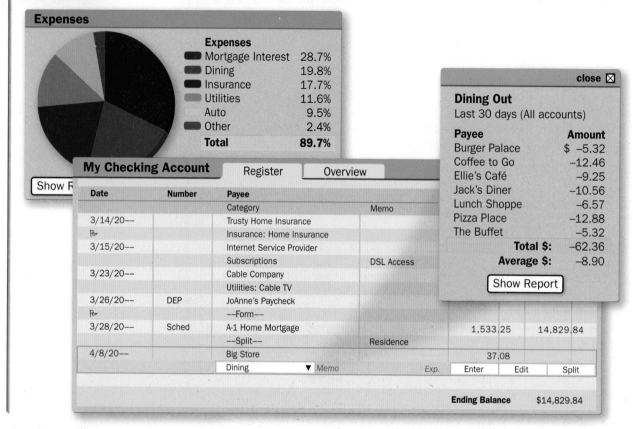

Figure 28.2 – *Managing Your Money*

● **Budgeting Software** You can use budgeting software to create reports, charts, and graphs that quickly show you when you paid a bill, how much you paid, and to whom. **How might budgeting software make preparing your taxes easier?**

Step 3: Budget for Unexpected Expenses and Savings

You have to plan for expenses such as food, rent, and clothing to satisfy your basic needs. An **expense** is an amount of money used to buy or do something. You must also plan for unexpected expenses, such as medical visits or accidents. Unexpected expenses could include rises in costs for items such as gasoline. **Figure 28.2** provides a glimpse of budgeting software.

A budget must also include a plan for savings. Savings make it possible for you to meet future wants and needs. They also protect you against expenses that you did not budget for, that are higher than you expected, or that are completely unexpected. You need a savings plan if your long-term goal is to make a **major** purchase, such as a new computer or a vacation.

When you develop your budget, make sure that the total income figure is the same as the total for planned expenses and savings. If your planned expenses and savings are more than your income, you will have to cut some expenses or find some other source of income.

As You Read

Think about some unexpected expenses you have had and how they affected your budget.

Step 4: Budget for Fixed Expenses

Fixed expenses are expenses that occur regularly and are regularly paid. They include payments for rent, insurance, and a car loan. The amount of a fixed expense might sometimes change, but it is usually about the same over long periods.

Step 5: Budget for Variable Expenses

Variable expenses are expenses that change and can be controlled more easily than fixed expenses. They include expenses such as food, phone charges, entertainment, and gifts. The amounts for these expenses usually vary from month to month.

Step 6: Record What You Spend

To find out how practical your budget is, you will need to keep track of your expenses during one month and revise your budget if necessary. The difference between the budgeted amount and the actual amount that you spend is the **budget variance**. This figure can be either a surplus or a deficit. A **surplus** is extra money that can be spent or saved, depending on a person's goals and values. A **deficit** occurs when more money is spent than is earned or received.

Step 7: Review Spending and Saving Patterns

Budgeting is a continual process. You need to review your budget each month and consider making changes.

Section 28.2

After You Read

Review Key Concepts
1. What are the seven steps to preparing a budget?
2. What is the difference between gross pay and net pay?
3. How are fixed expenses and variable expenses different?

Academic Skills

4. **English Language Arts** Interview someone who is responsible for a budget for a club, business, or other organization. How do goals drive the budget? How often is it revised? How is it monitored? Write a story about your interview for the organization's newsletter.

5. **English Language Arts** What are your goals for the future? Write a description of where you see yourself living and what you see yourself doing in 10 years. Then write a short plan describing the money management techniques you will use in order to meet your goals.

 Go to **connectED.mcgraw-hill.com** to check your answers.

Section 28.1 *Summary*

Personal Financial Planning Everyone must make financial decisions. Identifying your financial goals and planning how to get the most from your money are part of personal financial planning. If you plan well and carry out those plans, you can reach your financial goals. To create a financial plan, you need to determine your financial situation; develop your financial goals; identify possible courses of action; evaluate your alternatives; implement a financial plan of action; and review and revise your plan. Often financial planning means you must research options so that you can evaluate risk and make wise choices.

Section 28.2 *Summary*

Money Management A budget is a tool for getting the most from your income. With a budget, you can estimate your income and expenses and track your financial progress over time. Income and expenses often vary over time, so a part of budgeting is reviewing your goals, revising them, and adjusting your budget as needed. To create a budget, you need to set your financial goals; estimate your income; budget for unexpected expenses and savings; budget for fixed expenses; budget for variable expenses; record what you spend; and review your spending and saving patterns. Budgeting is an ongoing process.

Vocabulary Review

1. On a sheet of paper, use each of these key terms and academic vocabulary terms in a sentence.

Key Terms

personal financial
 planning
goals
opportunity cost
money management
budget
income
gross pay

deductions
net pay
expense
fixed expenses
variable expenses
budget variance
surplus
deficit

Academic Vocabulary

sources
achieve
revise
resources

utilize
hence
intermediate
major

Review Key Concepts

2. Explain the steps involved in the financial planning process.

3. Identify sources of financial information.

4. Discuss sources of risk.

5. Discuss the consequences of choices.

6. Discuss the importance of budgeting.

7. List the steps for preparing a budget.

8. Why is it important to plan for spending, saving, and investing your money?

9. "People always have a choice: to use their money on a good or service, or to invest or save the money." Do you think this statement is true? Why or why not?

10. Sometimes people are willing to delay making a purchase so they can buy something better later. This concept is known as delaying gratification. What effect do you think delaying gratification can have on budgeting?

11. Some people think of their income as the total amount that they earn, not the amount that they actually receive in their paycheck. What effect will that thinking have on their ability to live within a budget?

12. What do you think is the most difficult part of budgeting? Why?

13. How do your spending habits affect your standard of living? What are some unexpected expenses that you may have that will affect your budget?

14. What suggestions would you give to someone who thinks that savings are not an important part of budgeting and money management?

15. Estimate how much money you need for an item you would like to buy in the future. Write a brief essay about items that you could forgo buying now to have that item. When do you think you can achieve your goal?

16. Some people think money is something that they can always get. Others think that money must be conserved and used wisely or it will not be available when needed. Write two or more paragraphs about your thoughts on each statement.

17. What are your goals? In two or more pages, describe where you see yourself living and what you see yourself doing in 10 years. What personal financial planning methods will you use to meet your goals?

18. Why is opportunity cost an important concept for people to consider in their decisions about personal financial planning? Explain your answer in two or more paragraphs.

19. Check in the yellow pages of your local phone book, a local newspaper, library, or online to find information about personal financial planning assistance available in your community. Write a summary of information you find.

Spreadsheet Software

20. Early planning for college or postsecondary training is important. Use a spreadsheet to prepare a summary of the costs of a college education or training program. Visit Web sites for training and education institutions to find tuition and fees, estimated room and board costs, and costs for books and supplies.

Family First or Strictly Business?

21. Suppose you work as a financial planner for a well-known novelist who is also very wealthy. Your duties include advising her on personal investments. You have a brother who owns a struggling online business. He asks you to advise your client to invest in his company, pitching it as a "hot new dot-com." What should you do?

Chapter 28 Review and Activities

Applying Academics to Business

English Language Arts

22. Look for a paragraph in this chapter that describes a cause-and-effect relationship. Find another paragraph that has a topic sentence supported by details. Finally, find an example of a sequence of events.

Mathematics

23. Find a picture of a big-ticket item you would like to own. Figure out the equivalent cost in movies (at $7 per movie) and in dining out (at $9 per meal) for the item. For example, if an MP3 player costs $149, its cost-equivalent is 21 movies or 16 restaurant meals. Assuming that you see three movies per month and eat out seven times, make a plan for saving enough money to purchase your big-ticket item by eliminating one or more monthly movies and restaurant meals. Write a few sentences describing your plan.

CONCEPT **Problem Solving** You might start by computing how much you spend on movies and dining out each month. Then decide what you are willing to eliminate to save to buy the item you have chosen.

English Language Arts

24. Based on the concepts you have read about in this chapter, write a word that means the opposite or almost the opposite of each of the following:

income
gross pay
variable
unplanned

Mathematics

25. Americans save less than 5% of their income. Other countries have a higher percentage of savings per capita, including Belgium (22%), Denmark (16.2%), and Japan (15.7%). Research the average per capita savings of at least 10 countries and display your findings in a bar graph.

CONCEPT **Bar Graphs** Bar graphs can be designed so that the bars are horizontal or vertical. Each bar represents the quantity associated with a different category, in this case, the per capita savings of a country.

Active Learning

Financial Planning Software

26. Interview two or more people who use budgeting or financial planning software to organize financial information. Ask them how technology has affected their records and financial planning. Do they believe they are better money managers because they use the software? Write a summary of the information you learned.

Business in the Real World

Investing in a Corporation

27. An annual report is a corporation's yearly review of activities, especially its financial dealings. Choose a corporation, and research its annual report, either online or by contacting the company. Read the report's overview and highlights. Did the company meet its goals? Why or why not? Would you consider investing in it? In a two-page paper, explain your answers.

Real LIFE skills

PREPARING A PERSONAL BUDGET

28. Select a college or technical school that you might like to attend after school. Obtain information on tuition and other fees. Add the cost of food, shelter, clothing, books, and any other items you think are part of the cost. Estimate the total cost of the education. Then estimate how you will pay for it. Prepare a budget for the time you will seek the education.

Business CAREERS

FIND YOUR DREAM JOB

29. Locate the Occupational Outlook Handbook Web site. Click on the "OOH Search/A-Z Index" link and enter "budget analysts." Write a one-page report about the job. Conclude your report with a list of things you could do now to prepare yourself to pursue the occupation.

Role Play

A BUDGET FOR YOUR MARCHING BAND

30. Situation Your school's marching band has asked for your help in preparing the band's budget for the upcoming year. You and three of your classmates are meeting to identify ways it can raise money and plan a budget.

Activity Hold a meeting to plan ways to raise money and to prepare a proposed budget. The band has $435 in the treasury.

Evaluation You will be evaluated on how well you meet the following performance indicators:

- Identify three or more ways the marching band can raise money.
- Prepare a list of expected expenses for the marching band.
- Prepare a proposed budget.
- List steps that the band members can take to meet their goals.
- Communicate with others, and use correct grammar.

Standardized Test Practice

Directions Choose the letter of the best answer. Write the letter for the answer on a separate piece of paper.

1. Which punctuation mark, if any, is needed in the sentence?

Samantha asked her accountant "Would it be better to cut my budget for housing, increase my income, or save less each month?"

A , (comma)

B . (period)

C ; (semicolon)

D The sentence is correct as it is.

TEST-TAKING TIP Keep your family members informed about your test schedule. They can help you with your studies and provide encouragement.

Checking Accounts

Ask AN EXPERT

Checking Accounts: Budgeting

Q: How do I get started managing my finances?

A: Basically, budgeting is about managing the money coming in (income) and the money going out (expenditures). In the business world, this coming in and going out of money is known as cash flow. The goal is to create an overall positive cash flow. Before you decide how to manage your finances, spend a month or two keeping careful track of your cash flow. Assess how you spend your money and decide where possible cutbacks can be made, for example making coffee at home in the morning or cutting down on eating out. Discipline is the key to saving money. After making cutbacks, consider your options for investing the money you've saved. You may choose to invest in physical assets, such as a car or real estate, or in financial assets, including stocks, bonds, CDs, money markets, and traditional bank accounts.

Mathematics Edward is analyzing his finances. He has determined that in the month of May he spent $625 on rent and utilities, $293 on food, $216 on gas, $254 on his car payment, and $422 on entertainment. He made only $1,595 freelancing and $50 on investments. Will Edward need to cut back on his entertainment expenditures in order to have positive cash flow?

CONCEPT **Adding and Subtracting Multiple Numbers** When you are adding or subtracting more than two numbers, do one operation at a time. First, line up all of the addends vertically. Add up the columns from right to left. Finally, make the necessary subtractions.

Floresco Productions/age fotostock

● **Bank Services** You can withdraw money from a bank account several different ways. Why is it a good idea to keep printed copies of all banking receipts and records?

The Basics of Checking Accounts

Reading Guide

Before You Read

Think about some types of bank services that would enable you to manage your finances.

Read to Learn
- Discuss the different types of checking accounts and how they work.
- Discuss other services and offerings that banks provide checking account holders.

The Main Idea

Checking accounts are tools that many people use to make payments. A checking account provides a way for consumers to manage their spending, make payments easily, and keep track of their funds. When they have a checking account, customers can access information online through the bank's Web site.

Key Concepts
- How Checking Accounts Work
- Account Services and Other Offerings

Vocabulary

Key Terms

check	overdrawn
direct deposit	overdraft protection
interest-bearing account	stop payment
signature card	debit card

Academic Vocabulary

You will find these words in your reading and on your tests. Make sure you know their meanings.

demand	compare
common	designed

Graphic Organizer

In a figure like the one below, describe ways you will use traditional checking services and the additional services banks now provide.

Traditional Checking Services	Additional Services

 Go to **connectED.mcgraw-hill.com** to print out this graphic organizer.

How Checking Accounts Work

It is hard to imagine how businesses and people would function without checks. A **check** is a written order directing a bank or other financial institution to pay money on **demand** to the person or company named on it. Checks are a **common** medium of exchange, or way to make payments for goods and services.

A customer opens a checking account by depositing money into a bank. The bank provides paper checks, which can then be used to pay for goods and services. The check is paid to the payee, the business or person to whom the check was written. The payee can either deposit the check or cash it. Once the money is paid, the check writer's bank voids, or cancels, the check. **Figure 29.1** shows both sides of a canceled check.

✔ **Reading Check**   **Explain**   What is a check?

Figure 29.1 — *Writing and Cashing a Check*

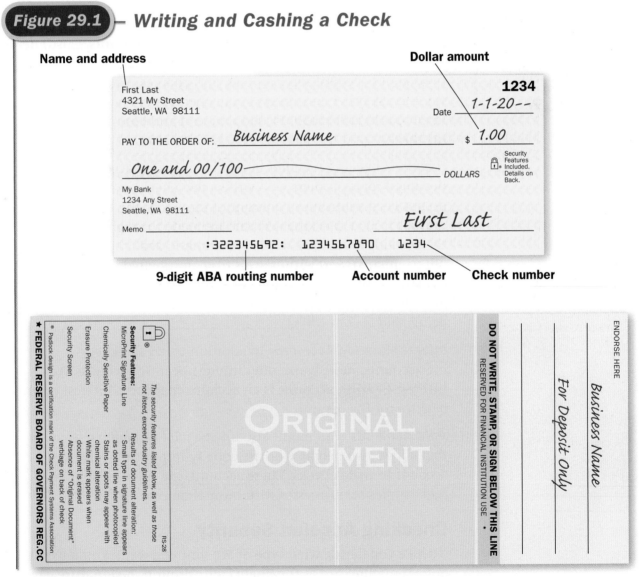

Name and address

Dollar amount

First Last
4321 My Street
Seattle, WA 98111

1234

Date *1-1-20--*

PAY TO THE ORDER OF: *Business Name* $ *1.00*

Security Features Included. Details on Back.

One and 00/100 DOLLARS

My Bank
1234 Any Street
Seattle, WA 98111

First Last

Memo

⑊322345692⑊ 1234567890 1234

9-digit ABA routing number

Account number

Check number

● An Endorsed Check Checks are a common medium of exchange. **Why is it sometimes a good idea to write a check instead of spending cash?**

● **As You Read**

Think about some reasons you would want a checking account.

Types of Accounts

Most banks offer several types of checking accounts. Customer service representatives at financial institutions can answer questions about account services, fees, and charges. You might also want to ask other consumers about their experiences with different banks and accounts. Shop around and **compare** financial institutions and the services they have to offer.

Regular Checking Account A regular checking account is **designed** for customers who write a few checks each month and do not keep a minimum amount of money in the account. Withdrawals from a checking account are made through checks that the account holder has written, automatic deductions (such as bill payments), and withdrawals from automated teller machines (ATMs). **Direct deposit** allows electronic transfers of payments directly from the payer's account to the account of the person being paid.

Interest-Bearing Accounts In addition to regular checking accounts, most banks offer interest-bearing accounts. An **interest-bearing account** is an account that earns interest on the balance for the depositor.

Joint Accounts You might also open a *joint account,* an account that allows two people who are equally responsible for the account to write checks. These accounts are often used by married couples or businesses with more than one owner.

Checking Account Security

Once you decide what type of account you want, you must fill out a signature card at the financial institution. A **signature card** is a record of an account holder's signature used to verify identity.

If someone takes a check that the account holder has written to him or her to the branch where the account was opened, the teller can verify the account holder's signature with the card. If the signature matches, then the check will be cashed. If it does not match, the check will not be cashed.

You must also provide your address, phone number, and the answer to a security question, such as your mother's maiden name. The bank then assigns you a checking account number and issues you a book of checks.

● **As You Read**

Think about some precautions you would take when opening a checking account.

Account Services and Other Offerings

Banks offer various services for checking accounts. Some of these services are offered as protection to the consumer. Other services are designed to make banking more convenient.

When an account is **overdrawn**, it means that the account owner has written checks for more money than the balance in the account. An *overdraft* is the amount that is overdrawn. **Overdraft protection** is a line of credit for overdrawn checks.

Business Case Study

Remaking the Checking Account

New features take checking accounts beyond paper and pen

Checking accounts have been around for decades, but new services are making them more appealing than ever.

Easy Payments. In 2014 Apple unveiled Apple Pay, which stores your account information and keeps it secure. Just hold your iPhone or Apple Watch by an enabled pay pad, and money is deducted from your linked checking account.

Low Fees, Great Service. Credit unions are offering students great deals on checking accounts. A recent study showed that credit unions offer more features, lower fees, and higher interest rates than national banks. One disadvantage to credit unions, however, is that they lack easy access to network ATMs.

Money for Charity. Did you know that many banks let you divert money into interest-earning accounts intended for charitable giving?

For example, an account offered at Marshfield Savings Bank in Marshfield, Wisconsin, pays 0.25 percent interest to your chosen charity. At year's end, your favorite nonprofit gets a check in your name!

Active Learning

Imagine that you want to give money to a favorite local charity and have two options to maximize your gift. Option 1 is to join a giving campaign run by the charity. If you give by the end of the month, an anonymous donor will match your donation and double the amount contributed. You can only afford to give $50 this month, however. Option 2 is to put $5 a month into a giving account through your bank. After 12 months, the bank will send the money to the charity with 0.75 percent annual interest added. Which option would generate the larger sum of money?

If you have overdraft protection and write a check for more than you have in the account, the bank will cover the check up to a certain amount. You may pay a service fee and interest for overdraft protection. A **stop payment** is an order for a bank not to cash a particular check. It also usually requires a fee. A **debit card** is a bank card that immediately takes money from a checking account when it is used. It is used like a credit card.

Online Banking

Technology allows consumers to handle many banking transactions over the Internet. Online banking allows consumers to check their account balances, transfer money, or pay bills at any time. With online banking, your checking account information is available to you from your home computer 24 hours a day, seven days a week. Online banking also allows you to save time and money. Banks offer the option of scheduling automatic payment of bills from the checking account, too.

You can use an Internet browser on your computer to handle online banking. With personal finance software, you can store information about your transactions for your records.

Section 29.1

After You Read

Review Key Concepts

1. How does a checking account work?
2. What are the three main types of checking accounts?
3. Discuss some additional services and offerings that banks provide checking account holders.

Academic Skills

4. **Mathematics** Vinita has a checking account at a local bank. This account pays 0.5% interest if she maintains an average balance of at least $1,500 during a month. In February, Vinita's average monthly balance was $1,120 more than the minimum. How much interest did she earn in February?

 CONCEPT **Percents Less Than One** To convert a percent to a decimal, multiply it by 100 by moving the decimal point two places to the left. Therefore, 0.5% = 0.005.

Math For math help, go to the Math Appendix.

 Go to **connectED.mcgraw-hill.com** to check your answers

Account Records

Reading Guide

Before You Read

Think about some ways you would manage a checking account effectively.

Read to Learn

- Describe how checking account holders manage their bank transactions.
- Describe the procedure for bringing your account into agreement with bank records.

The Main Idea

You must manage your checking account so that you have an accurate picture of your finances. A bank provides you with a bank statement showing all transactions. You should check your checkbook records against that statement regularly.

Key Concepts

- Keeping Track of Financial Transactions
- Reconciling Your Account Records

 Go to **connectED.mcgraw-hill.com** to print out this graphic organizer.

Vocabulary

Key Terms

check register   canceled checks
endorsement   bank reconciliation
bank statement   outstanding checks

Academic Vocabulary

You will find these words in your reading and on your tests. Make sure you know their meanings.

route   valid
traces   alteration

Graphic Organizer

In a figure like the one below, write a check to Tina's Hair Salon for $25.00.

First Last 4321 My Street Seattle, WA 98111	1234 Date_____
PAY TO THE ORDER OF:_____	$_____
_____ DOLLARS	
My Bank 1234 Street Seattle, WA 98111	
Memo_____	_____

:322345692:   1234567890   1234

Keeping Track of Financial Transactions

An advantage of checking accounts is that they enable consumers to keep records of their financial transactions. The different elements of a check provide information that can be used in financial record keeping. Financial institutions also provide forms and reports (see **Figure 29.2** for an example of a checking account statement) that consumers can use to keep their checking account in order. With these records, account holders can keep track of their income and expenses.

The Parts of a Check

There are usually three people, or parties, named on a check. The *payee* is the party to whom the check is written, or who is cashing the check. The *drawer* is the party who wrote the check and is paying the money, or drawing it from an account. The third party is the *drawee,* the financial institution where the drawer has an account.

Banks and other companies use the information printed on checks to **route** a check to your account for payment. A check must include an account number and a bank route number, which **traces** the check back to the account on which it was written. A check includes the name and location of the drawer's bank, a check number, and security features. A check presented for payment must include a **valid** date, the drawer's signature, the payee's name, and matching numerical and written amounts.

Science/Tech TRENDS

Biometrics
   With identity fraud becoming more prevalent, authorities and organizations have started looking for new ways to protect the consumer. One of the more promising technologies involves using biometrics to grant account access to consumers. Many parts of the body form patterns that are unique to each individual. The patterns formed by fingerprints, DNA, and characteristics of the eye form patterns that can last throughout a person's life. In the future, these technologies will be a highly accurate way of verifying customers' identities.

   Locate Web sites where you can research how biometric technologies may change the security industry. Write a paragraph describing other applications of biometrics.

Louis and Ling Chung
121 Bayside Road
Fall River, OH 42119-0120

Account Number: 211-37-065

Date of Statement: 3/31/20--

PREVIOUS BALANCE	CHECKS AND CHARGES	NO. OF DEPOSITS	NO. OF CHECKS	DEPOSITS AND CREDITS	BALANCE AT THIS DATE
$535.80	$1,011.25	1	5	$814.10	$338.65

DATE	CHECKS AND OTHER CHARGES		DEPOSITS AND OTHER CREDITS	BALANCE
			Beginning Balance	*$535.80*
	Check No.	Amount		
3/13	*106*	*50.00*		*485.80*
3/19	*M – Bob's Grocery*	*75.10*		*410.70*
3/23	*107*	*120.00*		*290.70*
3/24			*814.10*	*1,104.80*
3/25	*M – The Cleaner's*	*58.25*		*1,046.55*
3/26	*111*	*23.90*		*1,022.65*
3/28	*114*	*650.00*		*372.65*
3/28	*115*	*28.00*		*344.65*
	Service Charge	*6.00*		*338.65*

Please examine your statement at once. If no error is reported in 10 days, the account will be considered correct and vouchers genuine.

All items are credited subject to final payment.

C – Certified Check   S – Service Charge   CR – Overdraft   R – Returned Check   M – Merchant Sales Draft

● **Transaction Record** Louis and Ling Chung received this bank statement. **What were their totals for checks and deposits for the month?**

Writing a Check

When you write a check, record the check number, the amount of the check, the date, and the name of the payee in a check register. A **check register** is a checkbook log in which an account holder records checking account transactions. If you do not record the check immediately, you might forget some of the information.

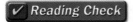 **Identify** Who are the three parties or people named on a check?

Making Deposits

To deposit cash or a check in your account, fill out a deposit slip. The deposit slip lists the amount of cash and checks and the total amount of the deposit. You may deposit your check at a bank, or through an ATM by using your ATM card without a deposit slip. You will usually receive a receipt for your transaction. After you make the deposit, record it in your check register.

To deposit or cash a check requires an **endorsement**, or the signature of the payee on the back of the check. Endorse the check on the back (on the lines printed for the endorsement). Sign your name exactly as it is written on the front of the check. Do not sign a check until you are ready to deposit or cash it. Then you have some protection in case it is lost or stolen. When making a deposit, write "For Deposit Only" as part of the endorsement so that it cannot be cashed if lost or stolen.

Bank Statements

Once a month, banks issue a **bank statement**, the bank's record of all the transactions in a checking account. The statement includes a record of all withdrawals, deposits, interest, and fees. It also includes a record of all **canceled checks**, or checks that have been cashed. A canceled check is proof that the money has been paid to a payee.

Handling Your Own Checks

Checks should be handled carefully. Do not print or write your driver license, Social Security, telephone, or credit card numbers on them. Keep checks, canceled checks, deposit slips, and bank statements in a safe place. Never leave your checkbook in the open or in a car. Check your bank statements for anything unusual. Make sure your checks have security features to protect against counterfeiting and **alteration**. Unless needed for tax purposes, destroy old documents that have your account number on them. Never make a check payable to "Cash." If "Cash" is written on the payee line, anyone who has the check can cash it.

● **As You Read**

Think about the importance of checking and keeping bank statements after receiving them.

● **Balancing the Checkbook** Michael and Conchetta Hamel received this bank statement. They need to reconcile the balance in the check register shown below with a bank balance of $830.89. The statement does not include check numbers 431 and 432. Also missing is a deposit in the amount of $27.85. The bank has charged a $6 service fee. **How would you reconcile their records?**

Figure 29.3 — *A Checkbook Register*

No.	Date	Description	Payment	Deposit	Balance
					$624.83
429	10/01	Old Navy	22.95		601.88
430	10/01	Kroger	15.86		586.02
--	10/01	Paycheck		350.77	936.79
--	10/02	Cash	50.00		886.79
431	10/04	Olive Garden	46.27		840.52
432	10/04	Amazon.com	37.48		803.04
--	10/06	Sam's check		27.85	830.89

Reconciling Your Account Records

Bank reconciliation is the process of seeing whether an account holder's records agree with the bank's records for the account. To reconcile is to bring into agreement, or balance. If the bank statement shows a different balance than your register, you should reconcile both records.

Balancing Your Checkbook

The first step to reconciling your account is to see whether the bank has processed all of your checks and deposits. With the bank statement and your check register, you can identify your **outstanding checks**, or checks that have been written but have not yet been cashed. The total dollar amount of outstanding checks should be subtracted from the balance shown on the bank statement. **Figure 29.3** shows an example of a checkbook register that must be balanced.

If you have made any deposits or ATM withdrawals that have not been recorded on the bank statement, those transactions should be factored into the bank statement balance. If the bank charged any service fees, you may not have recorded them in your check register. Subtract the service fee from the balance in your check register. If your account earns interest, add the interest shown on the bank statement to your check register.

Once the balance on the bank statement and the balance in your check register are the same, you have reconciled your check register balance with the bank statement balance.

Finding Errors If your balance differs from the bank's balance after you reconcile your account, double check the amounts in your records and all your additions and subtractions. Then check the bank's additions and subtractions. If you find a mistake, report it immediately. *Why is it important to reconcile your bank account?*

Section 29.2

After You Read

Review Key Concepts
1. What kinds of financial records help people manage their checking accounts?
2. What are some guidelines to consider when ordering and handling personal checks?
3. Describe the purpose of reconciling a bank statement and a check register.

Academic Skills
4. **English Language Arts** Work with a group of four to plan and design storyboards for a documentary called "Travels of a Check" that describes a check's life. Present your storyboards as visuals in an oral documentary.

5. **English Language Arts** Research how to balance a checking account using the monthly bank statement and check register. Write step-by-step instructions that are clear and concise describing the process.

 Go to **connectED.mcgraw-hill.com** to check your answers.

Section 29.1 *Summary*	Section 29.2 *Summary*
The Basics of Checking Accounts Banks, credit unions, and other financial institutions provide checking account services for individuals and businesses. Customers can write checks to transfer money easily to others. Banks offer a selection of checking accounts to meet their customers' needs. Some accounts are designed for those who need to write only a few checks. Others are designed for those who need more extensive banking services. Many banks offer their checking account customers additional services, such as overdraft protection, stop-payment services, debit cards, and online banking.	**Account Records** A checking account provides a way to keep track of financial transactions. There are usually three people, or parties, named on a check. There are specific steps that must be followed to write and deposit checks and to keep blank checks safe. A bank periodically sends each customer a record of all transactions recorded for the customer's account. With those statements, customers can reconcile the bank's records with their own records. This enables customers to find possible errors. It also helps them to manage their money and determine the correct information to start the next month.

Vocabulary Review

1. On a sheet of paper, use each of these key terms and academic vocabulary terms in a sentence.

Key Terms

check	debit card
direct deposit	check register
interest-bearing account	endorsement
signature card	bank statement
overdrawn	canceled checks
overdraft protection	bank reconciliation
stop payment	outstanding checks

Academic Vocabulary

demand	route
common	traces
compare	valid
designed	alteration

Review Key Concepts

2. Discuss the different types of checking accounts and how they work.

3. Discuss other services and offerings that banks provide checking account holders.

4. Describe how checking account holders manage their bank transactions.

5. Describe the procedure for bringing your account into agreement with bank records.

6. Banks may disregard the date written on a check that has been postdated, that is, dated for a future date. Why do you think banks have this policy?

7. What types of personal information do you think banks need and for what purposes?

8. How would you answer a person who is concerned that banking online is risky?

9. Most banks offer overdraft protection to their customers, sometimes for a fee. Would you consider taking overdraft protection? Why or why not?

10. How long do you think checking account records should be kept? Explain your answer.

11. Why is overdrawing a checking account poor financial management?

12. What effect do you think customer deposits in checking accounts have on the economic system?

13. Do you think people who have a joint checking account should each have a checkbook, or should they share one? Give reasons for your opinion.

14. In two or more paragraphs, discuss the factors to consider when deciding whether the fees associated with overdraft protection are worthwhile.

15. How would you endorse a check if your name is misspelled as the payee? How would you endorse a check if you wanted to send someone to the bank to deposit it for you? Write an example of an endorsement in each case.

16. Write a short article for your school newspaper on the precautions people should take when handling a checking account and keeping account records.

17. What effect do you think ATMs have had on customers' use of banks? Write a brief essay on your observations.

18. Why should you shop around before opening a checking account? What are some features that would appeal to you? Write a brief explanation of your response.

19. Think about the differences and similarities between debit cards and credit cards. Discuss them in at least one page.

Word-Processing Software

20. Use your local phone book, newspaper advertisements, bank Web sites, or brochures to prepare a report about banks. Include information such as the number of checking accounts offered, the minimum amount needed to open an account, interest rates offered on interest-bearing accounts, transaction fees charged, service fees, and other services offered with checking accounts.

Is the Bank's Loss Your Gain?

21. Suppose you have a regular checking account. One day you make a deposit at an ATM machine for $100. While your records show that you should have $500 in the account after the deposit, your ATM receipt shows a new balance of $5,000. You figure that the ATM has made a mistake and wonder what would happen if you did not tell the bank. What should you do?

Applying Academics to Business

English Language Arts

22. Credit cards and debit cards look alike, but they are very different when it comes to consumer protection. Find out more about the differences in how consumers are protected when they use the two types of cards. Write a few sentences informing others about these differences.

Mathematics

23. You and your friend Sal spend Saturday shopping. Sal uses checks to make purchases but needs help writing out the dollar amounts. Write the following dollar amounts as you would write them on a check: $36.45, $152.79, $16.14, and $1,311.35.

> **CONCEPT** **Writing Numbers** When writing the name of a number in words, avoid using the word *and* except to signal the decimal point. For example, write the name in words for 1,034.5 as "one thousand thirty-four *and* five-tenths."

English Language Arts

24. The following words have specific meanings in the context of banking and financial activity, but they have other meanings as well. Write a sentence for each word identifying its part of speech and describing at least two meanings.

interest   draw   account

Mathematics

25. Your bank statement shows an ending balance of $844.71. You have recorded in your checkbook register a deposit of $131.25 that does not appear on your statement, and two checks for $50 apiece that were not returned with the statement. What is your actual balance?

> **CONCEPT** **Credits and Debits** Deposits are additions to your account, and checks written against the account are reductions.

Active Learning

Online Bill Paying

26. Work in teams. Survey people in your neighborhood or school about online bill paying. Ask them: Do you pay bills online? If not, why? Do you write fewer checks than you did three years ago? Will you write fewer checks in the future? What do you like most about online bill paying? What concerns you about it? Summarize your information in a short report.

Business in the Real World

Check Scanning

27. Some banks provide scanning services for businesses to make check deposits. A business can transmit customers' check images from their business location to their bank. The process saves time and costs. Research check scanning by going online or calling some banks. You could also ask local businesspeople you know about it. Write a brief report of your findings, and share it with the class.

Real LIFE skills

USING THE RIGHT ACCOUNT

28. A routing transit number (RTN) is the nine-digit code on the bottom of checks that identifies which financial institution it is drawn upon. This code is also used to process direct deposits and other automated transfers. There are two other numbers on the bottom of every check. Research companies that print personal check blanks and fill out an order form so that the printer can print them with all of the parts of a standard check.

Business CAREERS

FIND YOUR DREAM JOB

29. Locate the Occupational Outlook Handbook Web site. Click on the "OOH Search/A-Z Index" link and enter the field of "banking." Then write a one-page report about this type of occupation. Conclude your report with a list of things you could do now to prepare yourself to pursue the occupation.

Role Play

USE OF ATMs

30. Situation You are a consumer who uses an automated teller machine (ATM) often. Your teacher has asked you to demonstrate ways to protect yourself and your bank information while you use an ATM.

Activity Prepare an outline of actions you can take to safeguard your personal information and account at an ATM, and then demonstrate the process.

Evaluation You will be evaluated on how well you meet the following performance indicators:

- Identify ways that theft can occur through ATM use.
- Explain steps to take when approaching and using an ATM.
- Demonstrate proper procedures to protect your personal information at an ATM.
- Prepare a written outline of points in your demonstration.
- Project your voice and use correct grammar.

Standardized Test Practice

Directions Choose the letter of the best answer. Write the letter for the answer on a separate piece of paper.

1. What is $2,952.11 rounded to the nearest hundred?

    A $2,900.00
    B $3,000.00
    C $2,952.00
    D $2,952.10

TEST-TAKING TIP Evaluate your test-taking savvy by answering these questions:
- Do I use my time well during a test?
- Does anxiety get in the way of doing my best on a test?
- How can I prepare better for my next test?

Chapter 30

Savings Accounts

Chapter Objectives After completing this chapter, you will be able to:

▶ **Section 30.1** *Savings Account Basics*
- **Discuss** the three reasons people save money.
- **Describe** compound interest.

▶ **Section 30.2** *Types of Savings Accounts*
- **Differentiate** a regular savings account from a CD, a money market fund, and a money market deposit account.
- **Explain** two advantages and two disadvantages of savings accounts.

Ask

AN EXPERT

Savings Accounts

Q: Which is best, passbook accounts, money markets, or CDs?

A: A basic savings account is sometimes referred to as a passbook account, since many banks provide account holders with little books used for keeping track of activity. The main advantage of a basic savings account is its accessibility—the money is pretty much there whenever you need it, and you're free to add or subtract at will. They can be opened with relatively little money, but of course, the disadvantage is that these accounts typically provide a comparably low rate of return. A money market account can be thought of as a restricted savings account since you're only allowed so many withdrawals per month. In addition, they tend to require a higher balance than a basic savings account. However, you will be rewarded with a higher interest rate. Finally, CDs, or certificates of deposit, usually provide investors with more favorable interest rates than most savings accounts and money markets. The downside is that your money would be locked away for a specific amount of time, anywhere from six months to a number of years.

Mathematics Patrick plans to open a savings account. He prefers a passbook account, but the interest rate of the money market account is 1.78% higher. How much more will he make if he puts $5,000 into a money market account?

CONCEPT **Percents Less Than One** Percents less than 1 represent values less than $\frac{1}{100}$. In other words, 0.1% is one-tenth of 1 percent, which can also be represented in decimal form as 0.001 or in fraction form as $\frac{1}{1,000}$.

● **Planning for the Future** Money people put aside for future use is called savings. **What are some things for which people save money?**

Savings Account Basics

● Before You Read

Think about how saving your money can be a way of being good to yourself.

Read to Learn

- Discuss the three reasons people save money.
- Describe compound interest.

The Main Idea

Money put aside for future use is called savings. Generally people use their savings for major purchases, emergencies, and retirement income. Savings accounts can earn either simple or compound interest. If one leaves money saved in an account that accumulates compound interest, interest is earned on both the amount saved and the interest earned.

Key Concepts

- A Guide to Saving
- Earning Interest on Savings

Vocabulary

Key Terms
savings
rate of return
compound interest

Academic Vocabulary

You will find these words in your reading and on your tests. Make sure you know their meanings.

experts   item
suggest   accumulate

Graphic Organizer

In a figure like the one below, list the reasons people need to save money in the left column. In the right column, give examples of reasons you will want to save in your own life.

Reasons People Save	Reasons I Should Save
1.	
2.	
3.	

 Go to **connectED.mcgraw-hill.com** to print out this graphic organizer.

A Guide to Saving

To achieve your financial goals, you will need a plan. Saving is putting money aside for future use. The money you save is called your **savings**. Savings plans include regular savings accounts, certificates of deposit, and money market funds.

The amount of money you save depends on how much of your income you are willing not to spend. Some personal finance **experts** say people should try to save about 10 percent of their take-home income. Many experts **suggest** that the amount to be saved should be taken from income as soon as it is received so that the saver is not tempted to spend it. However you save, it should be a part of your budget.

All savings involve some sacrifice. When you save money, you are putting off spending that money on an **item** that you might want right now. This sacrifice is called the *opportunity cost* of saving. The opportunity cost of a decision is the same as the benefit of the choice that is given up when one decision is made instead of another.

Saving is a way of being good to yourself. It helps to ensure that you will have money when you need it. People set up and maintain a savings plan for three reasons: to make major purchases, to provide for emergencies, and to have income for retirement.

✔ **Reading Check** **Identify** What are the three major reasons for setting up and maintaining savings plans?

> ● **As You Read**
>
> Think about whether waiting for something you want is worth giving up something else that you want.

International Business

Guarding Savings Security

Swiss banks have a reputation for providing customers with a secure and discreet banking environment. Accounts at banks such as Credit Suisse and UBS can be accessed worldwide. The Swiss Federal Banking Commission works to enhance this reputation by licensing banks and supervising their activities. This organization can act to protect the financial interests of account holders. The security of deposits is often a crucial feature to customers because of the important role savings accounts play in helping individuals to provide for emergencies.

Examples of Languages Across Cultures

Q: In French, how do you say: "May I have the check, please."
A: L'addition, s'il vous plait.
(pronounced: Lă-ă-dēē-sēē-ōn sēēl vōō plā)

Why is the security of money deposited one of the most important issues for account holders?

Figure 30.1 – *The Value of Starting Early*

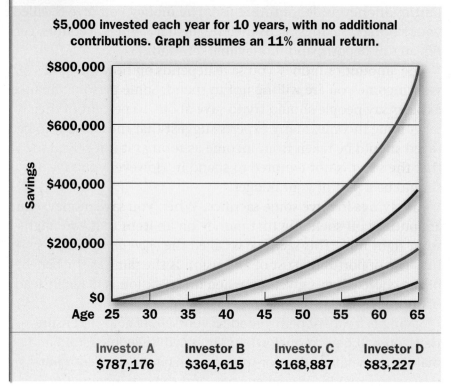

$5,000 invested each year for 10 years, with no additional contributions. Graph assumes an 11% annual return.

Investor A	Investor B	Investor C	Investor D
$787,176	$364,615	$168,887	$83,227

Making Major Purchases

Most people need to save money before they can make major purchases. Common reasons people save money are to buy a home or to pay for a college education. You might also decide to save money because you want to purchase a less expensive item, such as a good sound system, a top-of-the-line guitar, or a car.

Providing for Emergencies

You might face financial emergencies in your life. Your car could break down, you could lose your job, or you could develop a health problem. Saving your money can help you deal with the financial burden that an emergency can create. Experts recommend that people set aside at least six months of income in case of an emergency.

Planning for Retirement

It might seem too early to think about saving for retirement, but it is best to begin early. **Figure 30.1** illustrates the average retirement account balances for people who start saving at different ages. Most U.S. workers receive Social Security income when they retire. Many people have some type of retirement plan where they work, which will provide additional income. Business owners may also set up retirement plans.

For most people, though, Social Security and retirement plans do not provide enough money to retire comfortably. They must rely on their savings. If you start early in your life, you can **accumulate** a sizable nest egg. For example, suppose you want to retire in 35 years. If you start putting away $100 per month in an account with a return of 6 percent, by the time you retire, you will have saved about $143,000. You will have put in $42,000 and earned $101,000 in interest.

Earning Interest on Savings

Not all savings earn income. If you put your savings into a jar, a piggy bank, or under a mattress, no income is earned. To earn income on savings, you must store it in a place that will provide you with interest, such as a bank or savings and loan association. The money you put into a savings account earns interest.

If you put money into a bank's savings account, you are actually lending the bank your money. In this case, *you* are the creditor with the same conditions for lending as other creditors. The bank uses your savings to make loans to other people. Part of the interest the bank receives is used to pay interest to you.

Business Case Study

Saving Money Socially

Earn interest toward a future purchase—and tell everyone about it

Saving money takes patience and discipline. A recent banking innovation, the social savings account, helps by turning the act of saving into a social experience.

Social saving can be done through websites such as SmartyPig.com, a free online piggy bank that enables you to create personal financial campaigns for short- or long-term goals. You make regular transfers from your checking account into your interest-bearing social savings account and track progress toward your goals.

Social accounts also encourage you to share your progress on social media. Friends and family can support you in your quest, and even donate money toward your goal.

Active Learning

Visit a social savings website such as SmartyPig® (SmartyPig.com) and learn how the process works. Write a short description of how you create goals, fund campaigns, share progress online, and cash out when you reach your goal. After your description, explain whether you would or would not be interested in social saving, and why.

The Rule of 72
Compound interest is usually earned daily, monthly, quarterly, or annually. The more often interest is compounded, the more you earn. The Rule of 72 is a rule used to calculate how long it will take to double the money in an investment. It is calculated by dividing 72 by the annual interest rate to get the number of years. For example, if you leave money in a savings account and let interest compound at 6%, you can double your savings in 12 years. *Why might knowing the Rule of 72 be useful?*

Saving is important to the economy because it generates loan money for people and businesses. Consumers use loans to buy houses and cars. Companies use loans to update their facilities and equipment. New equipment and buildings for business can enable a company to produce more goods and services. This often means that the company will need to hire more workers, which leads to economic growth.

Rate of Return

Earnings on savings can be measured by the rate of return, or yield. The **rate of return** is the percentage of increase in the value of your savings from earned interest.

Compounding

Simple interest is interest earned only on money deposited into a savings account, called the principal. When principal and interest are left in an account, it earns compound interest. **Compound interest** is interest earned on both the principal and any interest earned on the principal. Compounding may take place every year, every quarter, every month, or even every day. For example, suppose you had $50,000 in a savings account at 6 percent annual interest. After one year, you would earn $3,000 in interest. With compound interest, the $3,000 would be added to the $50,000 and you would start earning interest on $53,000. After 15 years you would earn almost $70,000, or about $20,000 more than your initial deposit.

Section 30.1

After You Read

Review Key Concepts
1. Name three savings plans.
2. List the three main reasons people save money.
3. How is interest compounded?

Academic Skills
4. **Mathematics** Kim put the $75 she earned from babysitting on New Year's Eve into a regular savings account last year. She earned $3 in interest. What was Kim's rate of return?

 Rate of Return To calculate the rate of return, divide the total interest by the amount of her deposit.

Math For math help, go to the Math Appendix.

 Go to **connectED.mcgraw-hill.com** to check your answers.

Types of Savings Accounts

Reading Guide

Before You Read

Think about some of the best places to save your money.

Read to Learn

- Differentiate a regular savings account from a CD, a money market fund, and a money market deposit account.
- Explain two advantages and two disadvantages of saving accounts.

The Main Idea

There are several types of savings accounts—common ones being the traditional savings account, the certificate of deposit (CD), money market fund, and money market deposit account. Each type of savings account has advantages and disadvantages.

Key Concepts

- Choosing a Savings Account
- Advantages and Disadvantages of Savings Accounts

 Go to connectED.mcgraw-hill.com to print out this graphic organizer.

Vocabulary

Key Terms

regular savings accounts
certificate of deposit (CD)
maturity date
money market fund
money market deposit accounts
liquidity
inflation risk

Academic Vocabulary

You will find these words in your reading and on your tests. Make sure you know their meanings.

institution   duration
set   mutual

Graphic Organizer

In a figure like the one below, write notes about each type of account.

Type of Savings Account	Notes
Regular Savings Account	
Certificate of Deposit	
Money Market Fund	
Money Market Deposit Account	

Choosing a Savings Account

Banks, savings and loans, savings banks, credit unions, and brokerage firms all offer several types of savings accounts. The three basic types are regular savings accounts, certificates of deposit, and money market funds. **Figure 30.2** offers a look at interest compounded in savings accounts.

✔ Reading Check **Identify** What are the three basic types of savings accounts?

● **As You Read**

Think about putting your savings in a bank account or keeping it at home. Which would you prefer?

Regular Savings Accounts

Banks, savings and loans, savings banks, and credit unions all offer regular savings accounts. Traditionally called passbook accounts, **regular savings accounts** allow consumers to deposit or withdraw money at any time and to earn interest on the funds. Generally, a low minimum deposit, such as $100, is required to open a regular savings account. The interest rate varies from one financial **institution** to another. The rate can also change over time at the same institution. With a savings account, you can withdraw money without any penalty. However, the interest rate is usually low. Many banks also charge a service fee if the savings account falls below a certain minimum balance.

Figure 30.2 — *The Power of Compound Interest*

	Simple Interest			Compound Interest		
Year	Principal	6% Interest Earned	Interest Total	Principal	6% Interest Earned	Interest Total
1	$50,000	$3,000	$3,000	$50,000.00	$3,000.00	$3,000.00
2	$50,000	$3,000	$6,000	$53,000.00	$3,180.00	$6,180.00
3	$50,000	$3,000	$9,000	$56,180.00	$3,370.80	$9,550.80
4	$50,000	$3,000	$12,000	$59,550.80	$3,573.05	$13,123.85
5	$50,000	$3,000	$15,000	$63,123.85	$3,787.43	$16,911.28
6	$50,000	$3,000	$18,000	$66,911.28	$4,014.68	$20,925.96
7	$50,000	$3,000	$21,000	$70,925.96	$4,255.55	$25,181.51
8	$50,000	$3,000	$24,000	$75,181.51	$4,510.89	$29,692.40
9	$50,000	$3,000	$27,000	$79,692.40	$4,781.55	$34,473.95
10	$50,000	$3,000	$30,000	$84,473.95	$5,068.43	$39,542.38
11	$50,000	$3,000	$33,000	$89,542.38	$5,372.55	$44,914.93
12	$50,000	$3,000	$36,000	$94,914.93	$5,694.89	$50,609.82
13	$50,000	$3,000	$39,000	$100,609.82	$6,036.59	$56,646.41
14	$50,000	$3,000	$42,000	$106,646.41	$6,398.79	$63,045.20
15	$50,000	$3,000	$45,000	$113,045.20	$6,782.71	$69,827.91
	Total Interest Earned: $45,000			Total Interest Earned: $69,827.91		

● **Interest on Interest** Compound interest makes your money grow faster when interest is left to accrue. **Which account earned more interest? What is the difference in the account totals after 15 years?**

● **New Construction**
Businesses that build new buildings usually do so with borrowed money. **What is the relationship between savings and loans?**

Certificates of Deposit

Another type of savings account, called a **certificate of deposit (CD)**, requires you to deposit a specified amount of money in an account for a set period of time. The length of time might be three months, one year, or five years. A CD has a **maturity date**, which is when the money becomes available to you. The interest rate on a CD is higher than that on a regular savings account, but a CD's interest rate does not change over the **duration** of the CD term. If you cash in the CD before the maturity date, however, you will lose interest and might have to pay a penalty.

Money Market Funds

Brokerage firms, which buy and sell stocks and bonds, offer a special type of savings account called a money market fund. A **money market fund** is a kind of **mutual** fund, or pool of money, put into a variety of short-term debt (loans of less than one year) by business and government. In a way, you are lending your money to a business or the government to invest. The interest rate on a money market fund varies from month to month. An advantage is that you can withdraw your money at any time. You can also write checks on the account. There are, however, two disadvantages. Money market funds usually require high balances. Also, account holders can write only a limited number of checks.

Money Market Deposit Accounts Banks, savings and loans, and credit unions have their own form of money market fund called **money market deposit accounts**. They have the same basic requirements and characteristics of a money market fund. One difference is that the federal government generally insures the money in a money market deposit account.

 **Reading Check** **Compare** How does a money market deposit account differ from a money market fund?

Tracking the Money You Save No matter how or where you save your money, you must find ways to *find* the money you want to save. Write down your savings every time you decide not to buy something. Putting every penny you find or dollar you have saved into the bank will add up. *How do you think tracking every bit of your savings can help you save?*

Advantages and Disadvantages of Savings Accounts

Besides earning interest, savings accounts offer other advantages. However, they also have disadvantages.

Insurance Against Loss

Banks, savings and loans, and credit unions are all insured. The Federal Deposit Insurance Corporation (FDIC), a government agency, insures bank accounts. Even if a bank fails, the FDIC will replace depositors' accounts for up to $100,000. Money market funds offered by brokerage firms are not federally insured, but most brokerage firms have insurance on their accounts.

Liquidity

Liquidity means the ability to quickly turn an investment into cash. An investment such as a car or a business is not very liquid because it has to be sold to be turned into cash. Savings accounts, however, are highly liquid because cash can easily be withdrawn.

Low Rates of Return

Since there is very little risk with a savings account, there is usually a low return. With saving and investing, there is a relationship between rate of return and risk. The lower the risk, the lower the rate of return. The higher the risk, the higher the possibility of getting a higher return.

Inflation Risk

Inflation is a general increase in the cost of goods and services. **Inflation risk** is the risk that the rate of inflation will increase more than the rate of interest on savings. Suppose you have $1,000 in a savings account that earns 2 percent interest. During the next year, inflation is 4 percent. That means it costs $1,040 at the end of the year to buy what you could have bought at the beginning of the year for $1,000. Interest rates on most savings accounts fluctuate with inflation. However, the main risk with CDs is that their interest rates are locked in for a specific period of time.

The Costs of Savings Accounts

Savings accounts earn interest, but they can also cost money. Some accounts charge a penalty for early withdrawal or if the account balance falls below a certain minimum during a given period. Other accounts charge a fee for each deposit and withdrawal. The money you earn in interest on a savings account is also considered income. As a result, you have to pay income tax on it.

Section 30.2

○ After You Read

Review Key Concepts

1. What is the difference between a regular savings account, a certificate of deposit, and a money market fund?
2. Discuss some advantages and disadvantages of savings accounts.
3. What is the Federal Deposit Insurance Corporation, and what does it do?

Academic Skills

4. **English Language Arts** Work in a group of four to write, design, and produce a brochure titled "Saving—the Key to Your Future." Develop the content of the brochure around ways to make saving a regular habit. Include testimonials from people for whom saving has made a difference in their lives.

5. **English Language Arts** Collect brochures or other printed material from local banks containing information concerning the method each uses to compute interest. Analyze each to determine which communicate most effectively and how others might be improved. Present your findings orally and visually.

 Go to **connectED.mcgraw-hill.com** to check your answers.

Section 30.1 *Summary*

Savings Account Basics Saving is putting aside money for future use. The three main reasons for saving money are to make major purchases, for emergencies, and for retirement. Financial institutions pay interest on savings accounts in return for using savers' money. As with a credit account, the amount of interest earned depends on the interest rate, the size of the account, and the length of time you keep the account. Savings accounts earn simple interest or compound interest. Savings can grow more quickly with compound interest.

Section 30.2 *Summary*

Types of Savings Accounts Banks, savings and loans, and other financial institutions offer several types of savings accounts. Regular savings accounts, certificates of deposit, and money market funds are the major types of savings accounts. Some financial institutions have their own form of money market fund called a money market deposit account. Savings accounts earn interest, are usually secure, and have high liquidity. However, they can also cost money in fees and taxes, and generally carry a low return that may not keep up with inflation.

Vocabulary Review

1. On a sheet of paper, use each of these key terms and academic vocabulary terms in a sentence.

Key Terms

savings
rate of return
compound interest
regular savings accounts
certificate of deposit (CD)
maturity date
money market fund
money market deposit accounts
liquidity
inflation risk

Academic Vocabulary

experts   institution
suggest   set
item   duration
accumulate   mutual

Review Key Concepts

2. Discuss the three reasons people save money.

3. Describe compound interest.

4. Differentiate a regular savings account from a CD, a money market fund, and a money market deposit account.

5. Explain two advantages and two disadvantages of savings accounts.

6. Why is saving a way of being good to yourself?

7. If you have $1,000 to put into savings, do not need it for a year, and think that interest rates on savings will decrease, what is the best savings plan for you?

8. What do you think would happen if the FDIC did not exist?

9. How does inflation affect your savings decision?

10. Why is it a good idea to know about the Rule of 72?

11. Why are financial institutions willing to pay a higher rate of interest for a CD than for a regular savings account?

12. Many people have their employer put aside money from their paycheck for savings. Why do you think they do this?

13. Why do you think economists call banks and savings and loan associations intermediaries between savers and borrowers?

14. Why are savings important for the individual consumer and the U.S. economy?

15. Research the savings rate of Americans compared to people in other countries. Write an e-mail to your teacher explaining the differences you note.

16. Interview a banker about the relationship between types of savings plans and the interest rates that are offered. Write at least one page about your findings.

17. Write two paragraphs about reasons people at different income levels save the same or different percentages of their income.

18. Determine the nature of the IRA, Roth IRA, and 40l(k) retirement plans. Find out how each of them works. In a one-page report, discuss whether these plans encourage or discourage people from saving.

19. People rely upon different sources of income throughout their lives including their savings. Write an e-mail to your teacher listing the sources of retirement income you will rely on to live comfortably.

Calculating Compound Interest
20. Compound interest is interest earned on both the principal (the money you deposit in your savings account) and any interest you earned on it. Create a spreadsheet and the formulas necessary to calculate interest compounded daily, monthly, and yearly. The spreadsheet should contain at least five different interest rates.

Risking Someone Else's Future
21. You are a financial planner for Dave, who is 67 years old and retired. He wants to move his retirement account to more high-risk stocks. You would gain a great deal in fees and service charges if he turns all of his savings into stocks. However, he would face more risk if he buys the stocks. What should you do?

Applying Academics to Business

English Language Arts

22. Write a paragraph or two about your savings habits. Are you currently saving money on a regular basis? For what are you saving? Do you have a plan for a regular program of saving for the future?

Mathematics

23. Research the maturity dates and related interest rates for CDs from a variety of banks or savings institutions. Make a scatter plot using your data and write a sentence or two about what it shows.

THEORY **Data Analysis** Scatter plots are similar to line graphs in that they use horizontal and vertical axes. Scatter plots show how much one variable is affected by another.

English Language Arts

24. Based on the meanings of the following words as they are used in this chapter, suggest a synonym and an antonym for each:

benefit   compound
inflation   deposit

Mathematics

25. Compute the total savings on a $1,000 deposit held for one year in each of the following types of accounts:

a. a regular savings account earning 3.5% annual simple interest

b. a CD earning 7% annual interest compounded quarterly

c. a CD earning 3.5% annual interest compounded monthly

THEORY **Interest Rates** When computing interest earned on an amount during a period, divide the yearly interest rate, expressed as a decimal, by the number of periods in the year.

Active Learning

Money Left Over

26. Obtain a large jar or other container and ask everyone in your family to "deposit" their change there each night when they come home. After one month, count the money. How much have you saved? As a family, decide what you would like to do with the money.

Business in the Real World

Rephrasing a Brochure

27. Businesses that offer savings accounts use brochures to convey information about their products and services. Obtain a brochure from a bank or brokerage firm that explains the different kinds of savings plans that it offers. Rewrite it so that it can be understood by a preteen.

Real LIFE skills

FIGURING PENALTIES ON A CD

28. You called a bank to ask about its rates on a $1,000 CD. A representative told you that it earns 3% compounded quarterly. You ask what would happen if you withdrew the principal after nine months. You would lose the last six months' of interest. How much interest would you give up and how much would you get if you withdrew the money after nine months? What would be the rate of return on your savings given the return that you received?

Business CAREERS

FIND YOUR DREAM JOB

29. Locate the Occupational Outlook Handbook Web site. Click on the "OOH Search/A-Z Index" link and enter the job category "securities, commodities, and other investments." Then write a one-page report about this area of occupation. Conclude your report with a list of things you could do now to prepare yourself to pursue the occupation.

Role Play

FINANCIAL ADVISER

30. Situation You are a financial adviser who encourages people to save.

Activity Make a presentation about why people should save, including why it is important to them individually, and why it is important to the economy.

Evaluation You will be evaluated on how well you meet the following performance indicators:

- Explain the reasons saving is important for individuals.
- Describe reasons saving is important to the economy.
- Organize your presentation logically.
- Answer questions about saving.
- Project your voice and use correct grammar.

Standardized Test Practice

Directions Choose the letter of the best answer. Write the letter for the answer on a separate piece of paper.

1. How much interest was earned during the first month on a deposit of $4,000 in an account earning 6% annual interest compounded quarterly?

A $240

B $60

C $40

D $20

 TEST-TAKING TIP When studying in small groups, make sure your study group includes only students who are serious about studying.

Chapter 31

Investing

> **Chapter Objectives**   After completing this chapter, you will be able to:

▶ **Section 31.1** *Bonds*

- **Discuss** two goals to set before you start making investments.
- **Name** five characteristics of bonds.
- **Differentiate** between types of federal, municipal government, and corporate bonds.
- **Describe** the advantages and disadvantages of investing in bonds.

▶ **Section 31.2** *Stocks*

- **Discuss** stocks and stock markets.
- **Identify** the advantages and disadvantages of owning stocks.

Ask

AN EXPERT   Corporate Financial Performance and the Effect on Credit Quality

Q: Are sectors of the U.S. economy that generate strong earnings for shareholders also a good choice for bondholders?

A: There is not always a direct correlation between what is good for shareholders and what is good for bondholders. Bonds represent the ownership of debt, and stocks represent the ownership of equity. A company may do well for its shareholders while leaving its bondholders less satisfied because acquisitions or divestures end up damaging its creditworthiness. Creditworthiness is important because bondholders assume credit risk, the chance that the bond issuer will default on its debt.

Mathematics Express the current yield of a bond as a percentage by dividing the price of the bond into the amount of the annual coupon, the interest rate stated on a bond when it is issued. What is the current yield for a $95 bond with a $6 annual coupon? Replace the variables in the algebraic expression and evaluate the expression.

$$\text{Evaluate } x \text{ if } x = 6 \div \$95$$

CONCEPT **Algebra: Variables and Expressions** A variable is a symbol, usually a letter, used to represent a number. Algebraic expressions are combinations of variables, numbers, and at least one operation. Once the variables have been replaced with numbers, you can evaluate, or find the value of, the expression.

● **The New York Stock Exchange®** The New York Stock Exchange provides a market for buying and selling stocks and has the highest dollar volume of any stock exchange in the world. **What are stocks?**

David R. Frazier Photolibrary, Inc./Alamy

Bonds

Reading Guide

Before You Read

Think about the different ways that governments and corporations use large sums of money.

Read to Learn

- Discuss two goals to set before you start making investments.
- Name five characteristics of bonds.
- Differentiate between types of federal, municipal government, and corporate bonds.
- Describe the advantages and disadvantages of investing in bonds.

The Main Idea

Investing is using money to participate in a business enterprise that offers the possibility of profit. Bonds provide income opportunities for investors. They also generate money to help governments and corporations operate.

Key Concepts

- Setting Investment Goals
- Investing in Bonds
- Government and Corporate Bonds and Securities
- Advantages and Disadvantages of Investing in Bonds

 Go to **connectED.mcgraw-hill.com** to print out this graphic organizer.

Vocabulary

Key Terms

investing	bond discount
security	savings bonds
yield	municipal bonds
bond	corporate bonds
coupon rate	

Academic Vocabulary

You will find these words in your reading and on your tests. Make sure you know their meanings.

participate	commission
eliminate	matures

Graphic Organizer

On a figure like the one below, write notes about the advantages and disadvantages of bond ownership.

Bond Ownership

Advantages	Disadvantages

Setting Investment Goals

As You Read

Think about how entrepreneurs and investors both face risk.

To some people, investing is an unpredictable world of formulas, symbols, and terms. Others think it is just a matter of luck and timing. Although these perceptions are generally incorrect, they are reasons some people do not invest their money. However, investing presents opportunities for people and businesses to increase their income. **Investing** is using money to **participate** in an enterprise that offers the possibility of profit. It usually involves careful planning and goal setting.

It is wise to use a practical approach when investing. You can spend money on some things that you enjoy and still save enough for an investment program. Even a small amount invested regularly can add up to a large amount over time.

As you set your investment goals, ask yourself these questions:

- How do I want to spend my money?
- How much money do I need to satisfy my goals?
- How will I get it?
- How long will it take to save it?
- How much risk am I willing to take when I invest?
- What conditions could change my investment goals?
- Are my goals reasonable, considering my circumstances?
- What will happen if I do not meet my goals?

Most people have more than one financial goal. A short-term goal might be to save enough money to pay for a vacation. A mid-term goal could be to buy a business or home. A long-term goal might be to plan for retirement. There are two goals that everyone should set before starting to invest. First, you should limit your credit card charges and reduce or **eliminate** credit card debt. In most cases, this debt generates interest charges that are higher than the investment returns you can expect to receive. Second, start an emergency fund and add to it as your income increases. It is recommended that people save enough money to cover at least six months of expenses. Once you achieve these two goals, start looking at the different investment options that are available to you.

The goals you establish when you begin to make investment plans are likely to change. It is a good idea to meet with a financial adviser annually to review your portfolio and goals.

Types of Securities

Investment options include securities. A **security** is a tradable document that shows evidence of debt or ownership. Securities include bonds, shares of stock and mutual funds, and stock options. The return on an investment is the amount of money the investment earns, or the **yield**.

Investing in Bonds

When corporations or governments need to borrow large amounts of money, they often issue bonds. A **bond** is a certificate issued by a government or company in which it promises to pay back borrowed money at a fixed rate of interest on a specified date (the *maturity date*). It is a debt, and the buyer of a bond is the creditor (or lender) to the company or government that issued it, the debtor (or borrower).

✔ **Reading Check** **Define** What is a bond?

Bond Prices Bonds are rated according to their risk by several agencies, including Standard & Poor's and Moody's®. They are usually rated from *secure* (the highest rating) to *speculative* (the lowest rating). Those with more risk carry a higher interest rate than those that are more secure. Most bonds are considered safe investments. *Would you invest in a bond rated as speculative? Why?*

Characteristics of Bonds

Investing in bonds is similar to putting money into a savings account. Both act as a source of funds to be used for business and personal loans. Both generate interest for consumers. There are several differences, though. Bonds have specific characteristics.

The rate of interest on a bond is referred to as the **coupon rate**. (This rate is also referred to as the yield.) Interest is usually paid once or twice a year. For example, a $1,000 bond with a 6 percent coupon rate will pay $60 once a year or $30 twice a year. Bonds may be sold at a discount, or below their face value. *Face value* is the value of a security that is set by the company or government that is issuing it. It is usually shown on the front of a bond. Bonds accrue interest until they reach their full value. The difference between the amount you pay for the bond and its face value is the **bond discount**. There are two types of bonds you can buy: government bonds and corporate bonds.

Government and Corporate Bonds and Securities

Federal, state, and local governments issue bonds to help raise the money to fund their regular activities. Government securities are considered almost risk-free because they are backed by our tax dollars. Because they are low risk, government bonds offer lower interest rates than other bonds. The interest paid on a bond can be higher than the interest paid on a savings account.

Federal Bonds and Securities

The U.S. Treasury Department issues four basic types of securities: Treasury bills (or T-bills), notes, bonds, and savings bonds. Investors can buy these securities through banks or brokerages, which charge a **commission**. **Figure 31.1** shows TreasuryDirect, a financial services Web site that lets investors buy and redeem securities directly from the U.S. Treasury Department without paying a commission.

Figure 31.1 — *Buying Treasury Bonds*

● **Direct from the Treasury Department** Individuals, institutions, and government agencies can buy U.S. bonds over the Internet. **Why might a government agency want to buy bonds?**

Treasury Bills Treasury bills are sold in units of $1,000. They may reach maturity in four, 13, or 26 weeks. T-bills are discounted securities, which means the purchase price that investors pay is less than the face value of the T-bill. On the maturity date, the investor receives the full face value of the T-bill.

To figure out the dollar amount of return on a T-bill, subtract the purchase price of the T-bill from the face value. For example, suppose you buy a 26-week T-bill for $950. On the day the bond matures, you receive the face value of $1,000. The dollar amount of your return is $50 ($1,000 − $950 = $50). To find the rate of return on your investment, divide the dollar amount of the return by the purchase price ($50 ÷ $950 = .0526 = 5.26%). The rate of return on your T-bill is 5.26 percent. A T-bill held until maturity can be reinvested in another bill or paid to the owner.

Treasury Notes and Bonds Treasury notes are issued in $1,000 units, with a maturity of between two and 10 years. Treasury bonds are issued in $1,000 units, with a maturity of 30 years. Generally, the interest rates on notes and bonds are higher than on T-bills because of the increased risk of the rates rising or falling during the length of time until the note or bond matures.

U.S. Savings Bonds **Savings bonds** are registered bonds that are sold in denominations of $50 to $10,000. They allow people to earn interest on the savings they entrust to the government in exchange for the bond. Savings bonds cannot be bought and sold once they are purchased. They can be redeemed after one year.

A *Series EE* savings certificate costs half the amount of its face value to buy. For example, a $100 bond costs $50. After a certain number of years, it becomes worth its full face value. The time it takes to reach its maturity rate depends on the rate of interest. On Series EE bonds, the interest rate stays the same throughout the life of the bond. If you cash in a Series EE bond within five years, you have to pay a penalty. However, if you keep an EE bond past its maturity date, it will continue to earn interest for up to 30 years and can become worth more than face value.

Another type of savings bond is the *Series I* bond. Investors pay the face value for Series I bonds. If you want to buy a $500 Series I bond, you must pay $500. The interest rate on this bond fluctuates with the rate of inflation over time. As inflation goes up, the interest rate on the bond increases. However, the interest does not fall if there is deflation during a period of time. You can lose interest if you cash it in, or *redeem* it before its maturity date. For example, if you redeem a Series I bond during the first five years of your investment, you will forfeit, or lose, three months of interest.

EE bonds and I bonds are attractive to people who want safe, guaranteed long-term investments. Both classes of bonds are often purchased to finance education, supplement retirement income, or give as gifts. Interest from savings bonds is not subject to state and local income taxes. Investors who buy them to pay for a college education, or whose income is below a certain level, pay reduced taxes or no taxes at all.

Bonds Issued by Federal Agencies Besides the securities issued by the Treasury Department, bonds are issued by other federal agencies as well. Agency bonds, such as the participation certificates issued by the Federal National Mortgage Association (sometimes referred to as Fannie Mae®) and the Government National Mortgage Association (sometimes referred to as Ginnie Mae®), are almost risk-free. However, they offer a slightly higher interest rate than treasury securities. Their maturities range from one to 30 years, with an average life of about 12 years. Generally, their minimum denomination is $25,000.

Municipal Bonds

Local and state governments issue municipal bonds. **Municipal bonds** are sold to finance city, town, or regional projects such as schools, highways, and airports. You can buy them from a broker or directly from the government that issued them. The main advantage of municipal bonds is that the federal government generally does not tax the interest earned on them. As with Treasury bonds, you do not have to hold on to a municipal bond until it reaches its maturity date. If you sell it before it **matures**, however, you might receive less than the face value of the bond.

Corporate Bonds

Bonds issued by corporations are called **corporate bonds**. Corporate bonds can be bought and sold through brokerage firms. They are usually used to finance construction and equipment. Construction of buildings and purchases of equipment can increase productivity, which then helps society maintain and improve the standard of living. These are ways that savings and investments contribute to the economy.

The value of a corporate bond fluctuates according to the overall interest rates in the economy. If you buy a corporate bond with a high interest rate and interest rates fall, the corporation may be able to *call* your bond, or buy it back before the maturity date. This way the company does not have to continue paying the higher interest rate. Many issue new bonds at lower rates.

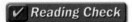 **Explain** How do corporate bonds help the economy?

?ETHICS in Business

Putting the Client First

■ **Critical Reading** Life is full of important decisions. Think about the kinds of decisions that you make as you read the question below.

You work as a stockbroker for a large brokerage firm, and a major portion of your salary comes from commissions. Every time someone buys or sells stocks or bonds, you receive a portion of the fee your firm charges for the trade. A client comes to you and wants to make a number of changes to his portfolio. In your opinion, these changes would decrease your client's wealth because they would cause him to incur brokerage fees that would exceed the value he would realize on the transactions. However, you would profit substantially from the commissions associated with the brokerage fees.

■ **Decision Making** Would you tell your client about the financial impact of the brokerage fees? Explain your answer.

Advantages and Disadvantages of Buying Bonds

Bonds have many of the same advantages and disadvantages as savings accounts. One advantage is that most bonds are secure, especially those from government and large, established businesses. In particular, bonds and other securities issued by the U.S. government enjoy the full faith and credit of the federal government. Bonds also pay interest.

Although they are liquid, one disadvantage of bonds is that an investor can lose money if a bond is sold or redeemed before it matures. Most bonds are written for a minimum of $1,000, which may make them out of reach for some investors.

Like savings accounts, bonds may not keep up with inflation. For example, if there is 4 percent inflation over the year, you must have 4 percent more money at the end of the year than at the beginning of the year to buy the same amount of goods and services. That means your bond must pay at least 4 percent a year after taxes if you are to keep up the purchasing power of your investment.

Section 31.1

After You Read

Review Key Concepts
1. What are the two goals you should consider before starting to invest?
2. Identify some characteristics of bonds.
3. Name the four types of securities issued by the U.S. Treasury Department.

Academic Skills
4. **Mathematics** The six members of the Canterbury Investment Club have pooled their money to invest in the stock market. They meet monthly to discuss stocks, do financial research, and choose purchases. Each club member pays an initial $200 to join, then $25 a month. All of the money is invested in the stock market. Write an expression showing how much money the club was able to collect by the end of the first year.

CONCEPT **Variables and Expressions** Use a symbol such as x to represent a variable or an unknown quantity in an expression.

 For math help, go to the Math Appendix.

 Go to **connectED.mcgraw-hill.com** to check your answers.

Stocks

Before You Read

Think about why stocks are generally considered more risky than bonds and other types of investments.

Read to Learn
- Discuss stocks and stock markets.
- Identify the advantages and disadvantages of owning stocks.

The Main Idea

A stock is a share of ownership in a corporation. Stock prices may change continuously. Though stocks offer the possibility of high rates of return on investment, they also carry a greater degree of risk.

Key Concepts
- Investing in Stocks
- Advantages and Disadvantages of Stocks

Vocabulary

Key Terms
stock
dividends
capital gain
capital loss
common stock
preferred stock
stockbroker
stock exchange
mutual fund

Academic Vocabulary

You will find these words in your reading and on your tests. Make sure you know their meanings.

indicates
illustrates
initiated
order

Graphic Organizer

In a figure like the one below, write notes about the advantages of owning stocks.

Stock Ownership

Advantages	Disadvantages

 Go to **connectED.mcgraw-hill.com** to print out this graphic organizer.

Investing in Stocks

A **stock** is a share of ownership in a corporation. When you buy stock, you receive a *stock certificate* that **indicates** ownership in a corporation. Stock prices may change throughout the day, every business day. There is no promise that a stockholder will get his or her money back or that he or she will receive income from owning stock. Therefore, stocks are generally more risky than bonds. Sole proprietorships and partnerships do not sell stock. **Figure 31.2 illustrates** types of investments and their levels of risk.

Companies that sell stock must follow rules set up by the Securities and Exchange Commission, or SEC. The SEC is a U.S. government agency that supervises the exchange of securities to protect investors from wrongdoing. The SEC also has strict guidelines that financial professionals must follow.

Return on Stocks

Just as bonds have specific characteristics, so do stocks. One is the return or yield on a stock. The amount of money the stock earns depends on its type of return and rate of return.

● **As You Read**

Think about the different types of investments. Have you ever had an investment? Did it make or lose money?

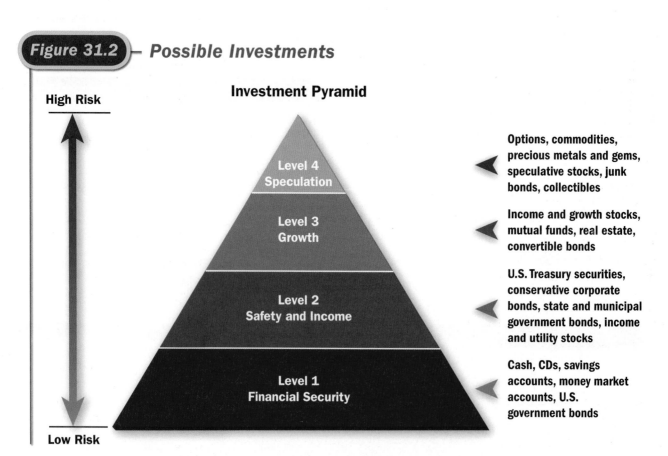

Figure 31.2 — *Possible Investments*

Investment Pyramid

High Risk

Low Risk

Level 4
Speculation

Level 3
Growth

Level 2
Safety and Income

Level 1
Financial Security

Options, commodities, precious metals and gems, speculative stocks, junk bonds, collectibles

Income and growth stocks, mutual funds, real estate, convertible bonds

U.S. Treasury securities, conservative corporate bonds, state and municipal government bonds, income and utility stocks

Cash, CDs, savings accounts, money market accounts, U.S. government bonds

● **Investment Pyramid** Building for your financial future takes a solid investment strategy. Without a solid foundation, you risk losing your investment. **What does this chart show about the possible risk and potential return for investing in stocks?**

● **Market Quotes** Every day that the market is open the stocks listed on an exchange are traded. The prices at which they are traded are broadcast to the public. **How would you find the names of stocks?**

Types of Returns on Stocks There are two ways that you can receive a return on stocks. One is through the payment of **dividends**, which is a share of profits given to stockholders. If a corporation makes a lot of money over a certain period of time, it can decide to distribute at least some of the profits in the form of dividends. Dividends are usually paid quarterly in cash or in more shares of stock.

Many stockholders receive a return on stock when they sell it. Selling stock for more than you paid for it results in a capital gain. A **capital gain** is a profit made from the sale of a financial asset such as stock or a bond. A **capital loss** is an amount lost when an asset is sold for less than its cost. As with other forms of income, the government taxes the amount received in dividends or capital gains.

The return on foreign stocks is a bit more difficult to determine since dividends are generally issued in the currency of the nation where the firm has its headquarters. For example, suppose you have stock in a firm based in England. The currency there is the pound. If a dividend of 2 pounds is announced and the exchange rate is 1 pound = $1.90, then the dividend would be 2 (pounds) × $1.90 = $3.80.

Rate of Return The rate of return on stocks is always expressed as a percentage of the original investment and figured on an annual basis. For example, suppose $1,000 earns $50 of interest in a savings account one year. The rate of return on the investment is 5 percent ($50/$1,000 = 0.05). A single share of stock whose value increases from $50 to $55 in a year and pays a $5 dividend during the year has a 20 percent rate of return ($10 return/$50 original investment = 0.20).

✔ **Reading Check** **Identify** What are the two ways you could receive a return on stocks?

©Corbis

Types of Stocks

When a company sells stock, it usually offers two different types. **Common stock** is stock that provides the most basic form of corporate ownership. It entitles the stockholder to voting privileges. All corporations must issue common stock. Many issue common stock only. For each share that is owned, the stockholder gets a vote in how to run the corporation.

Preferred stock is stock that gives the owner the advantage of receiving cash dividends before common stockholders receive any. This is important if a company is having financial problems. If the company pays dividends, preferred stockholders will receive their dividends before common stockholders. Preferred stockholders do not vote on company issues. Many preferred stocks stipulate the limit on what can be paid as far as a dividend. A dividend does not have to be paid each year.

Stocks carry different levels of risk. *Blue-chip stocks* are stocks in large, well-established companies that have a good track record of success and profitability. *Speculative stocks* are stocks in new firms without an established track record. They are often small firms that are developing new goods and services.

✔ Reading Check **Contrast** How do common stocks and preferred stocks differ?

● As You Read

Think about purchasing stock from a stockbroker compared to buying over the Internet. Which method would you choose? Why?

Stockbrokers

A **stockbroker** is a person who buys and sells stocks, bonds, and other securities for clients. Stockbrokers act as a link between buyers and sellers. They facilitate transactions. Many give financial advice. As a fee for their services, stockbrokers charge a *commission,* which is either a percentage of the value of the stock or a set amount for each transaction.

Many people lower their investment fees by buying and selling securities using the Internet. With online trading, the trade is **initiated** by the individual via a computer. The **order** is sent to a brokerage firm. Online brokerage houses, such as E*Trade® and TD AMERITRADE®, tend to charge less for each trade because there usually is no stockbroker involved. Some of the largest and more traditional brokerage firms provide online trading. They include Merrill Lynch®, Charles Schwab®, and others.

Stock Exchanges

Most stocks are bought and sold through a trading market known as a stock exchange. A **stock exchange** is an organized market for buying and selling financial securities. When people sell stocks or bonds through their stockbroker, their order is sent to the broker's representative on the stock exchange floor. An auction takes place at a booth where the stock is bought and sold.

Some of the best-known exchanges are the New York Stock Exchange (NYSE®) and the American Stock Exchange (Amex®). There are also regional exchanges such as the Chicago Stock Exchange. Only companies listed on an exchange can have their stocks traded there. Companies are listed on exchanges with codes called *stock symbols,* or ticker symbols. These codes are used to identify the stock. For example, the stock symbol for Walt Disney Company® is DIS, and for FedEx® it is FDX. Stock symbols and closing prices are listed in print and online in financial news sections.

Over-the-Counter Markets

Over-the-counter securities are not listed or sold through stock exchanges. They are traded directly between buyers and sellers in person or via computer. The transactions may be facilitated by individual dealers. Many over-the-counter securities can be bought and sold through the National Association of Securities Dealers Automated Quotations (NASDAQ®) market. The NASDAQ is an electronic stock market system that quotes over-the-counter securities.

Mutual Funds

Mutual funds lessen the risk of investing in the stock market. A **mutual fund** is a fund created by an investment firm that raises money from many shareholders and invests it in a variety of stocks or other investments. A mutual fund has great buying power. If the investments owned by the mutual fund make a profit, then the mutual fund's shareholders are likely to earn a dividend.

Mock Portfolios
Before investing money in the stock market, practice first. Build a mock portfolio by choosing at least three companies that interest you. Write each company's ticker symbol next to its name and the date. Document their prices each day to track their performance. Read stories about them. *If you are a teen, how can you buy stock when you are ready?*

Science/Tech TRENDS

Stock Tickers

Stock tickers were first used in the 1870s as a means of conveying stock prices over long distances. Before the ticker, information concerning stocks was delivered by hand in either written or spoken messages. Because the length of time individual stock information remains useful is short, it had not been sent over long distances. Instead, summaries of the day's trading were sent. Stock tickers are the ancestors of the modern computer printer allowing text to be transmitted over a wire to a printing device. Today, stock tickers are transmitted electronically and can be monitored on the Internet and on many news programs.

WebQuest

Locate Web sites where you can research electronic stock tickers. Write a few sentences about your experiences viewing electronic stock tickers.

Short- and Long-Term Investing

Most people who are investing for retirement will own individual stocks or bonds for a number of years. Long holding periods are an excellent way to build wealth while minimizing risk. Other investors buy and sell more often in an attempt to benefit from day-to-day fluctuations in the value of a stock. *Day traders* are people who buy and sell stock, usually on the Internet, based on minute-by-minute changes in the price of the stock. This is extremely risky. Day traders not only risk losing their original investment, but they also could face additional losses if they borrowed money to buy stocks whose prices fell.

> ✔ **Reading Check** **Explain** How can you purchase stocks that are not listed on a major exchange?

Business Case Study

Hedging Bets on Funds

There's a hot new product on Wall Street, but is it worth the risk?

Investing always involves risk—and investments with the biggest potential returns usually involve the most risk.

Hedge funds are one type of high-risk investment. They pool money from sophisticated investors and use a variety of risky strategies, such as betting on stocks and buying with borrowed money. Because hedge funds are not sold to the general public, they are free from some of the government regulations designed to protect investors. The failure of some high-risk hedge funds played a role in the U.S. financial crisis that began in 2007.

Today's "alternative mutual funds" borrow strategies from hedge funds. Like hedge funds, they buy a wide variety of assets, often with borrowed money. Unlike hedge funds, they are available to regular investors.

Many investors who are attracted to alternative mutual funds do not fully understand how risky they can be. In response, in 2014 the Securities and Exchange Commission launched an examination to see whether such funds are following all regulations and laws.

> **Active Learning**
>
> Divide into small groups. Your group has $1,000 to invest and can pick from three options: 1. A conservative mutual fund that over time has yielded a 4 percent annual return; 2. Stock in an established tech company that is selling for $100 per share (the stock has fallen recently but your broker projects a possible 15 percent gain in the next year); and 3. Investment in an alternative mutual fund that could increase as much as 150 percent in the next year, but that also has equal potential to lose half its value. Discuss your options, calculate your possible gains, and decide which investment option to select. Tell the class why you selected this option.

Advantages and Disadvantages of Stocks

A general principle when investing is that the greater the risk, the greater the possibility of a larger return. A major disadvantage of stocks is that you have more risk of losing your investment when putting money into them rather than a savings account or bonds. You also are not guaranteed a return each year with a stock. However, a big advantage of stocks is that long-term comparisons of returns on stocks and returns from savings accounts or bonds show stocks do better over time. Common-stock ownership allows stockholders to help make decisions about the company in which they are investing.

If a company declares bankruptcy, its stockholders may receive little or none of their investment back. Bondholders must be paid before stockholders. If anything is left, preferred stockholders are paid. Common stockholders are only paid if any money remains.

Liquidity refers to how easily an investment can be turned into cash. Most stocks can quickly be turned into cash by selling them. You are not guaranteed to get all the money out of your investment, however, because the value of the stock might have gone down since you bought it. Stock returns generally keep up with inflation, meaning that the value of an investment in them does not decrease when inflation rises.

Section 31.2

After You Read

Review Key Concepts
1. Discuss stocks and stock markets.
2. Identify an advantage and a disadvantage of stocks.
3. Why is it important to discuss your financial goals with a financial professional?

Academic Skills
4. **English Language Arts** Work with a group of students to research investment tips and guidelines for beginning investors. Create a poster display or bulletin board entitled "Top 10 Investment Tips for New Investors." When writing the ten tips, use parallel construction. For example, begin each tip with a verb.

5. **English Language Arts** Work with a group of three or four other students to search local newspapers for advertisements for investments such as stocks, bonds, mutual funds, CDs, and so on. Highlight or circle terms such as *rate of return, yield, fixed rate,* and *variable rate.*

 Go to **connectED.mcgraw-hill.com** to check your answers.

Section 31.1 *Summary*

Bonds Investing is using money to participate in an enterprise that offers the possibility of profit, especially buying bonds and stock. A bond is a certificate issued by a government or company promising to pay back borrowed money at a fixed rate of interest on a specified date. Like savings accounts, bonds earn interest. Most bonds are considered a safe investment. Governments issue bonds to help raise the money to fund their regular activities. The federal government sells a variety of bonds and other securities. State and local governments sell municipal bonds. Corporations usually sell bonds to pay for construction and equipment.

Section 31.2 *Summary*

Stocks Stocks are shares of ownership in a business. Only corporations sell stock. When a company sells stock, it usually offers two different types: common stock and preferred stock. Brokers buy and sell stock through stock exchanges. Unlike stocks on organized exchanges, over-the-counter stocks are not traded in a specific place. They are traded directly between buyers and sellers. Mutual funds are created by investment firms by raising money from many shareholders and investing it in a variety of stocks. One major advantage of stocks is their potential for high returns on investment. A disadvantage is their higher rates of risk.

Vocabulary Review

1. On a sheet of paper, use each of these key terms and academic vocabulary terms in a sentence.

Key Terms

investing	savings bonds	capital loss
security	municipal bonds	common stock
yield	corporate bonds	preferred stock
bond	stock	stockbroker
coupon rate	dividends	stock exchange
bond discount	capital gain	mutual fund

Academic Vocabulary

participate	indicates
eliminate	illustrates
commission	initiated
matures	order

Review Key Concepts

2. Discuss two goals to set before you start making investments.

3. Name five characteristics of bonds.

4. Differentiate between types of federal, municipal government, and corporate bonds.

5. Describe the advantages and disadvantages of investing in bonds.

6. Discuss stocks and stock markets.

7. Identify the advantages and disadvantages of owning stocks.

Critical Thinking

8. Why are Series EE savings bonds popular with the public?

9. Why do people invest in stocks and bonds?

10. Why do you think the federal government offers different types of investment options with various denominations and maturity dates?

11. If you have only a small amount of money, would you invest in a high-risk stock or a low-risk bond? Explain why?

12. Imagine you own 100 shares of common stock in a corporation. What will happen to your investment if the company declares bankruptcy?

13. Stocks that are not listed on exchanges or traded over the counter may be traded via the company's main office. The company will then try to sell them for the stockholder. Do you think this type of stock is more or less liquid than those on an exchange? Explain your answer.

14. Why do federal, state, and local governments not issue stocks?

Write About It

15. "Some bonds are riskier than some stocks." Write two or more paragraphs indicating how this might be true.

16. Contact a brokerage firm, or go online and research one. Find out about how various mutual funds are classified. Write an e-mail to your teacher on your findings.

17. Write at least two paragraphs either agreeing or disagreeing with the following statement: "As people grow older, they should put more of their money in bonds rather than stocks."

18. List the advantages and disadvantages of buying a corporate bond instead of putting savings in a CD. After reviewing the list, would you buy a corporate bond or a CD? Explain your answer.

19. Review Figure 31.2 on page 554, which discusses the investment pyramid. Then create your own investment pyramid showing how you would choose to invest money based on the levels of risk indicated in the chapter. Write a brief statement explaining your choices.

Technology Applications

Online Research

20. When considering an investment, it is important to make wise tactical decisions despite the hype you might hear in the media. Most technology stocks are traded on the NASDAQ. Find out more about the NASDAQ. What does the name mean? Where is it located? What is its history? How many different stocks are traded on it? Write a one-page report on your findings. Then discuss your report with your classmates.

Business Ethics

Help Your Clients—or Help Yourself?

21. Imagine that you are being interviewed for a job as a financial adviser for an investment firm. The interviewer says the company's average clients with the most savings are over the age of 55. However, this group includes the most conservative investors. Your job would be to encourage this group to invest in high-risk stocks, which would bring in more commissions but could possibly lead to major losses for the investors. Should you take the job?

Applying Academics to Business

English Language Arts

22. Research one of the leading stock exchanges in the world. Examples include the NYSE, the London Stock Exchange, and the Nikkei Exchange in Tokyo. Write a two-page essay telling how the exchange was started and how it has changed over the years. Include such information as the volume of trading that occurs and the process used to buy and sell stocks.

Mathematics

23. Sarah buys 500 shares of stock at $18 and sells the holding for a capital gain of $3,000. What was the share price at the time of the sale?

> **CONCEPT** **Capital Gain or Loss** The difference between how much you invest initially and the current value of that investment is called a *capital gain* if the current value is greater than the initial investment. If the current value is less than the initial investment, the difference is called a *capital loss*.

English Language Arts

24. Explore at least three Web sites devoted to helping the young investor. Write a few paragraphs comparing and contrasting their features. Tell what you think about the graphics, the appropriateness and accuracy of the information they provide, and the ease of use of the sites. Rank the three sites in order listing the best site first.

Mathematics

25. Locate the financial section of the newspaper. Choose three different stocks and study the stock listings for the following information:

Which stock traded the most shares on this day? How many shares were traded?

If you buy 100 shares of each stock you selected, how much would it cost you today? How much would it have cost you yesterday?

> **CONCEPT** **Reading a Chart** Charts are generally organized into rows and columns. Read down the column and across the row to find specific information.

Active Learning

Conducting a Survey

26. Conduct a survey of your family and friends to find out if they have ever invested in bonds. If yes, what kind? How did they purchase the bonds? What do they think about savings bonds as an investment? If they have never purchased a bond, why not? Prepare a report on your findings.

Business in the Real World

Research a Local Brokerage Firm

27. Investigate a brokerage firm. Ask about the services it provides, the educational outreach it offers, and the fees it charges. If possible, invite a stockbroker to your classroom to discuss his or her job. Ask the stockbroker about the skills and other requirements needed to become a stockbroker.

Real LIFE skills

WHICH BOND IS BETTER?

28. Maria has $10,000 to invest. She is considering purchasing a $10,000 corporate bond that offers 7% or a $10,000 municipal bond that offers 5%. Additional income from the corporate bond that she might receive would be taxed at 33%. Which of the investments will result in the greatest gain? Be sure to consider any taxes that might apply.

 **Business CAREERS**

FIND YOUR DREAM JOB

29. Locate the Occupational Outlook Handbook Web site. Click on the "OOH Search/A-Z Index" link and enter the job category of "financial managers." Then write a one-page report about this type of occupation. Conclude your report with a list of things you could do now to prepare yourself to pursue the occupation.

Role Play

ADVISING AN INVESTOR

30. Situation Your 40-year-old aunt would like to invest part of the $300,000 she has saved in CDs. She has asked you and two of your friends to look at the various investment options that she could consider and help her to decide which would be best.

Activity Your presentation should focus on comparing the different types of bonds and stocks to CDs.

Evaluation You will be evaluated on how well you meet the following performance indicators:

- Discuss the investor's financial situation and goals.
- Describe the different types of government and corporate bonds.
- Describe the differences between common stock and preferred stock.
- Describe the various types of CDs.
- Choose the best investment.

Standardized Test Practice

Directions Choose the letter of the best answer. Write the letter for the answer on a separate piece of paper.

1. Which is NOT true about a non-terminating, non-repeating decimal?

A   It is a rational number.
B   It can be expressed using an exponent.
C   It can be expressed using integers.
D   It is part of the system of real numbers.

 TEST-TAKING TIP Test anxiety can lower your test score. Talk with your family, teachers, and counselors about ways to manage and reduce test stress.

Real Estate and Other Investment Options

After completing this chapter, you will be able to:

▶ **Section 32.1** *Real Estate*
- **Describe** the three types of residential property.
- **Discuss** aspects of home buying that a potential home owner should know.
- **Determine** the differences between rental property and undeveloped property.

▶ **Section 32.2** *Other Investment Options*
- **Describe** how precious metals, precious gems, and other commodities as well as collectibles can impact an investment plan.
- **Discuss** the advantages and disadvantages of buying and selling collectibles online.

Ask AN EXPERT

Investing in Bonds and Real Estate: Credit Quality and Volatility

Q: How do you evaluate whether a bond fund is right for your portfolio?

A: When you buy bonds, you are basically lending your money to the issuer of the bond. A bond fund is like a mutual fund that aims to earn income without taking on unreasonable risk by investing in bonds. Bond funds also pay out regular income dividend distributions to shareholders. Although there is a common misconception among investors that bonds and bond funds are low-risk, there are a number of risks associated with both. These include credit, prepayment, and interest rate risks. Credit risk is the possibility that the issuers of the bonds may default, or not pay back the debt. Prepayment risk is the chance that the issuers will prepay at a time when interest rates have declined. Interest rate risk involves the risk that the market value of the bonds owned by a fund will fluctuate as interest rates do. The prospectus of a bond fund should disclose these and any additional risks.

Mathematics John is comparing his credit score with his friends' scores. His friends' scores are 723, 591, 645, 614, and 702, and his score is 661. Is his above or below the mean average of his friends'?

CONCEPT **Measures of Central Tendency** Single numbers can represent a whole list of numerical data. Three of these measures are the mean, the median, and the mode. The mean is the sum of the data divided by the number of items in the set.

● **The American Dream** Buying a home is the most expensive purchase most Americans will make. **Why do you think home ownership is so popular if it is so expensive?**

Ariel Skelley/Blend Images LLC

Real Estate

Reading Guide

Before You Read

Think about the different types of homes, commercial buildings, and other properties in which you could invest.

Read to Learn

- Describe the three types of residential property.
- Discuss aspects of home buying that a potential home owner should know.
- Determine the differences between rental property and undeveloped property.

The Main Idea

Real estate is an investment option. Residential property, such as single-family homes, is usually considered a good investment. Property can also generate income.

Key Concepts

- Investing in Real Estate
- Buying a Home
- Income Property

Vocabulary

Key Terms

real estate
residential property
real estate agent
equity

income property
rental property
undeveloped property

Academic Vocabulary

You will find these words in your reading and on your tests. Make sure you know their meanings.

attached
fluctuate

assembled
nevertheless

Graphic Organizer

List some types of real estate in a chart like the one below.

Types of Real Estate

Homes	Income Property

 Go to **connectED.mcgraw-hill.com** to print out this graphic organizer.

Investing in Real Estate

Real estate has always been a favorite investment for Americans. **Real estate** is land and anything **attached** to it, such as buildings or natural resources. Unlike stocks and bonds, a piece of property is something you can use. You can take pride in owning it. However, if you are new to the real estate market, you may be confused by the different choices you face.

For most Americans, a home is their largest financial asset. A home is usually considered a good investment because, generally, home prices have risen steadily over the years. This does not necessarily mean that the return on home ownership is better than on other types of investments. It also does not mean that everyone finds it to be a good investment. For example, some people buy homes in unpopular locations, where home values are stagnant or do not rise much. In other cases, people buy when the price is extraordinarily high and sell when prices have fallen. Homes **fluctuate** in value, just like other investments.

Buying a house is the most expensive purchase and major investment most people make in their lives. Before buying a home, there are a number of factors to consider.

Types of Homes

Residential property is property in which an individual or family lives. Single-family homes, multi-unit housing, and manufactured homes are forms of residential property. The type of residential property that people pick depends on their income and needs.

Tax Advantages
Homeowners can deduct the mortgage interest they pay each year on their federal income tax forms. This allows homeowners to lower their reported income, which decreases the amount of tax they owe. Property taxes are also deductible. *What are some other advantages of owning a home?*

 **Reading Check** **Identify** What are the three types of residential properties?

International Business

International Real Estate
International real estate can be complicated and should not be purchased on impulse. As appealing as an Italian villa might be, there are risks and regulations to consider. Currencies can be unstable, the political climate might not be receptive to foreigners owning property, and ownership laws can be complex. Potential buyers need to put thought and research into their purchase.

Examples of Languages Across Cultures
Q: In Greek, how do you say "How do you do?"
A: χαίρω πολύ. (pronounced: 'khai-ro po-'lēē)

Research some of the precautions people need to be aware of when buying real estate in Italy. What are some of the laws and restrictions Italy has when it comes to foreigners buying property?

As You Read

Think about the different types of homes you have seen. What type would you like to own?

Single-Family Homes The most popular residential property is the single-family house. It is usually on its own lot with its own yard. It is separate from other buildings and provides privacy. Single-family houses range from modest two-bedroom homes to huge mansions. **Figure 32.1** includes median home costs in different parts of the United States.

Multi-Unit Housing Multi-unit houses are usually single buildings divided into various units, with a separate person or family living in each unit. Multi-unit housing includes duplexes, townhouses, condominiums (or condos), and cooperatives (or co-ops). A *duplex* is a house that is divided into two halves and is inhabited by two families with separate entrances. A *townhouse* is usually a single-family house of two or three stories that shares a wall with a similar house. A *condominium* is a building or complex in which units of property, such as apartments, are owned by individuals. Each owner pays a monthly fee for maintenance and renovations of common areas. A *cooperative* is a jointly owned apartment building. Each co-op owner pays a monthly fee to pay for maintenance renovations of common areas, and, real estate taxes.

Manufactured Homes A manufactured home is usually one of two types. Prefabricated houses are partly **assembled** at a factory. The pieces are then transported to a building site and put together there. The other type is a mobile home. Mobile homes are usually fully assembled in factories. Generally small, they **nevertheless** contain many of the features of larger houses, such as fully equipped kitchens, bathrooms, and fireplaces. Mobile-home owners often do not own any land but rent space for the house. Because manufactured homes can be inexpensively mass-produced, they usually cost much less than other types of houses.

Building Equity As you pay down the principal of your home, your equity increases. For example, if you make a $30,000 down payment on a $150,000 house and pay $3,000 of principal over four years, your equity will increase from $30,000 to $33,000. Your equity also increases as the value of your home increases. *What would your equity be if the value of your home increased by $20,000 over those four years?*

Buying a Home

Few people have enough money to pay for a house in full. Most have to finance it with a *home mortgage loan,* or a long-term property loan. To buy a house also requires a down payment, which is usually 20 percent. The down payment is money that a potential home buyer must provide to obtain the loan. That means if you want to buy a house for $100,000, you need $20,000 for the down payment. The higher the down payment, the lower the mortgage loan will be.

Homebuyers often obtain a real estate agent to help them find a home. A **real estate agent** is a person licensed to arrange the buying and selling of homes and other types of real estate. Real estate agents usually charge their fees to the seller and not the buyer. You must be at least 18 years old to buy real estate on your own.

Figure 32.1 — Housing Costs

Location	Median Household Income	Median Home Price	Price-to-Income Ratio
Atlanta, GA	46,466	192,900	4.15
Baltimore, MD	39,241	150,100	3.83
Boston, MA	51,642	370,400	7.17
Chicago, IL	45,214	211,700	4.68
Dallas, TX	41,354	133,200	3.22
Detroit, MI	23,600	39,100	1.66
Houston, TX	42,847	124,600	2.91
Los Angeles, CA	46,803	421,700	9.01
Miami, FL	28,301	193,300	6.83
New York, NY	50,895	478,400	9.40
Philadelphia, PA	35,386	142,300	4.02
San Francisco, CA	73,012	727,600	9.97

Source: citi-data.com

● **The Cost of Living** The value of housing in different regions of the country can vary considerably. Review the average household income, median home price, and the price-to-income ratio for selected metropolitan areas. **In which three areas will the average person use the most income for housing? In which area will a person pay the least?**

Home Values

Several factors affect the value of a house, including its size, condition, quality, and location. Location is especially important. The distance between your home and work, available public transportation, and the quality of your local school system and public services also affect a home's value.

Home Equity The amount of equity you have in a home is very important. **Equity** is the value of a piece of property less the amount still owed on the money borrowed to purchase it. It is the amount on the house you actually own as opposed to how much you owe.

✔ **Reading Check** **Analyze** Would it be a good investment to buy a house at a very low price in an area where the major employer has moved away?

Income Property

Another reason for buying real estate is to obtain **income property**, or property used to generate income. With income property, the owner can produce income in two ways, depending on the property. They can collect rent or sell the property for a profit.

Rental property is any type of dwelling unit or other property rented for a length of time. An apartment building is a common form of rental property. Commercial property is another type. Commercial properties are rented to businesses. They include buildings for warehouses, offices, and restaurants. Sometimes land is rented to produce crops, graze cattle or sheep, or harvest natural resources, such as timber.

Undeveloped property is unused land intended only for investment purposes. The land usually does not have utility services. It cannot be farmed because it has not been cleared. Most people who invest in undeveloped property hope that its value will increase over the years. In some cases, though, the land's value stays the same or decreases. For example, a planned highway might never be built, leaving the land along its proposed route undeveloped. With undeveloped land, there is no rent paid to the owner. The financial gain earned on undeveloped property comes through the sale of the property after it has risen in value.

Section 32.1

After You Read

Review Key Concepts

1. Describe different types of residential property.
2. What are some factors to consider before buying a home?
3. Discuss the two forms of income property.

Academic Skills

4. **Mathematics** Maria is thinking of investing $300,000 in bonds that would pay 7% interest annually or using the money to buy rental property. How much money would she have to receive in rent for the rental property to give her a higher return on her investment than on the bonds?

CONCEPT **Problem Solving** When solving a word problem, carefully examine the knowns and the unknowns. Then determine how to write an equation that answers the question.

 For math help, go to the Math Appendix.

 Go to **connectED.mcgraw-hill.com** to check your answers.

Other Investment Options

Reading Guide

Before You Read

Think about the different types of items that you could collect that might make good investments.

Read to Learn

- Describe how precious metals, precious gems, and other commodities as well as collectibles can impact an investment plan.
- Discuss the advantages and disadvantages of buying and selling collectibles online.

The Main Idea

Investment plans should include a variety of investments. Aside from real estate, stocks, and bonds, a diversified portfolio might include commodities, such as precious metals and precious gems, as well as collectibles.

Key Concepts

- Diversifying Your Investment Plan
- Investing in Collectibles

Vocabulary

Key Terms

diversify
precious metals
precious gems
commodities exchange
collectibles
fraud

Academic Vocabulary

You will find these words in your reading and on your tests. Make sure you know their meanings.

finally   sites
despite   schemes

Graphic Organizer

List four diversified investments you can investigate in a graphic like the one below.

```
┌─────────────┐     ┌─────────────┐
│             │     │             │
│             │     │             │
│             │     │             │
└─────────────┘     └─────────────┘

      Diversified Investments

┌─────────────┐     ┌─────────────┐
│             │     │             │
│             │     │             │
│             │     │             │
└─────────────┘     └─────────────┘
```

 Go to **connectED.mcgraw-hill.com** to print out this graphic organizer.

Diversifying Your Investment Plan

There are many different types of investments from which to choose, allowing people to diversify their plan. To **diversify** means to vary investments in order to spread risk or to expand. A diversified investment plan (or portfolio) might include real estate, stocks, bonds, and commodities. It could also include precious metals, gems, and collectibles.

● **As You Read**

Think about some different uses of precious metals and precious gems.

Investing in Precious Metals

Many people invest their money in precious metals as a hedge against inflation. A *hedge* is a means of protection or defense against loss. **Precious metals** include valuable ores such as silver, gold, and platinum. They are commodities that are usually valued by the ounce. The price of gold rises when people believe that war, political unrest, or inflation may be near. For example, in 1979, the price of gold was about $100 per ounce. As inflation and political tensions grew, the price of gold rose to an all-time high of more than $850 an ounce in 1980. As international tensions ease or the political situation stabilizes, the price of gold falls.

Business | Case Study

Hidden Savings in Your Home

Investing in energy efficiency brings long-term gains

To be a smart investor, it pays to start at home. Switching to energy-efficient appliances can save you tens of thousands of dollars in the long term.

Do you have a second refrigerator? Fifteen percent of American households have a second fridge that's at least 20 years old. Older refrigerators are energy inefficient, so the convenience of fewer trips to the store can cost hundreds of dollars per year in energy bills. Today's refrigerators cost half as much and use two-thirds less energy than those made in 1980.

Another source of avoidable expense is old furnaces, air conditioners, and water heaters. Newer models use significantly less energy, making them good long-term investments that also pay off immediately in the form of lower bills. Your local power company might even offer appliance-upgrade rebates through green-energy programs, saving you even more.

Active Learning

The Database of State Incentives for Renewables & Efficiency, known as DSIRE (dsireusa.org), is a source of information on government financial rewards and policies that support energy efficiency in the United States. Using the map on DSIRE's website, research residential energy incentives in your state, county, and city. Pick an incentive program in your area and write a short report about it. Outline the eligible products and services offered, the specific incentives offered, and the application process.

Science/Tech TRENDS

Eco-Friendly Building

Eco-Friendly building is a term that is used when natural materials, rather than man-made materials, are used in the construction of buildings and homes. Differentiating between man-made and natural material can be difficult in today's world, where technology is present in almost every production process. Since it is tough to completely remove workers from the building process, it is more accurate to define eco-friendly building as construction that minimizes the use of materials that require large amounts of energy for their manufacture. It doesn't mean that you have to live in a log cabin to call your home eco-friendly. The goal of eco-friendly building is to use materials and techniques that don't add to pollution, waste fossil fuels, or misuse the resources of the environment.

Web Quest

Locate Web sites where you can research how eco-friendly building can be used to lessen the environmental impact of construction. Look for information on different types of materials and how they are used. Write a few paragraphs about the materials and how structures can be designed to save energy.

Investing in Precious Gems

Throughout history people have prized the precious gems that lie embedded in rock below the earth's surface. **Precious gems** (or gemstones) are rough mineral deposits (usually crystals) that are dug from the earth by miners and then cut and shaped into brilliant jewels. These gems include diamonds, sapphires, rubies, and emeralds. They appeal to investors because of their small size, beauty, ease of storage, durability, and potential as a protection against inflation.

Whether you are buying precious gems to store in a safe-deposit box or to wear as jewelry, you will want to keep in mind the risks associated with this type of investment. First, you cannot easily convert diamonds and other precious gems into cash. Also, as a beginning investor, you may have difficulty determining whether the gems you are buying are of high quality. Political unrest in gem-producing countries can affect supply and prices. **Finally**, you will likely have to buy your gems at higher retail prices and sell them at lower wholesale prices. The difference is usually 10 percent to 15 percent and sometimes as high as 50 percent.

The best way to know exactly what you are getting in an expensive precious gem is to have the stone certified by an independent geological laboratory, such as the Gemological Institute

Real World

"Precious" Investments

Investing in precious metals and precious gems can be simple and fun. You can buy them as jewelry from a trusted company, and then wear your investment. You can also buy shares of stock in companies that mine, process, and sell them. The New York Mercantile Exchange is a trading forum for precious metals. Other exchanges trade stock in precious-gem and metal companies. *Which method of investing in precious metals and precious gems would you prefer? Why?*

of America®. The certificate should list the stone's characteristics, including its weight, color, clarity, and quality of cut. The grading of gems, however, is not an exact science. Experiments have shown that the same stone submitted twice to the same laboratory may get two different ratings.

Despite the attraction of precious metals and gems, the investment risks are sizable, and metals and gems can fluctuate greatly in value.

> ✔ **Reading Check**   **Explain** What are some risks to investing in precious gems?

Investing in Commodities

Some people like to "play the market" for commodities such as oil, corn, and coffee. Through a **commodities exchange**, investors can buy contracts for quantities of a given commodity for delivery at a future date. Most investors want to sell their contract before the delivery date. They hope that the price of the commodity will rise in the world market. If it does, they can make a significant return. However, if prices decrease, they can lose a great deal. Even when you think you know the market very well, an unexpected event—for example, a freeze during the time coffee beans are about to be picked—can spell the difference between rags and riches.

Investing in Collectibles

Collectibles are items that appeal to collectors and investors. They can include rare coins and books, works of art, antiques, and stamps. Each of these items offers the knowledgeable collector or investor both pleasure and an opportunity for profit. Many collectors have been surprised to discover that items they bought for their own enjoyment had increased greatly in value while they owned them.

Collectibles on the Internet

Before the Internet became popular, finding items to add to a collection could be time-consuming. Collectors had to pore over magazines for collectors to research the values of items they wished to buy. Then they had to go to shows, sometimes far away, where collectors met to buy and sell their items. That process has changed. The Internet has made buying and selling collectibles efficient and convenient, and the number of Web **sites** for collectors has exploded. Today, eBay is the biggest online auction site.

The Pros and Cons of Online Collecting It is easy to see why the Internet has such appeal. With a few keystrokes, buyers can search for items to add to their collection. Sellers can reach people around the world. Prices are not necessarily lower on the Internet. Still, it is easier to do comparison shopping, and most Web sites do not charge a commission.

Collecting on the Internet has its drawbacks. Collectibles do not offer interest or dividends. You may have a hard time selling items in your collection at a good price on short notice. If your collection grows significantly in value, you will have to purchase insurance against damage and theft. As an online buyer, you cannot size up a dealer in person or easily examine objects for flaws or trademarks. Furthermore, fraud is an ever-present danger.

Staying Aware of Fraud

Collecting on or off the Internet can be a satisfying hobby and a good investment. Nevertheless, a wise collector must always be alert to **schemes** and scams. **Fraud** is the crime of obtaining money or some other benefit by deliberate deception. How do you know that the baseball glove you bought was actually signed by Mickey Mantle? Could your Civil War-era postage stamp be counterfeit? Is that old Barbie® doll, Lionel® train, or Darth Vader® action figure really authentic? The safest way to steer clear of fraud is to learn everything you can about the items you collect and to buy and sell only with reputable dealers.

Section 32.2

After You Read

Review Key Concepts

1. How can precious metals, precious gems, and other commodities as well as collectibles impact an investment plan?
2. Describe the function of a commodities exchange.
3. What are some pros and cons of online investing?

Academic Skills

4. **English Language Arts** Unlike stocks, collectibles can be hard to valuate and research. Work with a partner to research some of the terms associated with collectibles. Write the definitions of the terms *new-in-box*, *mint condition*, and *fair condition*.

5. **English Language Arts** Create a poster of your dream house. Use magazines, the Internet, or your own drawings to depict the features it will have, where it will be located, and what it will look like. Write captions and callouts describing your home and its features. Then find a real home that looks like your design using a newspaper or the Internet.

 Go to **connectED.mcgraw-hill.com** to check your answers.

Section 32.1 *Summary*

Real Estate Real estate has always been a popular investment for many people in the United States. Unlike stocks and bonds, a piece of property is something that an investor can use. Real estate investments can be in your own home and in income property. With residential property, one can choose from single-family homes, multi-unit housing, and manufactured homes. Income property offers the opportunity to earn money by collecting rent from the property or by selling it for a profit. A major disadvantage of investing in real estate is the difficulty of converting it to cash quickly.

Section 32.2 *Summary*

Other Investment Options Investing in precious metals, gems, and other commodities, or collectibles can be another way to diversify your investment portfolio. With these types of investment, the only way an investor can profit is to sell the item for more than the purchase price. With any of these investments, there is considerable risk. Investors should be sure to develop an understanding of the market and the items in that market. Being aware of possible fraudulent practices in the areas of gems and collectibles is important. This is especially true for online collectors.

Vocabulary Review

1. On a sheet of paper, use each of these key terms and academic vocabulary terms in a sentence.

Key Terms

real estate	diversify
residential property	precious metals
real estate agent	precious gems
equity	commodities exchange
income property	collectibles
rental property	fraud
undeveloped property	

Academic Vocabulary

attached	finally
fluctuate	despite
assembled	sites
nevertheless	schemes

Review Key Concepts

2. Describe the three types of residential property.

3. Discuss aspects of home buying that a potential home owner should know.

4. Determine the differences between rental property and undeveloped property.

5. Describe how precious metals, precious gems, and other commodities as well as collectibles can impact an investment plan.

6. Discuss the advantages and disadvantages of buying and selling collectibles online.

Critical Thinking

7. Why do you think some people prefer to buy a condominium instead of a single-family home?

8. Why do you think people are willing to go into debt to buy a home?

9. Some people think that land will always increase in value because there is a limited amount of it and an increasing number of people to use it. Do you think this is true? Why or why not?

10. Why might someone who has money to purchase a home opt to rent instead?

11. What warnings would you give a friend who is interested in putting most of his savings into baseball cards?

12. Why might it be better to sell a collectible through eBay than an antiques dealer?

13. Indicate whether investing in commodities is a low- or high-risk type of investment. Support your position.

Write About It

14. Research precious and semi-precious stones. Choose at least two each. In a one-page paper, discuss what makes them more valuable or less valuable than others.

15. Write at least two paragraphs indicating the advice you would give a friend who is thinking of buying a home.

16. In two or more paragraphs, discuss the risks associated with buying income property, precious gems, or other commodities.

17. Watch a TV program or go to an auction that focuses on collectibles. Write at least one page indicating what you have learned about collectibles.

18. What effect do anti-fraud laws have on the art market? Develop a paragraph supporting your answer.

19. In at least two paragraphs, explain what would happen to investments in precious gems and metals if the economy were strong. How would the results differ if the economy suffered a decline?

Technology Applications

Internet

20. Suppose you are a potential real estate buyer or seller. Go to the Web sites of at least three real estate firms in your area. Scan the listings that they have. What did you see at the Web sites that you think was helpful? Write at least 250 words about what you liked about the listings and what you think should be improved.

Business Ethics

Finding a Valuable Item

21. Imagine that you own a secondhand shop. One day, a man brings in a box of trinkets from his grandmother's attic. He says it is all junk and asks for $10. You glance through it and agree. After he leaves, you notice a pocket watch buried in the corner. You realize it is worth thousands of dollars. What should you do?

Chapter 32 Review and Activities

Applying Academics to Business

English Language Arts

22. Choose a character from a novel or play you have read. Research homes in your region that are for sale, and choose one you think might be appropriate for your character. Think about whether your character would be likely to live in the country or in the city, in a modest cottage or in a mansion. Write a paragraph or two about why the house you have chosen fits the character.

Mathematics

23. Wanda purchased an income property for $100,000. Her annual expenses were about $14,400, and the monthly income from rent averaged $1,500. She sold the property after three years for 17% more than the amount she paid for it. What was her net gain?

CONCEPT **Net Gain** Net gain is the difference between the original value of an asset, or what you paid for it, and the value of all cash generated from owning it.

English Language Arts

24. Property can refer to possessions, land, or products of the mind, called intellectual property. Find synonyms or examples for the word *property*, and list them under the three categories.

Mathematics

25. Imagine that you have $5,000 to invest and you decide to invest in three different precious metals. Using the Internet, you track the prices daily for a month and then display your data in a graph. Tell what type of graph would be best to display the data you have gathered. Explain why it is appropriate and other types are not.

CONCEPT **Data Analysis** Different types of graphs are suitable for displaying different types of data. Types of graphs include pie or circle charts, line graphs, bar graphs, scatter plots, and histograms.

Active Learning

Selling a House

26. Identify a person in your family or neighborhood who has just sold a house. Interview that person, asking the following questions: What did you do to the house before putting it on the market? Did you use a real estate agent? Why or why not? What did you find most difficult about selling your home? Indicate your findings in a one- to two-page paper.

Business in the Real World

Profile a Career

27. Research the careers associated with the real-estate profession. Choose one of the following: sales agents, brokers, real-estate lawyers, appraisers, and urban planners. Interview someone in the profession. How did he or she prepare for it? What type of education or training is required to do the job? Write a one-page paper on your findings.

Real LIFE · skills

DEVELOPING HOME-BUYING SKILLS

28. Interview someone who owns a house about what is involved in home ownership. Ask the following questions: What was the main reason you purchased a house? What are the difficulties that you had in purchasing a house? What are the costs of owning a home? If you sold it, would you buy another one? Write a report of at least one page on your findings. Discuss your report with your classmates.

 Business CAREERS

FIND YOUR DREAM JOB

29. Locate the Occupational Outlook Handbook Web site. Click on the "OOH Search/A-Z Index" link and enter the job category "jewelers and precious stone and metal workers." Then write a one-page report about this area of occupation. Conclude your report with a list of things you could do now to prepare yourself to pursue the occupation.

Role Play

REASON FOR BUYING INCOME PROPERTY

30. Situation You are a real estate agent meeting with someone who has money to invest. This person would like to invest in real estate, stocks, or bonds.

Activity You are trying to encourage this investor to put his or her money into rental income property instead of stocks or bonds.

Evaluation You will be evaluated on how well you meet the following performance indicators:

- Discuss the advantages and disadvantages of owning income property.
- Identify the advantages and disadvantages of owning stocks and bonds.
- Develop your arguments in an organized way.
- Use correct English and project your voice.

Standardized Test Practice

Directions Choose the letter of the best answer. Write the letter for the answer on a separate piece of paper.

1. Which is the best synonym for the word *gem* as it is used in this chapter?

   A   delight
   B   dear
   C   jewel
   D   find

 TEST-TAKING TIP Eat well before taking a test. Have a good breakfast or lunch and avoid junk food. Studies show that you need good nutrition to concentrate and perform your best.

John Calhoun
Rod Hill

CEO & COO, Integrated Management Services Engineers

Based in Jackson, Mississippi, IMS offers civil engineering services. IMS is one of only a handful of minority-owned engineering firms in the United States. This interview is with John Calhoun. John Calhoun and Rod Hill founded the firm.

Q & A

Describe your job responsibilities.

John: As CEO, I am responsible for the success and failure of the company's operations, marketing, strategy, financing, and creation of company culture. My main duty as CEO is formulating a strategy and vision. The CEO ultimately sets the direction. The CEO's second duty is building culture. Work gets done through people, and people are profoundly affected by culture. Culture is built in dozens of ways, and the CEO sets the tone.

What skills are most important in your business?

John: Resourcefulness, good listening and communication skills, a sharp and inquisitive mind to probe for answers, and the ability and discipline to maintain a meaningful and healthy lifestyle.

What is your key to success?

John: A broad education, broad curiosity, boundless enthusiasm, belief in people and teamwork, willingness to take risks, devotion to long-term growth, rather than short-term profit, commitment to excellence, readiness, and vision.

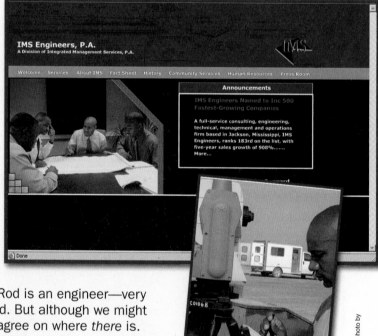

Some entrepreneurs start their companies alone. IMS was developed as a partnership. Do you see any challenges in partnerships versus going it alone?

John: Rod and I knew we wanted to create a quality engineering firm. Our partnership is based on mutual respect and friendship. We were best friends at college. We bring different strengths to the partnership. Rod is an engineer—very methodical. I'm much more free spirited. But although we might disagree on how to get there, we both agree on where *there* is.

What advice would you give students interested in starting a business?

John: Have big dreams and never stop dreaming of more. Know how to define success for yourself. Don't have someone define it for you. Establish excellent networks of people who support what you are doing. View obstacles as challenges and, at times, welcome them. Walk through fear and take calculated, or sometimes bold, risks.

Critical Thinking   *What consequences might result from launching a niche company?*

Some Qualifications Needed to Own a Civil Engineering Firm

Academic Skills and Abilities

Physics; engineering; mathematics (especially algebra, geometry, trigonometry, and calculus); interpersonal skills; general business management skills; verbal and written communication skills; multitasking, organizing, and planning skills

Academic Skills Required to Complete Tasks at Integrated Management Services Engineers			
Tasks	Math	Science	English Language Arts
Hold meetings			◆
Assign duties			◆
Design to meet customer needs	◆	◆	◆
Oversee construction	◆	◆	◆
Maintain safe work sites	◆	◆	◆
Schedule employees	◆		◆
Order supplies and equipment	◆		◆
Analyze financials	◆		◆

Education and Training

For a typical bachelor's degree in engineering, the first two years are spent studying mathematics, basic sciences, introductory engineering, humanities, and social sciences. In the last two years, most courses are in engineering, usually with a concentration in one specialty.

Career Path

The major civil engineering specialties are structural, water resources, construction, environmental, transportation, and geotechnical engineering. Many civil engineers hold supervisory or administrative positions, from supervisor of a construction site to city engineer. All 50 states and the District of Columbia require licensure for engineers who offer their service to the public. Independent of licensure, various certification programs are offered by professional organizations to demonstrate competency in specific fields of engineering.

Preparing for a Career
Self-Assessment Checklist
Use this self-assessment checklist to help determine ways you can build a successful career path.

✔ Keep your work area neat and organized to enhance safety and efficiency.

✔ Be professional. Limit personal phone calls, non-work-related e-mail, and distractions.

✔ Plan your day's schedule, keeping in mind any meetings and duties that require you to be considerate of other people's time.

✔ Complete the most important work first— don't get caught up in minor details.

✔ Avoid procrastinating— it may prevent you from producing top-quality work on schedule.

✔ Tackle one task at a time, and do not get side-tracked.

✔ Try to empathize with customers and co- workers to gain a better understanding of the situation.

✔ Pay attention to body language. Be alert to facial expressions, which often give clues to a person's inner feelings.

Building a Financial Future

You want to make your future as secure as possible. You want to plan for the future by building and managing your personal finances, making and living within a budget, and planning your financial future.

Thematic Project Assignment

In this project you will write a personal financial plan that describes how you want to plan for your financial future. Your plan might include a savings account, investments in bonds or stocks, or a retirement fund.

Step 1 Brainstorm Skills You Need to Complete This Activity

Your success in writing a personal financial plan will depend on your skills. Preview the activity, then brainstorm a list of the skills you will need to use to complete the activity and describe how you will use them. Skills you might use include:

Academic Skills reading and writing

Basic Skills speaking, listening, and thinking

Technology Skills word processing and keyboarding

 SKILLS PREVIEW Go to connectED.mcgraw-hill.com to download a graphic organizer you can use to brainstorm the skills you will use to complete the project.

Step 2 Think About the Financial Future You Want

Think about what you want your future to be like. Do you want to own a home someday? Would you like to have a family? Do you want to someday retire from your job? Would you like to travel? Think about how much money you will need to do some of the things you want in the future.

Step 3 Build Background Knowledge

Preview information on building a financial future.

Building a Financial Future

Dreaming about what the future holds for you is one thing. Being practical and building a financial future is quite another. Building a secure financial future takes research, careful planning, and discipline. First, you must research to be able to make wise choices about where to invest or to put your money. Second, you must plan how you are going to save and put money away for investments. Third, you must have the discipline to put money into a savings account or some other investment account.

Building a financial future is an important part of adulthood and should be an important part of everyone's life. No one knows what the future holds. The more secure you are financially, the better your future will be.

Step 4 Connect with Your Community

Interview two adults in your community about how they have planned for their financial future. Ask the adults how they learned about financial planning. Think about how important it is to plan for your financial future.

Step 5 Research How to Plan for Your Financial Future

Use library and Internet resources to research ways you can plan for your financial future. Use the checklist as a guide to your research. Keep records of your sources of information.

Step 6 Develop a Plan for Your Financial Future

Use word-processing and spreadsheet software to develop a plan for your financial future that includes all of the information described in the project checklist.

Developing a Plan for Your Financial Future

✔ Make a list of two things you want for your future. These might include a new vehicle, a home, a vacation, a college education, or a family.

✔ Use library and Internet resources, phone calls, or personal interviews to research the cost of each of the things on your list. For example, contact a local college to learn what the cost is of a two-year or four-year degree. Write this amount next to "a college education" on your list.

✔ Visit local banks in your area to learn about savings accounts, CDs, special college savings accounts, and other ways to save money. Also, use the Internet to research other types of investments, such as stocks and U.S. savings bonds.

✔ Create a chart that illustrates the items you want for your future, the amount you predict you will need, how you plan to obtain the money (such as through a savings account or by buying U.S. savings bonds), and when you will need the money.

Self Connections

✔ Describe the results of your research with the adults you interviewed.

✔ Explain what the investigation and its results mean to you.

Step 7 Evaluate Your Presentation

 RUBRIC Go to connectED.mcgraw-hill.com to download a rubric you can use to evaluate your final report.

Advanced Physical Therapy offers physical therapy services at outpatient clinics and work conditioning centers. At the end of this unit, you will learn about Advanced Physical Therapy founder JoAnne Jonathan and how she achieved her success.

Decision Making Do you take any steps to manage risk in your life?

Unit 11 Thematic Project Preview

Understanding Risk After completing this unit, you will research ways that insurance can help you protect valuable property.

Project Checklist As you read the chapters in this unit, use this checklist to prepare for the unit project.

✔ Think about what valuable property you might want to have in the future.

✔ Think about why you will need to have insurance for your property.

✔ Look for insurance agents in your community to learn more about the different types of insurance.

✔ Think about the types of jobs and careers available in the insurance industry.

Chapter 33

The Basics of Risk Management

Chapter Objectives After completing this chapter, you will be able to:

▶ **Section 33.1** *Types of Risk*
- **Discuss** risk and risk management.
- **Describe** different types of risk.

▶ **Section 33.2** *Handling Risk*
- **Describe** four ways that individuals and businesses can handle risk.
- **List** types of insurance protection.

Ask

AN EXPERT

The Basics of Risk Management: Credit Risk Assessment

Q: How does a bank assess its risk when making a large loan to a company?

A: Credit risk is the possibility that a company may not make timely payments on its outstanding debt. In the worst cases, the company never pays back what it owes. Banks must assess a company's credit risk before they decide whether to grant a loan to the company. Using various credit risk assessment templates, banks determine the credit scores, the probabilities of default, and rating estimates of the company. Based on this information, they may grant the loan or decide not to if the risk is too great.

Mathematics Danielle has $1,800 in credit card debt and still owes $6,200 on her car. Her annual income is $32,000. She has requested a credit line from the bank. Before granting her the credit, the bank must calculate her debt-to-income ratio. If the bank's cutoff for granting credit is 0.35, will she be eligible?

CONCEPT **Calculating Ratios** A ratio is a comparison of two numbers using division. Ratios are usually written in simplest form, so the ratio "8 out of 10" is written 4 to 5, 4:5, or $\frac{4}{5}$. Sometimes a ratio is represented as one number as either a percent or a decimal.

Managing Risk Businesses face many different types of risk. **Why do you think it is important for people to know what risks a business might face?**

Types of Risk

Reading Guide

Before You Read
Think about the various types of risk that you face in your daily life.

Read to Learn
- Discuss risk and risk management.
- Describe different types of risk.

The Main Idea
Everybody faces risk that can lead to loss, injury, or even death. Individuals and businesses can use strategies to manage risk as ways to reduce or avoid loss.

Key Concepts
- Risk Management
- Types of Risk

Vocabulary

Key Terms
risk
risk management
insurable risk
insurance
uninsurable risk
controllable risk
uncontrollable risk
pure risk
economic risk
human risk
natural risk

Academic Vocabulary
You will find these words in your reading and on your tests. Make sure you know their meanings.
criteria
minimize
decade
occurrences

Graphic Organizer
In a figure like the one below, give examples of each of the four types of risk.

Types of Risk	Examples
Insurable	
Uninsurable	
Controllable	
Uncontrollable	

 Go to **connectED.mcgraw-hill.com** to print out this graphic organizer.

Risk Management

All people and businesses make decisions that create risk. A **risk** is the possibility of loss or injury. You face risk daily. Some types of risk may be easier for you to tolerate than others. For example, if you ride in a car, bus, train, or plane, you take the risk of having an accident. You can also fall down the stairs at home or at school. *Business risk* is risk that businesses specifically face, such as the potential for financial loss. You cannot eliminate all risk, but you can reduce and manage it. **Risk management** is the systemic process of managing risk to achieve your objectives.

✔ Reading Check **Define** What is risk?

Types of Risk

There are several different types of risk. Risk may be insurable or uninsurable, as well as controllable or uncontrollable. Risk can be further identified as pure, economic, human, or natural risk.

An **insurable risk** is a risk that meets an insurance company's **criteria** for insurance coverage. **Insurance** is paid protection against loss due to injury or property damage. Drivers who have vehicle insurance present insurable risk. **Uninsurable risk** is a risk that is unacceptable to insurance carriers because the likelihood of loss is too high. A store owner might have difficulty finding insurance for a shop that is located in a flood zone.

Figure 33.1 — **Planning to Manage Risk** ——

● **Are You Prepared?** Being prepared to face risk is an important way for businesses to manage the possible consequences. **Which step do you think is most important?**

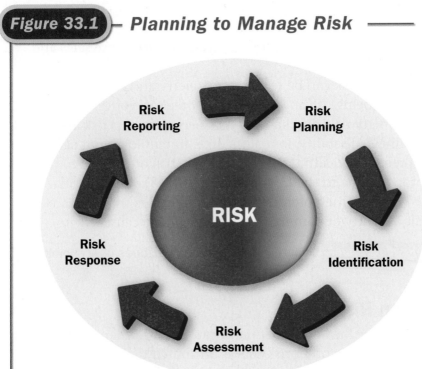

ETHICS in Business

Conduct in the Workplace

■ **Critical Reading** Life is full of important decisions. Think about the kinds of decisions that you make as you read the question below.

You are the head of the human resources department for a small company. Your company has experienced a rash of thefts. Several employees have mentioned their suspicions about one particular employee. However, no one has come forward with evidence against the employee.

■ **Decision Making** Should you confront this employee or conduct a search of his or her work area? What should you tell the police? Explain your answer.

As You Read

Think about the losses businesses can incur from bad checks.

Controllable risk occurs when conditions can be controlled to **minimize** the chance of harm. Environmental damage is a controllable risk that, in many cases, can be prevented. An **uncontrollable risk** cannot be controlled. For example, risk involved in doing business in the global marketplace cannot be controlled.

Pure Risk

A **pure risk** is the threat of a loss with no opportunity for gain. If you drive a car, for example, you run the risk of being in an accident and suffering loss and/or injury. Your insurance company will not issue you funds for avoiding an accident. Therefore, if you avoid an accident, you do not have an opportunity for gain. Of course, you would still try to drive carefully and avoid accidents. Businesses run the risk of loss from employee theft, burglary, bad checks, and accidents involving customers and employees. Businesses do not receive insurance funds for avoiding financial losses due to these occurrences. The purpose of insurance is to hedge against the risk of potential financial loss.

Economic Risk

Economic risk occurs when there is likelihood of economic loss. Even if you are very careful, you will not be able to avoid all risk. You can, however, protect yourself against economic loss. For businesses, economic risk results from changes in overall business conditions. If businesses fail to change their products when competitors offer more features, they may lose sales and face economic harm.

Economic risk can be related to property and to your own personal well-being. It can be placed in three categories: personal risk, property risk, and liability risk. *Personal risk* is risk associated with illness, disability, loss of income, unemployment, aging, and premature death. *Property risk* is the risk of damage to or loss of property due to theft, wind, fire, flood, or some other hazard. *Liability risk* is the potential for losses to others that occur as a result of injury or damage that you may have caused.

✔ **Reading Check** **Identify** What are the categories of economic risk?

Human Risk

Human risk is the risk of harm caused by human mistakes, dishonesty, or another risk that is attributed to people. Risk may be caused by people who are careless or dishonest. A friend might borrow something from you and damage or lose it. You might lose money to someone who snatches your wallet or purse. For businesses, human risk ranges from the financial impact of theft or embezzlement to job-related injury or illness.

Customer Dishonesty Human risk can be caused by customer theft, fraudulent payment, or nonpayment. Losses due to shoplifting are passed on to consumers through higher prices. Price increases are needed to pay for inventory shortages, security personnel, and the installation of theft prevention systems. Other examples of customer dishonesty include nonpayment of accounts or the use of stolen checks or credit cards.

Employee Risk Employees represent another human risk to businesses. Employees may cause loss. Companies depend on employees to do their job well. For example, commercial airlines prepare crews for emergencies caused not only by mechanical problems but also by human factors. If a flight attendant fails to keep an aisle clear, a passenger could trip and fall, break an arm, and sue the airline. Accidents like these can be financially devastating to a small business. The possibility of employee theft poses another risk to businesses.

Computer-Related Crime Over the past decade, computer-related crime has emerged as a significant new human risk to business. Malicious programs called computer worms or viruses can be inadvertently downloaded by employees and can wreak havoc on internal computer networks and communication systems. Hackers may break into computer systems to gain access or information for mischievous or criminal purposes.

● **Natural Disasters** Damage from a tornado can be devastating. **What type of risk does a tornado represent?**

Computer crime is committed by many different kinds of people—from current or past employees to professional cyber thieves. Businesses can reduce computer crime by keeping computer networks secure and using passwords, encoded firewall programs, and virus detectors. Employees can be trained on privacy policies and proper handling of confidential information.

Crime Prevention People try to avoid risks associated with crime by taking precautions at home and in public. To protect against theft, many businesses install closed-circuit TV systems and point-of-service terminals that generate reports. They also thoroughly review job applicants. To protect against losses due to bad checks and credit cards, they use check-reader and credit-authorizer machines. Companies hire security guards and install high-quality locks, proper lighting, and alarm systems.

Natural Risk

A **natural risk** is the possibility of a catastrophe caused by a flood, tornado, hurricane, fire, lightning, drought, or earthquake. These natural occurrences can cause damage or loss of property. Some risk is caused by people and is also called natural risk. Power outages, oil spills, arson, terrorism, and even war are classified as natural risk.

Weather Disasters
The United States sustained 133 weather-related disasters between 1980 and 2011, in which overall damages and costs reached or exceeded $1 billion at the time of each event, according to the National Climactic Data Center. *How can businesses and people prepare for such disasters?*

Section 33.1

After You Read

Review Key Concepts
1. Why do businesses and individuals practice risk management?
2. What are the four main types of risk discussed in the chapter?
3. Describe some types of human risk.

Academic Skills
4. **Mathematics** Your auto insurance policy has a bodily injury ratio of 1:4. This ratio describes the relationship between the maximum coverage for individual bodily injury and all bodily injury. If the most the policy pays for individual bodily injury is $150,000, what is the most it will pay for all bodily injury?

CONCEPT **Ratios** A ratio is a comparison of two quantities. A ratio of 1:2 means one part of the first quantity to two parts of the other. If the first quantity is 10, find the second quantity by multiplying by 2 to get 20.

For math help, go to the Math Appendix.

 Go to **connectED.mcgraw-hill.com** to check your answers.

Handling Risk

Reading Guide

● Before You Read

Think about what you do to handle the risk you face in your day-to-day life.

Read to Learn

- Describe four ways that individuals and businesses can handle risk.
- List types of insurance protection.

The Main Idea

Risk of loss can be avoided, reduced, retained, or transferred. Insurance is a way to transfer the risk of loss to an insurance company, which agrees to cover you economically if certain types of risk result in a loss.

Key Concepts

- Handling Risk
- Insurance Protection

Vocabulary

Key Terms

premium	hazard
peril	insurance policy

Academic Vocabulary

You will find these words in your reading and on your tests. Make sure you know their meanings.

retain	undergo
mode	conversely

Graphic Organizer

In a figure like the one below, list and describe four ways individuals and businesses can handle risk.

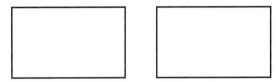

**Ways Businesses
Handle Risk**

 Go to **connectED.mcgraw-hill.com** to print out this graphic organizer.

Handling Risk

Since you cannot completely avoid all risk, you must learn to handle it. There are four ways to handle risk. You can avoid, reduce, **retain**, or transfer risk. Most people and businesses use a combination of all these methods.

Risk Avoidance

Avoiding risk involves thinking about the consequences of decisions. For example, you could avoid the risk of a train accident by never riding a train. However, this would eliminate a **mode** of transportation that is considered very safe. In many cases you can avoid risk, but sometimes it is not practical to do so. For a business, risk avoidance means refusing to engage in a particularly hazardous activity. For instance, market research can lead a business to conclude that investment in a product or service is not worth the risk. All business decisions should be made with consideration of the potential for benefit and for risk.

Business Case Study

Smart Cybersecurity

Companies get serious about IT to protect their customers and employees

Cyberattacks against businesses can result in crippled computer systems, leaks of business secrets, and theft of customers' personal information. The FBI estimates the financial damage alone at billions of dollars a year.

Many companies use firewalls and anti-virus software to defend their computer networks. But this is often not enough. Devastating cyberattacks struck the Target Corporation in 2013 and Sony Pictures Entertainment in 2014, despite their security measures.

Who is behind these cyber-assaults? Everyone "from computer geeks looking for bragging rights," says the FBI, "to businesses trying to gain an upper hand in the marketplace."

To respond to this threat, companies are deploying tools to detect and stop in-progress attacks. Some are even setting up Security Operations Centers that include around-the-clock monitoring and alerts.

Active Learning

Divide into teams. Pick one of the following types of cybersecurity challenges: malware, ransomware, denial of service attacks, corporate security breaches, phishing, social media fraud. Define your term, describe a case in which it negatively affected a business, and list specific measures a company could take prevent it. Assess how these cybersecurity measures are part of risk management. Share your ideas with the class.

Risk Reduction

Some risk cannot be avoided entirely. Instead you may need to practice risk reduction. For instance, your home should have smoke alarms and fire extinguishers. They can reduce the risk that a fire will cause damage. When you use equipment or tools, follow safety rules, wear protective glasses, and work in a properly designed work area to reduce the risk that you will be hurt.

Businesses practice risk reduction, too. For example, retail stores place electronic tags on expensive merchandise to discourage theft. This may not eliminate shoplifting, but it can reduce it. Business owners reduce risk by designing work areas to lower the chances of accidents or fire. They educate their employees about the safe use of equipment and keep safety equipment ready for use. Businesses also provide information about the correct use of products and warn customers about possible hazards.

Screening and Training Employees For most businesses, the best way to reduce risk from employee carelessness and incompetence is through effective employee screening, orientation, and training. Businesses screen applicants' backgrounds and check references. Some companies now require prospective employees to **undergo** drug testing before being hired. Drug abuse can increase human risk by making employees careless and more likely to ignore or forget safety rules.

Real World

Workplace Safety
The financial impact of workplace accidents is staggering. To manage this risk, businesses design work areas to avoid accidents. They also provide safety training. They try to address hazards before accidents occur. They comply with state and federal health and safety regulations and place first-aid kits throughout the workplace. *What are some things that companies can do to protect employees who work with hazardous materials?*

Risk Retention

It may be impossible to avoid certain types of risk. Bearing financial responsibility for the consequences of loss is called *risk retention*. For instance, suppose that your watch is valuable, but you enjoy wearing it anyway. If you take your chances on losing or damaging it, you will have to pay to replace it if necessary. You have chosen to retain the risk of the economic loss that you will lose or damage the watch.

A business may retain the risk that customer tastes will change and merchandise will not sell. They can underestimate the risk and stock too much merchandise. If consumer demand for that merchandise changes, they may have a greater loss than planned.

✔ **Reading Check** **Define** What is risk retention?

Risk Transfer

Insurance provides a way to transfer a risk of loss to an insurance company. Insurance divides a possible loss among large numbers of people or companies. Economic risk is shared most effectively when many people or businesses are involved. Each individual or company then pays a fee for protection.

Insurance Protection

Insurance protection requires careful planning and decision making. Choosing the right insurance plan is an important step. Insurance companies provide almost any kind of insurance you might want. How do you make your insurance choices? You must look at your individual situation and then choose the protection that fits your needs.

With insurance protection, no one person or business has to bear a loss alone. A **premium** is the price an insured person or business pays for insurance protection for a specified period of time. Insurance works on the "principle of large numbers," which means many share a loss so that no one person or business carries all the risk.

Risk, peril, and *hazard* are important terms in insurance. In everyday life, these terms have almost the same meanings. In the insurance business, however, each word has a distinct and special meaning. While risk is the chance of loss or injury, **peril** is anything that may possibly cause a loss. It is the reason someone takes out insurance. People buy insurance against a wide range of perils, including fire, windstorms, explosions, robbery, and accidents. **Hazard** is anything that increases the likelihood of loss through peril. For example, defective electrical wiring in a house is a hazard that increases the chance that a fire will start.

Individuals and businesses can insure property and people against potential loss by purchasing insurance policies. An **insurance policy** is a contract between a person and an insurance company to cover a specific risk. In return for the premium, or price for insurance coverage, the insurance company agrees to protect the policyholder against financial loss in case of an accident or loss that is covered in the policy.

Types of Insurance

There are several types of insurance for consumers. *Life insurance* offers protection for family members after someone dies. *Property insurance* covers damages or losses to your property. **Conversely,** *liability insurance* covers damages that you may have caused accidentally to someone else or to someone's property. *Health insurance* provides money to pay medical bills in case of accident or sickness.

Many businesses offer life and health insurance coverage to their employees. They also carry liability and property insurance to protect their property. Companies carry *workers' compensation insurance* to protect workers who are injured on the job. Workers' compensation insurance is required by the government and paid for by employees. It provides medical and income benefits to employees injured on the job. Job-related illnesses, such as carpal tunnel syndrome, are also covered.

Government Protection The federal government handles protection for some kinds of disasters or risk that private companies cannot cover. For example, lost crops or widespread destruction from floods or tornadoes can be costly. If necessary, the federal government can step in to declare a federal disaster area and provide financial aid. *What are some other ways that government helps people and businesses deal with financial risk?*

Section 33.2

After You Read

Review Key Concepts
1. What are four ways to handle risk?
2. What is the difference between risk retention and risk transfer?
3. Identify some types of insurance.

Academic Skills
4. **English Language Arts** Look at the terms below. Cross out the one that does not belong with the others. Circle the term that could be used as the heading in a list with the others.

   liability   property damage
   bodily injury   safety

5. **English Language Arts** Write a letter to your state's commissioner of insurance asking for information on the minimum automobile insurance requirements for your state. Write a paragraph about the response you receive.

 Go to **connectED.mcgraw-hill.com** to check your answers.

Section 33.1 *Summary*	**Section 33.2** *Summary*
Types of Risk Every person and business risks loss. Risk may be controllable or uncontrollable and insurable or uninsurable. Economic risk includes personal risk, property risk, and liability risk. Human risk caused by human mistakes or dishonesty is a particular problem for businesses. Natural risk caused by the weather can result in financial loss and damage.	*Handling Risk* Risk can be avoided, reduced, retained, or transferred. Individuals and businesses try to avoid and reduce risk whenever they can, but some risk is inevitable. Both businesses and people can transfer risk. Insurance provides a way to transfer risk to an insurance company. Insurance enables a large number of people to share a possible loss.

Vocabulary Review

1. On a sheet of paper, use each of these key terms and academic vocabulary terms in a sentence.

Key Terms

risk
risk management
insurable risk
insurance
uninsurable risk
controllable risk
uncontrollable risk
pure risk

economic risk
human risk
natural risk
premium
peril
hazard
insurance policy

Academic Vocabulary

criteria
minimize
decade
occurrences

retain
mode
undergo
conversely

Review Key Concepts

2. Discuss risk and risk management.

3. Describe different types of risk.

4. Describe four ways that individuals and businesses can handle risk.

5. List types of insurance protection.

6. Some people would rather take their chances than to try to avoid risk. Do you think this is a good or bad approach to risk?

7. What types of anti-shoplifting measures have you observed in stores?

8. Tornadoes, hurricanes, and floods have caused devastating losses in recent years. What do you think can be done to reduce losses from disasters?

9. Explain the difference between "economic risk" and "economic loss."

10. Some people do not take precautions to avoid risk because they think that their insurance company will reimburse them for any losses that they incur. What do you think?

11. How can businesses take precautions against customer dishonesty without offending their honest customers?

12. What advice would you give business owners to make their computer systems safer?

13. What problems can insurance companies face because of natural disasters?

14. Research uninsurable risk. What types of risk are uninsurable? Why? Is there a way to avoid an uninsurable risk? In at least one page, discuss your answer.

15. In at least two paragraphs, discuss some of the safety measures that your school has in place to reduce the risk of loss or injury.

16. Many employees take company property for their personal use. Write a brief e-mail to your teacher about the impact this can have on a business.

17. One way to reduce risk is to increase safety. List guidelines for people to reduce their risk of property loss, injury, or death on the road.

18. Choose a business in your community. Research the risk that this type of business might encounter. Write at least two paragraphs on your findings.

19. An insurance agent helps people to identify the purposes of their insurance plan and develops a program for them. Research the job of insurance agent. Write a report on the qualities that a good insurance agent should have.

Spreadsheet Software

20. Injuries and illnesses in the workplace can result in lost wages, increased medical expenses, and higher workers' compensation payments. Research the number of injuries and illnesses and their sources among U.S. workers. Prepare a spreadsheet and chart summarizing the information you obtain. Use the Internet or reference books in your library to find information.

Should She Return the Check?

21. Imagine that someone broke into your friend Teresa's home and stole her jewelry box. Teresa files a police report as well as an insurance claim for the stolen items. In both reports, she lists several pieces of jewelry as stolen, including a diamond necklace insured for $1,000. In a few days, the insurance company issues her a check for $1,000. The following week, she finds the necklace hidden in a closet. What should she do?

Applying Academics to Business

English Language Arts

22. Work with a group of three or four students to research the different types of vehicle insurance coverage. Create an outline for a short presentation, and give it to the class.

Mathematics

23. You recently purchased a used car for $5,000 with help from a bank that loaned you the money with a 6% simple interest loan. If your insurance costs you $230 quarterly, how much will the insurance and interest cost you in the first year?

CONCEPT **Problem Solving** Before solving a word problem, decide which operations you will use and how they relate to each other.

English Language Arts

24. Make a list of items you would want to have covered by insurance. Write a paragraph discussing why these items are important to you.

Mathematics

25. You are billed for insurance quarterly, or every three months. Your first bill gives you the option of paying the total or a lesser amount every month. If the total quarterly amount is $215 and the optional monthly amount is $79, what is the difference in the amount you would pay if you chose the monthly option?

CONCEPT **Comparing Rates** In a problem such as this, you will need to choose whether to compare the cost on a monthly, quarterly, or yearly basis.

Active Learning

Attitudes About Risk

26. People have different ways of handling risk. Work in teams. Survey at least 10 people in your neighborhood or school about their attitudes toward risk. Which risk do they run each day at home, at school, or at work? What are some ways they avoid or reduce each risk? Compile your findings, and share the results with the class.

Business in the Real World

Sick-Leave Policies

27. Time off from work because of employee illnesses is a huge cost to businesses. Many companies have wellness policies in place to promote good health. Interview a local business owner about his or her sick-leave policy. Ask about the number of sick days each employee is granted. Does the business also offer exercise and fitness programs? Write a report of your findings, and share it with the class.

Real LIFE skills

DEALING WITH UNCONTROLLABLE RISK

28. Suppose you have a retail store that sells imported furniture. Your main supplier is in a country that is undergoing major economic and political changes. These changes are being closely watched by your federal government, which may adjust its trade policies with the country. In one page or more, discuss the types of risk you might encounter and how to address them.

 **Business CAREERS**

FIND YOUR DREAM JOB

29. Locate the Occupational Outlook Handbook Web site. Click on the "OOH Search/A-Z Index" link and enter the job title "insurance underwriter." Then write a one-page report about this type of occupation. Conclude your report with a list of things you could do now to prepare yourself to pursue the occupation.

Role Play

REDUCING RISK FROM HAZARDS IN THE SCHOOL

30. **Situation** You have been asked to present a plan for reducing risk at your school. With three of your classmates, prepare a list of risks and ways to reduce or eliminate them.

Activity As a group, create a presentation for your school administrators on risk: Include your suggestions for reducing or eliminating risks.

Evaluation You will be evaluated on how well you meet the following performance indicators:

- Describe the process your group followed to identify risk in school.
- List the causes of various risks.
- Suggest ways to reduce or eliminate each risk.
- Prepare a written report using presentation software.

Standardized Test Practice

Directions Choose the letter of the best answer. Write the letter for the answer on a separate piece of paper.

1. Which best completes the sentence?

_____ insurance covers damage done to another person's vehicle or property.

A   Collision
B   Property damage liability
C   Bodily injury liability
D   Miscellaneous coverage

 TEST-TAKING TIP When studying for a test, write important ideas, definitions, and formulas on flash cards. Make a tape of your notes. Use these tools to review and prepare for test day.

Chapter 34

Vehicle and Property Insurance

> **Chapter Objectives** After completing this chapter, you will be able to:

▶ **Section 34.1** *Vehicle Insurance*

- **Describe** types of vehicle insurance.
- **Identify** laws that make vehicle insurance protection a necessity.
- **Give** examples of factors that affect the cost of vehicle insurance.

▶ **Section 34.2** *Property Insurance*

- **List** some examples of insurance for real and personal property.
- **Describe** protection provided by homeowners insurance policies.

Ask AN EXPERT

Vehicle and Property Insurance: Risk Management

Q: How do companies protect themselves against risk?

A: A company protects its assets through insurance, so that in the event of an emergency, the insurance, rather than the company, will cover the cost. Depending on the function the company serves, different types of insurance are necessary or at least recommended for risk management and reduction. For example, environmental and pollution liability insurance is a necessity for contractors, wastewater treatment facilities, and the power industry. Other types such as worker's compensation, management liability, and primary casuality insurance are important to numerous companies. Companies must also consider the types of health insurance packages they will provide their employees. Of course, all of these insurance options carry heavy costs, but without them, a company could go under as a result of a single crisis.

Mathematics You are house shopping and are trying to choose between two different neighborhoods. Insurance for the house you looked at in the first neighborhood will cost $2,348, and for the one in the other neighborhood will cost $3,652. Use front-end estimation to make a quick estimate of the difference in these costs.

CONCEPT **Front-End Estimation** Front-end estimation can be used to quickly estimate sums and differences before adding or subtracting. To use this technique, add or subtract just the digits of the two highest place values, and replace the other place values with zero. This will give you an estimate of the solution of a problem.

Chris Ryan/age fotostock

● **Insurance Against Loss** Insurance protects families against loss of their property. **Why do you think it is important to insure your car and your home?**

Vehicle Insurance

Reading Guide

Before You Read

Think about the reasons you would want to buy insurance for your vehicle.

Read to Learn

- Describe types of vehicle insurance.
- Identify laws that make vehicle insurance protection a necessity.
- Give examples of factors that affect the cost of vehicle insurance.

The Main Idea

With so many vehicles on our streets and highways, vehicle insurance is a necessity. Drivers must decide what types of coverage they need and can afford, and they have many decisions to make about their insurance needs.

Key Concepts

- Insuring Your Vehicle
- Laws on Vehicle Insurance
- The Costs of Insurance

Vocabulary

Key Terms

actual cash
  value
depreciation
financial
  responsibility law

compulsory
  insurance law
no-fault insurance
claim
deductible

Academic Vocabulary

You will find these words in your reading and on your tests. Make sure you know their meanings.

issues
quote

exceed
vary

Graphic Organizer

In a figure like the one below, give reasons the following types of protection are important considerations in purchasing vehicle insurance.

Vehicle Insurance Protection	Reasons for Buying Coverage
Bodily Injury Liability	
Property Damage Liability	
Collision	
Medical Payments	
Comprehensive Coverage	
Uninsured/Underinsured Motorists Protection	
Miscellaneous Coverage	

 Go to **connectED.mcgraw-hill.com** to print out this graphic organizer.

Insuring Your Vehicle

Not only does being a safe driver benefit everyone on the road, but having vehicle insurance also provides protection in a number of situations.

There are several ways drivers can reduce the risk of financial losses that result from accidents. One way is to buy insurance, paid protection against losses due to injury or property damage. To get insurance, the driver purchases a policy from an insurance company. The policy explains how much and what kinds of protection he or she has. The company that **issues** the policy is the *insurer,* and the buyer of the policy is the *policyholder.*

Types of Vehicle Insurance

The type and amount of protection you have with an insurance policy depends on how much you are willing to pay. Vehicle insurance offers seven types of protection:

- bodily injury liability coverage
- property damage liability coverage
- collision insurance coverage
- medical payments coverage
- comprehensive coverage
- uninsured/underinsured motorists protection
- miscellaneous coverage

The most basic type of coverage (required by most states) is *liability insurance.* Liability insurance protects vehicle owners from claims of injury or property damage to others in case they are held responsible for an accident. A driver should at least have liability insurance and then add other types of coverage. An insurance agent can help you choose the protection you need.

 **Identify** What are the seven types of vehicle protection?

Bodily Injury Liability Coverage Bodily injury liability insurance covers injuries to someone else. All drivers must have this type of coverage. The policy states the amount of protection in thousands of dollars. One figure applies to injuries to one person, and the second is a total for one accident. For 100/300 bodily injury coverage, the insurer pays up to $100,000 for injuries to one person. For one accident, insurance pays claims up to a total of $300,000. A good rule is to buy as much coverage as you can afford. Once you have basic insurance, it does not cost that much to increase protection.

Figure 34.1 – Vehicle Insurance

Coverage	Limits
Personal Liability (per accident)	$500,000
Medical Expense	$5,000
Uninsured/Underinsured Motorists	$500,000
Comprehensive	$50 deductible
Collision	$500 deductible
Towing	$50
Rental Reimbursement	$26 a day/maximum of $900

Property Damage Liability Coverage Property damage liability insurance covers damage to another person's vehicle or other property caused by the insured. All drivers should have property damage liability insurance. A policy might **quote** all liability limits together. The figure 100/300/50 means the insurer will pay $100,000 for injuries to one person, a total of $300,000 for one accident, and $50,000 for property damage. **Figure 34.1** shows an example of types and amounts of coverage for a policyholder.

Collision Insurance Coverage While property damage liability insurance covers damage to someone else's vehicle, collision insurance covers damage to the policyholder's vehicle. The maximum amount covered is based on the **actual cash value** of the policyholder's vehicle, which is the value of the automobile when it was new minus depreciation. The actual cash value of a vehicle is the amount it is worth used. **Depreciation** is the decline in value of an asset, such as a house, equipment, or a vehicle, because of use.

Medical Payments Coverage Medical payments coverage is also called personal injury protection. It covers injuries to drivers and anyone else in their vehicle.

Comprehensive Coverage Comprehensive insurance covers damage to a policyholder's vehicle caused by things other than an auto accident. It covers losses from falling objects, theft, flood damage, vandalism, and other causes. Comprehensive coverage cannot **exceed** the actual cash value of a policyholder's vehicle.

Uninsured/Underinsured Motorists Protection This coverage protects drivers from people who cause accidents but cannot pay for the damages. With this coverage, anyone riding with you is also protected. It also protects you if you are hit by a vehicle while walking or if you are in an accident caused by a hit-and-run driver. Most states require this coverage.

● **As You Read**

Think about why some states require drivers to buy coverage against people who have little or no vehicle insurance.

Miscellaneous Coverage Drivers can add other types of protection to their policies, such as coverage for a rental car. Vehicle owners must also add insurance to cover someone else who uses their car. People who are required to drive a vehicle for their job can add that vehicle to their policy. Those who ride motorcycles, motor scooters, or snowmobiles need insurance, too. Most policies will not cover damages caused as a result of racing.

Laws on Vehicle Insurance

Vehicle insurance laws **vary** from state to state. All states have some form of financial responsibility law. A **financial responsibility law** requires drivers to pay for any damages or injuries they cause in an accident. Most states also have some form of compulsory insurance law. A **compulsory insurance law** requires drivers to have a minimum amount of car insurance. With **no-fault insurance**, drivers involved in accidents collect damages from their own insurer no matter who is at fault.

Business Case Study

Preparing for a Business Career

This school club develops your work and life skills

If you're looking for an extracurricular activity to prepare for a career in business, check out the Future Business Leaders of America. FBLA, a nonprofit organization formed in 1940, educates and encourages students as they transition from school to the work world. Your school may already have an FBLA club you can join.

FBLA projects are usually advised by local business leaders. You can pursue a leadership role with your school's FBLA and take part in the Business Achievement Awards, a self-directed accelerated learning program. Participating in FBLA activities also gives you a leg up in college and scholarship applications.

FBLA places a high priority on giving back to communities. You can work toward achieving three levels of the Community Service Awards Program: Community (50 hours), Service (200 hours), and Achievement (500 hours). All the while you'll be engaging your community, building a network, and learning valuable skills that will serve you in any career path.

Active Learning

The FBLA is divided into five U.S. regions: Western, Mountain Plains, North Central, Southern, and Eastern, with state chapters in each region. Go online to research your state's FBLA chapter and write a short summary of its functions and events. Summarize the benefits of FBLA membership and how you could get involved in your school and community. Does FBLA appeal to you? Why or why not?

The Costs of Insurance

A **claim** is a request for payment from an insurer for any damages covered by a policy. The more money insurance companies pay in claims, the more they charge for insurance to make up for it.

Insurance Premiums

The premium an insurance company charges a policyholder covers the policyholder for a limited period of time. The amount of a premium depends on characteristics of the driver and the vehicle, different policy provisions, and other factors. At the end of the period, the policy can usually be renewed. The insurance company may cancel a policy or refuse coverage for someone with a record of accidents.

Deductibles

Most collision insurance has a deductible. A **deductible** is an amount in damages a policyholder must pay before the insurance company pays a claim. For example, suppose you get into an accident and it costs $700 to repair the damage to your car. If your deductible is $200, you must pay $200 of the damages, and the insurer will pay the other $500. Deductibles make drivers responsible for small losses. Insurance helps pay for larger losses.

Section 34.1

After You Read

Review Key Concepts

1. Identify seven types of vehicle insurance coverage.
2. List and describe three types of laws that affect vehicle insurance.
3. What factors affect the cost of vehicle insurance?

Academic Skills

4. **Mathematics** Several years ago, Stacy bought a home for $123,000. This year, she insured it for 150% of the purchase price. If the home is destroyed, how much will she receive from her insurance company?

CONCEPT **Percents Greater than 100**
Convert a percent greater than 100 to a decimal in the same way you convert any percent. Multiply the percent by 100 by moving the decimal point two places to the left.

 For math help, go to the Math Appendix.

 Go to **connectED.mcgraw-hill.com** to check your answers.

Property Insurance

Before You Read

Think about the types of coverage that are available for other property, including homes.

Read to Learn

- List some examples of insurance for real and personal property.
- Describe protection provided by homeowners insurance policies.

The Main Idea

Property owners can buy insurance to protect their real property, such as a house or business, and their personal property, such as furniture, jewelry, and equipment. Insurance companies write policies for homeowners, renters, and business owners to protect against many kinds of risk.

Key Concepts

- Insuring Your Property
- Homeowners Policies

Vocabulary

Key Terms

real property
personal property
renters insurance
standard fire policy

extended coverage
homeowners policy
rider
replacement value

Academic Vocabulary

You will find these words in your reading and on your tests. Make sure you know their meanings.

consists   civil
injured   nuclear

Graphic Organizer

In a figure like the one below, give reasons the following types of protection are important considerations in purchasing property insurance.

Property Insurance Protection	Reasons for Buying Coverage
Renters Insurance	
Standard Fire Policy	
Liability Protection	
Additional Living Expenses	
Business Insurance	
Homeowners Policy	

 Go to **connectED.mcgraw-hill.com** to print out this graphic organizer.

Insuring Your Property

Each year property is destroyed by earthquakes, fires, and other disasters. Property is also destroyed or damaged by lesser causes, such as accidents, theft, and vandalism. Property insurance provides protection from financial loss on property.

Types of Property Insurance

The two kinds of property you can insure are real property and personal property. **Real property** is property attached to land, such as a house, business, garage, or other building. **Personal property** consists of possessions that can be moved, such as furniture, jewelry, and electronic equipment. Insurance companies offer different kinds of protection for real and personal property.

✔ **Reading Check** **Contrast** What is the difference between real property and personal property?

Renters Insurance Suppose you live in an apartment. Your possessions inside the apartment are worth about $10,000. The owner of the building will probably have property insurance, but the owner's insurance will not pay for loss or damage to your personal property. Apartment renters can buy **renters insurance**, which covers loss or damage to a renter's personal possessions. Renters insurance covers items such as TVs, large appliances, and furniture. It can also include liability protection in case someone is **injured** in a renter's apartment. The cost of renters insurance depends on the amount of coverage, the type of the building, and the location of the apartment.

Real World

College Bound If your plans include college after high school and you will live off campus, you should consider renters insurance. *What steps do you need to take before getting renters insurance?*

Science/TechTRENDS

Autonomous Underwater Vehicles

Autonomous underwater vehicles or AUVs are unmanned, robotic vehicles used to explore oceans. Around 200 AUVs have been built since the mid-1970s. The main purpose of AUVs is to carry a payload. The type of payload depends on the mission. However, it can include things such as instrumentation to map the sea floor or equipment needed by underwater pipelines. Scientists use cameras in conjunction with AUVs to discover evidence of ancient civilizations on the sea floor.

WebQuest

Locate Web sites where you can research the applications of AUVs. Write a few paragraphs about other underwater vehicles and how they compare with AUVs. Then describe a business start-up idea using AUVs to provide a service.

● **Property Damage** Fires are the number one cause of property damage to homes. **How does property insurance protect homeowners?**

Standard Fire Policy Property owners can buy individual insurance policies to protect themselves against specific types of threats. Fires pose the greatest threat to property. They account for a large share of all property damage in the United States. Many people buy a **standard fire policy** to insure against damage due to fire or lightning. A policyholder can add other types of protection to this basic policy with **extended coverage**.

Liability Protection Liability insurance protects property owners from the costs of injuries to others on their property. It pays for two things: actual damages for which property owners are held liable, such as medical expenses, and legal expenses for the accident in case they are sued.

Coverage for Additional Living Expenses Additional living expenses insurance provides coverage for the cost of renting another place to live if a home is damaged. The amount of coverage might be limited to 10 percent or 20 percent of the coverage on your home. If the coverage on your home is $150,000, additional living expenses insurance may cover only up to $15,000 or $30,000 of your costs while you live somewhere else. The length of time you are covered might also be limited to six months or a year.

Business Insurance Business owners need property insurance just like renters and homeowners. Business owners can get insurance to cover the costs of damage to or loss of property. They can get liability insurance to protect themselves from claims by anyone injured on the premises. It is important for business owners to carry insurance because of the potential loss of income if they have to close for a while.

● **As You Read**

Think about liability protection for a business you may own one day. What other kind of liability protection might you consider other than insurance for injuries of employees or customers?

As You Read

Think about what you might need to prove to your insurance company that you sustained a loss. What types of proof would you need?

Homeowners Policies

Many insurance companies offer a combination policy with essential protection called a homeowners policy. A **homeowners policy** covers damage to property and personal property, additional living expenses if a home is destroyed, and liability protection. Policies are fairly standard in all states and protect against loss from fire, windstorms, explosions, riot or **civil** commotion, and other perils. **Figure 34.2** shows an insurance company's Web page for policyholders to file a claim.

These policies offer four types of protection. Structural protection covers the cost to repair or rebuild the house if it is damaged or destroyed. Most standard policies also cover garages or sheds that are detached from the house. The policies offer protection for personal belongings, such as furniture and clothes. Items such as jewelry and silverware are covered, but usually for a limited amount. Liability protection in homeowners policies protects against costs of injury or property damage to other people. If a home is badly damaged, additional living expenses protection pays the costs to live elsewhere while it is being rebuilt.

Homeowners policies do not cover loss from floods, earthquakes, landslides, acts of war, or **nuclear** hazards. However, riders can be added for them. A **rider** is an addition to a policy that covers specific property or damages. Insurance for natural disasters costs more where they are known to occur regularly.

Amount of Insurance

Insurance companies usually recommend that homeowners insure their home for 80 percent of its market value. Even a large fire or flood does not destroy a building completely. The land and the building's foundation will not be destroyed and will hold their value.

You can also insure property for either its actual cash value or its replacement value. The actual cash value is the value of the property new minus devaluation from use. For example, suppose you bought a home for $100,000, but it has depreciated in value by $20,000. If the home is destroyed by a mudslide, the insurer will pay only $80,000. The **replacement value** is the full cost of repairing or replacing the property, regardless of the depreciation value. In this case, the insurer would give you the full amount to repair or replace the destroyed home. As in any situation that might involve insurance, it is important to remember that without it, you would have to pay the full cost to replace the house, which could be $100,000 or more.

Property insurance has many of the same costs as vehicle insurance. The number of claims insurers pay each year affects the overall cost of insurance. Premiums depend on the amount of coverage and the type of policy needed. The amount of a premium is also determined by specific factors, such as the amount of the deductible and the location of the property. The type of home, the building materials in it, and preventive measures that the property owner takes are also key factors.

Real World

Homeowners Coverage A homeowners policy usually offers basic coverage, which provides protection for a dwelling and personal property. Additional coverage can be added to basic protection. Special coverage can be added for special items, such as jewelry, for up to $500. A homeowner can also buy extra coverage with a rider. The extra cost is usually low. *What are some items that a homeowner might protect with a rider?*

Section 34.2

After You Read

Review Key Concepts

1. In addition to vehicles, what types of property can be insured?
2. What types of coverage are included in homeowners policies?
3. What factors affect the cost of property insurance?

Academic Skills

4. **English Language Arts** Make a list of at least five different types of property insurance. Pair up with another student and discuss what the function of each type of insurance is and who would purchase it.

5. **English Language Arts** In groups of three, discuss and make a list of the things that might lower your homeowners insurance costs. Then make a poster using pictures and graphics from magazines illustrating those concepts.

 Go to **connectED.mcgraw-hill.com** to check your answers.

Section 34.1 *Summary*

Vehicle Insurance Vehicle insurance is a necessity for drivers. Insurance companies offer protection from bodily injury and property damage liability, medical payments, and collision expenses. They also offer comprehensive coverage, uninsured/underinsured motorists coverage, and miscellaneous coverage. All states require drivers to prove their financial responsibility in case of an accident. Vehicle insurance is the best way to demonstrate financial responsibility. The costs of vehicle insurance depend on several factors, including characteristics of the policyholder and the vehicle, and the amount of the deductibles.

Section 34.2 *Summary*

Property Insurance Renters, homeowners, and business owners need property insurance. Many different kinds of property insurance protect both real property and personal property against threats such as earthquakes, fires, floods, and various other disasters. Property owners can buy individual insurance policies to cover specific types of threats. Property insurance protects against loss of property, liability for injuries on the property, and additional living expenses in case a home is damaged or destroyed. A homeowners policy is a standard policy that combines various types of protection into one policy. Homeowners can insure their home for either its actual cash value or its replacement value.

Vocabulary Review

1. On a sheet of paper, use each of these key terms and academic vocabulary terms in a sentence.

Key Terms

actual cash value	personal property
depreciation	renters insurance
financial responsibility law	standard fire policy
compulsory insurance law	extended coverage
no-fault insurance	homeowners policy
claim	rider
deductible	replacement value
real property	

Academic Vocabulary

issues	consists
quote	injured
exceed	civil
vary	nuclear

Review Key Concepts

2. Describe types of vehicle insurance.

3. Identify laws that make vehicle insurance protection a necessity.

4. Give examples of factors that affect the cost of vehicle insurance.

5. List some examples of insurance for real and personal property.

6. Describe protection provided by homeowners insurance policies.

Critical Thinking

7. Why do teens pay more for vehicle insurance than most drivers?

8. Vehicle insurance will not cover a driver in a motorcycle-racing contest. Why do you think this is so?

9. Why can teen drivers be included on an adult's insurance policy?

10. Why would a bank or mortgage company insist that a new home owner buy homeowners insurance?

11. Why is it important for businesses to be able to buy insurance to cover profits that would have been earned if a disaster had not occurred?

12. What do you think is the purpose of a deductible in property insurance?

13. What are some examples of homeowners who should add special riders to their property insurance coverage?

14. Why do you think the number of claims that a property owner has over a period of time affects the cost of insurance and renewal?

Write About It

15. Write two or more paragraphs describing features of vehicles that help to reduce the cost of vehicle insurance.

16. In at least two paragraphs, describe ways that teen drivers can get the best rates for vehicle insurance.

17. Prepare a poster with a list of safe driving rules and a list of safe passenger rules that you can display in your school.

18. Insurance companies recommend that policyholders prepare an inventory of insured items they own and the replacement cost of each item. Make a list of your personal property and replacement costs. Summarize the type of insurance you need.

19. Research business insurance in the library or online. Write a short paper describing the types of insurance available for small-business owners. Include insurance policies related to buildings, vehicles, inventory, employees, and customers.

Technology Applications

Spreadsheet Software

20. Collect data from a family member, a neighbor, or a library or online source about the premiums charged by insurance companies for vehicle coverage. Prepare a spreadsheet that shows the types of coverage and the premium charged for each type. Create a chart that shows the percentage of the total premium for each type of coverage.

Business Ethics

Insurance Reimbursement

21. Imagine that your small business was burglarized, and expensive appliances and merchandise were stolen. The insurance company has asked you for an itemized list of stolen items. Your partner offered to help you "pad" the figures for the inventory. What could be the consequences of this unethical behavior?

Applying Academics to Business

English Language Arts

22. Find two insurance companies that offer renters insurance and are located in different areas. Find out what the insurance costs and what it covers. Make note of how and why the prices might differ. Give a presentation summarizing what you have found.

Mathematics

23. Imagine you are going to buy insurance for the contents of your room. Take an inventory of the items. Make a list or chart categorizing the items under appropriate headings, such as furniture, clothing, electronics, and books. Estimate the total cost to replace each item. Figure a total replacement cost for each category. Make a pie chart showing the relative values of the categories of items.

CONCEPT **Pie Charts** Pie charts are useful for showing how the parts of a whole relate to each other.

English Language Arts

24. Look at the list of terms below. Cross out the one that does not belong with the others. Circle the term that could be used as the heading in a list with the others.

fire
explosion
eleven perils
earthquake
aircraft

Mathematics

25. Eva's insurance agent told her that if she installed an alarm system in her home, she could reduce her annual premium by $\frac{1}{3}$. If Eva pays \$810 now, how much would she pay if she installed the alarm system?

CONCEPT **Inverse Operations**
Multiplication and division are inverse operations. Multiplying one number by another is the same as dividing the first number by the inverse of the second.
$a \times b = a \div \frac{1}{b}$

Active Learning

State Requirements for Vehicle Insurance

26. Research the laws in your state about motor vehicle insurance. Find answers to questions such as: Are drivers required to carry insurance? What type of coverage is required? What are the penalties for drivers who do not carry vehicle insurance? What types of discounts do companies have available for drivers who qualify for discounts?

Business in the Real World

Graduated Driver Licensing Systems

27. Research whether your state has a graduated driver licensing system for teen drivers. Interview several 19- to 23-year-olds and parents about their experience with the program. If your state does not have this system, read about it in the library or online, and interview young adults and parents about their licensing experiences. Summarize the opinions of both groups.

Real LIFE skills

PLANNING FOR THE FUTURE

28. Insurance cannot protect you from life's accidents, but it can help protect you financially. Proper insurance can help to put people back in the position they were in before an accident. The most common types of insurance are health, life, homeowners, and auto insurance. Write an e-mail to a family member or friend discussing the type of insurance that you think is most important.

Business CAREERS

FIND YOUR DREAM JOB

29. Locate the Occupational Outlook Handbook Web site. Click on the "OOH Search/A-Z Index" link and enter the job category "real estate brokers and sales agents." Then write a one-page report about these types of occupations. Conclude your report with a list of things you could do now to prepare yourself to pursue the occupation.

Role Play

THE VALUE OF INSURANCE

30. Situation You have been asked to give a presentation on the value of vehicle insurance. Include information on the kinds of vehicle insurance available and recommendations for coverage for teen drivers.

Activity With a partner, create an outline of information on vehicle insurance for teens for your presentation.

Evaluation You will be evaluated on how well you meet the following performance indicators:

- Identify types of coverage available for vehicles.
- Explain amounts of coverage that teen drivers should consider.
- Prepare a list for recommended insurance coverage for teen drivers.
- Create a written outline of points for your presentation.
- Project your voice and use correct grammar.

Standardized Test Practice

Directions Choose the letter of the best answer. Write the letter for the answer on a separate piece of paper.

1. $\frac{11}{24} - \frac{5}{12} =$

   A $\frac{5}{8}$ C $\frac{1}{4}$

   B $\frac{6}{24}$ D $\frac{1}{24}$

TEST-TAKING TIP Analyze multiple-choice questions very carefully. Note key terms. Use your knowledge and anticipate what the answer should be. Find an answer choice that looks like the one you predict.

Chapter 35

Life and Health Insurance

> **Chapter Objectives** After completing this chapter, you will be able to:

▶ **Section 35.1** *Life Insurance*
- **Identify** ways to protect your family financially.
- **Describe** the different types of life insurance.
- **Discuss** the costs of life insurance.

▶ **Section 35.2** *Health Insurance*
- **Analyze** reasons it is important to protect your health.
- **Determine** ways to pay for various health-care costs.

Ask

AN EXPERT

Life and Health Insurance: Whole Life vs. Term Insurance

Q: How do I evaluate life insurance options?

A: There is one major difference between term and whole life insurance: a term policy is just life coverage. When the insured dies, a term policy pays the face amount of the policy to the beneficiary. Term insurance can be bought for periods of one to 30 years. On the other hand, whole life insurance combines an investment component with a term policy. The investment could be in the form of bonds and money market accounts or stocks. The policy builds cash value against which you can then borrow. Three of the most common types of whole life insurance are traditional, universal, and variable. With both term and whole life insurance, you have the option of locking in the same monthly payment over the life of the policy.

Mathematics You have been offered two different health insurance options. You can pay either $154 a month or $1,600 for the year. What will be your percent savings if you chose the year-long option?

CONCEPT **Change a Decimal to a Percent** A percent is a number that compares a number to 100. Changing a decimal to a percent is easy—just multiply by 100 and add a % sign. You could also move the decimal point two places to the right.

● **Taking Care of Your Family** Life insurance and health insurance are available to help people of all ages take care of their families. **Why do you think life insurance and health insurance are important to your family?**

Blue Jean Images/Alamy

Life Insurance

Reading Guide

● Before You Read

Think about your family's expenses and the main person who makes sure that those expenses are paid.

Read to Learn

- Identify ways to protect your family financially.
- Describe the different types of life insurance.
- Discuss the costs of life insurance.

The Main Idea

Life insurance is a way to protect a family's standard of living after the person who is financially responsible for the family dies. There are several types of life insurance. Some of them also build savings.

Key Concepts

- Protecting Your Family
- Types of Life Insurance
- Costs of Life Insurance

Vocabulary

Key Terms

life insurance
proceeds
beneficiary
cash-value insurance
term insurance

Academic Vocabulary

You will find these words in your reading and on your tests. Make sure you know their meanings.

estate
purpose
survivor
features

Graphic Organizer

In a figure like the one below, list three types of cash-value life insurance in the left column and some notes about each type in the right column.

Life Insurance Type	Notes

 Go to **connectED.mcgraw-hill.com** to print out this graphic organizer.

Protecting Your Family

As You Read

Think about your family's expenses and how they are paid.

People provide for their future by saving money and wisely investing their funds. They provide for their families with investments and **estate** planning. No matter how well they plan, investments and a well-written will may not be enough. Just as vehicle insurance and property insurance protect against losses to property, life insurance and health insurance protect people.

Types of Life Insurance

Life insurance is insurance that is paid to a person or people designated to receive the funds when the insured person dies. The **purpose** of life insurance is to protect the standard of living of the survivors.

Buying life insurance can help you protect the people who depend upon you from financial losses caused by your death. Those people could include a spouse, children, an aging parent, or a business partner. Upon the policyholder's death, the insurance company pays the survivors the value of a life insurance policy, or the **proceeds**. A **beneficiary**, who is a **survivor**, is someone who receives part or all of the proceeds. The person who buys life insurance names one or more beneficiaries for the policy.

There are several types of life insurance to fit different needs. The cost of life insurance varies, depending on the type of coverage and characteristics of the policyholder.

✔ **Reading Check**   **Define** Who is a beneficiary?

?ETHICS in Business

Gambling on Self-Insurance

■ **Critical Reading** Life is full of important decisions. Think about the kinds of decisions that you make as you read the question below.

Insurance contracts are often seen as a form of gambling. The insurance company is gambling that you will not suffer the kind of loss against which you are insured. In return for taking on this risk, the company receives your premium. People who believe health insurance should be mandatory say that when people without health insurance gamble that they will not get sick, society ends up paying the bill.

■ **Decision Making** Do you agree that people should be forced to buy health insurance? Explain your opinion.

● **Life Expectancy** This chart shows life expectancy in the United States. **How many more years may a 15-year-old female expect to live compared to a 15-year-old male? What effect do these figures have on the cost of life insurance?**

Source: *World Health Organization*

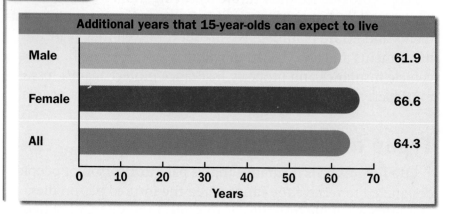

Figure 35.1 — **Length of Life**

Additional years that 15-year-olds can expect to live

	Years
Male	61.9
Female	66.6
All	64.3

Cash-Value Insurance

Cash-value insurance, or permanent insurance, provides both savings and death benefits. Part of the premium pays for death benefits, and the rest builds up cash value like a savings account. The cash value increases throughout the life of the policy. If a policyholder cancels the policy, he or she can receive the amount of the cash value. In an emergency, this person can borrow part or all of the cash value, but must pay interest on it. Policyholders can buy different forms of cash-value insurance.

Whole Life Insurance

With whole life insurance, a premium that stays the same is paid throughout the policyholder's lifetime. The policy remains in force until the insured dies, as long as the premiums are paid. Whole life insurance provides savings during the policyholder's life and pays benefits at death. **Figure 35.1** shows the number of years a person in the United States can expect to live. One of the factors in the cost of life insurance is the number of years a person will pay premiums.

✔ **Reading Check** **Compare** How are cash-value insurance and whole life insurance similar?

Universal Life Insurance

With universal life insurance, a policyholder has more flexibility in premium payments and benefits once the policy has built cash value. Premium payments are applied to three areas: insurance protection, expenses of the insurance company for the policy, and interest-earning investments for the policyholder. The investments earn interest and build savings. A policyholder may be able to increase the death benefit after passing a physical examination or change premium payments. Policyholders purchase universal life insurance if they want flexibility in premium payments and death benefits as their financial situation changes.

Variable Life Insurance

With variable life insurance, the cash-value part of the premium is used for investments such as stocks, bonds, and mutual funds, rather than savings. Like other types of cash-value insurance, the rest of the premium is used for guaranteed death benefits. The cash value is variable because it can increase or decrease in value, depending on how well the investments do. For example, if a portion of the premium is used to invest in stocks and the stocks double in value, the cash value may be doubled.

Policyholders can buy a policy that has **features** of both universal and variable life insurance. Variable-universal life insurance has the investment features of variable insurance as well as premium and death-benefit adjustments of universal life insurance.

Term Insurance

Term insurance covers a person for a specific period of time. The length of the term might be five, 10, or 20 years. Term insurance pays benefits only if the insured dies during the term of the policy. If the insured person lives beyond the term of the policy, the policy has no value. It can be renewed, but usually with a higher premium. Term insurance is sometimes called "pure protection," since it is used only to pay death benefits and does not build cash value. The major advantage of term insurance is its low cost, compared to cash-value insurance.

How does term insurance work? If Gabriel buys a five-year, $10,000 policy, he has protection for five years. If he dies during the term of the policy, his beneficiary will receive $10,000. After five years, his coverage ends. Gabriel can then renew the policy. As he gets older, however, his premium will increase.

Policyholders often have term insurance as a part of group life insurance. An employer or organization might provide term insurance for employees or members. One master insurance policy covers everyone in the group. When a member of the group leaves, the coverage ends for that person. For example, if you work for a company that provides term insurance as a benefit, you lose that coverage if you leave the company.

● **High-Risk Occupations** Some occupations are riskier than others. **Why is insurance for a high-rise construction worker more expensive than for other workers?**

Lloyd Sutton/Alamy

Workers or their companies usually pay less for a group policy than for individual policies. If the company provides coverage as a benefit, the employee usually pays a small part of the cost for the coverage. The employer pays the rest of the cost of the insurance. Some companies may pay the entire cost as a benefit to their employees.

● **As You Read**

Think about the importance of life insurance as people age.

Costs of Life Insurance

As with any type of insurance, the amount of the premium on a life insurance policy depends on the type of policy and the amount of coverage. Term insurance costs less than cash-value insurance. A policy for $100,000 costs more than a policy for $50,000.

Factors such as the policyholder's age, health, and occupation also affect the cost of the premium. Many people have to take a physical before they are sold an insurance policy to ensure that they are in good health. The older a person is, the higher the premium will be because of the likelihood the company will have to pay benefits sooner. Life insurance also costs more for people in dangerous occupations, such as a firefighter or a stunt pilot.

Section 35.1

○ *After You Read*

Review Key Concepts
1. What are the different types of life insurance?
2. How is term insurance different from whole life insurance?
3. What are three factors that affect the cost of life insurance?

Academic Skills
4. **Mathematics** Drew has a health insurance plan with a deductible of $750. The cost Drew paid for a doctor's appointment was $120, and the prescription he was given costs him $90 each time he gets it filled. After how many refills will he reach his deductible?

CONCEPT **The Deductible** The deductible in an insurance policy is the portion of any claim that is not covered by the insurance provider. It is usually a fixed amount that must be "met," or paid by the insured, before the full benefits of a policy can apply. Adding each out-of-pocket expense the insured makes will indicate how close he or she is to reaching the deductible.

For math help, go to the Math Appendix.

 Go to **connectED.mcgraw-hill.com** to check your answers.

Health Insurance

● Before You Read

Think about the steps you can take to protect yourself in case of illness or injury.

Read to Learn

- Analyze reasons it is important to protect your health.
- Determine ways to pay for various health-care costs.

The Main Idea

Health-care costs are often more than the average consumer can afford. Health insurance provides protection in case of illness or accident. Insurance companies and government health insurance programs are sources consumers turn to for help with their medical expenses.

Key Concepts

- Protecting Your Health
- Paying for Health-Care Costs

Vocabulary

Key Terms

coinsurance
copayment
pre-existing condition
health maintenance
  organization (HMO)

preferred provider
  organization (PPO)
Medicare
Medicaid

Academic Vocabulary

You will find these words in your reading and on your tests. Make sure you know their meanings.

medical
mental

percentage
stress

Graphic Organizer

In a figure like the one below, note some types of health insurance.

Types of Health Insurance

 Go to **connectED.mcgraw-hill.com** to print out this graphic organizer.

Protecting Your Health

● **As You Read**

Think about the importance of health insurance.

Many people are concerned about what would happen if they became sick or disabled. Health care for a serious illness or accident is very expensive. Few people have enough savings to pay for **medical** costs on their own. Health insurance provides protection against the costs of illness and accidents.

The *Patient Protection* and *Affordable Care Act* (ACA) of 2010 requires everyone to have health insurance and provides financial subsidies for those who qualify. There is a financial penalty for those who choose to remain uninsured and tax return filings now require proof of health insurance coverage. People can purchase private health insurance policies or compare options for health insurance on an online Health Insurance Marketplace. Because of the ACA, insurance companies can no longer refuse to insure people, cancel a person's health insurance if they become sick, or set certain limits on coverage.

✔ **Reading Check** **Explain** Why is health insurance important?

Business Case Study

What Does Success Mean to You?

A fulfilled life looks different for everyone

Money, power, and status are not all there is to success. Here is how five famous people have defined success in their own lives. Do any of these statements ring true for you?

• "Well-being, wisdom, wonder, and giving."
—Arianna Huffington, media mogul
• "Peace of mind, which is a direct result of self-satisfaction in knowing you did your best to become the best you are capable of becoming." —John Wooden, sports coach
• "Living in accordance with your values."
—Tony Hsieh, online retailer

• "The continued expansion of happiness and the progressive realization of worthy goals."
—Deepak Chopra, writer
• "Liking yourself, liking what you do, and liking how you do it." —Maya Angelou, poet

Active Learning

Working with a partner, brainstorm a list of actions, accomplishments, feelings, possessions, and relationships that individuals might use to define success. Discuss with your partner which matter to you.

Paying for Health-Care Costs

Many health insurance policies have **coinsurance**, a percentage of medical expenses that a policyholder must pay beyond the deductible. For example, you may have to pay 20 percent of the medical expenses for a serious illness. Many policies also require a **copayment**, or a fee paid each time a service is used. You might pay between $5 and $15 every time you visit a doctor or have a prescription filled. Another factor is the number of people covered by a policy, such as a family with children. The more people covered by a policy, the higher the premium.

Some services, such as dental, vision, or **mental** health care, might not be covered by a health insurance policy. In those cases, people must pay themselves or pay for additional insurance. Because of the ACA insurance policies will cover **pre-existing conditions**, serious health conditions diagnosed before a person obtained health insurance.

Major Medical Insurance

Major medical insurance, sometimes called catastrophic insurance, is the most important coverage for a serious illness or accident. It pays for most kinds of care in and out of a hospital, including hospital care, doctors' fees, tests, x-rays, and nursing care. Most policies have a deductible of several hundred dollars. With some plans, the insured also must pay coinsurance.

Online Health Help Health insurers have launched campaigns to get their members healthy. A recent survey of three large insurer sites, WellPoint®, UnitedHealth Group®, and Aetna®, evaluated their services to determine if these sites are helpful. The survey found that the information, health assessments, and personalized interactive tools help people fashion specific plans tailored to their needs. *Why do you think health insurers are making these tools available online?*

Major medical insurance is intended to cover health-care costs not covered by other types of insurance. The insurance company usually pays 75 percent or 80 percent of the costs and the policyholder pays the other 20 percent or 25 percent. For example, suppose your insurance has a $1,000 deductible and a coinsurance payment of 20 percent. If you are hospitalized and your medical bills come to $6,000, you will pay $2,000 ($1,000 deductible plus 20 percent of $5,000).

Hospital Expense Insurance

Hospital expense insurance pays for hospital care for a given period of time. It covers room and board, tests and x-rays, operating room costs, nursing care, and fees for medicine and treatments. Like major medical insurance, it might have a deductible. Some policies set a limit for each specific expense. Others set a maximum amount per day for a certain number of days. Hospital expense is the most popular type of health insurance because hospitalization is very expensive.

 **Explain** Why is hospital expense insurance the most popular type?

Surgical Expense Insurance

Surgical expense insurance pays part of a surgeon's fee for an operation. Most policies set a maximum payment for a particular surgical expense. A policy lists the surgical procedures and the costs allowed. In many cases, major medical insurance picks up where this coverage ends. Surgical expense insurance is usually bought with hospital expense insurance.

Medical Expense Insurance

Medical expense insurance covers the costs of a doctor's care *not* involving surgery. It might cover visits to a doctor's office or a doctor's calls at a hospital. This insurance is usually bought with hospital and surgical expense insurance. Insurance companies often combine all three types into basic health coverage plans.

Group Health Insurance

A group health insurance plan is the least expensive form of health insurance for most people. A company or organization may provide group insurance for its employees or members. The company pays for part or all of the cost for the plan, and employees may be able to add coverage at their own expense.

A **health maintenance organization (HMO)** provides health care at its own health center for a fixed fee per month. With an HMO, policyholders must go to a designated clinic. If they pick a doctor who is not part of the HMO, the patient must pay additional costs. HMO plans **stress** preventive health care to keep down medical costs.

A **preferred provider organization (PPO)** is a group of doctors and hospitals that agree to provide specified medical services to members at prearranged fees. With PPOs, members receive more coverage if they choose health-care providers approved by or affiliated with the plan. PPO health-care providers agree with the insurer to provide health care at reduced rates. While HMOs offer limited referrals to outside specialists, PPOs allow policyholders to choose their own physicians and hospitals within certain limits.

Government Health Insurance

Medicare is the U.S. government's major health insurance program for the elderly. With Medicare, the government partially pays for the health-care costs of people over age 65. **Medicaid** is a federally and state-funded health-care plan for people who are unable to pay for insurance or health care. It provides coverage for the aged, blind, and disabled, and for low-income families who qualify.

Medicare Part D
Medicare coverage Part D was introduced in 2006 to provide prescription drug coverage. Many insurance companies and organizations offer Part D plans. People covered by Medicare pay a deductible, copayment or coinsurance, and a monthly premium for their medical insurance. Some medical services are not covered by Medicare. Plan costs vary. *Do you think it is important for someone with Medicare to also have private medical insurance? Why or why not?*

Section 35.2

After You Read

Review Key Concepts
1. What are the different ways to provide insurance for health-care costs?
2. How might policyholders be required to pay for part of their health-care costs?
3. What types of health-care programs are available?

Academic Skills

4. **English Language Arts** Find and read an article about managed health care. Write a few paragraphs about it. Discuss what it means to consumers in terms of quality and accessibility of medical care.

5. **English Language Arts** In groups of three, identify and define three types of health insurance. Give a brief presentation on the one you feel would be the most beneficial.

 Go to **connectED.mcgraw-hill.com** to check your answers.

Section 35.1 *Summary*

Life Insurance Just as vehicle insurance and property insurance protect against losses to property, life insurance and health insurance protect people. Life insurance provides protection for a policyholder and survivors. Cash-value insurance provides both protection and savings. A policyholder can borrow the cash value of a policy, if needed, and will pay interest on the loan against the policy. With whole life insurance, a premium that stays the same is paid throughout the policyholder's lifetime. Term insurance provides protection but does not build cash value. Since it does not build savings, term insurance is less expensive than cash-value insurance.

Section 35.2 *Summary*

Health Insurance Health-care costs for a serious illness or accident can be financially devastating to a family. Insurance companies provide various types of health insurance. Major medical insurance, sometimes called catastrophic insurance, is the most important coverage for a serious illness or accident. Hospital expense insurance, surgical expense insurance, medical expense insurance, and group health insurance are also available. Most policies offer a combination of protection. A policy may combine major medical, hospital expense, and surgical expense insurance. Federal and state governments also offer health-care insurance through Medicare and Medicaid.

Vocabulary Review

1. On a sheet of paper, use each of these key terms and academic vocabulary terms in a sentence.

Key Terms

life insurance
proceeds
beneficiary
cash-value insurance
term insurance
coinsurance
copayment

pre-existing condition
health maintenance
   organization (HMO)
preferred provider
   organization (PPO)
Medicare
Medicaid

Academic Vocabulary

estate   medical
purpose   mental
survivor   percentage
features   stress

Review Key Concepts

2. Identify ways to protect your family financially.

3. Describe the different types of life insurance.

4. Discuss the costs of life insurance.

5. Analyze reasons it is important to protect your health.

6. Determine ways to pay for various health-care costs.

Critical Thinking

7. Describe a person for whom you think life insurance is not necessary.

8. Why are companies willing to provide health insurance plans for employees?

9. Should people consider buying some life insurance while they are young? Explain your answer.

10. Why do you think insurance companies offer a wide variety of life insurance policies?

11. Which type of health insurance do you think is most important? Why?

12. Is it fair that employees who hold term life insurance lose that coverage when they leave their company? Explain your answer.

13. Should the government provide health coverage for retired people? Why or why not?

14. If someone cannot afford all types of insurance, in what order of importance would you put the different types? Explain your thoughts.

Write About It

15. If you applied for life insurance, who would you list as beneficiaries? Explain your choices in at least two paragraphs.

16. Suppose the parents of two small children would like to buy life insurance for themselves. In at least two paragraphs, outline a plan for life insurance that you think would be suitable for them.

17. You are a health columnist for a newsletter aimed at people in the entertainment industry, such as dancers, actors, and writers. Write an article explaining why these artists should have adequate disability insurance coverage.

18. How might your lifestyle affect your life expectancy? In at least one page, discuss how your choices could affect your insurance rates.

19. Research the idea of national health-care coverage. Include information about the political, social, and economic issues involved. Then write a two-page paper on your findings.

Technology Applications

Presentation Software

20. Suppose your family would like to purchase health insurance. Research at least three insurance companies. Use the Internet, or contact the companies directly to obtain quotes. Find out if a deductible, copayment, and/or coinsurance are required. What are their policies regarding pre-existing conditions? Based on your findings, which (if any) plan would you choose? Prepare a slideshow of your information for the class.

Business Ethics

Should One Price Fit All?

21. Suppose you visit your doctor. In the waiting room, you overhear a conversation between an elderly patient and a medical assistant. The assistant tells the patient that his insurance will not cover an emergency procedure that cost $3,000. The patient says he cannot pay the whole amount. After discussing the situation with the doctor, the patient is told that the cost will be lowered to $1,500. With a partner, discuss the ethical issues involved.

Applying Academics to Business

English Language Arts

22. Look at the list of terms below. Cross out the one that does not belong with the others. Circle the term that could be used as the heading in a list with the others.

    government health insurance
    Medicaid
    health maintenance organization
    Medicare

Mathematics

23. Amber lost her job, but she could continue her health insurance through COBRA. Her monthly cost for the plan with COBRA is 23% higher than an insurance plan she could purchase herself. If the plan she could purchase on her own would cost $163 a month, what would the COBRA plan cost her?

    CONCEPT **Percents Greater than 100** Percents greater than 100 represent values greater than 1. If something is 23 percent greater than the original value, it equals 100 percent of the original value plus 23 percent of that value. Percents can be converted to decimals, as follows: $1.00 + 0.23 = 1.23$.

English Language Arts

24. In groups of four, choose one of the following insurance topics: cash-value life, term life, government health, or group health insurance. Research the topic and prepare a short presentation.

Mathematics

25. Jenn's medical bills total $11,000. Her insurance policy states that the policyholder has a $100 deductible and the insurance company will pay 75% of the remaining balance. Write and solve an equation to find how much of the $11,000 Jenn will have to pay.

    CONCEPT **Solving Equations** To solve an equation, use the correct order of operations. First, simplify within the parentheses, and then evaluate any exponents. Multiply and divide from left to right, then add and subtract from left to right.

Active Learning

Insurance Company Investments

26. Go to a library or check the Internet for information about how insurance companies invest the premiums they collect from policyholders. Prepare a chart or poster on your findings, and share it with your class.

Business in the Real World

Health-Care Plans

27. Interview someone you know who has health care through an HMO or a PPO. Ask for his or her opinion on the advantages and disadvantages of the plan. Share your findings through an oral report to your class.

Real LIFE skills

CONNECT WITH ECONOMICS AND LAW

28. Many companies that once sold just life insurance have "reinvented" themselves as financial services companies. Some promote themselves as "one-stop shops" for all your financial service needs. Access the Web site of your state's insurance regulatory agency. Find out what requirements insurance agents must meet to be able to sell other financial products, such as mutual funds. What are the pros and cons of buying financial products from an insurance company versus a stockbroker?

 **Business CAREERS**

FIND YOUR DREAM JOB

29. Locate the Occupational Outlook Handbook Web site. Click on the "OOH Search/A-Z Index" link and enter the job title "actuaries." Then write a one-page report about this type of occupation. Conclude your report with a list of things you could do now to prepare yourself to pursue the occupation.

Role Play

RESEARCHING LIFE INSURANCE

30. Situation You have been asked to prepare a presentation on various types of life insurance, such as term, whole life, and variable life insurance. Research different types of insurance, and present your ideas to your classmates.

Activity Prepare an outline of your presentation on the different types of life insurance.

Evaluation You will be evaluated on how well you meet the following performance indicators:

- Prepare a written outline of your presentation.
- Contrast the types of life insurance you have researched.
- Describe the type of person for which each type might be suitable.
- Discuss the factors that a consumer should consider when choosing among types of life insurance.
- Answer questions about life insurance.
- Project your voice and use correct grammar.

Standardized Test Practice

Directions Choose the letter of the best answer. Write the letter for the answer on a separate piece of paper.

1. $2\frac{4}{9} \times \frac{3}{16} =$

A $\frac{33}{67}$

C $\frac{1}{2}$

B $1\frac{3}{8}$

D $\frac{11}{24}$

 TEST-TAKING TIP If you are allowed to use a calculator at a testing site, make sure it is one that is authorized. Turn off other electronic devices, such as phones, pagers, and alarms.

JoAnne Jonathan

President and CEO, Advanced Physical Therapy, P.C.

Advanced Physical Therapy offers physical therapy services. The Indianapolis-based company's services are available at 10 outpatient clinics and three work conditioning centers.

Q & A

Describe your job responsibilities.

JoAnne: I meet with department heads throughout the company to include finance, marketing, billing, and regional directors of clinics. I review past business and future trends, solve current problems and create new opportunities for business growth.

What skills are most important in your business?

JoAnne: People like doing business with people they like. Being a problem solver is also important so you can anticipate problems with corrective action.

What is your key to success?

JoAnne: My success comes from the people I've hired and trained. Some of them have been with us for 17 or more years. They do a good job, and we provide ongoing training for all of the staff. Our goal is to make you feel better and to try to have fun while doing it, for both the patients and the staff.

What skills did you learn in high school that helped you become a successful entrepreneur?

JoAnne: I learned something from just about every subject, but especially math and statistics. School teaches you how to figure out problems. It also gives you discipline—you learn how to learn. I apply that to launching and running a business. You also learn communication at school, whether it's reading and writing skills that I use in understanding contracts or public speaking, doing conference calls, or interviews.

What advice would you give students interested in starting a business?

JoAnne: Read books and journals, take classes, and talk to mentors. Have financial backing for worse-case scenarios. Hire the best-qualified people. Partnerships may have their advantages, yet I chose to start my company alone. Prepare to put in a lot of time building, refining, and working in the business. You have to love and have a passion for your business. Maintain honesty and integrity in all that you do.

Critical Thinking
What might be the benefits and disadvantages to starting a company alone versus building a partnership?

Some Qualifications Needed to Own a Physical Therapy Clinic

Academic Skills and Abilities

Biology; chemistry; interpersonal skills; general business management skills; verbal and written communication skills; multitasking, organizing, and planning skills

Academic Skills Required to Complete Tasks at Advanced Physical Therapy			
Tasks	Math	Science	English Language Arts
Hold meetings			◆
Assign duties			◆
Develop patient treatment plans		◆	◆
Assess patient progress		◆	
Customer service			◆
Schedule employees	◆		◆
Order supplies and equipment	◆		◆
Analyze financials	◆		◆

Education and Training

All states require physical therapists to pass a licensure exam before they can practice, after graduating from an accredited physical therapist educational program.

Career Path

Physical therapists are expected to continue their professional development by participating in continuing education courses and workshops. In fact, a number of states require continuing education as a condition of maintaining licensure.

Understanding Risk

You will most likely own a vehicle someday. Your vehicle will be a valuable piece of property that you will want to insure. Vehicle insurance will help cover costs of the vehicle in case of an accident.

Thematic Project Assignment

In this project you will make a chart that compares vehicle insurance policies.

Step 1 Brainstorm Skills You Need to Complete This Activity

Your success in making a chart that compares vehicle insurance policies will depend on your skills. Preview the activity, then brainstorm a list of the skills you will need to use to complete the activity and describe how you will use them. Skills you might use include:

Academic Skills   reading and writing

Basic Skills   speaking, listening, and thinking

Technology Skills   word processing, keyboarding, and graphic software

 SKILLS PREVIEW Go to connectED.mcgraw-hill.com to download a graphic organizer you can use to brainstorm the skills you will use to complete the project.

Step 2 Think About the Type of Vehicle You Want

Think about the type of vehicle you dream of having. You work hard for the money to pay for the vehicle, so you want to make sure you have insurance to cover the vehicle in case it is stolen or damaged in an accident.

Step 3 Build Background Knowledge

Preview information on comparing vehicle insurance policies.

Insurance *Is a* **Must** *for* **Car Owners**

Are you thinking of buying your first car? Before you sign your name on the dotted line, make sure you have already arranged for insurance coverage. An insurance agent can help you choose which kind of insurance is best for you. Check with more than one agent to make sure you are getting the right coverage for the best price.

What type of insurance should you consider? Your agent will know the minimum requirements for your state. Ask an adult to help you decide what you need to protect your property and yourself, your passengers, and other people in case you have an accident.

Step 4 Connect with Your Community

Interview two adults in your community. Ask them about the type of vehicle insurance coverage they have. Ask them who their agent is, the name of the company that insures them, and why they chose this company. Think about how important insurance is to help you manage risk.

Step 5 Research Vehicle Insurance

Use library and Internet resources, phone calls, or personal interviews to research vehicle insurance. Use the project checklist as a guide to your research. Keep records of your sources of information.

Step 6 Develop a Chart Comparing Vehicle Insurance

Use word-processing and spreadsheet software to develop a chart that compares vehicle insurance that includes all of the information described in the project checklist.

Developing a Chart Comparing Vehicle Insurance

✔ Make a list of five different vehicle insurance companies. Vehicle insurance may be listed as car insurance. Use the Internet, phone book, or personal interviews to find the names of insurance companies.

✔ Choose a vehicle that you would like to own someday.

✔ Use a computer spreadsheet program to keep track of the information you are going to gather.

✔ Use the Internet, or call or visit five insurance agents or insurance companies to ask what coverage is recommended for the vehicle of your choice. Also, ask the cost of each type of coverage. Take detailed notes. Ask about the following coverage: bodily injury liability, property damage liability, collision coverage, medical payments coverage, comprehensive coverage, uninsured and underinsured motorists protection, and miscellaneous coverage. Use this information as the base for comparisons with other insurance companies.

✔ Make a chart that shows the type of vehicle, the coverage, and the cost of the coverage for the five different insurance companies. Also, add a column that shows any recommendations for different coverage and the cost of that coverage.

Self Connections

✔ Describe the results of your research with the adults you interviewed.

✔ Describe the type of vehicle insurance they have.

✔ Explain what the investigation and its results mean to you.

Step 7 Evaluate Your Presentation

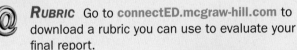

Rubric Go to connectED.mcgraw-hill.com to download a rubric you can use to evaluate your final report.

Number and Operations

▶ **Understand numbers, ways of representing numbers, relationships among numbers, and number systems**

Fraction, Decimal, and Percent

A percent is a ratio that compares a number to 100. To write a percent as a fraction, drop the percent sign, and use the number as the numerator in a fraction with a denominator of 100. Simplify, if possible. For example, $76\% = \frac{76}{100}$, or $\frac{19}{25}$. To write a fraction as a percent, convert it to an equivalent fraction with a denominator of 100. For example, $\frac{3}{4} = \frac{75}{100}$, or 75%. A fraction can be expressed as a percent by first converting the fraction to a decimal (divide the numerator by the denominator) and then converting the decimal to a percent by moving the decimal point two places to the right.

Comparing Numbers on a Number Line

In order to compare and understand the relationship between real numbers in various forms, it is helpful to use a number line. The zero point on a number line is called the origin; the points to the left of the origin are negative, and those to the right are positive. The number line below shows how numbers in fraction, decimal, percent, and integer form can be compared.

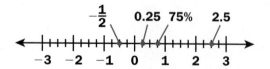

Percents Greater Than 100 and Less Than 1

Percents greater than 100% represent values greater than 1. For example, if the weight of an object is 250% of another, it is 2.5, or $2\frac{1}{2}$, times the weight.

Percents less than 1 represent values less than $\frac{1}{100}$. In other words, 0.1% is one tenth of one percent, which can also be represented in decimal form as 0.001, or in fraction form as $\frac{1}{1,000}$. Similarly, 0.01% is one hundredth of one percent or 0.0001 or $\frac{1}{10,000}$.

Ratio, Rate, and Proportion

A ratio is a comparison of two numbers using division. If a basketball player makes 8 out of 10 free throws, the ratio is written as 8 to 10, 8:10, or $\frac{8}{10}$. Ratios are usually written in simplest form. In simplest form, the ratio "8 out of 10" is 4 to 5, 4:5, or $\frac{4}{5}$. A rate is a ratio of two measurements having different kinds of units—cups per gallon, or miles per hour, for example. When a rate is simplified so that it has a denominator of 1, it is called a unit rate. An example of a unit rate is 9 miles per hour. A proportion is an equation stating that two ratios are equal. $\frac{3}{18} = \frac{13}{78}$ is an example of a proportion. The cross products of a proportion are also equal. $\frac{3}{18} = \frac{13}{78}$ and $3 \times 78 = 18 \times 13$.

Representing Large and Small Numbers

In order to represent large and small numbers, it is important to understand the number system. Our number system is based on 10, and the value of each place is 10 times the value of the place to its right.

The value of a digit is the product of a digit and its place value. For instance, in the number 6,400, the 6 has a value of six thousands and the 4 has a value of four hundreds. A place value chart can help you read numbers. In the chart, each group of three digits is called a period. Commas separate the periods: the ones period, the thousands period, the millions period, and so on. Values to the right of the ones period are decimals. By understanding place value you can write very large numbers like 5 billion and more, and very small numbers that are less than 1, such as one tenth.

Scientific Notation
When dealing with very large numbers like 1,500,000, or very small numbers like 0.000015, it is helpful to keep track of their value by writing the numbers in scientific notation. Powers of 10 with positive exponents are used with a decimal between 1 and 10 to express large numbers. The exponent represents the number of places the decimal point is moved to the right. So, 528,000 is written in scientific notation as 5.28×10^5. Powers of 10 with negative exponents are used with a decimal between 1 and 10 to express small numbers. The exponent represents the number of places the decimal point is moved to the left. The number 0.00047 is expressed as 4.7×10^{-4}.

Factor, Multiple, and Prime Factorization
Two or more numbers that are multiplied to form a product are called factors. Divisibility rules can be used to determine whether 2, 3, 4, 5, 6, 8, 9, or 10 are factors of a given number. Multiples are the products of a given number and various integers.

For example, 8 is a multiple of 4 because $4 \times 2 = 8$. A prime number is a whole number that has exactly two factors: 1 and itself. A composite number is a whole number that has more than two factors. Zero and 1 are neither prime nor composite. A composite number can be expressed as the product of its prime factors. The prime factorization of 40 is $2 \times 2 \times 2 \times 5$, or $2^3 \times 5$. The numbers 2 and 5 are prime numbers.

Integers
A negative number is a number less than zero. Negative numbers like −8, positive numbers like +6, and zero are members of the set of integers. Integers can be represented as points on a number line. A set of integers can be written {..., −3, −2, −1, 0, 1, 2, 3, ...} where ... means "continues indefinitely."

Real, Rational, and Irrational Numbers
The real number system is made up of the sets of rational and irrational numbers. Rational numbers are numbers that can be written in the form a/b where a and b are integers and $b \neq 0$. Examples are 0.45, $\frac{1}{2}$, and $\sqrt{36}$. Irrational numbers are non-repeating, non-terminating decimals. Examples are $\sqrt{71}$, π, and 0.020020002....

Complex and Imaginary Numbers
A complex number is a mathematical expression with a real number element and an imaginary number element. Imaginary numbers are multiples of i, the "imaginary" square root of −1. Complex numbers are represented by $a + bi$, where a and b are real numbers and i represents the imaginary element. When a quadratic equation

does not have a real number solution, the solution can be represented by a complex number. Like real numbers, complex numbers can be added, subtracted, multiplied, and divided.

Vectors and Matrices

A matrix is a set of numbers or elements arranged in rows and columns to form a rectangle. The number of rows is represented by m and the number of columns is represented by n. To describe the number of rows and columns in a matrix, list the number of rows first using the format $m \times n$. Matrix A below is a 3×3 matrix because it has 3 rows and 3 columns. To name an element of a matrix, the letter i is used to denote the row and j is used to denote the column, and the element is labeled in the form $a_{i,j}$. In matrix A below, $a_{3,2}$ is 4.

$$\text{Matrix A} = \begin{pmatrix} 1 & 3 & 5 \\ 0 & 6 & 8 \\ 3 & 4 & 5 \end{pmatrix}$$

A vector is a matrix with only one column or row of elements. A transposed column vector, or a column vector turned on its side, is a row vector. In the example below, row vector b' is the transpose of column vector b.

$$b = \begin{pmatrix} 1 \\ 2 \\ 3 \\ 4 \end{pmatrix}$$

$$b' = \begin{pmatrix} 1 & 2 & 3 & 4 \end{pmatrix}$$

▶ *Understand meanings of operations and how they relate to one another*

Properties of Addition and Multiplication
Properties are statements that are true for any numbers. For example, $3 + 8$ is the same as $8 + 3$ because each expression equals 11. This illustrates the Commutative Property of Addition. Likewise, $3 \times 8 = 8 \times 3$ illustrates the Commutative Property of Multiplication.

When evaluating expressions, it is often helpful to group or associate the numbers. The Associative Property says that the way in which numbers are grouped when added or multiplied does not change the sum or product. The following properties are also true:

• **Additive Identity Property:** When 0 is added to any number, the sum is the number.

• **Multiplicative Identity Property:** When any number is multiplied by 1, the product is the number.

• **Multiplicative Property of Zero:** When any number is multiplied by 0, the product is 0.

Rational Numbers
A number that can be written as a fraction is called a rational number. Terminating and repeating decimals are rational numbers because both can be written as fractions.

Decimals that are neither terminating nor repeating are called irrational numbers because they cannot be written as fractions. Terminating decimals can be converted to fractions by placing the number (without the decimal point) in the numerator. Count the number of places to the right of the decimal point, and in the denominator, place a 1 followed by a number of zeros equal to the number of places that you counted. The fraction can then be reduced to simplest form.

Writing a Fraction as a Decimal

Any fraction $\frac{a}{b}$, where $b \neq 0$, can be written as a decimal by dividing the numerator by the denominator. So, $\frac{a}{b} = a \div b$. If the division ends, or terminates, when the remainder is zero, the decimal is a terminating decimal. Not all fractions can be written as terminating decimals. Some have a repeating decimal. A bar indicates that the decimal repeats forever. For example, the fraction $\frac{4}{9}$ can be converted to a repeating decimal, $0.\overline{4}$

Adding and Subtracting Like Fractions

Fractions with the same denominator are called like fractions. To add like fractions, add the numerators and write the sum over the denominator. To add mixed numbers with like fractions, add the whole numbers and fractions separately, adding the numerators of the fractions, then simplifying if necessary. The rule for subtracting fractions with like denominators is similar to the rule for adding. The numerators can be subtracted and the difference written over the denominator. Mixed numbers are written as improper fractions before subtracting. These same rules apply to adding or subtracting like algebraic fractions. A fraction that contains one or more variables in the numerator or denominator is called an algebraic fraction.

Adding and Subtracting Unlike Fractions

Fractions with different denominators are called unlike fractions. The least common multiple of the denominators is used to rename the fractions with a common denominator. After a common denominator is found, the numerators can then be added or subtracted. To add mixed numbers with unlike fractions, rename the mixed numbers as improper fractions. Then find a common denominator, add the numerators, and simplify the answer.

Multiplying Rational Numbers

To multiply fractions, multiply the numerators and multiply the denominators. If the numerators and denominators have common factors, they can be simplified before multiplication. If the fractions have different signs, then the product will be negative. Mixed numbers can be multiplied in the same manner, after first renaming them as improper fractions. Algebraic fractions may be multiplied using the same method described above.

Dividing Rational Numbers

To divide a number by a rational number (a fraction, for example), multiply the first number by the multiplicative inverse of the second. Two numbers whose product is 1 are called multiplicative inverses, or reciprocals. $\frac{7}{4} \times \frac{4}{7} = 1$. When dividing by a mixed number, first rename it as an improper fraction, and then multiply by its multiplicative inverse. This process of multiplying by a number's reciprocal can also be used when dividing algebraic fractions.

Adding Integers

To add integers with the same sign, add their absolute values. The sum then takes the same sign as the addends. The equation $-5 + (-2) = -7$ is an example of adding two integers with the same sign. To add integers with different signs, subtract their absolute values. The sum takes the same sign as the addend with the greater absolute value.

Subtracting Integers

The rules for adding integers are extended to the subtraction of integers. To subtract an integer, add its additive inverse. For example, to find the difference $2 - 5$, add the additive inverse of 5 to 2: $2 + (-5) = -3$. The rule for subtracting integers can be used to solve real-world problems and to evaluate algebraic expressions.

Additive Inverse Property

Two numbers with the same absolute value but different signs are called opposites. For example, −4 and 4 are opposites. An integer and its opposite are also called additive inverses. The Additive Inverse Property says that the sum of any number and its additive inverse is zero. The Commutative, Associative, and Identity Properties also apply to integers. These properties help when adding more than two integers.

Absolute Value

In mathematics, when two integers on a number line are on opposite sides of zero, and they are the same distance from zero, they have the same absolute value. The symbol for absolute value is two vertical bars on either side of the number. For example, $|-5| = 5$.

Multiplying Integers

Since multiplication is repeated addition, $3(-7)$ means that −7 is used as an addend 3 times. By the Commutative Property of Multiplication, $3(-7) = -7(3)$. The product of two integers with different signs is always negative. The product of two integers with the same sign is always positive.

Dividing Integers

The quotient of two integers can be found by dividing the numbers using their absolute values. The quotient of two integers with the same sign is positive, and the quotient of two integers with a different sign is negative. $-12 \div (-4) = 3$ and $12 \div (-4) = -3$. The division of integers is used in statistics to find the average, or mean, of a set of data. When finding the mean of a set of numbers, find the sum of the numbers, and then divide by the number in the set.

Adding and Multiplying Vectors and Matrices

In order to add two matrices together, they must have the same number of rows and columns. In matrix addition, the corresponding elements are added to each other. In other words $(a + b)_{ij} = a_{ij} + b_{ij}$. For example,

$$\begin{pmatrix} 1 & 2 \\ 2 & 1 \end{pmatrix} + \begin{pmatrix} 3 & 6 \\ 0 & 1 \end{pmatrix} = \begin{pmatrix} 1+3 & 2+6 \\ 2+0 & 1+1 \end{pmatrix} = \begin{pmatrix} 4 & 8 \\ 2 & 2 \end{pmatrix}$$

Matrix multiplication requires that the number of elements in each row in the first matrix is equal to the number of elements in each column in the second. The elements of the first row of the first matrix are multiplied by the corresponding elements of the first column of the second matrix and then added together to get the first element of the product matrix. To get the second element, the elements in the first row of the first matrix are multiplied by the corresponding elements in the second column of the second matrix then added, and so on, until every row of the first matrix is multiplied by every column of the second. See the example below.

$$\begin{pmatrix} 1 & 2 \\ 3 & 4 \end{pmatrix} \times \begin{pmatrix} 3 & 6 \\ 0 & 1 \end{pmatrix} = \begin{pmatrix} (1\times3)+(2\times0) & (1\times6)+(2\times1) \\ (3\times3)+(4\times0) & (3\times6)+(4\times1) \end{pmatrix} = \begin{pmatrix} 3 & 8 \\ 9 & 22 \end{pmatrix}$$

Vector addition and multiplication are performed in the same way, but there is only one column and one row.

Permutations and Combinations

Permutations and combinations are used to determine the number of possible outcomes in different situations. An arrangement, listing, or pattern in which order is important is called a permutation. The symbol P(6, 3) represents the number of permutations of 6 things taken 3 at a time. For P(6, 3), there are $6 \times 5 \times 4$ or 120 possible outcomes. An arrangement or listing where order is not important is called a combination. The symbol C(10, 5) represents the number of combinations of 10 things taken 5 at a time. For C(10, 5), there are $(10 \times 9 \times 8 \times 7 \times 6) \div (5 \times 4 \times 3 \times 2 \times 1)$ or 252 possible outcomes.

Powers and Exponents

An expression such as $3 \times 3 \times 3 \times 3$ can be written as a power. A power has two parts, a base and an exponent. $3 \times 3 \times 3 \times 3 = 3^4$. The base is the number that is multiplied (3). The exponent tells how many times the base is used as a factor (4 times). Numbers and variables can be written using exponents. For example, $8 \times 8 \times 8 \times m \times m \times m \times m \times m$ can be expressed $8^3 m^5$. Exponents also can be used with place value to express numbers in expanded form. Using this method, 1,462 can be written as $(1 \times 10^3) + (4 \times 10^2) + (6 \times 10^1) + (2 \times 10^0)$.

Squares and Square Roots

The square root of a number is one of two equal factors of a number. Every positive number has both a positive and a negative square root. For example, since $8 \times 8 = 64$, 8 is a square root of 64. Since $(-8) \times (-8) = 64$, -8 is also a square root of 64. The notation $\sqrt{}$ indicates the positive square root, $-\sqrt{}$ indicates the negative square root, and $\pm\sqrt{}$ indicates both square roots. For example, $\sqrt{81} = 9$, $-\sqrt{49} = -7$, and $\pm\sqrt{4} = \pm2$. The square root of a negative number is an imaginary number because any two factors of a negative number must have different signs, and are therefore not equivalent.

Logarithm

A logarithm is the inverse of exponentiation. The logarithm of a number x in base b is equal to the number n. Therefore, $b^n = x$ and $\log_b x = n$. For example, $\log_4(64) = 3$ because $4^3 = 64$.

The most commonly used bases for logarithms are 10, the common logarithm; 2, the binary logarithm; and the constant e, the natural logarithm (also called $ln(x)$ instead of $\log_e(x)$). Below is a list of some of the rules of logarithms that are important to understand if you are going to use them.

$$\log_b(xy) = \log_b(x) + \log_b(y)$$
$$\log_b(x/y) = \log_b(x) - \log_b(y)$$
$$\log_b(1/x) = -\log_b(x)$$
$$\log_b(x)y = y\log_b(x)$$

▶ **Compute fluently and make reasonable estimates**

Estimation by Rounding

When rounding numbers, look at the digit to the right of the place to which you are rounding. If the digit is 5 or greater, round up. If it is less than 5, round down. For example, to round 65,137 to the nearest hundred, look at the number in the tens place. Since 3 is less than 5, round down to 65,100. To round the same number to the nearest ten thousandth, look at the number in the thousandths place. Since it is 5, round up to 70,000.

Finding Equivalent Ratios

Equivalent ratios have the same meaning. Just like finding equivalent fractions, to find an equivalent ratio, multiply or divide both sides by the same number. For example, you can multiply 7 by both sides of the ratio 6:8 to get 42:56. Instead, you can also divide both sides of the same ratio by 2 to get 3:4. Find the simplest form of a ratio by dividing to find equivalent ratios until you can't go any further without going into decimals. So, 160:240 in simplest form is 2:3. To write a ratio in the form 1:n, divide both sides by the left-hand number. In other words, to change 8:20 to 1:n, divide both sides by 8 to get 1:2.5.

Front-End Estimation

Front-end estimation can be used to quickly estimate sums and differences before adding or subtracting. To use this technique, add or subtract just the digits of the two highest place values, and replace the other place values with zero. This will give you an estimation of the solution of a problem. For example, 93,471 − 22,825 can be changed to 93,000 − 22,000 or 71,000. This estimate can be compared to your final answer to judge its correctness.

Judging Reasonableness

When solving an equation, it is important to check your work by considering how reasonable your answer is. For example, consider the equation $9\frac{3}{4} \times 4\frac{1}{3}$. Since $9\frac{3}{4}$ is between 9 and 10 and $4\frac{1}{3}$ is between 4 and 5, only values that are between 9×4 or 36 and 10×5 or 50 will be reasonable. You can also use front-end estimation, or you can round and estimate a reasonable answer. In the equation 73×25, you can round and solve to estimate a reasonable answer to be near 70×30 or 2,100.

Algebra

▶ *Understand patterns, relations, and functions*

Relation

A relation is a generalization comparing sets of ordered pairs for an equation or inequality such as $x = y + 1$ or $x > y$. The first element in each pair, the x values, forms the domain. The second element in each pair, the y values, forms the range.

Function

A function is a special relation in which each member of the domain is paired with exactly one member in the range. Functions may be represented using ordered pairs, tables, or graphs. One way to determine whether a relation is a function is to use the vertical line test. Using an object to represent a vertical line, move the object from left to right across the graph. If, for each value of x in the domain, the object passes through no more than one point on the graph, then the graph represents a function.

Linear and Nonlinear Functions

Linear functions have graphs that are straight lines. These graphs represent constant rates of change. In other words, the slope between any two pairs of points on the graph is the same. Nonlinear functions do not have constant rates of change. The slope changes along these graphs. Therefore, the graphs of nonlinear functions are *not* straight lines. Graphs of curves represent nonlinear functions. The equation for a linear function can be written in the form $y = mx + b$, where m represents the constant rate of change, or the slope. Therefore, you can determine whether a function is linear by looking at the equation. For example, the equation $y = \frac{3}{x}$ is nonlinear because x is in the denominator and the equation cannot be written in the form $y = mx + b$. A nonlinear function does not increase or decrease at a constant rate. You can check this by using a table and finding the increase or decrease in y for each regular increase in x. For example, if for each increase in x by 2, y does not increase or decrease the same amount each time, the function is nonlinear.

Linear Equations in Two Variables

In a linear equation with two variables, such as $y = x - 3$, the variables appear in separate terms and neither variable contains an exponent other than 1. The graphs of all linear equations are straight lines. All points on a line are solutions of the equation that is graphed.

Quadratic and Cubic Functions

A quadratic function is a polynomial equation of the second degree, generally expressed as $ax^2 + bx + c = 0$, where a, b, and c are real numbers and a is not equal to zero. Similarly, a cubic function is a polynomial equation of the third degree, usually expressed as $ax^3 + bx^2 + cx + d = 0$. Quadratic functions can be graphed using an equation or a table of values. For example, to graph $y = 3x^2 + 1$, substitute the values −1, −0.5, 0, 0.5, and 1 for x to yield the point coordinates (−1, 4), (−0.5, 1.75), (0, 1), (0.5, 1.75), and (1, 4). Plot these points on a coordinate grid and connect the points in the form of a parabola. Cubic functions also can be graphed by making a table of values. The points of a cubic function form a curve. There is one point at which the curve changes from opening upward to opening downward, or vice versa, called the point of inflection.

Slope

Slope is the ratio of the rise, or vertical change, to the run, or horizontal change of a line: slope = rise/run. Slope (m) is the same for any two points on a straight line and can be found by using the coordinates of any two points on the line:

$$m = \frac{y_2 - y_1}{x_2 - x_1}, \text{ where } x_2 \neq x_1.$$

Asymptotes

An asymptote is a straight line that a curve approaches but never actually meets or crosses. Theoretically, the asymptote meets the curve at infinity. For example, in the function $f(x) = \frac{1}{x}$, two asymptotes are being approached: the line $y = 0$ and $x = 0$. See the graph of the function below.

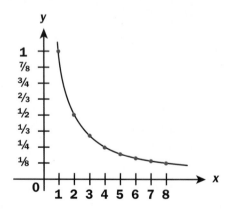

▶ Represent and analyze mathematical situations and structures using algebraic symbols

Variables and Expressions

Algebra is a language of symbols. A variable is a placeholder for a changing value. Any letter, such as x, can be used as a variable. Expressions such as $x + 2$ and $4x$ are algebraic expressions because they represent sums and/or products of variables and numbers. Usually, mathematicians avoid the use of i and e for variables because they have other mathematical meanings ($i = \sqrt{-1}$ and e is used with natural logarithms). To evaluate an algebraic expression, replace the variable or variables with known values, and then solve using order of operations. Translate verbal phrases into algebraic expressions by first defining a variable: choose a variable and a quantity for the variable to represent. In this way, algebraic expressions can be used to represent real-world situations.

Constant and Coefficient

A constant is a fixed value unlike a variable, which can change. Constants are usually represented by numbers, but they can also be represented by symbols. For example, π is a symbolic representation of the value 3.1415…. A coefficient is a constant by which a variable or other object is multiplied. For example, in the expression $7x^2 + 5x + 9$, the coefficient of x^2 is 7 and the coefficient of x is 5. The number 9 is a constant and not a coefficient.

Monomial and Polynomial

A monomial is a number, a variable, or a product of numbers and/or variables such as 3×4. An algebraic expression that contains one or more monomials is called a polynomial. In a polynomial, there are no terms with variables in the denominator and no terms with variables under a radical sign. Polynomials can be classified by the number of terms contained in the expression. Therefore, a polynomial with two terms is called a binomial ($z^2 - 1$), and a polynomial with three terms is called a trinomial ($2y^3 + 4y^2 - y$). Polynomials also can be classified by their degrees. The degree of a monomial is the sum of the exponents of its variables. The degree of a nonzero constant such as 6 or 10 is 0. The constant 0 has no degree. For example, the monomial $4b^5c^2$ had a degree of 7. The degree of a polynomial is the same as that of the term with the greatest degree. For example, the polynomial $3x^4 - 2y^3 + 4y^2 - y$ has a degree of 4.

Equation

An equation is a mathematical sentence that states that two expressions are equal. The two expressions in an equation are always separated by an equal sign. When solving for a variable in an equation, you must perform the same operations on both sides of the equation in order for the mathematical sentence to remain true.

Solving Equations with Variables

To solve equations with variables on both sides, use the Addition or Subtraction Property of Equality to write an equivalent equation with the variables on the same side. For example, to solve $5x - 8 = 3x$, subtract $3x$ from each side to get $2x - 8 = 0$. Then add 8 to each side to get $2x = 8$. Finally, divide each side by 2 to find that $x = 4$.

Solving Equations with Grouping Symbols

Equations often contain grouping symbols such as parentheses or brackets. The first step in solving these equations is to use the Distributive Property to remove the grouping symbols. For example $5(x + 2) = 25$ can be changed to $5x + 10 = 25$, and then solved to find that $x = 3$.

Some equations have no solution. That is, there is no value of the variable that results in a true sentence. For such an equation, the solution set is called the null or empty set, and is represented by the symbol $\varnothing$ or {}. Other equations may have every number as the solution. An equation that is true for every value of the variable is called the identity.

Inequality

A mathematical sentence that contains the symbols < (less than), > (greater than), ≤ (less than or equal to), or ≥ (greater than or equal to) is called an inequality. For example, the statement that it is legal to drive 55 miles per hour or slower on a stretch of the highway can be shown by the sentence $s \leq 55$. Inequalities with variables are called open sentences. When a variable is replaced with a number, the inequality may be true or false.

Solving Inequalities

Solving an inequality means finding values for the variable that make the inequality true. Just as with equations, when you add or subtract the same number from each side of an inequality, the inequality remains true. For example, if you add 5 to each side of the inequality $3x < 6$, the resulting inequality $3x + 5 < 11$ is also true. Adding or subtracting the same number from each side of an inequality does not affect the inequality sign. When multiplying or dividing each side of an inequality by the same positive number, the inequality remains true. In such cases, the inequality symbol does not change. When multiplying or dividing each side of an inequality by a negative number, the inequality symbol must be reversed. For example, when dividing each side of the inequality $-4x \geq -8$ by -2, the inequality sign must be changed to $\leq$ for the resulting inequality, $2x \leq 4$, to be true. Since the solutions to an inequality include all rational numbers satisfying it, inequalities have an infinite number of solutions.

Representing Inequalities on a Number Line

The solutions of inequalities can be graphed on a number line. For example, if the solution of an inequality is $x < 5$, start an arrow at 5 on the number line, and continue the arrow to the left to show all values less than 5 as the solution. Put an open circle at 5 to show that the point 5 is *not* included in the graph. Use a closed circle when graphing solutions that are greater than or equal to, or less than or equal to, a number.

Order of Operations

Solving a problem may involve using more than one operation. The answer can depend on the order in which you do the operations. To make sure that there is just one answer to a series of computations, mathematicians have agreed upon an order in which to do the operations. First simplify within the parentheses, and then evaluate any exponents. Then multiply and divide from left to right, and finally add and subtract from left to right.

Parametric Equations

Given an equation with more than one unknown, a statistician can draw conclusions about those unknown quantities through the use of parameters, independent variables that the statistician already knows something about. For example, you can find the velocity of an object if you make some assumptions about distance and time parameters.

Recursive Equations

In recursive equations, every value is determined by the previous value. You must first plug an initial value into the equation to get the first value, and then you can use the first value to determine the next one, and so on. For example, in order to determine what the population of pigeons will be in New York City in three years, you can use an equation with the birth, death, immigration, and emigration rates of the birds. Input the current population size into the equation to determine next year's population size, then repeat until you have calculated the value for which you are looking.

▶ Use mathematical models to represent and understand quantitative relationships

Solving Systems of Equations

Two or more equations together are called a system of equations. A system of equations can have one solution, no solution, or infinitely many solutions. One method for solving a system of equations is to graph the equations on the same coordinate plane. The coordinates of the point where the graphs intersect is the solution. In other words, the solution of a system is the ordered pair that is a solution of all equations. A more accurate way to solve a system of two equations is by using a method called substitution. Write both equations in terms of y. Replace y in the first equation with the right side of the second equation. Check the solution by graphing. You can solve a system of three equations using matrix algebra.

Graphing Inequalities

To graph an inequality, first graph the related equation, which is the boundary. All points in the shaded region are solutions of the inequality. If an inequality contains the symbol $\leq$ or $\geq$, then use a solid line to indicate that the boundary is included in the graph. If an inequality contains the symbol $<$ or $>$, then use a dashed line to indicate that the boundary is not included in the graph.

▶ Analyze change in various contexts

Rate of Change

A change in one quantity with respect to another quantity is called the rate of change. Rates of change can be described using slope:

$$\text{slope} = \frac{\text{change in } y}{\text{change in } x}$$

You can find rates of change from an equation, a table, or a graph. A special type of linear equation that describes rate of change is called a direct variation. The graph of a direct variation always passes through the origin and represents a proportional situation. In the equation $y = kx$, k is called the constant of variation. It is the slope, or rate of change. As x increases in value, y increases or decreases at a constant rate k, or y varies directly with x. Another way to say this is that y is directly proportional to x. The direct variation $y = kx$ also can be written as $k = \frac{y}{x}$. In this form, you can see that the ratio of y to x is the same for any corresponding values of y and x.

Slope-Intercept Form

Equations written as $y = mx + b$, where m is the slope and b is the y-intercept, are linear equations in slope-intercept form. For example, the graph of $y = 5x - 6$ is a line that has a slope of 5 and crosses the y-axis at $(0, -6)$. Sometimes you must first write an equation in slope-intercept form before finding the slope and y-intercept. For example, the equation $2x + 3y = 15$ can be expressed in slope-intercept form by subtracting $2x$ from each side and then dividing by 3: $y = -\frac{2}{3}x + 5$, revealing a slope of $-\frac{2}{3}$ and a y-intercept of 5. You can use the slope-intercept form of an equation to graph a line easily. Graph the y-intercept and use the slope to find another point on the line, then connect the two points with a line.

Geometry

▶ *Analyze characteristics and properties of two- and three-dimensional geometric shapes and develop mathematical arguments about geometric relationships*

Angles

Two rays that have the same endpoint form an angle. The common endpoint is called the vertex, and the two rays that make up the angle are called the sides of the angle. The most common unit of measure for angles is the degree. Protractors can be used to measure angles or to draw an angle of a given measure. Angles can be classified by their degree measure. Acute angles have measures less than 90° but greater than 0°. Obtuse angles have measures greater than 90° but less than 180°. Right angles have measures of 90°.

Triangles

A triangle is a figure formed by three line segments that intersect only at their endpoints. The sum of the measures of the angles of a triangle is 180°. Triangles can be classified by their angles. An acute triangle contains all acute angles. An obtuse triangle has one obtuse angle. A right triangle has one right angle. Triangles can also be classified by their sides. A scalene triangle has no congruent sides. An isosceles triangle has at least two congruent sides. In an equilateral triangle all sides are congruent.

Quadrilaterals

A quadrilateral is a closed figure with four sides and four vertices. The segments of a quadrilateral intersect only at their endpoints. Quadrilaterals can be separated into two triangles. Since the sum of the interior angles of all triangles totals 180°, the measures of the interior angles of a quadrilateral equal 360°. Quadrilaterals are classified according to their characteristics, and include trapezoids, parallelograms, rectangles, squares, and rhombuses.

Two-Dimensional Figures

A two-dimensional figure exists within a plane and has only the dimensions of length and width. Examples of two-dimensional figures include circles and polygons. Polygons are figures that have three or more angles, including triangles, quadrilaterals, pentagons, hexagons, and many more. The sum of the angles of any polygon totals at least 180° (triangle), and each additional side adds 180° to the measure of the first three angles. The sum of the angles of a quadrilateral, for example, is 360°. The sum of the angles of a pentagon is 540°.

Three-Dimensional Figures

A plane is a two-dimensional flat surface that extends in all directions. Intersecting planes can form the edges and vertices of three-dimensional figures or solids. A polyhedron is a solid with flat surfaces that are polygons. Polyhedrons are composed of faces, edges, and vertices and are differentiated by their shape and by their number of bases. Skew lines are lines that lie in different planes. They are neither intersecting nor parallel.

Congruence

Figures that have the same size and shape are congruent. The parts of congruent triangles that match are called corresponding parts. Congruence statements are used to identify corresponding parts of congruent triangles. When writing a congruence statement, the letters must be written so that corresponding vertices appear in the same order. Corresponding parts can be used to find the measures of angles and sides in a figure that is congruent to a figure with known measures.

Similarity

If two figures have the same shape but not the same size they are called similar figures. For example, the triangles below are similar, so angles A, B, and C have the same measurements as angles D, E, and F, respectively. However, segments AB, BC, and CA do not have the same measurements as segments DE, EF, and FD, but the measures of the sides are proportional.

For example, $\dfrac{\overline{AB}}{\overline{DE}} = \dfrac{\overline{BC}}{\overline{EF}} = \dfrac{\overline{CA}}{\overline{FD}}$.

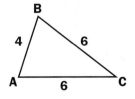

Solid figures are considered to be similar if they have the same shape and their corresponding linear measures are proportional. As with two-dimensional figures, they can be tested for similarity by comparing corresponding measures. If the compared ratios are proportional, then the figures are similar solids. Missing measures of similar solids can also be determined by using proportions.

The Pythagorean Theorem

In a right triangle, the sides that are adjacent to the right angle are called legs. The side opposite the right angle is the hypotenuse.

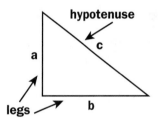

The Pythagorean Theorem describes the relationship between the lengths of the legs a and b and the hypotenuse c. It states that if a triangle is a right triangle, then the square of the length of the hypotenuse is equal to the sum of the squares of the lengths of the legs. In symbols, $c^2 = a^2 + b^2$.

Sine, Cosine, and Tangent Ratios

Trigonometry is the study of the properties of triangles. A trigonometric ratio is a ratio of the lengths of two sides of a right triangle. The most common trigonometric ratios are the sine, cosine, and tangent ratios. These ratios are abbreviated as *sin*, *cos*, and *tan*, respectively.

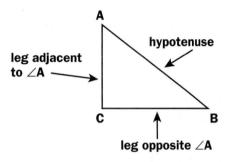

If ∠A is an acute angle of a right triangle, then

$$sin \angle A = \frac{\text{measure of leg opposite } \angle A}{\text{measure of hypotenuse}},$$

$$cos \angle A = \frac{\text{measure of leg adjacent to } \angle A}{\text{measure of hypotenuse}}, \text{ and}$$

$$tan \angle A = \frac{\text{measure of leg opposite } \angle A}{\text{measure of leg adjacent to } \angle A}.$$

► **Specify locations and describe spatial relationships using coordinate geometry and other representational systems**

Polygons
A polygon is a simple, closed figure formed by three or more line segments. The line segments meet only at their endpoints. The points of intersection are called vertices, and the line segments are called sides. Polygons are classified by the number of sides they have. The diagonals of a polygon divide the polygon into triangles. The number of triangles formed is two less than the number of sides. To find the sum of the measures of the interior angles of any polygon, multiply the number of triangles within the polygon

by 180. That is, if *n* equals the number of sides, then $(n - 2)180$ gives the sum of the measures of the polygon's interior angles.

Cartesian Coordinates
In the Cartesian coordinate system, the *y*-axis extends above and below the origin and the *x*-axis extends to the right and left of the origin, which is the point at which the *x*- and *y*-axes intersect. Numbers below and to the left of the origin are negative. A point graphed on the coordinate grid is said to have an *x*-coordinate and a *y*-coordinate. For example, the point (1,−2) has as its *x*-coordinate the number 1, and has as its *y*-coordinate the number −2. This point is graphed by locating the position on the grid that is 1 unit to the right of the origin and 2 units below the origin.

The *x*-axis and the *y*-axis separate the coordinate plane into four regions, called quadrants. The axes and points located on the axes themselves are not located in any of the quadrants. The quadrants are labeled I to IV, starting in the upper right and proceeding counterclockwise. In quadrant I, both coordinates are positive. In quadrant II, the *x*-coordinate is negative and the *y*-coordinate is positive. In quadrant III, both coordinates are negative. In quadrant IV, the *x*-coordinate is positive and the *y*-coordinate is negative. A coordinate graph can be used to show algebraic relationships among numbers.

► **Apply transformations and use symmetry to analyze mathematical situations**

Similar Triangles and Indirect Measurement
Triangles that have the same shape but not necessarily the same dimensions are called similar triangles. Similar triangles have corresponding angles and corresponding

sides. Arcs are used to show congruent angles. If two triangles are similar, then the corresponding angles have the same measure, and the corresponding sides are proportional. Therefore, to determine the measures of the sides of similar triangles when some measures are known, proportions can be used.

Transformations

A transformation is a movement of a geometric figure. There are several types of transformations. In a translation, also called a slide, a figure is slid from one position to another without turning it. Every point of the original figure is moved the same distance and in the same direction. In a reflection, also called a flip, a figure is flipped over a line to form a mirror image. Every point of the original figure has a corresponding point on the other side of the line of symmetry. In a rotation, also called a turn, a figure is turned around a fixed point. A figure may be rotated 90° clockwise, 90° counterclockwise, or 180°. A dilation transforms each line to a parallel line whose length is a fixed multiple of the length of the original line to create a similar figure that will be either larger or smaller.

▶ *Use visualizations, spatial reasoning, and geometric modeling to solve problems*

Two-Dimensional Representations of Three-Dimensional Objects

Three-dimensional objects can be represented in a two-dimensional drawing in order to more easily determine properties such as surface area and volume. When you look at the triangular prism, you can see the orientation of its three dimensions, length, width, and height. Using the drawing and the formulas for surface area and volume, you can easily calculate these properties.

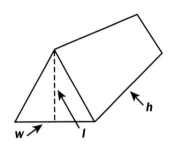

Another way to represent a three-dimensional object in a two-dimensional plane is by using a net, which is the unfolded representation. Imagine cutting the vertices of a box until it is flat then drawing an outline of it. That's a net. Most objects have more than one net, but any one can be measured to determine surface area. Below is a cube and one of its nets.

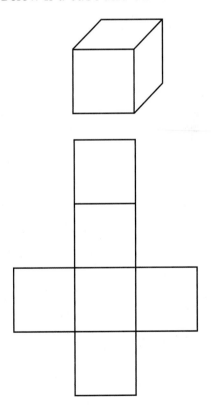

Measurement

▶ *Understand measurable attributes of objects and the units, systems, and processes of measurement*

Customary System

The customary system is the system of weights and measures used in the United States. The main units of weight are ounces, pounds (1 equal to 16 ounces), and tons (1 equal to 2,000 pounds). Length is typically measured in inches, feet (1 equal to 12 inches), yards (1 equal to 3 feet), and miles (1 equal to 5,280 feet), while area is measured in square feet and acres (1 equal to 43,560 square feet). Liquid is measured in cups, pints (1 equal to 2 cups), quarts (1 equal to 2 pints), and gallons (1 equal to 4 quarts). Finally, temperature is measured in degrees Fahrenheit.

Metric System

The metric system is a decimal system of weights and measurements in which the prefixes of the words for the units of measure indicate the relationships between the different measurements. In this system, the main units of weight, or mass, are grams and kilograms. Length is measured in millimeters, centimeters, meters, and kilometers, and the units of area are square millimeters, centimeters, meters, and kilometers. Liquid is typically measured in milliliters and liters, while temperature is in degrees Celsius.

Selecting Units of Measure

When measuring something, it is important to select the appropriate type and size of unit. For example, in the United States it would be appropriate when describing someone's height to use feet and inches. These units of height or length are good to use because they are in the customary system, and they are of appropriate size. In the customary system, use inches, feet, and miles for lengths and perimeters; square inches, feet, and miles for area and surface area; and cups, pints, quarts, gallons or cubic inches and feet (and less commonly miles) for volume. In the metric system use millimeters, centimeters, meters, and kilometers for lengths and perimeters; square units millimeters, centimeters, meters, and kilometers for area and surface area; and milliliters and liters for volume. Finally, always use degrees to measure angles.

▶ *Apply appropriate techniques, tools, and formulas to determine measurements*

Precision and Significant Digits

The precision of measurement is the exactness to which a measurement is made. Precision depends on the smallest unit of measure being used, or the precision unit. One way to record a measure is to estimate to the nearest precision unit. A more precise method is to include all of the digits that are actually measured, plus one estimated digit. The digits recorded, called significant digits, indicate the precision of the measurement. There are special rules for determining significant digits. If a number contains a decimal point, the number of significant digits is found by counting from left to right, starting with the first nonzero digit. If the number does not contain a decimal point, the number of significant digits is found by counting the digits from left to right, starting with the first digit and ending with the last nonzero digit.

Surface Area

The amount of material needed to cover the surface of a figure is called the surface area. It can be calculated by finding the area of each face and adding them together. To find the surface area of a rectangular prism, for example, the formula $S = 2lw + 2lh + 2wh$ applies. A cylinder, on the other hand, may be unrolled to reveal two circles and a rectangle. Its surface area can be determined by finding the area of the two circles, $2\pi r^2$, and adding it to the area of the rectangle, $2\pi rh$ (the length of the rectangle is the circumference of one of the circles), or $S = 2\pi r^2 + 2\pi rh$. The surface area of a pyramid is measured in a slightly different way because the sides of a pyramid are triangles that intersect at the vertex. These sides are called lateral faces and the height of each is called the slant height. The sum of their areas is the lateral area of a pyramid. The surface area of a square pyramid is the lateral area $\frac{1}{2}bh$ (area of a lateral face) times 4 (number of lateral faces), plus the area of the base. The surface area of a cone is the area of its circular base (πr^2) plus its lateral area (πrl, where l is the slant height).

Volume

Volume is the measure of space occupied by a solid region. To find the volume of a prism, the area of the base is multiplied by the measure of the height, $V = bh$. A solid containing several prisms can be broken down into its component prisms. Then the volume of each component can be found and the volumes added. The volume of a cylinder can be determined by finding the area of its circular base, πr^2, and then multiplying by the height of the cylinder. A pyramid has one-third the volume of a prism with the same base and height. To find the volume of a pyramid, multiply the area of the base by the pyramid's height, and then divide by 3. Simply stated, the formula for the volume of a pyramid is $V = \frac{1}{3}bh$. A cone is a three-dimensional figure with one circular base and a curved surface connecting the base and the vertex. The volume of a cone is one-third the volume of a cylinder with the same base area and height. Like a pyramid, the formula for the volume of a cone is $V = \frac{1}{3}bh$. More specifically, the formula is $V = \frac{1}{3}\pi r^2 h$.

Upper and Lower Bounds

Upper and lower bounds have to do with the accuracy of a measurement. When a measurement is given, the degree of accuracy is also stated to tell you what the upper and lower bounds of the measurement are. The upper bound is the largest possible value that a measurement could have had before being rounded down, and the lower bound is the lowest possible value it could have had before being rounded up.

Data Analysis and Probability

▶ *Formulate questions that can be addressed with data and collect, organize, and display relevant data to answer them*

Histograms

A histogram displays numerical data that have been organized into equal intervals using bars that have the same width and no space between them. While a histogram does not give exact data points, its shape shows the distribution of the data. Histograms also can be used to compare data.

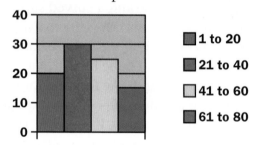

■ 1 to 20
■ 21 to 40
□ 41 to 60
■ 61 to 80

Box-and-Whisker Plot

A box-and-whisker plot displays the measures of central tendency and variation. A box is drawn around the quartile values, and whiskers extend from each quartile to the extreme data points. To make a box plot for a set of data, draw a number line that covers the range of data. Find the median, the extremes, and the upper and lower quartiles. Mark these points on the number line, then draw a box and the whiskers. The length of a whisker or box shows whether the values of the data in that part are concentrated or spread out.

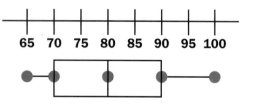

Scatter Plots

A scatter plot is a graph that shows the relationship between two sets of data. In a scatter plot, two sets of data are graphed as ordered pairs on a coordinate system. Two sets of data can have a positive correlation (as x increases, y increases), a negative correlation (as x increases, y decreases), or no correlation (no obvious pattern is shown). Scatter plots can be used to spot trends, draw conclusions, and make predictions about data.

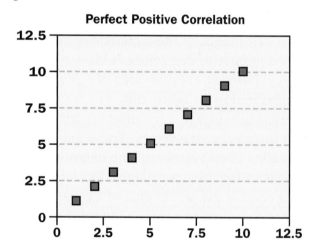

Randomization

The idea of randomization is a very important principle of statistics and the design of experiments. Data must be selected randomly to prevent bias from influencing the results. For example, you want to know the average income of people in your town but you can only use a sample of 100 individuals to make determinations about everyone. If you select 100 individuals who are all doctors, you will have a biased sample. However, if you chose a random sample of 100 people out of the phone book, you are much more likely to accurately represent average income in the town.

Statistics and Parameters

Statistics is a science that involves collecting, analyzing, and presenting data. The data can be collected in various ways—for example through a census or by making physical measurements. The data can then be analyzed by creating summary statistics, which have to do with the distribution of the data sample, including the mean, range, and standard error. They can also be illustrated in tables and graphs, like box-plots, scatter plots, and histograms. The presentation of the data typically involves describing the strength or validity of the data and what they show. For example, an analysis of ancestry of people in a city might tell you something about immigration patterns, unless the data set is very small or biased in some way, in which case it is not likely to be very accurate or useful.

Categorical and Measurement Data

When analyzing data, it is important to understand if the data is qualitative or quantitative. Categorical data is qualitative and measurement, or numerical, data is quantitative. Categorical data describes a quality of something and can be placed into different categories. For example, if you are analyzing the number of students in different grades in a school, each grade is a category. On the other hand, measurement data is continuous, like height, weight, or any other measurable variable. Measurement data can be converted into categorical data if you decide to group the data. Using height as an example, you can group the continuous data set into categories like under 5 feet, 5 feet to 5 feet 5 inches, over 5 feet 5 inches to 6 feet, and so on.

Univariate and Bivariate Data

In data analysis, a researcher can analyze one variable at a time or look at how multiple variables behave together. Univariate data involves only one variable, for example height in humans. You can measure the height in a population of people then plot the results in a histogram to look at how height is distributed in humans. To summarize univariate data, you can use statistics like the mean, mode, median, range, and standard deviation, which is a measure of variation. When looking at more than one variable at once, you use multivariate data. Bivariate data involves two variables. For example, you can look at height and age in humans together by gathering information on both variables from individuals in a population. You can then plot both variables in a scatter plot, look at how the variables behave in relation to each other, and create an equation that represents the relationship, also called a regression. These equations could help answer questions such as, for example, does height increase with age in humans?

▶ Select and use appropriate statistical methods to analyze data

Measures of Central Tendency

When you have a list of numerical data, it is often helpful to use one or more numbers to represent the whole set. These numbers are called measures of central tendency. Three measures of central tendency are mean, median, and mode. The mean is the sum of the data divided by the number of items in the data set. The median is the middle number of the ordered data (or the mean of the two middle numbers). The mode is the number or numbers that occur most often.

decide to group the data. Using height as an example, you can group the continuous data set into categories like under 5 feet, 5 feet to 5 feet 5 inches, over 5 feet 5 inches to 6 feet, and so on.

Univariate and Bivariate Data

In data analysis, a researcher can analyze one variable at a time or look at how multiple variables behave together. Univariate data involves only one variable, for example height in humans. You can measure the height in a population of people then plot the results in a histogram to look at how height is distributed in humans. To summarize univariate data, you can use statistics like the mean, mode, median, range, and standard deviation, which is a measure of variation. When looking at more than one variable at once, you use multivariate data. Bivariate data involves two variables. For example, you can look at height and age in humans together by gathering information on both variables from individuals in a population. You can then plot both variables in a scatter plot, look at how the variables behave in relation to each other, and create an equation that represents the relationship, also called a regression. These equations could help answer questions such as, for example, does height increase with age in humans?

▶ Select and use appropriate statistical methods to analyze data

Measures of Central Tendency

When you have a list of numerical data, it is often helpful to use one or more numbers to represent the whole set. These numbers are called measures of central tendency. Three measures of central tendency are mean, median, and mode. The mean is the sum of the data divided by the number of items in the data set. The median is the middle number of the ordered data (or the mean of the two middle numbers). The mode is the number or numbers that occur most often. These measures of central tendency allow data to be analyzed and better understood.

Measures of Spread

In statistics, measures of spread or variation are used to describe how data are distributed. The range of a set of data is the difference between the greatest and the least values of the data set. The quartiles are the values that divide the data into four equal parts. The median of data separates the set in half. Similarly, the median of the lower half of a set of data is the lower quartile. The median of the upper half of a set of data is the upper quartile. The interquartile range is the difference between the upper quartile and the lower quartile.

Line of Best Fit

When real-life data are collected, the points graphed usually do not form a straight line, but they may approximate a linear relationship. A line of best fit is a line that lies very close to most of the data points. It can be used to predict data. You also can use the equation of the best-fit line to make predictions.

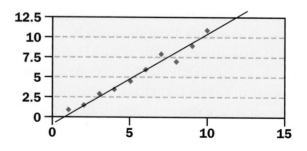

Stem and Leaf Plots

In a stem and leaf plot, numerical data are listed in ascending or descending order. The greatest place value of the data is used for the stems. The next greatest place value forms the leaves. For example, if the least number in a set of data is 8 and the greatest number is 95, draw a vertical line and write the stems from 0 to 9 to the left of the line. Write the leaves from to the right of the line, with the corresponding stem. Next, rearrange the leaves so they are ordered from least to greatest. Then include a key or explanation, such as $1|3 = 13$. Notice that the stem-and-leaf plot below is like a histogram turned on its side.

```
0|8
1|3 6
2|5 6 9
3|0 2 7 8
4|0 1 4 7 9
5|1 4 5 8
6|1 3 7
7|5 8
8|2 6
9|5
```

Key: **1|3 = 13**

▶ Develop and evaluate inferences and predictions that are based on data

Sampling Distribution

The sampling distribution of a population is the distribution that would result if you could take an infinite number of samples from the population, average each, and then average the averages. The more normal the distribution of the population, that is, how closely the distribution follows a bell curve, the more likely the sampling distribution will also follow a normal distribution. Furthermore, the larger the sample, the more likely it will accurately represent the entire population. For instance, you are more likely to gain more representative results from a population of 1,000 with a sample of 100 than with a sample of 2.

Validity

In statistics, validity refers to acquiring results that accurately reflect that which is being measured. In other words, it is important when performing statistical analyses, to ensure that the data are valid in that the sample being analyzed represents the population to the best extent possible. Randomization of data and using appropriate sample sizes are two important aspects of making valid inferences about a population.

▶ Understand and apply basic concepts of probability

Complementary, Mutually Exclusive Events

To understand probability theory, it is important to know if two events are mutually exclusive, or complementary: the occurrence of one event automatically implies the non-occurrence of the other. That is, two complementary events cannot both occur. If you roll a pair of dice, the event of rolling 6 and rolling doubles have an outcome in common (3, 3), so they are not mutually exclusive. If you roll (3, 3), you also roll doubles. However, the events of rolling a 9 and rolling doubles are mutually exclusive because they have no outcomes in common. If you roll a 9, you will not also roll doubles.

Independent and Dependent Events

Determining the probability of a series of events requires that you know whether the

THE BUSINESS PLAN:
YOUR ROAD MAP TO ENTREPRENEURIAL SUCCESS

Developing a good business plan can put you on the track to success in a small business. A business plan summarizes an entrepreneur's proposed business venture. It provides an organized report of a company's goals and how management intends to achieve those goals. A business plan is a continuing work in progress that should evolve as your business evolves. Developing a business plan is like outlining a strategy for turning your business idea into a reality.

What Is a Business Plan?

- A guide to the company's operations
- A document presenting your company's strategic vision
- A tool to persuade lenders and investors to finance your business
- A standard by which you can measure and improve business performance
- A plan to use as a basis for making sound business decisions

BUSINESS PLAN ELEMENTS

The Business Plan Appendix explains the content requirements for the essential elements of a business plan.

BUSINESS PLAN TEMPLATE

 Go to **connectED.mcgraw-hill.com** to print out this graphic organizer.

ASSIGNMENT

Select a business that you are interested in starting. Then develop a business plan for the venture. When you are finished writing the business plan, package the business plan using the guidelines on pages 672–673. Then present it and defend it in an oral presentation.

MANAGEMENT TEAM PLAN

In the Management Team section of the business plan, you will present your management team's qualifications for making the venture a success.

KEY MANAGEMENT

- Describe each management team member, including title, salary, abilities, duties, responsibilities, educational experience, previous industry and related work experience, and past successes. Describe the benefits that team members will provide to the company.
- Provide copies of the owners' tax returns, personal financial statements, and résumés.

ADVISORS AND PROFESSIONAL SERVICE PROVIDERS

- Describe the role, responsibilities, and members of the advisory board, if you have one.
- List the outside consultants the company will use. Include accountants, attorneys, bankers, insurance agents, technology advisors, Web developers, security contractors, and payroll specialists.

COMPANY DESCRIPTION

The Company Description outlines the company's basic background information, business concept, and goals and objectives.

BUSINESS HISTORY AND DESCRIPTION

- Explain your reasons for starting a new business or expanding an existing business.
- Describe the entrepreneurial opportunity.
- Provide a history of the business with development milestones that have been completed to date and the current status of the business.
- Describe the legal structure of the business and why you chose it.
- Include details about prior funding, royalty, partnership, and joint venture agreements.

GOALS AND OBJECTIVES

- Establish the business's goals and objectives and relate them to the investment you seek.
- Explain why you think the venture will succeed.

PRODUCT AND SERVICE PLAN

The Product and Service Plan describes the features and benefits of the business's products and services.

OVERVIEW OF PRODUCTS AND SERVICES
- Describe the product or service, including purpose, size, shape, colors, features, benefits, cost, functionality, design, quality, capabilities, technology, protections, and unique selling points.
- Describe competing and similar technology.
- Describe the need the product or service addresses in the market and how it benefits customers.
- Explain briefly how the products and/or services will be produced, the materials required, and the type of labor needed.

PRODUCT DEVELOPMENT STATUS
- Discuss the history and current status of product development.
- Provide projected dates for achieving other stages of development.

VISION AND MISSION STATEMENTS

The Vision and Mission Statements section of the business plan sets forth the guiding principles by which a company functions. These statements and vision statement should be clear and concise. They communicate what the business stands for, what its founders believe in, and what the company intends to achieve.

VISION STATEMENT
- Write a vision statement that establishes the scope and purpose of your company and reflects its values and beliefs.
- Express the company's vision in broad terms so that it will stand the test of time.
- Convey the future of the company as its founders see it.
- Develop strategies for achieving the vision of the business.
- Establish criteria for monitoring achievement of the vision.

MISSION STATEMENT
- Write a mission statement that expresses the specific aspirations of a company, the major goals for which it will strive.
- Define the direction in which the company will move.
- Convey a challenging yet achievable mission that the organization will be dedicated to accomplishing.
- Develop strategies for achieving the mission of the business.
- Establish criteria for monitoring achievement of the mission.

INDUSTRY OVERVIEW

Your business plan must address basic trends and growth within the industry. Think of your industry as those companies providing similar, complementary, or supplementary products and services.

INDUSTRY TRENDS AND GROWTH

- Describe the industry, including size by both revenue and number of firms.
- Describe how the industry functions, including a general explanation of the industry's distribution system.
- Describe the barriers of entry to the industry.
- Describe the positive and negative trends in the industry.
- Describe the past and future trends in the industry.
- Discuss growth trends and how many companies are expected to enter the industry in the future.
- Explain the factors that are influencing growth or decline in the industry.
- Include the failure rate in the industry.
- Describe the typical profitability in the industry.
- Describe the government regulations that affect the industry in general and your business in particular.
- Describe the local, national, or international industry standards with which your business will need to comply.
- Include current and historical industry employment data.
- Provide visualizations of industry data (charts, tables, graphs).

MARKET ANALYSIS

The Market Analysis section of the business plan is important because it presents your market research and features a customer demographic profile that defines the traits of the company's target market. Information about potential target markets should originate from primary and secondary research resources.

TARGET MARKET DEMOGRAPHIC PROFILE

- Write a demographic profile of the company's target market.
- Identify and explain market segments.
- Describe the market niche served.
- Describe the size of the target market.
- Explain if your market is domestic or international and describe the cultures and ethnicities within it.
- Describe the geographic statistics of your target market; where are your customers from and where do they live?
- Describe what members of the target market do for a living, their level of income, their social and economic status, and their level of education.
- Describe the ages, genders, family structures, lifestyle, and leisure activities of the target market.
- Explain what motivates the target market.

- Answer specific questions about your target market that are directly related to your products or services.
- If your product or service is marketed to businesses, describe the target market in terms of industry, product and/or service, geographic location, years in business, revenue, number of employees, and buying motivations.
- Describe how you analyzed your target market.
- Provide visualizations of demographic, geographic, and psychographic data (charts, graphs, tables).

TARGET MARKET PROJECTIONS

- Describe the proportion of the target market that has used a product or service like the company's product or service before.
- Project how much of the product or service the target market will buy (gross sales and/or unit sales).

MARKET TRENDS AND GROWTH

- Describe current trends and trends that have been forecast to occur within the target market.
- Describe the historical growth, current market size, and the growth potential of the market.
- Provide visualizations of market trend statistics (charts, graphs, tables).

CUSTOMER NEEDS ANALYSIS

- Conduct market research to uncover customers' wants and needs and to survey their impressions of the business and its promotions.
- Use the market research results to write a customer needs analysis that interprets and prioritizes the needs of the business's current and future customers.
- Prepare a visualization that presents highlights from the results of your customer needs analysis.
- Explain how the company will meet the target market's needs.

⬤ COMPETITIVE ANALYSIS

The Competitive Analysis section of the business plan should focus on demonstrating that the proposed business has an advantage over its competitors. You can gather information on competitors by viewing their Web sites; by talking to their customers, vendors, suppliers, and employees; by attending trade shows; and by searching newspaper and magazine databases.

COMPETITIVE OVERVIEW

- Identify, investigate, and analyze your top direct competitors, businesses that are offering identical or similar products or services as your business.
- Identify, investigate, and analyze your top indirect competitors, businesses that are offering products and services that are close substitutes.

- Identify, investigate, and analyze your top future competitors, existing companies that are not yet in the marketplace but could enter the marketplace at any time.
- Explain whether the business will have nonlocal competitors.
- State the locations of your top competitors.
- Describe how long your competitors have been in business.
- Describe the products and services your competitors sell and how much they sell (in units and sales dollars).
- Evaluate your competitors' product selection, product quality, and product availability.
- Describe the markets or market segments your competitors serve.
- Describe the benefits offered by the competition.
- Describe your competitors' images and their level of growth and success.
- Describe your competitors' advertising and promotion strategies and branding, packaging, and labeling strategies.
- Describe your competitors' pricing policies and pricing structures.
- Explain competitors' customer service and after sale service policies.
- Assess your competitors' financial condition and level of debt.
- Evaluate your competitors' equipment and production capacity.
- Outline the strengths and weaknesses of each of your competitors.
- Include charts or pie graphs showing the market share among your competitors as well as trends and changes over time.
- Prepare a grid or table that presents highlights from the results of your competitive analysis.

COMPETITIVE ADVANTAGE
- Describe the competitive advantage of your venture.
- Explain the key assets that your business has and its competitors do not have.
- Differentiate your company's products and services from your competitors' products and services.
- Describe how your business strategies and marketing mix strategies (product, place, price, promotion, and people decisions) will help you to attract and defend market share.
- Explain the percentage of the market the business intends to capture and how the business will achieve this market penetration.

MARKETING PLAN

A Marketing Plan describes a company's marketing mix strategies or how it plans to market, promote, and sell its products or services.

MARKETING MIX STRATEGIES
- Write a marketing plan, including an Internet marketing plan if appropriate, with product, place, price, promotion, and people strategies.
- Describe the marketing mix strategies and explain the message they are meant to convey.

- Describe the company's plan for finding the best market.
- Explain how the marketing mix strategies will be implemented and evaluated for effectiveness.

PRODUCT STRATEGY

- Describe your product, including how it functions, its design, image, appearance, packaging, labeling, warranties, service, and support.
- Describe the product's branding, including brand name(s), brand marks, trade names, trade characters, trademarks, logos, and corporate symbols.

PLACE STRATEGY

- Explain how your product will be made available to customers and where it will be sold.
- Describe channels of distribution and how they will help to foster market penetration.

PRICE STRATEGY

- State your company's pricing objectives and pricing strategy goals.
- Develop a pricing structure that takes into account fixed and variable costs, the competition, company objectives, proposed positioning strategies, the target market, and the consumer's willingness to pay.
- Describe the typical prices in the industry and how your business's prices compare.
- State whether you will accept checks, credit, debit cards, or other forms of payment.

PROMOTION STRATEGY

- Explain the company's promotional goals and promotional messages and how they will appeal to the target market.
- Develop a pre-opening promotional plan to establish a positive image and promote interest.
- Detail the promotions to be used, such as advertising, publicity and public relations, sales promotion, personal selling, direct mail, and e-mail.
- Describe the specific marketing mediums the company will use to deliver the promotional message to the target market. Include how often each will be used, what they will cost, why you chose them, and why they will appeal to the target market.
- Describe the marketing materials you will need, who will design them, how much they will cost, and how they will be designed to appeal to the target market.
- Describe the sales team, the sales process, and the sales incentives the company will offer.
- Provide your media budget and detail the cost of marketing materials per prospect.
- Provide examples of marketing materials.
- Describe how you will evaluate the effectiveness of promotional strategies.

PEOPLE STRATEGY

- Explain how you will recruit, hire, and train the people and employees who will help you to achieve business success.

OPERATIONAL PLAN

The Operational Plan section of the business plan includes information about all the processes that take place in the business.

LOCATION

- Describe where your business will be located, the number of locations, the zoning, the square footage needed, the layout and type of space, and renovations needed.
- Explain why you chose the location.
- State the average traffic count in front of the outlet.
- Describe any factors that hinder or help accessibility to the business and visibility of the site.
- Describe the businesses near your business's site, including target markets.
- Describe any community sign laws and local parking laws.
- Identify tax rates and state how they compare to other sites you considered.
- Project costs associated with the location.
- Describe how much the business can expand before it will need to relocate.
- Provide a map of the business location and facility layout blueprints.

PROPERTY OWNERSHIP OR LEASE TERMS

- Detail the terms of the lease or purchase of the property.
- Provide a copy of the proposed lease or building space purchase agreement.

EQUIPMENT NEEDS

- Describe and provide blueprints and specifications for the machinery and equipment needed.
- Explain whether you will purchase or lease the equipment.

MANUFACTURING PROCESSES AND COSTS

- Describe the manufacturing process and the technology requirements.
- Assess the manufacturing process in terms of direct and indirect costs.

SUPPLIERS AND PURCHASING

- Outline your key suppliers and the purchasing process.
- Provide copies of purchase orders and letters of intent from suppliers.

STORAGE AND INVENTORY

- Analyze the inventory needed to open and operate the business.
- Describe storage needs, space required, and costs involved.
- Explain inventory control procedures, equipment, and technology.

CHANNELS OF DISTRIBUTION

- Describe the channels of distribution and the associated costs.
- Explain the degree of difficulty in gaining industry distribution access.

QUALITY MEASURES AND SAFETY
- Describe how quality will be measured, controlled, and improved.
- Explain security precautions and health and safety regulations.

ORGANIZATIONAL PLAN

The Organizational Plan offers information about the business's legal structure, methods of and responsibilities for record keeping, and legal and insurance issues. It also covers the people aspects of the business, including staffing and training of personnel, and the organizational structure of the planned business.

LEGAL STRUCTURE
- Describe your legal structure and why it is advantageous for your company.
- Describe any legal agreements governing how owners can exit the company, how the company can be dissolved, how profits will be distributed, and who will have financial responsibility for losses.
- Project future changes in the company's legal structure and how such changes would benefit the company.
- Provide a copy of your partnership agreement if you have formed a partnership.
- Provide a copy of the Articles of Incorporation if the company is formed as a corporation.
- Provide a copy of the franchise contract and supporting materials if the company is a franchise.

RECORD KEEPING
- Describe the accounting system that will be used and why it was chosen.
- Describe what record keeping will be done internally and who will be responsible for keeping internal records.
- Explain when the business will use an outside accountant, such as to finalize monthly/year-end statements.
- Describe who within the company has the expertise to read and analyze the financial statements provided by outside accountants.
- Describe how you will use your financial statements to implement changes to make your company more profitable.

LEGAL AND INSURANCE ISSUES
- Describe any legal considerations that will impact your business, such as legal liability issues, government regulations, environmental regulations, zoning matters, or licensing requirements.
- Identify the insurance company the business will use, the types of insurance the business will need, and the costs involved.

LABOR, STAFFING, AND TRAINING
- Outline human resource policies, including staffing and personnel management procedures.
- Diagram and describe the organizational structure of the business.

- Provide an organizational flowchart.
- Develop a job description for each position on the organizational flowchart, including skill sets needed and salaries offered.
- Describe how many employees the business will have and in what types of positions.
- Outline hours of operation, scheduling policies, and types of shifts worked by employees.
- Complete a work schedule for a typical work week.
- Develop charts or graphs that classify employees by function, skill set, hourly pay, and part-time or full-time status.
- Identify situations where outsourcing should be used for hiring needs.

FINANCIAL PLAN

The Financial Plan presents past and current finances and financial forecasts and explains the assumptions made when calculating forecast figures. It includes the investment proposal and three key financial statements: a cash flow statement, income statement, and balance sheet.

INVESTMENT PROPOSAL
- Describe why you are applying for financing and how you plan to raise and use the money.
- Describe various investment structures and project when investors can expect to earn a profit.
- Identify, categorize, and analyze the start-up costs and fixed and variable operating expenses.
- Project the total cash needed to start the business.
- Include details about revenue streams and prior funding agreements.

EXIT STRATEGY
- Outline the business life cycle and explain your long-term plans for the business.
- Explain how your investors can expect to recoup their investment and earn a sufficient return.
- Define how investors can cash out their investment and achieve liquidity.

CASH FLOW PROJECTION
- Plan a cash budget that forecasts cash inflow (cash revenue from sales) and outflow (cash disbursements) projections for the first year and quarterly or yearly projections for the second and third years.

PROJECTED THREE-YEAR INCOME STATEMENT (PROFIT AND LOSS STATEMENTS)
- Prepare a three-year income projection that includes monthly projections for revenues, expenses, and profits (Revenues – Expenses = Profit or Loss) for the first year and quarterly or yearly projections for the second and third years.

PROJECTED BALANCE SHEET

- Prepare a projected balance sheet (assets, liabilities, and net worth) with quarterly projections for the first year and yearly projections for the second and third years.

BREAK-EVEN ANALYSIS

- Prepare a break-even analysis detailing when the company's expenses will match the income.
- Present the data in a graph format with sales on the X-axis and units sold on the Y-axis.

HISTORICAL FINANCIALS

- Provide cash flow statements, income statements, and balance sheets from the last three years if the company is an existing business.

FINANCIAL ASSUMPTIONS

- State the assumptions on which the financial projections are based.
- Explain how you derived forecasts for sales, costs of goods sold, operating expenses, accounts receivable, collections, accounts payable, inventory, taxes, and other items.
- Disclose whether the financial statements have been audited by a certified public accountant.

FINANCIAL RATIOS

- Calculate liquidity ratios to measure creditworthiness.
- Calculate profitability ratios to show operational performance.
- Calculate turnover ratios to measure changes in certain assets and to expose nonincome-producing assets.

 ## GROWTH PLAN

Planned growth can be very rewarding, and unplanned growth can be chaotic. The Growth Plan looks at how the business will expand in the future. Investors and lenders like to know that a business has plans to deal with growth in a controlled way.

GROWTH STRATEGIES

- Describe how and when the business owners would like the business to grow.
- Describe the products or services the business will develop to achieve growth.
- Describe the planned growth cycle.
- Describe how the business's growth strategies focus on the business's areas of expertise.
- Describe whether market research will be used to support and justify growth strategy decisions.
- Identify the critical skills that are needed to effectively manage growth.
- Explain how you will evaluate and initiate revisions to growth strategies.

BUSINESS LOCATION ISSUES

- Assess the current business location and how it can accommodate growth.
- Explain if growing the business will mean having to relocate the business to a larger facility.
- Analyze the costs involved in expanding or upgrading current facilities and/or moving to new facilities.
- Evaluate whether the business's lease agreement allows for modifications to the building and facilities.
- Describe alternative affordable premises.
- Explain if and when warehousing and storage facilities will be expanded to accommodate growth.

EFFECTS OF GROWTH

- Explain how planned growth will affect human resource expenses and management and staffing needs.
- Describe how planned growth will affect company goals and objectives.
- Assess if the business's target market will be affected by the growth plan.
- Describe how planned growth will affect technology and equipment needs.
- Describe how planned growth will affect the manufacturing process and costs.
- Explain how planned growth will affect financial control procedures, record keeping policies, and legal and insurance issues.
- Evaluate how planned growth will affect the sales team and sales process.
- Describe how planned growth will affect promotional goals and messages and marketing mix strategies (product, place, price, promotion, and people decisions).

GROWTH FINANCING

- Examine how growth costs will affect the overall financial health of the business in the short term and the long term.
- Evaluate growth financing options and describe the best plan to finance growth.
- Provide visualizations of growth projections (charts, tables, graphs).

 CONTINGENCY PLAN

The Contingency Plan examines the assumptions in the business plan and the greatest risks to the business and suggests plans to minimize the risk.

- List and examine the assumptions in the business plan.
- Examine risks that could cause the business to fail.
- Categorize business risks as human, natural, or economic; as speculative, controllable or uncontrollable; and as insurable or uninsurable.
- Identify the most significant risks that the new venture faces and describe plans the business owners have developed to deal with any of the situations should they arise.

- Describe how the company will respond to changes in market conditions caused by demographic shifts, socioeconomic trends, economic events, energy costs, and changes in government policies.
- Explain how the company will anticipate and respond to competitive threats from expected and unexpected sources, price cutting by competitors, and the introduction of new products by competitors.
- Explain how the company will handle cost overruns.
- Outline contingencies to meet staffing challenges and limit problems due to a dependence on key people.
- Describe how the company will respond if projected sales and revenue targets are not achieved.
- Describe the company's contingency plan in case of a major accident, event, or disaster that interrupts cash flow.
- Explain how the company will respond to product liability lawsuits.

EXECUTIVE SUMMARY

The Executive Summary recounts the key points in the business plan. It is written last because it summarizes the most important information from the business plan. Investors rely on it to decide if the business concept interests them. The executive summary should be just two pages long, and it should answer who, what, where, why, when, and how.

- Describe the company's mission, goals, objectives, current stage of development, owners, and key management team members.
- Describe the company, business model, legal structure, industry, product or service, target market, and the unique opportunity.
- Include evidence that justifies the soundness and future success of the opportunity.
- Describe the strategies the company will use to beat the competition.
- Include financial highlights such as:
  - The investment you are seeking
  - How much equity you would be willing to transfer
  - Collateral offered
  - How the funds will be used
  - How and when any loans will be repaid
  - Three-year projections of sales
  - Estimated annual after-tax profits

COVER PAGE

Every business plan should have a Cover Page. It is the first page the investor sees when he or she reads the business plan. Include this information:

- The company name, address, phone number, Web site address, e-mail address, and company logo

 TITLE PAGE

The page following the cover page is the Title Page. It includes this basic information about the business and the business plan:

- The company name
- The names, titles, and addresses of the owners
- The date the business plan was issued
- The name of the person who prepared the business plan

TABLE OF CONTENTS

The Table of Contents details the components of the business plan and the page numbers where they can be found within the business plan. Include this information in the Table of Contents:

- The titles of the major sections and subsections of the business plan
- The page number where each section and subsection is located

SUPPORTING DOCUMENTS

The Supporting Documents section of the business plan includes items, exhibits, and documentation relevant to the business. Include these items:

- Copies of the owners' résumés, personal financial statements, and tax returns
- For franchised businesses, a copy of franchise contract
- For franchised businesses, all supporting documents provided by the franchisor
- For partnerships, a copy of the partnership agreement
- For corporations, a copy of the Articles of Incorporation
- Photos, blueprints, and detailed specifications of products
- An organizational blueprint
- Photos and blueprints of the layout of the business's facilities
- Photos, blueprints, and detailed specifications for all equipment and machinery
- A map of the business location
- Copy of proposed lease or purchase agreement for building space
- Copy of contracts, licenses, and other legal documents
- Copies of purchase orders and letters of intent from suppliers
- Business cards
- Market research highlights
- Marketing materials
- Press releases
- Visualizations of industry data, demographic data, and market trend statistics

Key Terms Glossary

A

ability Skill that an individual has already developed

accounting The function of business that involves maintaining and auditing records, sending out and paying bills, and preparing financial reports for a business; The systematic process of recording and reporting the financial position of a person or an organization

accounting equation A concept that states that assets must always equal the sum of liabilities and owner's equity

accounts payable The total amount a business owes to creditors

accounts receivable The total amount of money owed to a business. It represents money to be received in payments after goods or services are sold on credit.

actual cash value Value of an automobile when it was new minus depreciation

ad campaign A series of ad messages that share a single idea and theme

advertising agency A business that specializes in developing ad campaigns and ads for its clients

advertising Paid, non-personal form of communication that businesses use to promote their products and services

ageism Discrimination based on age

annual percentage rate (APR) Cost of credit on a yearly basis

antitrust laws Laws that allow the federal government to break up monopolies, regulate them, or take over them

aptitude Potential for learning a skill

assets Property or other items of value owned by a business

audience The number of homes or people exposed to an ad

autocratic leadership A leadership style in which one person runs everything and makes all decisions without consulting others

B

baby boom generation Persons born in the United States between 1946 and 1964

background check The process of verifying certain information provided by a job applicant

bait and switch Sales tactic in which buyers are tempted by an advertised bargain but are then persuaded to buy a more expensive item instead

balance of trade The difference in value between a country's imports and exports over a period of time

balance sheet A report of the balances in all asset, liability, and owner's equity accounts at the end of an accounting period

bank account A record of how much money a customer has deposited into or withdrawn from a bank

bank reconciliation Process of seeing whether an account holder's records agree with a bank's records for an account

bank statement The bank's record of all the transactions in a bank account

bankruptcy Legal process in which a borrower is relieved of debts after showing an inability to pay

banner ads Ads displayed across the top or bottom of a computer screen

beneficiary Someone who receives all or part of the proceeds of an insurance policy, or a survivor of a deceased policyholder

benefits Extras that workers receive, such as health and life insurance, sick leave, retirement plans, and holiday pay

Better Business Bureau (BBB) Nonprofit organization that collects information on local businesses and handles consumers' complaints

body language Nonverbal communication that includes posture, eye contact, facial expressions, and gestures

bond discount Difference between the amount you pay for the bond and its face value

bond Certificate issued by a government or company promising to pay back borrowed money at a fixed rate of interest on a specified date

boycott A refusal to buy a company's goods or services

brand name Trade name for a product or service produced by a particular company

breach of contract The failure of one party to live up to the terms of a contract

break-even point The point at which total revenues, or sales, equal total costs and expenses of making and distributing a product or service

brick-and-mortar Actual buildings, such as stores and warehouses

brokerage firms Financial institutions that sell stocks and bonds and also may offer a wide range of financial services to clients

budget A plan specifying how money will be issued or spent during a particular period

budget deficit When the government spends more on programs than it collects in taxes

budget surplus A situation in which a government's revenue exceeds its expenditures during a one-year period

budget variance Difference between the budgeted amount and the actual amount that is spent

bureaucracy Formal organization with several levels of management

business Any commercial activity that seeks profit by providing goods and services to others in exchange for money

business cycle The rise and fall of economic activity over time

business ethics Rules based on moral principles about how businesses and employees ought to conduct themselves

business etiquette Conduct that is considered socially acceptable in business

business plan A written description of a new business venture that describes all aspects of the business

C

capital Money supplied by investors, banks, or owners of a business. Start-up capital is the money used to pay for the various assets and expenses of a new venture or business.

canceled checks Checks that have been cashed

capital gain Profit made from the sale of a financial asset such as stock or a house

capital loss Amount lost when an asset is sold for less than its cost

capital resources The things used to produce goods and services

career Work history of one or more jobs in the same or related fields of interest

cash advance Loan given in cash by a credit card company in anticipation of the borrower's being able to repay it

cash flows The amount of money that is available to a business at any given time

cash-value insurance Insurance that provides both savings and death benefits; also called permanent insurance.

centralized organization An organization that puts authority in one place—with top management

certificate of deposit (CD) Type of savings account that requires a specified amount of money be deposited for a set period of time

channel of distribution A pathway to direct products to consumers

charge account Credit provided by a store or company for customers to buy its products

check Written order directing a bank to pay money on demand to the person or company named on it

check register Checkbook log in which an account holder records checking account transactions

chronological résumé A list of your achievements in time order

claim Request for payment from an insurer for any damages covered by an insurance policy

Key Terms Glossary

clearance sale Sale to clear out goods that are going out of season or are no longer profitable

clicks-and-mortar The use of both the Internet and buildings, such as stores and warehouses, to conduct business

code of ethics A set of guidelines for maintaining ethics in the workplace

coinsurance Percentage of medical expenses that a policyholder must pay beyond the deductible

collateral Property or goods pledged by a borrower to use as security against a loan if the loan is not repaid

collectibles Items that appeal to collectors and investors

collection agent Person or business that collects payments for overdue bills

command economy An economic system in which a central authority makes the key economic decisions

commercial banks Banks that offer the entire range of banking services, such as checking and savings accounts, loans, and financial advice; also called full-service banks

commercial credit Credit used by businesses

commodities Items that are traded, especially unprocessed materials such as oil, food grains, and metals

commodities exchange Exchange where investors can buy contracts for quantities of a given commodity for delivery at a future date

common stock Stock that provides the most basic form of corporate ownership

comparative advantage The ability of a country or company to produce a particular good more efficiently than another country or company

comparison shopping Comparing the prices of competing brands or stores

compensation Pay and benefits

competition The contest between businesses to win customers

compound interest Interest earned on both the principal—the money deposited into a savings account—and any interest earned on it

compulsory insurance law Law that requires drivers to have a minimum amount of car insurance

computer An electronic device that accepts, processes, stores, and outputs data at high speeds, based on programmed instructions

computer-aided design (CAD) Software for designing products with a computer

conflict of interest Conflict between self-interest and professional obligation

conservation The process of preserving, protecting, and planning the management of resources

consolidation loan Loan that combines all your debts into one loan with lower payments

consumer Person who uses goods and services

consumer advocates Groups and individuals who work to protect, inform, and defend consumers

Consumer Credit Protection Act or Truth in Lending Act Federal law that requires creditors to inform consumers about the costs and terms of credit

consumer credit Credit used by people for personal reasons

consumer movement Movement to pass laws protecting consumers from unfair and unsafe business practices

consumer rights Protections included in the Consumer Bill of Rights. They are: the right to be informed, the right to choose, the right to safety, the right to be heard, the right to have problems corrected, the right to consumer education, and the right to service.

contract A legal agreement between two or more parties to do business

controllable risk Risk that can be controlled to minimize the chance of harm

controlling Keeping the company on track and making sure goals are met

cookies Bits of information about a computer user that are stored on the computer user's hard drive

cooperative Organization that is owned and operated by its members

copayment Fee paid each time a service is used

copyright The exclusive legal right given to artists to own their creations

corporate bonds Bonds issued by corporations to finance things such as construction and equipment

corporate culture A company's shared values, beliefs, and goals

corporation Company that is registered by a state and operates apart from its owners

cosigner Someone who agrees to be responsible for a debt if the main applicant does not pay it

cost per thousand (CPM) The media cost of exposing 1,000 readers or viewers to an advertising impression

coupon rate Rate of interest on a bond

cover letter Letter that accompanies a résumé and tells the employer about an applicant, explaining why the person is applying for a job

credit An agreement to get money, goods, or services now in exchange for a promise to pay in the future

credit counselor Someone who helps consumers work out a plan for getting out of debt and managing their money

credit limit The maximum amount a card holder can charge on a credit card

credit rating A measure of a person's ability and willingness to pay debts on time

credit report Document showing a person's credit history, including a record of past borrowing and repaying

credit unions Not-for-profit banks set up by organizations for their customers to use

creditor Person or organization that lends money or provides credit

culture The beliefs, customs, and attitudes of a distinct group of people

current assets Assets that are either used up or converted to cash during the normal cycle of the business

D

database management A computer program used to store data organized especially for rapid search and retrieval

debit card Bank card that immediately takes money from a checking account when it is used

debtor Person who borrows money or uses credit

decentralized organization An organization that gives authority to a number of different managers

deductible Amount in damages a policyholder must pay before the insurance company pays a claim

deductions Amounts that are taken from pay before a worker receives a paycheck

deficit Situation that occurs when more money is spent than is earned or received

deflation A general decrease in the cost of goods and services

delegating Giving managers and employees the power to run things and make decisions.

demand The amount or quantity of goods and services that consumers are willing to buy at various prices

democratic leadership A leadership style in which managers work with employees to make decisions

demographics Facts about the population

departmentalization Dividing responsibility among specific units, or departments

deposit The money put in a bank account

depreciation Decline in value of an asset

depression A deep recession that affects the entire economy and lasts for several years

desktop publishing Software used to produce publications such as reports, newsletters, and magazines

digital workflow Linking all the steps in a process digitally

direct deposit The electronic transfer of a payment directly from the payer's bank account to the account of the person being paid

direct distribution Distribution of goods or services from the producer directly to the customer

direct-mail advertising Ads sent by mail to people's homes

discrimination Unfair treatment of a person or group, usually because of prejudice about race, ethnicity, age, religion, or gender

diversify To vary investments in order to spread risk or expand

diversity A variety of employees with different backgrounds and identities

dividends A share of profits given to stockholders

down payment A portion of the total cost that is paid when a product or service is purchased

E

e-commerce Electronic commerce, or business conducted on the Internet

economic risk Risk that involves the likelihood of economic loss

economic system The method that a society chooses to use and distribute resources

economics The study of how individuals and groups of individuals strive to satisfy their wants and needs through making choices

e-learning Electronic learning; the process of learning online

electronic funds transfer (EFT) Allows money to be transferred from one bank account to another through a network of computers

embargo A ban on the import or export of a product

employability skills Basic skills that are needed to get, keep, and do well at a job

endorsement Signature of the payee on the back of the check

entrepreneur A person who recognizes a business opportunity and organizes, manages, and assumes the risks of starting and operating a business

entrepreneurial resources The people who recognize opportunities and start businesses

entrepreneurial Acting like an entrepreneur or having an entrepreneurial mindset

entrepreneurship The process of recognizing a business opportunity, testing it in the market, and gathering the resources necessary to start and run a business

entry-level job Job suitable for a worker who is new to a job, field, or subject

Environmental Protection Agency (EPA) A federal agency that enforces rules that protect the environment and control pollution

Equal Credit Opportunity Act Federal law stating that credit applications can be judged only on the basis of financial responsibility

Equal Pay Act Law passed in 1964 that requires men and women be paid the same wages for doing equal work

equilibrium price The point at which the quantity demanded and the quantity supplied meet

equity Value of a piece of property less the amount still owed on the money borrowed to purchase it

ergonomics Design factors for the workplace that are intended to maximize productivity by minimizing a worker's discomfort

e-tail Electronic retail

ethics Moral principles by which people conduct themselves personally, socially, or professionally

e-tickets Electronic tickets

e-workforce People who work with computers while doing business

exchange rate The price at which one currency can buy another currency

executive summary A brief recounting of the key points contained in a business plan

expense Amount of money used to buy or do something

exports Goods and services that one country sells to another country

express warranty Warranty that is explicitly stated, in writing or verbally

extended coverage Other types of protection added to a basic insurance policy

extracurricular activities Activities that students do besides schoolwork

extranet An extension of the intranet of a company or organization that gives authorized outsiders controlled access to the intranet

F

factors of production All the economic resources necessary to produce a society's goods and services

Fair Credit Billing Act Federal law that requires creditors to correct billing mistakes brought to their attention

Fair Credit Reporting Act Federal law that allows individuals to examine and correct information used by credit reporting agencies

Fair Debt Collection Practices Act (FDCPA) Federal law that serves to regulate collection agencies

Federal Deposit Insurance Corporation (FDIC) Government agency that insures bank accounts

Federal Reserve System The central bank of the United States

Federal Trade Commission (FTC) Agency that enforces antitrust laws and regulates interstate trade

finance The function of business that involves money management

finance charge The total amount it costs a borrower to have the lender finance the loan

finance companies Financial institutions that offer short-term loans to businesses and consumers, but at much higher interest rates than banks charge

financial forecast An estimate of a business's financial outlook for each of the next few years

financial institution A firm that manages money

financial plan A set of documents that outline the essential financial facts about a new firm or venture

financial responsibility law Law that requires drivers to pay for any damages or injuries they cause in an accident

financial statements Documents summarizing the changes resulting from business transactions that occur during an accounting period

fixed assets Items of value that are held for more than one year

fixed expenses Expenses that occur regularly and are regularly paid

fixed rate An interest rate that always remains the same

Food and Drug Administration (FDA) A federal government agency that protects consumers from dangerous or falsely advertised products

franchise Contractual agreement to use the name and sell the products or services of a company in a designated geographic area

fraud The crime of obtaining money or some other benefit by deliberate deception

free trade Few or no limits on trade between countries

free-rein leadership A leadership style that requires the leader to set goals for managers and employees and then leaves them alone to get the job done

frequency The number of times an audience sees or hears an ad

full warranty A guarantee about the quality of goods or services.

full-time job A job that requires at least 40 hours of work each week

Key Terms Glossary

G

garnishment of wages A court order to take all or part of a debtor's paycheck if he or she stops making payments

generally accepted accounting principles (GAAP) Rules that provide a way to communicate financial information to others

generic products Plainly labeled, unadvertised products that are sold at lower prices than brand-name goods

global economy The interconnected economies of the nations of the world

goals Things to be accomplished

goods Physical products

grace period Amount of time allowed to repay a debt without having to pay interest charges

grade labels Labels indicating the level of quality of foods

gross domestic product (GDP) The total value of the goods and services produced in a country in a given year

gross pay The total amount of money a worker earns for a specific time

group training Teaching several employees together

H

hacker A person who illegally gains access to and sometimes tampers with information in a computer system

hardware The physical components of a computer system

hazard Anything that increases the liklihood of loss through peril

health maintenance organization (HMO) Organization that provides health care at its own health centers for a fixed fee

hierarchy A formal chain of command with one person at the top who makes all the decisions

homeowners policy Insurance that covers damage to property and personal property, additional living expenses if a home is destroyed, and liability protection

human relations The study of how people interact in the workplace and how communication can be improved

human resources The people employed in a business, commonly referred to as personnel

human resources management The process of finding, selecting, training, and evaluating employees

human risk The risk of harm caused by human mistakes, dishonesty, or another risk that is attributable to people

I

identity theft Theft of a person's financial information for the purpose of committing fraud under that person's identity

imports Goods and services that one country buys from another country

impression A single exposure to an advertising message

impulse buying The act of making unplanned purchases

income The actual amount of money earned or received during a given period

income property Property used to generate income

income statement A report of the revenue, expenses, and net income or net loss for an accounting period

indirect distribution Distribution involving one or more intermediaries

inflation A general increase in the cost of goods and services

inflation risk Risk that the rate of inflation will increase more than the rate of interest on savings

infomercial A 30-minute commercial

information technology (IT) Using computing, electronics, and telecommunications to process and distribute information in digital and other forms

initiative The ability to act and make decisions without the help or advice of others

installment loans Loans repaid in regular payments over a period of time

insurable risk Risk that meets an insurance company's criteria for insurance coverage

insurance Paid protection against loss due to injury or property damage

insurance companies Financial institutions that provide protection against problems such as fire and theft

insurance policy A contract between a person and an insurance company to cover a specific risk

integrity An adherence to a code of ethical values, such as honesty, loyalty, and fairness

interest A fee charged for the use of money

interest-bearing account An account that pays earns interest on the balance for the depositor

interests An individual's favorite activities

intermediary A business that moves goods from one business to another

international trade The exchange of goods and services between nations

Internet A global computer network that connects many computer networks to allow information to flow freely around the world

internship A temporary paid or unpaid position that involves direct work experience in a career field

interstate commerce Business that takes place between states

intranet A computer network within an organization

intrastate commerce Business within each state

investing Committing money or capital in order to gain a financial return

J

job Work that people do for pay; also known as an occupation

job description A detailed outline of the duties, qualifications, and conditions required to do a specific job

job interview A formal face-to-face discussion between an employer and a potential employee

job objective A statement about the type of job a job applicant wants

job shadowing The act of following another worker for a few days on a job

L

labor resources Individuals who make the goods and services for which they are paid

leadership Taking a company and its employees in a direction based upon a vision

leading Providing direction and vision

legal monopoly A company that is allowed to operate without competition

liabilities Creditors' claims to the assets of a business

licenses Legal permits to conduct business

life insurance Insurance that is paid to a person or people designated to receive the funds when the insured person dies

limited liability A claim that holds a firm's owners responsible for no more than the capital that they have invested in it

limited warranty A warranty that covers only certain parts of a product or requires the customer to bear some of the expense when repairs are needed

line and staff authority An organizational structure with direct lines of authority as well as staff who advise line personnel

line authority An organizational structure in which managers at the top of the line are in charge of those beneath them, and so on

liquidity The ability to quickly turn an investment into cash

loss leaders Advertised products that sell at a loss to bring customers into a store

Key Terms Glossary

M

management The process of achieving company goals by planning, organizing, directing, controlling, and evaluating the effective use of resources

manufacturers Businesses that make finished products out of processed goods

market A group of customers who share common wants and needs

market economy An economic system in which economic decisions are made in the marketplace, where buyers and sellers meet to exchange goods and services, usually for money

market research The gathering and analysis of information on the size, location, and makeup of a product market

market segmentation The division of a market for a product into groups of customers who have the same needs and traits

marketing The process of planning, pricing, promoting, selling, and distributing ideas, goods, and services

marketing concept The process of determining the wants and needs of customers and providing them more efficiently and effectively than competitors

marketing mix The four main elements of marketing, also called the four Ps: product, place, price, and promotion. It sometimes includes a fifth P, for people.

mass media Means of communication, such as television, radio, and newspapers

maturity date The date when the money deposited into a certificate of deposit becomes available to the depositor

media planning The process of selecting advertising media and deciding the time and space in which the ads should appear

Medicaid Federally and state-funded health-care plan for people who are unable to pay for insurance or health care

Medicare U.S. government's major health insurance program for the elderly

middle managers Managers who carry out the decisions of top management

mission statement A statement that expresses the specific aspirations of a company, the major goals for which it will strive

mixed economy A combination of a market economy and a command economy

monetary system A system in which goods and services are directly exchanged using money

money A standard of value and a means of exchange or payment

money management A method of planning to get the most from one's money

money market deposit account A form of money market fund offered by banks, savings and loans, and credit unions

money market fund A type of mutual fund, or pool of money, put into a variety of short-term debt (less than one year) by businesses and governments

monopoly A company that controls an industry or is the only one to offer a product or service

mortgage An agreement in which a borrower gives a lender the right to take property if a loan is not repaid

mortgage companies Financial institutions that provide loans specifically for buying a home or business

multi-channel retailer A company that uses several means to sell products

multinational corporation A company that does business in many countries and has facilities and offices around the world

municipal bonds Bonds issued by local and state governments to finance city, town, or regional projects such as schools, highways, and airports

mutual fund A fund created by an investment firm that raises money from many shareholders and invests it in a variety of stocks or other investments

N

national debt The total amount of money a government owes

natural resources Raw materials from nature used to produce goods

natural risk The possibility of a catastrophe such as a flood, tornado, hurricane, fire, lightning, drought, or earthquake

needs Things that you must have in order to survive

net pay Gross pay minus deductions

networking The practice of building informal relationships with people whose friendship could bring advantages such as job or business opportunities

no-fault insurance Insurance that requires drivers involved in accidents to collect damages from their own insurance companies no matter who is at fault

nonprofit organization A type of business that focuses on providing a service rather than making a profit

O

occupation Activity in which one engages; also known as a job

Occupational Safety and Health Administration (OSHA) A division of the U.S. Department of Labor that sets and enforces work-related health and safety rules

oligopoly A small number of companies that control an industry

on-the-job training Learning a new job by actually doing it

operating system Software that controls the operation of a computer and directs the processing of programs

operational managers Managers who are responsible for the daily operations of a business

opportunity cost What you give up when you make one choice instead of another, sometimes called a tradeoff

organizational chart A chart that shows how the firm is structured and who is in charge of whom

organizing Getting resources arranged in an orderly and functional way to accomplish goals and objectives

orientation The process of helping new employees adjust to a company

outsourcing Using outside sources to do tasks traditionally handled by internal staff

outstanding checks Checks that have been written but have not yet been cashed

overdraft protection A line of credit for overdrawn checks

overdrawn Having written checks for more money than the balance in the account

owner's equity An owner's claims to the assets of a business

P

partnership A business owned by two or more people who share its risks and rewards

patent A legal grant for the sole right to own an invention

performance appraisal An evaluation of how well an employee is doing a job

peril Anything that may possibly cause a loss

personal financial planning Spending, saving, and investing money to assure a certain kind of lifestyle as well as financial security

personal property Possessions that can be moved, such as furniture, jewelry, and electronic equipment

personality The sum total of a person's feelings, actions, habits, and thoughts; characteristics that make someone special

planning The act or process of creating goals and objectives as well as the strategies to meet those goals and objectives

pollution The contamination of air, water, and land

pop-up ads Ads that appear for a few seconds when a computer user first logs on to the Internet or clicks on to a Web site

Key Terms Glossary

precious gems Rough mineral deposits (usually crystals) that are dug from the earth by miners and then cut and shaped into brilliant jewels

precious metals Valuable ores such as silver, gold, and platinum

pre-existing condition Serious health condition diagnosed before a person obtained health insurance

preferred provider organization (PPO) Group of doctors and hospitals that agree to provide specified medical services to members at prearranged fees

preferred stock Stock that gives the owner the advantage of receiving cash dividends before common stockholders receive any

premium The price an insured person or business pays for insurance protection for a specified period of time

presentation program Software for creating slide shows for presentations

price discrimination Act of charging various prices for the same product or service in different markets or to different customers

price The amount of money given or asked for when goods and services are bought or sold

prime time The time period when the TV or radio audience is the largest

principal The amount of borrowed money that is still owed and on which interest is based

privatization Hiring a business to offer a public good or service

proceeds The face value of a life insurance policy

processors Businesses that change raw materials into more finished products

procurement The buying and reselling of goods that have already been produced

producer A business that gathers raw products in their natural state

product liability The legal responsibility that manufacturers have to make a safe product

production The process of creating, expanding, manufacturing, or improving goods and services

profit The money left over after a business has paid the cost of providing its goods and services

promotion A move to a higher-level job that has more authority, responsibility, and pay

promotional sale A sale that offers a special buy on a new product or product that is in season

property Anything of value that is owned or controlled

prosperity A peak of economic activity

protectionism The practice of the government putting limits on foreign trade to protect businesses at home

pure risk The threat of a loss with no opportunity for gain

Q

qualifications Education, skills, and work experience needed to do a particular job

quota A limit placed on the quantities of a product that can be imported

R

random access memory (RAM) A computer memory used to hold all of the data and instructions required during operations

rate of return The percentage of increase in the value of savings from earned interest

real estate Land and anything attached to it, such as buildings or natural resources

real estate agent A person licensed to arrange the buying and selling of homes and other types of real estate

real property Property attached to land, such as a house, business, garage, or other building

recall An order to take back and repair or replace a product that has defective parts

recession A slowdown of economic activity

recovery A rise in business activity after a recession or depression

recruitment Actively looking for qualified people to fill a job

recycling The collecting of products for processing so that they can be used again

reference Someone who comments on a job applicant's character and qualifications for a job

regular savings account A savings account that allows consumers to deposit or withdraw money at any time and to earn interest on deposited funds

relationship marketing A strategy to build customer relations

rental property Any type of dwelling unit or other property rented for a length of time

renters insurance Insurance that covers loss or damage to a renter's personal possessions

replacement value The full cost of repairing or replacing property, regardless of its depreciation value

repossess To take back

reserves Funds set aside for emergencies, such as a rush of withdrawals at a bank

residential property Property in which an individual or family lives

resources Items that people can use to make or obtain what they need or want

résumé A summary of an individual's skills, education, and work experience

retailer A business that purchases goods from a wholesaler and sells them to the consumer, the final buyer of the goods

revenue The income that governments get from all sources; the money that comes into a business from the sale of goods and services

rider An addition to an insurance policy that covers specific property or damages

risk The possibility of loss or injury

risk management The systemic process of managing risk to achieve your objectives

S

safe-deposit box A secure box in a bank's vault for the safe storage of a customer's valuables

salary A fixed amount of pay for each week, month, or year

saving Putting money aside for future use

savings and loan associations Financial institutions that hold customers' funds in interest-bearing accounts and invest mainly in mortgage loans

savings bonds Registered bonds that are sold in denominations of $50 to $10,000

scarcity A shortage of resources

search engine A computer program that searches for specific words on the Internet and returns a list of documents in which they were found

secured loan A loan backed by collateral

security A tradable document that shows evidence of debt or ownership

self-managed teams Work groups that supervise themselves. With these teams, the manager's role is replaced by the team leader's role.

separation Leaving a company for any reason

services Tasks that businesses perform for consumers

signature card A record of a bank customer's signature used by the bank to verify the customer's identity

simple interest Interest earned only on money deposited into a savings account, called the principal

skill The ability to perform a task based on training and experience

small business An independently owned business that usually has the owner as its manager

Small Business Administration (SBA) A U.S. agency that protects the interests of small businesses

social responsibility The duty to do what is best for the good of society

Key Terms Glossary

software A computer program that contains a set of instructions that tell a computer what to do

sole proprietorship A business owned by only one person

spreadsheet A computerized worksheet for entering and charting data

standard fire policy Insurance that covers damage due to fire or lightning

standard of living The level of material comfort as measured by the goods and services that are available

start-up A newly formed business that usually is small

statement of cash flows A financial report that shows incoming and outgoing money during an accounting period (often monthly or quarterly)

stereotype To identify a person by a single trait or as a member of a certain group rather than as an individual

stock exchange An organized market for buying and selling financial securities

stock Share of ownership in a business

stockbroker A person who buys and sells stocks, bonds, and other securities for clients

stop payment An order for a bank not to cash a particular check

subsidies Grants given to lower costs

supply The amount of goods and services that producers will provide at various prices

surplus Extra money that can be spent or saved

sweatshop A shop or factory in which workers are employed for long hours at low wages and under unhealthy conditions

T

target marketing Marketing that helps companies focus on the people most likely to buy their goods or services.

tariff A tax placed on imports to increase their price in the domestic market

tax An amount of money people and businesses pay governments to help run a nation, state, county, city, or town

tax incentives Reductions in taxes that a government gives to a business or an individual to encourage a particular behavior

telecommunications The transmission of information over communication lines

telecommuting An arrangement that allows employees to work at home while communicating with the workplace by phone, fax, or modem

term insurance Insurance that covers a person for a specific period of time

test-market Offering a product in a limited market for a limited time

top-level managers Managers who are responsible for setting goals and planning for the future as well as leading and controlling the work of others

trade The activity of buying and selling goods and services in domestic or international markets

trademark A name, symbol, or characteristic that identifies a product

transfer A move to another job within a company at the same level and pay

transit advertising Posters placed on the sides of buses, in subway stations, inside trains, and at airports

trust A group of companies that band together to form a monopoly and cut out competition

turnover The number of employees who leave an organization and are replaced over a certain period

U

uncontrollable risk Risk that cannot be controlled to minimize the chance of harm

undeveloped property Unused land intended only for investment purposes

uninsurable risk Risk that is unacceptable to insurance carriers because the likelihood of loss is too high

unlimited liability A liability that holds the owner fully responsible for a company's debts

unsecured loan A loan that is not backed by collateral

usury law A law restricting the amount of interest that can be charged for credit

V

values Important beliefs and ideas that guide a person's decisions and life

variable expenses Expenses that change and can be controlled more easily than fixed expenses

variable rate An adjustable interest rate charged by financial institutions such as banks

virtual business or **dot-com company** A business that operates on the Internet

virtual reality An artificial, three-dimensional visual world created by a computer

virus A program that is part of another and inserts copies of itself, often damaging the stored data

vision statement A statement that establishes the scope and purpose of a company and reflects its values and beliefs

volunteerism Working without pay

W

wage An amount of money paid to an employee on an hourly basis

wants Things that a person does not have to have to survive, but would like to have

warranty A written guarantee from the manufacturer or distributor that states the conditions under which a product can be returned, replaced, or repaired

wearable computer A small portable computer that is designed to be worn on the body during use

Web browser A computer program used for displaying and viewing Web pages

webcast A broadcast made on the Internet

wholesaler A business that distributes goods; also known as a distributor

withdrawal The money taken out of a bank account

word processing Writing, editing, and producing documents, such as letters and reports, through the use of a computer program

World Wide Web A system for accessing, changing, and downloading a large set of hypertext-linked documents and other files located on computers connected through the Internet

Y

yield The amount of money an investment earns

Academic Vocabulary Glossary

A

access The act of approaching or entering; to get at

accommodation The provision of what is needed; adaptation or adjustment

accumulate To increase gradually in quantity or number

accurate Free from error, especially as the result of care

achieve To carry out successfully; accomplish

achievement A result gained by effort

acquire To get as one's own

adaptable Capable of changing

adequate Sufficient for a specific requirement

adjust To adapt or conform

administrator One who manages or supervises

affect To produce an effect upon

allocate To apportion for a specific purpose or to particular persons or things

alteration The act of making something different

alternative One of two or more things, courses, or propositions to be chosen

analyze To study or determine the nature and relationship of component parts

annual Occurring or happening every year or once a year

anticipate The act of looking forward

approach The taking of preliminary steps toward a particular purpose

area A geographic region

assemble To bring together for a particular purpose

assess To determine the importance, size, or value

assignment A specified task

associate To connect one thing with another in the mind

assurance A statement intended to inspire confidence

attach To fasten one thing to another

attitude A feeling or emotion toward a fact or state

author One who originates or creates

authority The power to influence or command thought, opinion, or behavior

authorize To invest with legal authority

automatic Done by machine; mechanical

available Present or ready for immediate use

aware Having or showing realization, perception, or knowledge

B

behalf In the interest of or to benefit someone else

benefit An advantage

bond An interest-bearing certificate of public or private indebtedness

bulk Not divided into parts or packaged in separate units

C

challenging Arousing competitive interest, thought, or action

civil Of or relating to citizens

comment To make an observation or remark expressing an opinion or attitude

commission A fee paid to an agent or employee for transacting a piece of business or performing a service

commit To pledge or assign

common Shared by two or more parties

communicate To transmit information, thought, or feeling so that it is satisfactorily received or understood

community A body of persons of common and especially professional interests scattered through a larger society

compare To examine and note the similarities or differences of

complement To fill out or complete

complex A whole structure (such as a building) made up of interconnected or related structures

Academic Vocabulary Glossary

comprehensive Covering completely or broadly

concept Something conceived in the mind

conduct A mode or standard of personal behavior

conflict Competitive or opposing action of incompatibles

consider To think about carefully

consist To be composed or made up— usually with *of*

constant Continually occurring or recurring

contact To get in communication with

contribute To play a significant part in bringing about an end or result

control To exercise power or influence over something

controversy A discussion marked especially by the expression of opposing views

conversely Reversed in order, relation, or action

convert To change from one form or function to another

convince To bring to belief, consent, or a course of action

cooperate To act or work with another or others

create To produce or bring about by a course of action or behavior

criteria Standards on which a judgment or decision may be based

crucial Of extreme importance

D

data Factual information used as a basis for reasoning, discussion, or calculation

decade A period of 10 years

decline The state of decreasing

demand An urgent request

demonstrate To illustrate and explain, especially with examples

design To devise for a specific function or end

despite In spite of

determine To settle or decide by choice of alternatives or possibilities

device A piece of equipment

display To put or spread before the viewer

dispose To get rid of

dispute A disagreement

distinct Distinguishable to the eye or mind as discrete; separate

distribute To divide among several or many

diverse Differing from one another

document A writing conveying information

duration Time during which something exists or lasts

E

edit To alter, adapt, or refine, especially to bring about conformity to a standard or to suit a particular purpose

element A constituent part

eliminate To put an end to; remove

emphasis Special importance or significance

enable To make possible, practical, or easy

encounter To come upon or experience, especially unexpectedly

enforce To carry out effectively

enormous Marked by extraordinarily great size, number, or degree

ensure To make sure, certain, or safe

error Something produced by mistake

establish To gain full recognition or acceptance

estate The assets and liabilities left by a person at death

estimate To determine roughly the size, extent, or nature of

ethnic Of or relating to large groups of people classed according to common racial, national, tribal, religious, linguistic, or cultural origin or background

evaluate To determine the significance, worth, or condition of, usually by careful appraisal and study

evident Capable of being seen or noticed

Academic Vocabulary Glossary

exceed To be greater than or superior to

expand To increase the extent, number, volume, or scope of

expert Someone with special knowledge or ability

F

facilitate To help bring about

factor One that actively contributes to the production of a result

feature A prominent part or characteristic

federal Of or relating to the central government or a federation as distinguished from the governments of the constituent units

fee A sum paid or charged for a service

finally Last in a series, process, or progress

flexible Characterized by a ready capability to adapt to new, different, or changing requirements

fluctuate To shift back and forth uncertainly

focus To concentrate attention or effort

formula A group of symbols associated to express facts or data concisely

function The action for which a person or thing is specially fitted or used or for which a thing exists

fund A sum of money or other resources set apart for a specific purpose

G

gender A sex, or the behavioral, cultural, or psychological traits typically associated with one sex

generate To bring into existence, produce

goal The end toward which effort is directed

grant To give or transfer formally

guarantee An assurance for the fulfillment of a condition

guideline An indication of policy or conduct

H

hence Because of a preceding fact or premise

I

identify To establish the identity of

illustrate To show clearly

image A visual representation of something

impact A significant or major effect

incentive Something that incites or has a tendency to incite to determination or action

incline To lean, tend, or become drawn toward

income A gain or recurrent benefit usually measured in money that derives from capital or labor

incorporate Unite or work into something already existent so as to form an indistinguishable whole

indicate To point out or point to

individual A single human being

initiate To cause or facilitate the beginning of

injure To inflict bodily harm

insert To put into something

instance A step, stage, or situation viewed as part of a process or series of events

institution An established organization or corporation

integral Essential to completeness

integrity The quality of possessing firm moral principles and values

interact To act together, toward others, or with others

intermediate Being or occurring at the middle place, stage, or degree between extremes

internal Of, relating to, or occurring on the inside of an organized structure

involve To engage as a participant

issue To put forth or distribute, usually officially

item A distinct part in an enumeration, account, or series; an article

J

justify To prove or show to be just, right, or reasonable

L

label To describe or designate with or as if with a label

labor Human activity that provides goods or services in an economy

link To couple or connect

locate To determine or indicate the place, site, or limits of

M

maintain Keep in an existing state

major Greater in dignity, rank, importance, or interest

manual A book that is conveniently handled; a handbook

mature To become due

mean To indicate or signify

media Channels or systems of communication, information, or entertainment

medical Of, relating to or concerned with physicians or the practice of medicine

medium Intermediate in quantity, quality, position, size, or degree

mental Of or relating to the mind

method A procedure or process for attaining an object

military Of or relating to soldiers, arms, or war

minimize To reduce or keep to a minimum

minimum The least quantity assignable, admissible, or possible

mode Particular form or variety of something

modify To make less extreme

monitor To watch, keep track of, or check

mutual Shared in common

N

network A group of radio or television stations linked by wire or radio relay

nevertheless In spite of that; however

nuclear Produced by a nuclear reaction (as fission)

O

objective Something toward which effort is directed

observe To watch carefully

obtain Gain or attain, usually by planned action or effort

occurrence Something that occurs; an event

option An alternate course of action; a choice

order A request or demand

overall Including everything

overseas Situated, originating in, or relating to lands beyond the sea

P

panel A group of persons who discuss a topic of public interest

participate Have a part or share in something

partner A member of a partnership, especially in a business

percentage The result obtained by multiplying a number by a percent

perform To carry out a function

period A portion of time determined by some recurring phenomenon

physical Having material existence

plus In addition to

policy A definite course or method of action selected from among alternatives and in light of given conditions to guide and determine present and future decisions

portion A part or share of something

pose To pretend to be someone else

Academic Vocabulary Glossary

potential Existing in possibility

predict To declare or indicate in advance

primary Of first rank, importance, or value

prime Having the highest quality or value

principle A rule or code of conduct

priority Something given or meriting attention before competing alternatives

process A series of actions or operations leading to an end

professional One who engages in a pursuit or activity professionally

prohibit Forbid by authority

project To plan, figure, or estimate for the future

publication A published work such as a magazine or journal

purchase To obtain by paying money or its equivalent

purpose The goal or intended outcome of something

pursue Employing measures to obtain or accomplish

Q

quote To state the current price of something

R

random Lacking a definite plan, purpose, or pattern

range A series of things in a line

region A broad geographic area distinguished by similar features

registered Enrolled formally

regulate To bring under the control of law or constituted authority

reject To refuse to accept or acknowledge

relationship The state of being related or interrelated

relaxed Easy of manner; informal

release To make available to the public

rely To be dependent

remove Get rid of; eliminate

require Demand as necessary or essential

research To collect information about a particular subject

resolved Cleared up, decided

resource A source of supply or support

respond To react in response

restore To bring back to or put back into a former or original state

restrict To confine within bounds

retain Keep in possession or use

reveal To make publicly or generally known

revise Look over again in order to correct or improve

role A function or part performed, especially in a particular operation or process

route An established or selected course, travel, or action

S

scenario An account or synopsis of a possible course of action or events

schedule A procedural plan that indicates the time and sequence of each operation

scheme An elaborate and systematic plan of action, especially a crafty or secret one

section A distinct part or portion of something written

sector A sociological, economic, or political subdivision of society

secure Free from risk or loss

seek Go in search of

series A number of things or events of the same class coming one after another in spatial or temporal succession

set Put into a position

shift To change the place, position, or direction of

significant Of a noticeably or measurably large amount

similar Having characteristics in common

simulate To give or assume the appearance or effect of

sole Having no sharer; being the only one

source One that provides information

specific Applying to, characterized by, or distinguishing something particular, special, or unique

stable Firmly established

strategy A careful plan or method

stress To emphasize

structure Coherent form or organization

submit Present or propose to another for review, consideration, or decision

sufficient Enough to meet the needs of a situation

suggest To mention or imply as a possibility

sum The result of adding numbers

summary An abstract, abridgment, or compendium

supplement Something that completes or makes an addition

survey A detailed critical inspection

survivor One who remains alive after death

sustain To give support or relief to

symbol Something that stands for or suggests something else by reason of relationship, association, convention, or accidental resemblance

T

task A usually assigned piece of work often to be finished within a certain time

team A number of persons associated together in work or an activity

technical Of or relating to proficiency in a practical skill

technique A method of accomplishing a desired aim

technology The practical application of knowledge, especially in a particular area

temporary Lasting for a limited time

theory A hypothesis assumed for the sake of argument or investigation

trace Discover signs, evidence, or remains of

tradition An inherited, established, or customary pattern of thought, action, or behavior

transferable The ability to be moved to a different place, region, or situation

transit The transportation of passengers by means of a local public transportation system

transmit To send or convey from one person or place to another

transport To transfer or convey from one place to another

trend A prevailing tendency or inclination

U

ultimate Last in a progression or series

undergo Submit to

unique Distinctively characteristic

utilize To make use of

V

valid Having legal efficacy or force

vary To make differences between items

vehicle A means of carrying or transporting something

version A form or variant of a type or original

via By way of

vision An image or concept in the imagination

visual capable of being seen; visible

W

welfare The state of doing well, especially in respect to good fortune, happiness, well-being, or prosperity

Index

Index

G

Index

Q

R

U

X

Y

Z